QUEST TO RESTORE GOD'S HOUSE
A THEOLOGICAL HISTORY OF THE CHURCH OF GOD
(CLEVELAND, TENNESSEE)

VOLUME I
1886-1923

R.G. SPURLING TO A.J. TOMLINSON
FORMATION-TRANSFORMATION-REFORMATION

QUEST TO RESTORE GOD'S HOUSE
A THEOLOGICAL HISTORY
OF THE CHURCH OF GOD
(CLEVELAND, TENNESSEE)

VOLUME I
1886-1923

R.G. SPURLING TO A.J. TOMLINSON
FORMATION-TRANSFORMATION-REFORMATION

WADE H. PHILLIPS

CPT Press
Cleveland, Tennessee

Quest to Restore God's House –
A Theological History of the Church of God (Cleveland, Tennessee)
Volume I, 1886-1923, R.G. Spurling to A.J. Tomlinson
Formation-Transformation-Reformation

Published by CPT Press
900 Walker ST NE
Cleveland, TN 37311
USA
email: cptpress@pentecostaltheology.org
website: www.cptpress.com

Library of Congress Control Number: 2014955973

ISBN-13: 9781935931447

Copyright © 2014 CPT Press

All rights reserved. No part of this book may be reproduced or translated in any form, by print, photoprint, microfilm, microfiche, electronic database, internet database, or any other means without written permission from the publisher.

Citations of Scripture are from the Authorized King James Version

Contents

List of Illustrations x
Foreword xiii
Preface xv
Acknowledgments xxv
Abbreviations xxvii

Introduction 1

Chapter 1
Baptist Roots 7
    One Born Out of Due Time 8
    Baptist Heritage 11
    Regulars, Separates, and United Baptists 13
    Migration to East Tennessee 15
    Old Landmarkism 19
    The Move to Lower East Tennessee 23
    Holly Springs Church 27
    Mountain Peculiarities 31
    Spurling Comes of Age 34
    Landmarkism Reasserts Itself 38
    Conflict with Pleasant Hill Church 40

Chapter 2
Christian Union is Born 42
    Valley of Decision 42
    Light Breaks Through 44
    Further Complaints Against Landmarkers 46
    Some Positive Aspects of Landmarkism 50
    A Glance in Other Directions 53
    Spurling's Vision 56
    Spurling's Eloquence 61
    Christian Union Set in Order 64
    The Role of Elder Richard Spurling 67
    Going Forward 72

Christian Union at Barney Creek 74
Christian Union at Shuler Creek 83
Christian Union at Piney Grove 84
Christian Union on Paul's Mountain 90
The Basis of the Union 91
Spurling's Leadership Position 94
Tomlinson's Record 96
Core Principles Discovered and Restored 97
Born with a Birth Defect 98

Chapter 3
Holiness-Pentecostal Transformation 106
Fire-Baptized Holiness Influence 119
   'Dynamite' 125
   'Lyddite' 131
   'Oxidite' 134
   'Selenite' 135
Origin of Modern Pentecostalism 136
Theologically Sound 144
Trinitarian Mysticism 145
Scholarly Characteristics 147
A Rational Mysticism 148
Martyrdom Complex 150
Fire-Baptized Revival at Camp Creek 152
Persecutions 156
Fire-Baptized Fanaticism 165
Holiness Church Established at Camp Creek 167

Chapter 4
Institutional Transformation 173
A Strong and Confident Leader 173
Complexity of Tomlinson 174
Quaker Roots 175
American Roots 179
Tomlinson at Culberson 185
Connection with Camp Creek 192
Influence of Frank W. Sandford and Shiloh 194
Persecution 202
Tomlinson Joins the Church 210
Tomlinson Pursues His Own Vision 216
Reaching Out on the Basis of Tomlinson's Vision 217

Centralizing the Government of the Churches 223
The Case of the Church of God (Holiness) 226
The Tomlinson Shift 229
Completing the Pentecostal Transformation 233
Disruption of 1909-1910 238
Development of an Episcopal Hierarchy 244
New Fields and Missions 248
Magnetic Attraction 255
The Case of the Church of God (Mountain Assembly) 256
The Evening Light and *Church of God Evangel* 257
Orphanage Work 259
The Lost Link Versus *The Last Great Conflict* 263
Fire-Baptized Spirituality 265

Chapter 5
Doctrinal Transformation 273
Trinity 276
The Bible 277
The Church 282
Full Plan of Salvation Restored 289
Apostolic Restoration 293
'The Covering Removed' 298
Modern-day Apostles 300
Divine Healing 309
Anabaptist and Quaker Influences 323
Plain Dress and Practical Holiness 326
On Oath Taking and Swearing 329
On Footwashing 332
Separation of Church and State 340
'Against Members Going to War' 343
Development of a Corporate Conscience 345
Snake Handling and Other Excesses 350
Tobacco Controversies 359
Important Teachings Codified 363
On Divorce and Remarriage 371

Chapter 6
The Road Back to Rome 379
The Magnanimity of Tomlinson 381
Feet of Clay 385
Carried by an Ancient Current 388

Tomlinson's Autocracy 410
Council of Elders 412
Cleveland – Seat of 'Theocratic Government' 418
Developing Exclusivity... 422
Growing Dissatisfaction... 425
The Case of Sam C. Perry 427
J.L. Scott Reformation... 433
The Case of R.G. Spurling.. 437
Christianized Communism 438
Further Reflections on the Church's Experiment in
    'Christian Communism'.. 453
Council of Seventy 455
Courts of Justice 457
Politics and Militarism 459
The Declaration... 460
Exchange and Indemnity Department....................................... 463

Chapter 7
Anatomy of a Disruption.. 466
The Rise of J.S. Llewellyn 468
The Constitution 483
Roots of Revolution... 492
The Faithful Standard... 493
An Explosive Elders' Council 495
A Combative Assembly 503
Tomlinson Resigns.. 520
Nothing Actually Settled 525
The New Government – A Freakish Arrangement............... 527
The Frame-Up 538
The Twelve Elders – Divided Loyalties 543
The Case of J.S. Llewellyn 548
The Case of F.J. Lee 551
The Case of E.J. Boehmer.. 560
The Case of M.S. Lemons.. 563
The Case of W.F. Bryant.. 567
The Case of A.J. Lawson.. 571
The June Council.. 574
Tomlinson Charged 593
Reflecting on the Charges 595
'Declaration of Independence' 602
The July Councils 608

    The August Council 616
    September-October Events 623
    Separate General Assemblies 628
    Summary Reflection 630
    What Could Have Been Done? 633

Bibliography 636
Index of Biblical References 646
Index of Names and Subjects 651

List of Illustrations

Figure 1   Wolf River Baptist Church
Figure 2   Joshua Frost c. 1864
Figure 3   J.R. Graves c. 1866
Figure 4   Richard Spurling (c. 1888)
Figure 5   I.B. Kimbrough (1826-1902)
Figure 6   Holly Springs Baptist Church c. 1890
Figure 7   Daniel E.L. Spurling Family c. 1891
Figure 8   Nathan (1838-1912), Brother of R.G. Spurling
Figure 9   Daniel (1841-1904), Brother of R.G. Spurling
Figure 10 Hiram (1849-1922), Brother of R.G. Spurling
Figure 11 R.G. Spurling c. 1875
Figure 12 R.G. Spurling and Family c. 1894
Figure 13 William R. Mulkey and wife (c. 1878)
Figure 14 Part of Pleasant Hill Baptist Church Congregation (c. 1902)
Figure 15 Map
Figure 16 Penelope (Paul) Tilley ('Aunt Nep')
Figure 17 R.G. Spurling and Family, c. 1897
Figure 18 Christian Union at Piney Grove (c. 1899)
Figure 19 Joseph Freeman and Family
Figure 20 Dorcas (Freeman) Bowers and Family
Figure 21 Larkin Evans and Family
Figure 22 Joab ['Jeeb'] and Omia [Spurling] Waldrop
Figure 23 Joseph and Nancy [Freeman] Prock
Figure 24 Pastor James Freeman
Figure 25 Andy Paul and Sarah [Freeman]
Figure 26 Committal of Andy Paul
Figure 27 William 'Billy' Martin
Figure 28 Robert Frank Porter and wife
Figure 29 Elias Milton ['Milt'] McNabb and Family (c. 1896)
Figure 30 Henry Clay and Minnie McNabb
Figure 31 W.H. Hickey Family
Figure 32 David and Zilphia Hamby
Figure 33 Ross and Emeline Allen and Family (c. 1902)
Figure 34 Walter Scott Kimsey (c. 1905)
Figure 35 The Shearer Schoolhouse (c. 1900)
Figure 36 Alexander ['Elic'] Hamby and Family (c. 1905)
Figure 37 W.F. Bryant and Family (c. 1905)
Figure 38 Billy Hamby and Family (c. 1902)

List of Illustrations   xi

Figure 39   A.J. Tomlinson and Family (c. 1898)
Figure 40   Tomlinson with Family and New Friends at Culberson (1900)
Figure 41   'The Hyatt House' (1900)
Figure 42   The Mission School at Culberson (1901)
Figure 43   R.R. McAllister's General Store
Figure 44   Railroad Depot at 'Zion Hill' (Culberson)
Figure 45   Abigail 'Abbie' Cress
Figure 46   James H. and Eliza Overstreet
Figure 47   Frank W. Sandford (1902)
Figure 48   Shiloh (1898)
Figure 49   Shiloh (1901)
Figure 50   Cabin home of W.F. Bryant at Camp Creek
Figure 51   Mountaintop Revelation
Figure 52   Site of the First General Assembly in 1906
Figure 53   Union Grove – Site of the Second Assembly in 1907
Figure 54   First General Assembly 'Delegates'
Figure 55   J.H. Simpson and Wife Julia [Maddox] (c. 1912)
Figure 56   A.J. Tomlinson (c. 1910)
Figure 57   Sam C. Perry
Figure 58   Miss Clyde Cotton
Figure 59   R.M. Evans
Figure 60   W.F. Bryant at Hillview (c. 1909)
Figure 61   Coconut Grove, Florida (1911)
Figure 62   'Pentecostal Worldwide Mission Band' (1911)
Figure 63   'Pentecostal Worldwide Mission Band' (1911)
Figure 64   W.F. Bryant in charge of the Orphanage in Cleveland (1911)
Figure 65   Miss Lillian Trasher – 'Mother of the Nile'
Figure 66   G.B Cashwell
Figure 67   M.M. Pinson
Figure 68   R.G. Spurling (c. 1915)
Figure 69   Mary Jane and A.J. Tomlinson (c. 1918)
Figure 70   Nora Chambers (c. 1912)
Figure 71   M.S. Lemons and Efford Haynes (c. 1920)
Figure 72   J.W. Buckalew (c. 1910)
Figure 73   Margaret Melissa Shearer (c. 1900)
Figure 74   A.B. Simpson
Figure 75   John Alexander Dowie
Figure 76   Bethesda (c. 1900)
Figure 77   A.J. Tomlinson (c. 1901)
Figure 78   Roy C. Miller (c. 1911)
Figure 79   H.L. Trim (c. 1914) and Flora E. Bower (c. 1911)
Figure 80   Homer Tomlinson in uniform
Figure 81   George W. Hensley and Others 'Taking up Serpents' (Used by permission of ETSU Archives of Appalachia)
Figure 82   Minnie Parker Handling a Snake (Used by permission of ETSU Archives of Appalachia)
Figure 83   Ordained Ministers c. 1913
Figure 84   Eighth Assembly, January 7-12, 1913

Figure 85   Tomlinson as he appeared in 1913
Figure 86   Council of Elders
Figure 87   First Session of Elders' Council – October 4-17, 1917
Figure 88   Sam C. Perry
Figure 89   J.L. Scott
Figure 90   A.H. Bryans
Figure 91   R.G. Spurling as he appeared c. 1916
Figure 92   Assembly in Session c. 1920
Figure 93   Bishops in attendance at the Assembly in 1913
Figure 94   J.S. Llewellyn c. 1921
Figure 95   Homer Tomlinson c. 1921
Figure 96   The Twelve Elders
Figure 97   J.S. Llewellyn, T.S. Payne, F.J. Lee c. 1924
Figure 98   M.S. Lemons c. 1922
Figure 99   A.J. Lawson c. 1922
Figure 100 Tomlinson, Llewellyn, and Lee formed the Executive Council
Figure 101 S.W. Latimer
Figure 102 S.J. Heath and wife, Annie
Figure 103 Tomlinson Family at the gravesite of Halcy Tomlinson Hughes
Figure 104 A.D. Evans and wife, Iris [Tomlinson] Evans
Figure 105 Evangel Offices and Publishing House 1920
Figure 106 F.J. and Eva Lee, and Jesse P. and Nellie Hughes (c. 1919)
Figure 107 M.W. Letsinger (c. 1930)
Figure 108 The new Assembly Auditorium (1920)
Figure 109 S.O. Gillespie
Figure 110 George T. Brouayer
Figure 111 Meeting of the Elders [Llewellyn-Lee faction] (August 1923)
Figure 112 Sunnyside Mission

Foreword

On July 31, 1993, Bishop Wade H. Phillips invited me to accompany him to the clerk's home of the Holly Springs Baptist Church in Monroe County, Tennessee. Bishop Phillips had gone to great lengths to locate the minutes of that congregation to which Richard Spurling belonged when he assisted his son, R.G. Spurling, in founding the Christian Union in 1886. Bishop Phillips had discovered the congregation, persuaded their clerk to retrieve their nineteenth-century records from a bank vault, and then received permission to make a photocopy. He later presented a copy of those minutes to the Hal Bernard Dixon Jr. Pentecostal Research Center, so they would be available to me and other scholars and students of the Church of God movement.

At that time I was on the library faculty of Lee College and completing a PhD dissertation at Vanderbilt University. It was an honor to spend the day with Bishop Phillips. Having lived in that region, he was familiar with the people and their culture; and I was grateful to be invited into their world. I was also awed by the opportunity to hold in my hands a document that was more than 100 years old and that no one in my denomination had ever seen – a document that I knew would rewrite our received history in a significant way.

The events that day revealed much about the author of *Quest to Restore God's House*. Wade Phillips recognized the value of primary historical resources, and he searched diligently until he found them. The minutes of the Holly Springs Baptist Church were not his first extraordinary find, and they would not be his last. *Quest to Restore God's House* is the fruit of those discoveries, of a careful reading of many previously unknown sources, and of a passionate journey to recover and interpret our common heritage. That Saturday trip to Monroe County in 1993 also revealed Bishop Phillips commitment to connect with the people of the region. By getting to know them and their communities he built relationships that led to even more discoveries and to a fuller understanding of the people, places, and culture out of which the Church of God developed. Further, his inclusion of a younger scholar and his donation of a copy of the Holly Springs minutes demonstrated his readiness to share what he was learning and his commitment to interact with others devoted to the mission of recovering and passing on our heritage.

Among those who have written about the birth and early development of the Church of God movement, no one has done more than Wade H. Phillips to recover, understand, and interpret their mission. Bishop Phillips is motivated by a love for God, an unwavering passion to comprehend our founders as they endeavored to follow their vision to restore God's Church, and a commitment to be faithful to their quest. One cannot read this book without being inspired by these men and women who devoted their lives to restore and build the Church of God.

David G. Roebuck, PhD
Church of God Historian
Director of Hal Bernard Dixon Jr. Pentecostal Research Center
December 17, 2014

Preface

I

This three-volume history is about a bold venture that was launched in 1886 in the Appalachian Mountains to restore God's house. The principal leaders believed they were being led by the Holy Spirit to build again the church that Christ had set in order during His earthly ministry. Having become dissatisfied and disillusioned with the religious status quo of their day, particularly the man-created and man-handled denominational system that the Reformation had spawned in the three previous centuries, the pioneers of the Church of God began to call upon God and to look afresh into the Scriptures for illumination and understanding on the subject of the church. The result set in motion one of the most powerful and unique traditions of faith in modern times.

The church has had its ups and downs, its triumphs and disappointments, and its divisions and defections. It has given birth to many heroes of the faith, and on occasion has had to discipline members and expel defectors. It has been applauded and ridiculed, acclaimed and denounced, admired and despised, exalted and brought low. It has stumbled on occasion and has had to recover itself, has drifted off course and has had to realign itself with the original charter. These historical developments make the Church of God and her pioneer fathers and mothers a fascinating story, full of intrigue and passion, charged with an inherent sense of profound purpose, and set aglow with visions of prophetic glory.

II

A true account of the history of the Church of God must necessarily include the set-backs and occasional defeats as well as the triumphs and moments of glory. Writing history with integrity requires the historian to acknowledge the 'warts' as well as to accentuate the 'beauty marks' in telling the story of the church. Accordingly, we have attempted in this history to understand and explain the ugly as well as to admire and magnify the lovely. As we move through the church's unfolding saga, some scenes do not make a pretty picture in historical time; but the prophetic picture always redeems the historical. It was this prophetic picture of the church – the ideal church – that impassioned and drove the pioneers in their quest to restore the Church of God of the Bible and fulfill its mission. They climbed the celestial mountain with the apostle and saw the awe-inspiring vision – 'the bride, the Lamb's wife' adorned in her wedding garment and arrayed in glory.

> And he carried me away in the Spirit to a great and high mountain, and showed me the great city, the holy Jerusalem, descending out of heaven from God, Having the glory of God (Rev. 21.9-11).

> Let us be glad and rejoice and give glory to God, for the marriage of the Lamb is come, and His wife has made herself ready. And to her was granted that she should be arrayed in fine linen, clean and white: for the fine linen is the righteousness of the saints (Rev. 19.7).

III

The period of time covered in this history spans little more than 125 years, compared to almost 3500 years if we had begun this history at Mount Sinai where the Bible church was first incorporated and set in order. Granted this is a relatively small slice of the church's captivating story, yet few periods in the church's long history are more fascinating and illuminating. The significant events that transpired during this period, and the personal and corporate experiences of the church's heroic leaders and people, including the advances made in understanding the Gospel and spreading its message and power around the world, are in many respects unparalleled in church history.

Volume I begins in the mountains of southern Appalachia in 1886 with a small group of Baptist reformers who adopted a restoration view of the church. They began their work under the name, 'Christian Union'. We will examine the origin and background of this group then follow its historical and theological growth and development into the twentieth century, and on to the disruption of the church in 1922-1923. Volume II will begin with the reform movement of A.J. Tomlinson and his followers, and trace the church's developments through most of the twentieth century. This period includes the remainder of the tenure of A.J. Tomlinson as General Overseer until his death in October 1943, and covers the tenure of Tomlinson's son, Milton, who succeeded him in the exalted office and served until 1990. Volume III will begin with the selection of Billy D. Murray Sr. who succeeded Milton in April 1990 and served until the Assembly in 2000. This period covers Murray's stormy tenure in the church's highest office and his resignation in 2000. It then continues with his successor, Fred S. Fisher Sr., and the radical changes and instability that followed. The 'falling away' that began under Murray's tenure and culminated during Fisher's tenure in 2004 will be carefully examined. Finally, the restoration and reorganization of the church in April 2004 under the name, 'Zion Assembly Church of God' will be taken up; this will be followed by the developments in Zion Assembly unto the present day. In conclusion, some reflection on the several divisions and restorations of the church will be evaluated, including the significant events that mark the bold claims of its pioneers on prophetic history and divine origin.

IV

Church of God pioneers believed they were chosen to fulfill the prophetic end-times restoration of the church. Were they? This is something the reader will have to evaluate and judge after making a fair appraisal of the prophetic and historical evidence presented in this book. Certainly the church's pioneers were bold to identify certain prophecies that they believed pertained to the restoration in which they were engaged. These prophecies not only gave them a sacred sense of corporate identity and a deep conviction in regard to the supreme value they placed upon their work, but the prophecies also illuminated their path forward. Certain passages in Isaiah are classic examples:

> 'So shall they fear the name of the Lord from the west, and his glory from the rising of the sun. When the enemy shall come in like a flood, the Spirit of the Lord shall lift up a standard against him' (Isa. 59.19).

> Arise, shine; for thy light is come, and the glory of the Lord is risen upon thee. For, behold the darkness shall cover the earth, and gross darkness the people: but the Lord shall arise upon thee, and his glory shall be seen upon thee. And the Gentiles shall come to thy light, and kings to the brightness of thy rising. Lift up thine eyes round about, and see: all they gather themselves together, they come thee … (60.1-5).

> 'For thou shalt break forth on the right hand and on the left; and thy seed shall inherit the Gentiles' (54.3).

> It shall come to pass in the last days, that the mountain of the Lord's house shall be established in the top of the mountains, and shall be

exalted above the hills; and all nations shall flow into it. And many people shall go, and say, Come ye, let us go up to . . . the Lord's house, to the house of the God of Jacob ... for out of Zion shall go forth the law, and the word of the Lord from Jerusalem (2.2, 3).

They saw the prophecy in Joel 2.28-32 – which depicts the Spirit being poured out in the last days on a prophetic 'remnant' of Israel – as being applicable to the restoration of the church in the twentieth century, though they acknowledged that it anticipated in the first instance the Pentecostal outpouring in Acts 2:

> And it shall come to pass afterward, that I will pour out my spirit upon all flesh; and your sons and daughters shall prophesy, your old men shall dream dreams, your young men shall see visions: And also upon the servants and upon the handmaids in those days will I pour out my spirit ... And it shall come to pass that whosoever shall call upon the name of the Lord shall be delivered: for in mount Zion and in Jerusalem shall be deliverance, as the Lord hath said, and in the remnant whom the Lord shall call.

An intriguing prophecy in Zechariah was interpreted in a similar way, which Church of God pioneers applied to the end-times restoration of the church: 'And it shall come to pass in that day, that the light shall not be clear, nor dark: But it shall be one day which shall be known to the Lord, not day, not night: but it shall come to pass, that at evening time it shall be light' (Zech. 14.6,7). Literally hundreds of prophetic passages were interpreted in this way. These prophecies gave Church of God pioneers great comfort, and deepened their conviction about the special call upon their lives; indeed, the prophecies informed and guided their path forward into the unfolding revelation of the church, and propelled them onward with thrilling expectations in anticipation of seeing the church's glorious end.

This view of the church in history and prophecy inevitably raises certain questions. Do the prophecies that tell of the church's restoration strictly confine themselves to a one-time event and fulfillment? Or do they have multiple applications that depict more than one restoration period of the church, for example, Isa. 54.3 and 60.1-5? If so, can we see this borne out in the history of the church in the New Testament and in these last days? A vast number of prominent scholars, ancient and modern, believe so; they maintain that inherent within inspired prophecy is the dynamic ability to speak uniquely to several generations of the church at the same time, yet also to a particular generation in its own peculiar circumstances.¹ The apostles in fact interpreted certain Old Testament prophecies in this manner. The apostle Paul, for example, applies Isa. 54.2 to the New Testament church, seeing in the prophecy a look forward to the Gospel age (Gal. 4.27); yet no one will argue that the prophecy had an immediate fulfillment in regard to Israel's Babylonian Captivity and the restoration of Jerusalem several centuries before the birth of Christ (cf. Isa. 49.18-22). Moreover, the passage alludes back farther to the time of Sarah in her barrenness and to her miraculous conception of Isaac (cf. 51.1-3 and Gen. 15.18-21); but also looks forward in anticipation of the church's glorious progress in the very last days (cf. 60.1-21), and finally to her ultimate fulfillment in the millennium (cf. 65.8-10, 17-25).²

The apostle Peter saw the outpouring of the Spirit on the day of Pentecost in Acts 2 as the fulfillment of Joel 2.28-32 (cf. Acts 2.14-18), yet his sermon anticipated men and women in every age of the church as having part in the fulfillment of this prophetic Pentecostal blessing (Acts 2.38, 39). Even some apostolic exhortations have prophetic implications: for example, Jude's exhortation to 'earnestly contend for the faith which was once delivered to the saints' spoke to the church in his generation, yet it anticipated the church's restoration and final victory in the end-times.

The pioneers of the Church of God believed they were on solid ground in interpreting biblical prophecy in this way. Their understanding was based on the belief that the Holy Spirit is the agent of prophetic inspiration, and that He, being one with the eternal Father and Son, transcends time and infinitely foreknows all things, and thus can reveal in a single prophetic utterance a snapshot of the church that in real time may take centuries to fulfill. Indeed, some of the visionary descriptions of Ezekiel, Daniel, and the apostle John function in this way. For example, the 'great multitude' that John saw 'come out of great tribulation'

---

¹ Wesleyan commentator, Adam Clarke, argued convincingly on this point in regard to the nature of Hebrew literature and prophecy (see 'Introduction to the Book of Isaiah', Clarke's *Commentary* (6 Vols.; Nashville: Abingdon Press), IV, pp. 7-16. Accordingly, the strict and static dispensational dichotomy between Israel and the church cannot be maintained when interpreting the prophetical writings, for some Old Testament prophecies have an extended application and fulfillment in the New Testament church.

² Again Clarke's comments are noteworthy on Isaiah 60. He maintains that this prophecy is too glorious and majestic to have been fulfilled in the first century church, or in any century up until the nineteenth when he wrote his Commentaries. He thus saw this passage as a prophecy which predicted the fall of the church in the first few Christian centuries, and envisioned its restoration and glory in the last days (*Commentary*, IV, pp. 222-24).

[Rev. 7.14] may imply the saints of all the successive ages. The Greek term ἐκ here may signify 'came out from' the great tribulation, not necessarily 'out of the midst of' it, and therefore the prophecy is not limited in its application to a single episode of tribulation in the last days, nor especially to the indignation in the last half of the post-rapture tribulation. Thus the Spirit captures in this single glance in John's vision the whole blood-washed throng of saints that had suffered [many of them by martyrdom] through the ages. It may include therefore all of the 'dead in Christ' in ages past along with the living saints ('we which are alive and remain') who will be 'caught up' together to meet the Lord in the air (1 Thess. 4.17).

It should be borne in mind that prophecy is given often from the perspective of God's infinite mind and eternal purpose, which may include in one infinite glance the church in every age and historical period including its perfection and final abode in glory. Part of a single prophetic passage therefore may address the church in one period of time, and another part of the same passage may pertain to the church in another period. Further, the dynamic of prophetic utterance is such that the same part may have multiple applications and therefore may describe and inform more than one period of time in the church's history.

Understanding prophecy in this way is vitally important if one is to catch the spirit and vision of the 'founders'[3] of the Church of God, and the restoration that they launched in the late nineteenth and early twentieth century: for this is what inspired their zeal and emboldened their mission. They saw themselves in this very light, that is, as a people answering a prophetic call and commission to evangelize the world with the 'whole counsel of God' – with the 'all things whatsoever' message that Christ had commanded (Mt. 28.19); and as their fellowship solidified in the early twentieth century, they sensed an acute self-awareness that they were God's 'peculiar people', and, therefore, that Christ's call to conform perfectly to His will 'in everything' was especially incumbent upon them (Eph. 4.11-16; 5.24-32; Phil. 1.27; 3.12-16; Col. 1.25-29; Rev. 19.7-9). They therefore looked back to the prophets and apostles, but they also looked forward; and, in fact, they looked back mainly to inform and measure their march forward. They lived the present in the light of the future. They rejoiced not so much that they saw themselves *in* history, but that they were in fact *making* history – a *future* history or-

---

[3] 'Founders' only in the sense that they discovered and restored the original pattern of the New Covenant church laid down by Christ and the apostles, not that they founded the church. The foundation was laid once for all time by Christ and the apostles (1 Cor. 3.10, 11; Eph. 2.20).

dained by the prescient mind of God and revealed in the prophetic Scriptures. This more than any other aspect of their faith captured their imagination and drove them furiously – and sometimes fanatically – to fulfill their prophetic purpose. It explains their hope and optimism: every challenge, every struggle, was seen in this light. This prophetic vision – foreseeing the future through the eyes of God – grounded their faith and hope in the imperfect present, and gave them a profound and convicting sense of eternal purpose that propelled them forward to do amazing exploits.

The questions that the pioneers asked themselves in the late nineteenth and early twentieth century, and, then, answered to their own satisfaction, were raised and answered again by succeeding generations. Granted, this on occasion caused a division, for it left no alternative to those who desired to remain faithful to the prophetic vision as originally understood and to underlying principles laid down by Christ. When a division happened, the faithful felt that they were fulfilling the apostle Paul's expectation in 1 Cor. 11.19: 'For there must be also heresies among you, that they which are approved may be made manifest among you'. Heresies and divisions therefore did nothing to diminish their confidence in their restoration work, but rather solidified their faith and sense of divine approval.

The essential questions – What is the church? What are the nature and characteristics of its government? How is the church formed? When did it begin? What is its mission? What is its end? What is the church's relationship to the kingdom of God? What are its basic and most important teachings? – had to be answered by each restoration remnant; but, amazingly, there remained a remarkable unity of thought and purpose in each remnant. It is true that each restoration brought added light and illumination that required certain existing practices and institutions to be modified or qualified, and sometimes new institutions had to be added to increase and perfect the government of the church, but these all worked together in moving the bride closer to her wedding day. What remained identical and constant in each faithful restoration of the church was the original spirit of the fellowship – which was centered in divine love – and the original understanding and vision of the church, particularly the unique perception that the word *church* signifies 'God's government on earth'.

These original principles in turn included the following premises that remained constant and unchanged: a) the church is visible and corporate; b) the church is composed of men and women who profess faith in Christ, and who manifest the fruit of the new birth; notwithstanding, however, that the church in its present imperfect and incomplete stage is spotted with some backsliders and 'false brethren brought in unawares'; c) the church is formed visibly and corporately by a church covenant; d) the church is distinct from the kingdom of God; e) the church is empowered to act for and with Christ in this present age until He returns; f) the Bible is the church's supreme objective authority and the final rule for faith and practice; g) the church's form of government is 'theocratic' in nature, which by definition signifies that the manifest approval of the Holy Spirit is necessary to authenticate the church's acts of business, including biblical interpretation; h) the church is ecumenical in its ministries and aims and therefore anticipates the union of all believers in one visible body of Christ; i) the church will finally adorn the wedding garment and be presented to Christ glorious in holiness.

The same questions that the fathers raised in the late nineteenth- and early twentieth century were raised again in recent years, and again answered to the satisfaction of those who reorganized the church in April 2004 under the name, Zion Assembly Church of God. This fellowship embodies the spirit of the pioneers and is fully committed to the basic principles of the original vision and mission of the church; hence the title of this book, *Quest to Restore God's House*. This theme attempts to capture the passion and vision that drove the several generations of ministers and members of this great tradition of faith. It moved each restoration remnant to consider afresh the principles and teachings of Christ and the apostles, and to rededicate itself to conform to the model of the exalted church revealed in prophecy. This has been the essential force behind the sacrifices and accomplishments, the passionate periods of dissent, the several restorations, and the spiritual struggle to keep the church truly apostolic and catholic (universal).

VI

Finally, our aim in this history is primarily three-fold: *First*, to identify and set forth the core principles upon which the church's founding fathers in the late nineteenth- and early twentieth century established the church; *second*, to identify these core principles in each successive generation of the church; *third*, to re-capture the prophetic vision of the church that impassioned the church's illustrious fathers and mothers to restore God's house – a vision that first poured forth from the pens and divine utterances of 'holy men of old' and which was revealed thereafter more fully to the New Testament apostles. David, Solomon, Isaiah, Peter, Paul, John and almost every prophet and apostle who were moved by the

Holy Ghost to write Holy Scripture had something to say of the church's exalted position in God's eternal plan.

> Glorious things are spoken of you, O city of God … The Lord loves the gates of Zion more than all the dwellings of Jacob (Ps. 87.3).

> My dove, my undefiled is but one; she is the only one of her mother, she is the choice one of her that bare her … who is she that looks forth as the morning, fair as the moon, clear as the sun, and terrible as an army with banners (Song 6.9, 10).

> Upon Your right hand did stand the queen [church] in gold of Ophir … So shall the king greatly desire your beauty: for he is your Lord … the king's daughter [church] is all glorious within: her clothing is of wrought gold … The virgins her companions … shall be brought unto you … They shall enter into the king's palace (Ps. 45.6-15).

> Arise, shine; for your light is come, and the glory of the Lord is risen upon you. For, behold, the darkness shall cover the earth, and gross darkness the people: but the Lord shall arise upon you, and his glory shall be seen upon you. And the Gentiles shall come to your light, and kings to the brightness of your rising. Lift up your eyes round about, and see: all they gather themselves together, they come to you … then you shall see, and flow together, and your heart shall be enlarged; because the abundance of the sea shall be converted unto you, the forces of the Gentiles shall come to you (Isa. 60.1-5).

> Let us be glad and rejoice, and give honor to him: for the marriage of the Lamb is come, and his wife has made herself ready. And to her was granted that she should be arrayed in fine linen, clean and white: for the fine linen is the righteousness of the saints (Rev. 19.7, 8).

These passages and a hundred more like them excited and filled with joy the hearts of our pioneers, for they opened to them the prophetic vision of the Bible church, revealing her incomparable beauty, majestic stature, and noble mission. More thrillingly, these same passages revealed to them the church's victorious conclusion – a perfected bride *caught up* to heaven by God's miraculous power – an exaltation that includes participation in 'the marriage supper of the Lamb'; the honor of returning to earth with Christ following the Great Tribulation to rule and reign with Him for a thousand years; and finally the honor of everlasting glory!

This triumphant and glorious vision of the church in biblical prophecy was the impetus that drove the Church of God's illustrious fathers and mothers to seek so passionately to identify with 'the vision'.

> And the Lord answered me, and said, Write the vision, and make it plain upon the tables, that he may run that reads it. For the vision is yet for an appointed time, but at the end it shall speak, and not lie: though it tarry, wait for it; because it will surely come . . . (Hab. 2.2, 3).

They saw themselves as having entered into this prophetic vision. This is why they so readily deprived themselves of the comforts of life and subjected themselves to ridicule and persecution. Like faithful Abraham, 'they went out, not knowing whither [they] went' on a quest to understand and restore the church of the Bible. 'The vision' drew them together to form one visible body of Christ, embodying one faith and one government. It inspired them to go forth in flaming zeal to proclaim the Gospel of regenerating grace, second-work sanctification, Spirit-baptism, the power of perfect love, practical holiness, and one church – one government and discipline – for all of God's people.

Finally, we hope, through this account of the church's militant history, to excite in our readers a contagious zeal to fulfill the mission of the church in this world – to complete what our illustrious fathers and mothers set out to do more than 125 years ago.

> Oh, may some wise and noble one
> Complete the work we have begun
> Oh, may it catch on every pen
> And trace the isles from end to end,
> And turn each foe into a friend
> And into one God's children blend.
> – R.G. Spurling[4]

---

[4] R.G. Spurling, *The Lost Link* (Turtletown, TN: self-published, 1920), p. 51.

Acknowledgments

This history of the Church of God is the result of more than 35 years of research and collecting of a vast amount of historical materials. Along the way, literally hundreds of people have assisted me in this endeavor, the great majority of whom must remain nameless here because of space and time limitations. Still, I wish to express my gratitude to anyone who may have contributed in some way to make this history possible.

Several of my co-workers in Zion Assembly have been especially helpful, not the least of these is my secretary, Marie (Spurling) Crook. She, not insignificantly, is the great granddaughter of R.G. Spurling. Marie assisted me for more than twenty years in researching and collecting materials, and spent many hours and months typing and retyping the manuscript. Her background among the Baptists in the mountains opened several doors that otherwise would have remained closed to outsiders – particularly to Church of God scholars. In some ways, I consider her the co-author of this work. Miss Wanda K. Busbee, an instructor in our School of Ministry, spent many hours proofreading the manuscript and offering helpful suggestions in regard to grammar and literary construction. The Assistant Presiding Bishop of Zion Assembly, E.A. McDonald, served as a sounding board for many of the historical and theological interpretations in this history, and encouraged me to pursue the task. Hundreds of other pastors and co-workers in Zion Assembly also encouraged me. Among these, several read portions of the manuscript and offered helpful comments, including Bruce Sullivan, L.W. Carter, and William R. 'Bill' James.

Outside of Zion Assembly, several friends and colleagues encouraged me to pursue this challenging task. Not the least of these are my colleagues in the Pentecostal Theological Seminary in Cleveland, Tennessee, particularly Dr. James M. Beaty, Dr. David G. Roebuck, Dr. John Christopher Thomas, and Dr. Lee Roy Martin; the latter three of whom read the manuscript and offered many helpful suggestions. Dr. Roebuck and I, fellow historians, have spent many hours exploring ideas and thoughts connected with our common heritage in the Church of God tradition. Dr. Roebuck is also the director of the Hal Bernard Dixon Jr.

Pentecostal Research Center in Cleveland, and was most gracious in making available many valuable source materials.

Dr. Vinson Synan and Dr. Stanley M. Burgess encouraged me to write this history while I was pursuing a PhD at Regent University under their supervision; and my good friend, Dr. Stan York, archivist for the International Pentecostal Holiness Church [Cornerstone Conference in North Carolina], also spurred me on to write this history. Scores of ministers and friends in the Baptist churches in the mountains of Tennessee, Georgia, and North Carolina, where much of this early history took place, also encouraged me to write this history and have patiently waited for it to appear in print.

I want to express here my gratitude to my wife, Dale, for her encouragement and patience. In a sense, she lived through this history; for often I brought the history home with me and she was forced to listen as I explained my interpretation on some new discovery. She also traveled with me to visit many of the people interviewed for this history, and walked with me through a large number of cemeteries to discover the whereabouts and birth and death dates of some of our illustrious pioneers.

Finally, I want to dedicate this history to the memory of my beloved son, Vincent Wade. The Lord saw fit in His great love and wisdom to take Vince home to be with Him in August 1993 while on his honeymoon in Cancun, Mexico. Vince had assisted me just a few months earlier in some of the research I had been doing in Morgan and Anderson Counties in Tennessee. I still recall vividly the joy we shared when we discovered the minutes of the Union and Clear Creek Baptist churches that were so revealing of Richard Spurling's life and ministry in the 1850s. On another occasion a few days later, he helped me to discover the newspaper article in the *Clinton Gazette* that reported Richard's death.

Wade H. Phillips

ABBREVIATIONS

AF	*The Apostolic Faith*
COGE	*The Church of God Evangel*
COGPH	Church of God Publishing House
FBHA	The Fire-Baptized Holiness Association of America
FS	*The Faithful Standard*
GAM	*Minutes of the Church of God General Assembly*
HAA	*Historical Annual Addresses* (3 Vols.; Cleveland, TN: White Wing Publishing House, 1971)
LCF	*Live Coals of Fire*
LGC	A.J. Tomlinson, *The Last Great Conflict*
PHA	*The Pentecostal Holiness Advocate*
TBM	*The Bridegroom's Messenger*
WHPC	Wade H. Phillips Collection
WWM	*White Wing Messenger*
WWPH	White Wing Publishing House
ZACG	Zion Assembly Church of God Archives

INTRODUCTION

In the latter half of the nineteenth century, ancient prophecies that foretold of a restoration of God's church still remained hidden from the understanding of common churchmen and run-of-the-mill church members. What Paul had said of natural Israel – that 'blindness in part is happened to Israel' – was a fitting description of the majority of Christians in the late nineteenth century in regard to the subject of the church. They lacked spiritual insight into its mystery, and thus what 'in other ages was not made known to the sons of men' still remained unknown to them. They had not entered into the full apostolic revelation of the church and, consequently, remained on the outside of the 'fellowship of the mystery' (Eph. 3.5-10).

But there were wide-awake saints whom God was illuminating, and to whom His plan for the end-times was unfolding. These chosen vessels believed that the fulfillment of the inspired prophecies that foretold of the church's restoration was near at hand; and they were waiting expectantly for the Lord's Zion to make her appearance again in the last days. Like Anna and Simeon in the New Testament, they 'looked for redemption in Jerusalem and waited for the consolation of Israel'. They could see Zechariah's prophecy of 'that day' upon the horizon, a time in which the Dark Ages would give way to the 'evening light' (Zech. 14.6, 7). These sons and daughters of Jehovah believed the 'evening time' of church history was upon them: a time in which the church – the government of God in the earth – would be restored, and the 'perfection of beauty' would shine out from the 'Zion of the Holy One' (Ps. 50.3; Isa. 60.14). Like the souls under the altar in the apostle's vision, they cried out, 'How long, O Lord?'

Nowhere was the hope and spirit of restoration more alive and expected than in America, for America was considered the 'New World' where one might make a new start in life, but also where utopian ideals might become reality and the church itself might be born anew. Quakers and Anabaptists poured into America for this very reason: to witness and to participate in the 'restitution of all things' (Acts 3.21). In general, Americans saw nothing but totalitarian tyrannies and religious corruption by kings and popes through the centuries of European and English rule, and thus longed for a religious as well as a political revolution. Drawing on biblical images, they saw Europe as their 'Egypt', the Atlantic Ocean as their 'Red Sea', and America as their 'Promised Land'.[1]

The American people as a whole were given to the restoration impulse. Statesmen, no less than radical churchmen, tended to skip over the previous two millennia of Europe's king-pope systems of government to establish their new nation upon the more ancient foundations of Greco-Roman republican ideals – ideals tempered, however, by the Judeo-Christian tradition, particularly the theocratic ideal of Israel in the Old Testament. General Washington, 'Father of Our Nation' – was perceived by many Americans as a modern Moses leading God's people out of British bondage and darkness into the light and freedom of the New World. During the Civil War, popular opinion cast President Lincoln as the savior of the nation. His words at Gettysburg – 'that this nation, shall have a new birth of freedom, and that government of the people by the people for the people, shall not perish from the earth' – immortalized his image in the minds of succeeding generations. In time, most Americans, north and south, saw Lincoln as the 'Great Emancipator' and savior of the nation. Indeed, the biblical images thrown over his life were nearly endless. Even his name, *Abraham*, was of divine origin, signifying 'the father of a multitude' or 'father of a nation'. And he himself could not have planned his death more dramatically, nor with more imagery and profound significance than being assassinated on Good Friday, April 14, 1865. Thus, his name and his message – 'a new birth of freedom' – captured the imagination of the American people, promising hope and deliverance to the 'teeming multitudes' coming to the 'land of the free and home of the brave'.

Lincoln's promises and prophetic expectations meant as much or more to radical-minded Christians as they did to slaves in the South, for their fathers had fled the Old World to come to the New for that very purpose – to worship God freely and to practice their faith and discipline without being hindered or encumbered by the state. Lincoln's new America – America on this side of the Civil War – promised to be truer to the Christian principles the Founders had articulated in the eighteenth

---

[1] Wade H. Phillips, *The Church of God: In the Light and Shadow of America* (unpublished manuscript, 1991), pp. 9-43. This manuscript may be obtained from International Offices of Zion Assembly Church of God, P.O. Box 2398, Cleveland, Tennessee 37320-2398.

century. There was therefore among the poor and disenfranchised a certain optimism and hopeful expectation, namely, that finally America's political creed – 'that all men are created equal and endowed by their Creator with certain unalienable rights' – would actually be lived out indiscriminately.

The Puritan ideal of a 'City Upon a Hill' had planted itself deeply in the American psyche and was as alive in 1900 as it was in 1630 when John Winthrop preached his 'Modell of Christian Charity' on board the *Arbella* en route to Massachusetts Bay. The Pilgrims at Plymouth ten years earlier, no less than the Puritans, had also envisioned the City of God in America: though, unlike the Puritans, they were Separatists and endeavored to restore a fallen church rather than to purify an existing one.

Notwithstanding their religious and political differences, Americans on the whole believed they were in the act of creating a 'new world', and so worked together toward that end. But the very soul of American society was overwhelmingly Christian, and the most determined and zealous Christians were of the radical stripe – men and women who were willing to fight and die, if necessary, for democratic freedoms, both civil and religious. There were reasons to criticize the extreme democratic idealism upon which America was founded, to be sure, as Alexis de Tocqueville did in his celebrated *Democracy in America* published in 1835-1840; but that idealism nevertheless explains in large measure why America developed as a 'nation with the soul of a church'.[2]

Radical Christians were passionate about restoring and imitating apostolic Christianity. They believed that Roman Catholicism and the Protestant reaction against Rome in the sixteenth century, which resulted in the church-state systems that dominated and governed life in Europe and England thereafter, had been established more on the authority of the early church Fathers than the inspired Scriptures, and, consequently, a disconnect existed between the primitive church in the New Testament and the religion of the 'Dark Ages'. In fact, Americans overwhelmingly considered Dark Age religion – particularly Roman Catholicism – to be apostate. The cry of radical churchmen was 'Forget the Fathers, give us the Grandfathers!' and 'Back to the Apostles!' Some said the so-called Church Fathers should be called rather 'Church Infants'. Typical of these groups were Quakers, Anabaptists, Mennonites, some

---

[2] Perry C. Cotham, *Politics, Americanism, and Christianity* (Grand Rapids: Baker, 1976), pp. 27-32; Phillips, *The Church of God: In the Light and Shadow of America*, pp. 8-42.

Baptist groups, Alexander Campbell and his followers (the 'Disciples'), and 'Mormons' (Church of Jesus Christ of the Latter Days Saints).

The restoration impulse was in fact a distinct mark of radical Christianity in America. Even Presbyterians, Puritans, and Congregationalists, though seeking to purge and purify an existing church (first the Roman, then the Anglican), were inclined toward a restoration vision. Somehow the contrasting ideas of restoring and purifying were more or less confused in the larger context of the American Dream. Thus mainline Protestants used biblical passages in both Old and New Testaments almost as readily as radical reformers to support a restoration view of the church in prophecy and history.

The Puritan postmillennial interpretation of prophecy prompted expectations of an imminent 'Golden Age' to begin in America. Jonathan Edwards in his sermon – 'The Latter Day Glory is Probably to Begin in America' – reasoned that as the Old World was given the honor of Christ's first advent, the New World would probably be honored with His second advent. He reasoned that the path of God's providential favor seemed to be unfolding through history from east to west, corresponding to the rising and setting of the sun. He cited the prophet's words in Isa. 59.19 to support his view – 'So shall they fear the name of the Lord from the west, and his glory from the rising of the sun'.[3] Malachi's view of Christ as the 'Sun of righteousness [arising] with healing in his wings' also fit well with his vision of God's unfolding scheme for the last days. Thus the rays of God's light, according to Edwards, shined first in Bethlehem; then emanated its rays to Judea and Palestine; thence to Greece, Rome, and all of Europe; thence to the British Isles; and finally the full Gospel light had burst on the scene in the New England colonies in the eighteenth century. Further, believers could rest assured on the basis of God's immutable decree that the brilliance of this noon-day Sun would not set until the whole American continent was covered with the Gospel's penetrating power. Only then should believers expect Christ's return to earth.[4]

At the heart of restoration theology, then and now, is the belief that the church may die and be restored to life again. Accordingly, this idea is one of the important aspects about the *mystery* of the church. Just as

---

[3] Jonathan Edwards, 'The Latter Day Glory Is Probably to Begin in America', in Conrad Cherry, *God's New Israel: Religious Interpretations of American Destiny* (Englewood Cliff, NJ: Prentice-Hall, 1971), pp. 55-59.

[4] Jonathan Edwards, *The Works of Jonathan Edwards* (2 Vols.; Carlisle, PA: The Banner of Truth Trust, 1987), II, pp. 283-90.

God can quicken one sinner to life, so He can restore a whole body of 'dry bones' and cause them to live again.

> And he said unto me, Son of man can these bones live? ... Prophesy unto these bones, and say unto them, O dry bones, hear the word of the Lord ... Behold I will cause breath to enter into you, and you shall live ... and the breath came into them, and they lived, and stood upon their feet, an exceeding great army ... these bones are the whole house of Israel (Ezek. 37.3-11).

It is true that this prophetic passage foretold of the imminent restoration of ancient Israel in Jerusalem following the Babylonian Captivity, but it also envisioned a more far-reaching fulfillment in the last days – a restoration of the New Testament church following a fall after the apostles and prophets had passed off the scene (Isa. 60.2; Acts 20.29-31; 2 Pet. 2; Jude 3, 4; Rev. 2.5; *et al.*). Who will deny that the Lord in an instant can establish a whole nation, and if that nation turns from God, may just as readily destroy it; and if it repents, He can just as easily plant it and build it up again (Jer. 18.7; Mt. 21.43)? He can break off branches from the Vine, and just as readily graft them in again (Rom. 11.19-24).

Like Christ, the church was born when 'the fullness of time was come' (Gal. 4.4; and compare Hab. 2.3), and again, like her Head, the church died and was buried and came forth from the grave of the Dark Ages (Isa. 60.1-3). And there is nothing preventing this pattern from being repeated. During her earthly pilgrimage the church has in fact on several occasions fallen and has had to be restored and has had to be built up again out of the ruins of its destruction. 'Thou shalt arise, and have favor upon Zion: for the time to favor her, yea, the set time, is come. For thy servants take pleasure in her stones, and favor the dust thereof' (Ps. 102.13, 14; Acts 3.21; Gal. 3.1-3; 4.19; Rev. 2.5). Much in the manner of the Shulamite woman in Solomon's love song who had gone away and then returned, the church, 'being predestinated according to the purpose of him who works all things after the counsel of his own will', was bound by God's foreordained purpose to answer the irresistible voice of the Bridegroom and the wedding guests echoing down through the corridors of time, crying, 'Return, return, O Shulamite; return, return, that we may look upon thee' (Song 6.13; see also Ps. 45.9-14; Mt. 25.6-10).[5]

Consistent with their restoration view of the church, the Church of God's fathers interpreted Solomon's phrase, 'As it were the company of

---

[5] A.J. Tomlinson, *The Last Great Conflict* (Cleveland, TN: Press of Walter E. Rogers, 1913), p. 161.

two armies', to signify the early church before the 'falling away' and her return in the last days. The 'two armies' – the early church and the restored church – were seen through the eyes of prophecy therefore as 'one company' that would be perfected in the endtimes and caught up in heavenly glory (1 Thess. 4.16, 17). Again, it was thought that the two armies might be an allusion to the Old Testament church (Jews) and the New Testament church (Gentiles) dancing together joyously in Pentecostal power and forming together 'one body' in Christ (Eph. 2.11-19; 3.6); for so the Hebrew word, *Mehanaim* [translated 'company' in Song 6.13] seems to indicate. If this be the prophet's meaning, it would be a fitting picture, for when David was delivered he exclaimed, 'Thou hast turned my mourning into dancing ... and girded me with gladness' (Ps. 30.11). Whatever more that may be implied in this cryptic phrase, the Shulamite without question prefigures the bride of Christ of whom the prophet wrote, saying, 'Who is she that looks forth as the morning, fair as the moon, clear as the sun, and terrible as an army with banners?' (Song 6.10).

1

BAPTIST ROOTS: 1755-1883

One of many mistakes that historians and scholars have made in telling the story of the Cleveland-centered Church of God has been to ignore or else to underestimate the fact that the founding fathers had been zealous Baptists, and that the Baptist tradition had a significant influence on the church's origin and early development. Many observers have assumed that because the Church of God metamorphosed into a holiness-Pentecostal body within twelve years of its birth and thereafter remained firmly fixed in that tradition, that it had originated in the Wesleyan-holiness tradition. But the fact remains that the church was conceived in a Baptist womb and came forth with distinct Baptist characteristics. It is not too much to say, in fact, that the establishment of the Church of God in 1886 was in one sense a reformation of a Baptist denomination, namely, the Missionary [Landmark] Baptist tradition, for almost all of the founding fathers were Landmark Baptists.

The Landmark influence may be seen especially in regard to the founding fathers' preoccupation with ecclesiological (church-related) themes. Thus, contrary to popular opinion, the Church of God's fathers were not focused at first on salvation themes, but rather on church-related themes. What they were seeking to understand was the biblical basis for Christian fellowship, both in regard to the local church and the universal church: for their deep roots in the Baptist tradition had already convinced them that the Bible church is visible: what remained was to reconcile the Baptist concept of local church independence with God's plan that plainly calls for the unity of all of God's people in one visible body (Song 6.8-10; Jn 10.16; 11.49-52; 17.20-23; Eph. 2.11-19; 4.4-6, 11-16).

This ecumenical vision weighed heavily upon the founding fathers of the Church of God, driving them to the Word of God and prayer for answers. But the burden of the vision, indeed the vision itself, was conceived at first about the year 1884 in the heart of a young Baptist preacher who was then living in the backwoods of the Unicoi Mountains in lower East Tennessee.[1] His name was Richard Green ('R.G'.) Spurling (1857-1935). It would be two years, however, before the mystery of God's church and the idea of Christian Union would unfold in his mind, and before he would understand what he was to do.

One Born Out of Due Time

Like many of the prophets of old, R.G. Spurling was a most unlikely prospect to fulfill such a high calling and noble purpose. In some ways he reminds us of David, for he was the youngest son of his father, and as such was overlooked by the elders and his brethren for the special role that God had ordained him to fulfill. But, unlike man, God looks on the heart rather than the outward appearance (1 Sam. 16.7) and saw in Spurling certain traits that He qualified by His grace and that he anointed to make him a leader of His people. Like David, Spurling proved to be 'a man after God's own heart', a chosen vessel to serve His eternal purpose – a man who loved 'the gates of Zion' and desired to rebuild the City of God. What David had said of Christ in a prophecy – 'The zeal of Your house has eaten me up' – could as well have been said of this young Baptist preacher.

Spurling was, like the apostle Paul, 'as one born out of due time'. A comparatively unknown 'prophet' with no formal education, he had little to commend him in the way of worldly preparation for the high calling of God that came upon him about the year 1877.[2] He could barely read and write, his parents being able to give him only about 'a month's schooling in "65"'.[3] Notwithstanding his lack of 'book learning', his father taught him in the ways of the Lord according to the faith and practices of the Baptist tradition, and, moreover, being an expert millwright and farmer gave him a valuable education in the skills of farming and building of sawmills and gristmills, trades that the young man readily applied to provide a living for his family and to help rebuild God's house. These skills were enhanced all the more by his personal ingenuity

---

[1] Tomlinson, *LGC*, p. 205.
[2] Spurling says in the original draft of *The Lost Link* that he had been preaching for '7 years' when he took his stand in 1884. The original hand-written draft of *The Lost Link* has within it a great deal of insight into Spurling's theology that was never published. The original manuscript will hereafter be cited as *Lost Link* [original].
[3] Spurling, *Lost Link* [original], p. 10.

and practical know-how which made him an efficient farmer and millwright. He even designed and constructed his own water turbine to turn his millstones, dispensing with the old water wheel that had made his millhouse operations cumbersome and less efficient.

Ironically, however, his remarkable skills and love of farming tended to distract him from his ministry. He admitted in later years that temporal interests had competed for his affections, and that too often his God-given gifts and talents had been 'buried in the earth' rather than spent on the more important call of God upon his life. Toward the end of his life, he gave instructions to his wife and children to bury him facing west toward the old home place, rather than east as the custom was: thus signifying his regrets for allowing earthly things to consume too much of his time.[4] Still, there was more in him to commend than to criticize. In spite of his shortcomings, God had shared His secret with him and raised him up to serve His eternal purpose.

Spurling grew up during the Reconstruction Period in the aftermath of the Civil War, being only seven years of age when Lee surrendered to Grant at Appomattox in April 1865. The deprivations and restrictions caused by the war, and the remoteness of his childhood home, located deep in the southern Appalachian Mountains, made life difficult for him. Adding more hardships to his already difficult situation, his father's health was broken during the war, and the burden of the family farm fell mainly upon him. Fortunately, he was gifted with a strong physical frame that made him equal to the task.[5] His circumstances forced him to grow up quickly and to bear the burden of manhood before his time. It is not surprising, then, that his demeanor was sober and his disposition much advanced for his years. Adversity had caused him to look to God for strength and comfort, and conditioned him with a robust sense of responsibility to fulfill the divine task laid upon him. He learned to master the trying circumstances of life and to overcome difficult obstacles thrown in his way; indeed, the adversities and challenges of life enabled him to achieve 'a far more exceeding and eternal weight of glory'.

---

[4] Interview, Allie Ledford, April 1995. Mrs. Ledford was the granddaughter of R.G. Spurling and lived with her grandparents until she was married at nineteen years of age. She was an outstanding Christian woman with an impeccable reputation. The record of her testimony is therefore highly credible. The story of Spurling's dying wishes is further confirmed by the situation of his grave in Turtletown, Tennessee: in contrast with the custom of being buried facing east, his headstone faces northwest toward his old home-place.

[5] The reputation for great physical strength that he and his brother Hiram had established as young men in the counties in which they lived (Monroe, Polk, and Scott counties in Tennessee) still lingered in the 1970s in the minds of eyewitnesses who had known them.

Spurling was saved when he was about twelve years of age and joined the Baptist church.⁶ Even before he was converted, he had expressed as a small boy a desire to serve God, and had shown a marked interest in church work.⁷ His parents and friends believed that God's hand was upon him to do a special work in His name, particularly because soon after his birth he had become deathly ill and was miraculously restored to life. In his brief autobiographical sketch, Spurling notes that the 'cold hand of death had taken hold of my tiny frame and soon life seemed to be entirely gone'.⁸ His poem written in 1897 dramatizes the scene:

> It was back before my memory's day,
> Before I'd even learned how to play,
> There on my infant bed,
> Which mother for her child did spread.
> There fearless of the doom of death,
> I yielded up my infant breath;
> My mother saw my awful doom,
> And for to weep she left the room.
> She sat down to weep and cry,
> Because she'd seen her infant die;
> But father lingered near the place,
> To gaze upon my pale white face.
> Then moved his hand with mournful sighs,
> And closed his little namesake's eyes;
> But God who all His purpose knew,
> Had something good that I might do.
> His gospel truths to unfold,
> Returned to me my little soul;

---

⁶ G.P. (Pinckney) Spurling (1877-1968) wrote a rough sketch of his father's life and ministry. This untitled sketch will hereafter be referred to as, *A Sketch of the Life and Ministry of R.G. Spurling* (Zion Assembly Church of God Archives hereafter will be noted as: ZACG Archives). Since Pinckney was born in 1877, he was an eyewitness to his family's early transitions and the events in his father's early ministry including the organization of Christian Union in 1886. Without this rough draft of only a few pages, many of the details and accomplishments in R.G. Spurling's ministry during this period would have been buried in oblivion, including his age at the time of his conversion and the year that he joined the Baptist church. There are some miscalculation of dates and a few facts that are blurred, but the events and other data in Pinckney's *Sketch* are otherwise consistent with county court records, marriages licenses, deed records, judicial records, death records, tax receipts, census records, eyewitness accounts, and Baptist church minutes, the latter of which show that most of the members of Christian Union had been Landmark Baptists.

⁷ Pinckney, *Sketch*, p. 1.

⁸ Spurling, *Lost Link*, pp. 45, 46

> Oh! may I all His truths proclaim,
> In honor to His glorious name.[9]
> – R.G. Spurling

Convinced of a divine purpose and destiny for his life, he applied himself diligently to the study of the Scriptures, and, in spite of his limited ability to read and write, boasted in God that eventually he was 'able to be counted a Bible scholar'.[10] His lack of formal education, moreover, did nothing to diminish his remarkable ability spiritually to discern truth and to think his way through complex theological issues and difficult situations. We see in him a little of Abraham Lincoln in this regard: he was self-educated, self-made, and a deep thinker. Though he was neither flamboyant, charismatic, nor striking in his physical appearance, yet he somehow captured the attention of a great many people who heard him teach and preach. His attraction was primarily in the content of his message and his vision of God's church. Like his Lord, 'he [had] no form nor comeliness ... that we should desire him; but the people were astonished at his doctrine'. We see in Spurling also vague impressions of Zerubbabel, Ezra, and Nehemiah – men raised up by the Lord and providentially prepared to bring God's people out of 'Babylon' and back to 'Jerusalem' to restore His house and rebuild the city of God. Reflecting on Spurling's life and ministry, we see no finer illustration of how God in His infinite wisdom '[chooses] the weak things of the world to confound the things which are mighty'.

Before we move on to Spurling's call into the ministry and the events that led to the restoration of the church, we should look a little deeper into his religious background, for the church he established in 1886 – Christian Union – was both a reaction against his Baptist tradition and at the same time a perpetuation of some of the central features of that tradition.

Baptist Heritage

Spurling's father, Richard (1810-1891), was an ordained minister in the Missionary Baptist church.[11] His grandfather, James (1769-1860), and at

---

[9] Spurling, *Lost Link*, p. 46
[10] Spurling, *Lost Link* [original], p. 10
[11] Tomlinson, *LGC*, p. 205. Tomlinson is careful to distinguish R.G. Spurling's status as a licensed minister from his father's status as an ordained minister. See also Spurling, *Lost Link*, pp. 10, 48. He is also careful to distinguish Richard Spurling from his son, Richard Green Spurling, the latter's middle name, Green, being given to him in honor of his maternal grandmother's family.

least three of his grandfather's thirteen brothers – Isaac, Elijah, Jeremiah – were also staunch Baptists[12] There are indications also that his great-grandfather, John (ca. 1738-1822), may have been a Baptist. We see then that his Baptist roots in America ran deep, extending into America's colonial period.

The Spurlings' interest in and zeal for the Christian faith were forged by the lingering influence of the First Great Awakening in the latter half of eighteenth century. R.G. Spurling's grandfather actually lived through the wave of the Second Great Awakening in 1790-1820 in North Carolina and Tennessee, and his father experienced its powerful influence as a child. Being zealous Baptists, his father and grandfather were therefore part of the significant Baptist influence that established the government and basic freedoms of the United States.

Baptists had in fact contributed immensely to the establishment of America. The story of Roger Williams in Rhode Island in the seventeenth century is well known, as well as the contributions of many other Baptists in the eighteenth century, including Separate Baptist pastors, Isaac Backus (1724-1806) and John Leland (1754-1841), both of whom were champions of religious freedom in America. These two ministers were architects of the principle of separation of church and state, having had a significance influence on the thinking of Thomas Jefferson and James Madison and the outcome of the Constitutional Convention in Philadelphia in 1787 as well as influencing and contributing to the content and adoption of the Bill of Rights in 1789.[13]

Regulars, Separates, and United Baptists

More strictly defined, the Spurlings were at first Separate Baptists, becoming United Baptists when Regulars and Separates merged in the late

---

[12] Wade H. Phillips, 'Richard Spurling and the Baptist Roots of the Church of God', paper presented to the Society of Pentecostal Studies, Guadalajara, Mexico, 1993, pp. 5-16; Phillips, *The Church of God: In the Light and Shadow of America*, pp. 28-32. The research of Larry, Ken, Norman, and Eleanor Spurling on their ancestors were helpful here, particularly the rough draft written and compiled by Norman Spurling ('Spurling and Sperling Family History: Virginia, North Carolina and Elsewhere') and the unpublished manuscript of Larry Spurling (*Spurling Family History: Their Life and Religion*). My own research, however, led to many significant discoveries showing the Spurlings' migrations and settlements on the frontier and other pertinent details regarding their religious roots, faith, philosophy, culture, and personal history.

[13] For a concise and excellent view of the Baptist contribution in the formation of religious and personal freedoms in America, see H. Leon McBeth, *The Baptist Heritage* (Nashville: Boardman Press, 1987), pp. 252-83.

1700s and early 1800s in Virginia, North Carolina, Kentucky, Tennessee, and along the northern border of South Carolina. The unification of these sub-species of Baptists was complete by about 1825.[14] These sects had argued with each other for years over doctrinal differences and church practices. Regulars ('Particulars' or 'Orthodox') were more strictly Calvinistic, creedal, and composed emotionally; whereas, Separates tended to be Arminian (or at least moderately Calvinistic), anti-creedal, revivalistic, and more free and emotional in worship. Separates also exhibited many characteristics that would later be identified with holiness-Pentecostalism: shouting, dancing, and falling to the ground under the power of the Spirit were not uncommon in their meetings. They observed the practice of footwashing, considering it to be a divine ordinance; laid hands on the sick and anointed with oil; encouraged plain dress, and discouraged the wearing of jewelry and make-up; and, though wanting the theological formula of the Wesleyan doctrine, they virtually taught and experienced entire sanctification.

United Baptists thus stood about mid-way between traditional Regulars and Separates, or between Calvinism and Arminianism. They were Arminian particularly in the sense of believing in a general atonement and in refusing to be bound too tightly to a creed. And although they agreed in their union with the Regulars to form Articles of Faith and Rules of Decorum for government and practice similar to the Regulars' tradition, they were emphatic in stressing that the Articles and Rules were not to be imposed dogmatically nor to be considered binding upon one's conscience. We give here the report of the General Committee of the Separates during the conciliatory meeting in 1787 that captures the conviction upon which Spurling would a hundred years later establish the Church of God:

> To prevent the confession of faith from usurping a tyrannical power over the conscience of any, we do not mean that every person is bound to the strict observance of everything therein contained; yet that it holds forth the essential truths of the gospel, and that the doctrine of salvation by Christ, and free and unmerited grace alone, ought to be believed by every Christian, and maintained by every minister of the gospel. Upon these terms we are united, and desire to hereafter, that the names of Regular and Separate be buried in obliv-

---

[14] For the best account of this historical development, see David Benedict, *A General History of the Baptist Denomination* (2 Vols.; Boston: Printed by Lincoln and Edmund, 1813); J.H. Spencer, *A History of the Kentucky Baptists* (2 Vols.; Cincinnati: J.R. Baurnes, 1885); and G.W. Paschal, *History of North Carolina Baptists* (2 Vols.; Raleigh, NC: Edwards and Broughton Co., 1930).

ion; and that from henceforth, we shall be known by the name of United Baptist Churches ...[15]

The Cumberland Mountains of southeastern Kentucky and northeastern Tennessee in the early 1800s was a stronghold for Separate Baptists These Baptists had their roots in western North Carolina in the 1750s under the leadership of one Shubal Stearns. It is almost certain that the Spurlings' Baptist roots extended to and perhaps began in the midst of the great revival initiated by Stearns in 1755 that spread from the Haw River in North Carolina to the Pee Dee River in South Carolina, a distance of about 60 miles (located east of the present-day city of Charlotte).[16] It is likely in fact that the Spurlings' Baptist heritage began in this famous revival. This is where John Spurling and his family lived and farmed (including his son James, the father of Richard Spurling) in the late eighteenth and early nineteenth century. This is where James met and married his wife Frances, and where four of his children were born. This great Separate Baptist revival swept thousands of families into its transforming power between 1755 and 1820, leaving scores of Separate Baptist churches in its path including those in the very vicinity where the Spurlings lived along Mountain River and Buffalo River.[17]

These same Baptists extended their revival west and became part and parcel of the great Camp Meeting revivals that set Baptists ablaze in the Green River Valley of Kentucky between 1800 and 1820, shooting burning ambers of revivalism into East Tennessee's Cumberland Mountains. In this region in the 1830s, Baptists were still shouting and quaking under the influence of the Spirit. The earliest Tennessee Baptists who formed the Holston Association in 1786 along the Holston River in the Knoxville region were the spiritual descendants of the original Separate Baptists from the Sandy Creek Association in North Carolina, even for a time putting themselves under the patronage and guidance of that body. Like most Baptists in the Cumberland Mountain region of Tennessee and Kentucky in the 1800s, these Baptists also observed footwashing and followed the missionary impulse.[18]

---

[15] Benedict, *History*, II, p. 62; Paschal, *History*, II, pp. 260-61. The Separates refused to be shackled with creeds, and for that same reason many did not unite with the Regulars on the United Baptist platform. The Spurlings did, however.

[16] See Morgan Edwards, *Materials Toward History of the Baptists*, pp. 91-97; Paschal, *History*, II, pp. 339-45.

[17] We are indebted to Larry R. Spurling, *Spurling Family History*, pp. 2-12, for his research in locating family deed records in Richmond and Lincoln counties.

[18] Cawthorn & Warnell, *Pioneer Baptist Church Records*, pp. 553-69; Benedict, *History*, II, pp. 214-18. The Holston Association Minutes shows that William Murphy in 1790 preached a missionary message from Mt. 28.19 ('Go ye therefore'). J.J.

Migration to East Tennessee

R.G. Spurling's ancestors rode the wave of Baptist migration from Lincoln County, North Carolina into East Tennessee in the early 1800s. This move was made apparently upon the death of his great grandfather, John, in 1822.[19] His father, Richard (then only a boy), and his grandfather, James, upon arriving with the family in Anderson County in the early 1820s immediately identified themselves with the churches in Tennessee that had their roots in the Sandy Creek Association in North Carolina. This move was only about forty years after the American Revolution and thirty years after Tennessee had become a state. The Spurlings (then spelled Spurlin) were apparently lured westward to the frontier by the prospects of cheap land and the excitement of the pioneer way of life, in addition to the call of God to spread the Gospel according to the Baptist interpretation of the faith.

When James moved his family from Anderson County to Fentress County in 1828, and then moved back in the 1840s to Morgan County (Morgan is situated between Fentress and Anderson Counties), his membership remained in United Baptist churches.[20] The Minutes of the Tennessee Association (whose mother was the Holston Association) show that he served as a delegate to the annual meeting from the New Salem church in Anderson County in 1825. Then, after moving to Fentress County, he and his family united with the Poplar Cove United Baptist church.[21] James served in 1832 as a delegate from the Poplar Cove

---

Burnett, *Sketches of Tennessee's Pioneer Baptist Preachers* (Nashville: Press of Marshall & Bruce Company, 1919), thus notes 'The Association was *missionary* from the beginning' (p. 563).

[19] We assume that Richard Spurling's grandfather died in 1822 since his will was attested that year; his father, James, then apparently migrated to East Tennessee after John's estate was settled. We know that he was in Tennessee by at least 1823 according to Baptist church records. In the 1830 Fentress County census record, a woman in her ninety-first year is listed in the Spurling household, which most likely was Richard's step-grandmother, Elizabeth. James and Frances apparently assumed responsibility for her upon the death of James' father, John, and perhaps according to his wishes.

[20] The Minutes of the several churches and Associations to which the Spurlings belonged between 1823 and 1891 have amazingly been preserved. See Ch. 1, notes 21-27 and Phillips, 'Baptist Roots', pp. 11-14.

[21] The Spurlings' migrations and whereabouts have been verified by the writer by property deed records, census records, marriage records, Baptist church minutes, and family records. For particular citations of these documents, see Phillips, 'Baptist Roots', pp. 5-16. Novella Cravens, great granddaughter of Richard's son, Nathan, worked in the local Fentress County library and was especially helpful to me in this area of my research, providing several documents verifying the location of the Spurlings' property and their arrival time in Fentress County.

church to the Stockton Valley Association.²² Interestingly this church had been constituted in 1822 with members from the old Wolf Fork church. Significantly, these churches along with the Wolf River church had battled with 'Campbellism' (Alexander Campbell's movement) through the 1830s and 1840s.

Figure 1

WOLF RIVER BAPTIST CHURCH

It is almost certain that Richard Spurling and his father and mother and siblings worshipped in this old log church house in the early 1830s. Spurling's church at Poplar Cove (later Clear Creek) was located just south about 5 miles from Wolf River, and both congregations belonged to the Stockton Valley Association. Richard's nephew, Lewis Spurling, moved back to this area after the Civil War and put his membership in this church. The clerk of this church, Everett Reagan, reported to the writer in 1995 that he believed this building was constructed in the late 1820s. The church was established in May 1821. This photo was at the time in the possession of Everett and his wife Bonnie at Byrdstown, Tennessee.

In 1838 the Poplar Cove church was dissolved apparently because of irregularities according to the rule of the Stockton Valley Association, and the faithful members were 'lettered off' to nearby churches.²³ The dissolution of the church may be explained in the context of the division

---

²² *Minutes of the Stockton Valley Association*, 1832.
²³ C.P. Cawthorn and N.L. Warnell, *Pioneer Baptist Church Records of South-Central Kentucky and the Upper Cumberlands of Tennessee 1799-1899* (published by authors, 1985; reprinted 1987 by Church History Research & Archives, Gallatin, TN) is helpful in its construction of the early history of the Baptist churches in Fentress County during this period. See particularly pp. 534-44.

at that time between 'missionaries' and 'primitives' or 'anti-missionaries'. The Stockton Valley Association had fallen at first under the influence of the anti-missionary element before recovering itself a few years later, whereas the Spurlings and it seems their pastor, Peter Reagan, were committed to the missionary position. Thus Reagan and the Poplar Cove church were said to have acted irregularly and illegally in several instances according to the anti-missionary position of the Stockton Valley Association. After the church was dissolved, it is difficult to know exactly what happened. Reagan apparently continued to report to the Association in behalf of a church called 'Clear Creek' which the Association said did not exist.[24] Reagan was finally dismissed as a disorderly minister.[25] Two churches seemed to have emerged out of the rubble of the Poplar Cove church – New Hope and Clear Creek. Reagan and the Spurlings had apparently formed a missionary church called Clear Creek which the Stockton Valley Association had refused to recognize.

About 1847 the Spurlings moved from Fentress County to Morgan County, a distance of about twenty-five miles. Here they became members of the newly organized Union United Baptist church.[26] In July 1852 they were dismissed with about twenty others in order to constitute the Clear Creek United Baptist Church.[27] These churches are still active today, located northwest and southeast of Wartburg, the county seat of Morgan County. The next year, 1853, the Clear Creek church and several other nearby churches became charter members of the Clinton Association of United Baptists. This new Association was formed out of

---

[24] Some further research may show a connection between the apparently mythological Clear Creek church in Fentress County and the Clear Creek church not far away in Morgan County, the latter of which the Spurlings helped to establish in 1852.

[25] *Minutes of the Stockton Valley Association*, 1844.

[26] The Union church was organized in November 1846. (*Union church Minutes*).

[27] The church was constituted on August 29, 1852. (*Clear Creek Church Minutes*). Besides the Clear Creek church records and minutes, I interviewed the oldest member of the church in 1992, Mrs. Greta Davis, then 86 years of age. Her grandfather was a charter member with the Spurlings. She was converted in the 1920s and recalled vividly the preaching and teaching that she received in those days. She said the people shouted and quaked under the power of the Spirit, and believed the Missionary Baptist church was the true bride of Christ. Alfred Agee and E.B. Walker constituted the presbytery to organize the Clear Creek church. Agee became the church's first pastor (*Clear Creek and Clinton Association minutes*). After Chesley H. Bootright had moved to Arkansas in 1849, Agee, Walker, and Joshua Frost were the most prominent and active ministers in the area. Frost was especially active in ordaining ministers in the Clinton Association. Agee must have had a great influence on Richard's son, James, for he named his first son, Richard Agee (b. 1857), reflecting the name of his father and his pastor, Alfred Agee.

the Northern Association of United Baptists.[28] The Northern Association was constituted in 1839 from the Powell Valley Association as a result of mission differences.[29] The Spurlings were thus identified as 'Missionary Baptists' from the beginning of the movement.

James Spurling's elder brother, Jeremiah, of Warren County, Georgia is listed as a subscriber in Benedict's *General History of the Baptist Denomination* published in 1813.[30] Jeremiah's subscription would have been taken by Benedict about 1810-1811. Most of the Baptists in this area of Georgia had migrated from North Carolina and also had their roots in the Sandy Creek Association. Thus, whereas Jeremiah and his family had migrated to Georgia, James and his family had migrated to East Tennessee. Hicks L. Spurling (ca. 1801-1879), Richard's older brother, whom we will meet again momentarily, was also a Baptist preacher living in northern Georgia in Murray County (not too distant from the Tennessee state line) with his family in the 1840s. He joined his father and brother in the move to Monroe County, Tennessee in the mid 1850s.

We have noticed that R.G. Spurling's grandfather, James, and his family brought with them from North Carolina the spirit of revivalism and missionary zeal that had characterized the Separate Baptists in that state in the late nineteenth century, and that many Separate Baptists had preceded them in coming to East Tennessee. Pastor Tidence Lane and his whole Separate Baptist congregation had migrated together from North Carolina and formed the first Baptist church in Tennessee in 1779,[31] seventeen years before Tennessee was admitted into the Union as a state. It is not strange then that James Spurling and his family were met in Tennessee with the same spiritual climate and familiar religious traditions that they had known in North Carolina. But Baptists in this region were also influenced by the revivalism and churchmanship that had affected eastern Kentucky and Middle Tennessee. The flaming cinders from the celebrated revival at Cane Ridge in Logan County, Kentucky in 1800-1801 had shot as far south as the Cumberland Mountains in Tennessee and were still burning in the churches in Anderson County when James and his family arrived there in the early 1820s.[32]

---

[28] For a good account of this, see Edith Wilson Hutton, *A Promise of Good Things, Longfield Baptist Church 1831-1981* (Oak Ridge, TN: Adroit, Inc., Office Products Printing, 1982), pp. 91-106.

[29] Hutton, *Promise*, pp. 31-38; and see Burnett, *Pioneer Preachers*, 'Joshua Frost', p. 164.

[30] Benedict, *History*, II, p. 574.

[31] Burnett, *Pioneer Preachers*, pp. 318-22.

[32] For an insightful view of the circumstances of the Baptist churches in this region at that time, see C.P. Cawthorn & N.L. Warnell, *Pioneer Baptist Church Records*

Old Landmarkism

A movement that swept Southern Baptists in the last half of the nineteenth century especially deserves our attention, for its influence, both negatively and positively, factored significantly into the events that led to the organization of Christian Union in 1886. This movement was called 'Old Landmarkism', having received its name from an essay published in 1854 by James Madison Pendleton, one of the principal advocates of the movement. His message, taken from Prov. 22.28, 23.10, and Jer. 6.16 distinguished the old landmarks of Baptist faith and practice and emphasized the need for contemporary Baptists to maintain them. J.R. Graves published Pendleton's message in tract form, renamed it 'An Old Landmark Re-set', and used it to lay out many of the principles that came to be known as 'Old Landmarkism'.

Graves was in fact the undisputed father of Landmarkism. He was an exceptionally gifted speaker and perhaps the most influential force in the development of Baptist thought and practice in the South throughout the latter half of the nineteenth century. His combative personality, however, as much as his doctrine tended to divide Baptists sharply, some holding him in highest esteem, others seeing in him little more than a fanatic and bigot. As editor of the influential *The Tennessee Baptist*, he used its wide circulation to spread Landmark teachings throughout the Southern Baptist Convention. Centered at first in Nashville and in Graves himself, the movement extended the tentacles of its influence to every quarter of Baptist life and experience in the latter half of the nineteenth century, aiming for nothing less than the establishment of a Baptist dominion in the South.

Motivated by what they perceived to be a 'departure from the faith' by Southern Baptist ministers and churches, Graves (1820-1893), Pendleton (1811-1891), and A.C. Dayton (1813-1865) – the 'Great Triumvirate' of the movement – and their followers met in Cotton Grove, Tennessee in 1851 and adopted the 'Cotton Grove Resolutions' which laid out the movement's principles. Besides holding to the inspiration and inerrancy of the Bible, Landmarkism maintained: 1) an exclusive view of Baptist churches that were in 'regular order', that is, churches that adhered closely to the principles of traditional Baptist government and polity as perceived by Landmarkers; 2) an unbroken succession of Baptist churches through history beginning with the kingdom of God being

---

of South-Central Kentucky and the Upper Cumberland of Tennessee 1799-1899; for a good local source that captured the spirit of the Baptists in this particular locality at that time, see Hutton, *A Promise of Good Things*, pp. 91-106.

established in the days of John the Baptist and followed by the churches established by Christ and the apostles in the New Testament; 3) a strict view of the church as a visible institution; 4) that only Baptist churches in regular order – Landmark churches – are true churches of Christ, all others being merely 'societies' and men-made organizations; 5) that true baptisms are by immersion only and are recognized by God only if performed by a regular Baptist church, all other baptisms even if performed by immersion being considered 'alien'; 5) in 'close communion', which excludes categorically non-Baptists from the Lord's Table, and also guards against members of sister Baptist churches who may not be in good standing; 6) that the church and kingdom are coterminous, the kingdom being the sum total of true Baptist churches; 7) in 'pulpit affiliation' with non-Baptists being strictly forbidden; 8) ordination being recognized only if authorized and performed by a Baptist church in regular order, otherwise considered to be 'alien ordination'. Thus preaching by non-Baptists was merely an exercise in 'speech-making', not true preaching, 9) missions was held to be an important part of the work of the church, but missionaries and missionary work were authorized only if commissioned by the particular local churches, not by mission boards, conventions, and para-church societies, the latter being considered unlawful and un-Scriptural.[33] Landmark churches thus came to be known as Missionary Baptist Churches, the names Missionary Baptist and Landmark Baptist being more or less synonymous and interchangeable.

The Landmark view of the church as being strictly a visible body, empowered by Christ with self-government, and all of the local churches together in regular order forming the kingdom of God, created the framework for an exclusive ecclesiology. Landmarkers saw themselves as 'a peculiar people' standing alone in proclaiming and practicing the pure Gospel. It followed naturally that all other religious bodies were more or less the Great Babylon envisioned by the apostle John in Revelation 17. Roman Catholicism was the Harlot Mother, and Anglicanism (called Episcopalism in America), Methodism, Lutheranism, Presbyterianism, Campbellism, and other Protestant bodies were the Harlot Daughters and Grand-Daughters of Rome. This was the view that Graves consist-

---

[33] For an understanding of Landmarkism, see J.R. Graves, *Old Landmarkism: What Is It?* (Texarkana, TX: Bogard Press, 1880). See also G.H. Orchard, *A Concise History of the Foreign Baptists* (Nashville: Graves & the Marks, Ag'ts of Tenn. Publication Society, 1885), particularly the 'Introductory Essay', pp. i-xxiii, by Graves; J.M. Pendleton, *Landmarkism* (Walker, WV: Truth Publications, 1899); *idem*, *Why I Am A Baptist*, (Nashville: Baptist Publishing House, 1853, reprint by Stacy Printing Co., Buffalo, Iowa, 1989). For a critical view of Landmarkism, see H. Leon McBeth, *A Sourcebook for Baptist Heritage* (Nashville, TN: Broadman Press, 1990), pp. 316-32.

ently expounded upon in the *Tennessee Baptist*, a view that was adopted by the majority of Southern Baptists in the nineteenth century. His remarks in a letter written in the 1850s addressed to Joshua Soule, Bishop of the Methodist Episcopal Church South, were typical of his constant bombardments against Roman Catholic and Protestant churches:

> Methodism is a sect, not of the Apostolic Church, but of Roman Apostacy; having the Church of England for her mother, and the woman in scarlet for her grand-mother ... Methodist ministers ... have one and all received their ordinations and authority from Rome – mystical Babylon, the 'Man of Sin' and son of perdition, through the Church of England!! Methodism, from its own testimony, belongs to the family of Mystical Babylon, a grand-daughter, and can the Churches of Christ, with any degree of right and propriety, recognize, by receiving, the acts of Mystical Babylon as Christian or Scriptural?[34]

It was this religious system – 'Old Landmarkism' – that informed and nourished R.G. Spurling in his formative years, and it was this same system, ironically, which he came into conflict with in the early 1880s.[35] It would be impossible in fact to understand Spurling and the circumstances that brought about his actions in 1884-1886, and conversely the actions taken against him, apart from understanding his roots in the Missionary ('Landmark') Baptist Church.[36]

Spurling was born about the time the Landmark movement was gaining a head wind in Tennessee and the South. His father and older brother, James J., were at that time especially active in the Clinton Association of United Baptists whose moderator, Elder Joshua Frost (1782-1865), was of Baptist fame – 'dean of Baptist preachers'.[37] Frost,

---

[34] J.R. Graves, 'Letter No. 6 (Revised Edition)', *The Tennessee Baptist*, October 9, 1852.

[35] The writer first connected Spurling with Landmarkism in 1992 after discovering that Spurling's reference to a Baptist historian named 'Archard' in *The Lost Link* is actually a misspelling of Orchard. The work he cites is G.H. Orchard's *History of the Baptists* that was re-published by J.R. Graves in Nashville in 1855. This was demonstrated by comparing Spurling's references to Orchard's history, pp. 22, 110, 175 with his quotes in *The Lost Link*, pp. 34, 35, 42. Since they are verbatim, we concluded that Spurling was citing Orchard's history. Interestingly, Orchard's history was re-published by Graves in order to support the position of the Landmarkers on historical succession and the sovereignty of each local church. This discovery led to numerous other discoveries enabling the writer to trace and interpret the faith tradition of the Spurlings back several generations.

[36] For further evidence that the Spurlings were Landmark Baptists, see Phillips, 'Baptist Roots', pp. 16-26.

[37] Hutton, *Promise*, pp. 13-22, 325-27.

affectionately known as 'Father Frost', had a great influence on Richard and the whole Spurling family, being the most prominent and influential Baptist minister in and around Anderson, Morgan, and Scott counties. He was the Spurling family's pastor at one point, having also performed the marriage between Richard and his wife Nancy Jane Norman on January 7, 1832.[38] Nancy's father was almost certainly the 'Brother Norman' mentioned by Burnett in his *Sketches of Tennessee's Pioneer Baptist Preachers* who donated an acre of land to build the 'Zion meetinghouse' in 1819 in Anderson County under Frost's direction.[39] Frost was a subscriber and contributor to *The Tennessee Baptist*, and, like its editor, J.R. Graves, was a moderate Calvinist and proponent of Andrew Fuller's theology, that is, he proclaimed a general atonement and was zealous for missionary outreach believing that God was not 'willing that any should perish, but that all should come to repentance'.[40]

Richard and Nancy worked closely with Father Frost, and followed him in reaching out to 'the destitute regions of Kentucky'.[41] It was during this time in July 1857 near the town of Willamsburg in Whitley County that R.G. Spurling was born. 'Father Frost' with perhaps Alfred Agee and others ordained Richard between 1853 and 1859 while his membership was in the Clear Creek church. We may assume this for the following reasons: first, it is not likely that Richard was ordained before 1853 since he was not one of presbyters who organized the Clear Creek church in 1852, and second, there are no evidences in any church or association minutes showing him to be an elder before this time. The Union church minutes do not show that Richard was ordained while his membership was there between 1847 and 1852, and the 'irregular' events at the Poplar Cove church in Fentress County would seem to have prevented his ordination there between 1838 and 1847. Since he was already recognized as an elder when he arrived in Monroe County in 1859,

---

[38] Marriage Records in Anderson County Court Minutes, pp. 76, 78. Phillips, 'Baptist Roots', pp. 12-14. An invaluable source in helping to piece together the Spurling story is Burnett, *Pioneer Preachers*. His sketches on Joshua Frost, I.B. Kimbrough, Zechariah Rose, M.C. Higdon, and other ministers connected with the Spurlings have been helpful.

[39] Burnett, *Pioneer Preachers*, p. 163. This needs further research, but the connection with Nancy's name, chronology, place, and the minister seems self-evident. The census records show Nancy's family lived in the vicinity of the Zion church and Joshua Frost's home. Henry and Aaron Norman were both prominent in the New Salem and Zion churches.

[40] Albert W. Wardin, Jr., *Tennessee Baptists: A Comprehensive History 1779-1999* (Brentwood, TN: Tennessee Baptist Convention, 1999), pp. 148, 204.

[41] See also *Clinton Association Minutes* 1853-1864; Burnett, *Pioneer Preachers*, p. 165; Pinckney, *Sketch*, p. 1.

it seems safe to assume therefore that he was ordained while he was active in the ministry at Clear Creek church and in the Clinton Association between 1853 and 1859, and most likely 'Father Frost' and Alfred Agee served as presbyters in his ordination.

Figure 2

JOSHUA FROST

c. 1864

Figure 3

J.R. GRAVES

c. 1866

The Move to Lower East Tennessee

Just before R.G. Spurling was born, his father in 1855-1856 ventured into the Springtown area of Polk County and the southern parts of Monroe County, Tennessee, reaching out to 'destitute regions' to proclaim the Gospel and the Missionary Baptist way of life.[42] This trip seems to have been made without the company of his wife and children, though he was accompanied for some reason by his older brother Daniel's sons, John, Clark, Hicks, and Lewis.[43] His older brother Hicks and

---

[42] In his *Sketch*, Pinckney says that his father lived in Morgan County until after the Civil War was over; however, the Minutes of the Spring Creek Baptist church and the Holly Spring's Baptist church show that his father was in Polk County and Monroe County during this time, and that he was also in McMinn in 1864. He was in Springtown in Polk County in fact as early as 1856 with his nephews, Lewis, Clark, Hicks, and John. Richard's wife was also in Monroe County in the middle of the Civil War, in 1863, and also his other sons – Daniel, Nathan, William, Hiram – three of whom fought in the war. See Phillips, 'Baptist Roots', pp. 14-16.

[43] We may assume this since all of them were in Spring Creek area together at the same time and were working together in the Spring Creek church. Richard's brother Daniel (b. 1799-1800) had died between 1848-1850 and his sister Sally and her husband, Anderson Tinch, assumed the responsibility of rearing the children.

his family from north Georgia joined him also in this venture, settling in the Towee area near the line that divided Monroe and Polk counties. When Richard arrived in the area, he was met with the fierce controversy still brewing between 'missionaries' (pro-convention advocates) and 'anti-missionaries' (anti-convention advocates) that had divided the Sweetwater Baptist Association in 1836-1837.[44] He came into conflict with the Springtown Baptist church and the Baptist elders in the area – Zechariah Rose, M.C. Higdon, Elijah Clayton, and others – who had sided with the anti-convention side of the controversy, some of whom also held to hyper-Calvinistic doctrines, for example, limited atonement, strict predestination (i.e. pre-necessitation), and reprobation. The anti-missionaries had declared a 'non-fellowship' with those who supported the Baptist State Convention, and finally in 1838 excluded those with whom they disagreed and formed their own Association,[45] claiming to be the true Sweetwater Baptist Association. Interestingly, the anti-missionaries then split among themselves over doctrinal issues, some standing on a hyper-Calvinistic platform, others holding to a more moderate Calvinism. Thus for many years there were actually three Sweetwater Baptist Associations: the 'missionaries', 'anti-missionaries', and 'go-betweens'.[46] Zechariah Rose seems to have been the most influential moderate of the anti-convention brethren, later becoming instrumental in helping to reconcile the divisions. Reflecting on the spectacle of these 'unfriendly divisions', the writer is reminded of the comment made by a Baptist friend some years ago who insisted that 'If any two Baptists agree on anything, they are no longer Baptists'.

By 1855-1856 all of the children were adults, except Lewis (b. 1842), and thus they may have followed their Uncle Richard to lower East Tennessee merely to venture out on their own. More likely, however, they were involved with him in the ministry, for all of them united with the Spring Creek Baptist Church in 1856.

[44] Glenn A. Toomey, *History of the Sweetwater Baptist Association and Its Affiliated Churches 1830-1980* (Madisonville, TN. Self-published, 1980), pp. 52-86. Toomey gives an excellent overview of the division and records many pertinent facts including a list of the churches on both sides.

[45] *Springtown Baptist Church Minutes*, 1844-1865.

[46] The best explanation on this development is a report given in the April 17, 1858 issue of the *Tennessee Baptist;* see also Toomey, *Sweetwater Baptist Association*, pp. 54-61.

But Richard found brethren of 'like precious faith' in the reputable I.B. (Isaac Barton) Kimbrough, T.J. Russell, J.S. Russell, John Shruggs, Robert Snead, and Thomas Smalling, among others. Kimbrough (1826-1902) was the pastor of the Spring Creek church when Richard arrived in the area. This church was located near the line separating Monroe and Polk counties. Kimbrough was destined to greatness among Baptists in Tennessee, serving as the moderator of the pro-convention Sweetwater Association for ten years, and as president of East Tennessee General Association for three years. He also helped to organize the Tennessee Baptist Convention in 1874, serving that body as vice president. In recognition of his labor and abilities, Carson College in 1876 conferred upon him an honorary Doctor of Divinity. He was a follower of Andrew Fuller in theology and a follower of J.R. Graves in faith and practice – a 'Landmarker'.[47] When Richard met him in 1856, Kimbrough had just completed a two-year appointment as missionary evangelist in the Sweetwater Association and had taken up his first pastorate at the Spring Creek church. Richard immediately got in the harness with him and went to work evangelizing the area and assisting Kimbrough with his pastoral duties. Richard's brother, Hicks, and two of his children, and three of his brother Daniel's sons united with the Spring Creek church. Richard assisted on occasion when Kimbrough was away, serving in the capacity of a 'ruling elder' and as 'pro-tem moderator' of business meetings.[48]

Figure 4

RICHARD SPURLING
(1810-1891)

Figure 4 (c. 1888) is the only extant photo of Richard Spurling known to exist. Identified by Ethel Kilby, a descendant of Richard who still lived near his old home place on Dry Creek in 1995.

---

[47] Burnett, *Pioneer Preachers*, pp. 302-308.
[48] There is no evidence that Richard ever held the position of a pastor. As a 'ruling elder' he assisted other pastors, performed marriages, baptized, conducted

Sometime late in 1856 or early 1857, Richard went back to Morgan County. There he resumed his missionary work under the guidance of 'Father Frost'. While reaching out into southern Kentucky with his wife Nancy now by his side, his last child, Richard Green, was born in July. After they returned to Morgan County, Richard prepared to move with his entire family permanently to Monroe County.[49] This move was made probably in early spring 1859 and included his aging father and mother. They settled on a farm on Dry Creek near Elder Kimbrough. Richard immediately went back to work with Kimbrough resuming the work he had begun in 1855-1856 promoting the missionary point of view.

Figure 5
I.B. KIMBROUGH
1826-1902)

Before Richard had left the area in late 1856 or early 1857, he seems to have led a number of Baptists in the area into missionary views. Some of those who had defected from Primitive Baptist views and joined the Spring Creek Missionary Baptist church were almost certainly influenced by Richard's ministry. In any case, the establishment of the Holly Springs church on Steer Creek August 1859 was partly the result of Richard's work.

Before we move on to examine more closely the Holly Springs church and Richard's ministry in southern Monroe County, it is important to note that he seems to have returned briefly to Morgan County with his wife and younger children during the Civil War. The primary reason for this move was the prevailing lawlessness in the region and the pillaging of marauding armies. It was indeed a dangerous and trying time, not only because of the invading armies but bushwhacking was prevalent. In addition, bitter rivalries sprang up within the communities, for the sons of some were fighting and dying for the cause of the Union, and the sons of others were fighting and dying for the Confederacy.[50]

---

funerals, served to mediate conflicts in the churches within a particular association, moderated business meetings, etc.

[49] Except for his son James J. and daughter Anne who were now married and settled in Morgan County.

[50] This is briefly mentioned by Spurling in *The Lost Link*, in which he says, 'Three of my brothers were driven into the war. Although my father was too old to be a soldier, he was driven from home and preaching and exposed to all kinds of weather which weakened his once strong and manly frame' (Spurling, *Lost Link*, p.

In the heat of the controversies, even Baptists turned upon themselves – 'brother against brother'. To make matters worse, three of Richard's sons – Daniel, Nathan, and William – joined the Union Army[51] when sympathies for the Confederate cause were especially high among the people of Polk County and southern Monroe County. We might well imagine that this made life more difficult for Richard and his family.

We have noticed that Richard was instrumental in helping to form in August 1859 the Holly Spring's Baptist Church on Steer Creek, and was active in the church from the beginning. This church (still existing today) is located about seven miles north of where the Spring Creek church stood in the 1850s. Richard's nephew, Lewis, was a charter member, and Richard and Nancy and Richard's father and mother, James and Frances ('Frankie'), formally united by 'letter' a few months later.[52] Here Richard's ministry would flourish, such as it was. He became active also in the larger circle of the Sweetwater Association and later the Eastanallee Association when it was organized in 1871. In his role as a 'ruling elder', he was asked on occasion to counsel and mediate disputes and difficulties within the area churches.[53] We have found no evidence that Richard ever served as a pastor anywhere.

Holly Springs Church

Some further comments here about the Holly Springs church and Richard's connection with it will be helpful in piecing together his life and ministry and the events that led to Christian Union in 1886. This church,

---

47). Spurling's three brothers who fought in the war were Daniel, Nathan, and William. They fought on the side of the North. The sons of Michael Higdon and Elijah Clayton, rival ministers of Richard Spurling, fought on the side of the Confederacy. The writer obtained the Civil War records of R.G. Spurling's brothers; these records coupled with local historical records reveal the bitter rivalries and awful contentions between the people in Polk and Monroe Counties. A family tradition says that Richard Spurling broke his hip during the war, which left him with a limp. This corresponds with R.G. Spurling's comments in *The Lost Link* and with the single extant photograph we have of Richard that reveals his injury and deformity.

[51] William enlisted with the Confederate army but was captured in 1862 and then deserted. He then enrolled with the Union army in 1863 (Civil War records – copy in ZACG Archives). Thereafter he was wounded and honorably discharged. See also note 56.

[52] James and Frances died about a year after the church was established, probably in late 1860, and we may assume are buried in unmarked graves in the Dehart cemetery.

[53] He served for example as one of the mediators in a conflict at the Shady Grove church in Monroe County in 1876, and was active in moderating conferences as well performing marriages and conducting funerals.

like all of the churches of which Richard was a member, adhered to Brown's 1853 covenant[54] – a covenant that had been adopted virtually by all Landmark Baptist churches. Holly Springs also ascribed more or less to the Articles of Faith and Decorum of the United Baptist Associations in East Tennessee. Like the Separate Baptists in North Carolina and in the Cumberland Mountain region of Tennessee, the members at Holly Springs practiced footwashing on a regular basis.[55] The first pastor was Elder Gamaliel Briant (also spelled Bryant), the grandfather of W.F. Bryant, whom we will meet again in the next chapter. Briant served as pastor at Holly Springs until 1863. He was followed significantly by Elijah Clayton whom Richard had come into conflict with over his pro-missionary and pro-convention views. Clayton (1786-1881) and M.C. Higdon (1823-1905) stood shoulder to shoulder in their faith, touting anti-convention views and tending to be harsh and difficult with those who disagreed with their opinions. They were passionate in their opposition to conventions, associations, and any kind of society that usurped or infringed upon the sole right of local churches to authorize mission work, most particularly if those societies solicited and collected funds to pay missionaries, even if that pay in 1840 was only fifty cents per day. They felt obligated, if not inspired, to charge missionaries sent out by conventions as being 'hirelings', and warning others not to 'partake in other men's sins by encouraging this kind of disorder and division.

Higdon had been mentored by Elder Elijah Clayton and looked on him as a father in the faith, honoring him by naming his first son, Elijah Clayton. But these men were also bonded together in their political views, declaring themselves passionately for the Confederate cause as the war approached. Now Richard disagreed with these men on political grounds as well as religious, and their disagreements only intensified as their sons enlisted on opposite sides of the conflict, with one of Higdon's sons, Clayton's namesake, paying the supreme sacrifice for the

---

[54] Brown's covenant is significant for J.M. Pendleton had incorporated it in his *Church Manual* which virtually all Landmark Baptist churches thereafter adopted as a rule of faith and order.

[55] The discovery of the Holly Springs Minutes was a glorious moment for the writer. For not only did these minutes open a wealth of information about Richard's life and ministry at Holly Springs, but opened the door also for many other discoveries related to his life and ministry. I attribute the discoveries to the special providences of the Holy Spirit; Apparently the Lord desired for the church's history to be uncovered and the story told. I will always be indebted to Mrs. Loweta Dockery, the clerk of the Holly Springs church at that time (1992) for being so gracious to extend to me several interviews and allowing me to photocopy the minutes.

Confederacy.⁵⁶ Clayton's appointment as pastor of the Holly Springs church in 1863 may explain in part why Richard requested by letter in April 1863 that he and his wife's names be 'stricken from the church Book'.⁵⁷ Higdon worked closely with Clayton in 1864-1866 in the Holly Springs church, often moderating business conferences and serving as 'supply' pastor. The influence of Higdon and Clayton seems to explain apparently why Holly Springs went to the anti-convention side of the controversy during the war.⁵⁸ This conclusion is further supported on the basis that Richard petitioned the church for a letter of 'recommendation' in July 1868 which the church agreed to 'postpone until some future time'.⁵⁹ Interestingly, there is no record that Richard's request was ever brought up again. Richard remained separated from the Holly Springs church until February 1875,⁶⁰ rejoining only after the church had committed itself again to pro-missionary and pro-convention views and had become active in the pro-convention Eastanallee Baptist Association.

During the Civil War and post-war years, Richard's sons and daughters married prominent persons in Monroe County, and their families became active in the Holly Springs church. Daniel and his family in particular became prominent in the church and in community and civil affairs. Daniel's son, Andrew, later served as the twenty-first pastor of the Holly Springs church and was prominent in community affairs.

---

⁵⁶ Two of Clayton's sons and three of Higdon's served the Confederacy. Higdon's son, Elijah Clayton, was wounded in April 1862 and died a few days later. His body was sent home and arrived not long before the news that Richard Spurling's son, William A., had deserted the Confederacy and joined the Union army.

⁵⁷ *Minutes of the Holly Springs Church*, April 1863.

⁵⁸ The fact that the Holly Springs church refused to give Richard a letter of recommendation to the Sweetwater Association in August 1867 seems to further support this view. *Holly Springs Church Minutes*, August 1867.

⁵⁹ *Minutes of the Holly Springs Church*, July 1868. It is interesting that Richard's son, Daniel, had become the church clerk the same month that Richard requested this letter of recommendation. Richard thought that Daniel's influence might help his case. But either Daniel had come to disagree with his father's missionary stand, or else his influence in favor of his father was just not enough to sway the opinion of the church. Either way, his request was denied.

⁶⁰ *Minutes of the Holly Springs Church*, February 1875. Richard apparently reconciled with the church at this time because in 1870 the anti-missionaries and missionaries reconciled their differences and united again into one association – the Sweetwater Baptist Association. In any case, at this point Richard became active again in the Holly Springs church and in the Sweetwater Baptist Association and also in the Eastanallee Baptist Association when it was formed out of the Sweetwater Association in 1871.

Figure 6
HOLLY SPRINGS BAPTIST CHURCH
C. 1890

Figure 7
DANIEL E.L. SPURLING FAMILY
C. 1891

Left: this was the second building constructed in 1872. It was located about 75 ft. from the present church house. The Masonic Lodge met regularly upstairs in this two-story building. Several members of the Holly Springs Church were Masons, including Daniel Spurling and his sons, Andrew and Colonel. *Right:* Daniel Spurling and wife, Mary (Dehart), with their children and grandchildren.

Figure 8
NATHAN
1838-1912

Figure 9
DANIEL
1841-1904

Figure 10
HIRAM
1849-1922

Elder Brothers of R.G. Spurling

(No photos available of James J., William A. or sisters, Anne, Elizabeth, and Nancy)

It was in and around Holly Springs that many of the families lived whose names will appear a little later in the Christian Union congregations. Most of them — Freemans, Procks, Irons, Pauls, Plemons, Waldrops, Millers, Bowers, Whites, Tiptons, *et al.* — were fellow members with Richard in the Holly Springs church or were members of one of the nearby churches: Springtown, Spring Creek, Maple Springs, Rural Vale, and Coker Creek. Some of them had intermarried with Richard's children and grandchildren and were all directly or indirectly influenced by his ministry. Richard's youngest son, R.G. Spurling, grew up among these families and had worshipped with them at Holly Springs and in the nearby churches. It is not surprising then that he was able to persuade many of them a little later to accept his vision of Christian Union.

Mountain Peculiarities

Before we move on to examine more closely the experience and ministry of R.G. Spurling and the events that led to Christian Union, a brief look at some of the peculiarities of southern Appalachian Mountain culture and the practices of Missionary Baptist churches in the mountains will give further insight into the religious psyche of the people, and add some flavor to the story of the Church of God in its early years.

One of the most striking peculiarities was the brogue and peculiar sayings that distinguished southern mountaineers. Since the majority of the people were of Scotch-Irish descent, it is said that the language of the mountaineers in Scotland and Ireland was handed-down and sequestered in the Appalachians. Again it is said that some of the peculiarities of the language of Shakespeare and Chaucer had been preserved from generation to generation in the isolation of the mountains. Be that as it may, the people commonly used 'hit' for it, 'haint' for 'am not' and 'have not', and 'taken' for took. They 'packed' their loads in 'pokes', and one was invited to 'light up' for a wagon ride. They said 'plague' for tease, and if one was willing, he was 'consentable'. One was said to be 'bad to drink', and another 'wicked to swear'. In regard to the weather, one might have heard a mountaineer say, 'Hit's blue cold out thar', or 'hotter'n the hinges on the gates of hell'. Naked was pronounced 'nekkid', and thus mountaineers would say, 'Nekkid as a jaybird', 'stark-nekkid', and 'bare-nekkid'. Hundreds of these linguistic peculiarities flavored the language in southern Appalachia. It is said that a young boy was making a speech in a class taught by a northern school mom in western North Carolina in the late 1800s. In the midst of a sentence that began 'I et seven apples and got sick', the school mom interrupted and said, 'you mean ate', to which the lad responded, 'maybe it was eight I et'.

Some of the peculiarities of the language doubtlessly developed for lack of formal education. Illiteracy was widespread in the mountains even in the early twentieth century, and even some who were considered somewhat 'larned' had only a few months of formal education. They wrote according to the way a word sounded in their Appalachian dialect.

Thus 'there' was spelled and pronounced 'thar', prayer was 'prair' or 'prar', and one's leg was a 'lag'. Hired was pronounced 'hard', thus 'the company *hard* me yesterday;' a fire was a 'far', thus 'that *far* surely is hot'; and the *tars* (tires) on that wagon are bent, or 'I've worked powerful long today and am really "tard"'.

Spurling was typical of this phenomenon. In his original draft of *The Lost Link*, written about 1896-1897, he explains,

> O ye churches that claim apostolac succation. I now summons you to testefy you Baptist and you Romenest who say yore church is the only church of Jesus Christ. Who authorized you to make laws and binding ruls that would sepperate gods children from Christs church ...[61]

More than thirty years later he wrote to A.J. Tomlinson:

> Dear Brother Tomlinson in mutch love I am sory that I hav not wrote sooner But I an wife hav bin so puney & flustrated not knowiny When one or the other might pass away But prais god we are Better at present But I am so nervies I hav to hold the pensel with Booth hands. Well I thought I might git to meet you and hav a hart to hart counsel with you and communicate serten things I hav learned and git the lay of the land.[62]

Reflecting on his experience as a boy in the mountain culture of eastern Tennessee and western North Carolina in the late 1890s, Homer Tomlinson recalled

> [The area in lower East Tennessee was] a ... moonshine country; most of the men 'toated' guns, most of the women used snuff. The chief social events were hoe-down dances, with drinking parties always in session simultaneously, and usually a few shots enlivened the evening. Few of the people could even read, with the exception of the children who were just about then beginning to have six weeks of school a year in some log cabin school house.

> The young men of the country hunted wild turkey, and pheasants. Husbands hunted while wives and children tilled the fields. The main ration in that part of the country was salt pork, except in hog-killing time ... But there were religious people. It made no difference if the preacher, who came around once a month, spit amber during his sermon, most of the people were 'churched'. Largely they were di-

---

[61] Spurling, *Lost Link* [original], p. 8.
[62] 'Letter to A.J. Tomlinson', dated December 2, 1930 (ZACG Archives).

vided into two camps, Methodists and Baptists But despite the theoretical good they did they seemed to spend a great deal of time in prejudiced practices. But among them, let it be said there were many sincere, God fearing people.⁶³

Many of the Missionary [Landmark] churches were spirited and lively, in spite of the fact that they taught and practiced a 'sinning religion'. Some of their outward manifestations in worship would later be identified with the holiness-Pentecostal movement. They spoke in terms that we now identify with Pentecostalism, with the exception of speaking in tongues. They testified to being 'caught up in the Spirit' and 'coming down out of the Spirit', as if returning to a natural or normal state of consciousness from a spiritual one. They were spirited and emotional in worship, often their whole bodies serving as organs to express and demonstrate their joy. They 'shouted' in the Spirit; sang exuberantly; prayed in great earnest, and cried especially during 'sacramentals', including foot washings.

Some of their peculiarities in worship and style grew out of the Appalachian culture itself. They embraced and shook hands with warm and decent affection; and some greeted with a holy kiss, invoking the label, 'kissing Baptists'. Spontaneity in worship was considered in order and natural; and preaching was often extemporaneous or impromptu, and always impassioned. Responsive shouts of joy and exuberant 'amens' often confirmed and intensified the delivery of the Word of God. As well, silence usually denoted disapproval.

There was always the effort for an Appalachian Baptist preacher to get in the rhythm of the Spirit in order to deliver the Word of God. Speed and rhythm were associated with 'anointing' and 'inspiration'. The lack of fluency and even a degree of intelligibility could more quickly be overlooked than the lack of exuberance and energetic delivery. Howard Dorgan in his *Giving Glory to God in Appalachia* describes colorfully his observation of preaching among the Baptists in southern Appalachia.

> … speaking at rates often exceeding two hundred words per minute, intoning his message in staccato bursts of rhetoric similar to the regular lines of unrhymed verse, with an occasional phrase that rises like an auctioneer's chant and approaches song, the preacher pours out such a torrent of words that at the end of each linear segment he emit's a sharp 'huuh' or 'haah', as he quickly exhales and inhales preparatory for his next flow of rhetoric. This 'huuh' or 'haah' constitutes the dominant beat of his rhythm and is usually thought of as

---

⁶³ Homer Tomlinson, 'History of Pentecost', *FS* (September, 1922), pp. 5, 6.

the hallmark of the Southern Appalachian sermon style ... the effect is a hypnotic rhythm that tends to dominate content, with congregations ... responding more to beat than to lyrics.[64]

Dorgan's observations adequately describe the Baptist churches in lower East Tennessee. This writer attended worship services in twelve Missionary Baptist churches in Monroe and Polk counties in Tennessee and in Cherokee County, North Carolina between 1992 and 1998 and can attest to the same. We may assume, moreover, that these same characteristics in worship and preaching were even more pronounced in the late nineteenth century when R.G. Spurling and the pioneers of the Church of God were laboring to restore the church of the Bible.

Spurling Comes of Age

The cultural characteristics and religious peculiarities just described formed the historical backdrop and life-setting from which R.G. Spurling emerged in the latter half of the nineteenth century. He grew up in the tri-county area of Monroe and Polk counties in Tennessee and Cherokee County in North Carolina. Religiously, this region was more or less immersed under the powerful influence of Landmark doctrines and practices. Many of the leading ministers in the region were Landmark advocates including Zechariah Rose, M.C. Higdon, and Elijah Clayton, the latter two leaning toward hyper-Calvinistic views and being rather rigid and harsh in their personal judgments.[65] These men stood shoulder to shoulder in their faith and execution of the ministry. It is not without significance that Clayton ordained Rose in 1841, and Rose ordained Higdon in 1847.[66] Together they formed a powerful and influential force in the region, holding tenaciously to traditional Baptist exclusiveness and the essential Landmark doctrines that forged that exclusiveness. What Burnett says of Higdon could be applied as well to Clayton and Rose: 'He doesn't work well in "union meetings", can pull better in "Baptist harness", and thinks that Baptists have to give account to their own Master in their own way'.[67]

---

[64] Howard Dorgan, *Giving Glory to God in Appalachia* (Knoxville: The University of Tennessee Press, 1987), p. 59.
[65] See Burnett's *Sketches* on these ministers. Where Burnett says that Rose was not as 'hard' as some of his brethren, we may assume that he refers to Clayton and Higdon, among others.
[66] Burnett, *Pioneer Preachers*, pp. 225, 431.
[67] Burnett, *Pioneer Preachers*, p. 226.

Zechariah Rose (1809-1886) was especially prominent in the region, helping to lay out Polk County in 1839; he also served as chairman of the first county court as a justice of the peace and taught in the first school in the county.[68] We mention Rose's prominence because he was a powerful influence in both civic and religious affairs in Polk County and in adjoining counties, promoting passionately and effectively J.R. Graves' Landmark agenda throughout the region. Graves and Rose mutually admired each other. Graves referred to Rose as the 'excellent Brother Rose',[69] and Burnett says Rose 'was a great admirer of Dr. J.R. Graves'.[70]

Now, as noticed earlier, Rose served as clerk of the anti-convention Sweetwater Baptist Association for more than twenty-five years, and Graves seems to have endorsed Rose's anti-convention position in publishing his report in the *Tennessee Baptist* in July 1853. Interestingly, M.C. Higdon served twelve years as Moderator of the anti-convention Sweetwater Association at the same time that Rose served as clerk. Rose argued that he and his Baptist association were not anti-missionary but against the state convention and its auxiliaries which he claimed usurped the authority of the churches in sending out missionaries, establishing Bible colleges, and devising programs to support them. These brethren – Rose, Higdon, Graves, *et al.* – saw in the convention system a drift toward apostate papal Rome, a usurping authority that supplanted the headship of Christ in the local churches. Thus Landmarkers criticized the president of the Southern Baptist Convention, Robert Howell, as severely as they had the Episcopal system of Methodism, calling Methodism 'the popery of Protestantism' and labeling Howell as 'the pope of Southern Baptists'.

Reflecting on the divisions among Baptists in the 1830s over the government and administration of missions, it is plain to see that the anti-convention side of the issues feared that Baptists were transgressing against their traditional democratic idealism and drifting toward a Roman Catholic-type of apostasy, surrendering gradually the authority and sovereignty of the local churches to a state-wide convention and hierarchical structure. They anticipated further that this state authority would in turn yield to a universal hierarchy and authority; hence, the apostasy of the early centuries all over again. While there was some basis for concern, the situation was magnified and distorted beyond any sense of

---

[68] Roy G. Lillard, *The History of Polk County, Tennessee 1839-1999* (Maryville, TN: Stinnett Printing Company, 1999), pp. 44, 78, 94, 99, 111, 112, 118, 126, 313.
[69] *Tennessee Baptist*, July 23, 1853, pp. 2-3.
[70] Burnett, *Pioneer Preachers*, p. 433.

reality. The truth is that the pro-convention advocates simply saw in the state convention a more effective way to evangelize and do mission work, and to help build up the local churches.

The differences between the factions, however, were not based purely on principle; there were personality conflicts and hidden works of the flesh that flared up and aggravated the peace and unity of the fellowship. The anti-convention advocates would have made a more favorable impact on the debate if they had fostered a more gentile attitude and Christ-like spirit. As it was, a great many of the anti-convention brethren tended to be stubborn, bitter, harsh, demanding, and narrow-minded in pushing forward their agenda.

Amazingly, however, the pro-missionary and pro-convention churches and the anti-missionary and anti-convention churches of the Sweetwater Association reunited in 1870 after thirty-three years of separation. Time had allowed the opposing sides to mellow and to think through their positions, and to realize that they were not so antagonistic after all, that in fact mountains had been made out of mole hills. Baptists on both sides of the issues yearned to be again one visible body of Christ, and on that basis reunited and proceeded on the traditional principles that they had held in common before the mission controversy in the 1830s had divided them.

The joyous reunion of the original Sweetwater Association inspired the formation of a daughter association in 1871 – the Eastanallee.[71] Now this Association was made up of the churches in the southern part of Monroe County, the northern part of Polk County, and the eastern part of McMinn County, and included virtually all of the churches with which R.G. Spurling was in fellowship, and which more or less governed his ministry in the late 1870s and early 1880s. Now the Eastanallee Association was zealously affected with Landmark sympathies, and, in fact, was virtually a Landmark Association. The appearance of Dr. W.A. Montgomery, one of the leading Landmark Baptists in the South,[72] sitting beside Dr. J.R. Graves in the Association's meeting in 1877 only helped to solidify Landmark convictions among the great majority of the ministers and churches in the region.[73] It is not surprising that the Association that year recommended that the ministers and members sub-

---

[71] Toomey, *History Sweetwater Association*, gives a good account of this development, pp. 82-88.

[72] Besides his great oratorical skills in the pulpit and abilities as a church administrator, Dr. Montgomery served as President of Carson-Newman College and was awarded several honorary doctorates, including an LLD from the University of Tennessee in 1876. He was also a lawyer and judge active in the Knoxville area.

[73] *Eastanallee Association Minutes* 1871-1921.

scribe to *The Tennessee Baptist* of which Graves was the editor and Montgomery the associate editor.

Figure 11

R.G. SPURLING
C. 1875

Figure 12

R.G. SPURLING AND FAMILY
C. 1894

In 1876 R.G. Spurling married Barbara Melinda Hamby[74] in Cherokee County, North Carolina whose family were members of the Pleasant Hill Missionary Baptist Church, a church that was governed and disciplined according to the general principles of Landmarkism. Now this church was under the influence of men like Elijah Clayton, Zechariah Rose, M.C. Higdon, William R. Mulkey, and later William Scott Kimsey, the latter two of whom we will meet again in the next chapter. It was in this church that Spurling accepted his call into the ministry, and in 1877 was set forth and licensed to preach.[75] The next year in June, Spurling's mother died, and there are indications that his father moved in with him and his family shortly thereafter. In 1879 Richard Green moved his family back to Monroe County about seven miles east of where he had lived as a child. In 1882 he and his father and his brother Hiram purchased 40-acre tracts of land side by side on Barney Creek, a small stream that flows west to east in southern Monroe County and empties into Coker

---

[74] Their wedding day was August 20, 1876. William R. Mulkey, the pastor of the Pleasant Hill church, officiated and administered the sacred vows. A copy of their wedding license is in 'Spurling File', ZACG Archives.

[75] See Ch. 1, note 2.

Creek. The Spurlings' properties were centered in the midst of three communities – Epperson, Coker Creek, and Ironsburg – each community being located about a mile from their properties. Here, Richard Green built a gristmill and sawmill and operated them to support his family, spending his remaining time studying and preaching the Gospel. Significantly, he and his wife's memberships remained in the Pleasant Hill church in Cherokee County, which was located about eight miles from where they lived on Barney Creek.

Landmarkism Reasserts Itself

In the mid 1850s, Robert Howell (1801-1868), president of the Southern Baptist Convention (1851-1859) and second only to Graves as the most influential Baptist preacher in the South in his day, began to take issue with Landmarkism. He had worked closely with Graves in the 1840s, and spoke of him at that time as 'our beloved Brother J.R. Graves'. But his relationship with Graves later deteriorated, which gave place for their theological differences to be magnified. Besides being the president of the Southern Baptist Convention, Howell was pastor of the prestigious First Baptist Church in Nashville in 1857 where Graves was a member. After their controversy became heated and made public, the church in Nashville sided with Howell and finally excluded the great Landmarker in October 1858. Never to be outdone, Graves fought back. At the end of the Civil War, he moved the *Tennessee Baptist* to Memphis and continued to press forward the Landmark vision, impacting

Figure 13

WILLIAM R. MULKEY AND WIFE (C. 1878)

Mulkey performed the marriage of R.G. Spurling and Barbara (Hamby) in 1876. He served as pastor of Liberty Baptist Church, and helped to organize the Pleasant Hill Church in 1875; was probably involved in Spurling's discipline in 1884.

particularly the South and Southwest and holding sway also over most of East Tennessee.[76]

Notwithstanding, in the 1870s some of the weaknesses in the Landmark system began to be exploited by Baptist scholars, and the movement began to lose some of its appeal. William H. Whitsett (1841-1911), a former student of J.M. Pendleton, and thereafter professor of church history and president of the Southern Baptist Theological Seminary at Louisville, began publishing articles discrediting the Landmark doctrine of the historical succession of Baptist churches, arguing rather that the Baptist tradition originated in the 1600s.[77] Landmark exclusivity also fell in Whitsett's writings, which stirred controversy throughout the decade. Many scholars agreed with Whitsett, but opinion at the grass roots level still largely favored Old Landmarkism, including the opinion of the majority of the ministers and churches in the Eastanallee Association in lower East Tennessee. In order to stimulate and revive the movement, the relentless Graves, with Howell now in his grave, rose to the occasion and published in January 1880, *Old Landmarkism: What Is It?*[78] Over 150,000 copies of this book were circulated, and it did in fact revive the movement.

It was in the midst of this Landmark reassertion in the early 1880s that R.G. Spurling's eyes were opened, and he began to challenge the *status quo* of certain Landmark doctrines. Whether he came to his conclusions independently or through the influence of the counter-Landmark movement initiated by Howell and Whitsett, we cannot be sure, but it is likely that the general stir against Landmarkism had some influence on him. In any case, Spurling came to embody the very complaint of Graves:

> It is freely admitted by reliable brethren who enjoy the widest outlook over the [Baptist] denomination in America, that for the last few decades of years the general drift has been, and now is, setting towards 'open communion' – it is boasted of as a 'broadening liberalism'. There are numbers in all our churches – and the number is increasing, especially in our fashionable city and wealthy town churches – who are impatient of the present restrictions imposed upon the

---

[76] The East Tennessee Generation Association in 1857 boldly announced its loyalty to Landmark principles.

[77] For a clear overview of this, see *Dictionary of Christianity in America* (Downers Grove, IL: InterVarsity Press, 1990), pp. 1253-54; *The Baptist Heritage*, pp. 457-58; *Encyclopedia of Southern Baptists*, II, pp. 756-57; and W.W. Barnes, *The Southern Baptist Convention*, pp. 136-39.

[78] J.R. Graves, *Old Landmarkism: What Is It?* has been republished by Bogard Press, Texarkana, TX 75503.

[Lord's] table ... and we refuse to allow [non-Baptists] to eat. The only ground upon which we can successfully meet and counteract the liberalizing influences, which are gently bearing the Baptists of America into the slough of open communion, is strict local communion, and the firm and energetic setting forth of the 'Old Baptist Landmarks' ...[79]

Spurling's unique theology of the church was formulated finally, however, quite independent of the influence of Howell and Whitsett, and it was also quite different. He rejected Howell's and Whitsett's idea of a universal spiritual church, but also the Landmark doctrine of the historical succession of New Testament churches, formulating in contradistinction to Baptists on both sides of the issue a restoration view of the church in history and prophecy.

Figure 14

PART OF PLEASANT HILL BAPTIST CHURCH CONGREGATION (C. 1902)

Conflict with the Pleasant Hill Church

The exclusive self-image of Landmarkism and the rigid polity and discipline held by the churches under Landmark influence, particularly in regard to open communion, alien baptisms, and the prohibition against Baptist ministers exchanging pulpits with ministers who were not licensed and duly recognized as 'regular Baptist ministers', became particularly troublesome for Spurling. The situation became critical when he began to preach on occasion at the nearby Methodist church in

---

[79] *Graves, Old Landmarkism*, p. 81.

Ironsburg and invited the Methodist people to worship with him in prayer meetings that he conducted in his gristmill on Barney Creek.[80] When he was called to account by the elders of the Pleasant Hill church for his actions, he found himself at odds with the Baptist establishment. He said, 'I soon found myself, so to speak, trying to run a broad gauge engine on a narrow gauge railway'.[81] When he refused to submit to the rigid regulations imposed, '[the elders and the church] demanded my license which I readily gave up'.[82] Not content with revoking his license, the elders then hounded him for preaching in other churches without a license. Finally he was driven altogether out of his Missionary Baptist Church. He wrote, 'I was again called into account for disobeying their rules … so I left them, choosing to obey God rather than man'.[83]

---

[80] These insights are more clearly revealed in the original draft of *The Lost Link*. The meetings at Barney Creek began in Spurling's gristmill, but shortly after Christian Union was organized there was a separate building constructed for worship. The construction of a separate building would not have been difficult since the Spurlings also operated a saw mill.

[81] Spurling, *Lost Link*, p. 47. R.G. Spurling's membership and ministry were in the Pleasant Hill Missionary Baptist Church in Camp Creek, Cherokee County, Tennessee, located on a hill overlooking the Hiwassee River. This church was formed ('armed-off') of the Liberty Missionary Baptist Church in 1875.

[82] Spurling, *Lost Link*, 47. In his *Sketch*, Pinckney noted that when the vote was taken to revoke his father's license there were not enough to carry it. Spurling then more or less gave up his license in order to avoid further contention. Thus, it was by his consent and encouragement that the congregation voted him out. Pinckney's testimony is consistent with his father's comments in the original draft of *The Lost Link*.

[83] Spurling, *Lost Link*, pp. 47, 48, 10.

2

CHRISTIAN UNION IS BORN: 1884-1895

So there Spurling stood in 1884, alone, without a fellowship, without the government of God's church. He explains in the original manuscript of *The Lost Link* that he 'had taken shelter in the Methodist Church until I could know what to do',[1] by which he meant merely that he had received some comfort in the friendship and hospitality of the Methodist people, not that he agreed with all of their faith and practices, nor especially that he had in any sense formally united with them.[2] Realizing the gravity of his situation, he wrote, 'Here it seemed to me that my little boat must forever sink as I was turned out of what I once thought was God's only true church. What shall I do? What can I do?'[3]

Valley of Decision

The situation was grievous and vexatious for him, for he knew God's church was visible and corporate, and that its constituents were 'members one of another'. The circumstances caused him to second-guess his decision and question his motives for separating himself from the church. In addition, his wife 'stood unmoved' in her relationship with the Pleasant Hill Baptist church; in fact, Spurling admitted that she 'was much humiliated at the thought of my defeat as a minister'.[4] It will be remembered that the Pleasant Hill church was Barbara's home church, and her parents, brothers, and sisters were prominent members there. So she was, understandably, severely torn. But the truth is that she was

---

[1] Spurling, *Lost Link* [original], p. 9.
[2] His further comments in *The Lost Link* pp. 23, 33-34 make it clear that he did not join the Methodist Church.
[3] Spurling, *Lost Link*, p. 48.
[4] Spurling, *Lost Link* [original], pp. 10-11.

never very enthusiastic about her husband's ministry, nor about his new venture in Christian Union; indeed, she seems to have tolerated and endured her husband's zeal for the ministry only because the social mores of the day more or less required a minister's wife to do so – to go along with her husband's ministry.[5]

To complicate matters, Spurling noted that 'the Baptists were saying come back and everything will be [alright], and the Methodists [were saying] stay with us and [we will] take the world for Christ and Methodism'.[6] He thus pondered his situation deeply and reflected inwardly, crying out in reflective prayer, 'Oh God ... Am I mistaken? Where is God's church? Where is His law? Where is Thy government? Oh, God, give me understanding, give me knowledge, give me the spirit of understanding and let me see the truth. There is something wrong and badly wrong.'[7] From that point on, Spurling began to pray and search God's Word and history for a more perfect understanding of the Bible church – a quest that would lead him to discover some of the core principles of the church and to initiate the restoration of God's house in 1886.

Still, however, even after he was convinced of the truths that God had revealed to him, he admitted, 'my manhood faltered' and 'my courage almost failed'.[8] He was intimidated by the prospect that his friends and the world around him 'would frown upon such a one ... if I tell my views ... even my own brothers and friends will mock at [my doctrine]'.[9] It was in this dark hour, under a cloud of doubt and confusion that God spoke to him, reassuring him and fortifying his vision through His Word. The Spirit drew his attention particularly to Jesus' parable of the Great Supper recorded in Mt. 22.2-14 and Lk. 14.16-24. In this parable, the servants of God invited the people [the house of Israel] to feast in God's kingdom, but the people made excuses and rejected the invitation; then the Master, being angry, commanded his servants, 'Go out quickly into the streets and lanes of the city, and bring in hither the poor, and the maimed, and the halt, and the blind [the Gentiles]'.

---

[5] Barbara's lack of enthusiasm for her husband's ministry was common knowledge in the family, affirmed by Allie Ledford and other family members interviewed by the writer. Allie, who lived with her grandparents, said her grandmother complained to her grandfather for 'going off to preach to the neglect of his family'. Pinckney says his mother supported his father's ministry (Pinckney, *Sketch*, p. 2), but the preponderance of evidence indicates that she supported him rather reluctantly and only half-heartedly.

[6] Spurling, *Lost Link* [original], p. 11.
[7] Spurling, *Lost Link*, p. 48.
[8] Spurling, *Lost Link* [original], p. 11.
[9] Spurling, *Lost Link* [original], p. 11.

With this encouragement from God's Word, the fear factor – the thought of failure – left the young preacher. He said I knew then 'I could fill my mission and do my duty'.[10] Spurling was now prepared to proclaim his revelation even if the people rejected his message.

We noticed earlier that Spurling's parents and their close friends believed that God had spared his life miraculously as an infant in order for him to perform a special work for the Lord. His parents had instilled this idea in his mind as a child. Now, having been called into the ministry and having been enlightened by the Word of God for his special mission, he was emboldened to go forward without fear. He was no longer unsure and timid, but bold and confident in his call and purpose. According to his own testimony, God had providentially spared his life and raised him up like Moses to lead His people out of bondage.

> Before the days I can remember
> Death took me in its cold dark grasp,
> With closed eyes and folded members,
> Behind death's curtain I did pass.
> Like Moses in his ark of rushes,
> God did not suffer me to stay,
> But raised me up to fulfill His purpose,
> And show His saints the way;
> Like Israel in Egyptian bondage
> Under Pharaoh's cruel hand,
> God has heard our cries and groaning,
> In those churches made by man.
> I've had to flee to Egypt
> And return at God's command,
> God is bringing out His people
> With a strong and mighty hand
> – R.G. Spurling[11]

Light Breaks Through

Once Spurling stepped out on faith to proclaim his revelation, he found to his pleasant surprise that many accepted the new light of his teachings. Among these was his blessed father of whom he wrote, 'Among the number [of those who accepted my message was] an elder or ordained minister who served the church until another was ordained on

---

[10] Spurling, *Lost Link* [original], p. 12.
[11] Spurling, *Lost Link*, p. 49.

Testament authority and qualifications'.[12] That 'ordained minister' was his father, Elder Richard Spurling, who served the church 'until another [a reference to himself] was ordained on Testament authority and qualifications', by which he signified that his authority and qualifications were based on the Bible, not on the Landmark Baptist tradition.

During this time, 1884-1886, Spurling created no small stir in the region where he lived in proclaiming the 'lost link' and the basic tenets of his newly enlightened faith. His vision for Christian Union and his denunciations of the established order of the Baptists, including charging them with being deficient in their love and spirituality, prompted a quick response from the churches in the Eastanallee Association. When the churches met in September 1884 at the Hiwassee Union church in Polk County, one of the queries brought before that body was obviously aimed at the Spurlings and those in sympathy with them. It was posed by the Salem church: 'Is ministerial affiliation and open communion in keeping with the New Testament?' The answer came back:

> As to pulpit affiliation, the Association answered that question years ago. Is it in keeping for a Baptist Church to call a Baptist minister to the pastoral care of a Church who advocates ministerial affiliation and open Communion? We answer, no.

Interestingly, Spurling's father and his brother, Daniel, were delegates at the Eastanallee Association meeting that had answered that question in September 1875 at the Cog Hill church in McMinn County. The resolution read:

> That the Eastanallee Association of Baptists disapproves of any Baptist Minister or Church holding to or practicing open Communion, it being a departure from the faith once delivered to the Saints and amounting to heresy. We, therefore, admonish all ministers and churches to refrain from such disorder.[13]

It has been said that 'An idea is the greatest force in the world'. If this is true, how much more powerful is an idea that originates in the mind of God. Certainly no force on earth can forever resist it. The prophet wrote: 'So shall my word be that goes forth out of my mouth: it shall not return unto me void, but it shall accomplish that which I please, and it shall prosper in the thing whereto I sent it' (Isa. 55.11). And again, 'My covenant will I not break, nor alter the thing that is gone out of my lips' (Psalm 89.34).

---

[12] Spurling, *Lost Link* [original], p. 12.
[13] *Eastanallee Association Minutes*, 1875.

How foolish, then, for the Baptists to slander Spurling and gather themselves together in an effort to destroy his work. They would have been wiser to have been guided by the wisdom of Israel's eminent rabbi, Gamaliel, who counseled the Jews not to seek to destroy the apostles nor hinder their efforts to build God's house, saying, 'You men of Israel, take heed to yourselves what you intend to do as touching these men ... let them alone: for if this counsel or this work be of men, it will come to nought [be overthrown]: But if it be of God, you cannot overthrow it; lest haply you be found even to resist God' (Acts 5.35-39).

Further Complaints Against Landmarkers

Before we move on to that historic day in which the church was actually restored and set in order in 1886, we should notice some other Landmark doctrines and practices with which Spurling took issue. This will enable us to see more insightfully the causes that moved Spurling toward the formation of Christian Union. We have already noticed several Landmark doctrines that he critiqued and rejected, particularly the rigid exclusivity upon which Landmarkers had built their system. Another Landmark doctrine with which he took issue was 'successionism', the idea that true Baptist churches had been established in the New Testament and had continued through history in an unbroken chain of succession up to the present day. True Baptist churches – Missionary (Landmark) churches – therefore embodied exclusively the faith and practices of the primitive churches. Historical succession was therefore tied inextricably with exclusiveness, with both ideas being embraced passionately by Landmark churches. Spurling saw the error in both of these doctrines – exclusivity and secessionism – and the compounded error formed by the two. He wrote in *The Lost Link*, 'Well, what about church identity, apostolic succession and ministerial authority? All such claims are a failure. Apostolic succession was alright as long as God's law was obeyed. But when the church began to make laws and to depart from God's law succession became a delusion'.[14]

Now it is clear that Spurling was in reference to Landmarkism as well as to the Roman Catholic Church when he spoke of 'apostolic succession', for he says in the original draft of *The Lost Link*, 'O ye churches that claim apostolic succession, I now summons [*sic*] you to testify: you Baptists and you Romanists who say your church is the only true church

---

[14] Spurling, *Lost Link*, p. 31.

of Jesus Christ'.[15] Spurling's rejection of exclusiveness and historical succession led him to develop, as we will see in a moment, a restoration view of the church in history and prophecy.

Ironically, most Anabaptists, from whom Landmarkers claimed to have descended in an unbroken line of succession, were restorationists. They did not see themselves as historical links in an unbroken chain of succession going back to the New Testament church, but rather as a spontaneous restoration of the fallen New Testament church. Indeed, they held that the church had fallen decisively under Constantine in the fourth century with the marriage of church and state, and had remained in a state of apostasy until Anabaptists came on the scene in the sixteenth century. The learned Anabaptist scholar, Frank H. Little, argues that the 'controlling idea in the Anabaptist concept of the church is the restoration of the primitive [apostolic] New Testament church'.[16] Leonard Verduin in his *The Reformers and Their Stepchildren* maintains that the Anabaptists believed that

> the Church had 'fallen' in the days of Constantine, with a 'fall' as calamitous and as fraught with evil consequences as the 'fall' in Eden. This 'fall' had made a fallen creature of the Church, one 'dead in trespasses and sins'. And just as the catastrophe in Eden had made a re-birth necessary, so did the 'fall' of the fourth century require a new creation ... they felt called therefore to reconstitute the Church, to start all over.[17]

By identifying themselves with the Anabaptists, the Landmarkers buried themselves in a quagmire of self-contradiction, for the Anabaptists themselves denied the succession theory. Spurling's restoration vision of Christian Union was therefore truer to the Anabaptist vision of the church than the Landmarkers doctrine of historical succession.

Whether or not Spurling and his followers knew Baptist professor, J.B. Gambrell, they nevertheless were in full agreement with his illustration of the 'lost horse'. Taking issue with the strict dogmatism of Landmarkism on the issue of historical succession, Dr. Gambrell said,

> I do not place much stress on historical succession – but the New Testament reads as though things were started to go on. Let me illus-

---

[15] Spurling, *Lost Link* [original], p. 8.
[16] Frank H. Little, *Anabaptist View of the Church* (Boston: Starr King Press, 1958); See also Harold S. Bender, 'Church', in *The Mennonite Encyclopedia* (4 Vols.; Scottdale, PA: Mennonite Publishing House, 1955), I, pp. 594-98.
[17] Leonard Verduin, *The Reformers and Their Stepchildren* (Grand Rapids, MI: Eerdmans, 1964), p. 40.

trate my idea of succession: A man lost a gray horse. He finds some horse tracks step by step for a hundred miles. Then he comes upon the horse – but it is a black horse. That is historical succession. Tracks are not worth a cent. If, on the other hand, you find the gray horse, it does not make any difference if you find any tracks. The whole business lies in the identity ... So, the man who takes the New Testament and finds a church in his neighborhood or elsewhere like the one in the Book, has succession.[18]

Like Dr. Gambrell, Spurling gave little or no ground for any historical identity, most particularly no ground for any historical continuity of the church. Accordingly, the church was a state of being – a state entirely contingent on the members being faithful and obedient to the teachings of Christ. Tomlinson reflected on the position of Spurling and his followers and noted, 'Besides the aforesaid points, they were awakened to the fact that God's church only existed where His law and government was observed by His children'.[19]

Spurling conceded later, however, virtually admitting that he did not comprehend at that time all of the implications and ramifications of his doctrine of the church. To his credit, he willingly modified his view in the coming years after other capable leaders united with the church and pointed out some of the shortcomings and impracticalities of his doctrine. But no radical changes were made until 1906 when the churches began to centralize their government and decision-making process. Indeed, the church would thereafter gradually come to identify itself with a distinct body of dogma and a unique view of 'theocratic government'. Ironically, the church would eventually adopt a system remarkably similar in some respects to that of papal Rome, thus standing Spurling's original idea of the church on its head. But we will elaborate on this development more fully in its place.

But Spurling's differences with the Landmarkers in the early 1880s were not purely based on doctrinal issues. His complaints had as much to do with the lack of grace and spirituality among the leaders and the churches. He saw the root of the problem more in the fact that there was 'jealousy already among the ministry'.[20] The highly esteemed Baptist historian, David Benedict, wrote in 1860 in his *Fifty Years Among the Baptists* that as early as the 1850s Baptists were losing their 'first love' and becoming colder, more worldly, and more formal in their worship and

---

[18] Burnett, *Pioneer Preachers*, p. 194.
[19] Tomlinson, *LGC*, p. 206.
[20] Spurling, *Lost Link*, 47; Pinckney, *Sketch*, p. 2.

inter-personal relationships. He lamented the fact that the waning of spirituality gave place to worldliness and a breakdown of church discipline.

> Fifty years ago it was contrary to Baptist rules for their members to frequent such places of amusement as multitudes of them now resort to without any official censure or complaint. Our people then made a broad distinction between the church and the world, and if any of their members went over the line to the world's side, they were at once put under church discipline ... Achans in the camp were then much dreaded, and church members were assiduously taught not to suffer sin upon a brother ... In our well regulated communities all the members of all grades, and of both sexes, felt bound to watch over each other, and become helpers in all matters of discipline, and all were held to a strict account in their moral conduct ...[21]

Certainly the Landmark movement in East Tennessee in the 1880s emphasized Baptist exclusiveness and the outward forms of church government and polity at the expense of spirituality and the cultivation of Christian graces in the heart. The high churchism of Landmarkism bent the movement in a legalistic direction and encouraged a 'Pharisaic' spirit and disposition in the ministers. Burnett in his *Sketches of Tennessee's Pioneer Baptist Preachers* cited repeatedly the harshness and rigidity of many of the ministers along with their pride and fleshly tendencies. In regard to the highly esteemed Dr. W.A. Montgomery, whom we met earlier, Burnett felt compelled to admit his faults, as well as to sing his praises, saying,

> He was ... a truly great preacher, but he was not perfect ... So, in candor I would have to say, he was always strong but not always sweet. He was not equally pleasing at all times, was not always gracious. He was sometimes caustic; sometimes dipped his pen in the 'waters of Marah'. He was ambitious and proud and had an infirmity of temper which he, no less than his friends, deplored. The writer has sometimes thought that the devil had a particular grudge against W.A. Montgomery, for sometimes, when he had preached like a seraph – preached as few men ever preached, and there was 'glory all around', the hand of some malignant spirit, appearing out of the

---

[21] David Benedict, *Fifty Years Among the Baptists* (New York: Sheldon & Company, 1860), pp. 77-78.

darkness, would dash the feast with pitch from the [sulfurous] regions below.[22]

In regard to Zechariah Rose, Burnett paid him a compliment in saying that he was 'not as "hard" … as some of his ministerial brethren'.[23]

Now the fact that Burnett, who wrote in praise of Baptist preachers, felt compelled by integrity to acknowledge the carnal characteristics of many of the ministers inclines us to accept more readily the validity of Spurling's criticism that the ministers lacked love and fell miserably short of the apostolic standards of charitable Christian fellowship. Indeed, Burnett's comments seem to have justified Spurling's charge that the Landmarkers tended to be guided more by their creed than by the Holy Ghost and the Word of God.

Some Positive Aspects of Landmarkism

Notwithstanding the Landmark doctrines that Spurling denounced and discarded, several concepts which he carried forward into Christian Union bore the distinctive influence of Old Landmarkism. These concepts were positive influences in many respects; and, overall, there was more to commend in Landmarkism than to criticize and condemn, particularly in respect to the Landmark view that the Bible church is necessarily visible in its nature and function, being actually 'the called out' and 'assembled body of Christ' on earth. Moreover, building on the principle that the church is God's visible government in the earth, it followed that the churches were responsible to discipline their members and to maintain a certain standard of order and outward righteousness. These teachings – that the church is a visible interdisciplinary body – were commendable and formed in Spurling a foundation for the Church of God. Like Landmark ministers and churches, Spurling concluded that there is no such thing as an 'invisible church' or 'spiritual church'. Nor is the true church the 'aggregate body of the redeemed'.[24] Landmarkers held that all truly saved people are in the 'family of God' but not necessarily in the church, for believers are not made members of the church automatically by the new birth. Spurling continued to hold in common with Landmarkers the strictly visible nature of the church, though he substituted the church covenant principle for the Landmark doctrine of water bap-

---

[22] Burnett, *Pioneer Preachers*, p. 376.
[23] Burnett, *Pioneer Preachers*, p. 433.
[24] Pendleton, *Why I am a Baptist*, pp. 1-121.

tism in regard to how the church is formed and how one is added to it.[25] Unfortunately, Landmark leaders overregulated their system and insisted on a strict observance of all Landmark rules and regulations. This pushed the movement into an exclusive mold, against which, unfortunately, as we will see, Spurling overreacted in building his liberal system in Christian Union.

In regard to a church covenant, Spurling either consciously or unconsciously had reached back deeper into Baptist and Anabaptist history to a principle practiced by groups called *Covenanters*. Scotch Reformers also in the middle of the sixteenth century had built their system on the principle of a church covenant. These radical reformers of the sixteenth century, having found themselves outside of the church of Rome and also outside the state churches of England and Protestantism in general, saw no other ground upon which to form their churches but a church covenant.[26] The covenant formula of English Separatist John Smyth and his followers in 1606 was typical:

> They shooke off this yoake of antichristian bondage, and as the Lords free people, joined them selves (by a covenant of the Lord) into a church estate, in ye fellowship of ye gospell, to walke in all his wayes, made known, or to be made known unto them, according to their best endeavours, whatsoever it should cost them, the Lord assisting them.[27]

This covenant tradition was still strong and viable in eighteenth and nineteenth-century Baptist churches in America. In his *Customs of Primitive Churches*, Morgan Edwards wrote in 1774: 'A covenant is the formal cause of a church: so that without a covenant, expressed or implied, a visible church cannot be'.[28] David Thomas expressed a similar lofty view of a church covenant. He identified several essential elements in the covenant principle, namely, that when faith has been confessed and repentance made, and baptism by immersion consented to or accomplished, that a church can be constituted by 'nothing else but mutual promise, or engagement to live together as brethren; and to help one

---

[25] In the original draft of the *Lost Link*, Spurling plainly says, 'Christian Union does not make baptism the door of the church' (p. 20). See also Pendleton, *Why I am a Baptist*, p. 196, and compare *Lost Link*, pp. 15, 17, 18, 23, 34.

[26] See Champlin Burrage, *The Church Covenant Idea: Its Origin and Its Development* (Philadelphia: American Baptist Publication Society, 1904); William R. Estep, *The Anabaptist Story* (Nashville: Broadman Press, 1963), pp. 190-225; Thomas N. Finger, *A Contemporary Anabaptist Theology* (Downers Grove, IL: InterVarsity Press, 2004).

[27] W.T. Whitley, *The Works of John Smyth* (Cambridge: University Press, 1915), I, lxii.

[28] Cited in Charles Deweese, *Baptist Church Covenants* (Nashville: Boardman Press, 1990), pp. 50-51.

another to their utmost, to serve God, to uphold His truth; and to promote the interest of His kingdom in the place where they dwell'.[29] This was the prevailing view among a large number of Baptists in the nineteenth century who found precedents in the Scriptures to confirm the same, for example, Exod. 19.5-8; 24.6-8; 2 Kgs 11.17, 18; 23.1-3; 1 Pet. 2.9. Spurling saw in Ezek. 16.8 – 'I … entered into a covenant with you … and you became mine' – a proof text for the idea of the church covenant.[30] He maintained further that 'Israel was God's chosen people, even before they went into Egypt', but 'the Jewish church was organized at Mount Sinai … It takes more than merely being a saint, or a child of God, to be the Church of God … [it takes] the covenant of visible unity and fellowship'.[31]

Another significant modification by Spurling of Landmarkism was to identify the family of God with the kingdom of God. Thus rather than identifying the aggregate of Landmark churches as the kingdom of God, he interpreted the kingdom as the mystical or spiritual realm of the redeemed.[32] This distinction saved Spurling and the Church of God in its early years from repeating the Landmark error of blowing one's own trumpet in claiming a strict exclusiveness, the same error that had been perpetuated by Roman Catholics and repeated by Campbellites and other groups. It also saved the Church of God from the tendency of de-Christianizing ministers and believers in other traditions of faith. Landmarkers were infamous for refusing to recognize any but regularly ordained Baptist ministers as being true Gospel ministers.

Spurling continued to hold in 1886 to the Landmark view that the local church is independent and autonomous and the only true form of God's church in the world; yet he yielded to the opinion of his fellow ministers in the Church of God in later years, with some reservations, working with them to develop a universal [catholic] polity in the church with a centralized form of government. Further, he continued to hold to the Landmark interpretation that the Great Whore in Revelation 17 was in fact the Roman Catholic Church, and that the Episcopalians, Presbyterians, Lutherans, Methodists, Campbellites, and other religious groups were the Harlot Daughters of the Great Whore. Ironically, he added the Baptists to the list of harlots, including the Landmarkers because they had bound men's minds and hearts to human creeds over against the law of Christ. In his view, Landmarkers, like other denominations, es-

---

[29] Deweese, *Baptist Church Covenants*, p. 51.
[30] R.G. Spurling, 'The Church', *COGE* 1.2 (March 15, 1910), pp. 1, 4.
[31] Spurling, 'The Church', p. 1.
[32] Spurling, *Lost Link*, pp. 40, 41.

tablished their churches on the basis of human legislation instead of love and divine revelation.

We see then that Spurling's Christian Union in 1886 was in many respects a reformation of Landmarkism, as well as a reaction against denominationalism in general, but its overarching aim was to restore the church of the New Testament.

A Glance in Other Directions

Spurling had looked at other religious traditions besides Landmarkism before he guided his followers into the formation of Christian Union. His writings reveal that he examined closely Alexander Campbell's Restoration Movement, and also the Methodism and Presbyterianism of his day.[33] But it is equally clear that he was not appreciably affected by any of these traditions. The heart and soul of his convictions were warmer and more spiritual than Campbellism, and more democratic and spiritual than the Methodist Episcopal system. He discerned that something vitally important was missing in these traditions, namely, the lack of a spiritual potency that identified them more with Babylon than Zion. His faith and vision would not allow him to settle for the dry bones of Campbellism and Methodism, for he knew that where there was no joy there was no love, and where there was no love and joy, there was no liberty; and where there was no love, joy, and liberty, there was no divine church. That was it! That's what was missing among these traditions – *love*, 'the lost link' – and this was vitally important to comprehend, for love, according to Spurling, was the primary and essential basis for Christian fellowship'.

Walter Scott, Alexander Campbell's partner and kindred spirit, had permeated their whole movement with a cool rationalism, denying original sin, and thus depriving the *Disciples of Christ* and *Churches of Christ* of the joy of spiritual regeneration. Landmarkers, most of whom were con-

---

[33] Spurling, *Lost Link*, pp. 17, 18, 23-25, 33-36. Interestingly, Spurling nearly always refers to Campbell as a major reformer; the same as Tomlinson does George Fox, for obvious reasons: Tomlinson and his ancestors had a long connection with Quakerism, and Spurling's father and grandfather almost certainly were influenced by Campbell's movement in the 1830s when they lived in Fentress County, Tennessee; for the Baptist churches in that area at that time were all affected by Campbell's movement, many in fact defecting to Campbell's movement. R.G. Spurling's grandfather, James, was a prominent member of the Poplar Cove church [also New Hope and Clear Creek] in the Stockton Valley Association in the 1830s, which along with other churches in the area were disturbed and disrupted by Campbellism for many years. See Cawthorn & Warnell, *Pioneer Baptist Church Records*, pp. 538-52.

fident debaters, had for a long time denounced Campbellism for teaching 'water salvation'. Graves, the champion Baptist debater, was greatly admired by Baptist preachers in the South for his 'preeminent abilities, gifts, and courage'. He skillfully denounced Campbellism and Methodism as well as Romanism, Episcopalism, and Presbyterianism for years in *The Tennessee Baptist* and in other published works. Campbellism and Methodism were especially the focus for his ceaseless tirades of polemics and denunciations because they were the major movements in his day contending for the loyalties of the people for 'the true church'. The Presbyterians, with their insistence on a formal, educated ministry were no longer competitive in the mountains in the latter half of the century, except in the Cumberland Mountain region: and the hundreds of holiness-Pentecostal bodies were still awaiting the last decade of the nineteenth century and the first decade of the twentieth for their emergence on the American scene. Thus Graves and the Landmarkers focused their merciless sarcasms and denunciations on the Campbellites for their religion of works and on the Methodists for their practice of infant baptism and mode of sprinkling, exalting Landmarkism as the divine alternative.

Spurling's faith was grounded in spiritual regeneration of the heart, not in a mere 'testimony' out of the head. On the one hand, to pour his spirit into Campbell's movement would have burst it asunder like 'new wine in old bottles', spilling the joy and life of his faith on the ground of apostasy. Methodism, on the other hand, was going through a drought in the latter part of the nineteenth century, and for decades had been departing from the Wesleyan principle of deep spirituality and the practice of holiness. The Methodist Church thus had little appeal to Spurling's hungry heart.[34] Still, how could he remain among the Landmarkers? For though there was a degree of love and spirituality in Landmark churches, love was not supreme. The Landmark system had been subjugated to arbitrary church rules and human legislation. Bigotry and arrogance connected with the high churchism of Landmarkism tended to crowd out love and compassion. It was the supremacy of human legislation over God's love that had Spurling defrocked and excluded from his Missionary Baptist church in 1883-1884, the same church he once believed was 'Christ's only true church'. He expressed his anguish at that point in his struggle to understand his dilemma and to know more perfectly the will of God for his life:

> Oh, God, are the days of murdering Christians not yet over? Am I a companion of John Huss at the stake amid the flames of persecu-

---

[34] Spurling, *Lost Link*, pp. 23, 33-35.

tions? Am I sold for nothing ... Oh, Jesus, is it Your law that has separated me from Thy people?[35]

So there the young man stood in 1886, a defamed Baptist minister with spiritual life in his soul, and with the concepts of Campbellism, Methodism, and other religious traditions in the corner of his eye. The outward form of Campbell's ecclesiology seemed more or less right, but it was dead: it was like a bridal gown thrown over a mannequin; like a shell wanting of a kernel. Methodism, conversely, was in outward form more or less Episcopalian and thus could not be countenanced as an acceptable system. Graves had called Methodism 'the popery of Protestantism', a charge with which Spurling agreed at least in sentiment. Landmark Baptist life came from God, but its exclusiveness and rigidity came from J.R. Graves, J.M. Pendleton, and other men. It was indeed a religious maze that vexed his spirit. His soul cried out, 'What shall I do? What can I do?'[36] Still, with his aged father, he searched the Scriptures and history, the Spirit working to give him peace with understanding, and to form the proper conception of the church in his mind. Like a divine seed planted deeply in his consciousness, struggling violently to germinate, yearning to grow and take proper form, the prophetic vision worked in him as a woman in pain to be delivered. He peered deeply into the Scriptures, and looked at the Christian traditions before him – Landmarkism, Methodism, Campbellism, and other traditions. He considered the Anabaptist tradition, which was so comparable to his Separate Baptist roots, being perhaps the very heritage of his English and European forebears.[37] He desperately desired to avoid ecclesiastical tyrannies, on one hand, and anarchy on the other. He wrote,

> Some think Christians ought not to be united in any bond of fellowship while others are not satisfied with the law and government of Christ and the Holy Spirit but must have a great many more laws and governments. So between the two extremes there is a wise and reasonable middle ground of truth which unprejudiced and honest Spirit-led Christians can surely find in the words and acts of the Savior and His followers under the leadership of the Holy Ghost.[38]

There between all these traditions somewhere, more or less, was the answer to the burden of his soul and spirit; there somewhere was relief from his spiritual anguish. There entangled in Landmark bigotry, Meth-

---

[35] Spurling, *Lost Link*, p. 48.
[36] Spurling, *Lost Link*, p. 48.
[37] See Phillips, 'Baptist Roots', pp. 9-15.
[38] Spurling, *Lost Link,* p. 41

odist episcopalism, and religious creeds was the spirit of the beautiful bride of Christ, and there among the Campbellites lay the divine corpse. Doubtlessly he thought it amazing how much Landmarkism, stripped of its successionism and rigid exclusivity, resembled his Anabaptist heritage.[39] Somewhere there among the Landmarkers, Methodists, Presbyterians, and Alexander Campbell's vision for Christian union was the figure of the bride, her spirit struggling to breath, travailing to be reborn! And there in Spurling and his followers was the desire and instrumentality to free her, to reform her, to restore her!

Spurling's Vision

We have seen that it was about the year 1884 that Spurling rejected the exclusive claims of his 'beloved Missionary Baptist church' and began to search the Scriptures and to study church history for an understanding of the Bible church.[40] Gradually he uncovered in biblical prophecy an important key in his quest, namely, that the church was predicted to fall and to be restored in the last days. He cited Isa. 60.1-3, Zech. 14.7, 2 Thess. 2.1-12 and other passages in support of his restoration theology. Thus, contrary to his Landmark Baptist tradition, he believed that during the Dark Ages, 'no church stood on God's law and government'.[41] In fact, after the church had fallen – which he concluded like the Anabaptists had culminated in 325 CE upon Emperor Constantine's exploitation of the church's confusion and lack of spirituality – what was built up in the church's place was 'Babylon'. Accordingly, in the fragmentation of Christianity and the developing denominationism, each denomination stood on a separate creed dividing God's people into a hundred camps,

---

[39] The close similarity of Spurling's doctrine of the church with the Anabaptist view of the church may be seen in the following: 1) the restoration concept of church in history, particularly interpreting the apostasy of the New Testament church with the marriage of church and state at Nicea in 325 CE (Spurling, *Lost Link*, pp. 16, 18-23); 2) the separation of church and state (pp. 18, 23); 3) the reservations with holding civil office (p. 46); 4] the strong anti-papal stand, including the anti-Catholicism, anti-episcopalism, and anti-creedalism (pp. 16-18, 23-25, 40); 5) the overall non-conformity with church-state polity and regulations; 6) the rugged independence and insistence on Congregationalist government and polity (pp. 34-35); 7) the tendency toward passivism (pp. 35-36); 8] the teaching and practice of covenanting and footwashing (p. 44); 9) the emphases on love and church discipline.

[40] Tomlinson, *LGC*, p. 205.

[41] R.G. Spurling, 'Address', Eighth Annual General Assembly 1913 (*GAM 1906-1914*), p. 195. Tomlinson reprinted this address in the *WWM* eulogizing Spurling following his death in 1935. See 'R.G. Spurling Passed Over The Tide' (*WWM*, June 22, 1935), p. 1.

thus frustrating Jesus' prayer for Christian union.[42] He felt so passionately about the evil associated with the religious arguments and divisions between the Roman Catholics and Protestants, and the Protestants against themselves, that he determined the whole denominational system was the fulfillment of what the apostle John envisioned through the Spirit, namely, 'MYSTERY, BABYLON THE GREAT, THE MOTHER OF HARLOTS, AND ABOMINATIONS OF THE EARTH'.[43] He noted in his 'Address' to the Eighth Annual General Assembly in 1913, 'The beautiful virgin became a harlot. The Church from its state of virginity drifted into Roman Catholicism'.[44]

This interpretation of Revelation 17 may seem absurd to the modern reader; but it should be borne in mind that ministers like Graves and Spurling in the nineteenth century were only three generations removed from the bloody persecutions that the Anabaptists had suffered at the hands of both Roman Catholics and Protestants in Europe and England. Graves was the grandson of a courageous Huguenot who fled to America after most of his ancestors had perished under Roman Catholic persecutions between 1685 and 1750.[45] More than 250,000 Protestants had perished or were forced to flee France during the attempted genocide under Catholic King Louis IV who boasted in 1715 that Protestantism had been exterminated from France.

We have not yet learned the roots of the Spurlings on the European side of the Atlantic; yet R.G. Spurling identified his faith, if not his blood, with the persecuted Anabaptists in Europe, claiming them as his spiritual ancestors. He spoke of the radical Anabaptists as 'our fathers'[46] and saw his spiritual heritage connected with the Anabaptists in Italy's Piedmont Valley and in the French, Swiss, and German Alps in the seventeenth and eighteenth centuries.[47]

The fathers and grandfathers of most Baptists in the nineteenth century had etched into the minds and spirits of their children the tales of the bloody and tortuous persecutions their ancestors had suffered. They instilled in them the knowledge of the precious gift of liberty, and warned them how easily the fragile state of religious freedom could disintegrate if it were not diligently nourished and maintained. For even in America, Baptists, Anabaptists, and Quakers had been persecuted by the

---

[42] Spurling, *Lost Link*, pp. 6, 13, 17-20, 23- 25.
[43] Spurling, *Lost Link*, pp. 5-6.
[44] Spurling, 'Address', *GAM 1906-1914*, p. 195.
[45] Burnett, *Pioneer Preachers*, p. 184.
[46] Spurling, *Lost Link*, p. 39.
[47] Spurling, *Lost Link*, pp. 16, 34. There may be a hint here that would corroborate a family rumor that the Spurlings' roots were in the mountains of Germany.

Anglican Church and the Puritans. And the persecutions did not cease until the Bill of Rights in 1789 had become the law of the land. Thus Spurling had little confidence in America as a nation in and of itself, warning in fact that America could as readily become a persecutor of God's people as had the state-church systems in Europe and England if Americans at any time were to allow the laws of antichrist to be substituted in lieu of the laws of Christ. Religious liberty could be lost as quickly as it had been obtained, and the old bigotry and persecuting spirit of the Dark Ages would again fill the land[48] – Babylon would rise again and immediately unleash her hordes of murderous demons against God's church in the last days. Spurling implied in fact that the murderous spirit of Babylon and her Harlot Daughters actually lay latent in modern Romanism and Protestantism, and was held in check only by a cultured civility – a civility that was superficial and that at anytime could crumble if not understood and diligently maintained. Having been 'horror stricken' by Charles Buck's bloody history of persecution in his *Theological Dictionary*[49] and G.H. Orchard's *History of Baptists*,[50] Spurling wrote: 'I turn from these awful scenes to the fair land of America and ask, Shall this fair land ever drink the blood of God's holy people, at the hand of some human creed? God only knows what the law of men will do when substituted instead of God's law'.[51]

> Through blood and through strife
> They hazarded their life,
> They were hunted and killed
> Over mountain and hill.
> Through prisons and fires,
> And beasts from the lyres,
> Though much trouble they saw,
> They clung to God's law.
> – R.G. Spurling[52]

As pointed out earlier, Spurling's view of the Harlot Church in Revelation 17 was formed as much by the influence of his former Landmark tradition as it had been by the inspiration of the Spirit and the Word of

---

[48] Spurling, *Lost Link*, pp. 5, 6, 15, 16, 21, 22, 34, 35.
[49] Charles Buck, *Theological Dictionary* (Philadelphia: William W. Woodward, 1825), pp. 437-43; G.H. Orchard, *History of Baptists*, pp. 254-340; compare *Lost Link*, pp. 33, 34.
[50] Spurling, *Lost Link*, p. 33.
[51] Spurling, *Lost Link*, p. 35.
[52] Spurling, *Lost Link*, p. 15.

God. The modification that Spurling made in the Landmark view was in denouncing religious systems without condemning the particular believers in those systems. As we will see further on in this work, unlike Landmarkism he recognized the prior baptisms of believers and accepted the ordination of ministers from other organizations who desired to unite with Christian Union.[53] He even allowed in Christian Union the individual member to decide according to his conscience the mode of his baptism, whether sprinkling or dipping (immersion), though he insisted on the uniform formula of 'in the name of the Father, Son, and Holy Ghost'.[54]

> I wonder as upon this band,
> I cast my wondering eyes.
> Each in their different churches stand,
> And ask not other nigh.
> I wonder as along their lines,
> Their fences I behold,
> Which seem to stop their love,
> From reaching all the fold.
> I wonder as upon their walls,
> Their mother's name I see;
> It almost makes my soul to shrink,
> Her name is mystery.[55]
> – R.G. Spurling

What was lost in the darkness of the Dark Ages more particularly was the mystery of the 'rock' upon which Jesus had at first established His church, namely, the Spirit-imparted revelation that Jesus is the Christ, the Son of the living God.[56] Further, the Holy Spirit in Spurling's theology of the church indwells and inspires believers and forms them into the body of Christ. For He writes God's laws upon the hearts of believers, enabling them to build up each other in the faith and to unite together spiritually and visibly in Christ.[57] Spurling illustrated this spiritual process by likening believers to stones in a quarry being hewn and dressed to fit together in a temple.

---

[53] Tomlinson, *LGC*, p. 208.
[54] Spurling, *Lost Link* [original], p. 20. Spurling admitted, however, that his preference was 'dipping'.
[55] Spurling, *Lost Link*, p. 25.
[56] Spurling, *Lost Link*, p. 7.
[57] Spurling, *Lost Link*, pp. 7-8.

> Like the temple of old ... every saint is a stone in the temple of God. Rev. 3.12. Thank God that you and I may be a part of God's church. Built by Christ – yes, here on earth is God's quarry and every stone that does not spoil in dressing in the quarry (visible church) will, when perfected through suffering like Jesus was, fit perfectly in the church triumphant – the temple of God.[58]

Equally important in Spurling's restoration vision of the church was his understanding of the law upon which Jesus had at first established the church, namely, the law of love; particularly love over against creeds. His theology of 'brotherly love' being derived from God's love, from *agape*, was the primary basis for 'Christian union' and the essential ingredient in genuine Christian fellowship.[59] In fact, it is only the dynamic of God's love working in and through the members that enables them to remain united together in Christ and to live and grow up together in the light and power of His government and teachings. Thus Spurling would exclaim after the church was restored, 'I am glad we ... have no other leader but God's Spirit; no other law but that which Jesus gave; no other rule of faith but the New Testament'.[60]

The lingering influence of Spurling's Baptist heritage may be seen in his radical sense of local church independence and the inviolability of the individual's conscience, the latter being exalted to an almost idolatrous status. These concepts, and the corresponding practice of them in the churches, created an unstable and volatile fellowship that made growth and coordination between the congregations of Christian Union, and even between the members themselves, virtually impossible. The movement was born therefore with a birth defect that hindered its growth and cohesiveness. Accordingly, as we will see further on, all of the churches of Christian Union would eventually go defunct or else remain stunted in their ability to grow and fulfill their noble vision for 'Christian union'.[61]

> The Lord of life from glory came,
> To make our minds and hearts the same;
> His gospel, law, and government
> Unto his children he has sent.
> No more the Gentile and the Jew,

---

[58] Spurling, *Lost Link*, p. 16.
[59] Spurling, *Lost Link*, pp. 20, 43.
[60] Spurling, *Lost Link*, p. 8.
[61] Wade H. Phillips, 'The First General Assembly: The Move Toward Centralized Government', *Church of God History & Heritage* (Winter Issue 2006), p. 2.

> But one man made of the two;
> The lines of strife no more to lay,
> But walk in love from day to day.
> The law of love He did command,
> That by it we should understand,
> And by it all His children know
> For out of it no strife can grow.
> Alas, where is this law today,
> From which the Church has gone astray?
> The law of Christ that have denied,
> By human laws they are supplied.
> Will Christians close their eyes and ears
> Against the light that now appears,
> Yet still to bow to human laws,
> Which God shall break like useless straws?
> O, brethren, for the sake of Christ,
> Leave off these laws that gender strife,
> Be by the Spirit ever led,
> He is the church's only Head.
> – R.G. Spurling[62]

Spurling's Eloquence

Spurling's lack of formal education took nothing away from his eloquence nor diminished in the least the effectiveness of his teaching and preaching. His pulpit ministry was persuasive, and though unlettered he had the ability to put in writing the vision that burned in his spirit. *The Lost Link* – his most extensive written contribution – is filled with stirring images, vivid metaphors, effective dialog, moving analogies, and well-placed parables. Though he frequently misspelled words, still he used them fluently and effectively, even large words like 'latitudinarianism'. He wrote of the early church as having 'organically fallen' and warned against 'political ecclesiasticism'; he spoke of a 'Christianized conscience' and of 'creed bound children'. Further, he demonstrated a remarkable grasp of church history, and drew upon that knowledge effectively to advance his vision of Christian Union.

His remarkable powers of persuasion illuminated the minds and stirred the passions of a few hundred people between 1883 and 1896, and a great many more after that including future leaders in the church

---

[62] Spurling, *Lost Link*, pp. 19-20.

such as W.F. Bryant, A.J. Tomlinson, M.S. Lemons, J.L. Scott, Sam C. Perry, and Nora Chambers. His ministry so touched Balford Abercrombie – who would be one of the twenty-one delegates in the first General Assembly – that he named his second son Sperling (b. 1905).

Included in Spurling's repertoire of oratorical skills was his use of sarcasm. He shrunk his opponents with his withering wit, and with penetrating sagacity, cut in half men who tended to be high-minded and puffed-up by position and education. He derided 'smart eleks' and 'self important preachers', and ridiculed church leaders who ruled with a 'self-assumed infallibility'. He wrote,

> The infernal regions never won a greater victory than when Satan gets a band of pious saints together and some 'smart elek' with self assumed infallibility gets up and says [he] won't ordain any man to preach unless he can teach their doctrine as they have set it up, and then they shout like Israel shouted when they saw Aaron's golden calf ...[63]

In another place he mocks 'the little preacher in the stand riding some hobby, branding all others as heretics or devils'.[64] He talked about denominations as being 'hatched', conjuring up the image of a mother serpent hatching her young – 'for every egg hatches a sect, and every sect is a daughter of the mother of harlots'.[65]

One of Spurling's most effective means of communication, however, was in his composition and recitation of poems. He seemed to especially wax eloquent through poetic expression, capturing in rhythmical verse his deepest thoughts and projecting the glorious vision of his heart. In his little book, *The Lost Link,* he composed no less than thirteen poems and fitted them appropriately to each subject to enhance his message and to touch the emotions of his readers. These same poems he used effectively in his pulpit ministry, expressing them on occasion in song. His address in the Eighth General Assembly in 1913 was typical of his effect upon his listeners. Following his message, there were 'shouts and tears of gratitude', and then he continued 'amidst shouts and cheers' to sing one of his poems that was fitted appropriately to enhance his message.[66] Then suddenly there was a mighty outpouring of the Spirit – 'the power fell and all were on their feet with uplifted hands, dancing and shouting and praising God. One played the organ under the power of

---

[63] Spurling, *Lost Link*, p. 26.
[64] Spurling, *Lost Link*, p. 37.
[65] Spurling, *Lost Link*, p.27.
[66] *GAM 1906-1914*, pp. 196-98.

the Spirit'. This glorious outpouring included about twelve persons who had 'fallen in love with the church' and came forward to become members.

Still there was something more in Spurling's eloquence that enabled him to influence and persuade men of the caliber of A.J. Tomlinson, M.S. Lemons, Sam C. Perry, J.L. Scott, and W.F. Bryant. It was his vision of God's church. Spurling was a man with a plan; he had systematized his vision, and was able to explain it with conviction and certainty. His words were thought through and weighty. According to Tomlinson, it took Spurling only 'five minutes' to change his mind – 'to knock out of me' – the idea of a spiritual or invisible church[67] and convert him to the doctrine of a visible church formed by a verbal covenant. Tomlinson introduced Spurling in the Eighth General Assembly in 1913 with these words:

> I was searching for the truth. I knew there must be some plan yet undiscovered for the government of God's people. It was in God's providence that I met brother Spurling who explained to me his vision of God's Church as he saw it in the Word. He showed me that we were received into the church by covenanting with each other to obey the laws of Christ.

There is still one more important quality that added to the eloquence of the Christian Union leader, and this quality conditioned all else. It was his love and fatherly disposition. Tomlinson said, 'I look upon him as my father', and hundreds of others felt that same way. And why not? For he was the first to conceive the revelation, and for many years thereafter travailed alone in prayer and in the ministry to give birth or rebirth to the Church of God. Moreover, he lived out the love that he preached, and delivered the message of Christian Union with charity and tender affections. He was charismatic in the true sense of the word. Tomlinson said in his eulogy of Spurling in the *White Wing Messenger* in 1935, 'I have pleasant memories of his blessed face ... my mind wanders back to the time when I sat at his feet and listened to his soft mellow voice as he opened the Scriptures to me about the Church of the Bible and our entrance to it by covenant and the right hand of fellowship'.[68] Again Tomlinson noted, 'His good and congenial spirit always made friends for him and he was loved by all who knew him'.[69]

---

[67] A.J. Tomlinson, 'R.G. Spurling Passed Over the Tide', *WWM* (June 22, 1935), p. 1.
[68] Tomlinson, 'Spurling Passed Over', p. 1.
[69] Tomlinson, 'Spurling Passed Over', p. 4.

Christian Union Set in Order

It was under R.G. Spurling's inspirational preaching and influence that eight souls stepped out by faith during that historic meeting on August 19, 1886 in Monroe County, Tennessee and agreed by covenant 'to set [*sic*] together as the Church of God to transact business as the same'.[70] Spurling's father, Richard, was one of those eight. The other seven men and women were John J. Plemons, Polly Plemons, Barbara Spurling, Margaret Loftis, Melinda Plemons, John Plemons, and Adeline Loftis.[71]

We noticed earlier that the elder Spurling was an ordained minister in the Missionary Baptist Church and had been under the impressions of Landmarkism,[72] but he was also particularly affectionate toward his youngest son and had formed a close bond with him; for besides being his natural father, he was yoked with him in the ministry. His paternal affections made him sympathetic toward his son's argument against the strict regulations and political discipline of the Landmarkers; and, moreover, he had joined with his son in worshipping with and befriending the Methodists in the Coker Creek area.[73] His love for the Methodists and other Christians would no longer allow him to maintain the separation demanded by the Landmarkers.

Now the elder Spurling was present on that fateful Thursday in August 1886 in the meetinghouse at Barney Creek and listened as his son preached the inspirational sermon that was destined to change the course of history. Unfortunately, a transcript of that sermon and its precise content has not been preserved, but we may be sure it contained

---

[70] Tomlinson, *LGC*, p. 205.

[71] Tomlinson, *LGC*, p. 207. Tomlinson got his information probably from Spurling himself or else from Barbara or Pinckney Spurling, all of whom witnessed the historic event. Tomlinson indicates that John Plemons and his son, John, were senior and junior, but actually they were not, at least not formally; the father's middle name was James, the son's Paul. Also in Tomlinson's account, Loftis is incorrectly rendered Lauftus.

[72] Phillips, 'Baptist Roots', pp. 16-31; *idem*, 'The Life and Times of Richard Spurling', *Church of God History & Heritage* (Summer/Fall 2002), pp. 6-7.

[73] Jeremiah C. Martin, a Methodist minister and prominent citizen in the Coker Creek area, was a local justice of the peace and friend of Spurling. In fact, he lived next door to Richard on Barney Creek. He performed the marriage of Richard to his second wife, Nancy Sue Smallen (formerly Nancy Sue Mitchell) in July 1887. Richard's first wife, Nancy Jane (Norman), born 1815, had died on June 10, 1878. Such was his relationship with the Methodists that he chose one of their number rather than a Baptist minister to ordain his marriage to his second wife. This Jeremiah C. Martin was the father of the William ('Billy') Martin, the same Billy Martin whom we will meet in the next chapter who conducted the revival in the Shearer schoolhouse in 1896 emphasizing sanctification and who would return in 1899 preaching the 'third blessing' – the baptism with the Holy Ghost and fire.

Spurling's complaints against Landmarkism and the need to establish a 'Christian Union' on the basis of mutual love, liberty, and respect. The message was probably *The Lost Link* in a kernel. In any case, Tomlinson says the sermon was 'full of force [that] proved effective' in regard to the need for a reformation.[74] In response to the message, the elder Spurling promptly stepped forward with the seven others mentioned above and covenanted himself with them to form Christian Union.[75] Then by virtue of his ordained status in his Missionary Baptist Church, he moderated the first business session and administered the covenant to his son, with the church extending to him the right hand of fellowship and accepting him into the fold. The church then chose R.G. Spurling as their pastor and his father ordained him the next month, September 2, 1886.[76] The elder Spurling was thus privileged to be the first ordained minister in the church, but R.G. Spurling was the church's first pastor.[77]

The name *Christian Union* expressed the vision and aim of the little flock, for R.G. Spurling and the few souls that stood with him intended to launch a movement that would bring about the visible union of God's 'creed-bound children' who were scattered throughout 'Babylon' – Mother Rome and her Harlot Protestant Daughters. Whether or not Spurling understood all of the implications of his actions on August 19, 1886, Christian Union was set in motion as an alternative to Rome's ecumenical aim. His alternative ecumenism was consistent with his understanding of the church as God's government in the earth. He envisioned a concrete union, a 'fold', formed on the basis of a covenant in which God's sheep could be fed the pure Word of God and be nourished up and disciplined in the faith. Further, he did not flinch because only eight souls started out with him on this ambitious venture, for, after all, God started the world over again in Noah's day with only eight souls.

---

[74] Tomlinson, *LGC*, pp. 206-207. One might wonder how Tomlinson came to this conclusion since he was not in the meeting and did not personally hear Spurling's sermon. It is likely that he just assumed it on the basis of the obvious effect and the results. It is possible that Pinckney Spurling or Barbara Spurling, both of whom were eyewitnesses in the meeting, may have shared with him their recollections.

[75] Tomlinson, *LGC*, p. 206.

[76] Tomlinson, *LGC*, p. 208. The date that Tomlinson gives here – September 26, 1886 – is likely a misprint or typographical error, for Spurling's license signed by his father gives the correct date: September 2, 1886.

[77] Tomlinson notes this distinction in 'Spurling Passed Over The Tide', p. 4.

Spurling anticipated that men would question his wisdom in trying to 'reform and build up a church at this late age in the world'.[78] His answer was, 'Suppose when the Jews were in Babylon that they had refused to go to their own land and rebuild the temple of God', and again, 'If our fathers had refused to make a reformation in the days of Luther we might be in the clutches of Rome today'. He thus encouraged his followers with the old proverb, 'it is never too late to do good'.[79] For Spurling, 1886 was the perfect time, 'the set time' (Ps. 102.13) to obey the prophetic call to come out of Babylon (Rev. 18.4).

God has His times and seasons for everything, and in the fullness of time the church came forth, not in a spectacular manner, nor with a riveting power that immediately drew the attention of the multitudes of Christians, much less the attention of the teeming masses of unbelievers; but with a steadfast and immutable purpose, the builders began to build again 'the tabernacle of David, which is fallen down' (Acts 15.16). And though the world and its great printing presses ignored the initial event, heaven rejoiced. The apostle's words 'as unknown, yet well known' (2 Cor. 6.9) might well be applied to that historic moment in 1886 when Spurling's little flock stepped forward in faith, and with a vision for Christian Union covenanted 'to [sit] together as the Church of God to transact business as the same'.[80]

Why would anyone familiar with Bible prophecy think it strange that the church should have such an uncelebrated beginning, or a new beginning in the last days? The apostle's words 'as unknown, yet well known' could be applied as readily to the occasion when Christ went up into a mountain and 'called unto him whom he would', and out of the multitude of disciples present on that day chose twelve and named them apostles (Lk. 6.13). Those Twelve formed the nucleus for His house in the last days (Ps. 72.16; Isa. 2.2-3; Micah 4.1; Mk 3.13-16; Lk. 6.12-17), being the initial remnant in the restoration of His church according to the prophecies (Isa. 1.9; 11.11; Jer. 23.3; 31.7-13; Amos 9.11; Micah 2.12; Acts 15.16, 17; Rom. 9.29). Yet this event, no less than the restoration of the church in 1886, went virtually unnoticed by the world, and even by the vast multitudes of believers at that time. Again, why should it seem strange to one familiar with the ways of the Lord? Saints know that God works on His own schedule according to a wisdom that transcends human comprehension. We should never underestimate the power of God, nor doubt the Almighty's resolve to fulfill His immutable counsel! On

---

[78] Spurling, *Lost Link*, p. 39.
[79] Spurling, *Lost Link*, p. 39.
[80] Tomlinson, *LGC*, p. 207.

May 13, 1948 there was no nation on earth called *Israel*, but the next day news flashed around the world that the nation of Israel had been reborn. 'Who has heard such a thing? ... Shall the earth be made to bring forth in one day? Or shall a nation be born at once?' (Isa. 66.8). Such a small thing for God to do!

Now if God can do such a marvelous thing in and through an unregenerate people – natural Israel – how much more wonderfully can He fulfill His eternal purpose for the Christian church? If a 'handful of corn in the earth in the top of the mountains' be planted by God, we may rest assured that eventually the 'fruit thereof [will] shake like Lebanon: and they of the city [will] flourish like the grass of the earth' (Ps. 72.16). So it was with the restoration of the church in 1886, and, as we will see in the succeeding chapters of this book, so it was again in 1923, and still again in 2004. In every instance, the church was restored with little notice by the multitudes of Christians and even less by the teeming multitudes of unbelievers.

Restorers have learned in every age not to 'despise the day of small things'; for they know that which invokes the hisses of the world the Lord may lay His hand on and bless and multiply. No power on earth can stop what the Eternal Word has ordained to be! The 'stone cut out of the mountain without hands' will go forth and conquer this world for Christ, and on that promise God's people may rest assured (Dan. 2.34, 44). The church may be weak in itself, but in God it is infinitely powerful. Never underestimate Zion, for she moves in the realm of the miraculous, having received from her Lord the 'keys to the kingdom'.

The Role of Elder Richard Spurling

Now the implications of the meeting on August 19, 1886 apparently had been thought-through by Spurling and his father for some time,[81] which we have every reason to believe included consideration that the elder Spurling's ordained status would lend weight to legitimizing the action of setting the church in order. Tomlinson's account in *The Last Great Conflict* seems to be carefully worded for this very purpose: to preserve the important details of the meeting anticipating the need in the future to show that the action was duly authorized.

> By virtue of the office he had held as a faithful ordained minister in the Missionary Baptist Church for a number of years, Elder Richard

---

[81] Tomlinson, *LGC*, p. 206. Spurling had related to Tomlinson that 'plenty of time for consideration' had been given to the time and place for the meeting.

Spurling was duly acknowledged and recognized as their minister, to do all the business devolved on him as such in the new order. He then having been placed in authority by the body, took his seat as moderator, and by prayer dedicated the infant church of God, imploring His guidance and blessings for it, and that it might grow and prosper, and accomplish great good. An invitation was then given for the reception of members, and they received Richard G. Spurling who was then a licensed minister. The church chose him as their pastor, and had him ordained the next month, September 26, 1886.[82]

Tomlinson's record makes plain also the fact that the vision and burden of Christian Union, contrary to all Church of God historiography,[83] was on the shoulders of the younger Spurling all along, and this agrees with the primary historical sources and data; for, first of all, soon after Christian Union was set in order, the elder Spurling returned to the Holly Springs church on Steer Creek and thereafter remained in fellowship with the Baptists until his death in 1891.[84] Second, Spurling's account in the original draft of *The Lost Link* says that his father was among the number that he persuaded to form Christian Union.[85] Third, there is no

---

[82] Tomlinson, *LGC*, p. 208. The preferred date for Spurling's license is September 2, 1886; for this date corresponds with his comments in *The Lost Link* [original] and the overall historical narrative. It is likely that a '6' was inadvertently added after the '2' in Tomlinson's manuscript.

[83] I first saw the error in Church of God historical accounts that confuse the roles of the two Spurlings while reflecting in 1992 on Tomlinson's account of the church's beginning in *The Last Great Conflict*. Looking afresh that year at his historical record, it became clear to me that he carefully maintains the distinction in the roles of the father and son, and that it was in fact the son that preached the sermon on August 19, 1886 that inspired the formation of Christian Union, and that it was primarily R.G. Spurling, rather than his father, who had the vision for the church. How and when were their roles reversed? It seems most likely that E.L. Simmons in his history – *The History of the Church of God* – published in 1938 was the first to confuse the son with the father and to reverse their roles; thereafter every historian assumed the veracity of Simmons' interpretation and followed suit, including Conn, *Like A Mighty Army;* Duggar, *Diary of A.J. Tomlinson;* and Davidson, *Upon This Rock*. It was then also that I first realized the clear distinction in their names, and thereafter discovered that Richard Green, the son, was named after his maternal grandmother's side of the family. Thus Richard Spurling and R.G. Spurling were not formally senior and junior, the father in fact had no middle name.

[84] Phillips, 'Baptists Roots', pp. 31-34. The Holly Springs Baptist Church Minutes shows clearly Richard's conflict with the church in September 1886 and his reconciliation two months later. In addition, his credentials as a Baptist minister were discovered in his pocket by the Anderson County coroner upon his death in 1891.

[85] Spurling, *Lost Link* [original], p. 12.

evidence that the elder Spurling had any impact upon the development of Christian Union after the church was set in order in 1886.

What seems clear is that Spurling used his father's ordained status to legitimize the organization of Christian Union, for, as we have noticed, it was a matter of importance according to Baptist polity and tradition for an ordained minister to effect a church organization and to moderate business sessions. It is noteworthy, however, that, contrary to all Church of God historiography, including Tomlinson's *The Last Great Conflict*, the elder Spurling did not die shortly after organizing Christian Union; in fact, he remarried in July 1887 (his first wife, Nancy, having died in June 1878),[86] sold his property on Barney Creek in Monroe County in 1889, and died on March 27, 1891 in Anderson County.[87] His death seems to have been the result of a stroke while en route back to his childhood homeland in the Cumberland Mountains.[88]

Richard's return to his Holly Springs Baptist church is understandable, if not justifiable. Almost his entire family was in the Holly Springs church at that time. We have noticed that his older brother, Daniel, died about 1849, and some of Daniel's children followed Uncle Richard and grandpa and grandma, James and Frances ('Frankie'), in their move to Monroe County in the spring of 1859. Several of them became members of the Holly Springs church after it was organized in August of that same year. Lewis became a deacon and was active in the Sweetwater and Eastanallee Associations. One of Richard's brothers, Hicks, from Georgia, and his children also had moved to Monroe County and had become active in the church. Richard's own sons, Daniel, Nathan, and William were all converted at Holly Springs and joined the church. Na-

---

[86] Nancy is buried in the Dehart Cemetery on Steer Creek about a mile from the Holly Springs church. Her stone gives the date of her birth and death: April 18, 1815 – June 10, 1878.

[87] E.L. Simmons' *History of the Church of God* (1938), Charles Conn's *Like A Mighty Army* (1955), Lillie Duggar's *Diary of A.J. Tomlinson* (1963), C.T. Davidson's *Upon This Rock* (1972-1975), all confuse R.G. Spurling with his father, and thus reverse their important roles. Further, they all follow Tomlinson's error in *The Last Great Conflict* showing that the father died shortly after the organization of Christian Union. Tomlinson's record, though otherwise a meticulously careful account of the origin and early development of the church, somehow completely distorts Elder Richard Spurling's birth, age, and death. It seems that he made certain assumptions on the basis of other information and recorded it as history.

[88] *Clinton Gazette*, April 2, 1891. This paper was published weekly on Thursdays. The article on Spurling's death states that he died on Friday. That Friday was March 27, 1891. The 'coroner's jury' ruled out heart attack as the cause of death. A stroke seems to have been the likely cause according to the circumstances; for he fell suddenly along a road known as Bucklick in the northwest part of Anderson County and was pronounced dead by the coroner.

than and William went back north to Morgan and Scott counties after the war, but Daniel remained and married into the prominent Dehart family. Daniel married William Jefferson Dehart's daughter, Mary, and his cousin, Hicks, married Mary's sister, Elizabeth. Dehart was probably the most prominent deacon and member of the Holly Springs church until he died, with the exception possibly of David E. Hedgecock.[89] The cemetery at Holly Springs where many of the Spurlings are buried is named Dehart Cemetery. Dehart was also a preacher. A surveyor working in the Holly Springs area in 1871 happened to go to church on a particular Sunday when Dehart was preaching, and reported: 'Went to meeting at 11 o'clock. Rev. Dehort [sic], 83 years of age, preached to a congregation of twenty persons, from Revelations 19:9, and though he murdered the King's English most horribly, he made some good points, and a great deal of noise'.[90]

Daniel's son, Andrew, became a deacon and later served for a short time as pastor at Holly Springs. Another of Daniel's sons, Colonel, became postmaster in Monroe County and later served as clerk of the County Court.[91] Daniel and Andrew and Daniel's cousin, Lewis, served as directors on the Monroe County Board of Education.[92] Daniel also served as a justice of the peace for the county, and as clerk of the Holly Springs church for many years, filling in on occasion as moderator of business conferences. He was also active in the Sweetwater and Eastanallee Baptist Associations. Moreover, Daniel had become a recognized, if not certified, 'medical doctor' and 'surgeon' in the area, though his qualifications seem to have been little more than the on-the-job training he received during the Civil War which included surgeries and amputations.[93]

We see then that by 1886 Richard's children and grandchildren were gaining prominence as a family in Monroe County, becoming involved in the political and business affairs of the region as much as the religious. It is not surprising then that none of Richard's family joined in the venture of Christian Union, all of them remaining in the Baptist tra-

---

[89] Hedgecock was a justice of the peace, the local postmaster at Towee Falls near Holly Springs, and he also donated the land on which the Holly Springs church was built.

[90] Lillard, *History of Polk County*, p. 118.

[91] Sarah G. Cox Sands, *History of Monroe County, Tennessee* (2 Vols.; Baltimore, MD: Gateway Press, Inc., 1980), II, p. 347.

[92] Sands, *History Monroe County*, II, p. 51.

[93] Daniel's headstone in the Dehart cemetery reads, 'Daniel E.L. Spurling, MD'. Allie Ledford shared with the writer what her grandfather, R.G. Spurling, handed down to her about his illustrious brother (Interview April 1995).

dition even through the next two generations. There was, it seems, simply too much to lose in social standing to get involved with the 'Wild Sheep Union' – a common slander used by the Baptists to denounce Christian Union and to discourage other Baptists from joining it.[94] We might well imagine that Daniel and the Deharts and Richard's in-laws and his grandson, Andrew, and other grandchildren pleaded with the Elder to reconsider his actions and return to his Baptist church.

Besides being confronted by his family, Richard would have been confronted by the elders and other members of the Holly Springs church and warned about the consequences of his actions. After all, he was disrupting his family, the church, and the community. They probably argued that what he had done in moderating the meeting that established Christian Union was illegal and irresponsible according to his own tradition of the faith, for it was customary among the Baptists that at least two, and preferably three or more ordained ministers come together to form a presbytery council to set a church in order and to ordain ministers. Richard himself had always practiced this form of government and polity. His family and the church might have reasoned with him also that his actions were contradicting the very love and unity he had so ardently preached and practiced. Was not the whole affair of Christian Union rather 'wild' and 'rebellious?' How could this 'church' be recognized by God? Surely none of these things could be right!

Moreover, Richard was now old and tired; his affections and interests were pulled from many directions, besides the fact that the Holly Springs congregation was speckled with the faces of his grandchildren and great-grandchildren. Yet his youngest son, Richard Green, and his little family were also dear to him. To complicate further his circumstances, he was likely contemplating by this time marrying again to a much younger woman with an intellectually-handicapped child, and making plans to return to Morgan or Scott County to live with one of his other sons.

There is still one more reason that might explain his return to the Holly Springs church; namely, he perhaps never intended to sever himself from his beloved Missionary Baptist church. While he sympathized with his son and desired to assist him in his ministry, and agreed with many of his complaints against the Landmarkers, he does not seem to have been as radical in his thinking nor as adventurous as his son: and thus he may have been coaxed more or less into participating in the action. But in any case, after some consideration the elder Spurling returned to Holly Springs to stabilize

---

[94] 'Wild Sheep Union' and 'Spurling's Church' were common slanders according to oral tradition handed down from members of Christian Union and some of the Spurling family members.

his family and make peace in the church. Yet his return must have been only half-hearted and mixed emotionally, for his deepest affections were with his youngest son whom he had fathered in his forty-seventh year and with whom he had bonded in the ministry.

We conclude, then, that though the elder Spurling was not as prominent in the restoration of the church in 1886 as historians and tradition have led us to believe, still, he was instrumental, and his part was important. The fact that he was 'honored with being the first ordained minister', and that he had the privilege to 'dedicate the infant church of God' and receive his son into the church in the new order, secured his immortality in the Church of God. Tomlinson wrote, 'To the sleepless nights of prayer and labors of love by this remarkable old saint and his son, Richard G. Spurling ... we attribute much of the success and advancement of later years'.[95] The present writer eulogized him in a presentation made to the Society of Pentecostal Studies in Guadalajara, Mexico in 1993:

> Thus ended the earthly pilgrimage of so great a warrior of grace and Christian liberty – a true descendant of Roger Williams! He was not especially gifted, but good; not flamboyant and colorful, but loving and just; not formally educated, but a thinker; not a dynamic leader, but a champion of Christian freedom – a holy terror against tyranny in every form. Unsung in this world, but well known in glory! He was buried by strangers without a stone above him to mark his grave, but the 'Rock' beneath him would not allow his name to lie in anonymity. A century after his pioneer spirit was laid to rest, millions of Church of God people would see in him their founding father.[96]

Going Forward

The events surrounding the elder Spurling's second marriage, his reunion with his Missionary Baptist church at Holly Springs, the selling of his property on Barney Creek, and finally his death left R.G. Spurling rather estranged and alone in the new venture. Nevertheless, the young man was determined to persevere and continued to preach the message of the 'lost link' and to share his vision for Christian Union. Tomlinson wrote, 'The little church grew very slowly. But few cared anything about the infant organization. The pastor, R.G. Spurling, continued his preaching, not only at the church, but wherever he was granted the liberty'.[97]

---

[95] Tomlinson, *LGC*, p. 209.
[96] Phillips, 'Baptists Roots', p. 37.
[97] Tomlinson, *LGC*, p. 209.

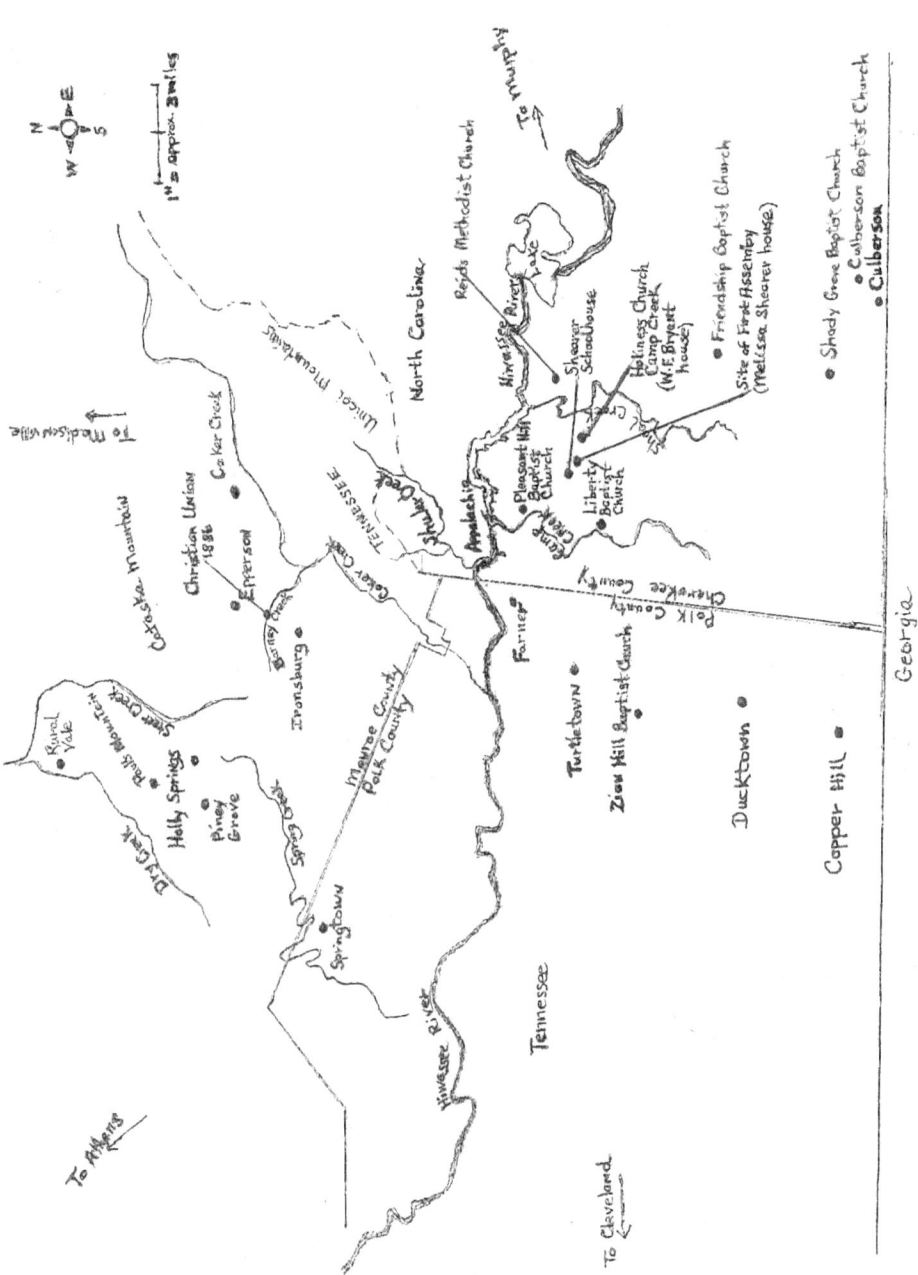

Figure 15

MAP

There was in fact some substantial progress made between the time the church was set in order at Barney Creek in 1886 and the organization of the Holiness Church at Camp Creek in 1902. Spurling set in order at least three more churches between 1886 and 1899, two located in the vicinity where he lived as a child on Dry Creek in the Rural Vale area and across the mountain on Steer Creek in the Holly Springs area, and one in Polk County near the banks of the Hiwassee River. We turn now to examine briefly the church at Barney Creek and the other three Christian Union churches in Monroe and Polk counties.

Christian Union at Barney Creek

We have noticed already the charter members who had composed the church at Barney Creek. These eight members were primarily from two families – the Plemons and Spurling families.[98] They had known each other for a number of years, all being members of the Baptist churches in the area. John J. Plemons (ca. 1818-1902)[99] was a member of the Springtown church in the 1850s and probably first met Elder Spurling when the latter arrived in the Springtown area in 1855-1856. John had been a Primitive Baptist[100] and was likely one of those whom Richard had persuaded to join the Missionary Baptist church at Spring Creek in the 1850s. John married Mary 'Polly' Adaline Irons (ca. 1820-1900) in 1839, and their son, John Paul Plemons (1854-1925) married Ester Melinda 'Linda' Thompson (1861-1915) in 1875.[101] Elder Spurling had

---

[98] The Loftis family could be included; but since the head of the family, William, did not join Christian Union, and his wife, Margaret, was a Plemons, the membership was composed basically of two families. Adeline of course was a Loftis and joined Christian Union; William did not join but may have attended services.

[99] The conflicting data in regard to the births and deaths of John J. Plemons and his wife, Mary 'Polly' (Irons) make it impossible to say with certainty when they were born and died. In addition, we do not know at this point where they were buried in order to benefit from a possible tombstone inscription. The best information may be in the census records which are fairly consistent in indicating that John was born in 1818 and Polly about 1820. It is almost certain that Polly died in the winter of 1899-1900 before the census was taken in the spring of 1900; a family tradition says that John died in 1902. He was living with his son John Paul and his family in 1900 in Madisonville (district 12) according to the census record, and is listed as a widower 82 years of age.

[100] The Springtown church was Primitive Baptist at that time.

[101] Again, there are conflicting dates in regard to the births of John Paul and Ester Melinda. Since no birth certificates were issued at that time, nor birth records kept (except in some instances in family Bibles), birth dates often became obscure. It was not uncommon for people in those days in the mountains not to know the dates of their births. Moreover, since both John Paul and Melinda were illiterate

performed and solemnized their marriage.¹⁰² If indeed Melinda's birth date on her tombstone is accurate, she wedded John Paul at fourteen years of age, not an uncommon practice in the mountains in those days. Margaret J. (Plemons) Loftis (1842-189-?) was John Paul's older sister.¹⁰³ She married William Loftis in 1868, and their union produced at least two girls including Mary Adeline 'Addie' (b. June 3, 1873) who became the youngest member of Christian Union.¹⁰⁴ She married Michael C. Higdon about 1893-1894 and their union produced six boys – Frederick, William, Lester, Robert Fletcher, Charlie, and Grady.¹⁰⁵ 'Addie' had a child before she married Michael – Cordia, born June 10, 1889.¹⁰⁶ Addie's husband, Michael, coincidentally was the nephew and namesake of Michael Columbus Higdon, the Baptist minister whom we met earlier in his opposition to the work and ministry of Richard Spurling. We will meet the Elder Higdon still again in the next chapter in his opposition to the holiness-Pentecostal movement in Polk County and at Camp Creek in Cherokee County.

(though a family tradition claims that Melinda learned to read a little), it is likely that they themselves were uncertain of their birth dates. John Paul's birth date on his tombstone is 1851, but descendants insist on 1854. The 1854 date also seems more compatible with census records and other data. Melinda's birth date in the 1900 census is September 1859, but elsewhere records indicate the 1861 date on her tombstone may be accurate. Her 1913 death date on her tombstone, however, is in conflict with her death certificate, which gives 5-14-1915. The death certificate date is of course preferred. The death certificate also says that she was 53 years old when she died, which corresponds to a birth date of September 1861.

¹⁰² Monroe County Marriage Records, Book D, page 228. Richard had also performed the marriage of John's older sister Sarah E. to Alvin Irons in 1873, Marriage Records, Book D, page 176. Alvin and Sarah were first cousins.

¹⁰³ Since William 'Bill' Loftis died in 1895 (court record) and was a widower at the time, Margaret must have died sometime between August 19, 1886 and 1895.

¹⁰⁴ 'Addie's' full name was Mary Adeline Ann; she seems to have been named in honor of her two grandmothers; she died August 29, 1940 and is buried beside Michael, Lester, and Cordia in the Ironsburg cemetery in Monroe County. Her sister's name was Texas Missouri (1878-1942). She married Thomas Cole and is buried in the Zion Hill Baptist church cemetery in Polk County. An oral tradition in the family claims that sometime after Bill and Margaret married, they went to Texas and then to Missouri before returning to Monroe County. During that time, their second daughter was born, hence her name, Texas Missouri.

¹⁰⁵ Monroe County census record, 1900; tombstone inscriptions; Michael's obituary in *Cleveland Daily Banner*, November 14, 1949.

¹⁰⁶ This raises a question in regard to Addie's marital status at the time that Cordia was born. Michael was clearly Cordia's stepfather, listed as such in the 1910 census record and verified by Michael's funeral notice in the *Cleveland Daily Banner*, November 14, 1949, p. 3. It is possible that Michael was Addie's second husband, but there is no record to verify a prior marriage. Cordia's death notice lists Michael as her father when clearly he was not, which may indicate that she was born illegitimately.

Immediately after the church was set in order at Barney Creek in August 1886 by Elder Spurling, who acted as moderator of the meeting by virtue of his standing as an ordained minister in the Missionary Baptist church,[107] the doors were opened and R.G. Spurling united with the church, and was thereupon selected as the pastor. But his appointment by the church was a foregone conclusion, for he was the inspiration behind the formation of the church and was its chief architect. Why did he wait until the church was set in order before joining? It was the customary protocol among Baptists that when believers in a particular place desired to be set in order as a church, they would form their union with a counsel of ordained ministers, a recognized presbytery, and then open the doors for the reception of new members and licensed ministers. Holding off until the believers had covenanted themselves together was therefore merely a formality. It may have been also that R.G. Spurling, who had just preached the instructive sermon that encouraged the church to be set in order, did not want to intimidate the prospective members or appear to be coercing them into forming the union, for he was still operating on the Baptist principle that a church is a 'voluntary association' of believers.

Following the organizational meeting, the church realized some growth. Penelope Josephine Paul (1853-1947), elder sister of Andy Paul, the latter of whom we will meet again in a moment, was one of the first to join the church at Barney Creek after it was set in order. She was living alone with her five-year old son, Elihu, in 1880,[108] but married William A. Tilley in 1887,[109] whose first wife, Susannah C. Irons, had died a few months earlier.[110] Penelope – called affectionately 'Aunt Nep' later

---

[107] Tomlinson, *LGC*, p. 208.

[108] Monroe County census record, 1880.

[109] Monroe County marriage records. They were married January 4, 1887: Book F, 257. A great granddaughter told the writer that Penelope had been married to Milas Stiles (ca. 1833-1899), who later abandoned her; but there is no record of such a marriage, besides Milas was still living when Penelope married William A. Tilley. Interestingly, when Penelope married William in 1887, Elihu (then eleven years of age) took the name Tilley.

[110] Much of this information was supplied by Fina (Tilley) Sheffield (1919-2009) who was an heir to the old Tilley property and still lived on it when I interviewed her on several occasions in 1993-1995. Her mother had died a few years earlier at 104 years of age. Fina was the granddaughter of Lewis Tilley whose first wife was Elder Richard Spurling's niece, Frances Omega 'Omie' Spurling (1838-1921), the daughter of Richard's brother, Hicks L. Spurling. Fina knew the family history well and spoke frankly about the downside as well as the upside of it. Her grandfather, Lewis, and his second wife attended Christian Union meetings. Fina's information corresponds with census records, deed records, marriage records, church records, and also the testimony of two elderly residents of Coker Creek – Neil Kelly and

in life by all who knew her – lived with the Tilleys and had attended to Susannah the last few years of her life. She became an outstanding Christian woman praised by all who knew her.[111] After William died in 1907, she never remarried.

Soon after Christian Union had been set in order in his gristmill, Spurling began to construct a separate building for worship services and the business of Christian Union.[112] The fact that he also owned and operated a saw mill or merchant mill on his property made construction of a separate building rather convenient. Here in this meetinghouse, a few more believers were added to the fold, but apparently the church never grew to more than twelve members; still, eyewitnesses reported that as many as fifty persons had attended worship services on occasion.[113] Pinckney Spurling recalled a revival meeting con-

Figure 16
PENELOPE (PAUL) TILLEY ('AUNT NEP')

Penelope Paul joined Christian Union probably before she married William Tilley in January 1887. She was at least half Cherokee Indian, as appears obvious in the photo. Affectionately known as 'Aunt Nep', she was reportedly 'an outstanding Christian woman'. She represented one of the highlights of Spurling's ministry at Barney Creek.

Harold Witt – both of whom lived in the area all of their lives and knew the local history well.
    [111] Neil Kelly: 'Aunt Nep was an outstanding Christian woman'.
    [112] Pinckney wrote, 'After the organization of the church in 1886, father furnished his own lumber and built a small church house (*Sketch*, p. 4). Neil Kelly, who lived about a mile from the Barney Creek meetinghouse, said he could remember the building still standing in the late 1930s.
    [113] Pinckney wrote that 'people would fill this church every meeting and pray', but admits few joined Christian Union because it was 'hard for people to give up their church creeds (*Sketch*, pp. 3-4). Other sources for this information were Neil Kelly, Harold Witt, and Fina Tilley, all of whom knew Pinckney Spurling and heard him speak on the beginnings of the church at Barney Creek. Neil Kelly and Harold Witt also knew R.G. Spurling personally and may have gleaned information from him. Kelly said Pinckney reported that they had as many as 40-50 people in the meetings.

ducted by his father at Barney Creek just before Christian Union was set in order in which 'the Holy Ghost fell on Fannie White and she began to speak in tongues'. Fanny L. White, wife of Henry H. White, postmaster at Epperson,[114] was about thirty-six years of age at the time and lived within walking distance of the Barney Creek meetinghouse.[115] It is possible that she afterwards united with the church, for according to reports she continued to worship in the new meetinghouse.[116]

Interestingly, though Richard and the Methodist ministers at Coco Creek (Ironsburg),[117] Jeremiah C. Martin and John F.M. Duggan,[118] had become good friends, and though Richard had 'taken shelter' for two years in 1884-1886 among the Methodist people there and had been invited to preach on occasion in the old log school house on 'Flint Hill' where they worshipped at that time, none of them followed him in the venture of Christian Union. He had even sawed and supplied the lumber for their new church house which they built in 1886-1887.[119] Still, it is

---

[114] Sarah G. Cox Sands, *History of Monroe County, Tennessee* (3 Vols.; self- published , 1980), II, p. 339.

[115] 1880 census record.

[116] Joe Abbot, *The Forgotten Church* (self-published manuscript, 1962), p. 44, says that she united with the church. Abbot from Bridgeport, Alabama came to the Coker Creek area in 1960-1961 to research and learn more about the founding of the church at Barney Creek in 1886; for he saw in Christian Union the origin of his own faith and heritage in the free holiness tradition. He collected much data through interviews with Pinckney Spurling and other eyewitnesses and second-generation descendants of Christian Union, recording the information in a crudely written but valuable little book called *The Forgotten Church*. He lists Fanny White as a member of Christian Union, having obtained the information apparently from Pinckney Spurling. Though we have no reason to question the veracity of Pinckney's record in regard to Fanny White, still he tended to collapse together events that took place in the church after 1895 with events that took place ten years earlier, including the church's holiness-Pentecostal development that began in 1895. If his recollection about Fanny White is accurate – that she indeed spoke in tongues – then it was almost certainly an isolated case before 1895.

[117] The area at that time was known as Coco Creek named for the famed Cherokee Indian princess, Betsy Coco. When the post office was established there in 1906, the area took the name Ironsburg in honor of the Irons' family. The larger area was still called 'Coker Creek' (an Anglicized form of Coco Creek), and thus there were three communities in this part of the Coker Creek basin area: Ironsburg, Epperson, and Coker Creek.

[118] Methodist Episcopal Church Journals of the Holston Conference, 1881-1889. The Presiding Elder's report in the 1883 journal shows that Rev. John Duggan (1835-1906) was a circuit rider in the area. Also unpublished historical sketch of the church called *History of the Ironsburg United Methodist Church* by Mary Etta Hawk affirms that John F.M. Duggan was the pastor of the church at this time and supervised the construction of the new building in 1886-1887. This data is further corroborated by Pinckney, *Sketch*, pp. 3, 4.

[119] Pinckney, *Sketch*, 3.

not surprising that the Methodists remained unmoved, for though Christian Union was a reformation of the Landmark Baptist tradition, it remained otherwise more or less compatible with the doctrine and polity of Baptists in general. The gulf between the Methodists and Christian Union apparently was just too wide to bridge – the Methodists being a highly formal hierarchical Episcopal system, and Christian Union a loosely knit fellowship of churches held together only by 'the ties of love and mutual respect'. Like Baptists in general, the members of Christian Union feared any system of hierarchy and centralization, and the Methodists feared any system that lacked these political features. Spurling maintained that 'Liberty of the soul is the breath and element of that religion inculcated in the New Testament and has been and will be preserved only by those who descend from all governments devised by human policy ... Liberty is what God's people want and must have it at any cost or hypocrisy will soon invade the church'.[120]

Pinckney Spurling in his *Sketch* says that though the Methodists worshipped with the members of Christian Union on occasion, it was simply too 'hard for [them] to give up their church creeds'.[121] Tomlinson says, 'The little church grew very slowly. But few cared anything about the infant organization'.[122] But actually the failure of Christian Union at Barney Creek seems to have been in part because the Coco Methodist church was doing so well in the 1880s. Local tradition and the Holston Methodist Conference records show that many souls were saved in the early and mid 1880s, and the church grew to about 200 members becoming one of the strongest Methodist churches in lower East Tennessee.[123] It looked indeed as if the Methodist people at Coco Creek were going to 'take the world for Christ and Methodism'. Thus, the dark picture that Spurling was painting at that time of denominational Christianity and 'creed-bound people' did not seem credible in light of the Coco Methodist church's spiritual fervor and apparent success.

Another reason that Christian Union did not succeed at Barney Creek was due to the opposition of Hezekiah Witt (ca. 1810-1892).[124] He was one of the most influential members in the Coco Methodist church at that time, the church having begun in his home and continued

---

[120] Spurling, *Lost Link*, p. 42.
[121] Pinckney, *Sketch*, p. 4.
[122] Tomlinson, *LGC*, p. 209.
[123] Hawk, 'History of Ironsburg Methodist church', p. 2; the Holston Conference records for the Coco Methodist church are consistent with local records and testimonies.
[124] Testimony of Neil Kelly and Harold Witt. Speaking of Hezekiah Witt and his family, Kelly said, 'The Witts did not care much for the Spurlings'.

there for a while under the leadership of Jeremiah C. Martin (1840-1898) in the early 1880s, and afterward under the pastoral guidance of John Duggan (1835-1906).[125] The relationship of Witt with the Spurlings apparently had been friendly while they worshipped together in his home and in the old Flint Hill schoolhouse, but once Christian Union was organized the relationship deteriorated and Witt used his influence to prevent the growth and success of the church. Apparently one reason for this deterioration was that Witt could not imagine with the Methodist church doing so well why Spurling would set up a rival church less than a mile away. He was perhaps among those who had said to Spurling, 'Stay with us and [we will] take the world for Christ and Methodism'.[126]

It is likely, however, that William 'Billy' Martin and his father, Jeremiah, would have been among the Methodists who worshipped on occasion with the members of Christian Union at Barney Creek, or at least attended for the sake of curiosity. We may assume this for the following reasons: first, the Martins' property joined the Spurlings' on Barney Creek making them next door neighbors; second, they had worshipped together in the Coco (Ironsburg)[127] Methodist church for two years where Jeremiah and his wife, Mary Letitia (Witt), were pillars, and where their son, Billy, was just then perhaps beginning to sense his call into the ministry; third, the Martins and Spurlings were on friendly terms. Jeremiah in fact, in his capacities as a minister and local magistrate, performed the wedding of Richard to his second wife, Nancy Sue Smallen, in July 1887.

It was Jeremiah's son, Billy, who sparked the holiness revival in 1895 in the vicinities of Ironsburg and Epperson that spread throughout the area transforming Spurling's Christian Union churches into holiness bodies. Still, between 1884 and 1895, it was Spurling who had laid the groundwork for this powerful revival. This is not to say, however, that he had formulated and preached a Wesleyan-type of holiness; rather he had succeeded to some degree to expose the spiritual inadequacies of the Methodist and Baptist churches in the region, and had encouraged the people to seek for a deeper spirituality and for freedom in the Spirit. Perhaps more importantly, however, he had charged the atmosphere

---

[125] Hawk, 'History of Ironsburg Methodist Church', p. 2. Actually the church's history dates back before the Civil War; but its worship facilities had burned down on two previous occasions. When Spurling moved into the area, the Methodist people were worshipping in the Flint Hill school.
[126] Spurling, *Lost Link* [original], p. 11.
[127] See Ch. 2, note 116.

with restoration ideals and a revolutionary spirit that encouraged the overthrow of the religious status quo.

Spurling moved to Polk County in 1889 and bought a farm on the north side of the Hiwassee River near his wife's parents. The reasons for this move are not clear, but perhaps one reason is that industry and commerce were beginning to boom in that part of Polk County; huge timber and logging companies had moved into the area, and the Marietta & North Georgia railroad was just then in 1888-1889 surveying and laying out the road for the emergence of passenger trains and the construction of the famous 'W' track, and where a little later in that same vicinity the famous L & N Loop would be built near his property. Spurling thus perhaps envisioned prosperity and a better life in that part of Polk County for his growing family. Another reason may have been that he had become alienated to some degree from his beloved father, who, then almost 79 years of age, had remarried in 1887 a woman nearly half his age who had a small handicapped child, and was planning to move back to the Cumberland Mountain region to live with or near one of his other sons – James J., William, or Hiram.

Still, however, Spurling's move to Polk County may have been from pressure by his wife, Barbara, who desired to be near her family, or perhaps it was because Christian Union had made so little progress at Barney Creek between 1886 and 1889 that he thought it was time to move on to riper fields. Perhaps God had spoken to him to move on. Doubtlessly it was a combination of all of the above reasons, but we are inclined to think that it was especially because of his interest in advancing the cause of Christian Union; for while he lived and worked at Barney Creek, he had continued to reach out in all directions proclaiming the need for a restoration of the New Testament church: certain fields seemed manifestly riper and more open to the message of Christian Union than the Coker Creek area.

Whatever the reasons for his move to Polk County, there is no indication that Spurling had become discouraged. Pinckney said that though the people at Coker Creek refused to give up their creeds, his father had 'never [become] discouraged'.[128] Reflecting on those early years, the Christian Union leader himself said that in spite of the opposition and lack of growth, 'The Lord was with me and gathered hundreds of people to hear about the new way, and so we went on'.[129]

In any case, the move to Polk County marked the end of Christian Union at Barney Creek. It is almost certain that by 1889 the work there

---

[128] Pinckney, *Sketch*, p. 4.
[129] Spurling, *Lost Link*, p. 49.

had dwindled to almost nothing. There had been very little growth apparently after the first few months. Some of the members either before or shortly after 1889 moved away and returned to their Baptist churches. Pinckney said, 'many of [the] members failed to endure and soon faded away'.[130] John and Melinda Plemons moved to Christiansburg and united with the Missionary Baptist church in that city,[131] and Aunt Nep joined a Missionary Baptist church in Tellico Plains.[132] When Adeline married, she and her family joined a Baptist church in Polk County,[133] and even Spurling's father had returned to his Holly Springs Baptist church shortly after Christian Union was organized.

Before we move on to examine the other Christian Union congregations, we should note here a particular characteristic of the Barney Creek church held in common by all Christian Union congregations and southern Appalachian people in general in the late nineteenth century. Many of the members in Christian Union could not read and write, and many more bordered on illiteracy. Typical was John Paul Plemons of the Barney Creek church and his wife, Melinda. John was completely illiterate while 'Linda' could read a little but could not write; further, several of their children even after they were grown could not read or write.[134] We draw attention to this deficiency not to reflect on the spirituality of the ministers and members in Christian Union, nor to suggest that a lack of formal education diminished their intelligence, for, as we have seen in the case of R.G. Spurling, one could be quite eloquent and not be formally educated. Indeed, Americans in general in the nineteenth century were accused of being anti-intellectual, but their pragmatic nature enabled them to excel in many ways. Still, it cannot be denied that the lack of formal education especially among the leaders of Christian Union was one of the reasons that the fellowship did not advance any farther than what it did. At some point, the lack of a structured education program hinders a body of people from moving forward.

---

[130] Abbot, *Forgotten Church*, p. 30.

[131] Confirmed by testimony of descendants. Also, John and Melinda Plemons and their children are buried in the Christiansburg Baptist church cemetery in Monroe County.

[132] Penelope 'Aunt Nep' is buried in the Druid Hills Baptist church cemetery near Tellico Plains.

[133] At one time Michael and Adeline, and Adeline's sister, Texas, were members of Zion Hill in Polk County, and when Michael died he was a member of the Southside Baptist church in Cleveland.

[134] Noted in 1910 census record; also these facts were common knowledge in the family confirmed by several of the relatives and grandchildren interviewed by the writer.

Figure 17

R.G. SPURLING AND FAMILY

This photo (c. 1897) was taken a few years after the Spurlings had moved from Shuler Creek to Turtletown in 1893. *Left to right standing (back row):* Goldsberry Pinckney [1877-1968], Sarah Elizabeth [1879-1910], Killis Green [1882-1964], Elijah Killis and Elizabeth [Dockery] Hamby (Barbara's parents). Standing in front of them are Barbara Emmaline [1886-1961] and Mary Jane [1888-1904]. *Sitting [front row],* R.G. Spurling [holding James Jackson, b. 1894], Richard Eli [b. 1891], and Barbara Melinda (Hamby) Spurling [1858-1939].

Christian Union at Shuler Creek

After selling out at Barney Creek in 1889, Spurling purchased a farm just north of Farner in Polk County not far from where Shuler Creek runs into the Hiwassee River. This farm was part of the old home place of his wife's family, E. Killis and Elizabeth [Dockery] Hamby. The testimony of Spurling's granddaughter, Allie (Spurling) Ledford, who lived with her grandparents until she was nineteen years of age, confirms other testimony that Spurling organized a small church here about 1890.[135]

---

[135] Abbot, *Forgotten Church*, p. 37. Interviews with Allie Ledford by the writer in 1992-1998. Mrs. Ledford traveled with the writer in 1993 and showed him the very spot where the church had stood in the 1890s. It was less than a mile from the old home-place where Barbara (Hamby) Spurling, R.G. Spurling's wife, was reared. It was located on the opposite side of the Hiwassee River from the Pleasant Hill Baptist church, the same church in Cherokee County, North Carolina that had revoked Spurling's license in 1884 and excluded him.

Pinckney says that his father had organized a church at this place before 1889 while he was still living on Barney Creek.[136] It is more likely, however, that his father had held prayer meetings in this area and had shared with the people the message of Christian Union without having actually set the church in order. In any case, the church was set in order with only five or six members[137] and did not realize much growth, if any, in spite of Pinckney's recollection (who was twelve years of age when they moved to Polk County) that the church had prospered while his family lived there between 1889 and 1893.

This area was deprived of public schools and offered little to advance the education of Spurling's children, and, as it turned out, offered little to advance the cause of Christian Union. Seeing no future there for his family and the ministry, Spurling decided in 1893 to move farther south about five miles to Turtletown. There he purchased a large tract of land and built a gristmill and farmed.[138] This area gave opportunity for his children to receive some schooling and for his ministry to be more productive. From his home in Turtletown he continued to pastor the church he had organized at Shuler Creek and began to evangelize in nearby Georgia and North Carolina.[139] W.F. Bryant was probably in reference to the church at Shuler Creek when he said, 'Brother R.G. Spurling ... organized a church over there with 5 or 6 members'.[140] However, like the church at Barney Creek, this church gradually died away; indications are that it did not survive beyond 1898. Bryant says in reference to this church, '[Spurling] came over and wanted me to help him in his meeting ... I went with him ... but the meeting went dead'.[141]

Christian Union at Piney Grove

After Spurling moved to Polk County in 1889, he organized a church on October 8, 1897 about ten miles northwest of Coker Creek at a place called 'Piney' or Piney Grove.[142] This church was located on what is

---

[136] Pinckney, *Sketch*, p. 4.
[137] Bryant/Lemons interview, p. 3.
[138] Polk County Deed Records, County Courthouse, Benton, TN.
[139] Abbot, *Forgotten Church*, p. 37; Allie Ledford interview, 1995.
[140] Bryant/Lemons interview, p. 3.
[141] Bryant/Lemons interview, p. 3.
[142] When the manuscript for this book was near completion (October 2013), the writer discovered a record kept by the Piney Grove church which includes the basic teachings and church covenant of Christian Union, and also the precise date that Spurling organized the church – October 8, 1897 (ZACG Archives). Some of the information in regard to this church has been preserved in Pinckney's *Sketch*

today called Reliance Road in the Rural Vale area about three miles from the Holly Springs Missionary Baptist church on Steer Creek. The Piney Grove church thrived for several decades, perpetuating itself mainly through the efforts of one family – Minter Freeman (1843-1929) and his sons and daughters and their children.[143] Freeman was a Civil War veteran and grew up with R.G. Spurling's older brothers, Nathan, Daniel, and William in the Dry Creek and Steer Creek areas of southern Monroe County.

The Freeman, Evans, and Miller families helped to get this church started under the guidance of Spurling. The leader of Christian Union had apparently held several meetings there between 1884 and 1897 exhorting the people to reform from creeds and to covenant together to form a true Gospel church on the basis of love and 'a right of way for the leadership of the Holy Ghost and conscience'.[144] Having persuaded a number of the believers in the area of his vision, Spurling set the church in order and ordained Andrew Freeman (1871-1910) into the ministry. The church then accepted this young minister to be their pastor. Andrew married Mary Haun, the daughter of a prominent Baptist minister in the region. Andrew's name would be memorialized in

---

and Abbot's *Forgotten Church*; but two second generation members of the Piney Grove church still living in 1993, shared with this writer many valuable insights and bits of data. Particularly helpful was Charlie Freeman (1902-2001), who served as the pastor of Piney Grove and whose father, James, served before him and his uncle, Andrew, before his father, the latter being the first pastor. Before the discovery of this church record, Charlie had told the writer that the church had been set in order in the 1890s, which conflicted a little with the data furnished by Pinckney's *Sketch*, the latter claiming the church at Piney Grove was established before 1889. But Charlie's testimony is now affirmed by the recent discovery. The Holly Springs Baptist Church Minutes also corroborate Charlie's testimony, supplying pertinent data and precise dates in regard to the circumstances leading up to the exclusion of members of Holly Springs Church, namely, they had joined Christian Union, or were in sympathy with the Holiness movement. In any case, the discovery of the recent document has given to us the definite date that Spurling set the church in order. It is likely that Spurling held meetings with the people at Piney Grove in the late 1880s and through the 1890s, but did not actually set the church in order until October 1897. It seems likely also that the people gathered together for worship and maintained the semblance of a church before Spurling actually set them in order. We may assume this because of the actions taken by the Holly Springs church in 1895 to exclude members who had apparently accepted holiness teachings and had gathered together to worship on that basis; and who were also apparently in sympathy with the basic principles of Christian Union. Since Andrew Freeman (b. 1871) was the first pastor at Piney Grove Christian Union, it is likely that Spurling ordained him about the same time that he organized the church, an assumption which also corresponds with the testimony of Charlie Freeman.

[143] Pinckney, *Sketch*, p. 4.
[144] Tomlinson, *LGC*, p. 206.

Church of God history as one of the twenty-one delegates who participated in the first General Assembly in 1906.[145]

Several of Andrew's brothers and sisters – George, Dorcas, and Sarah – were members of the Holly Springs Baptist church, as were also Andy Paul and his sister Sarah, the latter having married William Thomas Freeman in 1887.[146] They had begun to attend holiness meetings at Piney Grove before the church was set in order, and eventually had become convinced of the message and vision of Christian Union. Accordingly, they began to proclaim the new light they had received, and, predictably, in July 1895 the Holly Springs church appointed a committee 'to visit Sisters Sarah Freeman, Sarah Paul, and George Freeman to investigate a rumor that has come to the church that they are practicing and teaching heresy'.[147] Having done their investigative work, the committee reported their findings to the church in the September business meeting, and as a result the church 'took up the case of G.W. Freeman and Sarah Paul and excluded them from the fellowship of the church for heresy'. In the November business meeting, the church also excluded Martha Freeman, and we may assume a number of others thereafter also defected and joined Christian Union.[148]

Thus, beginning in 1897, there was an inflow of believers into Christian Union at Piney Grove most of whom, if not all, defected from Holly Springs and other Baptist churches in the area. George W. Freeman (1869-1967) became a great assistant to his brother Andrew serving more or less informally in the capacity of a deacon.

Included in the number that joined the church at Piney Grove was Andrew's and George's sister, Dorcas Louiza [Freeman] Bowers (1877-1962). She was later set forth to preach and licensed by Spurling,[149] becoming the Church of God's first female minister. She married Levi Bowers in 1894 and sometime after 1915 moved to Ohio. She re-

---

[145] Charlie Freeman interview, 1995; *GAM Minutes 1906-1914*, p. 19.

[146] Sarah Paul, Andy Paul's sister, married William Thomas Freeman in 1887 and thus became Sarah Freeman, and Sarah Freeman, Andrew's sister, married Andy Paul in 1891 and thus became Sarah Paul.

[147] *Holly Springs Minutes*, July 1895.

[148] According to the testimony of Charlie Freeman; the Holly Springs minutes also seem to indicate so.

[149] Dorcas was the sister of Andrew and James, and the aunt of Charlie Freeman. Charlie reported that it was common knowledge that 'Spurling licensed Aunt Dorcas'. Reflecting on this period, Spurling wrote a letter to Tomlinson, dated November 6, 1932, 'I think you were the fifth or sixth preacher I ordained' (ZACG Archives). Tomlinson was apparently in fact the sixth; the other five being Andrew Freeman, James Freeman, Dorcas Freeman, and Andy Paul, all licensed apparently between 1897 and 1902, and W.F. Bryant on May 15, 1902.

turned to Tennessee in the early 1940s and lived out her days in Madisonville; dying in fellowship with the Piney Grove church.[150] Andrew's brother, James (1879-1923), was also ordained by Spurling sometime between 1898 and 1902, and became the pastor of the church after Andrew died in 1910. Andrew's brother, Joseph, and his large family also worshipped at Piney Grove.

This church flourished for several years with more than one hundred attending services at its peak in 1897-1905. Included in the number who attended this church on a regular basis was Joseph M. Tipton whom we will meet again in the next chapter. He was a member of the Rural Vale Baptist church which was located less than two miles from the Christian Union church at Piney Grove and became one of the leaders in promoting the holiness movement in the area beginning in 1895. His sister, Eliza, married Larkin Evans; this couple became pillars at Piney Grove.[151] William Andrew ('Andy') Paul, who lived next door to Joe Tipton and his wife, Eglantine, would also factor significantly into the development of Christian Union, becoming the pastor of the Christian Union church on Paul's mountain. We have noticed that Paul's sister Sarah married William Thomas Freeman in 1887. Their family became active in the church at Piney Grove and assisted Andy also in the church on Paul's Mountain.

Most of the members of the Piney Grove church in the late 1890s were not new converts, but rather defectors from the Baptist churches in the area. But this was true of all the churches in Christian Union. The excitement of the vision of 'Christian Union' drew a great many in the beginning from the Baptist churches in the region, but the novelty of the movement eventually wore off and after 1905 attendance began to wane. The church at Piney Grove revived under the ministry of Charlie Freeman in the 1920s, but was not identified with the Cleveland-centered Church of God. After the Church of God came under the leadership of A.J. Tomlinson in 1903 and began to move toward centralization, Piney Grove chose to remain independent. By 1907 all formal ties between the church at Piney Grove and the Church of God in Cleveland had been severed. Interestingly, the members of Piney Grove adopted the name 'Church of God' in 1907 on the counsel of Joe. M. Tipton, but continued to distinguish themselves from what they then called 'The Assembly Church of God'.

---

[150] The name 'Church of God' is inscribed on her tombstone in the Sunset Cemetery in Madisonville according to her wishes.
[151] Abbot, *Forgotten Church*, p. 44.

Figure 18

CHRISTIAN UNION AT PINEY GROVE (C. 1899)

These young people and children were part of the Sunday school. Back left standing, George Freeman, the brother of Andrew. Andrew attended the first Assembly in 1906 and served as pastor of Piney Grove until his death in 1910.

Figure 19

JOSEPH FREEMAN AND FAMILY

Figure 20

DORCAS (FREEMAN) BOWERS AND FAMILY

Dorcas has the distinction of being the first woman licensed to preach in the Church of God. She was a member of Christian Union at Piney Grove with her father, mother, and brothers and sisters. She was licensed by Spurling probably about the time the church was organized in October 1897. Her brothers Andrew and James served successively as pastors.

Christian Union is Born: 1884-1895 89

Figure 21

LARKIN EVANS AND FAMILY

Figure 22

JOAB ['JEEB'] AND
OMIA [SPURLING] WALDROP

Larkin's wife, Eliza Jane [Tipton], was the sister of Joe Tipton. Omia was the daughter of Richard Spurling's brother, Hicks. 'Jeeb' and 'Omie' were members of Holly Springs Baptist Church and later joined Christian Union at Piney Grove.

Figure 23

JOSEPH AND
NANCY [FREEMAN] PROCK

Figure 24

PASTOR JAMES FREEMAN

Nancy [Freeman] Prock was the sister of Andrew and Dorcas. James had a large family and farmed for a living. Joseph was a descendant of John Prock who had served as pastor at Holly Springs Church. Joseph and Nancy joined Christian Union.

Christian Union on Paul's Mountain

Some little distance from Piney Grove on 'Paul's Mountain' or 'High Top' (located between Dry Creek and Steer Creek), Spurling organized another church ca. 1898-1899 and ordained Andy Paul to preach. The church accepted him to serve as their pastor.[152] Paul (1868-1959) had been saved through the influence of Richard Spurling's ministry in November 1886 and had become a member of the Holly Springs Baptist church.[153] But sometime afterward he backslid, and in October 1893 was excluded on the charge of 'swearing'. Shortly thereafter he was restored in a Christian Union meeting at Piney Grove. We have already noticed that his wife, Sarah (Freeman), and a number from the Freeman family accepted holiness teachings and left the Holly Springs church, eventually joining Christian Union in 1897. It will be remembered also that 'Aunt Nep', eldest sister of Andy, had earlier joined Christian Union at Barney Creek.

Significantly, Andy Paul was divorced and remarried. He had married Rebecca Hodges in 1888, but this marriage ended in divorce in 1890.[154] Then in 1891 Andy married Sarah L. Freeman, the daughter of Minter Freeman and sister of Andrew, James, George, Joseph, and Dorcas (Freeman) Bowers. Andy and Sarah were married thereafter for almost seventy years, and, according to the testimony of Charlie Freeman, she diligently supported his ministry. Joe Tipton preached on occasion also in the church on Paul's Mountain. This Christian Union congregation flourished for a few years and then gradually died away. It seems to have ceased to exist at least by 1910.[155] Paul and a few of his followers later

---

[152] In addition to Pinckney's *Sketch* and Joe Abbott's *Forgotten Church*, the writer interviewed in 1994-1995 two second generation descendants of Christian Union – Charlie Freeman and Joshua Prock – both eyewitnesses of many of the events in the early history of Christian Union in Monroe County. Charlie Freeman's father, James, and his uncle, Andrew, served as pastors of the Christian Union at Piney Grove. There is an amazing correspondence between Pinckney's *Sketches*, Abbot's *Forgotten Church*, and the eyewitness accounts of Freeman and Prock. Together with church minutes and county records – property deeds, tax records, census records, marriage records, and family histories -- we have been able to piece together and reconstruct the early events of Christian Union following the 1886 organization. All of these sources are preserved in ZACG Archives.

[153] Testimony of Charlie Freeman (Interview 1995) confirmed by the Holly Springs Church Minutes, November 1886. Charlie knew Andy for over fifty years and worshipped with him in the Christian Union church at Piney Grove.

[154] Marriage and court records: Madisonville, Monroe County.

[155] We base this estimate on testimony of Charlie Freeman and Joshua Prock (Freeman/Prock interviews 1994-1995). Charlie said he could remember attending the church on Paul's Mountain as a child.

fell into the 'Jesus Only' doctrine and formed an independent Oneness church.[156]

Figure 25
ANDY PAUL AND
SARAH [FREEMAN]

Figure 26
COMMITTAL OF ANDY PAUL

Paul was licensed by Spurling and served as pastor of the Christian Union on Paul's Mountain. This church was located between the Holly Springs Baptist church on Steer Creek and the Piney Grove church near Dry Creek on what was called Paul's Mountain, known also as 'High Top'.

Paul died in April 1959 at the age of 91. He is buried in the Dehart Cemetery at Holly Springs near Nancy and Daniel Spurling's graves, the wife and son of Elder Richard Spurling.

The Basis of the Union

Up to this point, the several churches in Christian Union were a loosely knit fellowship seeing themselves as independent churches 'united only by the ties of faith and charity'.[157] Spurling wrote in *The Lost Link*, 'We here give [the] agreement or basis of union as it stood in 1895'. This covenant consisted of a brief list of teachings that governed each church and that gave some vague sense of identity to the fellowship of the churches.[158] The tenets of the 'agreement' were few indeed, and the spirit of the covenant extremely democratic, bordering on a system of

---

[156] Freeman/Prock interviews 1994-1995.
[157] Spurling used Orchard's *History of the Baptists*, republished by J.R. Graves in Nashville in 1855, to support his position of the independence of the churches (cf. Spurling, *Lost Link*, pp. 34, 35, 42, with Orchard, *History*, pp. 22, 110, 175).
[158] Spurling, *Lost Link*, p. 44.

individualism; but Spurling and the members of Christian Union considered the freedom and individualism necessary in order for the fellowship to be truly 'theocratic', that is, to allow God preeminence in each person's conscience. Pinckney says that his father 'always stood ... for a Bible church with a theocratic form of government'.[159] It is doubtful, however, that R.G. Spurling used the word 'theocratic' before Tomlinson; and it is clear that other leaders began to use it only after 1906. Still the principle was present in Spurling's teaching, but it meant something different for Spurling than it did for Tomlinson and some other leaders in the church: for Spurling, 'theocratic government' signified individual freedom in the Spirit and the manifest leadership of the Holy Ghost, not a centralized political system with a chief executive officer.

In regard to the covenant as it stood in 1895, Spurling says further,

> We invite to union and fellowship all persons who avow faith in Christ and love to God and His people and a willingness to live a Christian life so as not to dishonor the cause of Christ, and we exclude only for known violations of God's Word or commands, Whereas each member shall give an account to God for [himself] and a Christianized conscience ... We reject all conscience binding creeds as being contrary to Scripture, also [to] religion and love ... Against such we do protest.[160]

The members of Christian Union were in this sense typically Congregationalists and more particularly Baptists, for the Baptist denomination universally and historically held the local church to be the New Testament form of church government, and congregationalism to be logically the best form of government for a regenerate people. The influential Baptist professor, Augustus H. Strong (1836-1921), spoke for almost all Baptists in the late nineteenth century in arguing that 'Since each local church is directly subject to Christ, there is no jurisdiction of one church over another, but all are on equal footing, and all independent of interference or control of the civil power'.[161] He argued further that 'this form of church government proceeds from the supposition that Christ

---

[159] Pinckney, *Sketch*, p. 2.
[160] Spurling, *Lost Link*, p. 44. Coincidentally, this is exactly the same wording in the document recently discovered from the Piney Grove Christian Union.
[161] Augustus Hopkins Strong, *Systematic Theology* (Valley Forge, PA: Judson Press, 1907), p. 898.

dwells in believers', and therefore 'Baptist polity is the best possible polity for good people'.[162]

Nevertheless, Baptists generally maintained that churches should be in communion with each other, though only on a free and autonomous basis. Again, representing the general consensus of Baptists in this regard, Strong insisted that

> Any number of believers, therefore, may constitute themselves into a Christian church, by adopting for their rule of faith and practice Christ's law as laid down in the New Testament, and by associating themselves together, in accordance with it, for His worship and service. It is important, where practicable, that a council of churches be previously called, to advise the brethren proposing this union as to the desirableness of constituting a new and distinct local body; and, if it be found desirable, to recognize them, after its formation, as being the church of Christ. But such action of a council, however valuable as affording ground for fellowship of other churches, is not constitutive, but simply declaratory; and without such action, the body of believers alluded to, if formed after the New Testament example, may be notwithstanding a true church of Christ.[163]

Still, however, most Baptists – Landmarkers and Primitives excepted – made a distinction between *Congregationalism* and *Independency*, a distinction that Spurling, being still under the influence of Landmarkism, did not make in Christian Union. Strong quotes the Congregational theologian, E.A. Park, to show the importance of making this distinction: 'Congregationalism recognizes a voluntary cooperation and communion of the churches, which Independency does not do. Independent churches ordain and depose pastors without asking advice from other churches.' Strong goes on to explain,

> In accordance with this general principle, in a case of serious disagreement between different portions of the same church, the council called to advise should be, if possible, a mutual, not a *ex parte*, council ... It is a more general application of the same principle, to say that the pastor should not shut himself in to his own church, but should cultivate friendly relations with other pastors and with other churches, should be present and active at the meetings of Associations and State Conventions ... His example of friendly interest in the welfare of others will affect his church. The strong should be taught to help

---

[162] Strong, *Systematic*, p. 904.
[163] Strong, *Systematic*, p. 902.

the weak, after the example of Paul in raising contributions for the poor churches in Judea.[164]

Again, this subtle but important distinction between *Congregationalism* and *Independency* was not made clear by Spurling, if indeed he believed in it at all; and, in any case, it was rejected by the only two Christian Union congregations that survived after 1900, namely, the Piney Grove and Paul's Mountain churches. Quoting G.H. Orchard in affirmation of Independency, Spurling says the churches in the New Testament were 'independent of each other, neither were they joined together by association, confederacy or any other bond but that of charity ... independence and equality formed the basis of their internal constitution'.[165] Moreover, whether or not he meant to do so, Spurling pushed the ideal of *Independency* into individualism, which worked finally to the detriment of what he otherwise hoped for in Christian Union.

The independent spirit and the bent toward individualism were inherent defects in the structure of Christian Union, to be sure; for they retarded the growth of the churches both spiritually and numerically, and otherwise prevented the noble aims of Christian Union from being realized, particularly the fulfillment of the ecumenical ideal which we will examine more critically in Chapter Four. Notwithstanding these defects, the covenant of Christian Union as it stood in 1895 served for the time being as the basis of fellowship for each congregation, and it gave some semblance of corporate identity to the fragile union between the churches. More importantly, notwithstanding the shortcomings in Spurling's vision and system, the core principle of the Bible church – divine government – was embedded deeply in Christian Union, and thus the believers had agreed to '[sit] together as the Church of God to transact business as the same'.

Spurling's Leadership Position

Spurling was the pastor of the church at Barney Creek, and held no other position in the fellowship of the churches in Christian Union. Later he also served as pastor of the church at Shuler Creek in Polk County. It is conceivable that he could have served as pastor of two churches at the same time, but he was not the overseer of all the churches, for there was no administrative hierarchy in Christian Union. The highest authoritative ministerial position was that of pastor, and each pastor was equal with

---

[164] Strong, *Systematic*, p. 928.
[165] Spurling, *Lost Link*, pp. 34, 35.

every other pastor; there was no office for a 'pastor of pastors', nor position for a 'first among equals'. It should be borne in mind that the several Christian Union congregations were independent democracies united only by the intrinsic qualities of love and mutual respect, not by any external political structure; moreover, the churches selected their pastors; they were not appointed by Spurling or by any kind of Episcopal or presbytery council. Christian Union churches did not even meet together in conventions or associations apparently for fear that these kinds of meetings might lead to a usurpation of the prerogatives of the independent churches.

The principle that the churches were 'independent of each other, neither were joined together by association, confederacy or any other bond but that of charity' was an important and cherished belief in Christian Union, and one which was guarded carefully. It was a principle apparently embraced, in fact, even more passionately by some of the members of Christian Union than by Spurling himself, for Spurling later yielded to the structure of the General Assembly and to at least a moderate form of centralization, whereas most of the ministers and members in Christian Union did not. It will be remembered that most of the members of Christian Union had been Landmark Baptists and some had been Primitive Baptists,[166] and thus the idea of the sovereignty and autonomy of the local church ran deeply in Christian Union. For this same reason, the pastors were esteemed but not exalted, for the ultimate authority of God resided in the churches themselves, not in the ministers. It was an old principle held dear among Baptists and carried forward into Christian Union, namely, that 'the government of Christ is with His body', that is, '[His] government shall be upon His shoulder' or in His body, the church (Isa. (9.6), and the ministers were thus merely part of this body.

There was then in Christian Union — as there were among the Baptists and among the people in Appalachia in general in the nineteenth century — a leveling egalitarianism. No one was allowed to rise too high, particularly in regard to position, for God had no shadow on earth, and Christ had no vicar. The exaltation of ministers to Episcopal and hierarchical positions was a contrivance of man and a product of apostate Christianity and religions like Islam and Mormonism, and thus, accord-

---

[166] John J. Plemons (the patriarch of the Plemons family), Minter Freeman (the patriarch of the Freeman family), Thomas Paul (Andy Paul's father), and Joab Waldrop, who married Richard Spurling's niece, Omega 'Omie', and joined the Piney Grove church had all been at one time Primitive Baptists.

ingly, could not be entertained by a people who were fully engaged in a quest to restore apostolic Christianity.

One wonders then how the ministers and members in Christian Union formed the basis of their agreement. We know how the first church was formed, for Tomlinson left us a record, but how was the Union formed on an extended basis between the churches? It is possible that they had fellowship meetings, though we have no record of such meetings; it seems more likely, however, that the covenant of Christian Union was mediated simply by Spurling himself as he itinerated among the individual ministers and churches and proclaimed and explained his vision of Christian Union.

Notwithstanding that Spurling did not hold a superior administrative position in Christian Union, he was nevertheless highly esteemed among the ministers and members; indeed he was looked upon as the founder of the movement, and thus his words and actions carried weight. He was perceived to have divine authority to ordain and to issue ministerial credentials, and he was looked to for counsel and advice.

Tomlinson's Record

A.J. Tomlinson declared in his short history of the Church of God in *The Last Great Conflict* that the 'little flock' set in order at Barney Creek in 1886 was the 'infant church of God', and therefore the moment the eight believers were incorporated and duly set in order, history was made and prophecy was fulfilled. 'That day', wrote Tomlinson, 'is a day worthy of remembrance'.[167] He viewed the event so profoundly important that he listed the names of the eight members and the particular terms of their covenant.[168] He stated further that 'Elder Richard Spurling was honored with being the first ordained minister', and credited him with assisting his son, R.G. Spurling, to 'launch this last great reformation'.[169] He acknowledged also that the work which followed, including the move that centralized the administrative authority of the church in Cleveland, Tennessee after 1906, grew out of that 1886 meeting and was organically tied to it. He obviously saw at the time the benefit of carefully recording for historical purposes that the Holiness Church at Camp Creek that he joined in 1903 was a 'continuation of that same organization that was started sixteen years before'.[170] His short

---

[167] Tomlinson, *LGC*, p. 206.
[168] Tomlinson, *LGC*, p. 207.
[169] Tomlinson, *LGC*, p. 208.
[170] Tomlinson, *LGC*, p. 213.

history published in 1913 shows clearly that the church which he himself was then overseeing was the same church that Spurling had set in order in 1886. Ironically, as we will see further on, Tomlinson's record in *The Last Great Conflict* would stand to contradict his reinterpretation of the church's origins after the division in 1923.

Some Core Principles Discovered and Restored

Reflecting on Spurling's doctrine of the church, several important principles stand out as foundational: 1) the church is a visible assembly of believers; therefore, there is no such thing as a spiritual or mystical body of Christ or so-called invisible church made up of all born-again believers; 2) the church is God's government in the earth, His *ekklesia*, and as such is authorized to 'bind' and 'loose' on earth in His name what has been bound and loosed in heaven; 3) the Holy Spirit must be given preeminence in the church, and the members must be allowed freedom to worship and interact with the Spirit; 4) God's church exists only where His law and government is observed by His children; 5) the supreme objective authority of the church is the Bible, particularly the New Testament, the latter being the final word on all matters of faith, government, and discipline; 6) the church assembly is 'a judicial body only', not a legislative nor executive body, and is authorized therefore only to interpret God's laws revealed plainly in the Holy Scriptures; 7) the church cannot legislate binding regulations that may injure or contradict the conscience of a particular member; 8) the church is distinct from the kingdom of God, the kingdom corresponding more or less to what some refer to as the 'invisible church', whereas the church is the visible and corporate body of believers; 9) the church is formed by a church covenant, not baptism, nor the new birth; 10) the particular members must be in unanimous agreement on doctrinal statements and disciplinary order considered binding upon the members; 11) the essential power and life of the church is in the Spirit of God – in His regenerating grace and supreme leadership; 12) the 'rock' upon which the church is founded is the personal revelation that Christ is the 'Son of the living God'. The church is thus centered in and built upon the members' common revelation of Christ and His teachings; 13) the preeminent attribute of the church is love, 'the lost link, which is the key to the successful restoration of the church and the fulfillment of its ecumenical purpose; 14) the fellowship of the churches is held together only by the ties of love and mutual respect, not by hierarchy nor centralized authority; 15) the New Testament church 'fell away' in 325 CE and necessarily had to be restored according to history and prophecy; 16) the 'falling away' resulted in the Dark Ages and the rise of the Roman Catholic Church and denominationalism, which together are identified in biblical prophecy with the Babylonian harlot and her offspring in Revelation 17-18; 17) the church's vision is ecumenical, and its mission, global; 18) the church will fulfill its prophetic purpose in the world and climax in the miracle of true believers being brought together in the unity of one fold – in a triumphant Christian Union!

Born with a Birth Defect

We have seen that the focus of Christian Union was almost entirely on the *church*, not on salvation themes, most particularly not on holiness-Pentecostal themes. Spurling and his followers were preoccupied almost entirely with finding and maintaining the biblical basis for Christian fellowship. It would be ten years before Christian Union would be swept into the holiness-Pentecostal movement. Indeed, the individualism inherent in the original covenant principle – 'giving each other equal rights and privilege to interpret for yourselves as your conscience may dictate' – actually prevented Christian Union from taking a stand on almost anything that smacked at governing the ethical behavior of its individual members, apart from what was commonly understood to be immoral. Spurling had said that 'we exclude only for known violations of God's Word or commands',[171] but one was left to wonder what those commandments or violations were. He maintained that stealing, cursing, fighting, and polygamy were 'violations of the New Testament', and thus '[could not] be upheld by the church'.[172] But apart from these prohibitions, and we may assume also flagrant cases of fornication, murder, etc., the members of Christian were encouraged to follow their conscience and not to judge one another.

Christian Union members were therefore at liberty to use tobacco and snuff if the practice did not offend their conscience, and we may assume the same was true in regard to drinking liquor for 'medicinal purposes',[173] for such practices were consistent with Baptist tradition,

---

[171] Spurling, *Lost Link*, p. 45.
[172] Spurling, *Lost Link*, p. 11.
[173] It was common knowledge in the Plemons' family that John Paul Plemons, a charter member of Christian Union at Barney Creek chewed tobacco, and his wife, Melinda, also a member used snuff (Ruth Plemons interview, 1992). Several of the members at Piney Grove and Paul's Mountain churches used tobacco and drank spirits for 'medicinal purposes;' and this seems to have been the case with some in these churches even after holiness views had been adopted in 1895. These observa-

and, as we have seen, Spurling had not ventured far from that tradition in establishing Christian Union. Spurling denied that tithing was a New Testament teaching,[174] and it is almost certain that the standard against divorce and remarriage in Christian Union was rather low; for the individual's conscience was considered the final judiciary in cases of divorce and remarriage. We may assume this on the basis that Spurling had ordained Andy Paul knowing full well that he had been divorced and remarried, and there are indications that at least two other couples in Christian Union at Piney Grove were divorced and remarried. Moreover, though divorce and remarriage was not prevalent among the Baptists in the mountains, and usually carried the stigma of a scandal, still the practice was allowed, and thus we have no reason to believe that divorce and remarriage was an issue in Christian Union.

It may be seen that Strong's justification of the Baptist position in regard to individual conscience in his *Systematic Theology* is almost identical to Spurling's: 'It is the very relation of the church to Christ and His truth which renders it needful to insist upon the right of each member of the church to his private judgment as to the meaning of Scripture'.[175] Spurling asked, 'Has [not] every member equal rights and privileges to read and understand and practice God's Word as they [*sic*] see it?'[176] He emphasized that for one to go against his conscience was hypocrisy. 'Does every Christian have the right to read the Bible? If they do then it is true they have a right to believe as they understand it. To teach them [to practice contrary to what they believe], it is hypocrisy and a sin'.[177] Again, the basis for this autonomy was the supremacy of the individual's conscience. He urged all individuals therefore to 'read and practice as you think will please God best'.

Notwithstanding the right of each member to interpret the Bible for himself, the members of Christian Union somehow had agreed on Baptism [though the choice between sprinkling and immersion was left up

---

tions were confirmed in interviews with Charlie Freeman and Joshua Prock. Charlie served as pastor of Christian Union at Piney Grove in the 1920s, and his father before him in 1910. Charlie said, '[These things were] left up to each member, how they felt about them'.

[174] In a letter to Tomlinson dated November 6, 1932, Spurling plainly states that he does not believe that tithing is taught in the New Testament. He reconciled with Tomlinson and joined the church on the basis that he would tithe only because the Bible says to obey 'every ordinance of man'. Tomlinson said, 'Well, that's good enough'.

[175] Strong, *Systematic*, p. 903.
[176] Spurling, *Lost Link*, pp. 10, 11; also p. 45.
[177] Spurling, *Lost Link*, p. 40.

the individual member],[178] and they agreed that the Lord's Supper [Communion] and Footwashing were also Gospel ordinances.[179] One wonders, however, if a member challenged these teachings, or changed his or her mind, having received in his or her opinion greater light, what would have been the outcome? And what if a believer desired to unite with Christian Union but did not ascribe to these ordinances? Would the doors of the church have been closed, for example, to a Quaker? What if one agreed with Baptism and the Lord's Supper, but disagreed with the practice of Footwashing? How was the church to judge? Most especially, what if the members of Christian Union 'discerned' that this particular believer had the love of Christ abiding in him, and that his life otherwise exemplified 'a willingness to live the Christian life so as not to dishonor the cause of Christ', would they have opened the doors of the church to him or her?

Spurling's sharp contrast between the outward law of the Old Testament and the inward law of the New Testament bordered on a kind of Quakerism, that is, it tended to exalt an 'inner light' revelation – conscience – as the supreme authority of the church. He maintained that the 'Christian law is not an outward law' but rather consisted altogether in love. To him, the basis of Christian fellowship is a 'discerning law' by which true believers know and respect each other, making them capable also to bond together in Christian Union. 'Therefore fellowshipping each other by the law of love [over against the 'law of faith'] is the lost link'.[180] Again he insisted that the mystery of the 'lost link' is the very key to Christian fellowship, that is, love is not merely a moral attribute that enables believers to bond together spiritually, but the very power and wisdom that enables believers to bond together corporately in one visible body of Christ. 'This great law of love stands out in God's Word with preeminence over all other laws as the law by which to know and fellowship each other.'[181]

> Many preachers preach about love and dwell on charity and think it no more than the natural element of religion, but fail to see it to be the law of the new covenant by which to infallibly know each other

---

[178] In the original manuscript Spurling makes it plain that the mode was optional, though the formula recommended was Trinitarian.
[179] Spurling, *Lost Link*, p. 45.
[180] Spurling, *Lost Link*, pp. 22, 23.
[181] Spurling, *Lost Link*, p. 22.

as members of God's church, and is the law by which God will judge the world.[182]

Spurling felt that he could best convey the profoundest mysteries of God through poetic expression, and so wrote the following poem in regard to love and Christian fellowship:

> Send forth Thy law in every heart,
> The law of God to us impart,
> Like Thee, dear Father, and Thy Son
> May we Thy children join in one.
>
> May now Thy holy law of love.
> Which cometh down from above,
> In strongest ties our hearts unite,
> That we may walk in gospel light.[183]
> – R.G. Spurling

The problem with Spurling's *Lost Link*, however, was that it tended to eliminate any sense of objectivity. It set love over against objective truth, over against outward standards, even if those standards were plainly Scriptural.

> It is no wonder that the once powerful Methodist Church has lost so much of her power with God and man. Her twenty-nine articles are enough to drive the Spirit-filled saints from her fold. Why are they not drawn from the Bible? Whether they be truth or error it differs not. If every article were as pure as gold it would break God's law as Moses broke the table of God's law.[184]

His criticism of Methodism and its articles of faith, therefore, could have been made contrariwise against Christian Union and her lack of articles; that is, someone could have as well said, 'it is no wonder' that the churches in Christian Union had failed to grow and persevere; for if the Methodist's articles were 'driving the Spirit-filled saints from her fold', so also the lack of definite articles of faith were apparently one reason Spirit-filled saints were not drawn to Christian Union.

The theology of the *Lost Link* simply left too much up to the individual; it was an ideal that could not be practically applied. It emphasized love at the expense of other principles in the New Testament that gave the church structure, government and discipline.

---

[182] Spurling, *Lost Link*, p. 44.
[183] Spurling, *Lost Link*, pp. 30, 31.
[184] Spurling, *Lost Link*, pp. 25, 26.

The difference between Spurling and the Baptists in regard to the democratic nature of the church and individualism was that he formulated the principle into a church covenant without going on to adequately qualify the principle as Strong did in his *Systematic Theology*:

> Each member while forming his own opinions under the guidance of the Spirit, is to remember that the other members have the Spirit also, and that the final conclusion as to the will of God is to be reached only by a comparison of views ... The church is in general to secure unanimity by moral suasion only; though, in case of willful and perverse opposition to its decisions, it may be necessary to secure unity by excluding an obstructive member, for schism.[185]

The supremacy of personal conscience was advocated by Spurling in the extreme; he even argued that Arius in the fourth century – who denied that Jesus was God and of the same divinity with the Father – should have been tolerated rather than corrected and disciplined for his heresy; and most certainly he should not have been excluded from the church, but rather embraced in love.[186] It was thus that the desire for 'liberty' in Christian Union gave place outwardly to a loose political structure, which allowed in turn for a loose moral discipline.

Spurling was typically Baptist in believing that Episcopal church systems which depend on church officers and an outward political structure for moral order and discipline are prone to conceal corruption. This is what he meant in saying, 'Liberty is what God's people want and must have it at any cost or hypocrisy will soon invade the church'.[187] Again, Strong captured the sentiments of Spurling in this regard: 'It is best that a church in which Christ does not dwell should by dissension reveal its weakness and fall to pieces; and any outward organization that conceals inward disintegration, and compels merely a formal union ... is a hindrance instead of a help to true religion'.[188]

It seems clear now that Spurling in establishing Christian Union was reacting against the legalism of his traditional Baptist faith; the problem was that he pushed the pendulum to the other extreme, building a system which gave place to liberalism. He was keenly aware of the arguments for and against legalism on one hand and liberalism on the other, and the tension that existed between the two; for he recalled that in 1884 the Baptist elders at Pleasant Hill and the nearby churches had

---

[185] Strong, *Systematic*, p. 904.
[186] Spurling, *Lost Link*, p. 23.
[187] Spurling, *Lost Link*, p. 42.
[188] Strong, *Systematic*, p. 904.

'[shook] their gray heads and [waved] their palsied hands [against him] and [cried] latitudinarianism'.[189]

But Spurling did not perceive himself to be a liberal; he believed he had established Christian Union on a 'reasonable middle ground' between two extremes. He wrote:

> Some think Christians ought not to be united in any bond of fellowship while others are not satisfied with the law and government of Christ and the Holy Spirit, but must have a great many more laws and governments. So between the two extremes there is a wise and reasonable middle ground of truth which unprejudiced and honest Spirit led Christians can surely find in the words and acts of the Savior and His followers under the leadership of the Holy Ghost.[190]

Time would prove, however, that he had not in fact found the middle ground, but had bent Christian Union toward the liberal side in pursuit of an ideal that could not fulfill the practical mission of the church. Moreover, his idealism stood in contradiction to and over against his emphasis that the church – God's true church – is 'God's visible government in the earth'. Yet for all the talk of 'visible government', where was it? We have no record that Christian Union churches keep records or minutes; it is almost certain in fact that they did not. We would not even know the names of the original charter members and the date and order of things at Barney Creek on August 19, 1886 if Tomlinson had not interviewed Spurling years later and left us a record in *The Last Great Conflict*.

Because no records and minutes were kept in Christian Union churches, we have had to reconstruct and piece together the story of Christian Union through oral testimonies, scant pieces of written information left by first and second generation witnesses, minutes of the Baptist churches in the area, county census records, marriage records, deed records, tax records, court records, family genealogical records, and Spurling's *The Lost Link* and Tomlinson's *The Last Great Conflict*. Further, we have no record that Christian Union churches appointed clerks and treasurers; and it is almost certain that they did not, for there was no financial system in Christian Union; the members did not tithe nor believe in any kind of systematic giving. There is no record that Christian Union appointed and licensed deacons, nor had a reporting system or any correspondence between the churches. There is no record that members moving from one place to another asked to be dismissed in order to be

---

[189] Spurling, *Lost Link*, pp. 39, 40.
[190] Spurling, *Lost Link*, p. 42.

received in good standing in another Christian Union church; again it is almost certain that they did not. Where was the government?

Further, there was no administrative authority in the churches of Christian Union, nor especially between the churches. Emphasis was almost completely on the administration of the Holy Ghost. 'Shall the Holy Spirit choose your field of labor, or shall some man say where you shall labor? Shall God say by His Spirit, Go ye into all the world and preach the gospel to every creature, while your elder says not so?'[191] Still further, there were no qualifications for the ministry, except the individual's declaration that he was called of God. No elder had the right or the responsibility to say to anyone, 'You must [not] go because you are not learned'.[192] Again, where was the government?

Since Christian Union did not believe in tithing and had developed no plan of systematic giving, it is not surprising that the ministers were not systematically paid, if in fact they were paid at all. Spurling received no pay for his ministry. In regard to Christian Union at Shuler Creek, Pinckney says his father 'kept watch over the work even though it was small, and took nothing for his services, but rather he gave to them'.[193] Charlie Freeman, who served as pastor of Christian Union at Piney Grove, and his father and uncle before him, said they received no support for their ministries. This was apparently not merely a charitable gesture on the part of the ministers, but a principle laid down in Christian Union. It was one way for Christian Union to 'draw the line between … a gluttonous and a self-denying ministry'.[194] Spurling pleaded, 'Oh, preachers … Do not be a hireling, do not look after pay instead of the flock'.[195]

> Go work in my vineyard today,
> The Master is calling for you;
> Why ask your poor brethren for pay?
> The Master will give you your due.
> The clusters are falling today.
> That should have been gathered by you,
> But when this old harvest is past,
> What use has the Master for you?
> The wolves now have entered the flock,
> The hirelings are hasting to flee;

---

[191] Spurling, *Lost Link*, p. 36.
[192] Spurling, *Lost Link*, p. 36.
[193] Pinckney, *Sketch*, p. 4.
[194] Spurling, *Lost Link*, p. 29.
[195] Spurling, *Lost Link*, p. 37.

> Before the great raid can be stopped,
> I fear much destruction we'll see.
> The flock now is starving for food,
> The fleece you're longing to sheer;
> But they that are perished and gone,
> Your labors can never restore.
> The people their offerings abhor,
> Because of the yearning for coin;
> Remember the sons of Eli,
> And fear lest their fate should be thine.
> Oh, Lord, do Thou pity the poor,
> And into Thy vineyard now send,
> Men like Peter and Paul,
> Unbought by the wages of sin.[196]
> – R.G. Spurling

While it was commendable that the ministers were willing to serve without pay, still it worked to the detriment of the growth and stability of the churches in Christian Union, for the ministers having to labor on farms and secular jobs were not able adequately to prepare themselves for the ministry – to feed and care for the sheep. Certainly the argument against a systematic financial plan for the church was not drawn out of the New Testament (cf. e. g. Mt. 23.23; Lk. 11.42; 1 Cor. 9.7-14; 1 Tim. 5.17, 18; *et al.*). Spurling and the ministers and members in Christian Union in regard to finances had again overreacted against the abuses or perceived abuses in the Baptist and Methodist churches.

Spurling's passionate opposition to creeds and his reluctance to form an adequate political and administrative structure left the infant Christian Union without the ability to develop a strong and healthy skeletal system necessary for growth, nourishment, and maturation of the members (Eph. 4.16; Col. 2.19). Thus, notwithstanding the important foundational principles upon which the initial restoration work began, Christian Union was born with a birth defect – a weak outward structure bent toward an individualism, a defect that would have to be modified before the church could move forward and be molded into the prophetic church in the Scriptures. It would be twenty years, however, before this inherent deformity would be corrected, and only after a new leader had come on the scene and gradually gained the preeminent influence in the church.

---

[196] Spurling, *Lost Link*, pp. 37-38.

3

HOLINESS-PENTECOSTAL TRANSFORMATION: 1896-1905

In May 1895, William B. 'Billy' Martin (1862-1944) whom we met earlier in connection with the Methodist Church at Coco Creek (Ironsburg), and Joseph M. 'Joe' Tipton (1853-1925), who had been working with the ministers and members in Christian Union at Piney Grove and on Paul's Mountain, became stirred in their spirits about the deplorable spiritual condition of the Baptist and Methodist churches in southern Monroe County. Martin had a vivid memory of the powerful revivals that he had experienced as a young man when his father, Jeremiah, and Elder John Duggan after him were pastors respectively in the 1880s at Ironsburg. It is almost certain also that Tipton had experienced the power of those revivals, for he lived within the geographical circle of influence of those great revivals.[1]

Martin and Tipton were joined in their concerns by Elias Milton ('Milt') McNabb (1860-1945) and William L. ('Billy') Hamby (1856-1908),[2] and a little later by a young preacher named Robert Frank

---

[1] Tipton's home was located between Steer Creek and Dry Creek only about six miles from the Ironsburg and Epperson communities. We have discovered recently evidence that in 1909-1910 Tipton had preached in the Ironsburg Methodist church (Charles Timothy Hawk, *Journal* 1906-1913: copy in ZACG Archives). This discovery indicates further that he may have preached there much earlier and worked with Spurling at Barney Creek and the Coker Creek area in the early 1880s.

[2] Tomlinson lists Martin, Tipton, and McNabb (Tomlinson, *LGC*, p. 209); Bryant mentions Hamby (Geneva Carroll, 'Youth Interviews Experience', *The Lighted Pathway* [July 1949], p. 14); and M.S. Lemons and Bryant mention Porter (Chesser *Interview*, pp. 16-18). Porter became prominent as head of the FBHA in Tennessee, but there are indications that he was active with Martin in the movement shortly after the revival began. Porter almost certainly influenced Lemons to join the fire-baptized holiness movement in 1899. He officiated the marriage between Lemons and his wife, Mattie, in 1900. Further, Porter assisted Spurling in

'R.F'. Porter (1879-1944). McNabb and Hamby were Baptists from Cherokee County, and Porter a Methodist from Dentville in Polk County. These ministers and laymen gathered about them a small following and began to pray for a move of God. Included in the number was Sarah A. Smith (1844-1918) who would in the years to come factor into the Church of God's holiness-Pentecostal transformation. So wrought upon by the Spirit of God, these men and women pushed aside their natural food and gave themselves incessantly to prayerful intercessions for the salvation of sinners, and for the awakening of the established churches from their apathy and spiritual indifference. They kept their petitions before God until suddenly the Holy Spirit descended upon them with manifestations similar to those on the day of Pentecost.[3] Immediately they began to realize a strange and wonderful anointing to preach the Gospel, and to witness to the transforming power of the Spirit.

Now these men and women, having been quickened and emboldened by the Spirit, began to hold prayer meetings from house to house in their communities in the southern part of Monroe County – in Ironsburg, Coker Creek, Epperson, Dry Creek, Steer Creek, Spring Creek, Maple Springs, Reliance, Piney Grove, and Rural Vale. God honored their sincerity and spiritual hunger with mighty outpourings of the Spirit similar to those recorded in the book of Acts.

Notwithstanding the Pentecostal manifestations exhibited in their meetings, 'speaking in tongues' was not at first recognized as a significant and distinct manifestation:[4] yet eyewitnesses later recalled occurrences of tongues speech in the meetings. The reason that early historical accounts fail to mention the manifestation of tongues speech seems to be that the attention of the believers was at first focused on the more sensational and obvious demonstrations of shaking, quaking, jerking, shouting, and dancing in the Spirit. They would often rejoice that 'God had put the dance upon them' and had exercised their bodies in peculiar ways, but they failed to see the significance of tongues-speech. It should

---

organizing the Holiness Church at Camp Creek in May 1902 (Chesser *Interview*, p. 18).

[3] *FS* 1.6, pp. 5-6.

[4] *FS* 1.6, p. 6. It is interesting, however, that Pinckney Spurling reports that Fanny White was baptized with the Spirit and spoke in tongues at Barney Creek sometime between 1885 and 1886 (*Sketch*, p. 4). Also, several second generation members of Christian Union congregations, including Charlie Freeman and Joshua Prock, testified that their fathers and mothers told them that the outpouring of the Spirit in 1895-1900 including manifestations of speaking in tongues. Charlie Freeman reported to this writer that, 'Aunt Dorcas was baptized with the Holy Ghost and spoke in tongues at Piney Grove'.

be borne in mind that the doctrine and significance of speaking in tongues, which had ceased to be understood and preached after the church's apostasy in the fourth century, had not come to light in modern times. Like many other doctrines and operations of the Spirit, the significance of speaking in tongues still lay under the darkness of the Dark Ages. Thus, even if speaking in tongues was prevalent in their meetings, the phenomenon simply was not recognized and identified as a distinct and important manifestation of the Spirit.[5]

In any case, it was reported that the Spirit would 'take hold' of the believers with such force and demonstrations that some of their neighbors declared 'they were going mad'.[6] Unmoved by the doubters and critics, those who were being blessed and empowered were fully convinced that this outpouring of the Spirit was a genuine move of God, and so they continued in the flow of the Spirit seeking the kingdom.

Was this revival connected to Spurling and Christian Union? It seems almost certain that it was not directly connected, yet it is as certain that it was the result in part of the groundwork laid by Spurling and his followers between 1884 and 1895. Tomlinson says the revival was the result of Spurling's earlier preaching in the area. He noted in *The Last Great Conflict* that although

> ... few cared anything about the infant organization [Christian Union] ... Spurling continued preaching, not only at the church, but wherever he was granted liberty. In this way the minds of the people were continually agitated, and gradually prepared for the work of the Spirit that was to follow. For ten years this servant of God prayed, wept and continued his ministry against much opposition and under peculiar difficulties, before seeing much fruits of his labor.[7]

Besides the connection already noticed between Martin and Christian Union, Spurling was associated also with Tipton in the ministry of Christian Union at Piney Grove and likely earlier at Barney Creek. As pointed out earlier, he had worshipped with Billy Martin and his father for two years in the Methodist church at Coco Creek; thus, it is almost certain that Martin had heard Spurling preach on occasion in the

---

[5] Christian Union members [James Freeman, Andrew Freeman, Dorcas Freeman, Andy Paul, G.P Spurling] reflecting on the meetings in 1895-1900 in the Coker Creek and Steer Creek areas of Monroe County testified that speaking in tongues was a regular part of the worship, though they identified the manifestation more clearly after the doctrine of tongues-speech was formulated between 1901 and 1906 in connection with the outpourings of the Spirit in Topeka and Los Angeles.

[6] *FS* 1.6, p. 6.

[7] Tomlinson, *LGC*, p. 209.

schoolhouse on Flint Hill and probably in the meetinghouse on Barney Creek. It will be recalled that the Barney Creek meetinghouse was located just over the hill less than a half mile from where the Methodists met for worship in the schoolhouse. Further, Martin was Spurling's neighbor and Tipton did not live far away; in fact, Tipton and Spurling had probably known each other since they were children, having been reared together in the same community on Dry Creek and having attended with their families the same Baptist churches – Holly Springs and Rural Vale. Just as intriguing, Billy Hamby was Spurling's brother-in-law and Milt McNabb his neighbor, both of whom were members of the Pleasant Hill Baptist church in Cherokee County, the same Baptist church that had defrocked Spurling in 1884 and excluded him.

However intimate and intertwined the ministries of Martin, Tipton, Hamby, and McNabb were before 1895, they had come together in the spring of that year more especially with a common concern for a spiritual awakening. In the following weeks and months, they began to pray and study the Scriptures together, and had come to identify their experiences with the Holiness movement. Immediately they began to proclaim the 'second blessing' which prompted mixed responses, some receiving their message with joyous acceptance, others violently rejecting it. Most of the believers in the Christian Union churches, which Spurling had organized between 1886 and 1899, accepted the new light and adopted holiness teachings, though the extremely democratic and autonomous nature of these churches produced a variety of interpretations of what actually constituted holiness and how entire sanctification might be identified. In this light, Christian Union churches between 1895 and 1900 were not Wesleyans, strictly speaking, in their interpretation of sanctification and holiness.

The denominational churches in the Coker Creek basin area, in any case, staunchly resisted the revival led by Martin and Tipton and entrenched themselves against holiness teachings. The lukewarm religious establishment began to criticize and ostracize these Gideon warriors of holiness-Pentecostal restoration, and, finally, after the old established churches had reprimanded and warned them, the saints were charged with heresy and excluded.[8] Nevertheless, undaunted by the spectacle of being excommunicated by their friends and fellow members, they actually rejoiced over the defamation, 'counting it all joy' to suffer for the true Gospel: and they continued to preach in proportion to the glorious illumination and powerful anointing that had come upon them.

---

[8] *FS* 1.6, p. 6.

These enlightened recruits of holiness were not content to remain in Monroe County but extended the scope of their ministry into adjoining counties, including Cherokee County, North Carolina – particularly in the extreme western part of Cherokee County located only about twelve miles south of where the revival first broke out at Ironsburg and Epperson in the Coker Creek basin area in Tennessee. Milt McNabb and Billy Hamby actually had returned home by coming to Cherokee County, their families having lived in the Camp Creek area of Cherokee County since before the Civil War. Milt's father, Edmund McNabb (1822-1912),[9] was a prominent deacon in the Pleasant Hill Baptist church. He had donated the land where the first place of worship was constructed, which was located originally on the hill just above the Hiwassee River where the Pleasant Hill cemetery is today. Billy Hamby's family was also a part of this church including his sister, Barbara, who had married R.G. Spurling. It was this church that had refused to ordain Spurling in the early 1880s, and eventually forced him to leave his 'beloved Missionary Baptist church' which resulted in the formation of Christian Union in 1886.

The Pleasant Hill Baptist church had been 'armed off' of the Liberty Baptist church in 1875, the latter having been established in 1848 about five miles south of the Pleasant Hill community. Camp Creek flowed north and meandered through these communities a distance of about six miles and emptied into the Hiwassee River. The area was thus called Camp Creek, though it was known more formally as Patrick named in honor of the Kilpatrick family which began to occupy the area soon after the removal of the Cherokees in 1838. The area post office was also called Patrick. The Bryants, Kilpatricks, McNabbs, Colemans, Shearers, Hambys, Picklesimers, Bridges, Elrods, Allens, Bruces, Burgers, Adams, Quinns, Crains, Ledfords, Paynes, Dockerys, Wests, Rapers and a few other families had moved into the area between the removal of the Cherokees and the Reconstruction Period following the Civil War. Between that time and the turn of the century, these families had intermarried until they had become to a great extent one blood. Nearly everyone was everyone else's uncle, aunt, cousin, nephew, niece, grandpa, grandma, or in-law.

With few exceptions these hearty pioneers of Scotch-Irish decent were Baptists, and as noticed earlier they had formed a tight knit fellowship of churches called the Liberty & Ducktown Baptist Association.

---

[9] Edmund McNabb had married W.F. Bryant's mother's older sister, Mattie. He was therefore Bryant's uncle, and thus 'Milt' McNabb was Bryant's cousin.

The few exceptions were Methodists, but the Methodists were subservient to the influence of the Baptists in the region. It should be borne in mind also that a kind of *quid pro quo* existed between the interests of religion and civil affairs, between spiritual and temporal matters. The same prominent families controlled the whole of life in the communities. The heads of the families were not only the ministers, deacons, clerks, and stewards in the churches, but the merchants, postmasters, magistrates, sheriffs, and leaders in the lodges. This created an almost impenetrable wall of defense around the community of Camp Creek, and the local patriarchs were determined to preserve the *status quo*. So much for the principle of separation of church and state at Camp Creek!

It was this mighty fortress, this powerful tradition – a virtual Jericho of mountain culture and Baptist dogma – that the holiness-Pentecostal movement attempted to penetrate in the late 1890s. When the revival first ignited at Camp Creek in the spring of 1896 in the Shearer schoolhouse located on a ridge above a small stream that fed the creek, there was widespread interest and enthusiasm. Hundreds of people were drawn to the meeting to witness the transforming power of the Holy Spirit at work. Hardened sinners were converted, and nominal church members were awakened to the dynamic power of the Gospel. W.F. Bryant Jr. was typical of the hundreds of skeptics who at first attended the meeting. He left the following testimony:

> At this time I was a member of the Baptist church and none of us believed in sanctification although I attended the revival. I noticed how those who claimed sanctification would go to their fellowmen and fix everything right, making their confession to one another ... Many times I mentioned to my pastor about getting mad and having malice in my heart. He would say to me, 'I see a higher experience but how to get there, I don't know'. That would make me hungry for more of God ... In 1896 I began seeking God definitely for an experience that I never had attained to. The spirit within me would cry out, 'Give me the blessing like those other few have received'. Oh, how I had to consecrate my life, dying out to my own selfish nature and forsaking all, including my earthly friends and giving up my Baptist church, in fact, making a clean breast of everything. But, thank God, when I got all on the altar, on Thursday morning, about 9:00 o'clock, I was sanctified while in my saddle on my horse. In that same year many of us received the Holy Ghost.[10]

---

[10] *FS* 1.6, p. 6.

The revival meeting in the Shearer schoolhouse in 1896 continued for ten days and brought forth a bountiful harvest. The entire region was affected. A large number claimed to have experienced the power of the second work of grace, including many of the members of the Liberty and Pleasant Hill churches. No one could deny the manifest effect of sanctifying grace, for the lives of known thieves, fornicators, and drunkards had been radically changed, some of whom were members of the spiritually shallow Baptist and Methodist churches. Area residents had witnessed with their own eyes hardened sinners transformed into saints. In a flash of sanctifying fire, thieves were made honest, fornicators were cleansed, drunkards sobered up. Yet the pastors and leaders of the churches remained unaffected by the revival, and in fact dug in their heels and set themselves in opposition to it; committing themselves with renewed vigor to maintain their traditional creed which denied the possibility of an instantaneous and complete work of sanctifying power.

The primary evangelists who conducted the meeting at Camp Creek – Martin and Tipton – moved on to other appointments in Monroe, McMinn, and Bradley counties, though they returned frequently to Camp Creek to encourage the saints and to hold meetings. Still, the newly sanctified believers at Camp Creek were unorganized, and this left them vulnerable to confusion and discouragement. They were 'as sheep having no shepherd'. It was in this vacuum that God raised up a man to fill the need. This man, whom we noticed earlier, was William Franklin ['Will'] Bryant, Jr.[11] Though Will had been converted when fourteen years of age under the preaching and pastoral guidance of R.A. ('Albert') Pinkerton, he soon backslid to his former habits. This was not so alarming to Baptists, however; indeed it was rather expected by a people who denied the possibility of sanctifying grace and the power to live above sin. Thus, accordingly, one remained saved and in good standing with his church even if backslidden as long as he did not deny the cardinal points of Baptist faith and order; and it was expected also that acknowledgment be made when one broke the commandments or committed open sin. The doctrine of *perseverance* or *eternal security* – 'once in grace always in grace' – insured the convert that he could 'never finally

---

[11] The distinction of W.F. Bryant as a junior has not been made in Church of God historiography for two reasons: first, it was not known: for Bryant himself did not make the distinction; second, W.F. Bryant Sr. had not factored into Church of God histories until now, and thus it did not seem important or necessary to draw attention to the distinction.

fall away'.¹² Though he might lose his joy and dignity and honor in this present world, he was assured he could not lose his salvation.

Will Bryant was under these impressions even after he returned to the illegal practice of making 'moonshine'. Baptists did not censure the making or drinking of alcohol for 'medicinal purposes', yet they attempted to discipline members for drunkenness and revelry. The Liberty & Ducktown Baptist Association in 1894 during their annual meeting was forced to answer the charge that 'more than three-fourths of the intoxicants manufactured in the county of Cherokee is the work of the members of Baptist churches'.¹³ Their response only made matters worse, for the leaders blamed other Baptist churches in the region for this stigma, and attempted to whitewash their own members' involvement, saying, 'As far as we are able to ascertain, the churches in the Liberty & Ducktown Association have sustained a credible rank of opposition to intemperance'. But it was all too obvious to observers that the practice was prevalent also within the bounds of the Liberty & Ducktown Association.

Allowing for the consumption of intoxicating spirits for 'medicinal purposes' created a real problem, namely, how were the elders and churches to distinguish between one who was drunk and one who was merely under the influence of 'medicine?' As one Baptist elder exclaimed, 'Some Baptists are taking too much medicine!' The problem was more complicated in the mountains because 'moonshining' and 'bootlegging' seemed to be a practical necessity – the means to preserve a corn crop and generate a little money for the operation of the particular households; at least, this was the excuse used commonly by those who indulged in the practices and it seemed to ease their collective conscience. Most people simply turned a blind eye to these practices in the mountains. Even the ministers indulged the habit of drinking 'spirits'. It is said that Will Bryant, before he was sanctified, got along better with his pastor if he gave him a jug of 'wildcat whiskey' now and again.¹⁴

But things changed on that fateful Thursday morning in 1896 when Will Bryant came under the influence and power of the Spirit of God. The blood of Jesus Christ penetrated deep into his heart and washed away the seed of Adam 'purifying his heart by faith'. Seated in his saddle,

---

¹² The doctrine of *Perseverance* – eternal security – was expressed as an important tenet of faith in almost all Baptist churches under Calvinistic influence, including Landmark churches and the churches in the Southern Baptist Convention.

¹³ *Liberty & Ducktown Association Minutes*, 1894. See under committee report on 'Temperance'.

¹⁴ David Lemons, 'Cradle of Pentecost', North Cleveland Church of God, 1983 (video tape).

quaking under the power of the Spirit, Will Bryant was sanctified and Spirit-filled in route to visit a neighbor.[15] At that moment 'old things passed away, and behold all things [became] new'. The 'old man' in Will Bryant was dead, a saint was born! This new man was anointed, empowered, gifted. Will Bryant was still uneducated and unpolished, to be sure, but he was now an instrument in the hands of the Almighty. What he lacked in natural abilities and cultured skills, the Holy Spirit compensated, equipping and empowering him with spiritual and charismatic gifts.

Sadly, William Franklin Bryant, Sr. (1835-1890)[16] did not live to see his son's spiritual transformation. Surely, he would have rejoiced, for he had been bitterly disappointed in him and felt reproached by his behavior;[17] for the Bryants had a proud family heritage that extended back several generations. Will's lifestyle was a contradiction of this admirable heritage: he was illiterate and indulged in the baser things of life – in the illegal and sinful practices of making moonshine whiskey and bootlegging, practices that strained his relationship with his father.

Will Sr. had ascended to prominence in his Baptist church and community during his relatively short stay on this earth. He had married into the well-to-do Kilpatrick family, was a deacon and clerk in the Liberty Baptist church, was comparatively well educated, and had become a postmaster and a justice of the peace. Further, he was selected by his peers to serve as clerk for the Liberty & Ducktown Baptist Association meetings. His father, Gamaliel, was a prominent minister in the region, including, as we noticed earlier, having served as the first pastor of the Holly Springs church in Monroe County in 1859-1863. Elder Richard Spurling was one of his members and fellow ministers.

But unknown to Will Sr., there was something deeper working in the spirit of Will Jr. – a spiritual hunger to be purified in his soul and transformed into the image of Jesus Christ. It would have been a great consolation to his father if he could have known that Will would be changed by the power of God in the years to come, and excel as a minister of the Gospel; though we are left to wonder if he would have accepted Will's holiness-Pentecostal interpretation of the Gospel, and especially his new light on the Bible church.

---

[15] *FS* 1.6, p. 6

[16] The Bryant's spelled their name 'Briant' until about 1880. Will Sr. is buried in the Liberty cemetery.

[17] Testimony of Nettie Bryant, pp. 2-4; interview of Nora (Bryant) Jones by the writer, May 1986.

The sincerity, passion, and courage of the new Will Bryant immediately attracted a following among those who had been sanctified or were sympathetic with the holiness movement. Though only a layman, and not knowing how to read and write,[18] the mantle of the Divine Shepherd fell upon him, partly of necessity, for no prominent licensed ministers in the area, Baptist or Methodist, joined in the holiness movement. Will was more than glad to accept the challenge and to do the best he knew how, looking to the infinitely wise and omnipotent One for assurance and guidance. Those who had spiritual discernment knew the Hand of God was upon Will Bryant, and apparently the recognition of this fact was the thing that magnified his stature in the eyes of the believers.

Figure 27

WILLIAM 'BILLY' MARTIN

With his mother, Mary, and sons shortly after his wife Callie died in 1902.

Figure 28

ROBERT FRANK PORTER AND WIFE

(c. 1928)

Following the revival in 1896, with the holiness evangelists now gone, the saints began to meet in homes where the message and experience of entire sanctification were welcomed. This enabled the spirit of

---

[18] The fact that Bryant could not read or write was widely known. He acknowledged it himself in Bryant/Lemons interview, p. 2. He soon, however, by divine providence learned how to read the Bible.

the revival to continue, and it occasioned the holiness believers to separate more obviously from the established congregations whose inflexible creeds and hard-shell Calvinistic dogmas 'quenched the Spirit' and discouraged their members from seeking deeper spiritual experiences. But the more the nominal churches complained and railed against the holiness believers because of their new found faith and experience, the deeper it drove the wedge between them. Moreover, the established churches met at places that were inconvenient for most of the holiness believers (three or four miles distance for many of them), which made their separation still more obvious and pronounced. Being now alienated from their traditional communities of faith, the holiness believers naturally gravitated toward each other, and this continued until an informal band was formed.

This little flock now consisting of about fifty to sixty believers rendered the homes of the individual members too small to accommodate their worship services.[19] This situation summoned the pastoral instinct of Will Bryant. Assessing the need for a place they could gather together, Will made arrangements to use the Shearer schoolhouse for worship services and to establish a Sunday school. This decision made the division between the holiness and non-holiness believers still more visible, though no action was taken by the established churches for over two years formally to exclude the holiness believers.[20] Not being much of a preacher and unable to read, Will directed the services mainly around worship – singing, praying, and testifying by those who had been sancti-

---

[19] John C. Jernigan, 'Rev. and Mrs. W.F. Bryant', *COGE* 36.6 (April 7, 1945), p. 3.

[20] The records and minutes of the Liberty and Pleasant Hill Baptist churches show clearly that the holiness believers were charged and excluded in 1899-1901. The misinformation and errors in the history books (e.g. Conn, *Mighty Army*, pp. 25-30; Davidson, *Upon This Rock*, I, pp. 294-300) in regard to the date of their exclusions and other events that took place at Camp Creek between 1896 and 1902 came about by the tendency of eyewitnesses to collapse together the several events of this period upon reflection 30-40 years later. Thus the initial revival in 1896, the formation of the holiness band 1896-1897, the fire-baptized influence in 1898-1901 with the manifestation of tongues-speech, the persecutions 1897-1903, the exclusions 1899-1901, and the court trial c. 1900, were all collapsed together as if they had happened within a few weeks or months, whereas actually they were distinct and sequential events that transpired over a period of six years. This blurring of history happened rather innocently on the one hand as eyewitnesses reflected on the period for historical purposes; but on the other hand several of the early historians prejudiced their interpretations to preserve, and sometimes to fabricate, denominational prestige; still others simply did not do the necessary work of searching out and scanning the actual records in order to give a credible account of the events.

fied and healed by the power of God.[21] Will exhorted on occasion the best he knew how according to what he had heard other holiness preachers proclaim; and though his exhortations were not pretty or poetic, they were anointed, moving, and effective. John C. Jernigan, a former General Overseer in the Church of God, reflected on Bryant's ministry: '[He] was an unlearned man, but during his evangelistic activities he was a great exhorter and had a powerful influence over sinners'.[22] Homer A. Tomlinson, who knew Bryant and his ministry intimately, recalled,

> I always marveled at the ministry of W.F. Bryant whom I was near much of the time in all those beginning years. While he could not read nor write, only later learning to read a large print New Testament, he was well established in the Scriptures, and this by his remarkable remembrance of the preaching from those about him. He became a mighty preacher, and one whom both my father and I, rejoicing in the power of the Holy Ghost upon him, were always blessed and thrilled when we heard him preach.[23]

Homer said on another occasion, in admiration of the deep spirituality and giftedness of Bryant, that he thought he was the first person in the church to be used by the Spirit with the gifts of 'interpretation of tongues' and 'discernment of spirits'. In regard to the latter, he noted,

> I was amazed at the accuracy of his judgment of the spirit manifested among the people, both in the church services, where wild spirits sometimes would appear, causing some to do unseemly things, say unseemly things; seemed to me almost clairvoyant in judging the characters of many both within and without the church.[24]

In regard to Bryant's character, A.J. Tomlinson endorsed him as a 'good and faithful man', by which he meant one who was sanctified and Spirit-filled and immersed completely in the work of the Lord. He noted in particular, in a kind of circular letter that he published in 1907, that 'Dear Brother Bryant, one of our faithful workers, is on a fifty mile tramp today from one point in the mountains where I left him yesterday

---

[21] Nettie Bryant/Ella (Bryant) Robinson interview, 4. W.F. Bryant's daughter, Louella 'Ella', was involved in the holiness revival from the beginning and became a charter member of the Holiness Church at Camp Creek. She and her mother are helpful sources in attempting to reconstruct the events in 1896-1903.
[22] Jernigan, 'Rev. and Mrs. W.F. Bryant', p. 3.
[23] Homer A. Tomlinson, *The Shout of a King* (Queens Village, NY: by author, 1968), pp. 45-46.
[24] Homer, *Shout*, p. 18.

to another for a meeting over Sunday, because I had no means to pay his fare around on the railroad. But he goes without a murmur'.[25] Tomlinson's comment captured the essence of Will Bryant. What he lacked in natural gifts and abilities, he made up for by his complete willingness and dedication to obey God and serve the church. He was 'an Israelite in whom [was] no guile'. Like Nathanael, his motives were pure, aiming only to serve the sanctified purposes of Christ.

Bryant loved the people in the mountains; he was devoted to them, and his devotion prompted him to make many personal sacrifices in order to be their minister. Not only did he minister to the spiritual needs of the mountaineers, but labored to appropriate and distribute clothing and sometimes food to the 'poorest of the poor'. In an appeal for assistance from Christian people in the north, Tomlinson wrote: 'The second-hand clothing can be used any and at all times in the year, but especially it is needed in cold weather. Bro. Bryant is a faithful man in putting it out right up in the mountains where it is so much needed'.[26] Will's main co-worker in these endeavors was J.B. Mitchell, the elderly Christian gentleman and colporteur from Sandusky, Ohio who first brought Tomlinson into the southern Appalachian Mountains in the mid 1890s. Mitchell had connections in the north with several Christian organizations including the Brethren in Christ, and through them was instrumental in appropriating most of the food, clothing, and literature that was distributed to the poor in the mountains. But Will Bryant was the primary distributor. It should be borne in mind also that Will's only reward for his sacrificial service was the blessings of God and a good name, the latter of which he esteemed 'far above rubies'.

Will's leadership at Camp Creek during those early years between 1896 and 1902 was sufficient to hold together the informal fellowship that had developed among the sanctified and Spirit-baptized. He invited guest preachers from the holiness movement to speak as often as he could get them. This made the saints feel that they were part of something greater than their little band at Camp Creek. At the same time, however, the guest preachers agitated the local mountaineers who were by nature suspicious of 'outsiders', especially those who encouraged the 'modern theory of sanctification'. Criticism began to mount from the old established churches including Reid's Chapel Methodist located about four miles east of Camp Creek in spite of the fact that Will's brother, Gamaliel, namesake of his grandfather, served as a minister in

---

[25] A.J. Tomlinson, 'Missionary Evangelism' (Cleveland, TN: December 31, 1907), p. 3 (a report of the work at Culberson).
[26] Tomlinson, 'Missionary Evangelism', p. 1.

this church. This put the little holiness flock in the midst of a triangle of churches that were antagonistic to the movement. Liberty Baptist congregated to the west, Pleasant Hill Baptist to the north, and Reid's Chapel Methodist to the east. Farther west from Liberty was the Turtletown and Zion Hill Baptist churches, and a little farther east of Reid's Chapel Methodist church stood Friendship Baptist. All of these churches, with the exception of Reid's Chapel, were part of the Liberty & Ducktown Baptist Association, the ministers and members forming a powerful coalition against the little holiness band. They finally, to their shame, conspired to commit violent acts against the Spirit-baptized saints. The evidence against Zion Hill, Liberty, Friendship, and Pleasant Hill churches betrayed their Christian profession – the names Babylon, Bondage, Spite, and Misery perhaps being better suited to their carnal and persecuting nature on this occasion.

Fire-Baptized Holiness Influence

We have seen how a Holiness revival that began in the hearts of a few ministers and members in the Methodist and Baptist churches in Monroe County beginning in 1895 transformed Spurling's Christian Union congregations. This revival, thereafter, spilled over into the adjoining counties of Bradley and Polk in Tennessee and into Cherokee County, North Carolina. But the phenomenon that would set ablaze this revival and bring it to a fever pitch was the fire-baptized holiness movement. This powerful movement inflamed the passions and captured the imagination of Billy Martin, Frank Porter, Milt McNabb, Joe Tipton, Billy Hamby, Sarah A. Smith, and others beginning in 1898-1899, the same ministers and laymen who had initiated the revival in 1895 in Monroe County that emphasized entire sanctification. It is still unknown when and where precisely these men came into contact with the fire-baptized holiness movement, but by spring 1899 they were fully immersed in it.[27]

The fire-baptized movement was destined to have a profound and lasting effect on the Church of God, so much so that it would be impossible to understand the spirit and developments in the church in the early twentieth century without a thorough knowledge of this movement; for the Church of God entered the twentieth century having been

---

[27] It is most likely that the primary source that informed Porter, Martin, Tipton, *et al.* about the fire-baptized holiness movement was J.M. Pike's *Way of Faith* magazine published from Columbia, South Carolina. This widely circulated holiness magazine carried sermons by B.H. Irwin and reported with favor his meetings in the Southeast.

transformed by this movement. By 1906 under the leadership of A.J. Tomlinson, the church moved its center to Cleveland, Tennessee which was located in the midst of a cluster of fire-baptized holiness congregations. The rapid growth of the church in the Cleveland area was due in fact in large part to Tomlinson's ability to incorporate the scattered bands of fire-baptized believers into the Church of God.

The fire-baptized movement had emerged out of the radical wing of the holiness movement beginning in 1895. It flourished on the basis of a radically new and enlightened understanding of the announcement by John the Baptist in Mt. 3.11, namely, that the imminent coming of Christ would mark the inauguration of a new age; but its influence spread also in protest against the compromises or perceived compromises of holiness standards in the National Holiness Association. More specifically, John's announcement of Jesus' baptism with the Spirit marked the beginning of the fulfillment of end-time events in which God would pour out His Spirit upon all flesh, and Christ would redeem and sanctify a peculiar people for His name, and gather together His elect from the ends of the earth into one bride of Christ.[28] The restoration of the doctrine and experience of the 'baptism with the Holy Ghost and fire' thus became the cornerstone of fire-baptized theology and experience. Each fire-baptized saint was a living witness of this eschatological hope.[29]

The fire-baptized holiness movement first ignited in the Oklahoma Territory in the fall of 1895, and thereafter spread like a prairie fire across the Midwest and then into the Southeast. In 1898 at Anderson, South Carolina, the movement was organized into a national body – The Fire-Baptized Holiness Association of America (FBHA), and in the ensuing months grew rapidly into an international fellowship with a global vision. By 1899, the FBHA had congregations in 13 states and two countries, with plans to send missionaries to Cuba, Africa, and India. In October 1899 the organization began to publish *Live Coals of Fire*, an 8

---

[28] The church–bride theology was still in its early stages of development in the FBHA between 1895 and 1900. But it is clear the organization was moving in the direction of a concrete ecclesiastical institution by 1899. After the FBHA was organized in 1898, the local churches began to function in the discipline laid down by Jesus in Mt. 18.15-20, and were moving in the direction of the discipline taught and practiced by the apostolic church in Acts 1.15-26; 15:28; 16.4, 5.

[29] It has been argued by some Pentecostal scholars that *eschatology* rather than *pneumatology* was the impetus and focus of early Pentecostalism. We see in the FBHA and its effect on the Church of God some justification for this view. Certainly what drove Irwin and subsequently Tomlinson was a vision of 'The Last Great Conflict'.

page monthly paper that by January 1900 boasted of subscribers throughout the United States and in several other countries.

In the same month that *Live Coals of Fire* was inaugurated, the movement acquired a valuable tract of land (75 acres) from Mrs. Cynthia 'Dollie' Lawson located two miles north of Cleveland.[30] The movement's extremely zealous and capable leader, Benjamin Hardin Irwin (ca. 1854-1926), envisioned an international center for the FBHA on this property, which was to include a 'School of the Prophets'. This school, designed to train ministers and missionaries to fulfill the FBHA's global vision, already had a small beginning in 1899 under the direction of Miss Emma Defriese, a recent convert to the movement from Birchwood. By 1900, fire-baptized evangelists were shooting in all directions like flaming cinders from a rumbling volcano. Several of the evangelists, including Billy Martin and his family, had taken up residence on the newly acquired property near Cleveland preparing to launch from this base their ministries throughout the world.[31]

Amazingly, the phenomenal growth in the FBHA happened in less than five years. Like a series of spiritual explosions set off by a divine spark, fire-baptized revivals swept the Midwest and Southeast similar to the outpourings of the Spirit recorded in the book of Acts. The movement was spontaneous, enthusiastic, and mystical. There were emotional excesses, Pharisaic legalisms, and theological aberrations, to be sure, which opponents magnified in order to stigmatize the movement with a negative image, but the core of fire-baptized holiness theology and experience was sound and spiritually wholesome. The movement bore all the marks of the prophetic 'latter rain' outpouring of the Holy Spirit promised in the Scriptures (e.g. Joel 2.28-32; Acts 2.1-21). Nothing less than a complete restoration of apostolic Christianity was envisioned in the fire-baptized holiness movement between 1895 and 1900, and for this same reason most fire-baptized believers were swept into the Pentecostal movement after the outpouring of the Spirit occurred in Los Angeles in 1906.

It may be observed that the physical and emotional excesses that attended fire-baptized meetings were not unlike the excesses and confu-

---

[30] Cynthia 'Dollie' (Curry) Lawson was coincidentally the sister-in-law of A.J. Lawson, the latter of whom joined the Church of God in January 1908 and later became a prominent deacon in the Cleveland church; and still later (after the church divided in 1923) was appointed by Tomlinson as the General Treasurer, a position that he held for 25 years. Cynthia had married Lawson's younger brother, Perry Neptune, in July 1899.

[31] Martin and his wife, Callie, and two of their children were preparing to move to Africa for missionary service as representatives of the FBHA.

sion manifested in the apostolic church (1 Cor. 12-14, e.g.), which have appeared in every great revival in every age since the first century. Indeed, the excesses in the FBHA may in one sense be interpreted simply as sincere and zealous, albeit overzealous, devotion to the vision of Christian responsibility and accountability, particularly in view of the expectation of Jesus' imminent return for a pure and spotless bride. Their deep spiritual experiences awakened in them an acute sense of contrasting spiritual realities: of heaven and hell, of the kingdom of God and the kingdom of Satan, of angels and demons, of holiness and sin, of salvation and eternal damnation. But most of all, fire-baptized saints were awakened to a penetrating vision of God himself. They thus walked circumspectly before God 'redeeming the time'.

What in retrospect may seem to have been foolish or unnecessary behavior, particularly in regard to some fire-baptized dress codes, ethical restrictions and physical demonstrations, could be considered commendable in the context of the saints' unparalleled spiritual experiences in the 1890s, which filled them with a beatific vision of God and His eternal purpose. A fair appraisal might rather see in them a sincere and humble people simply responding in faith and obedience without question to what they believed was the will of God and a restoration of apostolic Christianity. They walked in the light they had, and were willing to abandon anything and everything to exalt God and to represent Christ ever more perfectly in the world. Their sincerity and complete abandonment to God added convicting testimony to the genuineness of their spiritual experiences, whether their theology was perfect or not. 'Thy people shall be willing in the day of thy power, in the beauties of holiness' (Ps. 110.3). Fire-baptized saints in fact were not so much against the wearing of gold and feathers, as they were the spiritual pride and monetary waste behind the gold and feathers. No doubt some fire-baptized pride showed up in the process,[32] and no doubt some of their ethical rigors were needless deprivations; but these shortcomings and excesses were more or less harmless theological aberrations. The only real damage was done against their own message and missionary purpose, namely, to restore a 'third blessing' theology and experience in the church in the last days – a baptism and theology of spiritual fire and dynamic power that would glorify God, and transform a peculiar people into the perfect image of Jesus Christ.

---

[32] Alexander the Great is reported to have come upon Diogenes, the celebrated Greek cynic who lived with the dogs in the city dumps of Athens, greeting him with these words: 'Diogenes, I can see your pride through the holes in your pants'.

By 1900 the fire-baptized vision had dilated to global proportions, and the movement had grown faster than Irwin and the evangelists could facilitate through the organization of the FBHA. That the movement transcended the limitations of human organization was in fact part of the fire-baptized euphoria and excitement. The ministers and members believed the movement was under divine direction, functioning on a miraculous and providential level of existence. The perception that God was at the helm guiding the movement into waters uncharted since the days of the apostles kept the ministers and saints in a perpetual state of prophetic anticipation. They lived with thrilling expectations believing that the fulfillment of apocalyptic events was at hand, and that the FBHA itself was being prepared to be the special agency for this prophetic end-times action. Thus fire-baptized ministers lived and worked in spiritual travail, seeking to give birth or rebirth to the original form and function of the apostolic church, envisioning the prophetic bride in her spotless wedding garment going out to meet her soon coming Bridegroom!

Then suddenly, almost as quickly as the fire-baptized movement had ignited in 1895, its flame seemed to vanish. The FBHA from the beginning had been tied too closely to the personality and vision of its passionate and dynamic leader, B.H. Irwin, and thus when Irwin's fall from grace became 'open and gross' early in 1900, the organization nearly fell with him. The moral failure of Irwin shook the organization to its foundation.[33] Fire-baptized ministers were disillusioned and confused, and

---

[33] J.H. King, Irwin's successor as General Overseer of the FBHA, said that Irwin had shown signs of an 'apostate condition of heart' as early as the summer of 1899; his backslidden condition became 'open and gross' by the spring of 1900, which forced his resignation. Reportedly, he would go from pulpit to brothel throughout his travels, indulging in revelry and drunkenness (J.H. King, 'History of the Fire-Baptized Holiness Church', *PHA* 4.49 (April 7, 1921), pp. 10-11. Irwin married his second wife, Mary Lee (Jordan), without having divorced his first wife, Anna, and more unscrupulously abandoned her in 1910 along with their three small children. Mary, who became a devout Christian under the guidance of Florence Crawford in Portland, said Irwin was 'definitely immoral' and 'a slave to his passions'. His son, Fenelon, remarked that 'He wanted to reform the world, but could not reform himself' (Vinson Synan, 'The Lives of Benjamin Hardin Irwin', unpublished paper, p. 7). The discovery of some recent evidence has removed the mist from Irwin's later years. Toward the end of his life, he had fallen back on his Old Calvinism and became a follower of Daniel Parker's 'Two-Seed-In-The-Spirit Predestinarian Baptist Church' (for a succinct view of this sect, see Elmer T. Clark, *The Small Sects in America* (New York: Abingdon-Cokebury Press, 1937, pp. 202-203). There are conflicting reports of Irwin's end in this world; but the weight of evidence indicates that he probably died in Palestine, Texas in 1926.

the saints were scattered; and though the FBHA ultimately survived, it continued without much of its original passion, intensity and character.

Figure 29

ELIAS MILTON ['MILT'] MCNABB AND FAMILY (C. 1896)

McNabb and his wife, Viney Josephine [Coleman], married 1879, were leaders in the holiness revival that began in Monroe County in 1895. They lived in Cherokee County and were instrumental in bringing the revival to Camp Creek in 1896. When this revival was swept into the Fire-Baptized Holiness Movement in 1898, McNabb and his family were immersed into it and helped to spread the fire-baptized message throughout the area. McNabb's sons, Henry Clay and William Oliver married Minnie and Mamie Simpson, daughters of J.H. Simpson. When John Alexander Dowie began to build his dream of Zion City north of Chicago in 1901 and began selling lots on his newly-acquired 6600 acres, McNabb moved his family to Zion City to live under the shadow of Dowie. With thousands of others, they had glorious expectations of the City of God on earth and looked for the soon coming of Christ to Zion. After Dowie's health began to fail in 1905, and he lost control of the ministry and property in 1906, Henry Clay and Minnie moved their family to Cleveland and joined the Church of God under the leadership of Tomlinson. Henry Clay spoke in the second Assembly on the 'Gifts of the Spirit' (*GAM 1906-1914*, p. 33). Still apparently unsettled, Henry and Minnie moved back to Zion City to live near his brother William Oliver and his family. He obtained a seat on the high school board and died in Zion in 1965. Milton [d. 1945] and Viney [d. 1936] moved to Hawthorne, California and were laid to rest there. This photo reveals McNabb's political persuasion. The poster on the wall is of Republican presidential candidate,

William McKinley, who was elected in spite of the sensation of William Jennings Bryan and his famous 'Cross of Gold' speech made in the 1896 democratic convention.

The 'fire' and 'power' of the FBHA nevertheless did in fact continue. Like electricity, which according to the laws of physics cannot be diminished in its total mass, the fire and power of the movement simply metamorphosed into a new form under a new name – the Pentecostal movement. But before we move on to discuss this intriguing transformation, we should examine the FBHA's theology and experience of multiple spiritual baptisms that were experienced subsequent to Jesus' initial baptism with the Holy Ghost and fire.

'Dynamite'

By spring of 1899 the experience of 'dynamite' subsequent to the initial baptism of fire had come to light.[34] Thereafter it became the most pronounced doctrine in the movement and the most sought after experience.[35] At that point in the developing fire-baptized theological scheme, the baptism of 'dynamite' was the apex of mystical experience. Dynamited saints

Figure 30
HENRY CLAY AND MINNIE

---

[34] The exact date of Irwin's 'dynamite' experience is difficult to determine. He claimed to have experienced the 'dynamite' during a meeting on the third floor of a building at 158 Simcoe Street in Toronto. This place had been appropriated for fire-baptized mission work, and several meetings had been held there between 1898 and 1899. It is most likely that Irwin received the baptism of dynamite during his trip to Toronto early in 1899; for in a sermon preached in November 1898, which Irwin later published in *Live Coals of Fire*, he says nothing of the new experience. It is inconceivable that if he had had the experience at that time he would have failed to mention it. Nor is the experience mentioned as a tenet of faith in the Constitution of the FBHA adopted in 1898, nor in the amendments added later at the meetings in Royston, Georgia.

[35] The doctrine of 'dynamite' seems to have come into its own at Moonlight, Kansas on August 18, 1899 during the event of a fire-baptized meeting in which Irwin preached a sermon by that title. Certainly the experience was popularized by that time. 'The Dynamite' was later published in *Live Coals of Fire* (November 10, 1899), pp. 2-3. At that time it became the culminating point of fire-baptized testimony and experience.

could then exclaim, 'I am saved, sanctified, filled with the Holy Ghost, baptized with fire and dynamited with all dynamite'.

Fire-baptized leaders made great ado over the Greek word for power, *dunamis*, drawing attention to the fact that the English word 'dynamite' is derived from it. This perception of dynamic force, of baptisms of divine energy,[36] was understood metaphorically or in a spiritual sense, and thus fire-baptized evangelists drew analogies between the way the Spirit works and the way chemicals interact and formulate to create powerful explosions. As we shall see in a moment, the experiences of 'lyddite', 'oxidite', and 'selenite', in addition to 'dynamite', were made possible in and through the initial baptism with the Holy Spirit and fire. The initial fire-baptism thus laid the foundation for a dynamic continuum of spiritual experience opening the way for unlimited possibilities into the infinite depths of God. We can only speculate if Einstein had split the atom a generation earlier what affect it would have had had on the fire-baptized imagination – perhaps the *atomic bomb baptism!*

In any case, these dynamic experiences, though essentially of the same spiritual nature, were considered 'distinct and definite' experiences rather than merely gradations of spiritual power. Somehow, through a new anointed super-consciousness, the fire-baptized believer was enabled both to recognize and classify his or her spiritual experiences. Similar claims would be made a little later in early Pentecostalism by those experiencing *glossolalia*. C.F. Parham would base his concept of Pentecostalism on the gift of *xenolalia* – the ability to speak in known languages – rather than 'unknown tongues', and would influence W.J. Seymour along these same lines. Accordingly, uneducated believers – some of whom could not read nor speak good English – claimed to be able to speak and recognize Chinese, Italian, French, Russian, Japanese, and scores of other languages through the Spirit. The novelty of this idea soon wore off, however, when newly Spirit-baptized believers sailed across the oceans with their new 'gift of tongues' (known languages) only to discover the natives could not understand a word they were saying.

Again, the misinterpretation of tongues-speech in Acts 2 and elsewhere in the New Testament as the gift to speak 'known languages' was a basic feature of Pentecostalism under the influence of Parham, and for a while of Seymour in Los Angeles; it was not the theology of Irwin and the fire-baptized movement. Fire-baptized evangelists interpreted the

---

[36] The dynamite experience was often qualified thus as 'heavenly dynamite' or 'divine dynamite'.

promise of Jesus' baptism in Mt. 3.11 and the tongues-speech manifested in Acts 2 as evidence of spiritual empowerment rather than the ability to speak known languages. If anything, the gift to speak in known languages was a special manifestation of the Spirit, not a normative accompaniment of Spirit-baptism. Irwin made this plain in a message in April 1899 in which he distinguished the manifestation of 'tongues like as of fire' in Acts 2.3, which he apparently understood as unintelligible speech or 'unknown tongues', from the manifestation of the dialects or known languages in Acts 2.4.[37]

Moreover, Parham, like Frank W. Sandford in Maine, was seeking for a more effective missionary method to reach the lost, and believed he had found the answer in the gift of tongues – the supernatural ability to speak in the languages of the various peoples and tribes of the earth; whereas, Irwin and the fire-baptized evangelists were seeking for dynamic anointing to proclaim the Gospel with power, and for supernatural enablement to stand against the wiles of the devil in prosecuting the mission of the church. Thus John E. Dull, a Quaker-turned-fire-baptized evangelist, was preparing himself in 1899-1900 through ardent study of the Spanish language to be able to preach to the Cubans in their own dialect:

> I will be here at Chadbourne [NC] two days studying De Tornos ... a practical and theological system for learning the Spanish language ... God is enabling me to master this language. I have promised never to speak a word in Spanish save for His glory, and I have the assurance in my soul that I will preach to the Cubans in their own dialect.[38]

Dull's understanding of the Spirit's enablement in this regard was typical of all fire-baptized evangelists: the baptism of fire gave the believer the desire and ability to learn languages; it was not a gift that enabled believers to by-pass the natural intellect or to do away with the need to apply oneself diligently to study in order to learn another language.

We have noticed that the 'baptism of fire' subsequent to entire sanctification occasioned the fire-baptized holiness movement to form a bridge that led to twentieth-century Pentecostalism. Even so, as we noticed a moment ago, this 'third blessing' with the possibility of subsequent experiences of increased power and anointing was not understood as a new method for missions, but rather as a dynamic enablement to

---

[37] Irwin, 'The Pentecostal Church', *LCF* (June 1, 1900), p. 3. This message was first preached at Royston, Georgia on April 15, 1899.
[38] 'Letter', *LCF* (December 1, 1899), p. 3.

strike holy terror and conviction in the hearts of sinners, which included apostate preachers and half-baked, 'tobacco-chewing', 'Sabbath-breaking', 'hog-eating', 'coffee-drinking', 'necktie-wearing', 'lodge-loving', 'theater-going', 'jewelry-adorned', 'pride-ridden' church members and 'Jezebels'. The *fire* was an earth-quaking, volcanic force of divine energy that originated in, and erupted from, the throne of God; it shot through fire-baptized saints in the form of 'thunder' and 'zig-zag lightning' in order to scourge the earth of sin and unbelief.

In contrast to Parham's 'tamed' Pentecostalism, there was an array of metaphors relative to natural phenomena used by fire-baptized saints to describe their explosive spiritual experiences. Besides their chemical images of dynamite, lyddite, oxidite, and selenite, fire-baptized experiences were called 'tornadic', 'cyclonic', and so on. Earthquakes were particularly useful because their power could be gauged by seismographs to determine how powerful they were. Irwin could not have exalted the former Quaker, John E. Dull, in any greater measure than by calling him the 'Earth-Quaker'.

The *fire* – particularly the *dynamite* – was considered 'the power [*dynamite*] of God unto salvation',[39] a power that could awaken a dead conscience, quicken a dead soul, and drop backsliders to their knees before the revelation of God's glorious holiness. At the same time, it was a power that could drive saints to deeper and more ecstatic experiences of mystical communion with God. Thus, the multiple baptisms of fire empowered the saints with ever increasing energy in the Spirit in order to blow away anything that stood in the path of the church's mission in the world, and at the same time enabled fire-baptized saints to go deeper in their communion with God. Sheer energy more than spiritual gifts was the primary reason for spiritual baptisms. The *charismata* thus became more and more relegated to the single attribute of *power*, the latter of which opened the door for the concept of an infinite number of baptisms that would plunge the believer ever deeper into God.

We have noticed that the *fire* was the means to Christian perfection. Unfortunately, perfection was often understood more in terms of personal deprivations – what one was willing to give up and do without – than in terms of inward graces that worked to benefit one's neighbor and to edify the church. This caused holiness to be interpreted negatively, sometimes in isolation from divine love, which tended to relegate the concept of holiness to rigid ethical standards. One sister wrote that the

---

[39] Irwin proclaimed that the 'eternal gospel of Jesus Christ is 'the dynamite of God unto salvation to everyone that believeth' ('The Dynamite', p. 2).

baptisms of fire and dynamite had empowered her to get rid of her 'feathers, flowers, silks, laces, ribbons, gold, and all the rest of the devil's rubbish that is ruining souls today'.[40] Another wrote, 'Oh the style and fashion there is in the churches! People cannot dress and act like the world and go to heaven in the end. Glory to God, I do not care about ribbons, feathers, laces, jewelry, ornaments, or any of the rest of those nice things of the devil.'[41]

Emphasizing the negative side of holiness, without balancing it with the positive power of divine love, caused fire-baptized saints to think and act in terms of isolation rather than separation. Involvement in politics was thus considered worldly,[42] including voting and the buying of bonds and insurance policies. Certain Mosaic legislation was incorporated into the fire-baptized repertoire of prohibitions, particularly dietary restrictions against pork and 'unclean' meats'.[43] An Old Covenant view of the Sabbath was maintained with legal and rabbinic-like restrictions, though the particular day was changed from Saturday to Sunday – 'the Lord's day'. Irwin reprimanded any 'minister professing to be Christian riding on the cars on Sunday, visiting on Sunday, and reading the Sunday newspaper and indulging in worldly pleasure'.[44] He added, 'who would not put him down as a hypocrite, and so they should?'

In addition, community dances were denounced, along with the theater, secret societies, card playing, 'joking and jesting', and in general all amusements and forms of recreation not in conformity with spiritual worship and the Lord's work. A brief editorial in *Live Coals of Fire* captured the attitude and vision of the fire-baptized movement's worldview:

> In what respect does the church of today differ from the world, and what is the essential difference between it and the outside world which 'lieth [sic] in wickedness'? Both use tobacco, both attend the theater, both belong to the lodge, both ridicule holiness, and both believe in and practice sinning religion.[45]

This view of the world and the church explains the fire-baptized movement's negative emphasis on power, that is, as a weapon to destroy

---

[40] Miss Ethel Allen, 'Testimony', *LCF* (March 9, 1900), p. 7.
[41] Miss Jennie Waters, 'Testimony', *LCF* (March 9, 1900), p. 6.
[42] Irwin, 'Faith in God', p. 3.
[43] Historians Joseph E. Campbell and C.T. Davidson list a number of other ethical prohibitions and peculiarities in worship. See Campbell, *The Pentecostal Holiness Church* (Franklin Springs, GA: The Publishing House of the Pentecostal Holiness Church, 1951), pp. 203-205; and Davidson, *Upon This Rock*, I, p. 290.
[44] Irwin, 'Faith in God', p. 3.
[45] *LCF* (November 3, 1899), p. 8.

Satanic powers and forces that oppose the extension of the Gospel. Irwin had been inspired by John Fletcher's *Works*, particularly his 'Portrait of St. Paul' and 'Checks Against Antinomianism' in which Fletcher boldly reprimanded backsliding preachers and mere professors of religion. Irwin thus applied Fletcher's boldness and enthusiasm to what he perceived to be the condition of professing Christianity in his own day, particularly his perception of the apostasy of the National Holiness Association. The *dynamite experience* thus magnified the voice of fire-baptized saints in greater measure like the prophets of old to denounce sin and ungodliness in the backsliding churches, and in the pagan world around them.

After Irwin discovered that the Greek word, *dunamis*, was the etymological root for 'dynamite', he began to proclaim that this *power* could be received as a definite spiritual experience. Thereafter the doctrine of the 'third blessing' became more clearly and emphatically identified with empowerment and service. Passages like Acts 1.8 were thereafter translated, 'But ye shall receive [*dynamite*] after that the Holy Ghost is come upon you and ye shall be witnesses unto me'.[46] 'Strengthened with all might' was translated 'dynamited with all dynamite', and the apostle's passage in Phil. 4.13 was translated, 'I can do all things through Christ which dynamiteth me'. Fire-baptized people began to seek to be 'dynamited with all dynamite' in order to 'blow up' the strongholds of the devil, to unearth hypocrisy, to expose sin and carnality, to purge 'the filth of the daughters of Zion', and to convict and melt the hearts of hardened sinners before the presence of the Almighty God.

'Heavenly dynamite' also enabled saints in a greater way to reveal the holy presence and power of God through manifestations of dancing, jumping, laughing, screaming, jerks, trances, hot chills, falling, fainting, healings, and exorcisms of demons. These manifestations of the Spirit not only witnessed to the approval of God in the fire-baptized movement, which they believed legitimatized fire-baptized authority, but were intended to frighten sinners to repentance or else drive them away from the fellowship of fire-baptized saints. In a remarkable camp meeting at Moonlight, Kansas, Anna M. Brechbill, the local fire-baptized pastor, thus remarked concerning her neighbors in the community: 'we have tried to get them right or make them go away'.[47]

Baptisms of empowerment were needed in ever greater measure to discern sin and the devil, and to sustain the witness of fire-baptized

---

[46] Irwin, 'The Dynamite', p. 2
[47] 'Grumblers', *LCF* (October 20, 1899), p. 2; see also John E. Dull, 'The Third Blessing', *LCF* (October 20, 1899), p. 2.

saints against the avalanche of criticism and persecutions coming in upon them from 'apostate preachers and dried up members of churchianity' who 'lodge like devils' in the branches of man-made religion. These deeper mystical experiences, however, were not limited to visions of God and heaven; fire-baptized saints were enabled also to see the devil and the ghastly sights of hell while in a trance or under the power of an ecstasy. A.K. Willis, from Montevideo, Georgia, described his experience on January 10, 1898. While lying flat on his back in a trance, and after having heard and seen many wonderful things in heaven including a vision of his mother-in-law and the prophet Elijah, Willis said he was 'permitted to see the torments and real flames [of hellfire], and the old devil and millions of lost spirits'.[48]

Once the fire-baptized saints declared war on Satan and the world held captive by him, including the multitudes huddled together in a lukewarm and carnal system of denominations, there would be hell to reckon with, and the saints would have to be especially empowered and equipped to succeed in the mighty conflict. This vivid, piercing, clairvoyant view of spiritual warfare against the powers of darkness and spiritual wickedness in high places was the catalyst that drove fire-baptized evangelists toward the last day's restoration of Pentecostal power. Responding to criticism from unbelievers in regard to the 'third blessing', John E. Dull ('the Quaker-shaking ex-Quaker') declared,

> It was a third work for me, and why not? What if it was a fourth or fifth, if it was from God? Who has the divine commission to put a numerical number on the works of God in the human heart? Or who has God delegated to harness the Holy Ghost, and thus deprive hungry souls of the deeper and richer manifestations of God?[49]

'Lyddite'

This view of ever-deepening, ever-loftier experiences into the infinite depths of God was bound to lead to experiences beyond the fire and dynamite. Accordingly, on February 21, 1900, Miss Jennie Watters of Toronto received the definite empowerment of the 'lyddite'. This, according to Irwin, was 'the first definite testimony to the lyddite'.[50] Later in this same issue of the *Live Coals of Fire*, the testimony of Miss Watters appeared:

> In the afternoon, while I lay on the floor, Sister Quant was reading a letter from one of the evangelists [A.E. Robinson], and I just got the

---

[48] 'Willis' Vision', *LCF* (October 6, 1899), p. 6.
[49] Dull, 'The Third Blessing', p. 5.
[50] B.H. Irwin, 'Editorial Correspondence', *LCF* (March 9, 1900), p. 1.

experiences right along as she mentioned them through the letter; first sanctification, then the Holy Ghost, the fire and the dynamite; I just seemed to have them and did not know what to call them, but as soon as she mentioned them I claimed them and shouted that I had them everyone. It was not me that claimed it, it was the Holy Ghost who spoke through me. I could no more help claiming these experiences than I could help claiming salvation, O, praise the Lord. When I got to the dynamite I asked if there was anything else; someone said, 'Lyddite', and I claimed it right straight. I knew I had it, glory, glory, glory to Jesus![51]

She went on to describe further her experiences,

I have salvation that makes me open my mouth; I could not keep it closed. I lay on the floor, jumped up and danced every little while, then fell to the floor again with a bang and did not get the least bit hurt nor know where I was falling, for my eyes were closed most of the time. I was dancing, shouting, and praising God all the time, and if my throat had not been healed I could never have shouted the way I did. This never ceased for about eleven hours, praise the Lord ... The power just leaped from my toes to my fingertips. I cannot praise the Lord enough.

Lyddite was a relatively new discovery made in the late nineteenth century near Lydd, England (hence 'lydd' + 'ite'), that was composed mainly of picric acid. The highly explosive nature of this substance is greater than that of dynamite; thus Irwin and his followers fitted it metaphorically to their theological scheme of ever-increasing power in the Spirit. The lyddite shell was first used with noticeable effect as a military weapon during the British-Boer war in South Africa which had begun in October 1899. This was coincidently about the same time that J.H. King was appointed by Irwin as the Ruling Elder in Ontario, Canada and as the pastor of the Toronto church. Since Canadian troops were sent to assist the British in South Africa, news of the war filled the Toronto papers. It was in these published reports apparently that King learned of the power of lyddite as a weapon of war from which he immediately drew an analogy to spiritual warfare.

Now in the British-Boer was going on in South Africa they have introduced lyddite, which proves to be the most dangerous of all materials for the destruction of human life. It tears up the largest pieces of

---

[51] Waters, 'Testimony', p. 6. Irwin informs us in the editorial of this issue that he is the one who said, 'lyddite'.

artillery, and blows up strongholds where the enemy is entrenched. At the Modder River battle the British with lyddite shells blew the water right out of the river and filled the air with sickening green smoke. The very force of a lyddite shell passing near some Boer soldiers killed them instantly even without exploding, and their faces turned green from the effect of it. The world has been taxed to manufacture these awfully destructive materials, and shall the world be wiser in their generation than the children of light? If the world is constantly exerting itself to the utmost in the manufacture of implements and destructive materials by which to destroy its enemies, shall not we as warriors in God's great army do our utmost to obtain all the destructive experiences that God can give us?[52]

Mattie Watters' experiences were attended by such dramatic manifestations of spiritual power that they exceeded and elevated even the expectations of Irwin and King. In response to Miss Watters' question, 'Is there anything more?' (See her testimony above), it was Irwin who said, 'lyddite',[53] whereupon Miss Watters instantly claimed the experience. Thereafter the general overseer declared,

> We are in full sympathy with this lyddite warfare. We have no time to stop and parley with the foe, our object is to crush him and blow him up. There are more things in God's great magazine than are dreamed of in the philosophy of these fire-fighting holiness people. We have the dynamite and hell-crushing lyddite, and still we are not satisfied. We are going in and down for the unspeakable, unnamable, 'exceedingly abundantly above' things, which can only be apprehended ... by an uncompromising child-like faith. Praise God for the lyddite![54]

About the same time that the lyddite experience had been discovered and restored, the experiences of 'selenite' and 'oxidite' were identified and began to be experienced. But whereas the dynamite and lyddite were understood more strictly in terms of quantitative power, the selenite and oxidite were understood in terms of higher mystical experiences, at least from the perspective of Irwin's son, Stewart.[55] *Dynamite* and *lyddite* were spiritual baptisms enabling one to proclaim the Gospel with greater

---

[52] J.H. King, 'Our Weapons of Warfare', *LCF* (May 18, 1900), p. 1.
[53] Irwin, 'Editorial Correspondence', p. 1.
[54] Irwin, 'Editorial Correspondence', p. 1.
[55] King, however, was apparently misinformed about the nature of selenite and thus interpreted it as a higher explosive than lyddite. He wrote, '[Lyddite] is not the highest explosive in nature, as we have learned. Our enemies tauntingly asked when we testified to the lyddite, 'Are you going to get the selenite?' [Selenite] is the next higher explosive in nature's kingdom' (King, 'Our Weapons of Warfare', p. 8).

power, to cast out devils, and to work miracles for the advancement of the kingdom; whereas, *selenite* and *oxidite* were gifts elevating saints to heavenly places in Christ Jesus, where they could see the unseen and breathe the pure air of heaven. Stewart Irwin explained the nature of the multiple baptisms in light of Acts 2.1-4:

> Then came – and that in rapid order – the dynamite and lyddite, for they spake with other tongues as the Spirit gave them utterance. This utterance of speech was beyond understanding by those who witnessed the awful scene, and they were utterly confounded and greatly amazed. This is not strange for they were 'strengthened with all might', and bursting forth with articulations of heavenly lyddite. They were actually viewing the heavenly inhabitants—had the selenite; and were breathing the pure atmosphere of heaven – had the oxidite. Hallelujah! O the grandeur of being in heavenly places, viewing heavenly things and breathing heavenly atmosphere.[56]

'Oxidite'

This remarkable and illuminating passage by the younger Irwin clearly reveals the developing theology of the FBHA. Stewart's studies in science, particularly botany, chemistry, and electricity, informed his theology and interpretations of spiritual experience. Though he apparently invented the word 'oxidite', yet his analogy to certain scientific discoveries relative to oxygen reveals the significance he attached to the new word. The natural air we breath on earth is only one-fifth oxygen, the rest being for the most part the elements of nitrogen, carbon dioxide, and argon. The air we breathe is thus corrupted, which reflects the results of sin and divine judgment. When the saints are glorified and the curse is lifted from nature, paradise will be restored and thus saints will again breathe the pure air of heaven. But even in this present fallen world, air can be purified through liquidation. In this process, air is cooled down to about -200 degrees F. At that point, the nitrogen, carbon dioxide, and argon are separated from the oxygen, leaving only a purified oxygen to breathe.

Irwin apparently had gained knowledge of this process while studying at the University of Nebraska and thus applied it metaphorically and analogically to describe how the Spirit elevates the believer through the power of a distinct and definite spiritual experience, which he denominated the 'baptism of oxidite'. Through this experience the consecrated saint is enabled to breathe the infinitely pure air of heaven while being

---

[56] 'The Breath of Jesus', *LCF* (June 1, 1900), p. 6.

yet in this present world. Irwin seems to have developed this theology by observing the way the Spirit works in healing certain diseases, particularly respiratory illnesses. Accordingly, a soul is lifted up through mystical communion with God and angels in celestial bliss, and thereby is enabled to miraculously inhale the healing and glorified atmosphere of heaven. This was indeed 'good news' to saints who had respiratory related illnesses and could believe in the supernatural work of God. Immediately, those already fire-baptized began to seek for these higher and deeper spiritual experiences.

'Selenite'

About the same time that the oxidite baptism was established, the *baptism of selenite* began to be proclaimed. It is difficult to determine who introduced this experience into the movement. It is likely that it was Stewart Irwin, though one report indicates that an outsider may have first suggested the name in jest. In any case, it had made its appearance in the FBHA at least by early spring in 1900. Again, it is from the pen of Stewart Irwin that we learn most about the nature and purpose of the baptism of selenite. We have already noticed that young Irwin had a penetrating intellect like his father's, and that he was learned in physics, botany, and science, particularly in the field of electricity.[57] Recent discoveries in electricity, particularly in regard to photoelectric cells, had been introduced at the World's Fair in Chicago in 1893, and these were exciting new topics in his studies at the University of Nebraska. This knowledge enabled Irwin to draw an analogy to how the power of God works in the realm of spiritual experience. Selenium, a chemical element of the sulfur group, which occurs in transparent crystals or crystalline masses, increases its electrical conductivity when light strikes it. In the form of selenite plates, selenium is able to polarize light and convert that light directly into electricity. Thus selenite began to be used in the late nineteenth century in photoelectric devices which eventually led to photographic exposures and the projection of human images and motion pictures.

The word 'selenite', derived from the Greek word for moon, *selene*, came into use because it was widely believed in the 1890s that the moon was a visible and hardened form of selenium, a kind of gigantic gypsum ball or massive sphere of plaster of Paris suspended in the heavens. With this in mind, it was easy for Irwin to draw parallels from the natural

---

[57] In rejoicing over his son's conversion and call into the ministry, B.H. Irwin noted, 'His electrical knowledge, and his willingness to do anything which may be required will make him of great service in the office' ('Our Working Force', *LCF* [October 20, 1899], p. 4).

phenomena in chemistry and astrophysics to how the Holy Spirit works in illuminating and empowering saints. Young Irwin thus advanced fire-baptized preaching to include the 'baptism of selenite', which we have every reason to believe he preached in his fire-baptized meetings at Camp Creek, North Carolina and in Cleveland, Tennessee in 1900.

Though Stewart Irwin does not explicitly mention the baptisms of *oxidite* and *selenite* in his reports of his meetings at Camp Creek, he posted notice in the April 1900 issue of *Live Coals of Fire* that he was departing for 'Bryant's schoolhouse' for a meeting,[58] and concluded his article proclaiming, 'Saved from all sin, and from sinning; sanctified wholly, soul, mind and body: filled with the blessed Holy Ghost: baptized with the living white fire of the Trinity and dynamited with all dynamite: healed and waiting for the premillennial coming of Jesus'.

After Irwin left the meeting at Camp Creek and returned to the movement's base at Beniah near Cleveland, he wrote an article for the paper concerning the disciples' baptism on the day of Pentecost, which included, according to Irwin, multiple baptisms of power. He noted, 'They received explosion after explosion of dynamite and lyddite ... while they moved in the way that God led, from place to place and from experience to experience'.[59]

Origin of Modern Pentecostalism?

Stewart Irwin's reference to unintelligible speech or unknown tongues raises again the questions of who introduced the doctrine of 'speaking in tongues' in connection with Spirit-baptism, and when did the modern-day Pentecostal movement begin? Irwin's reference to 'ecstatic speech' as the result of the baptism of *lyddite* predates by eight months Charles Fox Parham's introduction of Spirit-baptism with its connection to speaking in tongues at Topeka, Kansas in January 1901. Indeed, we have every reason to believe that Parham himself was introduced not only to a post-sanctification 'third work blessing' but also to *glossolalia* in fire-baptized meetings which had been blazing across Iowa, Kansas, Nebraska, Missouri, Texas, and Oklahoma since Irwin had inaugurated the movement in 1895. Parham's biographer, James R. Goff Jr., acknowledges that Parham was deeply affected and influenced by the FBHA.[60] The same writer, however, says that Parham was introduced

---

[58] Stewart T. Irwin, 'Letter', *LCF* (April 6, 1900), p. 6.
[59] Stewart T. Irwin, 'The Breath of Jesus', *LCF* (June 1, 1900), p. 6.
[60] James R. Goff Jr., *Fields White Unto Harvest* (Fayetteville: University of Arkansas Press, 1988), pp. 54-57.

to tongues-speech at Frank W. Sandford's 'Holy Ghost and Us' Bible school in Shiloh, Maine in 1900,[61] but this supposition may be questioned on the basis that Parham dismissed the *glossolalia* in fire-baptized meetings as mere 'chatter', 'jabber', and 'babble', for he claimed the ability to distinguish between known languages and mere 'gibberish', the latter being, according to Parham, sheer nonsense and nothing less than sensationalism and fanaticism with no practical value. He rejected the revival at Azusa Street on this same basis, denouncing the meetings as being filled with 'absurd exhibitions' which were for the most part little more than 'gymnastic contortions of Holy Rollers, who throw fits, perform somersaults, roll and kick in the straw or dust or upon the floor of the meeting house'.[62] He claimed that 'two-thirds of the people professing Pentecost are either hypnotized or spook-driven'.[63]

More importantly, B.H. Irwin's theology of tongues-speech was superior to Parham's in that it was more consistent with Scripture and the Pentecostal movement, particularly as the Pentecostal experience was defined under the leadership of W.J. Seymour and the saints at the Azusa Street Mission after they had separated from Parham in 1906-1907. At least by December of 1906, the official position of the Azusa Mission distinguished between the 'gifts of tongues' and the 'witness of tongues'. The lead article in *The Apostolic Faith* stated,

> The baptism with the Holy Ghost makes you a witness unto the uttermost parts of the earth. It gives you power to speak in the languages of the nations. So everyone ... receives the witness of speaking in tongues as the Spirit gives utterance. You may not receive the gift of tongues when you receive the baptism with the Holy Ghost, but you receive the witness of tongues, that is to say, – you will speak in tongues when you are baptized with the Holy Spirit.[64]

Gradually between 1907 and 1909, as Seymour and the saints in the Azusa Street Mission studied the subject of tongues-speech more carefully, they articulated more clearly the differences between 'unknown tongues' and 'known tongues' and the gift of 'interpretation of tongues'. Thereafter, Pentecostals universally came to accept 'unknown tongues' – which 'no man understands' (1 Cor. 14.2) – as the initial vocal evidence of Spirit-baptism. Noticeably, more and more emphasis was put on

---

[61] Goff, *Fields*, pp. 74-75.
[62] Goff, *Fields*, p. 129.
[63] Sarah E. Parham, *The Life of Charles F. Parham* (Joplin, MO: Tri-State Printing Co., 1930), p. 130.
[64] 'Pentecost With Signs Following', *AF*, December 1906, p. 1.

'unknown tongues' and 'interpretations' as the movement progressed, and less and less on the gift to speak known languages, the latter being understood as an extraordinary gift.

The developing theology of tongues-speech in the Pentecostal movement thus began to sound remarkably similar to what Irwin taught in 1899-1900. As pointed out earlier, Irwin had distinguished as early April 1899 the manifestation of 'tongues of fire' on the day of Pentecost in Acts 2.3 from the manifestation of the various dialects in verse four.[65] Moreover, he identified 'tongues of fire' as the manifestation of fire-baptism subsequent to the experience of entire sanctification. His explanation in his message at Royston, Georgia in April 1899 is perfectly consistent with the interpretation of Spirit-baptism at Azusa Street except that the term *baptism of fire* is substituted for the *baptism with the Holy Spirit*. Both movements proclaimed a 'third blessing' subsequent to entire sanctification and both interpreted Acts 2 as empowerment for service and the anointing to proclaim the Gospel with power. Irwin describes the manifestations on the Day of Pentecost as 'a case of real spiritual intoxication' in fulfillment of the prophecy of Joel 'who foretold of these wonders'. Finally, he says in reference to Acts 2.3, 'These were tongues of fire. The dialects were another thing. God put mighty power upon these people, and the Holy Ghost enabled them to speak with other tongues'.[66] This is why J.H. King said years later that the last days Pentecostal outpouring actual began in the fire-baptized movement. Reflecting on the history of the FBHA in its early years, King wrote:

> The church was both Scriptural and unscriptural in that it taught and maintained that the Pentecostal Baptism was subsequent to sanctification; unscriptural in that it set forth two baptisms in the Pentecostal outpouring. This unscriptural teaching with all that followed in its train turned the church aside from its providential purpose, and its distinctive mission was largely lost. It could and would have been used to usher in the great Pentecostal baptism in its reality and fullness had it not fallen into this mischievous error.[67]

It becomes apparent when King's comments are carefully weighed that he surrenders the fire-baptized movement's claim on the origin [or restoration] of the Pentecostal Movement only on the basis of its com-

---

[65] Irwin, 'The Pentecostal Church', *Live Coals of Fire*, June 1, 1900, p. 3.
[66] Irwin, 'The Pentecostal Church', p. 3.
[67] King, 'History of the Pentecostal Holiness Church', *PHA* 4.50, 51 (April 14, 1921), p. 11.

plicated theology of multiple baptisms and the excesses and distortions connected with certain Mosaic legislation and ethical rigors. Otherwise, every element of the Pentecostal baptism in Acts 2, which was espoused later in the Azusa Street Mission after December 1906, was manifested in fire-baptized meetings between 1895 and 1900. Moreover, the link to the Azusa Street Mission, namely Charles Fox Parham and his Apostolic Faith movement in Kansas, was directly influenced by Irwin and the FBHA. What seems apparent now on reflection is that between 1895 and 1909 the theology of Spirit-baptism was simply better understood and more clearly defined, but the experience itself was present from the beginning in Irwin's fire-baptized movement.

This was precisely the conclusion of the Church of God in 1922. Homer Tomlinson writing about the outpouring of the Spirit at Camp Creek in the church's *Faithful Standard* magazine explained:

> We do not say that this was a part of the Latter Rain outpouring, because those who received the Baptism did not realize what it was until after 1906, when they heard of the Los Angeles outpouring. But looking back they realized it was the same thing, the same Spirit, the same power and the same manifestation.[68]

Further research and reflection in recent years on the historical and theological evidence has led us to conclude that the beginning of the Pentecostal movement should indeed be located in the fire-baptized holiness movement, particularly in light of what was proclaimed and experienced in 1899-1900 with the proliferation of *glossolalia* and other spiritual gifts. The testimony of W.F. Bryant and Sarah A. Smith adds weight to this conclusion, namely, that Billy Martin came back to Camp Creek teaching the baptism with the Holy Ghost and speaking in tongues.[69] Martin's return to Camp Creek preaching the baptism with the Spirit was at least by 1899 and possibly as early as 1898, for after the 1896 revival in the Shearer schoolhouse he and Tipton returned 'frequently' to Camp Creek to hold meetings.[70] We have noticed that Martin and Frank Porter had learned of the baptisms of fire and dynamite in fire-baptized meetings, or through fire-baptized literature, and consequently had joined the FBHA by1899 and possibly as early as 1898. These two men traveled together to Nebraska to meet with Irwin in

---

[68] 'History of Pentecost', *FS* 1.6, p. 5.
[69] Bryant and Lemons, 'Chesser Interview', p. 2; 'Youth Interviews Experience', *The Lighted Pathway* (July, 1949), p. 14.
[70] Testimony of Sarah A. Smith in B.F. Lawrence, *The Apostolic Faith Restored* (St. Louis, MO: Gospel Publishing House, 1916), pp. 45-46.

1899, and thereafter returned to the Southeast preaching the experiences in Tennessee and North Carolina, Porter being appointed as the ruling elder of the FBHA in Tennessee. Daniel Awrey, another fire-baptized evangelist, testified that about a dozen persons had been baptized with the Spirit and spoke in tongues in a meeting at Beniah in 1899.[71]

At least by May 1900 Martin was with Stewart Irwin and Tipton at Camp Creek in Cherokee County, North Carolina teaching the experiences of lyddite, oxidite, and selenite in 'Bryant's schoolhouse' which included the manifestation of ecstatic speech ('unknown tongues'). The fact that more than one hundred persons were said to have been Spirit-baptized during the Camp Creek revival in 1899-1900 with the manifestation of *glossolalia*[72] further supports the argument that the Pentecostal movement in the twentieth century had its origin in the FBHA before 1900, rather than in the Azusa Street mission in 1906, or in Parham's meetings in Kansas in 1901.[73]

Sarah A. Smith (1844-1918) who had been working with Billy Martin and his wife, Callie, and with Tipton, McNabb, and Hamby since the revival broke out in Coker Creek in Monroe County in 1895, claimed that she was baptized with the Holy Spirit in a meeting in the Epperson community and spoke in other tongues with about forty others in 1900.[74] This was apparently following a glorious two-week revival in April at Epperson and another outpouring at Camp Creek the first week in May 1900 which she and Martin's wife attended after the meeting had begun. Martin was apparently the minister in charge. In regard to the meeting at Epperson she said, 'Sunday April 22d was the greatest day of

---

[71] Lawrence, *The Apostolic Faith Restored*, p. 45.

[72] Tomlinson, *LGC*, pp. 210-12. Here Tomlinson notes that, 'While the meetings were in progress one after another fell under the power of God, and soon quite a number were speaking in tongues ... Men, women and children received the Holy Ghost and spoke in tongues under the mighty Spirit of God' (pp. 210-11). And again, 'It is estimated that more than one hundred persons really received the baptism as the evidence during that revival' (p. 212). Tomlinson's statements here are based on the personal testimonies of those were in the meetings, for example, W.F. Bryant and Margaret Melissa (Shearer) Murphy, but Tomlinson himself was in some of the meetings after 1899.

[73] This was in fact the testimony of Irwin in December 1906 after he professed to have recovered from his fall through the ministry of Florence Crawford in Portland, Oregon, and was again baptized with the Holy Ghost and spoke in tongues. Irwin would later denounce the Pentecostal experience and, as noted earlier, would end his days as a 'two-seed-in-the-Spirit' Baptist.

[74] Stanley H. Frodsham, *With Signs Following* (Springfield, MO: Gospel Publishing House, 1941), pp. 16-17.

all; the meeting lasted most of the day, and the wonderful manifestations that God put upon His little ones were indescribable'.[75]

Still it seems the meeting in which she and about forty others were baptized with the Holy Ghost at Epperson was in the summer of 1900 after the fall of Irwin had become common knowledge. Apparently after receiving the news of Irwin's fall, those who had been living at Beniah – the Martins, Smith, *et al.* – returned to their homes. It was during this time also that many decided to go to Zion City, Illinois – including Milton McNabb – to work with John Alexander Dowie in his sensationalized ministry in the Christian Apostolic Church. In any case, it was later in the summer of 1900 apparently that the greatest outpouring happened at Camp Creek while Martin and Tipton were there. Smith reflected in 1915,

> I can remember hearing them [Martin and Tipton] say that nearly everyone fell under the power (that is, over in North Carolina), and the thought came to me that I had been unwilling to fall, for the Lord had been trying me by putting His power on me in a peculiar way, so that I would spin around like a top; two or three times He had done it, and every time I would back up to the wall to keep from falling. But when I heard their testimony, I told the Lord I would fall or do anything, but I wanted what He had for me ... Of course, He tried again, and ... I yielded and fell and spoke in tongues.[76]

This was the same meeting at Epperson in which about forty or fifty others were baptized with the Holy Spirit and spoke in tongues. The timeline corresponds also with Bryant's testimony that Martin came back to Camp Creek in 1899-1900 'preaching the Baptism of the Holy Ghost and talking in tongues'.[77]

The only justification given by those holding that the Pentecostal movement began with Parham in 1901 in Topeka or with Seymour in 1906 in Los Angeles is on the basis that speaking in tongues was both anticipated and consciously understood to be the initial and conclusive

---

[75] Sarah A. Smith, 'Letter', *LCF* (May 18, 1900), p. 2. In her report, Smith says further that immediately following the glorious outpouring at Epperson, that she and Martin's wife, Callie, came on to Patrick (Camp Creek) to join in the glorious meeting that was going on there. Smith is a reliable witness, for she joined the Church of God and later served on the staff of Lillian Trasher's orphanage in Egypt until her death in 1918. She had an impeccable reputation as a Christian and servant of the church.

[76] Smith, *The Apostolic Faith Restored*, p. 46.

[77] Bryant/Lemons interview, p. 2.

evidence of Spirit-baptism.[78] But this interpretation relegates the origin of the Pentecostal movement to a correct theology of speaking in tongues in regard to Spirit-baptism, an idea that in itself is problematic, for it is certain that the apostles had not known what to expect on the day of Pentecost, and in fact defined their theology retrospectively in light of their experience, not vice versa. Moreover, we have seen that Parham's theology of tongues was in error, for he relegated the initial evidence of Spirit-baptism to known languages,[79] and otherwise tended to suppress the free exercise of the Spirit, going so far even to usurp authority to 'tame' saints whom he deemed to be too emotional and irregular in worship.

Parham claimed to be able to tell the 'difference between a clear language and a chatter and jabber', for, said he, 'a language has certain tones to it that makes you know'.[80] Under this exalted opinion of human ability to discern and comprehend the distinct sounds of hundreds of languages and thousands of dialects, and conversely his distorted impressions of God's power, including limiting the Infinite Spirit to speak only in known human languages, caused Parham to hinder and even to prevent multitudes from being actually baptized with the Spirit; for his inclination was to quench what he could not comprehend. Still further, Parham embraced and proclaimed many strange and erroneous doctrines including annihilation of the sinner's soul ('conditional immortality'), Zionism, Anglo-Israelism, the superiority of the white race, and a bewildering concept of the bride and the church.[81]

Seymour, while still under the influence of Parham, began the meetings at Azusa Street in April 1906 under the impression that speaking in tongues was for the most part the gift to speak in known languages, and thus *glossolalia* was understood to serve primarily as a divinely-ordered and miraculous missionary method enabling the church to spread the Gospel more speedily throughout the world. Seymour's theology and spirit of ministry otherwise, however, bore little semblance to Parham's; indeed, Seymour parted ways with Parham after the latter showed up in Los Angeles in October 1906 and reproved the Azusa Street elders and saints for what he considered to be emotional excesses, denouncing also the tongues-speech he had heard as being mere 'chatter, jabber, [and]

---

[78] Goff, *Fields*, pp. 71-72.
[79] Parham, *Voice Crying in the Wilderness*, pp. 28-38.
[80] Parham, 'The Baptism of the Holy Spirit', in Robert L. Parham, *Selected Sermons of the late Charles F. Parham and Sarah E. Parham*, 1941, p. 67.
[81] These doctrines are explained in Parham's *A Voice Crying in the Wilderness*, pp. 86-118.

sputtering'. He attempted further in a stuffy and high-handed manner to impose his ideas on the ministry and outreach of the Azusa Street Mission,[82] which the elders met with stout resistance and insisted that Parham depart from them.

Parham did depart and started his own mission in another part of town under his authority as 'Projector' of the Apostolic Faith movement. Thereafter Seymour's relationship with Parham continued to deteriorate resulting finally in a complete schism. The positive side of this division was that Seymour, having been weaned from Parham's influence and ideas, was now free to develop a broader and sounder biblical theology of Spirit-baptism. Between 1907 and 1909 Seymour led the way in developing the general parameters of classic Pentecostal theology and experience in the twentieth century.

The moral failure of B.H. Irwin and his resignation as General Overseer of the FBHA in June 1900 devastated the fire-baptized movement. This seems to explain why the doctrines of *glossolalia* and Spirit-baptism were not more fully developed theologically by the scattered remnant of fire-baptized saints; for the movement from the beginning had been dependent almost entirely on the leadership of Irwin and his theological constructions. But for all practical purposes the Pentecostal movement had begun in the FBHA, proliferating during the meetings in East Tennessee and at Camp Creek, North Carolina in 1898-1900.

On reflection what seems plain now is this: Parham had merely formulated in 1900-1901 a theology of what had been suggested to his mind by observing the outpourings of the Spirit with tongues-speech in fire-baptized meetings and other religious movements,[83] and by experiencing the same himself in 1901.[84] But, as we have seen, his relegation of tongues-speech to known languages caused him to misinterpret the doctrine and primary purpose of speaking in tongues in the Scriptures. This fact alone would seem to disqualify Parham from being the 'father' of the Pentecostal movement, for he actually denied the true biblical evidence of Spirit-baptism – tongues spoken in a mystery 'unto God [which] no man understands' (1 Cor. 14.2). Seymour also would have to

---

[82] Parham, *Life*, pp. 164-202; Vinson Synan, *The Holiness-Pentecostal Movement in the United States* (Grand Rapids, MI: Eerdmans, 1971), p. 112.

[83] Parham had also visited the meetings at Shiloh in Maine conducted by Frank W. Sandford and the meetings conducted by John Alexander Dowie in Zion City, Illinois both of which produced manifestations of *glossolalia*.

[84] Parham in fact taught the 'baptism of the Holy Ghost and fire' in 1899. See *Apostlic Faith* (Topeka) (March 22, 1899), p. 8; and Goff, *Fields White Unto Harvest*, p. 57.

be denied the prestigious title – 'father of the movement' – on this same basis, for as we have seen he had been indoctrinated by Parham and thus guided the Pentecostal movement in Los Angeles at first along the lines of Parham's theology of Spirit-baptism. It is true that Seymour, after separating from Parham, gradually developed a broader and more biblical theology of Spirit-baptism, particularly in regard to defining the initial evidence of tongues-speech as being basically unintelligible to man, over against the gift to speak in known languages. Moreover, he had concluded that this unintelligible speech ('unknown tongues') was the sign of empowerment for Christian service upon the sanctified life. Again, it is intriguing that this development in Seymour's theology of Spirit-baptism was so similar to Irwin's theology, particularly in the light of Irwin's evolving understanding of Spirit-baptism and tongues-speech in 1898-1900. A strong argument may be made therefore that Irwin's theology of Spirit-baptism flourished in Seymour after 1906 by accident through Parham, that is, a correct view of Spirit-baptism and tongues-speech had emerged out of Parham's erroneous view ironically through Seymour; but the seeds of modern Pentecostalism had been planted first by Irwin and the fire-baptized evangelists between 1895 and 1900.

Theologically Sound

In spite of some of the strange-sounding ideas and terms used by fire-baptized evangelists, the FBHA was basically sound theologically. What now may seem strange or extreme to outsiders who can only reflect on the history and theology of the movement from a distance was nevertheless spiritually transforming and deeply convicting to those actually immersed under the power of the Spirit then and there. Further, the extremes might be excused on the basis of the freshness and newness of fire-baptized experiences and the saints' child-like curiosity to explore the deeper realms of God. Fire-baptized leaders were innovators and restorers of apostolic Christianity, plowing up old ground and cleaning out wells that were first dug by the prophets of old and experienced by the apostles in the New Testament.

In any case, in spite of the fact that the fire-baptized movement plunged deep into the ocean of mystical experience, it retained an orthodox view of the Wesleyan *via salutis* of conviction, repentance, pardon, justification, regeneration, and sanctification. Moreover, the Holy Spirit was distinguished as the third person of the 'blessed trinity', and His office work was distinguished in the Trinitarian economy especially in regard to His role in the unfolding of eschatological events.[85] Irwin designated the age between the Day of Pentecost and the Second Coming of Christ as the dispensation of the Holy Spirit, a concept that he borrowed from the writings of John Fletcher. The fundamental orthodoxy of the FBHA particularly in regard to second work sanctification and holiness is noteworthy, for it distinguishes it from the great majority of Pentecostals who beginning in the second decade of the twentieth century distanced themselves from the holiness tradition. Most so-called 'second wave' and 'third wave' Pentecostals since the 1960s (charismatics and neo-charismatics) have in fact emerged from or else have fallen back on the historical elements in Roman Catholic, Eastern Orthodox, Lutheran, and Episcopalian traditions. It is a 'Pentecostalism' that has little semblance to the classical Pentecostalism of the late nineteenth- and early twentieth century. It sprang from a wholly different seed, with a different message and a different vision.

This neo-Pentecostalism is even more intriguing in view of its courtship with the high church traditions and the modern currents of Eastern mysticism. It is a movement that has been absorbing the mystical abstractions of Eastern philosophy for several decades, being gradually lured into web of the mysterious woman envisioned by the apostle John, namely, MYSTERY, BABYLON THE GREAT, THE MOTHER OF HARLOTS AND ABOMINATIONS OF THE EARTH (Rev. 17.1-5). What is at stake are the essential truths of the Gospel of Christ as they have been understood and defined in the light of Reformed and Wesleyan theology for almost three hundred years – truths that will be espoused and embodied finally only in the bride of Christ and the saints who make up God's kingdom (Rev. 19.7-9, 11-14). But here we are jumping ahead of our narrative; let us return to the theological development of the fire-baptized holiness movement between 1895 and 1900.

Trinitarian Mysticism

Fire-baptized experience revived an intriguing aspect of the mysticism in the Middle Ages, namely, that deeper experiences in the Spirit that enable the devout to discern and commune with each person in the Trinity separately. These intra-Trinitarian revelations swept fire-baptized believers up into the glory of the celestials enabling them to penetrate into the very depths of the Divine Mystery. While in the power of these ecstatic

---

[85] J.H. King wrote in *Live Coals of Fire* a masterful five-part thesis on the order and purpose of eschatological events. His academic preparation particularly shined in these articles.

experiences, the consciousness of the fire-baptized saint was quickened by the Spirit, enabling him or her to focus – or rather the 'fire' focused for him or her – more clearly each person in the Trinity so that each divine person could be recognized in His distinct office.

Irwin and other fire-baptized evangelists used the experiences and writings of Roman Catholic mystics like Monsieur de Renty, Francois Fenelon, and Madam Guyon (though Guyon was detached institutionally from the Roman Church), and early Methodist mystics like John Fletcher, Hester Ann Rogers, William Bramwell, and Lady Maxwell to support their mystical experiences and doctrines. Irwin, after having read the journal of Lady Maxwell, was confident that she

> … had the real baptism of fire, and how the Lord did reveal Himself to her – the personal Father, and the personal Holy Ghost, and the personal Son, each separately, and she was so taken into God that she knew when the Father visited her heart, and when the Son visited her heart, and when the Holy Ghost visited her heart'.[86]

The writings of the Puritan divine, John Owen, were also used to support the experiential practice of mystical communion[87] in order that the 'saints might have communion distinctly with the Father, and distinctly with the Son, and distinctly with the Holy Ghost'.[88] In quoting Owen, as well as Wesley and Fletcher, Irwin proved his thoroughly orthodox view of the Trinity. He drew heavily on Owen's interpretation of the Father being the logical source and fountain of the Trinity.[89] Thus, fire-baptized experience related especially to the revelation of the Father, the fountain of all pure love and power. The 'fire' burned its way through into the very 'bosom of the Father'. E.D. Wells, from Oklahoma City, expressed the accepted position of the FBHA:

> It is not the office of celestial fire to cleanse from sin. It accompanies the reception of the Father into the soul which has been washed white as snow in the blood of the Lamb. When we receive this abiding experience we can walk as did Jesus: 'In the power of the Spirit'.[90]

In other words, the *fire* enabled saints to walk in perfect obedience to God and to proclaim with greater boldness and effect the true Gospel.

---

[86] B.H. Irwin, 'The Eradication of Sin', *LCF* (November 3, 1899), p. 5.

[87] B.H. Irwin, 'Editorial', *LCF* (October 6, 1899), p. 7. Owen is here quoted but not cited. We discovered the quote in *The Works of John Owen* (16 Vols.; London: The Banner of Truth Trust, 1966, reprint), II, p. 34.

[88] Irwin, 'Editorial', p. 7.

[89] Owen, *Works*, II, pp. 9-46.

[90] E.D. Wells, 'The Real Fire', *LCF* (October 6, 1899), p. 6.

The two-fold baptism with *the Holy Ghost and fire* – cleansing and empowerment – opened the way for the saints to plunge into unfathomable depths and unspeakable intimacies in the Spirit, into the 'secret places' of intra-Trinitarian glory. Fire-baptized experiences and claims of extraordinary powers immediately raised the question of accountability – how was one to judge what was truly of God or merely imagined? This problem was all the more complicated for fire-baptized saints, because the movement had emerged for the very purpose of discrediting and overthrowing religious organizations that made private revelations and deeper mystical experiences accountable to a body of judicial review. Thus the moment the FBHA set itself to discipline what it considered to be erroneous or excessive, it seemed to be contradicting its own *raison d'etre* – that is, acting in self-contradiction to its own message and practice. This paradox was resolved, however, by claims of exclusivity. Someone had to be right and fully enlightened to the truth, and that someone was the FBHA.

Accordingly, God had raised up the FBHA for this very purpose: to establish right doctrine, order, and discipline, and to fulfill the great commission. It happened quite naturally therefore that what had begun as a movement gradually crystallized into an ecclesiastical institution. By 1898 the term *ecclesia* (Latin form of the Greek, *ekklesia*) was being used, and by 1899 Irwin was using the term almost exclusively in reference to fire-baptized congregations. It was only a matter of time until the word 'church' would replace 'association' in the official title of the organization. Doubtlessly Irwin would have seen to this himself if he had not fallen, but as it was the name FBHA became the Fire-Baptized Holiness Church (FBHC) in 1902 under the oversight of Irwin's successor, J.H. King.

King, however, proceeding without his mentor's vision, partly because he had been disillusioned by Irwin's moral failure, gradually began to turn the FBHC's developing ecclesiology in a different direction.

Scholarly Characteristics

We have already noticed the intellectual and scholarly emphasis of the fire-baptized holiness movement in its formative years. This was personified in several of its early leaders beginning with Irwin. He was educated in law and practiced as an attorney for several years before giving himself completely to the ministry. Besides his formal education in law, he was naturally inclined to study in many areas of science and literature. Irwin's appetite for knowledge was turned toward theology upon his conversion, and his intellectual bent colored the whole movement while under his influence and leadership.

The intellectual and academic emphasis in the FBHA was further encouraged by J.H. King after he succeeded Irwin at the helm of the movement. Though not as gifted and charismatic as his mentor, King was intelligent and academically prepared to rise quickly in the structure of the movement. He was formally educated at the U. S. Grant Theological Seminary in Chattanooga (now the University of Tennessee at Chattanooga). His articles in *Live Coals of Fire* fully expressed his theological education. While under Irwin's influence and authority, King continued to emphasize intellectual and academic excellence. Further, the overall demographic of the FBHA was in general favorable for the advancement of education, for the movement originated in the North where formal education was normative and highly valued. And, though the momentum of the movement quickly shifted to the South, its leadership remained in the North; and, in any case, its leadership in the South was also at first comparatively well educated and prepared for ministry. This is reflected in many of the articles in *Live Coals of Fire* authored by both men and women. They were in general theologically sound, creative, and well written. Indeed, the writers often referred to the Greek text both for originality and emphasis, and took to task certain words and phrases in the King James Version.[91] This reflected the scholarly bent of the early leaders of the movement, but also the Northern influence; for it was in the South mainly that the King James Version was exalted to infallibility. Accordingly, fire-baptized preachers and teachers felt it necessary on occasion to go behind the text of the King James Version to the original Hebrew and Greek texts in order to clarify and establish their interpretations of entire sanctification and fire-baptism.

A Rational Mysticism

We have noticed the mystical inclination of the fire-baptized movement. Yet the mysticism was not extravagant and full blown; rather it was consistent with what John Fletcher called 'rational mysticism' – a prudent spirituality that covers 'the naked truth to improve her beauty, to quicken the attention of sincere seekers, to augment the pleasure of discovery,

---

[91] B.H. Irwin, 'Editorial', *LCF* (April 6, 1900), p. 1.

and to conceal her charms from the prying eyes of her enemies'.[92] Fletcher employed the term, 'evangelical mysticism', to explain what he considered to be a 'judicious' and 'necessary' mysticism, in contrast with philosophical and speculative mysticism, the latter of which does 'violence to sound criticism, in quitting, without reason, the literal sense of the Scriptures, and running into ridiculous and forced allegories'.[93] Speculative mysticism 'resolves all into spirit ... [or else] turns everything into body or matter throughout the universe',[94] whereas 'evangelical mysticism' insists that experience conform to reason, tradition, and experience, and, above all, to the Holy Scriptures.

This so-called 'Wesleyan Quadrilateral' – reason, experience, tradition, Scripture – kept the feet of Methodism on the ground during its most intense and heightened spirituality in the eighteenth century. It was also the foundation that kept the fire-baptized movement from plunging into a full-blown mysticism. Thus, notwithstanding its excesses and fanatical tendencies in regard to certain dress codes and Mosaic legislation, the fire-baptized movement was basically sound theologically. The fundamental doctrines of God, trinity, humanity, the Holy Scriptures, salvation in Christ, faith, repentance, justification, regeneration, sanctification, Spirit-baptism, divine healing, spiritual gifts, and the chronological order of eschatological events, were all sound and defensible by the rule of evangelical standards. But the FBHA was unique in that it judged all religious experience and testimony by holiness standards consistent with the Wesleyan tradition, and insisted that the baptism with the Holy Spirit and fire was subsequent to entire sanctification and necessary for the most efficacious proclamation of the Gospel.

Further, the fire-baptized scheme of multiple baptisms – 'fire', 'dynamite', 'lyddite', 'oxidite', 'selenite' – were not so absurd as might seem at a glance. The names were simply metaphors used to explain and encourage deeper experiences in God. J.H. King had made an intelligent, if not theologically sound, defense of these multiple baptisms by drawing parallels to natural phenomena.

> If the combination of certain substances in nature constantly increases the power of destruction, is there not a corresponding higher destructive power in the divine kingdom which if obtained will enable us to be more and more powerful in our opposition to the devil's forces? All laws in nature were instituted by the Lord, in all their in-

---

[92] John Fletcher, *The Works of the Reverend John Fletcher* (4 Vols.; Salem, OH: Schmul Publishers, 1974), II, p.7.
[93] Fletcher, *Works*, II, p. 9.
[94] Fletcher, *Works*, II, p. 11.

numerable varieties and degrees of operation, and the laws of the natural and spiritual kingdoms are largely analogous, so what is found to exist in the lower has its counterpart in the higher. And upon this basis, as well as the Word of God, many of the dynamited saints sought and received the addition of power to their souls called the heavenly lyddite ... Glory to God! As long as the devil opposes and severely denounces this new experience it is all the evidence we desire, and it is the only apology we have in testifying to and preaching it.[95]

The error was in declaring that these multiple baptisms were prescriptive and normative as well as definite and separate experiences, rather than understanding them simply as various operations and intensities of the same spiritual baptism, namely, the *baptism with the Holy Ghost*. We have already noticed that King later admitted this while reflecting on the history of the FBHA:

The church was both Scriptural and unscriptural. Scriptural in that it taught and maintained that the Pentecostal Baptism was subsequent to sanctification; unscriptural in that it set forth two baptisms in the Pentecostal outpouring. This unscriptural teaching with all that followed in its train turned the church aside from its providential purpose, and its distinctive mission was largely lost. It could and would have been used to usher in the great Pentecostal baptism in its reality and fullness had it not fallen into this mischievous error.[96]

Martyrdom Complex

Irwin saw himself and his fire-baptized regiment in an extremely hostile world, indeed the world was a battleground on which Satan and his forces were waging war against the FBHA on two fronts: unbelievers on one flank and apostate Christianity on the other, with the latter serving Satan's purposes with the most skill and ability. Thus, when Irwin discovered that the Greek word for 'witness' is *martyr*, he immediately conditioned the movement with a martyrdom complex. He noted in a message in *Live Coals of Fire*:

The cause of the Fire will not take on its full proportions until some seraphic Stephen of the Fire Baptized Holiness Movement shall ac-

---

[95] King, 'Our Weapons of Warfare', p. 8.
[96] King, 'History of the Fire-Baptized Holiness Church', *PHA* 4.50, 51 (April 14, 1921), p. 11.

tually become a martyr for the truth and the fire. Who bids for a flaming crown of martyrdom?[97]

In Irwin's mind, this was the reason God had raised up the fire-baptized movement, namely, to meet the devil in the heat of combat, to triumph over the forces of darkness or die trying, until at last the white clad armies of Jehovah had prevailed in the 'last great conflict'. Irwin and his followers were determined to give the principalities and powers of darkness no quarter in their fellowship, and to drive Satan's forces into the hell that had been prepared for them.

Irwin's view of Christ's imminent return with its consequent judgment created a sense of extreme urgency within the FBHA. Moreover, the supposition that only a relatively few would be saved only added to the frantic disposition of fire-baptized believers. It was believed that the time had come, or was near at hand, that those who were going to be saved were already saved, and the rest would remain under the power and control of Satan. Relatively few indeed would be pulled out of the fire. He declared in a message in *Live Coals of Fire,*

> God is bringing the movement down to the water's edge, and preparing for Himself a Gideon's band that will go forth with Torch and Trumpet, burning and blazing for God, and blowing, with no uncertain sound the old Pentecostal ram's horn. Already we are too many – we need to be reduced in number or improved in quality. We need to get rid of these 'fearful and afraid' ones (Judges 7.3), who see nothing but dangers, and blunders, and mistakes, and perils, and disaster ... we want those, and those only, who see nothing but victory, and conquest, and glory ahead, and who have never learned the language of disaster and defeat. We want men and women with the definite experience of the fire, and literally surcharged with the diving dynamite from the upper skies, who can be trusted anywhere on the field of carnage.[98]

Perfection was thus the goal and primary purpose of the FBHA, but it was perfectionism that became tainted with excesses and needless deprivations in contradistinction of the Wesleyan view of perfection that was centered in God's love. This error tended to cause fire-baptized saints to run off and leave the weak and timid: for the FBHA perceived itself not as a refuge for the tired, discouraged, or fearful; but rather as an army engaged in war, recruiting only able bodied men and women

---

[97] B.H. Irwin, 'A Declaration of War', *LCF* (December 1, 1899), p. 1.
[98] B.H. Irwin, 'Let the Sifting Continue', *LCF* (December 1, 1899), p. 1.

willing to be trained and equipped for battle. Only those who would seek to be 'dynamited with all dynamite' were the right kind of stuff for this noble endeavor.

It is not our intention here to psychoanalyze Irwin or the movement, yet it is apparent that the spiritual disposition of the movement developed in part out of frustration from the passionate opposition it received almost everywhere it went. Violent persecutions were commonplace in Irwin's meetings. The ridicule and belittling received from the movement's staunchest critics, which eventually included almost all the respected holiness leaders of the day, were particularly hurtful. Irwin and his followers took these rejections hard and personal. But the more they pressed their fire-baptized doctrine and position, the more they were shunned and ridiculed. Almost everywhere the evangelists conducted meetings, declaring war on the devil and the 'apostate churches', they were met with equal or greater resistance. Their declared purpose was to tear up communities and rebuild them for God. The communities, conversely, were just as determined not to be 'torn apart'. Ironically, many fire-baptized places of worship were burned or dynamited, and not in a metaphorical sense.

The small band of fire-baptized preachers and laymen began to develop an attitude of 'us against the world'. They became defensive and exclusive. Denominational churches were considered apostate and, in fact, everything outside the fire-baptized movement was denounced and excluded, in their view, from fellowship in the bride of Christ. The apparent impatience of Irwin, who became ever more frustrated as his high expectations for the movement were stalled or hindered, only added to the negative and denunciatory disposition of the movement. In addition, as we shall see further on, Irwin was beginning to tire, and with his weariness he neglected to replenish his own spirituality.

Fire-Baptized Revival at Camp Creek

Now all of this – the whole fire-baptized experience with its profound insight into the mysteries of God along with its excesses and aberrations – came in on the revival at Camp Creek that had begun in 1896. We have noticed that beginning in 1899 and possibly as early as 1898, fire-baptized theology and experience transformed the nature and tone of the little holiness band that had formed under the lay leadership of Will Bryant following the revival in the Shearer schoolhouse in 1896. The leaders of the fire-baptized revival – Billy Martin, Joe Tipton, Milt McNabb, and Frank Porter – had been fire-baptized and dynamited in

1898-1899, and Martin and Porter had become leaders in Irwin's FBHA after it was organized in Anderson, South Carolina in August 1898. These two young ministers, former Methodists, were bright and shining lights in the movement, praised and exalted by Irwin, having blazed a fire-baptized trail of holiness in 1898-1900 across lower East Tennessee, including Cleveland (the county seat of Bradley County) and the surrounding communities of Birchwood, Charleston, Drygo, Beniah, Luskville, Dentville, Dare, Let, and Union Grove.

The flaming cinders shooting out from fire-baptized meetings in Tennessee spread *the fire* also across the state line into the Baptist and Methodist churches in Cherokee County, North Carolina, transforming the holiness revival that had begun there in 1896 into a fire-baptized meeting. This is especially significant, for the fire-baptized movement revived Spurling's struggling Christian Union congregations and transformed them into Pentecostal dynamos proclaiming radical righteousness. Thus, when Spurling finally convinced Bryant and the little holiness band at Camp Creek to organize in May 1902, they called the name of the new church, 'The Holiness Church at Camp Creek' rather than Christian Union. This title signaled that Spurling's Christian Union had been immersed into the holiness-Pentecostal movement, setting the stage for the emergence of the Church of God in the twentieth century.

It is particularly significant that the FBHA was climaxing in its fervor and apocalyptic expectations under the leadership of Irwin about the same time that it impacted the holiness revival at Camp Creek beginning in 1899. The fiery preacher from Coker Creek, Billy Martin, was still a minister in the Methodist Episcopal Church when he conducted the revival meeting in the Shearer schoolhouse in 1896. In fact, Martin had remained active and in good standing with the Holston Conference of the Methodist Episcopal Church (Eleazer Circuit) until he was fire-baptized in 1898-1899.[99] He came back to Camp Creek in 1899 with Porter and others to preach his new light on the line of the fire-baptized movement, which included the multiple baptisms of 'dynamite', and 'lyddite', and in 1900 the baptisms of 'oxidite', and 'selenite'. Porter had become the ruling elder of the FBHA in Tennessee in 1899 and worked closely with Martin. Like Martin, he was also a minister in the Methodist Episcopal Church. Porter apparently introduced M.S. Lemons into the fire-baptized movement, and to the revival that

---

[99] *The Holston Annual Official Record of the Holston Annual Conference*, Cleveland, Tennessee. October 1896, p. 9; *Holston Annual Conference Record*, Bristol, TN. October 6-13, 1897, p. 9.

was going on at Camp Creek in 1899-1900.[100] Lemons' future wife, Mattie Carver, was in 1899 already fire-baptized and dynamited and fully entrenched in the movement.[101]

It was the baptisms of fire, dynamite, lyddite, oxidite, and selenite that Martin, Porter, and Stewart Irwin preached in that powerful meeting at Camp Creek in May 1900. Sarah A. Smith described her eyewitness account of the meeting in a report published in *Live Coals of Fire* in May of that same year. 'Sister Martin and I came on to Patrick [Camp Creek], N.C., to assist in the meeting in progress here, and God is with us in great power, and sinners are in a rage, but we trust God to give us the victory. Praise God for the fire, and dynamite, and lyddite'.[102]

Whether or not the holiness band at Camp Creek had the faintest idea of what the fire-baptized preachers were talking about in regard to 'lyddite', oxidite', and 'selenite', they knew nevertheless that these 'baptisms' had to do with the deeper things of God, and they were eager and ready to 'be filled with all the fullness of God'.

There are no recorded instances of selenite 'moon dust' materializing and falling on the saints in fire-baptized meetings at Camp Creek, but there is oral testimony that lingers to this day among the older Baptists and Methodists in that area that 'the holiness people would throw powders on the people and cause them to jerk, faint, and convulse'.[103] Others claimed that the holiness people had the power to hypnotize their victims and cause them to 'bark like dogs' and 'writhe like serpents'.[104]

Knowledge of Irwin's fall in the spring of 1900 had a devastating effect on Martin, Porter, and Irwin's son, Stewart, all of whom admired and worked closely with the 'charismatic' and capable General Overseer. With Irwin's fall, the work of the FBHA in lower East Tennessee was debilitated and scattered. The vision and high hopes for the School of

---

[100] Porter performed the marriage of Lemons to Miss Mattie Carver on November 1, 1900 (copy of marriage certificate, 'M.S. Lemons File', ZACG Archives). He resided at that time not far from where Porter lived in Luskville, TN. Lemons wrote articles in *LCF* (Dec. 29, 1899 and Feb, 1900) and left record of attending the fire-baptized meetings at Camp Creek in 1900-1901 (M.S. Lemons, *Story of the Church of God*, unpublished manuscript 1937, p. 11). He maintained that the Holiness church at Camp Creek was organized by R.G. Spurling and R.F. Porter in May 1902 (Lemons, *Story*, p. 4).

[101] 'Mattie Carver's Letter', *LCF* (April 6, 1900), p. 5.

[102] Sarah A. Smith, 'Letter', *LCF* (May 18, 1900), p. 2.

[103] While doing research at Camp Creek in 1991-1993, the writer was informed by several of the children and descendants of these mountain folk that the stories about the holiness people and hypnotic powders were true, and cautioned me to be careful when interviewing the holiness people 'lest a spell be put on you'.

[104] Bryant was investigated by his Baptist church 'to see if I had hypnotic powders!' 'History of Pentecost', *FS* 1.6, p. 6.

the Prophets at Beniah were dashed, and the trips envisioned for Africa and South America to plant the fire-baptized banner on those continents were canceled or postponed.

Figure 31

W.H. HICKEY FAMILY

Figure 32

DAVID AND ZILPHIA HAMBY

W.H. Hickey married Laura Shearer, the daughter Drury and Melissa Shearer. David Hamby married Zilphia, the sister of Laura. Another sister, Norma, was also Spirit-baptized. They all became staunch supporters of the holiness-Pentecostal Movement, and were excluded from the Liberty Baptist Church in 1899-1901. Melissa was Spirit-baptized and joined the Holiness Church when it was set in order in May 1902. She became an influential force in the church and in the Camp Creek community. Hickey became a magistrate, which helped to abate some of the persecution in 1897-1900. Drury Shearer died c. 1901 and Melissa married J.C. Murphy in 1903 [first marriage performed by A.J. Tomlinson]. They moved into Melissa's cottage and hosted the first General Assembly in their house in 1906. Laura, Zilphia, and Norma were raised in this historic house. The cottage home was in 1941 purchased and restored by Tomlinson and his followers. It has been preserved as a monument to the restoration of New Testament church government – the General Assembly, the 'highest tribunal of authority for the interpretation of the Scriptures'.

J.H. King, who succeeded Irwin in July 1900, reported years later in *The Pentecostal Holiness Advocate* the sordid story of Irwin's apostasy:

> As to when he did backslide cannot be definitely determined. Even at Anderson, S.C. when the State Associations were centralized into one organization he did that which caused misapprehension as to his uprightness and sincerity. During the year 1899 he in various meetings gave evidence of an apostate condition of heart, and those that possessed a degree of discernment could see in him such a spirit that proved conclusively that he was far from possessing the experience of sanctification. In the spring of 1900 he was guilty of open and gross sins such as could not be farther hidden or palliated. Confes-

sions that he made afterwards revealed that he had been leading a double life for many years.[105]

Persecutions

We have noticed that following the glorious revival in the Shearer schoolhouse, Will Bryant and about 50-60 members of the Baptist and Methodist churches[106] formed a loosely-knit holiness fellowship in order to embrace and proclaim the light they had received on entire sanctification. This caused no small stir in the area, alarming Baptist elders against the holiness movement. The doctrine and experience of holiness not only contradicted Baptist faith, it disrupted the traditional order of the communities, which were more or less extensions of the government and order of the Baptist churches. The Liberty Baptist church minutes (1898-1901) are replete with references against 'the modern theory of sanctification'.[107] The church 'demanded of the modern sanctificationists [*sic*] whether they [would] subscribe to the faith and principles of the Baptists or not'.[108] Twenty-five members of the Liberty church did not, and were excluded 'for contempt of the church; departing the faith of Baptist; and endorsing the modern ... theory of sanctification'. Among those excluded were W.F. and Nettie Bryant.

Between March 1899 and June 1901 the Pleasant Hill church (located about five miles from the Liberty church) excluded fifteen of their members for 'teaching and harboring erroneous doctrines' and 'for dis-

---

[105] King, 'History of the Fire-Baptized Holiness Church', *PHA* 4.49 (April 7, 1921), p. 10.

[106] Though only 40 members were eventually excluded from the churches for embracing holiness doctrines, there were many others who stood with the holiness band for a while. Bryant said that more than fifty were baptized with the Holy Ghost and spoke in tongues in home prayer meetings ('History of Pentecost', *FS* 1.6, p. 20). Several of these believers later returned to their Baptist and Methodist churches, several more became discouraged and went back into the world, and a few left for Alexander Dowie's movement in Zion City, Illinois to await the soon coming of the Lord.

[107] Before the writer acquired the minutes of the Liberty, Pleasant Hill, and Zion Hill Baptist churches while doing research in the mountains in 1991-1993, Church of God histories had been written almost entirely on the basis of oral testimony. Obtaining these minutes has enabled us to give a more accurate account of the events that took place between 1896 and 1902.

[108] *Liberty Baptist Church Minutes*, November 1898. Several were excluded on the charge of 'heresy', including Justice of the Peace, W.H. Hickey, and his wife, Laura (Shearer), the daughter of Melissa (Shearer) Murphy. The charge was 'contempt of the church ... and endorsing the modern theory of sanctification which disannuls the Baptist church its faith and principles'.

obedience toward the church'.[109] Among those excluded were M.D. ('Uncle Dick')[110] Kilpatrick and his wife, Betty (Coleman), Jesse and Lucy Coleman, Alexander ('Elic') Hamby, and Margaret Melissa Shearer who in 1903 married J.C. Murphy and hosted in her house on Camp Creek the first General Assembly in 1906.

Persecutions had begun at least by the summer of 1897.[111] The first legal document that confirms the oral tradition of early persecutions was discovered by the writer in 1998.[112] This document is a warrant for the arrest of Ambers Rogers for 'disturbing public worship'. It was issued on August 26, 1897 by W.H. Hickey, justice of the peace for Shoal Creek Township (Camp Creek was part of Shoal Creek Township). Interestingly, Hickey had married in 1887 Laura Shearer, the daughter of Melissa Shearer (Murphy); and their family joined in the holiness movement.[113] The document further states that Rogers 'was at the church house intoxicated and swearing and cursing during the time of preaching against the form and statute in such cases made and provided and contrary to the law and against the peace and dignity of the state'. W.F. Bryant brought the complaint the same night that the disturbance took place. Witnesses to the complaint were Luther Coleman, Hayes Robertson [Robinson], Elic Hamby, Evert Shearer, Rastes Hensley, and Osco Shearer, all of whom were involved in or sympathetic with the holiness movement.

Abuses against the holiness people escalated in 1898-1900. 'Night Caps' – a vestige of the Ku Klux Klan still active in the mountains at that time – tried in vain to stamp out the holiness movement with threats, whips, buckshot, fire, and dynamite. Bryant himself was shot on more than one occasion, his livestock killed, wells poisoned, and family threatened.

---

[109] *Liberty Baptist Church Minutes*, December 1898.

[110] Bryant's mother, Nancy, was the sister of M.D. 'Uncle Dick' Kilpatrick. Most historical records, including local, mistakenly assume that 'Dick' is short for Richard (so does Conn in *Like a Mighty Army*), but in fact M.D. are initials for Miles Dickson. It is said that when he was born, the family had just moved 'miles away from Dickson County, Tennessee to Cherokee County, North Carolina', and that his name was given to recall their time in Dickson County. Falsely assuming that 'Uncle Dick' is short for Richard has caused some to confuse him with another Kilpatrick named Richard.

[111] 'History of Pentecost', *FS* (September 1922), pp. 5-6, 20-21; 'W.F. Bryant', *COGE* 40.31 (October 8, 1949), pp. 6-7; Tomlinson, *LGC*, pp. 210-11.

[112] The document was discovered by the writer in the North Carolina state archives at Raleigh under 'Criminal Actions Papers 1895-1897'.

[113] The Hickeys were excluded from the Liberty Baptist Church for joining in the Holiness movement. It was in Laura's childhood home that the First General Assembly was held.

Among the leading women in the holiness band was Emeline (Bridges) Allen (1859-1955). She and her husband, Ross, were fire-baptized and hosted meetings in their home on Camp Creek. On one occasion about the year 1900, some twenty-five to fifty hooded and robed 'Night Caps' armed with clubs, guns, and knives paraded up and down the road in front of their house threatening and cursing; whereupon Emeline (spelled also Emelyne), full of the Spirit, went out to meet them. With the meekness of a lamb and boldness of a lion, she informed them that their hoods and masquerade had not concealed their identity from her and that in fact she knew them all by name, but that if they would disrobe themselves and be at peace she would prepare them something to eat. In any case, nevertheless, she assured them that the meetings were going to continue.[114] And with those words and her courageous spirit she disarmed them and the mob dispersed.

Emeline's husband, Ross (1861-1915), joined in the holiness movement in the beginning and had apparently preached a little,[115] but afterwards recanted his holiness testimony and joined the crowd of holiness fighters. In December 1903 Tomlinson had him arrested for disturbing the worship services at Camp Creek.

> Last Sunday our meeting was disturbed and broken up at Camp Creek ... by Ross Allen, a ranter. The next day he was arrested and after trying every way we could to get him to leave us alone, all in vain, he was tried, convicted and sentenced to jail for an indefinite time. I offered to pay him out ... if he would only promise to let us alone, which he would not do. I was so sorry to send the poor man to jail, but it seemed it was the only way to deal with him ...[116]

The persecutions at Camp Creek reached a climax sometime in the summer of 1900. During the glorious revival conducted by Stewart Irwin and Billy Martin in Bryant's make-shift tabernacle near his house at Camp Creek in April-May 1900, Sarah A. Smith reported that she and Billy Martin's wife, Callie, were in that glorious revival and that the 'sinners [were] in a rage'.[117] Tomlinson wrote that when the persecutions arose 'four or five houses were burned', and that

---

[114] A.E. Kilpatrick, *Thoughts and Memories* (unpublished manuscript, 1980), pp. 25-27; John L. Sherrill, *They Speak with Other Tongues* (New York: Pyramid Books, 1964), p. 48; Conn, *Mighty Army*, p. 36; Nettie Bryant/Ella (Bryant) Robinson interview, pp. 3-4; Phillips, personal interviews with Allen descendants (1991).

[115] A.E. Kilpatrick, *Thoughts and Memories*, p. 26.

[116] Tomlinson, *Diary*, December 9, 1903.

[117] Sarah A. Smith, 'Letter', *LCF* (May 18, 1900), p. 2.

At one time the storm of persecution broke in with such fury that one hundred and six men, composed of Methodist and Baptist ministers, stewards and deacons, one justice of the peace and one sheriff, banded together to put down the revival, even by violence, if that was the only way it could be accomplished. They deliberately tore down and burned the house, where sinners were getting saved in nearly every service, in open daylight.[118]

The actions by this violent mob made up of churchmen, civil officers, moonshine peddlers, murderers, and other sordid characters, boastfully calling themselves the 'One Hundred and Six', represented the climax of the persecutions at Camp Creek. Among the leaders of the infamous One Hundred and Six were Sanford Ledford, George Quinn, and W.F. Bryant's brother, W.G. 'Gay' Bryant, the latter of whom was a Methodist minister. Thereafter the persecutions began to subside, for Bryant and some of the brethren in the holiness band succeeded in bringing the leaders of the One Hundred and Six to justice. Several were arrested and called to account by the Cherokee County justice system in Murphy, and would have been sent to prison if Bryant had not pleaded with the court to dismiss the case if the men would solemnly promise to end the violence.[119]

The persecutions had in any case succeeded only to scatter the fires of revival, which by 1899 had spread to nearby counties in Tennessee and Georgia. Evicted from the Shearer schoolhouse, and burned out of the log building they had erected for worship across the road from the schoolhouse, the holiness band began to meet in private homes around the area.[120] Bryant built a crude 'tabernacle' next to his house for worship which apparently hosted the fire-baptized meeting in the spring of 1900.[121]

---

[118] Tomlinson, *LGC*, p. 211; see also Bryant's personal report on this mob and the persecution, 'History of Pentecost', *FS* 1.6, p. 20.

[119] 'History of Pentecost', *FS* 1.6, p. 20; Nora Bryant testimony; Phillips interview, May 1993; Nettie Bryant/Ella (Bryant) Robinson interview, p. 2. Lake Ledford, the grandson of Sanford Ledford and the husband of Allie Ledford, R.G. Spurling's granddaughter, said the story of the persecutions was well known in his family, and that many of his family members were proud of it. He related to the writer that two of the most zealous leaders in the persecutions was his grandfather, Sanford, and George Quinn a neighbor. W.F. Bryant's brother, Gamaliel, also was an instigator and leader in the persecution.

[120] Tomlinson, *LGC*, pp. 210-12; 'History of Pentecost', *FS* 1.6, p. 20.

[121] Lemons noted in an interview, 'Brother Bryant had a little shack that we had meetings in' (Bryant/Lemons interview, p. 19). Bryant himself called it a 'log church in my yard' ('History of Pentecost', *FS* 1.6, p. 21). Elsewhere it is referred to as 'Bryant's tabernacle' and 'Bryant's schoolhouse'.

Figure 33
ROSS AND EMELINE
ALLEN AND FAMILY (C. 1902)

Figure 34
WALTER SCOTT KIMSEY
(C. 1905)

When it became apparent that the movement could not be stopped by brute force, Baptist elders began to exercise the power of their creedal disciplines to bring members in line with Baptist faith and practice. Walter Scott Kimsey was pastor of both the Liberty and Pleasant Hill Baptist churches in 1898-1900[122] when the revival and doctrines of holiness were rocking these churches. Kimsey was born the same year as R.G. Spurling, and preceded him in death by only a few months. They had been fraternal Baptists since their youth, and had become members of the same association – Liberty & Ducktown Baptist Association – after Spurling married Barbara M. Hamby in 1876 and united with the church at Pleasant Hill.[123]

The Pleasant Hill Baptist Church was a thriving mountain church that met in a log building just above the banks of the Hiwassee River in Cherokee County near the Tennessee state line.[124] Kimsey was a firm

---

[122] Kimsey (1857-1934) was serving as pastor of the Zion Hill and Liberty churches in 1898 and also assisted E.A. Deweese at Pleasant Hill. In addition to these, he accepted the pastorates at Pleasant Hill and Shoal Creek in 1899. See 'Statistical Tables', *Liberty & Ducktown Baptist Association Minutes*, 1898-1900; *Liberty Baptist Church Minutes*, 1898; and *Pleasant Hill Baptist Church Minutes*, 1899.

[123] Kimsey was born and reared in Polk County. He had known Spurling at least since the latter had married Barbara Hamby and began to attend the Pleasant Hill Baptist Church in 1876. Thus when Spurling bought the farm at Turtletown in 1893, he and Kimsey were well acquainted. Doubtlessly Kimsey was also aware of the incidents that led to Spurling's exclusion from the Pleasant Hill church in 1884.

[124] The writer acquired in 1993 the original deed to this church, which is now in the Archives of Zion Assembly Church of God. See also, Phillips, 'Richard Spurling and the Baptist Roots of the Church of God', p. 17 n. 43, and p. 34.

and zealous Baptist and, like many Baptists in the mountains of lower East Tennessee in the late nineteenth century, was fully convinced of the basic tenets of Landmarkism, which we noticed in the previous chapter advocated that only Missionary [Landmark] Baptist churches were true churches of Christ.

Kimsey's actions against those who defected from Baptist faith and order to embrace holiness was thus sparked by his zeal for the Landmark tradition. His ministry was part of the legacy of the revered Zechariah Rose (1809-1886), whom we met in the previous chapter. Kimsey believed the mantle of Rose and other revered Landmark champions like Elijah Clayton had fallen upon him: and he was determined that the Landmark banner would continue to fly in the tri-county area during his watch.

Kimsey was influenced also by Rose's disciple, Michael Columbus Higdon (1823-1905), whom we met in the previous chapter.[125] In 1898 Higdon had married Kimsey's niece, Melinda, and moved to Ducktown in Polk County.[126] While there, Higdon became active in the churches in the Liberty & Ducktown Association, and was elected to the pastorate in Kimsey's home church at Zion Hill in Turtletown.[127] Higdon excited Kimsey's passions for Baptist faith and order, reinforcing his views that the Baptist faith was perfectly consistent with God's eternal plan and purpose, and thus was exclusive of all 'man-made systems' and 'human societies'.

We have noticed that the Landmark tradition ran deep in the region and was widespread. Since the 1860s four generations of Landmark preachers – Clayton, Rose, Higdon, Kimsey – had forged a powerful

---

[125] Burnett's biography of Higdon is particularly helpful. Higdon was ordained by Zechariah Rose and two other presbyters at the Friendship Baptist Church in Polk County in 1847 ('M.C. Higdon', *Pioneer Baptist Preachers*, pp. 225-26). He quickly became a prominent pastor and later was elected moderator of Sweetwater Baptist Association [anti-convention]. Rose served as the clerk of that association for many years, including the years that Higdon moderated. After the two branches of the Sweetwater Association were reconciled in 1870 and the Eastanallee Association was formed, Higdon served as moderator of that association for several years.

[126] Higdon was 75 years of age when he married the 32 year-old Melinda. She died in childbirth the next year.

[127] *Zion Hill Baptist Church Minutes*, 1898-1900 (copy in ZACG Archives). Higdon was appointed as messenger to the Liberty & Ducktown Association meeting in 1899 from Zion Hill church ('Statistical Table', Liberty & Ducktown Association, *Minutes*, 1899, p. 11). He was recommended to the association with high praises: 'Whereas, Rev. M.C. Higdon has been a faithful soldier of the Lord and has of late moved from the bounds of the Eastanala [sic] Association, we hereby certify his ministerial standing as regular and of high esteem among us ... adopted by this body in session this Sept. 16th, 1899'.

coalition of influence. We have noticed that Rose had mentored Higdon, and Higdon had married into the Kimsey family later in life. Rose's cousin, Gideon, was pastor of the Turtletown Baptist Church and had served as a presbyter when the Pleasant Hill church was set in order in 1875. Higdon, as we noticed in the previous chapter, had opposed R.G. Spurling's father, Richard, during the lingering controversies over 'missions' in the 1850s-1860s which had divided the Sweetwater Baptist Association in Monroe and Polk counties in 1837-1839. He stood with Zechariah Rose, William Carroll Lee, Elijah Clayton, T.A. Higdon (Michael's brother) and others against Richard and those who had taken the pro-convention ('pro-missions') position. These anti-convention brethren believed the East Tennessee State Convention and the Southern Baptist Convention threatened the traditional Baptist view that the local church is the only true expression of God's church, and the only medium through which the Great Commission could be duly fulfilled.[128] We have noticed also that Higdon and Elijah Clayton had influenced the decision of Richard Spurling's home church at Holly Springs to join the anti-convention branch of the controversy shortly after the war began in 1861.

Clayton had followed W.F. Bryant's grandfather, Gamaliel, as pastor at Holy Springs church in the early 1860s. The influence of Higdon and Clayton seems to explain why Richard and Nancy abruptly requested by letter in 1863 to have their names 'stricken' from the [church] books'.[129] In 1864-1866 Higdon had worked closely with Clayton at Holly Springs moderating business conferences and serving as an assistant in pastoral work, which seems to explain in part why Richard's family, in-laws, and friends requested letters of dismissal from the Holly Springs church in May 1865.[130] Higdon and Clayton continued to hold the superior influence in Holly Springs and among area churches until about 1880.

Civil War differences and animosities magnified the tension between Richard Spurling and the Higdon/Clayton faction at Holly Springs. Higdon and Clayton were passionate and active supporters of the Confederacy. Clayton (1786-1881) had fought with 'Old Hickory' (Andrew Jackson) in the Indian Wars, and was a veteran of the war of 1812.[131] And although Clayton was seventy-five years of age when the Civil War

---

[128] See Toomey's treatment of this controversy in *History of the Sweetwater Baptist Association and Its Affiliated Churches 1830-1980* (published by the author, 1980), pp. 52-88.

[129] *Holly Springs Church Minutes*, February, 1863.

[130] *Holly Springs Church Minutes*, January 1865.

[131] See Revolutionary and Civil War military and pension records in 'Elijah Clayton' File (copies in ZACG Archives).

began, he 'endeavored to raise a company of volunteer soldiers for the Rebel army' which occasioned the suspension of his government pension in 1872.[132] Higdon also served in the Confederacy with two of his sons, one of which was killed in 1862.[133]

Richard Spurling, conversely, had three sons – Daniel, Nathan, William – who fought with the Union.[134] William had enlisted with the South in 1862 but in July 1863 was captured at Vicksburg and defected from the Confederacy to join the Union.[135] These differences between the North and South were bitter and passionate in East Tennessee during the awful conflict, affecting everyone in and out of uniform including Richard Spurling. Richard Green noted, 'Although my father was too old to be a soldier, he was driven from his home and preaching and exposed to all kinds of weather which weakened his once manly frame'.[136]

Kimsey, like his mentor, Higdon, was said to be a 'dyed in the wool Baptist'.[137] What Baptist historian, J.J. Burnett, said of Higdon was equally true of Kimsey: he did not work well in 'union meetings', pulled better in 'Baptist harness', and believed 'that Baptists [had] to give account to their own Master, and, therefore, ought to do their own work in their own way'.[138] Thus, in the late 1890s Kimsey was a young minister with a powerful denominational heritage and a bright future, offering promise to be a champion of conservative Baptist views for the next generation.

Those who had become involved in the holiness movement thus represented in Kimsey's view a disorderly and contemptuous band of sedition against divine government. He promptly led his churches beginning in 1898 to take action against all those 'harboring the modern theory of sanctification', charging them finally with 'heresy' and 'contempt for the Baptist faith'.[139] Higdon doubtlessly encouraged Kimsey

---

[132] Revolutionary and Civil War military and pension records of Elijah Clayton; military and pension records of Elijah Clayton (copies in ZACG Archives).

[133] Military and genealogical records of M.C. Higdon (copies in ZACG Archives).

[134] *Lost Link*, p. 47.

[135] Civil War military and pension records of Daniel Spurling, Nathan Spurling, and William A. Spurling (copies in ZACG Archives).

[136] Spurling, *Lost Link*, pp. 47-48.

[137] Alga B. Kimsey, a descendant of Walter Scott Kimsey, recalled that 'he prayed long prayers ... was stern ... and was a dyed in the wool Baptist' (Interviews by the writer, October 1996; March 1998). It is not without significance that the epitaph on Kimsey's tombstone, which also marks his wife's grave, reads: 'They were of the Baptist faith'.

[138] Burnett, 'M.C. Higdon', *Pioneer Baptist Preachers*, p. 226.

[139] *Liberty Baptist Church Minutes*, 1898-1900; Pleasant Hill Baptist, *Minutes*, 1899-1900; *Liberty & Ducktown Baptist Association Minutes*, 1898-1899.

in his pursuit to bring the holiness band at Camp Creek into submission. He had preached a 'protracted meeting' at Pleasant Hill on July 9-13, 1898,[140] and in December of that same year Kimsey was elected to the pastorate at Pleasant Hill.

Figure 35

THE SHEARER SCHOOLHOUSE (C. 1900)

Several holiness meetings were conducted here in 1896-1897 including the initial revival led by Billy Martin, Joe Tipton, Milton McNabb, and Billy Hamby in the spring of 1896.

As pastor of both the Liberty and Pleasant Hill churches, Kimsey proceeded to direct the congregations to appoint committees to confront and admonish the members who 'harbored sympathy' for the holiness movement, and to exclude those who remained firm in their holiness convictions. Between 1898 and 1901 forty members were excluded from the two churches.[141]

---

[140] *Pleasant Hill Baptist Church Minutes*, July 1898.
[141] Oral accounts of the number excluded ranged from 26 to 37. Having obtained in 1991-1993 the minutes of the Liberty and Pleasant Churches, we now know the number was 40 – twenty-five from Liberty and fifteen from Pleasant Hill.

Fire-Baptized Fanaticism

Notwithstanding the fact that Kimsey and the religious establishment in the region are to be blamed for the persecution and violence against the holiness people, still there seemed to be a sincere concern on their part for the stability and general welfare of their communities. Seeing in the holiness movement little more than 'wild-fire and 'emotional absurdities', particularly after the movement had come under the influence of the FBHA, the pastoral instincts of the Baptist elders urged them to take matters into hand. To be sure, the excesses and fanaticism that attended fire-baptized meetings were allowed to escalate and go in all directions. The notion of multiple baptisms and ever deeper cleansings through the Spirit seemed to have no end. Fire-baptized believers professed not only to be delivered from coffee, pork, pork by-products (especially lard), pepper, tomato soup, buttermilk, and so on, but they tended also to press their peculiar views on others. It could have been said of them what the apostle Paul said of the Jews who attempted to establish righteousness on the basis of the law, 'that they have a zeal for God, but not according to knowledge'. One of the leaders of the fire-baptized movement, W.S. Foxworth, in an effort to help curtail some of the excesses wrote in *Live Coals of Fire* in 1900,

> It is possible for good people to get under bondage to their own ideas, whims, and vows ... I know of a precious sister who will not eat anything that is cooked on Sunday ... I know of others who will not eat fish, beef, chicken, bread, vegetables, or anything where bacon or lard is used in the cooking, [and they make themselves also] an offence by asking questions at the table, and insulting the courtesy of the people who are kind enough to entertain them ... One brother denounces another for blackening his shoes ... another for trimming his beard ... One sister denounces another for wearing a corset or artificial teeth ... others are in bondage to some rash vow that they made ... ignoring the fact that it would be much better to confess their mistake ... than to go on under the galling yoke which they had made for themselves ...[142]

Irwin endorsed the 'spirit and wisdom' of Foxworth's article in an editorial, saying 'May God save our people from all self-imposed bondage to unscriptural vows, and from mere external and legal observances'.

In addition to the nonsensical practices and needless deprivations in regard to eating, drinking, hair styles, dress codes, etc., there were ex-

---

[142] *LCF* (March 23, 1900), p. 4.

cesses in regard to emotional and physical demonstrations in the meetings at Camp Creek. The doctrine of multiple baptisms offered infinite possibilities for ever new spiritual experiences. Certain experiences like the 'Wheel-In-A-Wheel' empowered and exercised fire-baptized saints to walk on the top of benches, do somersaults, leap supernaturally high, etc.[143]

In view of these fanatical indulgences, it is not surprising that the Baptists and Methodists and other denominational people had difficulty in seeing the good in the underlying message and experience of the fire-baptized movement. But there was another reason that the ministers and community leaders at Camp Creek believed that 'this crazy religion' had to be 'stomped out'. They charged that this 'crazy stuff' was disrupting their orderly society. And indeed it was. For Irwin had emboldened the fire-baptized evangelists to go into the communities for the express purpose of blowing up unbelief and opposition with Spirit-inspired 'dynamite' and 'lyddite', and to do this in order to reform the communities according to the vision of the FBHA. Irwin instructed his evangelists to declare war! The FBHA was therefore aggressive, confrontational, and even combative.

The warlike disposition of the FBHA, along with the haughty attitude that it tended to engender, did not sit well with the mountain folk at Camp Creek. The religious and community leaders – preachers, merchants, lodge leaders, and civil officials – felt challenged and threatened; for they believed that their monolithic authority was divinely ordained to govern and guide the people. Surmising that they were being invaded by a foreign power, they reasoned that after their counsel and warnings had gone unheeded, they were justified in responding to the fire-baptized 'dynamite' and 'lyddite' with real bullets and real dynamite.

But it is clear that even if the fanaticisms and excesses of the FBHA could have been removed or curtailed, the doctrine and power of entire sanctification would have remained, and it was the latter that most egregiously offended and infuriated the Baptists; for they knew that if the fire-baptized saints had their way, not only would their Baptist faith and order be overturned but their whole culture would have to be reordered; for the very nature of holiness theology and experience called for a re-orientation of the traditional authority that the Baptists held so dear. It was like Jesus overturning the tables of the money changers and cleansing the temple: the gesture signified that Christ was not only purifying the worship but reordering the priestly authority of the temple – that is,

---

[143] Davidson, *Upon This Rock*, I, p. 290; Conn, *Mighty Army*, pp. 39-43.

Jesus cleansed the temple in order to reestablish God's house on the foundation of the Gospel. The religious establishment at Camp Creek sensed that the fire-baptized holiness movement was calling for this same kind of radical transformation, and therefore proclaimed that the preaching of entire sanctification was a 'dangerous heresy' that could not be tolerated.

Again, although the doctrine and experience of holiness was overstated by fire-baptized evangelists,[144] it is apparent that the Baptists would have firmly rejected any doctrine that offered grace to take away completely and forever tobacco habits, profanity, intoxicants, and the internal disposition of the soul that harbored anger, bitterness, envy, malice, and the fleshly characteristics of the 'body of sin'. The fact is, the greater part of the people at Camp Creek loved their carnal culture; it was for them a way of life – a way of life grown up around the traffic of moonshine whiskey and a religion that was compatible with the fallen nature of man. Simply put, the people had affectionately embraced 'sinning religion'.

Holiness Church Established at Camp Creek

In the course of these events, R.G. Spurling, who at that time was living at Turtletown about four miles from the Camp Creek community came into the midst of the holiness band on occasion attempting to persuade Bryant and the saints to organize and come under the government and vision of Christian Union.[145] Bryant recalled that 'Brother Sperling [sic] kept coming to me and saying 'Let's set a church in order. We need it.'[146] The reason for Spurling's insistence was primarily his vision of God's church, but also because he was grieved in his spirit to see so many who had been blessed in the great revival between 1896 and 1902 fall by the wayside because of persecution and lack of government and sound teaching. Tomlinson wrote,

> During these years of revival and persecutions, Mr. Spurling often came in their midst, and in vain tried to show the precious people the

---

[144] There are indications that some in the holiness band at Camp Creek taught sanctification not only as a 'second definite work of grace' but as a state of 'sinless perfection'. 'History of Pentecost', *FS* (September 22, 1922), p. 20. This error may be assumed, moreover, on the basis that many fire-baptized preachers at first preached that one could attain to a state of sinless perfection in God through the *baptism of fire*.
[145] Tomlinson, *LGC*, p. 212.
[146] Bryant/Lemons interview, p. 4.

need of God's law and government. Everything moved on smoothly among themselves for several months, even years, and they were able to endure all the persecutions ... with grace and love. But in the absence of government and authority, false teachers crept in and led many humble, sincere, unwary souls into error. Factions began to show themselves, and fanaticism took possession of some who were more easily duped by Satan than others.[147]

Bryant and the others however resisted, believing that church government was man-made and resulted always in confusion and bondage.[148] Many under the influence of the FBHA believed in fact that church authority and government was antichrist, and that putting one's name on a church book, or for that matter on a lodge book or a union book, was the mark of the beast. Notwithstanding, the counsel of Spurling finally prevailed, and on May 15, 1902 in Bryant's cabin home the Holiness Church at Camp Creek was set in order with sixteen members.[149] Tomlinson notes that, 'under the instructions and supervision of Mr. Spurling, an organization was effected ... one of the officers, W.F. Bryant, was set forth by the church and ordained, which made the church permanent'.[150] Lemons informs us that R.F. Porter, who had been the ruling elder of the FBHA in Tennessee, participated in setting the church in order, and Bryant adds that Porter assisted Spurling in ordaining him on that same day.[151]

Five important points are worthy of note here in regard to the establishment of the church at Camp Creek in 1902. First, Spurling's vision for Christian Union was revived and perpetuated, for this congregation represented a link between the work begun at Barney Creek in 1886 and the establishment of the church in Cleveland in 1906. Tomlinson notes that the Holiness Church at Camp Creek 'was a continuation of the same organization that was started sixteen years before,[152] and Lemons says the church in Cleveland in 1906 was a 'continuation of the Holiness

---

[147] Tomlinson, *LGC*, p. 212.
[148] Bryant/Lemons interview, p. 4.
[149] Bryant remembered late in life that the church was set in order with 'about seventeen members' ('A Little Church History', *The Lighted Pathway* [November 8, 1941], p. 7). Tomlinson, reflecting on the event in his annual address in 1928, noted: 'the Church of God was built up from one church with sixteen members ... to a membership of 21,076' (*Historical Annual Addresses* (3 Vols.; Cleveland, TN: WWPH, 1971), II, p. 13. Tomlinson's account is preferred because he knew the importance of maintaining precise historical records and because he is definite on the number.
[150] Tomlinson, *LGC*, p. 213.
[151] Bryant/Lemons interview, p 18.
[152] Tomlinson, *LGC*, p. 213.

Figure 36

ALEXANDER ['ELIC'] HAMBY AND FAMILY (C. 1905)

Hamby and his wife joined in the holiness-Pentecostal Movement and later the Holiness Church at Camp Creek when it was organized in May 1902. He attended and participated in the First General Assembly in January 1906 and was ordained a bishop in the second Assembly in 1907 (*GAM 1906-1914*, p. 33).

Church at Camp Creek'.[153] Second, though Spurling's Christian Union congregations had been swept into the holiness-Pentecostal movement between 1895 and 1902, the establishment of the church at Camp Creek under the title, Holiness Church, more emphatically declared that Christian Union had metamorphosed into a holiness body. Third, the establishment of the Holiness Church shifted the center of the Christian Union movement from Monroe County, Tennessee to Camp Creek in Cherokee County, North Carolina where it would remain until the center was moved again to Cleveland, Tennessee after the first General Assembly in January 1906.[154] Fourth, it marked the fact that the work of

---

[153] Bryant/Lemons interview, p. 14.

[154] It could be argued that the church was centered in Tomlinson after June 1903, and thus when Tomlinson moved to Cleveland in December 1904 the center of the church moved with him. But inasmuch as the first General Assembly represented a new form of government for the church, and it was held at Camp Creek, apparently the majority of the ministers and members still felt that the center of gravity was at Camp Creek. However, between that first General Assembly at Camp Creek and the second one held in January 1907 at Union Grove near Cleveland,

the Spirit at Camp Creek between 1896 and 1902 had culminated in the Spirit's ultimate objective, namely, to form the New Testament church and incorporate believers into one visible body of Christ. Fifth, there is a sense in which Pastor Walter Scott Kimsey and his Baptist co-workers unwittingly helped to establish the Church of God. Their firm and unyielding insistence on strict compliance to Baptist faith and discipline demanded more of those who had experienced entire sanctification and Spirit-baptism than they could endure. The persecutors left the followers of holiness with no alternative except to organize a separate body under the pastoral care and vision of R.G. Spurling.[155]

Figure 37

W.F. BRYANT AND FAMILY (C. 1905)

Back Row from left: Agnes, Winnie, Luther, Frank Roberson [Robinson], Julius. *Front row left:* Lowell, W.F. Bryant, Nora, Nettie [holding Ernest] Ella [Bryant] Robinson [holding Olen].

Setting the church in order at Camp Creek was significant, to be sure, particularly in regard to perpetuating Spurling's vision for Christian Union and marking more distinctly the church's holiness transformation. For it is almost certain that the church at Camp Creek would have suffered from the same infirmities that the other Christian Union congrega-

---

almost everyone had come to recognize Cleveland as the center of the church's authority and activities.

[155] The writer was privileged to be the guest speaker for an 'old-fashion day' celebration at the Pleasant Hill Baptist church in 1993. He congratulated the congregation for 'helping to start the Church of God', reasoning with a note of humor that if the good Baptists had not kicked our fathers and mothers out of their churches, they might not ever have gotten the Church of God started.

tions in Monroe and Polk counties had suffered if significant changes had not been made in the months and years ahead in regard to the leadership and political structure of the church. The church at Camp Creek had already demonstrated its inability to grow and flourish. Even fourteen months after it had been organized, not a single member had been added to the fold, and the charter members '[struggled] to keep the work alive'.[156] The original church on Barney Creek had gone defunct in 1889, and the church on the north side of the Hiwassee River near Shuler's Creek in Polk County had fizzled before 1902. The only two Christian Union congregations remaining were at Piney Grove on Reliance Road in Monroe County and on Paul's Mountain in Rural Vale.

Figure 38

BILLY HAMBY AND FAMILY (C. 1902)

Hamby and his family were active in the fire-baptized holiness movement at Camp Creek. With the McNabbs and Simpsons and others they moved to Zion City in 1902 to be under the 'great Alexander Dowie', but returned to Camp Creek after the grand illusion evaporated. Billy's wife, Sarah, [center] attended the first General Assembly in 1906.

The fundamental flaw in Spurling's theology of the church was rooted in the individualism that his mountain religion and culture had encouraged, a flaw which we will examine more closely in the next

---

[156] Tomlinson, *LGC*, p. 214.

chapter. Indeed, not only were the Christian Union churches more or less autonomous but also the individual members. Christian Union had been established on the basis of an extreme democratic idealism.

What was lacking in Spurling's vision for Christian Union was basically four things: 1) a firm and objective basis for fellowship, both in regard to the members' relationship to one another and the churches' relationship to one another; 2) a clear understanding of the church's universal character and mission in the world; 3) a centralized government to coordinate and harmonize the local churches together in faith and worship, and in decision-making and mission work; 4) an inspirational leader with the organizational skills to bring about these results.

4

INSTITUTIONAL TRANSFORMATION: 1906-1915

Several important developments took place between 1902 and 1906 that set the stage for the institutionalization of the church and its transformation into a universal body with a global vision, not the least being the decision to meet together once a year in a General Assembly. But perhaps the most significant event happened on June 13, 1903, for that was the day that Ambrose Jessup Tomlinson joined the church. Without question, the centralization of the church and the institutional transformation that followed was in large part due to Tomlinson's leadership and vision. The moment he joined the church, the work that Spurling had begun in 1886 and nourished until 1903 'revived and took upon it a new impetus'.[1]

A Strong and Confident Leader

What had been lacking in the church since 1886 was strong and gifted leadership, not in the sense of setting the church in order and projecting an idealistic vision for Christian Union, for Spurling had been sufficient for that task; but leadership in the sense of a personality who could take charge and command a following, in addition to exemplifying a passion for evangelism and possessing the ability to bring the churches together in a tighter and more workable union in order to fulfill the universal mission of the church. That kind of leadership was supplied by A.J. Tomlinson (1865-1943), an ex-Quaker and farmer from Indiana who had come into the mountains to do missionary work under the auspices of the American Bible Society and the American Tract Society.

---

[1] Tomlinson, *LGC*, p. 214.

The Complexity of Tomlinson

The significance of Tomlinson's joining the church cannot be overstated, for his charismatic personality and leadership abilities so overwhelmed the church that it became more or less an extension of his ideas and vision. It is not too much to say that without Tomlinson the church would not have advanced with the great success that it did between 1903 and 1923, yet with him it was bound to divide; for his autocratic style of leadership, along with his conviction that he was 'God's Anointed – Prophet of Wisdom'[2] allowed for little or no resistance to his authority. Tomlinson consequently gave no quarter to anyone who disagreed with the vision that burned in his imagination; for he believed his vision was one with the prophets' and apostles' vision. His temperament and disposition, as we will see in the chapters ahead, inspired men and women to follow him, but repelled and provoked others; he endeared thousands, but disappointed tens-of-thousands.

Tomlinson's impact on the church makes for an interesting study because he brought with him the ideas and experiences of several radical religious traditions, along with the ideals and principles of American government. Embodied in Tomlinson to one degree or another were the doctrines and experiences of George Fox and traditional Quakerism, the ideals and vision of Frank W. Sandford and his 'Holy Ghost and Us Bible School' in Shiloh, Maine,[3] the ideals of A.B. Simpson and his ministry in Nyack, New York, the ministry and vision of John Alexander Dowie in Zion City, Illinois, the doctrines and vision of God's Bible school in Cincinnati, Ohio, and the doctrines and experiences of radical holiness leaders such as Stephen Merritt, George D. Watson, Martin Wells Knapp, Seth C. Rees, A.M. Hills, William Godbey, B.F. Taylor, Reuben 'Bud' Robinson, Henry Clay Morrison, J.M. Pike, and B.H. Irwin.[4] In addition to these men, he was inspired indirectly by the minis-

---

[2] Tomlinson's son-in-law and co-worker, A.D. Evans, edited a book published by the church in 1943 that featured Tomlinson's writings. Evans gave it the title, *God's Anointed – Prophet of Wisdom*. In his own words, Tomlinson claimed that he was mentioned in the Bible, citing Jer. 30.21 and Isa. 66.2 as proof references to himself.

[3] Phillips, *Quakerism and Frank W. Sandford*, pp. 1-30, notes 1-12; *idem*, *Corruption of the Noble Vine*, pp. 1-10.

[4] Homer A. Tomlinson, *The Great Vision of the Church of God* (Cleveland, TN: WWPH, 1939), pp. 3-7; Tomlinson, *Diary*, May 10, 1903; Evans, *God's Anointed – Prophet of Wisdom*, 'Introduction'. Tomlinson also subscribed to religious periodicals such as J.M. Pike's *The Way of Faith* in Columbia, SC; the Brethren in Christ's *Evangelical Visitor* in Harrisburg, PA; Frank W. Sandford's *Tongues of Fire* in Shiloh, ME;

tries of John Wesley, John Fletcher, George Mueller, and Charles Finney,[5] and the ideals and vision of American presidents and statesmen.[6] Thus one could say after a certain fashion that specific elements of all these traditions, for better or worse, joined the church with Tomlinson on that eventful day in 1903.

Quaker Roots

A.J. Tomlinson was born into at least a sixth generation Quaker family. Some of his ancestors apparently knew and worked with George Fox himself,[7] and perhaps came to America with William Penn in 1682.[8] His great-grandfather, William (1749-1813), and grandfather, Robert (1793-1875), migrated from Ireland in the late eighteenth century, settling in Randolph (now Guilford) County in the Piedmont Valley of North Carolina.[9] Though pacifists, they were sympathetic to the cause of America's independence and, of course, being Quakers, relished the principle of religious liberty. Active in the movement to emancipate slaves in the eighteenth and early nineteenth century, they migrated first to Ohio and then to Indiana in 1822 seeking the 'American Dream', but also in protest against the 'unjust and inhumane' Southern institution.[10] In Indiana, Tomlinson's grandfather joined the 'Antislavery Party' and his family including his father, Milton, became involved in the Underground Railroad. It was a matter of family pride years later that the hideaways they and other Quakers provided for runaway slaves became

---

and *God's Revivalist* in Cincinnati. Many of the books of these holiness ministers were recommended in *Samson's Foxes* and later in *The Way*.

[5] Tomlinson, *Diary*, March 10, 1901; April 14, 1901. Tomlinson's friend and missionary co-worker, J.B. Mitchell had been taught by Finney at Oberlin College, and through Mitchell, Tomlinson became familiar with Finney's ministry.

[6] Tomlinson's writings and annual addresses as General Overseer are peppered with inspirational stories about American heroes and exploits and the ideals and visions of American presidents and statesmen.

[7] Asher K. Tomlinson, *Genealogy of the Tomlinson and Kellum Families*, (published by the author, 1925); Book Two introduced by Sam Tomlinson, pp. 68-69.

[8] Tomlinson, *Genealogy*, p. 69

[9] Tomlinson, *Genealogy*, pp. 8-14. Coincidently, some of R.G. Spurling's ancestors were in Randolph County at this same time. It is possible that they were acquainted with the Tomlinsons since the population there was sparse in the late 1700s.

[10] A.K. Tomlinson, *Genealogy*, pp. 15-18, 28-29, 75-79. See also Charles Fitzgerald McKiever, *Slavery and the Emigration of North Carolina Friends* (Murfreesboro, NC: Johnson Publishing Company, 1970), pp. 50-54; Phillips, *Corruption of the Noble Vine*, p. 34.

known as 'Grand Central Station' for the Underground Railroad.[11] Here in this Quaker-dominated region, amidst political and religious activism, Ambrose was born and reared.[12]

Though Tomlinson's father and mother, Milton and Delilah, were not born again nor attending Quaker worship services when he was growing up,[13] his grandparents and several of his aunts and uncles and cousins were devout Quakers and members of the Society of Friends. His grandparents in fact had been instrumental in establishing the Chester church.[14] Thus when Tomlinson was converted he joined the Quaker church (or *meeting* as they called it) in Chester, a small community located two miles north of Westfield in southern Indiana.

Significantly, Tomlinson united with a branch of Quakers that in 1850-1870 had been swept into a renewal movement led by Joseph John Gurney – a movement that emphasized Bible study and a distinct new birth experience. Tomlinson was thus more or less a 'Gurneyite' – an evangelical Quaker.[15] Space does not allow here a full examination of his Quaker faith and tradition; suffice it to say that he was deeply influenced by Quakerism, including the Quaker bent toward mystical experience, perfectionist ideals, plainness in appearance, Spirit-centered faith and worship, pacifism, lay leadership, the education and care for orphans and poor children, works of charity, and the Quaker's connection with the American Bible Society.[16] Even after he left the Quakers, the

---

[11] Phillips, *Corruption of the Noble Vine*, pp. 37-39; one of Tomlinson's relatives married Levi Coffin's sister, Ann, before they left North Carolina and came to Indiana (A.K. Tomlinson, *Genealogy*, pp. 17-19, 29, 79).

[12] Indiana was the home of more than one-third of all the Quakers in America in the late nineteenth century (McKiever, *Slavery and Emigration,* pp. 51-53; Rufus Jones, *Later Periods of Quakerism*, p. 887). Tomlinson's hometown, Westfield, had the largest population and concentration of Quakers in the world in the 1880s. His grandfather, Robert, and his sons, were active in the Quaker faith, and in politics and community affairs in general. Milton, Tomlinson's father, however, fell out with the Quakers in the 1840s.

[13] The research of Roger Robins in his biography of A.J. Tomlinson has unearthed some new information on the Tomlinson family's Quaker background, particularly in regard to the religious experiences of A.J. Tomlinson's father and mother, Milton and Delilah, and their former connection with the Quaker church. His work also probes deeper into the Quaker roots of Tomlinson's wife, Mary Jane (Taylor). His access to the minutes of the Chester and Westfield church minutes has given documented evidence for Tomlinson's early life and religious experiences. See R.G. Robins, *A.J. Tomlinson, Plainfolk Modernist* (Oxford; New York: Oxford University Press, 2004), pp. 65-88.

[14] Phillips, *Corruption of the Noble Vine*, p. 31, n. 44.

[15] Phillips, *Corruption of the Noble Vine*, pp. 36-42.

[16] Some of the standard works on Quakerism that doubtlessly influenced Tomlinson were: *The Journal* and *Works of George Fox*; the classical theological work was

Quaker tradition did not leave him, not altogether at least; evidences of Quakerism, for better or worse, can be seen in him and his leadership years later in the Church of God. In Tomlinson, George Fox found a place in the Church of God.

Even Tomlinson's holiness transformation in the early 1890s happened within the context of his Quaker experience.[17] A great many evangelical Quakers had been swept into the holiness movement beginning in the 1870s; but in the late 1880s a radical breakthrough happened about the same time that Tomlinson was converted and united with the Quakers. Tomlinson's celebrated Quaker neighbor in Westfield, Seth Cook Rees (1854-1933), was transformed by the holiness movement in 1883; he, in turn, became instrumental in spreading the holiness message among Quakers throughout eastern United States. Rees, along with Martin Wells Knapp, would have a major impact on Tomlinson's Christian development in the late 1890s.[18] These two holiness firebrands established the International Apostolic Holiness Union and Prayer League centered in Cincinnati in 1897,[19] which sponsored God's Bible School, Salvation Park, and the widely-circulated magazine, *God's Revivalist*. Tomlinson attended God's Bible School, was a subscriber to *God's Revivalist*, and digested the teachings of many of the leaders connected with that ministry, including G.D. Watson, A.M. Hills, and Bud Robinson.

The Quaker influence on Tomlinson and the Church of God may be seen in a variety of trends and specific institutions, much of which iron-

---

Robert Barclay's *Apology for the True Christian Divinity*, first published in 1675; republished as *Barclay's Apology* by Knowles, Anthony & Co. in Providence in 1856. Though much of Barclay's theology was modified by Quakers in the twentieth century, the *Apology* remained the standard in Tomlinson's day, and one can see its influence on Tomlinson's thinking before and after he joined the Church of God. Some of the standard works on Quakerism that were published in the twentieth century are: William C. Braithwaite's two volumes, *The Beginnings of Quakerism* published in 1912, and *The Second Period of Quakerism* published in 1919 (London: MacMillan and Co., Limited); Rufus M. Jones, *The Later Period of Quakerism* (2 Vols.; London: MacMillan and Co., Limited, 1921); and D. Elton Trueblood, *The People Called Quakers* (Richmond, Indiana: Religious Society of Friends, 1975).

[17] An excellent work explaining Quakerism in the context of Tomlinson's upbringing and his conversion and holiness transformation between 1865 and 1898 is Thomas D. Hamm, *The Transformation of American Quakerism, Orthodox Friends 1800-1907* (Bloomington and Indianapolis: Indiana University Press, 1988); see also Phillips, *Corruption of the Noble Vine*, pp. 26-35, and Robins, *Plainfolk Modernist*, pp. 89-101;

[18] Homer in fact says his father first heard of entire sanctification through the ministries of Seth C. Rees, Martin Wells Knapp, George D. Watson, *et al.* connected with God's Bible School (*Shout of a King*, p. 17).

[19] Paul S. Rees, *The Warrior Saint* (Indianapolis, IN: The Pilgrim Book Room, 1934), pp. 54-56.

ically overlapped with Spurling's teachings on one hand, and, as we will see further on, with Frank W. Sandford's on the other. The Quaker influence was stronger and more noticeable in Tomlinson's early ministry, but it was never completely purged from his mind and spirit; which in some ways was a good thing, for many noble and commendable principles were espoused by the Quakers.

First, we see the Quaker influence on Tomlinson in some of the church forms and practices that he introduced into the Church of God; for example, in his practice of allowing the congregation to raise questions in response to sermons; in the roles of the church clerk, elder, and overseer; in the intra-subjectivity of group experience; in the reverence for consensus opinion and the ideal of unanimity in regard to faith declarations; in his idealistic egalitarianism;[20] in his democratic dialogs; in the role of the moderator in business meetings to discern the 'sense of the meeting' and make rulings accordingly; in the hierarchy of church government; in the polity and administration of the whole Quaker system. *Second*, we see the Quaker influence in Tomlinson's personal and collective habits; for example, in his meticulous habit of keeping records, minutes and journals; in his simplicity and plainness of dress and speech [e.g. Tomlinson in typical Quaker tradition seldom referred to the days of the week and months of the year by their names, but said simply 'first day', 'second day' ... 'first month', 'second month', etc]; in his censorship of wearing jewelry; in the frequent use of the term 'friend;' in the reverence for George Fox and the Quaker tradition in his writings; in the paradox of his anti-intellectualism in regard to mystical experience and yet his emphasis on education; in his disdain and sometimes denunciation of theology. *Third*, we see the Quaker influence in his doctrinal concepts; for example, in his Christological weaknesses and distaste for

---

[20] The egalitarianism and democratic nature of the church had already been established by Spurling and the members of Christian Union through the influence of their Baptist roots; but Quakers were more extreme than the Baptists in this regard, especially early in their history. They were famous (or infamous) for refusing even to tip their hats to authority or bow to dignitaries for fear of showing respect to persons. They would not recognize titles such as 'king', 'lord', 'doctor', and 'bishop', and even avoided the term 'sir' as an address, giving occasion for the peculiar usage of 'thee' and 'thou'. In George Fox's view every man was a 'friend' which seemed to him the best form of address and most consistent with the theology and teachings of Jesus (see *Quaker Family in America*, p. 25; George Fox, *Journal*). Again, Tomlinson mellowed with the passing of time on some Quaker peculiarities, modifying some extremely narrow views in favor of a broader evangelical worldview – e.g. on faith healing; yet, ironically, he descended into an extremely narrow view on some other points – e.g. in regard to his position as General Overseer and posture over the church.

theological reflection; in his dualistic and docetic tendencies; in his deistic concepts; in his absolutism in regard to the covenant of marriage and corresponding denunciation of divorce and remarriage; in his perfectionist ideals; in his anti-creedalism; in his concept of apostolic restoration; in his emphasis on spiritual gifts, prophesying, etc.; in his emphasis on mystical experience; in his emphasis on the anointing, power, and revelatory work of the Holy Spirit.

American Roots

The American experience with its colorful pageant beginning in the James and Plymouth colonies, paraded and celebrated from Boston and Charleston to the Mississippi, and across the Oregon Trial to the Pacific, spanning four centuries from its genesis in the early seventeenth century to well into the twentieth, was personified in Tomlinson, and in the men whom he at first considered to be the founding fathers of the Church of God – R.G. Spurling and his father, Richard. The Spurlings, however, lived more in the practical reality of America, Tomlinson more in the Dream.

It would be difficult to exaggerate how deeply and thoroughly the founders and early pioneers of the Church of God were influenced by American idealism and the political system of the United States, particularly in view of America's courtship with Christianity and the mysterious civil-religious system that grew out of that courtship. The currents of Americanism – so idealistic, fascinating, passionate, triumphant, and invigorating – were too strong for the church's pioneers to resist.[21] In many ways they emulated the American system, and sometimes superimposed American political ideals and strategies over the biblical design of the church. This was most flagrantly demonstrated in the years 1917-1921 when the church adopted a kind of bi-cameral system of government with a 'Council of Twelve' and 'Council of Seventy' that composed the 'official assembly' of the church. The parallel between the United States' upper house (senate) and lower house (congress) was obvious. In 1921 the church adopted a Constitution that began with the words, 'We, the Church of God ... In order to form a more perfect union'. Included in the Constitution (Article 5) was a Judicial System with lower courts that answered finally to a Supreme Court.[22] Like many

---

[21] For an in-depth look into the American influence on the Church of God, see Phillips, *The Church of God: In the Light and Shadow of America*, and *idem*, 'Our American Heritage', *Church of God History & Heritage* (Winter 1999), pp. 1-6.

[22] *GAM*, 1921, p. 63; see also Phillips, 'Our American Heritage', pp. 1-6.

American churches, the Church of God was carried by the tide of the New World's ideals, experiences, and visions, and later by the patriotism of the American state.

It would be almost impossible in fact to understand the nature and character of the Church of God, particularly in regard to the church's historical development in the first half of the twentieth century, without some knowledge of the American state and American history: for the forerunners and forefathers of the Church of God were in their generations intertwined with the most significant events in America's history, including the colonists' natural inclination toward independence; their reaction to 'taxation without representation' climaxing in the Revolutionary War; the establishment of a constitutional-democratic form of government with the unique feature of a 'wall of separation' between church and state; the controversies and events leading to and climaxing in the Civil War; the adventure and romance of Western expansion and frontier life; and the excellence of America in the late nineteenth and early twentieth century as the most progressive and powerful nation on earth. Through all of these national metamorphoses, the Church of God was being conceived and formed, becoming in large measure the embodiment of American ideals and the historical American experience.

No one in the church embodied and romanticized America more than Tomlinson; he was himself a 'melting pot' of American idealism. His first impressions of America were formed by his Quaker family and friends, and later by the Quaker-dominated Union Academy in Westfield that he attended as a young man. Quakers themselves generally romanticized the American Dream and contributed significantly toward making that Dream come true. Ever since the renown Quaker, William Penn, had left England in 1682 and attempted his 'Holy Experiment' in Pennsylvania ('Penn's Woods'), Quakers were in the forefront in expressing and promoting American ideals. Penn's attempt was virtually a microcosm of American ideals of self-government, religious liberty, and personal and property rights, which a century later – after the Revolutionary War had ended and the Constitution and Bill of Rights had been adopted – found permanence in the American state. Though Penn's 'Holy Experiment' failed in Pennsylvania, Quakers ever after endeavored to restore the Edenic paradise in the New World, and Tomlinson was an heir to this idealistic heritage.[23]

---

[23] His vision at Culberson in 1900 was to restore the 'Garden of Eden, where God can come and talk with us in the cool of the day' (*Diary*, April 14, 1901).

Coming of age in the Midwest in the late 1880s, precisely at the time and in the glory of Nebraska's rising star, William Jennings Bryan – the 'magnetic orator' and 'peerless leader' of the Populist Party – Tomlinson inhaled American mythology and breathed in its idealism. Like many nineteenth and twentieth-century Americans, he believed that Christopher Columbus' life and work were providential, that his explorations particularly the discovery of America were chartered more by God than Ferdinand and Isabella, all in fulfillment of biblical prophecy.[24] He and his followers would eventually see Columbus' discovery as part of a single plan of Divine providence to restore the fallen church of the Bible.[25] In this manner, Tomlinson endeavored to extend the Church of God's restoration roots nearly four-hundred years deep in history, comprehending the whole Reformation Period in Europe and England. America was, however, peculiarly the 'chosen land' in which the church was actually found and restored to her primitive glory in the New Testament.[26] Accordingly, America was foreordained in God's design to encompass the earth with her brightness and glory.[27] This perception or 'vision' attempted to bestow upon the Church of God a catholicity and dignity that transcended its more humble roots in the rather isolated setting in the Appalachians.

Again, when Tomlinson came into the mountains of southern Appalachia, he came embodying the idealism of America and the American Dream. In that decade – the 1890s – big ideas and high hopes ruled the day in America. It was a period of railroad expansion and big city building. The transcontinental railroad having been completed in 1869 was connecting major cities from east to west. The population in America had escalated from 32 million in 1860 to 75 million in 1900. The appearance of skyscrapers began to loom on the horizon – the first being

---

[24] Thirty-First Annual Address, 1941, *HAA*, III, pp. 215-17; Thirty-Third Annual Address, 1943, *HAA*, III, p. 265; Twenty-Fifth Annual Address, 1935, *HAA*, II, pp. 223-37. Charles T. Davidson, *America's Unusual Spot* (Cleveland, TN: White Wing Publishing & Press, 1954), pp. 126-38; Evans, *God's Anointed – Prophet of Wisdom*, p. 24.

[25] Evans, *God's Anointed – Prophet of Wisdom*, p. 24 – 'Christopher Columbus is honored because he was the person that discovered America and America had to be discovered first, before the bible prophecies could be shifted from the old world to the new'.

[26] Thirty-First Annual Address, *HAA*, III, pp. 215-17.

[27] Isaiah 60 became a favorite passage used to support this interpretation of the church in prophecy. Tomlinson especially focused on America (particularly North Carolina and Tennessee) during his sentimental years, particularly after his stroke in 1937. He strained the meaning of passages in order to magnify his personal experiences and the great love of his life – 'the Church of God'. See, e.g. his last five annual addresses, 1939-1943, *HAA*, III, pp. 136-275.

raised in Chicago in 1890; by 1900 New York had twenty-nine. Industrialization was increasing – factories were transforming American life and culture. Scores of inventions in steam and electricity were changing the face of society. Communications – particularly the telephone system – were networking the nation in one way, railroads in another. The first telephone message was transmitted in 1876, the year R.G. Spurling married Barbara M. Hamby. In 1892, the year that Tomlinson was sanctified, a line was opened from New York to Chicago. And the nation's geographical boundaries were changing. In 1889, the year Tomlinson married Mary Jane Taylor, Montana, North and South Dakota, and Washington were added as states to the Union. The next year Idaho and Wyoming added stars to Old Glory; and in 1896 Utah became a state when Mormons agreed, at least in theory, to give up their practice of polygamy. It was a time when Indians (native Americans) and thirteen million buffalo roamed the plains; cowboys were driving herds across the frontier; wagon trains with loads of settlers were pioneering western expansion; Tombstone was burying her dead in Boot Hill; and gold miners were sifting for wealth in the high Sierras. It was a day of political activism; almost everyone got involved in public life in one way or another. People actually thought they could change things, and thus paraded with torchlights and shouted themselves hoarse at political conventions and rallies.

And things were changing. The year 1900 marked not only the turn of the century but also the emergence of a triumphant and transformed America. Just before the century closed, the United States emerged victorious in its war with Spain. The victory 'dazzled the country and flattered its national vanity' magnifying its already growing pride as a world power. It emerged from the war with newly acquired territories off the shores of the Pacific – the Philippines, Guam, Hawaii – and in the Caribbean, America took on the role of protectorate over Cuba and Puerto Rico. The young nation's new international presence and world status, with the accompanying global responsibilities, more or less ended the old policy of isolation. For a moment America was an empire, with imperialism in her eye! By the turn of the century the American frontier had nearly vanished; sprawling cities were rising and rural communities diminishing. The simple agrarian nature and character of the country in the first half of the nineteenth century were transformed and complicated by the wheels of industry – particularly in the North. Concrete was pouring into America's rustic valleys like lava from Vesuvius.

Two years after the Spanish-American War, President McKinley was assassinated shortly into his second term by a half-crazed anarchist named, Leon Czolgosz. Significantly, this brought to the nation's highest office the extremely energetic and aggressive Theodore 'Teddy' Roosevelt, and with him the air of imperialism that was already taking hold of the country since its victory over Spain. Roosevelt – in his day perhaps 'the most popular and best loved man in America' – ran the country the same way he charged up San Juan Hill. He carried a 'big stick' and often used it. Many hoped that his strong and inspiring leadership would expand American boundaries and lead her to rule the entire Western Hemisphere.

The image and influence of the new president, the increasing health of the economy, and the success of the war with Spain, with the newly acquired colonies around the world, and the apparently fulfilled concept of Manifest Destiny, all contributed at the turn of the century to a subtle but general acceptance of Anglo superiority. The not-so-subtle arch-imperialist and supremacist himself, Rudyard Kipling, expressed in 1899 in *The White Man's Burden* the inner, and sometimes bold, sentiments of most Americans.

> Take up the White Man's burden –
> Send forth the best ye breed –
> To bind your sons in exile
> To serve your captives need;
> To wait in heavy harness,
> On fluttered fold and wild –
> Your new-caught, sullen peoples,
> Half-devil and half child.

Roosevelt was probably the most able man to sit in the White House since Lincoln.[28] He was rugged and vigorous like Jackson and learned like Jefferson. He was born the same year as R.G. Spurling, and went to the White House the year before Spurling organized the Holiness Church at Camp Creek in North Carolina. He was flamboyant and self-assertive, and in some ways show-offish. Roosevelt was awed by the glory of being President, as much or more than by the excellence of being an American.[29] The 'Rough Rider' was bold, brash, sporty, fearless, and carried a pistol to warn the public that he would not go down as easily as McKinley. His presidency (1901-1909) led the way into the Progressive Era of American history, an era in which important developments happened in the Church of God. His tenure would see the

---

[28] Hugh Barogan, *The Longman History of the United States of America* (New York: William Morrow & Company, Inc. 1985), p. 462.

[29] Barogan, *Longman History*, p. 463.

emergence of the Church of God in North Carolina; its reemergence in Tennessee; the rise to prominence of A.J. Tomlinson; the nature of the church metamorphose from Baptist, to Holiness, to Pentecostal; and the polity of the church was transformed from a loose federation of independent congregations into a body of churches under a centralized government. Roosevelt's magnification of the American state and the glory of its government, and his own flamboyant and ostentatious personality and style, certainly influenced Tomlinson, and through Tomlinson influenced the development of the government and polity of the Church of God.[30]

Figure 39

A.J. TOMLINSON AND FAMILY (C. 1898)

This photo was taken in Indiana not long before Tomlinson moved his family to Culberson in 1899. From left: Homer, Ambrose, Halcy, Mary Jane, Iris.

---

[30] Phillips, *The Church of God: In the light and Shadow of America*, pp. 41-44.

Tomlinson at Culberson

Tomlinson had been saved in 1889[31] and was swept into the radical holiness movement in July 1892.[32] About two years later, he felt that God had called him to an exalted position of leadership – to 'gather together a company of people' to evangelize the world. He composed a contract in 1909 for this purpose, the preamble of which reads:

> Pursuant to a call of God about the year 1894, emphasized again and again since that time by the Spirit of the Lord ... I, A.J. Tomlinson, promised the Lord that I would gather together a company of people, men and women who feel called of God, to be in the company, and whom God has satisfied me by revelation, conversation, providence, or otherwise, that they are suitable persons and faithful for service ...

---

[31] Tomlinson himself never pin-pointed the exact date of his conversion, but noted on several occasions that it was shortly after an experience in a severe thunderstorm during the first year of his marriage (Tomlinson, *LGC*, p. 223), which would have been between April 1889 and March 1890. In that storm, his conscience was awakened to the reality of God's presence, and soon afterwards he was saved. Homer, however, nailed down his conversion to the year 1889 (*The Great Vision of the Church of God* [Queens Village, NY: published by the author, 1919], p. 1); and this date is confirmed by Duggar, *Tomlinson*, p. 20.

[32] There is some room for speculation in regard to the exact date of Tomlinson's sanctification experience; but the preponderance of evidence strongly favors July 1892. I base this on five pieces of evidence: 1) Tomlinson wrote *The Last Great Conflict* for the most part in 1911-1912, though it was not concluded and published until February 1913. In this book he relates that his sanctification experience happened 'about twenty years ago' (p. 226). This would date his experience between 1891 and 1893; 2) Homer is emphatic in his *The Great Vision of the Church of God* that his father was converted in 1889 in the first year of his marriage (p. 20); yet years later in an editorial he says his father was converted in 'July 1892' (*Diary* I, p. 15). It seems almost certain that his later account confuses the date of his father's sanctification experience with his conversion experience (see Homer *Diary*, II, p. 23 and compare I, p. 15). Homer's emphatic date of July 1892, coupled with the fact that he links it with his father's spiritual experience while working in a cornfield, agrees with his father's testimony that he was sanctified while he was working the corn crop in the field (A.J. Tomlinson, *Answering the Call of God* [Cleveland, TN: WWPH, 1933], pp. 5-7); whereas he was saved in 1889 at the altar in the Quaker meetinghouse in Chester; 4) further, the July 1892 date seems to agree with his father's activities in the Chester and Westfield churches as Sunday school superintendent in 1890-1891, for he relates that 'some little time after [these appointments] I fell into a tremendous conflict with the "old man"' (*LGC* p. 225; see also *Answering the Call of God*, pp. 5-6). We conclude then that according to the preponderance of evidence, Tomlinson was sanctified at 'about twelve o'clock in the day' sometime in July 1892 (*Answering the Call of God*, p. 6).

This contract was formulated to establish the 'Pentecostal Worldwide Mission Band', obligating those who enlisted in the company to abandon almost completely all temporal concerns, and to submit wholly to the leadership of A.J. Tomlinson.

> We and each of us whose names are affixed below, enter into this company realizing to some extent what it means, and because I feel it is God's will for me at this time with the understanding that I will do my utmost to be true to my God, true to each member of the company and true to A.J. Tomlinson, who is recognized by me as the leader, under God, of this God-called and God-sent company of saints of the most high God ... I further agree that while I recognize said A.J. Tomlinson as the divinely appointed originator and propagator of this company or band of crusaders, I also agree to accept his counsel and advice, respect and obey him while I remain in said company, and that if I at any time become dissatisfied with the work or feel led of the Lord to discontinue the work in the company contrary to the wishes and advice of said A.J. Tomlinson or wish for any cause to disconnect myself from said company and A.J. Tomlinson its leader, I hereby agree to give thirty days' notice of the same, and when I depart I will not say or do anything to hinder or interfere with the work for God done by the company. I also admit that said A.J. Tomlinson reserve the right to dismiss me from the company at any time that I refuse to comply with this contract.[33]

While Tomlinson did not put this contract into operation until 1909, yet the spirit of it had been embodied in him since 1894. Thus, when he joined the church in 1903 and was put in as the pastor at that same time, the content of this contract formed his vision and the disposition of his leadership. He had believed since 1894 that he was especially called and anointed by the Lord to 'gather together a company of people' on the premise that they would sacrifice everything to evangelize the world and fulfill the mission that Christ gave to His church.

Tomlinson believed he was destined to accomplish some great thing for the Lord; yet it would be several years before he would find his niche in life, and before the vision of his ministry would become clear to him. The years leading up to his joining the church in 1903 were therefore important ones, for they impacted his development as a leader. We turn now to consider these formational years.

---

[33] 'Contract for the Pentecostal Worldwide Mission Band' (document in 'A.J. Tomlinson File', ZACG Archives).

After Tomlinson was converted in 1889, he spent several years attending Bible schools in Nyack, New York, Shiloh, Maine, and Cincinnati, Ohio, and came under the influences of such men as A.B. Simpson, Stephen Merritt, Frank W. Sandford, Martin Wells Knapp, Seth C. Rees, and G.D. Watson.[34] About this same time he became acquainted with J.B. Mitchell, a missionary and colporteur for the American Bible Society and American Tract Society, who had ventured into Tomlinson's hometown of Westfield to raise funds to sponsor one of his trips into the southern Appalachian Mountains. They quickly became good friends and co-workers in missionary and colporteur work, and beginning in 1895-1896 made several trips together into the southern Appalachians of Kentucky, Georgia, Tennessee, and North Carolina.[35] After surveying the landscape, he felt led to move to the extreme western corner of North Carolina near the Tennessee and Georgia state boundaries to establish a mission and build his dream of Zion – to 'make a Garden of Eden, where God can come and talk with us in the cool of the day, and we will not be ashamed like Adam [was], but only be too glad to meet Him'.[36]

In July 1899 Tomlinson with J.B. Mitchell de-boarded a train in Murphy, North Carolina searching for a suitable place to reach out to the poor and spiritually destitute people of southern Appalachia. He settled in October at Culberson, a small community located about twelve miles west of Murphy along the L & N Railroad, choosing this community probably because public opinion at that time was forecasting that Culberson would soon become a thriving metropolis. He made friends with one John W. Ballew and his wife, Gussie, almost as soon as he had arrived at Culberson and they invited him to hold services in their home. The Ballews and their in-laws, the Hyatts, Withrows, and Andersons, were some of the first settlers in Culberson.

---

[34] *Homer*, Diary, I, pp. 9-10; Evans, *God's Anointed – Prophet of Wisdom*, 'Introduction'; Robins adds David Updegraff, Dougan Clark, and others who almost certainly had some influence on Tomlinson's Christian experience: see *Plainfolk Modernist*, pp. 89-116. We have no conclusive proof that Tomlinson attended Simpson's camp in Nyack, but it is almost certain that he did, for he was in New York on more than one occasion and the traces of Simpson's 'Four-Fold Gospel' and ministry are strikingly present in his writings (e.g. Tomlinson, *LGC*, pp. 101-102), and he plainly attributes some of his thinking to Simpson's influence (Tomlinson, *LGC,* p. 156). If he was not influenced personally by Simpson, he certainly was indirectly via Seth C. Rees, Martin Wells Knapp, Stephen Merritt, and Frank W. Sandford.
[35] Homer, *Diary*, I, p. 15
[36] Homer, *Diary*, III, p. 19.

Soon Tomlinson rented a house and began to proclaim the message of entire sanctification and radical righteousness, being supported only by gifts from persons like Abigail Cress, a member of the Brethren in Christ church in Abilene, Kansas. 'Dear Mother Cress', as Tomlinson affectionately referred to her, responded to his pleas for help in publications like the Brethren's *The Evangelical Visitor* and after 1901 Tomlinson's own *Samson's Foxes*. Abigail (1855-1933)[37] and some of her children had accepted the fire-baptized message in B.H. Irwin's meetings in Abilene[38] and had become part of the movement among the Brethren in Christ to promote radical holiness, including the Wesleyan view of an instantaneous second crisis experience – entire sanctification.[39] Her eldest son, Clifford and his wife, Sarah (Zook), went to South Africa as missionaries in 1898, Sarah dying there not long afterward of a fever, along with her unborn child.

Inspired by men like Frank W. Sandford and George Mueller, Tomlinson was determined to fulfill his ministry completely on the basis of faith, for he had been taught in the Holy Ghost and Us Bible School at Shiloh, Maine to stand uncompromisingly on a literal interpretation of the Pauline principle to 'owe no man anything'.[40]

---

[37] Abigail, whom Tomlinson refers to as 'Dear Mother Cress' in *Samson's Foxes*, helped to form a bridge between the Brethren in Christ and the Holiness Movement early in the century, being influenced by B.H. Irwin's fire-baptized holiness movement. Abigail got involved in the Missionary Movement that swept the Brethren in Christ and most holiness churches in the latter part of nineteenth century. She became a great supporter of Tomlinson and J.B. Mitchell in their work at Culberson, having become acquainted first with Mitchell in the early 1890s. She solicited money, clothes, and literature in the Brethren churches in and about Abilene, and also through the Brethren's *Evangelical Visitor* in order to support the work at Culberson. Tomlinson and Mitchell reported regularly of their work to the *Visitor*: see April, 1890; October 15, 1892; July 1, 1893; February 1, 1895; June 15, 1895; May 1, 1899; October 1, 1899; May 1900; October 15, 1900; July 15, 1901; December 1, 1901; July 1, 1902; August 15, 1902; August 1, 1904; July 1, 1905; December 15, 1905; March 15, 1907; August 1907; January 1908; February 1, 1908; September 1, 1908; August 23, 1909; August 22, 1910; October 1, 1910. These issues give pertinent details about Tomlinson's and Mitchell's work and of goods and services received. Cress is mentioned also in Tomlinson's 'Missionary Evangelism', a report of the work at Culberson published January 1, 1907, and also in 'A Brief Report of Mission Work', 1902; and Phillips, *Corruption of the Noble Vine*, p. 135.

[38] G. Clifford and Sarah Cress, 'Hearts Set for the Field', *Evangelical Visitor* (June 1, 1898), p. 216.

[39] Carlton O. Wittlinger, *Quest for Piety and Obedience: The Story of the Brethren in Christ* (Nappanee, IN: Evangel Press, 1978), pp. 236-53, 321-41.

[40] Homer, *Diary*, III, p. 22 and compare Nelson, *Fair, Clear, and Terrible*, p. 83; Frank W. Sandford, *Seven Years with God* (Mount Vernon, NH: The Kingdom Press, 1957), pp. 58-69.

Institutional Transformation: 1906-1915 189

Figure 40

TOMLINSON WITH FAMILY AND NEW FRIENDS AT CULBERSON (1900)

From left sitting: Ella 'Willa' [Withrow] Hyatt, Mary Jane Tomlinson, A.J. Tomlinson; *second row standing:* Homer Tomlinson, Dolly Anderson, Iris Tomlinson; *third row:* Luther Bryant (son of W.F. Bryant), Iowa Aletha [Hyatt] Anderson, Halcy Tomlinson, Julius Bryant [son of W.F. Bryant], J.B. Mitchell, and [in buggy] Miles Dickson ['Uncle Dick'] Kilpatrick. All of these became active in the Tomlinson mission and school for children.

Soon he started a Sunday school in a rented house.[41] In October 1900, S.D. Anderson and his wife Iowa Aletha,[42] sold him a lot (about two acres) for the nominal fee of two dollars. His co-workers helped him to build a crude structure on this property for a school and orphanage, and he planted and raised a garden to help feed the staff and students. Tomlinson had this property deeded to 'God Almighty, and

---

[41] The school was first opened on April 9, 1900 (Tomlinson, *A Brief History of Mission Work*, p. 1).
[42] This Culberson couple, along with the Ballews, Hyatts, and Withrows were assisting Tomlinson in his mission. Their adopted daughter, Dolly, attended the school, and later became a school teacher in Culberson.

A.J. Tomlinson, [His] steward or agent'.[43] In January 1901 he began to publish *Samson's Foxes*, a four page monthly paper that proclaimed holiness and informed readers in several states of the work and progress of his missionary work in the mountains. On March 7, 1901 he inquired about 600 acres offered for $3800. He spent nearly the whole day walking over the property and dreaming; and though he was financially broke, he feigned he would purchase it.[44]

Figure 41

'THE HYATT HOUSE' (1900)

From left: Isaac Bruce; Arthur Ballew; John and Gussie [Hyatt] Ballew; Carl and Ella [Withrow] Hyatt; S.D. Anderson, Dolly Anderson, Iowa Aletha [Hyatt] Anderson; Zinnia and Hezekiah Burchfield Hyatt. Tomlinson boarded in this house at Culberson for a short time until he was able to make other arrangements. He was befriended by John Ballew and his wife, Gussie [Hyatt] Ballew, the sister of Iowa Aletha Anderson. They with several others worked with and helped to support Tomlinson while he was in Culberson in 1899-1904.

In spite of near destitution and the lack of the basic necessities of life, the work continued to progress a little – the staff and students living more on the 'bread of life' than cornbread. Tomlinson was joined in the

---

[43] Cherokee County Deed Records, Murphy, NC: Book 33, p. 354; see also *Diary*, May 13, 1901.
[44] Tomlinson, *Diary*, May 1, 1901.

work between 1900 and 1902 by ministers and teachers whom he had met in his earlier travels through the mountains as a colporteur, among whom were J.H. Overstreet and his wife, Eliza, from Kentucky, W.D. McGraw and his wife, and Homer Burroughs and his wife, also from Kentucky. He was also assisted by members of the Hyatt, Ballew, and Withrow families who lived in and about Culberson. Evangelistic endeavors were launched by willing workers inspired by Tomlinson's vision, faith, and indefatigable energy. The whole commune lived day by day on a spiritual plane also, seeking always deeper intimacy with the Spirit and endeavoring to do His bidding; for the Spirit spoke to them individually and corporately in prayer services. The saints in the Zion Hill Mission seemed to have a running conversation with God, not unlike Sandford and his followers at Shiloh.

Figure 42

THE MISSION SCHOOL AT CULBERSON (1901)

Tomlinson and Mary Jane are standing to the left on back row; left of them Carl and Ella [Withrow] Hyatt; seated right front center, John Ballew [with beard and cane], his wife Gussie standing to his right]; seated to his left and right are mission workers, Overstreets and Burroughs, who were drawn to the mission by the call of God and Tomlinson's vision.

The yearning for a farm remained passionate, but still the earnest was not evident. Time and again Tomlinson recorded in his diary the cry of his heart, 'O, God give us the farm. O God give us $5000 at once'. But it seemed the providences of heaven were shut up against him for some infinite reason known only to God. Finally, however, in May 1901 he was enabled to purchase for $500 from his friend, John W. Ballew, a tract of 75 acres on a hill that included a five-room house on it overlooking the rail station in Culberson. He named the property 'Zion Hill'.[45] In August 1902 he began to lay the foundation on this property for the 'industrial school' and the 'main Mount Zion building', hauling granite and marble stone from a nearby quarry to build the basement walls.[46]

Figure 43
R.R. McAllister's Store

Figure 44
Railroad Depot

Tomlinson's mission school and house were located on the hill [which Tomlinson named 'Zion Hill'] just above the railroad depot where he received clothing and goods from supporters for the mission school. A hundred yards north was R.R. McAllister's general store. In the photo above [ca. 1900] R.R. McAllister is third from left; his son, John, is fourth from right [with hat in hand]. The photo of the depot was taken c. 1904. Dolly Anderson who attended Tomlinson's mission is standing third from right.

His Connection with Camp Creek

On one of his treks through the mountains with his colporteur wagon and horse team, Bill and blind Barney,[47] Tomlinson came upon two boys at a place called Shoal Creek. He shared the Gospel with them and sold them a copy of the New Testament. These boys turned out to be W.F. Bryant's son, Luther, and his nephew, Milt Anderson.[48] Luther

---

[45] The money to purchase the property came from the settlement of his father's estate after his death in 1899 (Homer, *Shout of a King*, p. 12). This property interestingly was deeded to A.J. Tomlinson and his wife, Mary Jane, not to God Almighty (Cherokee County Deed records, Book 37, Page 38).

[46] Homer, *Diary*, III, pp. 26, 32; idem, *Great Vision of the Church of God*, pp. 3-4.

[47] Tomlinson's colporteur wagon was a covered hack; on both sides were written in large letters the words, 'Have Faith in God'.

[48] *Citizen-Times*, North Carolina (August 14, 1955); Tomlinson, *Diary*, I, pp. 54-55. Conn's version of this story is slightly different (*Mighty Army*, p. 50); he has Bryant's other son, Julius, in the place of Bryant's nephew, Milt Anderson. The *Citizen-Times* account here is preferred because it is corroborated by Homer Tom-

promptly invited him to his home about a mile away on Camp Creek to meet his father, urging him in his mountain brogue, 'Ye ort to meet ma pa. He's powerful religious.'[49] Tomlinson accepted the invitation, and via Bryant became acquainted with the fire-baptized revival then going on at Camp Creek.

Figure 45
ABIGAIL 'ABBIE' CRESS

Figure 46
JAMES H. AND ELIZA OVERSTREET

Brethren in Christ member in Kansas, Abigail Cress faithfully supported the mission at Culberson. James H. and Eliza Overstreet were faithful workers with Tomlinson in 1901-1902. Eliza was reportedly an excellent teacher.

The significance of this meeting cannot be overemphasized, for seeds were planted that would produce eventually a harvest of holiness-Pentecostal believers throughout the world: and friendships were forged by men who would soon become preeminent leaders in the Church of God. This meeting took place apparently sometime in the fall of 1899,[50] and thereafter Tomlinson became more or less identified with the holiness band; he being a frequent speaker in their meetings at Camp Creek, and Bryant and others at Camp Creek visiting often his meetings in Culberson.[51] There had been in fact a spiritual affinity real-

---

linson's account in *Diary*, I, pp. 54-55, and Homer gives a more elaborate and detailed account of the story, and he was also raised with the boys since childhood. It is likely that Julius was at home and became part of the story after Tomlinson arrived at his house and recalled the event from that perspective.

[49] Homer, *Shout of a King*, p. 7.

[50] Tomlinson says he had been acquainted with Bryant and the people at Camp Creek for 'four or five years' before he joined the church in June 1903. That would locate the meeting in 1899. Since he had settled in Culberson on October 16, 1899, it is therefore most likely that this meeting happened in late October or in November 1899.

[51] Bryant's wife, Nettie (Anderson), was in fact from the vicinity of Culberson and had been a member of the Shady Grove Baptist church before their marriage.

ized between him and the holiness believers from the beginning, particularly in regard to their passionate pursuit for spiritual purity and an ever-deepening mystical relationship with God. They were connected also in their passionate dislike and fear of denominational Christianity, and in fact all religion that was organized and governed by men. Overall, the thinking and experiences of the fire-baptized holiness band at Camp Creek fit well with Tomlinson's roots in Quakerism and his recent connections with radical holiness preachers like A.B. Simpson, Frank W. Sandford, Martin Wells Knapp, Seth C. Rees, B.H. Irwin, and George D. Watson.

During the same period of time that Tomlinson was meeting with Bryant and the saints at Camp Creek, he was building up his ministry and mission work in Culberson which was located about fourteen miles east of Camp Creek. We have noticed that he had already established a school and orphanage and was sending out missionaries through the mountains to proclaim the Gospel of radical righteousness. In addition, he was laying the groundwork for an industrial school, and in January 1901 began publishing *Samson's Foxes*, a four-page paper (11 x 16-inch sheets). The masthead of the paper read: 'Samson's Foxes is published monthly in the interest of the "Hundred-Fold" gospel, and the speedy evangelization of the mountain districts of North Carolina, Georgia and Tennessee, and the world'.

Influence of Frank W. Sandford and Shiloh

The headline on *Samson's Foxes* shows plainly the link between Tomlinson's work at Culberson with that of Frank W. Sandford's ministry in Shiloh, Maine, for it reflected Sandford's 'Hundred-Fold Gospel' concept and replicated almost word for word the subtitle on the masthead of Sandford's *Tongues of Fire*, which read, 'published semi-monthly in the interests of the speedy evangelization of the world on Apostolic Principles'.[52] Tomlinson, in fact, had been baptized twice at Shiloh, once on October 30, 1897 by N. Ralph Gleason, an assistant of Sandford, and the second time by Sandford himself on October 1, 1901 in response to

---

She probably took the opportunity to visit her family and relatives while assisting Tomlinson in his work there.

[52] For a sympathetic view of Sandford's life and ministry, see Frank S. Murray, *Sublimity of Faith* (Amherst, NH: The Kingdom Press, 1981); for critical views, see William G. Hiss, *Shiloh, Frank W. Sandford and the Kingdom, 1893-1948* (PhD thesis; Tufts University, Ann Arbor, MI, 1978), and Shirley Nelson, *Fair, Clear, and Terrible: The Story of Shiloh* (Latham, NY: British American Publishing, 1989).

his message that he was the prophetic 'Elijah', called and anointed to restore the 'Church of the Living God'. Both baptisms had a profound impact on Tomlinson, but each in its own way.[53] His first baptism meant that he would have to resign or face excommunication from his Quaker church (for water baptism represented a serious breach of Quaker faith); it meant also that his relationship with his natural family – grandparents, aunts, uncles, cousins – would be to some degree strained. His second baptism committed him to a new set of spiritual regulations and government – namely, the regulations and government of 'The Church of the Living God', and more particularly the government and peculiar mindset of Sandford himself; for according to Sandford (1862-1948), the divine mantle of the prophetic end times 'Elijah' had fallen upon him, and he had been sent by God to establish and cleanse 'The Church of the Living God'.[54]

Tomlinson's entries in his *Diary* for July-October 1901 in regard to Sandford's ministry show plainly that he had been intimately connected with Shiloh since his first baptism there in October 1897. His entry for July 25, 1901 – 'I feel that all "Shiloh" is at my back pushing me on, and I dare not go back on the teaching I received at Shiloh (Maine)' – reveals conclusively that he was fully engaged in upholding the faith as interpreted by Shiloh at that juncture in his Christian experience. This entry also strongly suggests that he had an on-going relationship with Shiloh either in person or through correspondence since 1897, and perhaps earlier still;[55] for if his acquaintance with Shiloh was merely casual, and

---

[53] Tomlinson would be baptized still again on August 13, 1913 by T.L. McLain in order to satisfy his desire to be baptized by a Church of God preacher. His wife was baptized at the same time. In addition, Homer says his father had also been baptized by Stephen Merritt, the Methodist minister and wealthy funeral home director from New York (Tomlinson, *Great Vision of the Church of God*, p. 6).

[54] Murray, *Sublimity*, pp. 287-95; Phillips, *Quakerism and Frank W. Sandford*, pp. 1-5, n. 9; Homer, *Diary*, III, pp. 13, 28-31.

[55] Tomlinson's testimony in his *Diary*, 'Received the Holy Ghost about March 1896' (October 30, 1897) is an indication that he was there at that time to visit Shiloh, for this terminology was used by Sandford, and Tomlinson refers to it in his connection with Shiloh. Further, his *Diary* shows that he had been in Maine before his baptism in October 1897, and it is almost certain that he would have visited Shiloh at that time. Still, Tomlinson may have made the confession – 'Received the Holy Ghost' – under the influence of Stephen Merritt whom he had spent some time with in New York; for this was Merritt's teaching before it was Sandford's; in fact, Merritt had convinced Sandford in a meeting at A.B. Simpson's Old Orchard campground in 1894 that there was a special reception of the Holy Ghost subsequent to regeneration and sanctification – an experience that could be received by faith in a rather unemotional and rationalistic way, simply on the basis of 'faith' and a confession (Murray, *Sublimity*, pp. 121-23; Sandford, *Seven Years with God*, p. 144).

he had not visited Shiloh again between 1897 and 1901, his Diary entry in July 1901 would be even more remarkable; for it would mean that the teachings of Shiloh and his experience there in 1897 were still holding sway over his life and ministry four years later. Further, the July 1901 entry was in response to two persons at Culberson who 'disagree much with our teaching'. The term 'our teaching' was said in connection with what he says directly afterwards, namely, 'the teaching I received at Shiloh'. In other words, 'our teaching at Culberson is the same teaching that I received at Shiloh'. There is in fact little or no room for doubt that his ministry at Culberson between 1899 and 1902 was more or less an extension of Sandford's ministry centered in Shiloh.

Figure 47
FRANK W. SANDFORD
(1902)

Figure 48
SHILOH (1898)

It is not without significance that when H.L. Chesser questioned M.S. Lemons in 1949 about Tomlinson's religious background, he recalled after a space of almost fifty years, 'He was with that fellow Frank up in Maine, that went to the penitentiary'.56 Tomlinson's four or five year connection with Sandford and his ministry at Shiloh,57 including

---

It is almost certain that Tomlinson's confession in March 1896 was along the line of Merritt's teaching either *via* Sandford or from the mouth of Merritt himself.

56 Bryant/Lemons interview, p. 19. This is more astounding in view of the fact that Lemons knew and worked intimately with Tomlinson for more than twenty years.

57 In addition to the volume of evidence that connects Tomlinson with Sandford during this time, the writer interviewed by phone and written correspondence (1988-1989) Sandford's biographer and great admirer, Frank S. Murray, who lived with Sandford the last eighteen years of his life. Murray said that William Gleason, brother of Ralph Gleason who had baptized Tomlinson in 1897, remembered 'Tommy' Tomlinson in relation to the early days of Shiloh's development and ministry (Frank S. Murray correspondence dated February 20, 1989). Murray notes that

his two baptisms there, his subscription to *Tongues of Fire* which kept him abreast with the ministry and activities at Shiloh between visits, his apparent theological orientation with the teachings, authority, and vision of Shiloh, including the radical concepts of apostolic restoration, and his apparent deep affections for Shiloh prove that he was under the powerful influence of Sandford and Shiloh between 1897 and 1902, and most likely his ministry during those years was an integral part, if not an organizational extension, of Shiloh.

Significantly, Tomlinson felt pressed to go again to Shiloh for the convention that was to begin September 25, 1901, apparently because with hundreds of others he was anxious to hear from the divinely-appointed 'Man of God' who was just then returning from England with exciting reports and fresh revelations from God. Shiloh was already abuzz with millennial expectations, but the atmosphere was all the more charged in anticipation of Sandford's report on what God had revealed to him England.

Figure 49

SHILOH (1901)

When Tomlinson arrived at Shiloh in September 1901, his heart was fluttering with excitement. He could hardly wait to hear Mr. Sandford expound on prophetic events, and to see the expansion of the magnificent 'Shiloh'. The flags on the towers were waving and the people were abuzz with millennial expectations and imminent end-time events. Tomlinson was moved with what he saw and heard; but, still, he was dreaming of his own 'Shiloh' at Culberson.

---

if Tomlinson was at Shiloh in 1897, he would have almost certainly helped to construct the great edifice there – the main Shiloh building.

Anyone, like Tomlinson, who was keeping up with the ministry and activities of Shiloh through *Tongues of Fire* and other religious and secular newspapers and through the holiness 'grapevine' knew that spectacular end-times events were unfolding at Shiloh – that it was time for the 'man of God' to 'remove the covering cast over all people' according to the words of the prophet Isaiah. It had already been announced that God had especially spoken to Sandford and said, 'Remove the Covering', and that the Lord had commissioned him to gather together and train an obedient army that would without question follow the orders of a divinely-ordained chain of command – a hierarchy of spiritual authority that culminated in a specially anointed 'man of God'. All of these spiritual regulations were necessary in order for the 'Church of the Living God' to fulfill her mission in the world, and to fit the prophetic picture of the bride of Christ in Solomon's love song – the 'undefiled dove' who 'looks forth as the morning, fair as the moon, clear as the sun, and terrible as an army with banners'.[58]

These prophetic themes – 'the covering removed', 'the hundred-fold Gospel', 'the city set on a hill', 'the restoration of all things', 'the perfection of the church', 'the last great conflict', 'the white clad army', 'the glorious millennium', etc. – had been unfolding at Shiloh since Tomlinson's first baptism there in 1897. 'The Holy Ghost and Us' Bible School that had begun in 1895 was little by little giving way to the greater and more important vision of the 'Church of the Living God'. But no one anticipated the astounding claims that would be made by Sandford in the convention in September 1901.

Tomlinson had arrived at Shiloh for the convention just in time to hear Sandford preach for over a week on the 'True Church'. Every day he focused on the 'seven golden candlesticks' in Rev. 1-3, whose mystery was rooted in the seven-pronged lampstand in Lev. 24.2-4. The week-long sermon culminated on the first day of October with Sandford leading the convention and student body down to the Androscoggin River for a special baptism service to pronounce more decisively the establishment of Church of the Living God. The means of organizing the church was the 'restored and authoritative baptism' that God had revealed to Sandford while he was in England. He preached the essential points of this baptismal message throughout New England in the days and weeks ahead.

---

[58] Hiss, *Shiloh*, I, pp. 259-75; Murray, *Sublimity*, pp. 234-96; Nelson, *Fair, Clear, and Terrible*, pp. 85-167.

> You must see that we have not had scriptural baptisms ... We have not baptized people into the Church for we have not had the Church set in order ... I never organized the Church because God never showed me how. I declared I never would have a church organization if I had to have a man-made one – if I had to organize it as men organize it.
>
> But at last over in England God showed me how to set the churches in order, and I came back across the seas with great gladness in my heart. God's sheep are going to be gathered in, and they are going to be blessed.
>
> I am glad to tell you today that I am here to wipe out all the past ... I promise you that the people I baptize will be all white. From this time on you are going to have a sweet orderly Church, and its is going to grow after this ...
>
> I suppose that no one who has been through these eight years of waiting on this line can understand the joy I had when I at last understood just how to gather the flock of God out of the wicked world and to separate them and care for them – they [the thirty- and sixty-fold Christians] having their place and the overcomers [the hundred-fold Christians] having their place and the two not conflicting.[59]

As Sandford prepared to baptize the willing and starry-eyed candidates on that first day of October, he declared,

> God is here, and the representative of God is here that has power and authority from God to remit your sins ... I declare that every one of your sins will be remitted today if you are baptized. Beware how you hear it! If you accept it, you accept the 'counsel of God'. If you reject it, you reject 'the counsel of God'. Hear the voice of a prophet. Hear the voice of a preacher of righteousness ... of one who is commissioned authoritatively to wash the Church and prepare them for the coming of Jesus Christ. God help you to 'press' into the kingdom.[60]

Of the vast number that attended that inaugural baptismal service, 218 stepped forth including Tomlinson, and were immersed by the 'man of God' in the waters of the Androscoggin. This same man would boldly

---

[59] Murray, *Sublimity*, pp. 287-88.
[60] Murray, *Sublimity*, pp. 290-91.

declare in the days to come that he was by divine appointment the prophetic end times 'Elijah' whom God had sent to 'restore all things'.

Ironically, this dramatic-filled baptismal service on October 1, 1901 seems to have both climaxed and ended Tomlinson's connection with Shiloh; certainly it marked the beginning of his separation from the movement. He remained at Shiloh through October 8th and seems to have mentally digested all that had been taught and that had transpired the previous two weeks. In the days and weeks ahead, he would read in *Tongues of Fire* and hear elsewhere of the extravagant claims made by Sandford including his announcement that he was the prophetic 'Elijah' spoken of by the prophet Malachi. He would learn also that Shiloh had taken an extreme turn to declare itself emphatically God's exclusive church and that a new policy had been adopted that forbade outsiders – that is, those who had not received the 'Elijah baptism' – to the Lord's Table. After reasoning it all out, with perhaps the counsel of his nameless 'friend' and traveling companion, who almost certainly was J.B. Mitchell, Tomlinson concluded that Sandford and Shiloh had gone too far. His October 9th entry in his *Diary* – 'Yesterday a friend and myself left Shiloh for the South' – conveyed, perhaps unwittingly, a symbolic as well as literal meaning, for Tomlinson 'left Shiloh' at that time spiritually as well as physically. How many days or weeks it took him to sever completely all ties with Shiloh we have no way of knowing with certainty; but after his October 9, 1901 entry he never mentions Shiloh or Sandford again.[61]

No doubt the public outcry against Sandford's authoritarian rule and abusive discipline reported in religious as well as secular newspapers between 1898 and 1903 affected Tomlinson's decision. Sandford was later found guilty of cruelty and manslaughter in 1904,[62] and again in 1911 he was tried and found guilty of manslaughter, being sentenced on this latter occasion to a term in a federal penitentiary.[63] But Tomlinson's decision was made ultimately when he sobered to the fact that Shiloh

---

[61] It is significant also that although *Samson's Foxes* clearly bears the marks of Sandford and Shiloh in 1901, thereafter *Samson's Foxes* and *The Way*, the latter of which was published by Tomlinson and M.S. Lemons in 1904-1905, promote the books and publications of preachers associated with God's Bible School in Cincinnati – Seth C. Rees, Martin Wells Knapp, G.D. Watson, A.M. Hills, J.J. Pickett, Beverly Carradine, *et al.*

[62] Murray, *Sublimity*, pp. 332-35.

[63] In his zeal to evangelize the world speedily, he was responsible for the exposure and deaths of several ministers and laymen on a missionary trip in the summer of 1911 aboard his schooner, the *Coronet*, and his barkentine vessel, the *Kingdom*. He was tried and found guilty of manslaughter in December of that year and locked away in a federal prison in Atlanta until 1918.

had become more or less a cult under the spell of Sandford's fantastic claims and fascinating machinations, and that the 'Church of the Living God' had been transformed suddenly from a universal spiritual body into a concrete visible organization with Sandford as its indisputable prophet and chief executive. In the weeks and months ahead, Sandford would claim that he was 'Elijah, the Restorer', the 'Lion of the Tribe of Judah', and the 'Son of God'. If A.B. Simpson has been quoted correctly, his remark in regard to Sandford was prophetic: 'Frank Sandford will never be satisfied until he is extra-plenipotentiary with the Almighty Himself'.[64] Looking back, there had been it seems a certain delirium latent in Sandford's psyche since the early days of Shiloh; but, by the end of 1901 he had become more obviously delusional and infected with a messianic complex. After the convention in October 1901, he seems to have been overcome with a malignant megalomania. Frank Bartleman in Los Angeles did not hesitate to mark him with John Alexander Dowie in Zion City as a charlatan who 'severely abused and fleeced the flock of God' and exalted himself to pad his own pockets.

Notwithstanding that Tomlinson by 1902 had broken ties with Sandford and the Church of the Living God, Shiloh left its imprint on him. Many of the ideas and the apocalyptic visions of that tradition were branded in his mind and spirit. Ever after his Shiloh experience between 1896 and 1902, he would have a preoccupation with ecclesiological (church-related) themes, including 'the covering removed', 'the city of God', 'restoration of all things', the 'apostolic office', 'perfectionism', 'the last great conflict', an absoluteness in regard to faith healing and faith living, and many other apocalyptic and militaristic motifs related to a victorious end-times army, not the least of these being Sandford's preoccupation with the 'Fair, Clear, and Terrible' description of the church in Solomon's prophetic vision. But none of these themes were engrained in Tomlinson's psyche more deeply than Sandford's teaching in regard to leadership, particularly the idea that God would raise up a specially-anointed man to gather His people together into a company, and who through the guidance of the Holy Ghost would lead them to the Promised Land – to perfection and millennial glory. In the years to come, Tomlinson regurgitated several of the ideas and themes that he had learned at Shiloh, and more or less followed them like a blueprint in constructing the Church of God.[65]

---

[64] Nelson, *Fair, Clear, and Terrible*, p. 165.
[65] Phillips, *Corruption of the Noble Vine*, pp. 36-68.

Persecution

Tomlinson's work in Culberson was located only a stone's throw from the Baptist and Methodist churches that stood adjacent to each other not fifty yards apart on the same ridge where he had established his school and orphanage. These churches became antagonistic to his ministry, though the Baptist church more fiercely opposed it, perhaps because a few of their members had become sympathetic to Tomlinson's message and vision and had begun to attend his meetings.

Tomlinson's entry in his diary for August 15-18, 1901 captures the situation then existing between himself and the antagonistic residents at Culberson, and reveals also a certain characteristic in his thinking and disposition:

> I was called to the front door and I there met a Baptist minister by the name of Davis and one of his brethren. I politely shook hands with them and invited them into the house, but they declined. They seemed to be somewhat agitated and quickly produced *Samson's Foxes*. The minister asked me if I claimed it as my publication. I said, 'yes sir'. He desired to show me some of the false statements in it concerning the condition of twenty-five percent of the southern people of the poor whites. I listened, with but very few words, for several minutes while he called me a fraud, deceiver, hypocrite, liar, etc. He finally run down with his tirade of abuse, after he repeatedly said our work would have to stop. I asked him if he was through. He said he was. I said I would not offer any defense, but gently and tenderly invited them in and we would pray about the matter. They refused and railed upon me for the insult as they seemed to take it as such. Then I asked that we might shake hands, they hesitated again, but I insisted saying that I had nothing but love for them for all they had said. I told them I would pray for them and asked them kindly to pray for me. They finally took my extended hand and departed. One of my co-workers kindly advises me to leave the town, but I am refusing to go. I am here to give my life for this people, if needs be, until I am delivered by God Himself. We are going right on with our work, although they said they were determined to stop us and to stop our supplies from the north. Poor things, they do not realize that they are fighting against God, and that their task is such a hard one. God pity and forgive them, they know not what they do.

The minister that confronted Tomlinson was almost certainly Elder W.H. Davis, a prominent minister that worked within the bounds of the

Liberty and Ducktown Baptist Association in 1899-1902 in the Culberson area, and who was close friends with several of the businessmen and leaders in the community. It should have been no surprise to Tomlinson that two days later another man showed up at his house, and called him out into the woods for a 'man to man' talk. This man 'turned and began a great tirade of abuse, cursed me to everything he could think of. Did all he could to get me to take my part and resent him so he would have a chance to commence a fight. I took it all quietly without a ripple in my soul. He went off, threatening and cursing'. The seriousness of this man's threat may be seen in the words that Tomlinson confided to his diary, 'I went very carefully in God'. It turns out that this man had challenged Tomlinson to a gunfight, which we will elaborate upon further in a moment.

Immediately following this sobering incident, Tomlinson went into his office and talked the situation over with three of his co-workers and then prayed. While in prayer, the Spirit whispered to him, 'depart'. He then records in his diary,

> We committed all to God, prayed for our enemies. When we arose, I told them I thought I had best absent myself from home for awhile. I began to get ready and, before I was wholly ready, a messenger came in saying they were forming a company of men to wait on me. I hastily kissed my wife and children goodby [*sic*] and slipped out into the woods and hills. Praise God, like Jesus, Paul and others I was permitted to escape their cruel hands, and when it was dark I slipped around the town and walked ten miles through mud and rain to the house of a friend.

Now the situation at Culberson was similar to that at Camp Creek in that the church elders and community leaders and merchants formed a monolithic system that ruled almost entirely the political and social life in the area; indeed the entire region was more or less under the same political-religious influence, including the county sheriff's office and the local justices of the peace.[66] One branch of this governing structure was the Liberty & Ducktown Baptist Association which brought together the Culberson and Shady Grove churches as well as the Shoal Creek and Camp Creek churches – Liberty, Pleasant Hill, and Friendship – and the churches across the state line in Ducktown and Turtletown. Tomlinson's

---

[66] The area was not altogether lawless, but those in law enforcement favored the ruling parties, which at Culberson were the very ones whom Tomlinson had antagonized.

work at Culberson was thus perceived by this body to be connected with the holiness movement at Camp Creek, and indeed it was.

It should be borne in mind that during the early years of Tomlinson's ministry at Culberson, he was still under the influence of radical holiness zealots like Sandford; and more recently had come under the influence of the bold and sometimes harsh preaching style of B.H. Irwin's fire-baptized evangelists, particularly in the person of W.F. Bryant. While Tomlinson was more polished than Bryant and could of course read and write, still he was impressed with the power and plainness of Bryant's preaching, which, although crude and blunt, was effective. Homer said sinners would 'wince' under conviction when Bryant preached, and that the saints would 'shout' and 'dance' in the Spirit and be 'exalted' as he proclaimed the simple truths of the Gospel.[67] He recalled being with his father as a small boy and hearing Bryant preach; said his father sat

> transfixed ... like one hypnotized at the undecorated, unvarnished and bold truth of it all. Never had he seen, back in the north, such zeal, such fearlessness, such a hard hitter. Here was a fearless zealot ... a preacher of bedrock righteousness.[68]

Besides the content of Bryant's preaching, Homer attempted to capture his mountain brogue:

---

[67] Homer Tomlinson in his 'Almighty God of the Mountains' preserves many of the details of Tomlinson's and Bryant's personal lives and ministries at Camp Creek and Culberson in 1899-1904. This story was published in parts each month in the January 1936 through February 1937 issues of *The Joyful News* magazine. Once Bryant, Tomlinson, and their families and co-workers are identified under the names of 'Malcolm Horner' (Tomlinson), his wife, 'Laura' (Mary Jane Tomlinson), his daughter, 'Mary' (Halcy Tomlinson), 'Preacher Coleman' or 'Old Man Coleman' (W.F. Bryant), his wife, 'Nellie' (Nettie Bryant), 'Fate Bruce' (John W. Ballew), his wife, 'Mandy' (Gussie Ballew), 'Big John Collins' (R.R. McAllister), *et al.* The story opens up and we are enabled to gain many insights and details into the events that transpired in Tomlinson's ministry at Culberson – insights and details that are found nowhere else. It is admitted that the story is 'embellished as a parable' (see advertisement for 'Almighty God of the Mountains' in Homer A. Tomlinson, *Amazing Fulfillments of Prophecy* (Cleveland, TN: WWPH, 1934), but where incidents are exaggerated it is acknowledged elsewhere so that the plain facts may be distinguished from embellishments, e.g. in regard to his father being called out for the gunfight in August 1901, Homer says in 'The Fanatic', *FS* (October 1923, pp. 21-23) that his account of the incident 'happened exactly as written'. We may assume this to be accurate because he published the incident knowing that eyewitnesses including his mother and father would read his account of the story.

[68] Homer, 'Almighty God of the Mountains' (February 1936), p. 5.

If you don't quit yore sinnen', God a-mightily send you into hell-fire and damnation. Ah hates sin, ah'll fight hit wherever ah meets hit, ah'll hit it as long as ah've got a fist, ah'll kick hit as long as ah've got a brogan shoe, ah'll butt hit as long as ah've got a head, ah'll bite hit as long as ah've got teeth, ah'll never stop till ah'm gwine ter heaven, and sin's done gone ter hell … Now you all thing ah'm powerful hard on ye. Ah don't aim to be. Yore my friends … God made me yore preacher and ah's gotta tell the truth. But ah love ye … Now, there's good news. 'The gift of God is eternal life through Jesus … Hain't that what hit says, brother? … That's why ah want youenses ter live right. Weeenses of the mountings have to wrassel out a thin livin' … We hain't got a good time hyer. Ah want you all to make shore yore ready on that line. Abraham's over thar, Isaac's over thar. Ah, Jacob's over thar, eternal life'.[69]

It was under the influence of Bryant and other fire-baptized evangelists that Tomlinson's ministry began to shift from missionary and colporteur work to preaching the Gospel and pastoral interests. His pastoral instincts of course became more obvious after he joined the church in 1903, but they were beginning to show up in his work at Culberson. It was about that time that Tomlinson began to shift the bulk of the colportage and orphanage work – including the soliciting and distribution of literature and clothing to the poor – to his good friend and capable co-worker, J.B. Mitchell.

When Tomlinson first began to preach, it was natural that his style was rather blunt and harsh, for he had been impressed by the 'hard hitting' preaching of Bryant and the fire-baptized mountaineers. Homer admitted that his father's 'invective upon sin and lawlessness was devastating'.[70] So strong and tactless was his preaching that, according to Homer, his mother 'chided him a bit', saying,

[Ambrose], I know you're right, and I'm for you, but sometimes I think you preach too hard. Why, you called some folks 'white-washed sepulchres', and you called moonshiners 'hounds of hell'. And you called the women who use snuff 'nasty-faced wenches'. Now it may all be true, but it sounds terrible. Now Big John is going to give a big dance and you say anybody that goes there'll go to hell. Don't you think you ought to be a little easier.[71]

Tomlinson's response was,

---

[69] Homer, 'Almighty God of the Mountains' (February 1936), p. 5.
[70] Homer, 'Almighty God of the Mountains' (April 1936), p. 5.
[71] Homer, 'Almighty God of the Mountains' (May 1936), p. 5.

> Now, [Mary], I've got to tell you about that. I seem to love these mountain folks so much I would be willing to die for them. I love Big John. He thinks I'm mad at him. But he's doing wrong. He's taking advantage of these ignorant people. It's not right. Things are not right here, and I've been made a sharp threshing instrument and I'm going to thresh these mountains, and fight sin where I find it. I'm going to …[72]

It should be borne in mind that Tomlinson at that time was inexperienced as a minister and missionary. Certainly as a leader and administrator he was a novice; as such, he made several mistakes in his zeal to reach out to the community at Culberson and surrounding communities. It is granted, however, that he may not have succeeded any better in converting the people at Culberson even if he had approached the situation in a milder and more moderate manner; for the greater part of the people were addicted to snuff and tobacco habits, and were in general acclimated to a culture that included making, drinking, and selling moonshine whiskey. And there were crooked merchants and businessmen who were bent toward maintaining their commercial interests by underhanded and shady business tactics. But, still, a meek and pastoral Tomlinson rather than a fiery and impatient Tomlinson might not have so incensed and infuriated the 'establishment'. As it was, he was determined to turn over the tables of the moneychangers, restraining only from using a cat-o'-nine-tails.

In any case, like Sandford and Irwin, Tomlinson saw himself as a spiritual warrior, and believed that he was commissioned by Christ to declare war on Satan and his followers. After all, he had been divinely enlisted into God's army in the midst of the 'Last Great Conflict', and, as a fearless captain in God's army, he felt it incumbent upon him to lead the troops into battle. His evangelistic tactics were therefore often immoderate and unwise – even threatening. Homer boasted that when his father first began his work at Culberson, he was a fanatic. Thirteen years before he wrote 'Almighty God of the Mountains', he told the story of his father's ministry at Culberson under another work that he titled, 'The Fanatic', published in four installments in the church's *Faithful Standard* magazine in August-November 1923. Using the fictitious names of 'Calvin Turner' (for his father) and 'Brown's Gap' (for Culberson) he revealed unwittingly the marks of Sandford's teachings and ministerial style upon his father's early ministry, and perhaps to a lesser degree the fanaticism of the fire-baptized movement. Unfortunately,

---

[72] Homer, 'Almighty God of the Mountains' (May 1936), p. 5.

only the October 1923 issue of the *Faithful Standard* is extant. But in this one issue there are significant bits of history found nowhere else.

Suffice it to say that Tomlinson's declaration of war in the name of holiness against the mountaineers in and about Culberson was met with fierce retaliation. The very carnality that he had sought to eradicate rose up against him, overturned his colporteur wagon, stripped him of his clothes except for his underwear, and left him alone in the woods. He was 'blasted from pulpits and religious publications as a fanatic and irresponsible zealot'.[73] The 'establishment' at Culberson, part of the same power structure that dominated Camp Creek and the region round about, was as determined and passionate to eradicate Tomlinson and his 'crazy religion' as Tomlinson was to eradicate sin.

It is not surprising then that Tomlinson and his family began to be severely persecuted at Culberson about the same time that the saints at Camp Creek were. His house was shot up on one occasion while his family was inside, and two of his teachers and evangelists were beaten. Homer Burroughs was beaten with a whip and tarred and feathered, dying two years later back in his home in Kentucky; James H. Withrow was badly injured from a head wound from which he never fully recovered, died a few years later in Atlanta.[74] We noticed a moment ago that Tomlinson himself was actually challenged to a duel – with real pistols! The man who called him out was apparently Richard R. McAllister (1848-1926), an influential man in the community.[75] He owned and operated with his son, John Milton (1883-1944), a general mercantile at

---

[73] Homer, *Shout of a King*, p. 13.
[74] Homer, *Diary*, I, pp. 56-65; *idem*, *Shout of a King*, pp. 12-13.
[75] Homer tells the story of McAllister relative to his father under the name 'Jim McCallister' in his story of the 'Fanatic' (*FS* [October 1923], pp. 21-23; see also Homer, *Diary*, I, pp. 58-59). Homer notes, however, that McAllister later befriended his father, and went on to become a successful businessman. His son, John, later obtained a position with the government. Further corroboration of the details of McAllister's life and incidents at Culberson were supplied to the writer by his granddaughter, Maude (McAllister) Gulledge (Phillips interviews with Maude (1993-1994). Mrs. Gulledge was the postmistress for Culberson for over twenty-five years, following in the footsteps of her father who had handled the mail as a young man when the post office was located in their mercantile store. According to Homer, McAllister used the cover of his store for the illegal traffic of moonshine, and was known to resort to violence to defend what he believed was necessary to preserve the status quo of the social order at Culberson. Interestingly, McAllister family portraits written by granddaughters correspond generally with Homer's data, though understandably they omit either purposively or for lack of knowledge the details of their father's and grandfather's interactions with Tomlinson in 1900-1903. See 'The R.R. McAllister Family' and 'John Milton McAllister' in *The Heritage of Cherokee County, North Carolina* (3 Vols.; Winston-Salem, NC: The History Division of the Hunter Publishing Co. 1987), I, pp. 313-14.

Culberson, which not insignificantly housed the post office where Tomlinson mailed out *Samson's Foxes*.[76] The store was located beside the railroad tracks less than a hundred yards from the railroad station, both of which were in sight of the Zion Hill Mission that sat on the top of the hill. McAllister was also, according to Homer, the prime mover behind the gang that had wrecked Tomlinson's colporteur wagon and left him out in the woods in his underwear. It was this same gang we may assume that was intending to bushwhack Tomlinson on August 17, 1901. Some of the men in this gang coincidentally were relatives of the infamous 'One Hundred and Six' that persecuted the saints at Camp Creek and burned down their places of worship.

The persecutions at Culberson became so severe that Tomlinson was forced to leave home for almost a year in 1901-1902 for the sake of his family's safety and for his own life.[77] Finally in late November 1902 under much duress from persecutions on one hand and unpaid bills on the other, he felt it necessary to return to Indiana.[78] He moved to the city of Elwood and went to work as a machinist in a glass factory. There he earned money to pay off his debts, and took time to reflect on God's call upon his life.

During this time, he was under a cloud of uncertainty and discouragement. He noted in his *Diary*, 'I must confess I have been laboring under peculiar difficulties, and have not had sufficient inspiration to write in my diary for quite a while'. But things were about to change. He attended a meeting in Indianapolis in May 1903 conducted by one of the celebrated holiness preachers of that day, G.D. Watson. In the very first service, Watson preached a message on the power of God's love; this message deeply touched the heart of Tomlinson. While Watson was preaching, Tomlinson said, 'A question arose in my mind as to whether I had yet been overshadowed, or covered over, or had put on the outer garment, viz., divine love. Col. 3.14.' The next day, he wrote in his diary, 'Today the question arises as to whether I want to die for Jesus. I have

---

[76] Tomlinson reported in several issues of *Samson's Foxes* that God had sent him to the mountains to help the 'poor ignorant whites' in the region. Unlike Mitchell, Tomlinson painted a less than flattering picture of the people in the area which infuriated McAllister and some of his cronies.

[77] Homer, *Diary*, I, pp. 56-67.

[78] In his Introduction to the reprint of his father's book, *The Last Great Conflict*, Milton Tomlinson admits that his father's comments in *Samson's Foxes* about the 'poor, uneducated mountain folk' at Culberson 'angered the denominationalists in the area. And so descriptive were his articles about the poverty-stricken plight of the backwoods Appalachian people, that he also incensed the well-to-do. Endless persecutions resulted and finally drove him to move his family – his wife and three children, Halcy, Homer, and Iris – back to Indiana.'

been willing to die, but now it comes with force, "do I want to die for Him?" I go down before God for all He wants in me.'[79]

Tomlinson had prayed through a crisis. His uncertainty in regard to his ministry in the mountains vanished as Watson proclaimed the power of a sanctifying and Spirit-filled Gospel. He was now ready to go back to Culberson to fulfill his calling amidst persecutions and whatever the enemy might throw at him – willing also to die if necessary for the sake of the Gospel!

But there was something else drawing him back to the mountains, namely, the Holiness Church at Camp Creek. While in Indiana, he had kept up a correspondence with Bryant, having formed a special bond with him since their first acquaintance in 1899. But their relationship had cooled a little since May 1902 when Bryant and the holiness believers at Camp Creek had yielded finally to Spurling's counsel and agreed to set the church in order. This caused great concern for Tomlinson, for it seemed to turn on its head everything he and Bryant and the fire-baptized believers had agreed upon up to that time in regard to faith and divine order. Tomlinson was in fact deeply entrenched in the doctrine of a spiritual church – an invisible body that was mystically composed of all born again believers. He simply could not relegate the lofty ideals he had attached to a spiritual church to an imperfect visible organization here on earth. To him, what men called the visible church was merely a man-made system of denominations – a thing that was rather to be despised and rejected than elevated and praised. And up to that point, Bryant and the saints at Camp Creek had agreed with him. Thus when Bryant told Tomlinson at his house on one occasion that he and Spurling were talking about setting a church in order, Tomlinson wrote him from Culberson a few days later saying, 'I am afraid of it ... Be careful about this church business. It is dangerous.'[80]

Still, there was a mystery in the Holiness Church at Camp Creek that intrigued and puzzled Tomlinson. He could not rid himself of the idea that there was something special in the move that had united Bryant and Spurling and the saints at Camp Creek in a church union. The fact that Bryant and Spurling were known to be men of God and sober and careful in judgment, and that they were standing 'shoulder to shoulder' haunted him. Reflecting on that time, Bryant recalled that '[Tomlinson] began to get interested in the church a little'.

---

[79] Tomlinson, *Diary*, May 10, 1903.
[80] Bryant/Lemons interview, p. 5.

Tomlinson Joins the Church

When Tomlinson met with Spurling and Bryant and others in Bryant's cabin at Camp Creek on June 12-13, 1903, he had believed up to that point that the church was spiritual and that one was automatically made a part of it by the new birth. But in the Bible study on June 13, the architect of Christian Union persuaded Tomlinson differently. In regard to the idea of a spiritual or invisible church, Tomlinson wrote, 'Brother Spurling knocked that idea out of me in five minutes'.[81] Spurling had convinced him that the church is a visible and corporate body formed on the basis of a church covenant, and that believers are united individually to the church on that same basis.[82] For how, according to Spurling's reasoning, could a false brother 'creep into the church unawares' (Gal. 2.4; Jude 3) if the church was spiritual and invisible? or how could one be 'cast out' of the church (3 John 9, 10) if it was anything but a visible and corporate body? He showed him further that the church is God's government in the earth, ordained to bind and loose in the earth what has been bound and loosed in heaven. He also distinguished the church from the kingdom of God, showing Tomlinson that the latter is spiritual and entered through the new birth, whereas the church is visible and that one is 'added' to it by covenant; in fact what Tomlinson had been calling the spiritual church was nothing more or less than the kingdom of God.[83] Jesus himself had made this distinction in His teachings – that the church is a 'city set on a hill that cannot be hid' (Mt. 5.14); whereas the kingdom of God 'comes not with observation' (Lk. 17.21). Accordingly, the so-called invisible or spiritual church is no more than a myth, a theological fiction. These were eye-opening and life-changing concepts for Tomlinson.

Spurling convinced Tomlinson further that the New Testament church had gradually 'departed from the faith' after the apostles had passed off the scene in the first century, and that this was according to prophecy and history. But he shared the 'good news' also that the church was destined to be restored according to prophecy. More specifically, Spurling dated the church's 'fall' at 325 CE during the reign of Constantine the Great. This date marked the event when Emperor Con-

---

[81] *WWM* (June 22, 1935), p. 4.

[82] See Tomlinson's comments in introducing Spurling to the Eighth Assembly, 1913, *GAM*, p. 97; also *WWM* (June 22, 1935), pp. 1, 4.

[83] This is shown plainly throughout Spurling's writings (e.g. Spurling, *Lost Link*, pp. 18, 19, 40, 41; *COGE* 1.2 (March 15, 1910), p. 3), and supported fully also in Tomlinson's writings (e.g. Tomlinson, *LGC*, pp. 144-203). See further *GAM 1906-1914*, pp. 227-28.

stantine manipulated the bishop of Rome, Sylvester I, and called for an ecumenical council to be held at Nicea near Constantinople ('New Rome') in present-day Turkey. The emperor then presumed himself upon the church and presided over the council, proceeding during the course of that historic meeting to unite the church and state under the authority of the emperor and on the basis of the Nicene Creed.[84]

> Come, children of the Light.
> Leave off your Babylonish strife.
> Her merchandise no longer buy.
> Nor heed the Babylonish cry.
> This mystery is the man of sin,
> In the Apostles' day it did begin,
> To diminish each other's faith,
> With days and years it kept apace.
> Until the days of Constantine,
> It then the church and state combined.
> Dominion to the state did give,
> And caused that horned beast to live.
> Against its powers reformers strove.
> Which caused them in strange lands to rove.
> Though many of them their blood have shed.
> Its lasso rests upon our head.
> – R.G. Spurling[85]

Tomlinson was of course already familiar with restoration theology, for Quakers taught the fall and restoration of the New Testament church,[86] and Sandford had made it the center of his teaching at Shiloh. B.H. Irwin and Charles Fox Parham and other radical holiness preachers also proclaimed a restoration of apostolic Christianity. The big difference in Spurling's restoration doctrine, however, was in regard to the church itself; for he was not so concerned with holiness-Pentecostal themes – second work sanctification, Spirit-baptism, faith healing, and other dynamics of the Gospel – but rather the visible unity and fellowship of God's people in one Christian Union; he envisioned visible un-

---

[84] Spurling, *Lost Link*, pp. 13-25.
[85] Spurling, *Lost Link*, p. 22.
[86] Tomlinson, *LGC*, pp. 165-72; *HAA*, I, pp. 39, 40, 119; and see Phillips, 'Quakerism', pp. 5-6, 10-12, notes 10-11. See also William C. Braithwaite's two volumes: *The Beginnings of Quakerism* [1912] and *The Second Period of Quakerism* [1919] (London: Macmillian and Co., Limited; Rufus M. Jones, *The Latter Periods of Quakerism* (London: Macmillan and Co. Limited, 1921; and D. Elton Trueblood, *The People Called Quakers* (Richmond, IN: Religious Society of Friends, 1975).

ion on the basis of love, freedom, and mutual respect, not hierarchy and creeds.

Spurling's focus on the restoration of the visible government and discipline of God's people as it turned out was thus unique and distinct from all that Tomlinson had ever heard. It remained, however, for Spurling to convince the ex-Quaker that the work he had begun in 1886 was a true restoration of the fallen apostolic church – the government of God for His people. This would seem to have been a difficult task, for Bryant recalled Tomlinson's disagreement with the setting of the Holiness Church in order at Camp Creek in May 1902:

> Tomlinson began to get interested in the church a little. I told him that we were going to set the church in order. He said, 'Who?' I said, 'Me and Brother Spurling'. He wanted to know who ordained us and I told him and he said, 'I am afraid of it'. He went back to his home and wrote me a letter and said, 'Be careful about this church business. It is dangerous.'[87]

But when Tomlinson met with Spurling in Bryant's cabin on the morning of June 13, his resistance was quickly broken down by the elder's wisdom and vision of the church. Tomlinson wrote of the memorable event, 'I poured in the questions and Bible answers were given which perfectly satisfied all my inquiries'.[88]

Still, however, Tomlinson needed something more – some further confirmation deeper in his soul, namely, a personal revelation from God. This he received while in prayer on the mountain behind Bryant's cabin early on Sunday morning, June 13. Bryant notes that when Tomlinson came back down the mountain after prayer, 'he was just a laughing and wanted to shake hands with me'. He said, 'I am satisfied'. I said, 'About what?' He said, 'The church is right ... I am a candidate for the church today'.[89]

The gravity and exuberance of Tomlinson's experience on the mountain transformed him, and as it turned out redirected his ministry and defined him as a leader. Thereupon he united with the church on the basis of Spurling's powerful arguments based on the Scriptures and the assurance of the Spirit in his soul during his mountain-top experience. Tomlinson recalled that special moment during a program conducted at the foot of Burger Mountain in 1941:

---

[87] Bryant/Lemons interview, p. 4.
[88] Tomlinson, *Answering the Call*, p. 17.
[89] Bryant/Lemons interview, p. 5.

I stood right there in front of the fireplace [pointing to the very spot where Bryant's cabin once stood), Brother Spurling, who is gone to heaven, took the Bible and gave it to me. He handed it to me and said, 'Will you take this Bible as the Word of God, believe it and practice it, obey its precepts and walk in the light as God is in the light'. I thought deeply. I remembered what a time I had on the mountain. I meant business. God meant business ... Right here I gave my hand to Brother Spurling ...[90]

Tomlinson had admitted that up until that time he had been like 'a ship at sea with no rudder by which it should be controlled'.[91] The questions that had haunted his spirit since he was saved in 1889 still perplexed his spirit in 1903, namely, Does God have a church, and where is it? His spiritual travail was reminiscent of Spurling's in 1884 when he cried out, 'Where is God's Church? ... Where is Thy government? Oh, God give me light ... give me understanding and let me see the truth'.[92] Reflecting on that moment after his conversion, Tomlinson wrote:

Then came the real conflict: What church should I join? If there had been but one, as was the case in the time of the apostles, I would have been saved from that trouble. I searched and prayed and sought for information from people, books and papers. I was perplexed ... at a crisis. I did not know what to do. They were all different, and none of them really satisfied me, but I felt I must be a member of some church. If I had only known the Bible Church then![93]

Tomlinson was aware that he lacked a firm grounding for his ministry, namely the Bible church's government and discipline. He had investigated many religious movements until he was nearly exhausted, all of them leaving him dissatisfied and confused. His family's local Quaker church in Chester, Indiana that he had joined shortly after his conversion did not fill the hunger in his heart to know and to be a part of the 'fellowship of the mystery', nor had Sandford's Church of the Living God at Shiloh satisfied and settled him. He admitted that he had joined the Quakers 'merely for convenience' and that his experience among them did little more than to help him get started in the ministry; and that his experience with Sandford and Shiloh had ended in disappointment. There were other groups, too, that he had investigated and befriended,

---

[90] Evans, *God's Anointed – Prophet of Wisdom*, pp. 12-13.
[91] Tomlinson, *Answering the Call*, p. 17.
[92] Spurling, *Lost Link*, p. 48.
[93] Tomlinson, *Answering the Call*, p. 5.

but all in vain; for they all denied the existence of a truly divine and visible church in the earth, teaching rather that the true church in its purity and power is ultimately spiritual and mystical.

Tomlinson had become at that point exasperated in his search for God's church. Recall his anguish and turmoil for lack of a firm grounding for his faith. He admitted, 'I had already searched and investigated many movements until my faith in them had completely exhausted. I seemed to be like a ship at sea with no rudder by which it should be controlled'.[94] But on that day – June 13, 1903! – in his meeting with Spurling, Bryant, and the church at Camp Creek – and on the mountain with God! – his heart was fixed and his feet planted in the Church of God. He was finally satisfied and settled.

Figure 50

CABIN HOME OF W.F. BRYANT AT CAMP CREEK[95]

---

[94] Tomlinson, *Answering the Call*, p. 17.

[95] This photo was discovered by the writer in a folder of artifacts connected with the church's early history and identified as the home of W.F. Bryant. Since it corresponds with descriptions of Bryant's house given by eyewitnesses, and otherwise fits perfectly the landscape where Bryant's house stood, it is assumed to be authentic. However, Bryant's daughter, Nora, who lived in the house as a child discounted the claim, recalling some ninety years later that the house seemed larger and more attractive. Three factors may call into question Nora's recollection: first, her ability to recall accurately in 1995 how the house appeared in 1905; second, the house doubtlessly deteriorated some when the photo was taken years later; third, Nora, recalling with a great deal of fondness for her childhood, may have unwittingly embellished the house in her imagination. Suffice it to say, that if the house in this photo is not Bryant's house, it is very similar to it. It is situated on the hill exactly as Bryant's cottage was; it is facing east with the chimney on the south end

Through all of the thrilling episodes of his religious experience among the Quakers, among the people at Shiloh, God's Bible School in Cincinnati and other movements, Tomlinson's thirst to find God's church was never quenched. His heart continued to long for the divine 'restingplace'. Finally in God's providence, and through his work with the American Bible Society, he came upon Spurling, Bryant, and the saints in the mountains of western North Carolina. There his years of searching for God's church would end. He had discovered it! In reference to his experience on the mountain and his revelation of the church, Tomlinson wrote,

> As the discovery was made a shout pierced through [my] soul, and almost before [I] was aware of it, [I] ... was shouting at the top of [my] voice, and leaping and clapping as [I] cried, 'The Church of God! The Church of God!' ...[96]

Figure 51

MOUNTAINTOP REVELATION

Tomlinson returned in November 1939 with some of his followers to the mountaintop behind Bryant's cabin where he had prayed and received his revelation of the church on June 13, 1903. The next November he persuaded Bryant – with whom he had broken fellowship in 1923 – to come with him to confirm the event. Tomlinson marked the spot where he thought he had prayed so earnestly thirty-seven years before. This was the beginning of the Burger Mountain and Fields of the Wood traditions among Tomlinson's followers.

---

exactly as Bryant's was; and it has wood shingles, rough board veneer, and a front porch the same as Bryant's house had.
[96] Tomlinson, *LGC*, p. 159

Tomlinson's experience on the mountain would loom larger and larger in his imagination in his later years, especially after the church divided in 1923 and more especially during his stroke years in 1937-1943. Eventually he would rewrite the church's history from the perspective of his personal revelation on the mountain, and would lead his followers in memorializing his revelation during annual celebrations on the spot where he had 'prayed and prevailed'. In 1939 he returned to Camp Creek with some of his followers to reflect on his mountaintop experience and to purchase property to construct a memorial to mark the event. That was the beginning of the Burger Mountain tradition which today is preserved in the 216 acre biblical theme park called 'Fields of the Wood' located in Cherokee County, North Carolina. But of this we will elaborate further in its place in Volume II.

Tomlinson Pursues His Own Vision

It is true that Spurling had opened Tomlinson's eyes to many important characteristics of the Bible church, and had received him into the church and ordained him; yet Tomlinson had not entered into Spurling's vision, nor was he ever a follower of Spurling. Rather he borrowed certain fundamental principles from Spurling's theology of the church in order to fulfill his own vision; and upon joining the church in 1903 and being appointed by the brethren to be their leader, he immediately went about to fulfill the vision of the church that burned in his own imagination, namely, to remove 'the covering cast over the nations' (Isa. 25.7) and to gather together God's scattered sheep into 'one fold' in answer to Jesus' prayer (Jn 10.16; 11.49-52; 17.20-23; Eph. 1.10; 2.11-19; 3.5).

We have noticed also the deep impression that Frank W. Sandford and the people at Shiloh made on Tomlinson. Anyone familiar with Sandford's ministry at Shiloh and Tomlinson's ministry in the Church of God will see the unmistakable similarities. Sandford's romantic interpretation of Solomon's vision of the prophetic bride – 'Who is she that looks forth as the morning, fair as the moon, clear as the sun, and terrible as an army with banners?' – rooted itself deeply in Tomlinson's imagination, and remained a lively expectation for him throughout his illustrious life and ministry. But, again, in the final analysis, Tomlinson pursued his own vision and sought to fulfill his own destiny. His sense of a peculiar call upon his life, and of being divinely ordained to a peculiar position in the church, precluded him from ever following anyone; for he believed he was ordained to sit at the pinnacle of a divine hierarchy, and it followed as a matter of course that all believers were called to come under his authoritative leadership.

Even before Tomlinson came to the mountains, he had sensed a special and profound call upon his life – a call that God had reaffirmed to him many times since 1894. When he was baptized in the Androscoggin River in October 1897 at Shiloh, he heard a voice say, 'This is my beloved son, in whom I am well pleased',[97] and this 'voice' was ever reassuring him of his special call and purpose in life. Thus when he joined the church at Camp Creek, it was to fulfill his own vision and his promise to God that he would 'gather together a company of people, men and women who feel called of God, to be in the company, and whom God has satisfied me by revelation … [to be] suitable persons and faithful for service'.

Reaching Out on the Basis of Tomlinson's Vision

Immediately upon uniting with the church, Tomlinson's special gifts and leadership abilities were recognized and he was chosen to pastor the church at Camp Creek. Under his zealous and visionary leadership, the church began to grow and expand. In 1904 churches were established in two adjoining states, one in Jones [Morganton], Georgia, and two in Tennessee at Union Grove near Cleveland and in Luskville where M.S. Lemons had already established the work. The church at Camp Creek also enjoyed some growth under Tomlinson's leadership. Four united with the church at the same time that he did in June 1903, one of whom was Tomlinson's co-worker at Culberson, Oscar Withrow, and another Tomlinson's son, Homer; the other two were also likely Tomlinson's co-workers at Culberson. The next year M.S. Lemons and Tomlinson's wife, Mary Jane, joined the church with twelve others.

In 1904-1905 Sunday schools and mission works were established at Wildwood in Cleveland and at Drygo, a small community located about three miles north of Cleveland (the log building where the Drygo church met was located in the middle of where today the Charleston access road intersects with Interstate 75). Also a mission was established in J.H. Simpson's house ('Simpson's Chapel') located north of Charleston, and Spurling had a work going in Isabella, Tennessee near Ducktown.[98] Together there were now four local churches and at least three missions with a total of about 150 members.[99] Now these churches and missions

---

[97] Homer, *Diary*, III, p. 13.
[98] Homer, *Diary*, III, p. 37
[99] Tomlinson, 'Deposition', p. 1708.

were organized and operating apparently under the government and political agreement of Christian Union as it stood in 1895,[100] that is, they were more or less independent bodies united only by the 'ties of love and mutual respect'. But there was a subtle dynamic at work that would soon transform the church, namely, Tomlinson's vision of the church over against Spurling's vision.

The transition of the church from being Spurlingian to Tomlinsonian actually began the moment Tomlinson joined the church in 1903. This may be seen in Tomlinson's obvious omission of the two active Christian Union churches that Spurling had established at Piney Grove and on Paul's Mountain in his history of the church in *The Last Great Conflict*, and in his reports in his dairy and other publications. His historical narrative of the church simply jumps from Barney Creek on August 19, 1886 to the Holiness Church at Camp Creek in May 1902, then jumps again to his union with the church on June 13, 1903. His account then follows the progress of the church under his oversight and never looks back to Spurling's work.[101] But were the churches at Piney Grove and on Paul's Mountain not part of the church at that time? Obviously they were, at least from Spurling's point of view and apparently also from the standpoint of the brethren in those churches, and also according to the Christian Union agreement in 1895. For why else would Andrew Freeman, the pastor of the Piney Grove church, have been recognized in 1906 as an elder and a 'delegate' in the first General Assembly? Granted, Freeman's presence in the first Assembly may have been in one sense that of an observer, in hopes of being able to report back to the brethren in Monroe County that Spurling had not compromised his vision of Christian Union, nor had agreed to centralize the government of the churches according to the rumors then circulating, nor had allowed the man from the North to usurp authority over all of the local churches. Whatever other reasons Freeman may have had in attending the Assembly in January 1906, certainly evaluating the nature of the event and reporting back to the brethren in Christian Union was one of them; for the ministers and members at Piney Grove were extremely skeptical of the call for a General Assembly and the possible implications.

As things turned out, the Christian Union congregations could not have been pleased with Freeman's report, for that Assembly took a stand against the use of tobacco, advised the local churches to start keeping records, and in many other respects 'advised and urged' the lo-

---

[100] Spurling, *Lost Link*, p. 45
[101] Tomlinson, *LGC*, pp. 206-14.

cal churches to conform to Assembly recommendations. Both the content and spirit of the Assembly represented a whole new direction for the churches, certainly a radical change in the 1895 agreement of Christian Union. Obviously, the visible and structural government and polity of the fellowship was going through a radical metamorphosis.

It is rather conspicuous that Freeman did not attend the Assemblies in 1907 and 1908 in Bradley County at Union Grove and Cleveland, and in fact he is never mentioned again after the Assembly in 1906.[102] Moreover, the Piney Grove and Paul's Mountain churches had no representation in the Assemblies after 1906, neither are they mentioned by Tomlinson nor do they appear in any Assembly reports. The only reference we have to these two churches is by implication in a report in the 1909 Assembly, and later in Tomlinson's reflections on the early developments of the church in his court deposition in 1924. Lemons' report of visiting the people on Steer Creek is almost certainly a reference to the church at Piney Grove. But by 1909, the Piney Grove church had already declared independence, and the church on Paul's Mountain had apparently ceased to exist or had been absorbed into the Piney Grove church. Lemons reported that 'some good work [was] done there and some good people but are in need of care and help'.[103] It is likely that Lemons and Spurling visited the Piney Grove people between 1906 and 1909 but apparently had not persuaded them to join in the movement to centralize the government and operations of the churches, virtually to form a universal church.[104] Indeed, it is certain that Spurling himself did not envision universality and centralization in the same way that Tomlinson and Lemons did, that is, as a universal institution with an authoritative center.

There were in fact three different ecclesiological views at work in the church in 1902-1906 represented in Spurling, Tomlinson, and Bryant. In the years to come, these three views would result in three separate organizations: the Original Church of God (represented in Spurling), the Church of God (represented in Bryant), and the Church of God of Prophecy (represented in Tomlinson). We will see in the chapters ahead how the intriguing differences in these three views played out in the di-

---

[102] Freeman died in 1910 at the age of 38; he is buried in the Dehart Cemetery about 3 miles from Piney Grove.

[103] *GAM 1906-1914*, p. 57.

[104] The *Journal* of Charles Timothy Hawk (1874-1960) of Ironsburg shows that Spurling and also Joe Tipton were still active in the Dry Creek, Steer Creek, and Coco Creek vicinities between 1906 and 1913. Tipton preached on occasion in the Coco Creek (Ironsburg) Methodist church during this time (recorded in Hawk's Journal (1906-1913): ZACG Archives).

visions in 1919-1920 and 1922-1923. But for the time being – between 1903 and 1919 – Tomlinson's views prevailed.

Tomlinson was serving in 1905 as pastor of three of the four churches that he counted as being part of the fellowship under his oversight. He was also overseeing the three missions that had been established, and was encouraging the evangelists to reach out into new fields. The unity of the ministers and members at this point was centered primarily in Tomlinson's personality and vision; but an increasing realization was dawning upon some of the leaders that the churches' basis for union was rather flimsy and inadequate. What was needed was a more perfect union formed on the basis of a better system of government and decision-making. Tomlinson wrote, 'Near the close of 1905 the work had so prospered that there began to be a demand for a general gathering together of members from all the churches to consider questions of importance and to search for additional light and knowledge. Accordingly, arrangements were made and a meeting called toward that end'.[105] This was the first step toward a centralized form of government. How well Tomlinson and the other leaders in the church understood at the time all of the implications of this move is not clear,[106] but there was a certain inevitability in centralizing the government of the church under a man like Tomlinson who had a forceful personality and a bent toward an autocratic style of leadership. It invited trouble, for a situation was created that would require special vigilance to avoid the development of the papal-catholic type system that had ruined the apostolic church in the third- and fourth centuries.

Whether or not Tomlinson and the leaders of the church were perfectly cognizant of the implications of their actions at that time is unlikely; but, in any case, a middle ground was being negotiated between Spurling's Baptist-type of government and the kind of papal-episcopal system that Tomlinson advocated. Ever after the call in 1905 to meet in a General Assembly, the church would struggle to hold in tension these two extreme forms of government: a congregational-independency on one hand, and a Roman-type of catholicity on the other; the latter of

---

[105] Tomlinson, *LGC*, pp. 214-15. In his annual address in 1912, Tomlinson recalled that in 1905 the leaders had counseled together in regard to the Scriptural precedent for a general gathering of the church, and had concluded that the annual gatherings of Israel were a pattern that continued in the grace dispensation; and further, that the council at Jerusalem in Acts 15 set the precedent for a General Assembly (*HAA*, I, p. 14).

[106] Homer is more or less right in estimating that about ten years after his conversion in 1889 the vision of the church 'began to dawn upon him', and after 1903, 'began to take form' (*Great Vision of the Church of God*, p. 1).

which was being recapitulated more or less particularly in the mind and actions of Tomlinson.

As early as 1912 a discussion on the Assembly floor revealed the ministers' and members' struggle to understand the apostles' system of government. In introducing M.S. Lemons to speak on the subject, Tomlinson noted that 'the form of church government [in the New Testament] was not democratic, that is, government by the people by majority vote, neither republican in form, that is, governed by the people by representatives selected by them, but it was theocratic in form, a government by the immediate direction of God'. Later, after Lemons had spoken on the question of ordination and church government, the Assembly requested the General Overseer to address the subject. Tomlinson in no uncertain terms suggested a new system of government for the church that was remarkably similar to the Episcopal system in Roman Catholicism. He even acknowledged the similarity, saying, 'Some may say "I know now what you are aiming at, you want to organize a body like the Catholic Church"'. He went on to try to explain away the obvious, but it remained that he and Lemons and others were supplanting Spurling's democratic-type system in Christian Union with a system similar in many respects to the Roman Catholic episcopal system.

Tomlinson was fully convinced in fact that a true theocracy could be built only on the basis of a unique and specially-anointed Man of God at the pinnacle of a hierarchy of executive authority. Again, those familiar with the theology of Frank Sandford and his ministry at Shiloh will see his mark on Tomlinson in this regard. Sandford seemed to exalt the Holy Ghost, but actually he exalted the man through whom the Holy Ghost spoke, namely, God's specially anointed messenger. Speaking in regard to himself, Sandford had declared,

> And you can well afford to hear the voice of the man who has always spoken in behalf of righteousness. I call upon you as you value your soul to heed the words of the man sent of God to warn you – of the man sent to prepare you for the awful presence of Jehovah. I declare to you it will be a fearful day when the Son of God comes ... When He shall say, What did you do with the man I sent? ... with my Forerunner? ... I am come to punish with everlasting destruction them that did not obey the gospel preached by My messenger![107]

We will see later that Tomlinson's effort to superimpose Moses' position in the 'church in the wilderness' over the Church of God was a page taken from Sandford's teaching. In fact, Sandford's pattern of de-

---

[107] Murray, *Sublimity*, p. 310.

velopment in establishing his preeminent position at Shiloh was virtually repeated by Tomlinson in Cleveland. Sandford had taught at Shiloh that the first battle to be fought in order to restore and establish God's church was the position of 'God's anointed leader'. He explained,

> So the very first battle to be fought is the battle of securing, training, and disciplining God's anointed leader, until Divinity can reckon on him, so that whatever God wants done He can be certain will be carried out without His purpose being turned aside by the failures of humanity.[108]

Figure 52

SITE OF THE FIRST GENERAL ASSEMBLY IN 1906

This was the house of Melissa's first husband Drury Shearer who died in 1901. Melissa was a prominent member of the church at Camp Creek. Tomlinson officiated the wedding of Melissa to J.C. Murphy in November 1903, his first such act as an ordained minister. The house became known thereafter as the J.C. Murphy house. Several months after the First Assembly, Murphy died and Melissa sold the house to T.C. Kilpatrick. Murphy had been connected with the mission at Drygo north of Cleveland; before that he had joined the fire-baptized holiness movement, along with J.H. and Julia Simpson and others who became prominent in the early development of the Church of God in Cleveland.

This battle – the effort to establish God's anointed leader – that Sandford had waged at Shiloh between 1893 and 1902, Tomlinson waged

---

[108] Frank W. Sandford, *The Art of the Christian Soldier* (Amherst, NH: The Kingdom Press, 1966), p. 25.

again successfully in the Church of God between 1903 and 1914. But here we are jumping ahead of our narrative; we will elaborate further on this intriguing development and its implications in its proper place.

Centralizing the Government of the Church

The first General Assembly was held in the cottage home of J.C. and Margaret Melissa (Shearer) Murphy at Camp Creek in the dead of winter on January 26-27, 1906 (see below). During the meeting, a snow storm hit the region that more or less shut in the twenty-one delegates to transact the business at hand.[109] The Assembly was based on the model revealed in the book of Acts, particularly in regard to the form of government demonstrated in Acts 15.1-16.5 in which the apostles and elders and the 'whole church' came together to interpret the Scriptures and to decide matters of import. The General Assembly gradually came to be considered the very essence of the church – the essence of the *ekklesia*. It was in particular the divine institution designed and authorized by Christ to 'bind and loose in the earth what is bound and loosed in heaven'. If the church was the 'government of God in the earth', the General Assembly was the 'highest tribunal of authority' for that government in action.

In his 1913 annual address, Tomlinson spoke of the General Assembly as if it had a life and identity of its own. Certainly it was the very voice of the church:

> The Assembly of the Church of God has reached a plane of stupendous immensity. It is no more the tender plant unknown and unknowing as at the time of its birth on the twenty-sixth and twenty-seventh days of January seven years ago ... At the time of its birth it was not known whether it would live or die: but time and evidences prove that it was destined to live and make its mark in the world. Its weak voice was unheard at the start, but it is now assuming such vast proportions that its voice is echoing around the world.

By the time the churches met in January 1907 at Union Grove near Cleveland for the second Assembly, many of the leaders considered the meeting to be indispensable in the church's unfolding venture:[110] and thus the 'officials' in that Assembly – Tomlinson, Bryant, and Lemons –

---

[109] Tomlinson, '[The General Assembly] was born in the midst of a snowstorm in the country home of J.C. Murphy and his faithful wife in Cherokee County ...' (*HAA*, I, p. 20).
[110] *GAM 1906-1914*, p. 17.

believed it was wise and apparently necessary to endorse R.G. Spurling's 1886 credentials that had been signed by his father. The endorsement read, 'We the undersigned in conference held at Union Grove, Tenn. Jan. 12, 1907 endorse the credentials of the above date and signature and hereby set our hands and subscribe to the same'.[111] Obviously they saw in the Assembly a new and higher tribunal of authority.

Many of the church's leaders in fact marked the church's beginning with the first Assembly in 1906 rather than 1886. F.J. Lee responded to an enquiry from a member in Galloway, Florida in 1926 saying, 'The Church of God, in its present existence was set in order January 26, 1906, in the home of J.C. Murphy, Cherokee County, North Carolina'.[112] Tomlinson and Bryant seemed to have believed this also early on, but then changed their views years later, Bryant insisting that the church began in his house on May 15, 1902,[113] Tomlinson going back to Spurling's meeting at Barney Creek on August 19, 1886. Tomlinson, however, would again change his view after the disruption in 1923 marking the beginning of the church with his revelation on the mountain on June 13, 1903 and his declaration, 'This is the Church of God', a concept that his followers would rally around after his death in 1943.

Notwithstanding, most of the ministers and members in 1906 were still inclined to reject centralized authority in the strict sense of the term, understanding the Assembly to be merely a counseling body and solely judicial in nature rather than executive and legislative.[114] Assembly 'findings' were considered more or less informational and imperfect or incomplete, and therefore were not considered 'binding' upon the churches and members. This was certainly the view of men like R.G. Spurling, Andrew Freeman, Joe Tipton, J.H. Simpson, and Alex Hamby, and later men like J.L. Scott and Sam C. Perry.[115] In fact, except for Spurling and Freeman, the ministers and members of the two Christian Union congregations in Monroe County – Piney Grove and Paul's Mountain – flatly rejected the notion of a General Assembly, celebrating

---

[111] A copy of Spurling's license with this endorsement is in 'R.G. Spurling File', ZACG Archives.

[112] 'Letter from Lee to Mrs. W.D. Clark', Galloway, Florida, July 13, 1926 ('F.J. Lee File', ZACG Archives).

[113] Bryant stated, 'The first church was set in order in my house – the Holiness Church of Camp Creek' (Bryant/Lemons interview, pp. 11, 12).

[114] This was a principle adopted in the first Assembly in 1906 and thereafter carefully maintained: 'We do not consider ourselves a legislative or executive body, but judicial only'.

[115] Tipton and Simpson did not attend the first General Assembly, but they were in the church and held the same view that Spurling did in regard to centralized authority and the General Assembly.

and marking more emphatically their independence from the churches under Tomlinson's oversight after the first Assembly in 1906. Thereafter they referred to the fellowship of churches under the governance of the General Assembly as the 'Assembly Church of God'.[116]

Fear of centralization was a legacy for the most part of the church's Baptist roots, particularly the Baptist idealism of local church independence and voluntary cooperation through associations and conventions. The history of persecution and tyranny in Europe's pope-king system of government was still a vivid memory in the minds of Church of God pioneers, and, in fact, in the minds of most Americans at the turn of the

Figure 53

UNION GROVE
SITE OF THE SECOND ASSEMBLY IN 1907

twentieth century. Indeed, the United States itself stood as a constant reminder of the grace and blessedness of religious and personal freedoms. Gradually, however, the General Assembly became authoritative and from it developed a hierarchy of Episcopal authority over the churches. The 'General Assembly of the Churches' eventually became the church's General Assembly, that is, the churches surrendered their autonomy and independence to the General Assembly – the church's 'highest tribunal of authority' – and to the officers representing this authoritative body. As centralization tightened between 1906 and 1919, some internal dissatisfaction emerged, for many held the church's original form of government and polity to be a sacred trust; and the dissatisfaction became stronger and more widespread as Tomlinson pressed for an even tighter centralized authority. Eventually the church would divide

---

[116] Freeman/Prock Interviews, 1992-1995.

over the issue of centralization, first in 1919-1920 and again in 1922-1923, though the latter division was more complicated.

The impact of centralized authority on the church cannot be overemphasized; for until the first Assembly in 1906 the ministers and members understood the church to be a visible and corporate fellowship, but not a universal body, particularly not a universal body that was centrally governed. They held rather that the local churches were virtually independent and autonomous, and that any counsel between the churches was merely advisory; Assembly 'decisions' were thus merely recommendations.[117]

The Case of the Church of God (Holiness)

We may assume that since Tomlinson and Lemons decided to discontinue *The Way* in 1905 and recommended in its place *The Church Herald* – the primary organ for the Church of God Holiness centered in College Mound, Missouri – that they were pretty much in agreement with the teachings of that organization, including more or less their view of the Bible church.[118]

The Church of God Holiness' view of the Bible church was remarkably comparable to Spurling's view including the modifications and adjustments that had been made under Tomlinson's leadership up to 1906. In an article on the Bible church written in 1894 by A.M. Kiergan and reproduced in *The Church Herald* in March 1907, the writer reflecting on the beginning of the 'Holiness Church' said that the 'Spirit-baptized followers of Christ' having been excluded from the common denominations for their stand on holiness

> found themselves without proper and Scriptural fellowship and co-operation. Then the question of the Church forced itself upon our attention, and then began an unprejudiced and conscientious search for the true apostolic church order. This search appealed to history and the New Testament, and has resulted in the development of a

---

[117] Spurling, *Lost Link*, pp. 33, 34. Clearly Spurling was to some degree in 1886 still under the powerful influence of the Baptist tradition, particularly his Missionary [Landmark] Baptist tradition, and almost all of the ministers and members in 1906 were still being governed and guided by a Baptist mind-set in regard to the local churches and general gatherings.

[118] For a fair appraisal of the Church of God (Holiness), see Clarence Eugene Cowen, *A History of the Church of God [Holiness]* (Overland Park, Kansas: Herald and Banner Press, 1949); for a more particular view of the church itself in this tradition, see John P. Brooks, *The Divine Church* (El Dorado Springs, MO: Witt Printing Company, 1891).

> Church polity which we conceive to be anti-sectarian and apostolic, and which has developed without the formulation of ecclesiastical counsels or drafting of a creed ...

The writer then went on to give a theology of the church that is worth quoting here in full, for it captures more or less – except for the church covenant doctrine and the omission of footwashing – the view of the ministers and members of the Churches of God under Spurling's and Tomlinson's leadership between the time the Holiness Church at Camp Creek was set in order in 1902 and the first General Assembly in 1906:

> We came to see that there is but one divine and heaven-sanctioned Church on earth – the Church of God; and so denominated in the Scriptures. We saw likewise that this divine Church is not a sect, and that no sect, as such, is the divine Church. We feel assured that denominational divisions are unwarranted in the Scriptures and unsanctioned by the Lord.
>
> In the Church of God is large liberty for the exercise of personal gifts, and yet an anarchal [*sic*] spirit is not tolerated, as liberty outside of Scripture limits is antichrist. The polity of the Church is very simple. The condition of fellowship in the Church is Scriptural experience of saving grace, and a holy life. Christ is the door into the Church; the passport is justification and regeneration, pure and simple, and not connectional only in the sense that one congregation is bound to all others by a common doctrine, common interest, and order in common with all other congregations of the Church of God. Churches are set in order with elders and deacons. Deacons are the temporal overseers; the elders are the male preaching ministry. Among us women are helpers in the Gospel, and also preach and conduct public services. Deacons are appointed by the congregations where they live or are known, to be ordained to the eldership. They are ordained by laying on of the hands of two or more elders, who also deliver them 'Letters of Commendation' to all the world so long as their life and doctrine comport with the Scriptures. They are not ordained to the ministry of any sect, but of the Church of God, apostolic and world wide. Yet the ministers are responsible to the congregations where they live and labor for their doctrine and conduct. For just cause the Church, by a body of elders, withdraws fellowship from an offending and incorrigible elder and annuls his letter of commendation. An offending layman is disciplined by the congregation according to the New Testament rule covering his case.

The Church of God formulates no creed and enacts no laws for its government. It is not legislative in any sense but purely executive, taking the New Testament as a full and sufficient statement of doctrine and practice.

The doctrines of the Church is what is commonly called evangelical – God the Father, merciful, gracious, and just; Christ the Redeemer of the world; the Holy Ghost, the quickener of conscience, enlightener of the mind, leader and comforter of those who trust in Christ, conviction for sins, salvation by faith, justification, regeneration, adoption, witness of the Spirit, death to carnality total and complete by entire sanctification subsequent to justification and regeneration, growth in grace and eternal glory in heaven to the pure in heart. We believe in the resurrection of the dead, eternal punishment of the wicked, and we practice the ordinances of the Lord's Supper and baptism of water. The local congregations hold property by boards of trustees in trust for the Church of God.

Our motto is 'The world for Christ'. To this end we insist upon personal salvation from all sin, encourage missionary zeal, publish papers, books, and tracts, and aid orphanage work.

Our ministers, like the apostles, have no stated salaries, but receive from the people what they freely contribute to their support. We repudiate as utterly out of keeping with the true spirit of Christianity all worldly expediencies for raising means for the support of the Church, such as festivals, suppers, shows, theatricals, socials and like revelings.[119]

As it turned out, however, the Churches of God now under the preeminent influence of Tomlinson became more aware of the significance and importance of Spurling's doctrine of the visibility of the church and its formation by covenant. Tomlinson enlarged upon the church covenant idea and applied it to his developing idea of a universal church; in fact, it became a doctrinal pillar that set apart the Churches of God from other holiness fellowships; for it incorporated the members and the several churches together into one visible fellowship, enabling them to observe and practice one government between them. Apparently, it was this realization that cooled the relationship between the Church of God Holiness centered in Missouri and the Churches of God

---

[119] A.M. Kiergan, *The Church Herald* (March 1, 1907), pp. 4-5.

centered in Cleveland. By 1906 the two organizations had aborted the move toward a possible union between them.

But was there in fact a union in-the-making between these two fellowships? Let the reader decide for himself. As co-editors of *The Way*, Tomlinson and Lemons wrote in announcing the discontinuance of the paper:

> We have arranged with Bro. George Smith, of College Mound, MO., to fill out your time with *The Church Herald*, a large paper and a weekly in place of a monthly, and full of good reading matter. We will contribute articles and give our reports in this paper. *The Herald* and ourselves are combining our interests more closely. We believe the results from this combination will be fruitful. We want to ask you all kindly to accept this change, as we feel it is the best thing to do.[120]

Notwithstanding the possibility of a merger in the making, or a church union, there were after 1906 no further communications between the two churches, and it seems that the primary reason for the discontinuance was over the doctrine of the Bible church itself, particularly the view of Tomlinson and his followers that the church is strictly visible in nature and is formed on the basis of a covenant; and further, as such, the true church ceased to exist in 325 CE with the usurpation of Emperor Constantine and the Council of Nicea, and it was not visibly restored until Spurling set in order Christian Union in 1886.

The Tomlinson Shift

Ironically, Tomlinson was at this same time pressing Spurling's basic ecclesial concepts and principles into a concrete universalism, and leading the Cleveland-centered churches in a different direction. By the end of 1905 there were subtle indications that certain radical modifications were in the making in regard to Spurling's original vision of the church – modifications that were being suggested in Tomlinson's preaching and actions, and also in Lemons' preaching, the latter of whom had become exceptionally close to Tomlinson and tended to echo and execute his ideas. It is clear in retrospect that Tomlinson was moving toward the formation of a universal church, whether or not he was fully cognizant of it, and that he was positioning himself to sit at the pinnacle of power in the hierarchy of its government. Spurling himself had sown the seeds for the concept of a universal church in his firm insistence on a visible

---

[120] *The Way* 2.9 (September 1905), p. 5.

church to the exclusion of an invisible church, and in his vision for Christian Union. It simply remained for Tomlinson to lead the way in combining Spurling's visible church idea with universality. It was in this manner that the church metamorphosed gradually from being Spurlingian to Tomlinsonian.

The fact that the churches were willing to meet together to discuss and resolve issues represented a major shift in the ministers' and members' understanding of what it meant to be 'the church'.[121] However, this shift was at first not so obvious; for most of the ministers and members understood the General Assembly to be only an 'advisory body', not a centralized controlling authority.[122] Moreover, the fact that the churches until 1911 were still selecting their pastors made the move toward a centralized authority less obvious and less threatening. Further, it seems apparent that the concept of centralized authority was at first in the minds and vision of Tomlinson and Lemons more than anyone else. They saw in the General Assembly the apostolic form of government for the church based on Acts 15.1-16.5, and therefore had committed themselves to reestablish the church on the basis of this model.

The institution of the General Assembly marked the beginning of the church's move toward a centralized and universal form of government and polity with a hierarchical administration, the latter of which emerged naturally out of centralization. It is important to grasp, however, that, while many of the church's pioneers saw the need for a hierarchical administration in the church, they maintained that the church itself was not hierarchical; for the highest authority in the church was not vested in the administration, but in the body of the church itself. It was only on this basis that the shift toward universality and centralization was tolerated, for the prevailing understanding was that each member stood on equal footing before Christ. Further, since every minister and member in good standing was filled with the Spirit of God – the chief Teacher and spiritual Guide of the church – each member was considered potentially

---

[121] Indeed, most of those in Christian Union congregations established by Spurling refused to attend and participate in the first General Assembly. Andrew Freeman was an exception. Charlie Freeman reported to this writer in June 1995 that Christian Union members identified the ministers and churches who aligned themselves with the General Assembly as the 'Assembly Church of God'. They considered the institution of the General Assembly to be an act of 'departing from the faith'.

[122] Thus the words 'recommend' and 'advise' are used many times in the First Assembly to express and convey the sense and counsel of the Assembly in regard to subjects considered.

Institutional Transformation: 1906-1915

Figure 54

FIRST GENERAL ASSEMBLY 'DELEGATES'

Twenty-one ministers and members attended the first General Assembly on January 26-27, 1906 in the home of J.C. and Melissa [Shearer] Murphy at Camp Creek, North Carolina. Photos of Theophilus Ellis, Nancy S. Ellis, and Andrew Freeman have not been discovered.

qualified to participate in the decision-making process. However, the church very early limited the decision-making process to male members, encouraging women to participate through their husbands and church elders. This policy revealed yet again the Baptist influence on the church in its formative years, accepting the traditional Baptist interpretation of such passages as 1 Cor. 14.28; 1 Tim. 2.11, 12. Assembly resolutions were adopted also only on the basis of the principle of 'one accord'.[123] The essential nature of the church therefore was not hierarchical, for all of the members were considered a vital part of the judicial process.[124]

But there was another factor considered to be indispensable in the government and decision-making process of the church, namely, the importance of the interaction of the Spirit of God with the ministers and members. Church of God pioneers understood that the dynamic presence of the Spirit, operating in harmony with the objective authority of the Holy Scriptures, is primarily what makes the church a *theocratic* form of government, particularly in contrast with other forms of government – monarchical, Episcopal, Presbyterian, democratic, republican, congregational, etc. They endeavored therefore to maintain the principle of 'it seemed good to the Holy Ghost, and to us' (Acts 15.28). The acute self-consciousness of this fact – that the Holy Spirit must be manifestly in charge – is what kept the early pioneers on their knees and sober before the Lord, for they held that 'God's church existed only where His law and government was observed by His children'.[125]

The importance of the pioneers' understanding of the church as being God's government in the world cannot be overstated; for it gave them their reason-for-being and governed almost their every decision and action. Their profound awareness that the term 'church' signifies God's 'government', kept them sober, prayerful, and keenly self-conscious of their responsibility as members of Christ and His government. Thus, when they assembled together to act *for* and *with* God, they consecrated themselves in order to be fit instruments – ambassadors, governors, ministers – of His government in the earth. Like Jacob,

---

[123] This was a vital principle of church polity established in the first Assembly in 1906, and carefully restated many times in succeeding Assemblies. See *GAM* of 1st Assembly, pp. 9, 10; also Phillips, 'The First General Assembly: The Move Toward Centralized Government', *Church of God History & Heritage* (Winter 2006), pp. 1-2.

[124] The following motto or ruling was the first order of business adopted in the First General Assembly: 'We do not consider ourselves a legislative or executive body, but judicial only'. Further, the Assembly was modeled on the basis of the council at Jerusalem recorded in Acts 15 in which apparently the 'whole church' – 'the apostles and elders and brethren' – participated (vv. 12, 22, 23, 25, 28).

[125] Tomlinson, *LGC*, p. 206

when he received the revelation of God's house and its purpose, they said, 'How dreadful is this place! This is none other but the house of God, and this is the gate of heaven' (Gen. 28.16, 17). Like father Abraham and all of the faithful in the Old Testament, they saw the promises of God 'afar off', including the perfection of the church and their reward of positions in the millennial government. They were thus 'persuaded of [the promises], and embraced them, and confessed that they were strangers and pilgrims in the earth' (Heb. 11.13). Indeed, they 'looked for a city which has foundations whose builder and maker is God' (Heb. 11.10).

Completing the Pentecostal Transformation

We have noticed that the seed for modern-day Pentecostalism was planted by the fire-baptized holiness movement in 1895-1900, and that this movement transformed Spurling's Christian Union congregations virtually into a holiness-Pentecostal fellowship in 1898-1902. Still, however, the popular view of modern Pentecostalism marked the beginning of the movement with the work of W.J. Seymour and the outpouring of the Spirit at the Azusa Street mission in Los Angeles in April 1906. Ironically, the leaders in Church of God accepted this popular interpretation,[126] and therefore did not claim to be a part of the Pentecostal movement before 1906. It was not until after the dispute over speaking in tongues in 1909-1910 between A.J. Tomlinson and his followers and the faction led by J.B. Goins and J.H. Simpson that the Church of God clearly identified itself with the Pentecostal movement.[127]

This intriguing fact forces us to rewind history and examine the events as they unfolded in the church at that time. We noticed that there was a theology of tongues-speech developing in the fire-baptized movement in 1898-1900 in connection with the baptism with the Holy Ghost and fire; but after Irwin's fall from grace became public knowledge in June 1900 and the fire-baptized saints were scattered, interest in the manifestation of tongues-speech faded, particularly in regard to connecting speaking in tongues with Spirit-baptism. Then too, the understanding of tongues-speech in the FBHA in 1898-1900 never evolved into the 'initial evidence' formula. *Glossolalia* was considered to be only one manifestation of the dynamic continuum of spiritual experience subsequent to entire sanctification, and possibly, as indicated in

---

[126] 'History of Pentecost', *FS* 1.6, pp. 6, 7.
[127] See 'Completing the Pentecostal Transformation' in Chapter 4.

Stewart Irwin's interpretation, the evidence that specifically identified the baptism of lyddite. But whatever theological interpretation was working its way out of the fire-baptized saints in regard to *glossolalia*, it was aborted by Irwin's fall from grace and resignation in the spring of 1900. Eventually J.H. King and the ministers in the FBHA ceased to teach and practice the doctrine of multiple baptisms subsequent to the two-fold baptism of the Holy Ghost *and fire*, and interest in the particular manifestation of speaking in tongues faded away along with the baptisms of lyddite, oxidite, and selenite.

Interest in the doctrine of speaking in tongues in the Church of God was not rekindled until news of the revival at Azusa Street in Los Angeles reached the southeastern states via the ministry of G.B. Cashwell beginning in late December 1906. A leading minister in the Pentecostal Holiness Church from Dunn, North Carolina, Cashwell had traveled to Los Angeles in November 1906 to investigate the news of the Pentecostal outpouring, and while there became fully convinced of the doctrine and experience and was himself Spirit-baptized. He returned to North Carolina full of the Spirit and began to publish the Pentecostal movement throughout the Southeast, becoming celebrated as the 'Apostle of Pentecost in the South'.[128]

The FBHA (FBHC after 1902),[129] led by J.H. King, accepted the Azusa Street interpretation of Spirit-baptism via Cashwell and in 1908 entered the Pentecostal movement. The movement swept the South like a swirling tornado; thousands of fire-baptized and radical holiness believers were Spirit-baptized with the evidence of speaking in tongues, and thousands more were awakened to the fact that they had already been Spirit-baptized, based on the light of the new Pentecostal formula of 'speaking in tongues as the Spirit gives utterance'.

Tomlinson, being a subscriber and regular reader of *The Way of Faith* magazine published by J.M. Pike in Columbia, South Carolina had almost certainly read the reports by Frank Bartleman and others of the Azusa Street outpouring, and thereby had become interested in the Pentecostal baptism.[130] In the second General Assembly held in January 1907 at Union Grove near Cleveland, Tomlinson included the 'Gifts of the Spirit' as one of the important subjects to study. Henry C. McNabb

---

[128] Vinson Synan, 'Gaston Barton Cashwell', in *The New International Dictionary of Pentecostal and Charismatic Movements* (Grand Rapids, MI: Zondervan), pp. 457-58.

[129] After King succeeded Irwin as General Overseer of the FBHA, he had the word 'Church' substituted for the word 'Association' – thus in 1902 the name of the organization became Fire-Baptized Holiness Church.

[130] A.J. Tomlinson, 'Letter to J.M. Pike', October 22, 1908, pp. 1, 3.

was assigned to address the subject, who, interestingly enough, was the son of Milton McNabb and the son-in-law of J.H. Simpson. Some comments and discussion by Spurling, Lemons, Bryant, and Alexander 'Elic' Hamby followed McNabb's message on the subject. McNabb then felt led to sing impromptu, and the power of God fell on the delegates amidst shouting and various other manifestations of the Spirit.[131] That evening, Tomlinson preached on the subject, 'The Baptism with the Holy Ghost and Fire'.[132] Unfortunately no record exists that reveals the precise content of his message, but we have every reason to believe that mention was made of the reports then circulating in regard to the mighty outpourings of the Spirit in Los Angeles and other places around the country. There is no indication, however, in the *Assembly Minutes* or in Tomlinson's *Diary* that he promoted at that time the Pentecostal movement's new formula for Spirit-baptism, that is, tongues as initial evidence; indeed, it is unlikely for he himself was still unsettled on the issue.

Nevertheless, his interest in the Pentecostal movement continued to build, and in June 1907 he traveled to Birmingham, Alabama with M.S. Lemons to observe the Pentecostal revival being conducted by M.M. Pinson and H.G. Rogers, future founders of the Assemblies of God. Cashwell showed up in this meeting and it is likely that Tomlinson met him at that time. In any case, it is apparent that Tomlinson and Lemons became fully convinced in this meeting that speaking in tongues is the evidence of Spirit-baptism, and they began to seek for the experience, bringing back the doctrine with them to Cleveland. Tomlinson recorded in his *Diary* for June 14, 1907, 'Returned home yesterday from Birmingham, Ala., where I have been for a week in a meeting with Bro. M.M. Pinson. Glorious results. Speaking in tongues by the Holy Ghost'. Lemons confirms in his interview with Chesser that it was in the Birmingham meeting that 'we really heard of the Holy Ghost and speaking in tongues', noting also that he and Tomlinson had prayed to be Spirit-baptized, but had failed to pray through at that time.[133]

Sometime after this meeting in Birmingham, Tomlinson wrote to J.M. Pike requesting his opinion of Cashwell.[134] After receiving a favorable response, Tomlinson invited Cashwell to speak in the Third Annual Assembly in the new tabernacle in Cleveland. The 'Apostle of Pentecost in the South' spoke on two occasions, and on January 12, 1908 while he was expounding on Spirit-baptism with the evidence of

---

[131] *GAM 1906-1914*, pp. 35, 36.
[132] *GAM 1906-1914*, p. 37.
[133] Bryant/Lemons interview, p. 15.
[134] Tomlinson, 'Letter to J.M. Pike', p. 1.

speaking in tongues, Tomlinson fell from his chair to the floor beside him under the power of God. He described in detail his dynamic Pentecostal baptism in a letter to Pike in October 1908:

> [Cashwell] came on the 10th of Jan. 1908. On the 12th of the same month, under the second sermon I heard him preach, I fell off my chair on the platform right beside him and from that moment the Holy Ghost took control and I yielded all to Him and I did not rise for about 3 or 4 hours and after I had received the full Pentecostal baptism, and according to reports, had spoken in about 10 different languages.
>
> Among the many different manifestations I was taken through was the following night. While lying flat of my back I was filled with wonderful joy and while I laughed on account of this great joy my hands and arms were completely controlled by an unseen force and they would rise to meet each other above my body and I could feel them as they were clapped together a number of times. At another time during the same experience a sheet of power seemed to come down all over and around me while lying flat of my back and enveloped me and lifted me up off of the floor and carried me in the air in the direction of my feet and gently let me down again in about the same position that I was in when taken up.
>
> I could feel the power take hold of me just as sensible as if some one touched me. Bro. Pike this is indeed wonderful, and instead of gradually wearing away as might be supposed it is constantly increasing. I don't mean by this that this special power is felt in the same way all the time but there is a real development in my life that has never appeared before. The effect of my ministry is so different ...[135]

Years later, while reflecting on his Spirit-baptism in 1908, Tomlinson added,

> Then came a very interesting part of the experience – 'They shall see visions'. In vision I was carried to Central America, and was shown the awful condition of the people there. A paroxysm of suffering came over me as I seemed to be in soul-travail for their salvation. Then I spoke in tongues as the Spirit gave utterance, and in the vision I seemed to be speaking the very same language of the Indian tribes with whom I was surrounded. Then, after a little rest, I was carried in vision to South America, and of all the black pictures that

---

[135] Tomlinson, 'Letter to J.M. Pike', pp. 1-3.

were ever painted that was surely the blackest. The vision settled on Brazil, and after another paroxysm of suffering or soul-travail the Spirit spoke again in another tongue; then after a little relaxation I was carried to Chili, with the same effects and results; then in like manner to Patagonia, away down among the illiterate Indians. Each place I was shown, I gave assent in my spirit to go to them. From Patagonia to Africa, and on to Jerusalem; and while there I endured the most intense suffering, as if I might have been suffering similar to that of my Savior on Mount Calvary. I never can describe the awful agony that I felt in my body. After every paroxysm of suffering came a tongue. From Jerusalem I was carried to Northern Russia, then to France, thence to Japan; and then I seemed to get back to the United States, but soon I was taken away North among the Esquimaux. While there, the language of the Spirit spoken through me seemed similar to the bark of a dog. I was carried to a number of other places in a similar manner. I must not fail to tell of the terrible conflict I had in the vision with the devil. I came into direct contact with him. While in this state, there came the most awful struggle of all. While talking in an unknown tongue the Spirit seemed to envelope me, and I was taken through a course of casting out devils ... and the last verses of Mark sixteen came very vividly before my mind.[136]

After this glorious immersion into the Spirit, Tomlinson began zealously to promote the Pentecostal movement's interpretation of Spirit-baptism and endeavored to transform the Church of God completely into a Pentecostal body. In June, Tomlinson began a meeting in the new tabernacle in Cleveland along Pentecostal lines. He noted in his report to Pike: in 'the fifth service the power of God fell and some [of the people] fell to the floor screaming. The next service three received the baptism of the Holy Ghost and spoke in tongues as the Spirit gave utterance'.[137] After this, Tomlinson arranged for the church to pitch a tent on Central Avenue 'and the work commenced in earnest, and continued every day and night for ten weeks ... The meetings were opened at 3 P. M. and would frequently continue until 12 and 2 o'clock at night'. Thousands attended this glorious revival, some from ten and fifteen miles distance. The revival resulted in 163 being baptized with the Holy Ghost and 228 making a profession of salvation.[138]

---

[136] Tomlinson, *Answering the Call*, pp. 11, 12.
[137] A.J. Tomlinson, 'Pentecostal Power and Manifestations at Cleveland, Tenn. 'Letter and report to J.M. Pike', October 22, 1908, p. 1.
[138] Tomlinson, 'Pentecostal Power and Manifestations', p. 3.

Notwithstanding the glory and transforming power in this revival, Tomlinson noted that there was much opposition including a great many which rejected speaking in tongues as the evidence of Spirit-baptism. 'Were it not for the tongues being the sign of the baptism, and had we not held down on that as the evidence in the teaching, no doubt many more would have claimed the Baptism. If we had wanted to count numbers in preference to genuineness we could have counted many more'.[139]

Among those who rejected tongues-speech as the sign of Spirit-baptism were the assistant pastor of the Cleveland church, John B. Goins, and the church's prominent deacon, J.H. Simpson, and their followers.

The Disruption of 1909-1910

Since very little is known about J.H. Simpson and J.B. Goins and the disruption of the church in 1909-1910, and almost nothing has been written about this important episode in the church's history, we will elaborate upon it here as it unfolded beginning early in 1900. Simpson and his wife had been connected with the fire-baptized holiness movement since 1899; before that, they had been staunch Baptists. Two of his daughters had married the sons of Milton McNabb,[140] the latter of whom was one of the three evangelists who had brought the fire-baptized message to Camp Creek in the late 1890s.[141] The Simpsons as well as the McNabbs were therefore prominent and active in the developing holiness movement. Simpson's wife, Julia, wrote in April 1900 in *Live Coals of Fire* an article revealing her and her husband's Baptist background and their transition into the fire-baptized holiness movement; Simpson's eldest daughter, Minnie, wrote in *The Way* in March 1905 an article showing the family's transition into the Church of God.[142]

Soon after Simpson moved to Cleveland, he established a general mercantile located at 101 East Central Avenue, dealing in 'dry goods, shoes, and groceries'.[143] The name of his business was 'J.H. Simpson &

---

[139] Tomlinson, 'Pentecostal Power and Manifestations', p. 3.
[140] Genealogical Records of Elias Milton McNabb and Jacob H. Simpson: (ZACG Archives).
[141] Tomlinson, *LGC*, p. 207.
[142] *The Way*, inaugurated in 1904 by Tomlinson and M.S. Lemons, was discontinued in September 1905.
[143] This was specified on the letterhead of Simpson's business stationary (ZACG Archives).

Son'. He began to worship with Tomlinson in private homes and became a charter member of the church in Cleveland when it was organized on October 10, 1906. He was ordained shortly thereafter as a deacon and became prominent in the church with his wife and fifteen children. He paid the token fee of one dollar, a legal formality, for the land donated by F.J. Loomis to the church on the corner of Eleventh and Peoples Streets,[144] and contributed substantially in time and labor as well as finances to the construction of the house of worship in 1907.[145]

Notwithstanding Simpson's prominence, Tomlinson received complaints constantly against Simpson's apparent harshness and domineering spirit, which created strained relationships between Simpson and some of the church's prominent leaders – W.F. Bryant, M.S. Lemons, H.L. Trim, *et al*.[146] – and made circumstances in the church in Cleveland difficult. The situation became more problematic after Pentecost came to Cleveland in 1908. Simpson never got in the spirit of it, rejected the revival from the beginning and grew sour. Tomlinson noted in January 1909, 'J.H. Simpson has been causing us trouble by division and offences and contentions for several months'.[147] His tendency to be legalistic and harsh showed up all the more against the joy and glory of the Pentecostal manifestations that filled the church. The church had grown from sixty members late in 1907 to more than two hundred by October 1908, and Simpson and his family were left behind clinging to a pre-Pentecostal mind-set. Unwilling to submit to the new light, he rose against it with a vengeance and created havoc in the church. Finally, on January 2, 1909, only four days before the fourth General Assembly, Simpson was brought before the church in conference. After 'considerable persuasion' by Tomlinson, and with tears and agonizing prayer by the church to no avail, Simpson was excluded based on the instruction in Rom. 16.17,[148] though Spurling apparently disagreed with the action.[149] Simpson did not take the decision lightly and began to campaign

---

[144] Testimony of Ethel [Simpson] Robertson, 'Letter to Tomlinson', dated November 18, 1984 ('J.H. Simpson File', ZACG Archives); see also A.J. Lawson, 'Deposition', p. 1558.

[145] Tomlinson, *Diary:* February 1, 1909; letter from Simpson to Tomlinson, March 1, 1909 (ZACG Archives).

[146] 'Letter from Eva M. [Simpson] Crittenden to Tomlinson', March 2, 1909 ('J.H. Simpson File', ZACG Archives).

[147] Tomlinson, *Diary*, January 2, 1909.

[148] Tomlinson, *Diary*, January 2, 1909.

[149] 'Letter from Simpson to Tomlinson', February 2, 1909: 'Brother Sperling sed [*sic*] you had no rite [*sic*] to turn me out and I can prove it by him and others' ('J.H. Simpson File', ZACG Archives).

against Tomlinson and those who sided with him in the dispute. He and his family sent a barrage of harsh letters to Tomlinson, accusing him of being unjust and a lord, and charging Bryant and others also with various indiscretions including abuse of their trust as stewards. He threatened further to sue the church if he was not reinstated.[150]

Simpson found a sympathetic ear in John B. Goins after the latter had moved to Cleveland in August 1909. Goins had been baptized with the Spirit on July 18, 1906 in Griffin, Georgia in another organization. Shortly thereafter his minister's license was revoked and he was excluded from that denomination.[151] He then established an independent Pentecostal church at Florence, Alabama in 1907.[152] He came in contact with Church of God ministers about that time, and while attending a Pentecostal convention in Memphis was ordained by Tomlinson and L.P. Adams on November 22, 1908.[153] On April 15 of the next year Tomlinson conducted a revival at Goins' church in Florence,[154] and made arrangements at that time to bring him to Cleveland to serve as his assistant pastor. Goins was fairly well educated and extremely zealous for the new Pentecostal experience and message and seemed to be a promising minister for the church; however, when he arrived in Cleveland he was met with the trouble still brewing over Simpson's exclusion.[155] Simpson's complaints and negative influence only magnified what already seemed to Goins to be fanatical behavior in the Cleveland church, particularly on the part of some of the leaders including Tomlinson, Bryant, and Lemons.[156] Further, he disagreed with the doctrine that the church is a visible body formalized by a church covenant.[157] Before he came to Cleveland he had written in *The Bridegroom's Messenger*, 'There is not a council of men on earth today that is able to set down rules to write out a discipline that will be able to govern the church of God. Men have tried to do that but have failed'.[158] Eventually Goins recanted his Pentecostal testimony, denounced speaking in tongues

---

[150] 'Letters from Simpson to Tomlinson', January 30, February 2, 22, March 1, 1909; 'Letters from Mamie and Ethel Simpson to Tomlinson', January 31, 1909; Julia Simpson to Tomlinson, n.d.; Eva M. [Simpson] Crittenden to Tomlinson, March 2, 1909. ('J.H. Simpson File', ZACG Archives).

[151] *TBM* 1.2 (Nov 1, 1907), p. 2.

[152] *TBM* 1.2 (Nov 1, 1907), p. 2.

[153] Tomlinson, *Diary*, November 26, 1908; John B. Goins' *Certificate of Ordination* (copy in ZACG Archives).

[154] Tomlinson, *Diary*, April 15, 1909.

[155] *Cleveland Herald* (January 13, 1909).

[156] *Cleveland Herald* (January 13, 1909).

[157] 'Letter from Goins to Tomlinson', April 1910 (ZACG Archives).

[158] *TBM* 2.30 (January 15, 1909), p. 2.

without an interpreter, questioned the operation of spiritual gifts in general, and denied that tongues-speech was a necessary evidence of Spirit-baptism.[159]

During the course of these things in Cleveland, serious accusations of adultery against Goins were coming to Tomlinson's office from the church Goins had left at Florence.[160] These accusations were supported by messages and interpretations which Tomlinson discounted as a means to charge Goins.[161] To what extent the rumors and accusations pushed Goins in the direction he already was headed, namely, to recant his Pentecostal experience and rebel against the government of the church, is difficult to tell; but certainly they weighed heavily upon him.[162] In any case, Goins gravitated toward Simpson and his faction of disgruntled members and soon realized complete affinity with them and became their leader. This was an opening for which Simpson had eagerly awaited. While Tomlinson was in Florida in October-November 1909 evangelizing and establishing churches, Goins denounced him as a heretic, went through the motions of revoking his ministry, and threatened to have him 'expelled' altogether from the church.[163] Now working closely with Simpson, P.A. Wingo, Ralph Aikman, and others, Goins made every effort to seize control of the church.[164] A.J. Lawson, Bryant, Lemons, Mary Jane, and Homer all wrote to Tomlinson about the trouble, advising him to return home as soon as possible.[165] During the confrontational business conference that followed, only forty-three stood with Goins; whereupon Goins turned in his license to Tomlinson and declared independence.[166] Tomlinson went home and burned his license. An ugly struggle followed, turning into a physical brawl at one point. In his typical fashion, Tomlinson described the awful scene as colorfully as he could:

---

[159] 'Letters from Simpson to Tomlinson', January 30, March 2, 1909 (ZACG Archives); Duggar, *A.J. Tomlinson*, p. 84; and Homer, *The Great Vision of the Church of God*, p. 10.
[160] Noah Patrick, Oak Waldrep, Joe Patrick to Tomlinson, August 11, 1909; Noah Patrick to Tomlinson, August 15, 1909; P.E. Cramblit to Tomlinson, August 23, September 3, 1909; L.O. Waldrep to Tomlinson, December 13, 1909, ('A.J. Tomlinson File', ZACG Archives).
[161] 'Letter from Tomlinson to Noah Patrick, Oak Waldrep, and Joe Patrick', August 30, 1909 (ZACG Archives)
[162] 'Letter from Goins to P.E. Cramblit', August 16, 1909 ('Tomlinson File', ZACG Archives)
[163] Homer, *Diary*, I, pp. 85-89; *idem*, *The Great Vision*, p. 10.
[164] Tomlinson, *Diary*, November 10, 1909.
[165] Homer, *Diary*, I, pp. 74-80. Bryant was illiterate and thus dictated his letter via Homer.
[166] Tomlinson, *Diary*, December 1, 1909.

I received a letter from home saying 'more trouble'. The Goins-Simpson crowd came into the meeting demanding the use of the house half the time. On being refused, Homer Simpson made for Bro. Bryant and Sr. Scoggins stepped between them. I don't know it all, but Bro. McMannen tried to preach and could not for the disorder caused by those parties, so they closed the meeting. The janitor [a relative of M.S. Lemons] began to put out the lights, when Homer Simpson forbid [sic] him, and as he was going on with it, Ralph Aikman grabbed him (the janitor). Lemons (janitor, and not even a Christian) gave Aikman a good shaking up, when the two Simpsons (Homer Simpson and his father, J.H. Simpson) and Goins piled on Lemons, and he was too much for all of them. Homer Simpson took up a chair and struck Lemons with it, and Lemons wrenched it out of his hands and ran the whole bunch off.[167]

The ordeal wound up in the courts and in the newspapers and brought a reproach upon the church.[168] The court ruled that the Goins-Simpson faction could use the church's facilities every other week. This was unacceptable to Tomlinson and the church, but the situation continued for nearly a year before the church finally won the legal right to have complete control of the building again.[169] Goins returned to Florence, Alabama and proceeded to divide the church there at Sunnyside. He named his independent organization, Sunnyside Street Holiness Church.[170] Goins came back to Tomlinson thirty years later, made restitution to the church and re-joined on March 26, 1939. The church rejoiced.[171] However, within a few days he regressed to his old complaints about fanaticism and on April 10th was again excluded.[172] Simpson remained in Cleveland, became active in politics, succeeding in 1920-1921 to obtain a seat in the Tennessee state legislature representing Bradley and Polk counties.[173] He died on November 3, 1936 and is buried in Fort Hill cemetery near Tomlinson.[174]

---

[167] Homer, *Diary*, I, p. 138.
[168] 'Holiness Preachers In Toils Of The Law', *The Journal and Banner* (July 23, 1909); 'Holiness Preachers Appeal Case To Court', *The Journal and Banner* (July 27, 1909).
[169] Duggar, *Tomlinson*, pp. 82-86; and Homer, *Diary*, I, pp. 88-89.
[170] 'Letter from Goins to Tomlinson', March 30, 1910.
[171] Tomlinson, *Diary*, March 30, 1939.
[172] Tomlinson, *Diary*, April 5, 14, 1939; Homer, *Diary*, I, p. 89.
[173] *Biographical Directory, Tennessee General Assembly 1796-1969* (Tennessee State Library and Archives), pp. 17-18.
[174] Interestingly, when Jacob died, Julia rode a train to California and married Milton McNabb [his wife having recently died]. They were reportedly happy for a

Notwithstanding the trouble and confusion caused by the Goins-Simpson schism, the Pentecostal wave that flooded the church in 1908 was too widespread and forceful to be abated by skepticism, ridicule, or theological contradiction. All resistance to the Pentecostal baptism was soon overwhelmed, and in August 1910 the church published in the *Evangel* a list of twenty-five 'prominent teachings' two of which were 'Baptism with the Holy Ghost subsequent to cleansing' and 'The speaking in tongues as the evidence of the baptism with the Holy Ghost'.[175] It was further agreed upon in the 1911 Assembly that these two teachings with twenty-three others be published in tract form.[176] The controversy and schism in 1909-1910 had settled the matter; the church ever after was firmly established in the classical Pentecostal tradition.

Figure 55

J.H. SIMPSON AND
WIFE JULIA [MADDOX] (C. 1912)

Figure 56

A.J. TOMLINSON
(C. 1910)

Some have confused the Assembly issue and discussion in 1911 in regard to the 'Abiding of the Holy Spirit' with the 'Baptism with the Holy Ghost'. However, it was commonly understood at that time by most holiness-Pentecostals including Church of God people that the 'Abiding of the Holy Spirit' had to do with salvation and more particularly with sanctification, not the 'Baptism with the Holy Ghost'. After a discourse by R.G. Spurling, and some further comments and discussion by a number of brethren, everyone 'seemed to see eye to eye [that] some manifestations of the graces, gifts and fruits of the Spirit would evidence

---

time and then Milton died. Julia returned to Cleveland and died at the age of eighty-three. Some of this information was received from Simpson's grandson, Harold Davis ('J.H. Simpson File', ZACG Archives).

[175] *COGE* 1.12 (August 15, 1910), p. 3.
[176] *GAM 1906-1914*, pp. 85-91.

the abiding of the Spirit'.[177] Again, this issue had to do with the manifest fruit of sanctification, not the baptism with the Holy Spirit.

Development of an Episcopal Hierarchy

We noticed earlier that the development of an Episcopal hierarchy naturally emerged after the church centralized its government. For just as a visible local church must have a pastor and deacons and ministers to function properly and efficiently, so a corporate universal church must have a pastor – a 'General Overseer' – and servants under him to operate and oversee the various ministries and business affairs of the church. Still, all hierarchies are not the same; Presbyterian bodies, for example, do not culminate at the top in a single office but in a council made up of a plurality of men and women. Early Presbyterians, in contrast with Congregationalists, saw in the New Testament an external government that unified and moderated between the churches, yet they devised their system so as to avoid the error of papal Rome, that is, in locating final authority in a solitary office occupied by one man – the pope. Interestingly, the Church of God's hierarchical system, which culminated at the top in the office of the General Overseer, resembled more the Roman Catholic hierarchical system than the Presbyterian system.

The development of the office of General Overseer in the Church of God, and the hierarchy built down from it, grew out of the pioneers' growing understanding of a visible universal church, but also out of Tomlinson's personal vision of his own peculiar calling and sense of prophetic destiny.[178] Like Sandford, Tomlinson disdained 'headless' systems like that of the Baptists and Congregationalists and independent 'free holiness' groups, believing that divine order requires necessarily a specially anointed man to be the head of God's government in this present world.

We noticed earlier that Tomlinson found in the writings of certain early church fathers – Eusebius, Hegessippus, *et al.* – justification for his theology of an exalted position atop the pinnacle of an Episcopal hierarchy. Unfortunately, it was these same church fathers and their writings that paved the road in the second, third, and fourth centuries that led to the Roman Catholic papal system. Tomlinson's admiration of these church fathers and their writings caused him unwittingly to follow their

---

[177] *GAM 1906-1914*, pp. 85-87.
[178] Phillips, 'Quakerism', pp. 2-7.

inspiration and counsel in developing a similar system in the Church of God.

The great majority of Tomlinson's followers did not at first see the similarity between the administrative structure that he was endeavoring to build and the Roman Catholic system; indeed, Tomlinson himself seemed to be blinded to the obvious similarity. What the pioneers were focused on was the need for divine government and order with able leaders who could administrate and coordinate the work to fulfill the church's mission in the world. And they saw in Tomlinson a gifted and prepared leader who seemed to be the natural choice to head up such a government and organization. Certainly Tomlinson's natural abilities and formal education put him head and shoulders above almost everyone in the church in its early years.[179] He was considered outstanding even by men of the stature of Lemons and F.J. Lee. Moreover, the office was being conceived and formed at the same time that great pains were being taken to restore the church's apostolic form of government and ministry. Now as Tomlinson was the chief architect and prime mover in this development, it was inevitable that Sandford's ideas would find their way in the construction of the Church of God's government and political system, for Tomlinson was still deeply affected by the teachings he had received at Shiloh. Accordingly, Tomlinson taught the church to look for modern-day apostles who could take the church 'on to perfection'. The office of apostle was considered by many in the church including Tomlinson to be needful for the church's full restoration, and thus the people were encouraged to watch for signs in ministers that could identify them as last days apostles.[180]

---

[179] He was educated at Westfield, Indiana's renowned Union Academy (Homer, *Diary*, I, pp. 1, 11). This school was rated as one of the best high schools in America in the late nineteenth century. John J. Baldwin wrote early in the century, 'One can hardly find a locality between the Atlantic and the Pacific where there is not someone who has heard of Westfield and Union High' (John F. Haines, *History of Hamilton County, Indiana*, 1915, p. 31). Haines noted that 'many graduates of Union High were as proud of their credentials as if they had graduated from Harvard, Yale, or Princeton. Records do show that men and women of "great moral fiber" did go out from the school to fill with distinction positions of honor and responsibility in life' (p. 33). See also Tomlinson, *Answering the Call*, p. 3; 'Union High School Graduation Program', 1883 (copy in ZACG Archives); 'Letter by Byford F. Inman', Westfield, IN, July, 23, 1927 (copy in ZACG Archives); 'The Aurora', Union High School paper, 1.1, 1899 (copy in ZACG Archives).

[180] Tomlinson, *LGC*, pp. 127-31, 236-40. Scores of renowned ministers in the first decade of the twentieth century like John Alexander Dowie in Chicago and Sandford in Maine were identifying themselves as apostles on the grounds that by their hands miracles were wrought, healings performed, and the dead were raised.

Beloved, we must press on and reach the original in all its phases. We have teachers ... pastors, evangelists, and prophets to a degree, but no Apostles are known yet. There is no doubt ... men living who will develop into Apostles ... For unmistakable signs will prove [them] the same as the sign of tongues proves the baptism with the Holy Ghost'.[181]

It followed, moreover, quite naturally in Tomlinson's mind that God-called and gifted apostles would appear on the scene, and there would arise also by divine design a supreme leader among the apostles who would be appointed to exercise final authority. In fact, at the same time that Tomlinson was laboring to restore the apostolic office, he was laboring also to establish a 'supreme and mediatorial throne' in the church – the office of General Overseer. He would claim in 1913-1914 that the office of General Overseer was a peculiar and solitary position atop the pinnacle of a hierarchy that included apostles and prophets. In order to support this view, he claimed that James, the brother of Christ, was not an apostle, but rather 'occupied a position superior in rank to any of the [apostles]' including the Twelve.[182] He thus searched and interpreted the Scriptures with these presuppositions in mind in order to establish his supreme position in the church.

Now the office of General Overseer developed in the following manner: in the General Assembly in 1909 Tomlinson was selected to serve as the General Moderator of the Churches of God. This position had limited authority that included little more than moderating the Assembly and licensing ministers. In 1910 the title of the position was changed to General Overseer and some further responsibilities were added, including the appointment of the pastors. By 1912 Tomlinson began to see the position as being a special and highly exalted office, magnified above even the apostolic office. We have noticed that he thought he had found this office in James, the Lord's brother, who moderated the council in Acts 15. He maintained that this James held a solitary office that antityped Moses' position in Israel, and as a matter of course filled the place of Christ in the church on earth after Jesus had ascended back to the Father.[183]

After Tomlinson developed this interpretation of the unique office and presented it to the General Assembly in his annual addresses in 1913 and 1914, it was accepted with enthusiastic support by most of the

---

[181] Tomlinson, *LGC*, pp. 127-28.
[182] *GAM 1906-1914*, pp. 297-98.
[183] See *GAM 1906-1914*, pp. 257-63, 296-309; Phillips, 'Quakerism', pp. 10-20.

prominent ministers, including Lee and Lemons.[184] In the 1914 Assembly, sentiments were expressed that lauded Tomlinson as being God's appointment for life.[185] Most everyone considered the office sacred with a special anointing and purpose. Tomlinson in particular maintained this opinion as long as he lived. In his nineteenth annual address in 1929, he rehearsed how the office of General Overseer had developed, showing that he had been selected by the Assembly year after year by unanimous agreement. But in reflecting on his selection in 1913, he notes significantly,

> When the time came for the selection of the General Overseer that year, the Holy Ghost seemed to wrest it out of the hands of the Assembly and took such complete charge of the affairs until it was believed, by perhaps all present, that the Overseer had been selected by the Holy Ghost and anointed for the position. Then the next year the Holy Spirit ... made it so clear that the selection was final that I was afraid to mention it any more for fear I would grieve the Holy Ghost.[186]

Tomlinson's view of his exalted station in the church, along with his absolute refusal to allow the office to be modified or his own selection to ever be reconsidered, created a fault in the very foundation of the church that would ever after be the occasion for envy and division. Complaints that the office was popish, monarchical, and dictatorial never ceased to aggravate the peace and harmony of the church between 1914 and 1923; and also ever after among Tomlinson's followers the same complaints arose on occasion and often ended in schism, a phenomenon that we will elaborate upon in the chapters ahead.

After the office of General Overseer had been established in 1909-1910, the need for a governmental position between the General Overseer and the churches became apparent. This need was met by the Assembly in 1911 and seven state overseers were appointed, and also an overseer for the Bahamas.[187] In 1913 the appointment of overseers became the responsibility of the General Overseer.[188] Thereafter, as the church expanded in the states and territories, the overseers were appointed by the General Overseer, and the state overseers began to make

---

[184] *GAM 1906-1914*, pp. 265, 313-14.
[185] *GAM 1906-1914*, pp. 314-15.
[186] *HAA*, II, p. 53.
[187] *GAM 1906-1914*, pp. 107-109.
[188] *GAM, 1906-1914*, pp. 267, 270.

most of the pastoral appointments in their respective states.[189] This established the basis for the general administration of the church in its Episcopal form.[190]

New Fields and Missions

The church's vision for restoration encompassed the world from the beginning. It was embodied at first in the idealism of R.G. Spurling whose vision had developed through his studies in church history and the missionary vision of nineteenth-century Landmark Baptists. His prayer in 1897 revealed his vision as well as his burden:

> Oh, may some wise and noble one
> Complete the work we have begun,
> Oh, may it catch on every pen,
> And trace the isles from end to end.[191]
> – R.G. Spurling

Spurling's visionary dream, however, as we have seen, was just that – a dream; his ideals always loomed larger on paper and in the pulpit than in reality. It turned out that the idea of the 'lost link' was easier to romance than to apply in any practical way. Further, he lacked the leadership ability and organizational skills to make his dream come true; and, according to his own admission, he lacked the kind of personal commitment needed to build a vibrant missionary organization.

The organizational development of the church and its global outreach awaited the coming of A.J. Tomlinson, a man gifted with leadership instincts and whose Christian experience had been informed and guided by radical evangelical-holiness groups that envisioned a global harvest of souls, and that had already organized and immersed themselves in missionary outreach.[192] Tomlinson too was a dreamer; but he was a man fully committed to make any sacrifice to transform his dream into a practical reality. Further, his wife, Mary Jane, was as fully commit-

---

[189] Churches that were mature and strong enough continued to call their own pastors, but in many cases the state overseers began to appoint pastors after the Ninth Assembly in 1913. Note the decision by Tomlinson in *GAM 1906-1914*, p. 270.

[190] The church vacillated between the overseers and the churches in the coming years in regard to the appointment of pastors, but finally the Episcopal form won out.

[191] Spurling, *Lost Link*, p. 52.

[192] Homer, *Diary*, I, pp. 1, 7-8, 16.

ted as he was; and their children also – all of them – were incorporated into the work of the ministry.

Figure 57
SAM C. PERRY

Figure 58
MISS CLYDE COTTON

Figure 59
R.M. EVANS

Sam C. Perry and Miss Clyde Cotton were Spirit-baptized and joined the Church of God – Cotton in 1906 and Perry in 1908. Both were dynamic evangelists and scattered the Pentecostal flame everywhere they went. Cotton had worked with Tomlinson in 1905, assisting him to get the church established in Cleveland. She and Flora E. Bower assisted Bryant in establishing the churches in the Tellico Plains vicinity – at Hillview and Red Knobs. R.M. Evans was baptized with the Spirit during the Florida Holiness Camp meeting in 1907 and joined the church during Tomlinson's celebrated meeting there in 1909. He subsequently became a missionary to the Bahamas and afterward was appointed to oversee that island nation in 1911.

Perhaps no Pentecostal pioneer was better prepared to launch and sustain a missionary endeavor than Tomlinson. We have seen that he had been educated at Westfield's renowned Union Academy, hailed as one of the best schools in America in the 1880s.[193] After his conversion, he attended the Bible and missionary schools of some of the most able men in America, including A.B. Simpson in New York and Martin Wells Knapp, the founder of God's Bible School in Cincinnati.[194] Tomlinson was young, able, energetic, determined, educated, and equipped with organizational skills and a natural ability for leadership. Thus, the moment he joined the church in 1903 he set out to evangelize and plant churches.[195]

---

[193] See note 179.
[194] Homer, *Diary*, I, pp. 7-17; Phillips, *Corruption*, pp. 1-18; *idem*, 'Quakerism', pp. 1-10.
[195] Besides the record we have in Tomlinson's *Diary* and his short history in *The Last Great Conflict*, we have discovered a report written in Tomlinson's own hand (August 16, 1904) that fills in much of the activity of the church in 1903-1904. This report was never published ('A.J. Tomlinson File', ZACG Archives).

After the Pentecostal message came to the Southeast from California in 1906, and took root beginning in 1907 in North and South Carolina, Georgia, Alabama, Tennessee and Florida, the Church of God simply rode the wave of the Pentecostal revival wherever it went. Pentecostal pioneers such as G.B. Cashwell, F.M. Britton, M.M. Pinson, Sam C. Perry, and J.H. King blazed a trail through the Southeast opening the way for the planting of Church of God congregations. By 1909 Church of God ministers led by Tomlinson were in the forefront of the movement.[196] As the Spirit ignited revivals across the land, Church of God ministers were there to harvest the souls and plant local churches.[197]

Florida was particularly a hotbed of Pentecostal fervor. The annual South Florida Holiness camp meeting at Pleasant Grove near Durant was introduced to the Pentecostal movement in 1907 through the ministry of F.M. Britton.[198] This great meeting was opened to the Church of God in 1909 when Tomlinson was invited to be the camp meeting speaker through a special call of the Spirit.[199] The meeting was powerful and fruitful. Pentecostal fire fell from heaven with all the manifestations of apostolic Christianity. Equally important, many of the people became convinced through Tomlinson's eloquence of the need for church government and discipline. Accordingly, 174 joined the Church of God in Florida before the meeting had closed, including many who had been stalwart opponents of church organization. Three bishops were also ordained and several evangelists licensed;[200] these ministers returned to

---

[196] The best source to see this development is *The Bridegroom's Messenger*, all issues from 1907 through 1910.

[197] Homer, *Diary*, I, pp. 7-8; Conn, *Mighty Army*, pp. 85-116.

[198] Stanley H. Frodsham, *With Signs Following* (Springfield, MO: Gospel Publishing House, rev. edn, 1946), pp. 41-42. Much of Britton's ministry is chronicled thereafter in *The Bridegroom's Messenger*, 1907-1910; see also Joseph E. Campbell, *The Pentecostal Holiness Church 1898-1948* (Franklin Springs, GA: The Publishing House of the Penteostal Holiness Church, 1951), pp. 207-335.

[199] Tomlinson's 'Address of Acceptance', *GAM 1906-1914*, p. 199: 'In making the selection of the man to conduct one of the great camp meetings at Durant Fla. they wrote me that the Holy Ghost had named me as that man'.

[200] Tomlinson, *Diary*, October 9-November 26, 1909; Mr. and Mrs. Howard Juilieart, 'Wonderful Meetings at Tampa and Pleasant Grove Camp Grounds, Florida' *TBM* 2.40 (June 15, 1909), p. 1, though Tomlinson and J.H. King and his fellow minister, F.M. Britton, strongly disagreed over the nature of the church and the operations and gifts of the Spirit. King and Britton at first denied that the church was visible and empowered with disciplinary authority. Conn notes that a pet slogan of Britton was 'No card to sign, no church to 'jine'; just come out from among them and be ye separate' (Conn, *Mighty Army*, p. 97 n. 12). Britton also at first resisted the gift of 'interpretation of tongues'. Homer gives a full report of Britton's differences with his father (*Diary*, I, pp. 102-103, 136-38).

their respective states and communities and brought several congregations into the Church of God.[201]

It is worthy of note here that Sam C. Perry was the president of the Pleasant Grove camp meeting and Mrs. R.M. Evans was the secretary and treasurer. One of them apparently wrote to Tomlinson inviting him to the meeting. Both Perry and R.M. Evans would become prominent in the church in the years to come. Perry rose through the ranks of the church's administration, and in 1917 was appointed to a seat on the prestigious Council of Elders when it was formed that year. Perry, however, became controversial and unruly after he was appointed to the Council of Elders, finally leaving the church in 1919 after disciplinary action was taken.

The Florida camp meeting had attracted the attention of Edmond S. Barr and his wife, Rebecca. Edmond was a native of the Bahamas Islands and his wife reportedly a native of Florida. They were baptized with the Spirit in 1909 and soon afterward made plans to take the Pentecostal message to the Bahamas.[202] R.M. Evans (1847-1924), a Methodist minister, had been baptized with the Spirit apparently during F.M. Britton's meeting at Durant in July 1907. He joined the Church of God during Tomlinson's meeting there in 1909.[203] He also felt a definite call to go to the Bahamas, and made plans with the Barrs to evangelize the Islands. He helped fund the Barrs' trip in November 1909, and later sold his home and livestock to provide passage for himself and his wife. Tomlinson officially appointed him as missionary to the Bahamas in 1910, and as the overseer in 1911. Early in January 1910, the Evans' and Carl M. Padgett landed at Nassau, thus becoming the first missionaries representing the Church of God outside the United States.[204] Tomlinson was excited about the venture and fully supported it.[205] He orga-

---

[201] Tomlinson, *Diary*, entries for October-November, 1909; and Conn, *Mighty Army*, pp. 96-99.

[202] R.M. Evans, 'Missionary', *COGE* 1.1 (March 1, 1910), p. 7.

[203] *GAM 1906-1914*, pp. 106-107, 129-30. Some of our information on Evans comes from research done by James E. Cossey which he compiled in a report in 1979, 'Search for R.M. Evans' ('R.M. Evans File', ZACG Archives).

[204] This has been challenged recently by Michael Swan, a pastor in the Bahamas who is writing a history of the Church of God in the Bahamas. He contends that though Edmond S. Barr himself was a native Bahamian, his wife, Rebecca, was a native and citizen of the United States. If his information is correct, then Rebecca would be technically the church's first missionary. She and her husband were ministers in the church in 1909 and went to Bahamas with the Pentecostal message, and with the intention of establishing the Church of God in that nation.

[205] *TBM* 1.13, p. 3. Evans had turned in his credentials to the Methodist Church and began to supervise a 'little orphanage' at Pleasant Grove Campground (Cossey, 'Search for R.M. Evans'). His wife served as secretary and treasurer for the Pleasant

nized a Pentecostal band of musicians and preachers in the spring of 1911 and set sail with a party of thirteen for the Bahamas to support and expand the work that had been launched by the Barrs and Evans. The band remained in the Bahamas for several weeks establishing a front for the church's world conquest. This venture marked the beginning of the church's world mission program.[206]

Figure 60

W.F. BRYANT AT HILLVIEW (C. 1909)

W.F. Bryant, after moving to Cleveland, continued to labor in the mountains. His old friends, Jesse Coleman and his family, had moved to Tellico Plains and Bryant worked with them to establish churches at Hillview and Red Knobs between 1906 and 1909. Clyde Cotton and Flora E. Bowers also assisted in getting these churches established.

Evans and some others were excluded from the church in Florida in 1913 for reasons unknown to the writer at this time. They appealed to the Assembly through J.S. Llewellyn for their case to be reconsidered,

---

Grove camp meeting in 1908-1909, and Perry served as president (cf. *TBM* [March 15, 1909], p. 2).

[206] Tomlinson, *Diary:* January-April, 1911. Evans' report to the General Assembly in 1912 gives additional information (*GAM 1906-1914*, pp. 129-30; and some further details about the missionary adventure are provided in Tomlinson's 'Brief Sketch of the Life and Works' of Roy C. Miller, *Classified Scriptures on the Church of God* (Cleveland, TN: Press of Church of God Evangel, 1913, pp. 12-21).

and the Assembly shuffled the matter to the General Overseer to investigate.[207] No data is available that reveals the details of the ordeal, but Evans was reinstated as a bishop in 1916.[208]

Figure 61

COCONUT GROVE, FLORIDA (C. 1911)

'The Pentecostal Worldwide Mission Band to Hasten the Gospel to Every Land' was organized by Tomlinson during the meeting at Coconut Grove in February 1911. J.W. Buckalew was the music director. The band practiced during the day in preparation for their mission trip to the Bahamas and evangelistic meetings in Florida. *Far left*: Roy C. Miller and future wife, Lula Williams; *far right*: Efford Haynes and wife, Clyde [Cotton] Haynes. A. J. Tomlinson is fifth from right.

While this initial missionary effort was being pursued in the Bahamas, a number of independent and denominational evangelists united with the church to help spread the holiness-Pentecostal Gospel and the peculiar message of the Church of God in the United States. New contacts were made in Mississippi, Kentucky, Arkansas, and Virginia. Tomlinson himself had connections in most of the mid-West states, and Sam C. Perry visited Cuba laying the foundation for the future of the work

---

[207] *GAM 1906-1914*, p. 321.
[208] Evans became mentally disabled a few years later and ended up in a mental health facility in Durant, Florida. He died in 1924.

Figure 62

Figure 63

'PENTECOSTAL WORLDWIDE MISSION BAND' (1911)

Driven by a vision for world evangelization, Tomlinson in 1911 organized the 'Pentecostal World-Wide Mission Band', consisting of preachers and musicians who were dedicated to the purpose of the new organization. Members were required to sign a document that called for strict discipline and a pledge of loyalty to the leader and the objectives of the band. After having had a successful meeting at Coconut Grove, the Pentecostal Band sailed from Miami to evangelize the Bahamas and establish the Church of God. Between 1911 and 1914, the band traveled throughout Florida evangelizing and establishing churches. Some of the more prominent men and women in the photo below are: front row: Roy C. Miller [left seated on ground]; J.W. Buckalew [holding trumpet]; A.J. Tomlinson [behind the banner]; R.M. Evans [holding child]; back row: third to right, Miss Flora E. Bower; Miss Lula Williams; Efford Haynes; Clyde [Cotton] Haynes.

there.[209] J.W. Buckalew, Efford Haynes, J.B. Ellis, H.L. Trim, J.A. Davis, C.R. Curtis, F.G. Chambers, M.S. Lemons, and others were dynamic evangelists with a vision to expand God's kingdom and build the Church of God. The Lord also raised up an army of women to evangelize, teach, and help to build the church, some of the more prominent of whom were Flora E. Bower, Clyde Cotton (who had been instrumental in the great Cleveland revival), Nora Chambers, and Sallie O. Lee. At the same time, men with gifts of administration and churchmanship like F.J. Lee, T.L. McLain, J.S. Llewellyn, E.J. Boehmer, and S.O. Gillaspie were rising to prominence in the developing government of the church. By 1911 all of the ingredients to build a flourishing organization were at hand. In the next few years churches were organized in Maryland, Pennsylvania, Ohio, Michigan, Oklahoma, and Texas. Between 1911 and 1918 the church's membership grew nearly 500 percent, and doubled again by 1922. The Assembly statistics in 1922 showed 21,076 members, 666 churches, and almost 1000 ministers.[210]

Magnetic Attraction

By 1911 the name, 'Church of God', was well on its way to becoming a household word in the South.[211] The zeal and unity of the ministers was magnetic; the church's order and government were attractive; and Tomlinson himself was dynamic and charismatic, his personality and vision attracting followers.[212] Though only five feet seven inches in height and about 165 pounds, there was an aura about Tomlinson that was striking, due in part to his charismatic personality, in part to his complete abandonment to God and His work, and in part to his vision and indefatigable energy to restore and build 'the last day's Church of God'.

---

[209] *GAM 1906-1914*, pp. 106-107.
[210] *GAM*, 18th Assembly, p. 47.
[211] Vinson Synan, *The Holiness-Pentecostal Movement in the United States* (Grand Rapids: Eerdmans, 1971), p. 80
[212] *GAM 1906-1914*, pp. 265, 314-15. The real or imagined signs of divine approval upon his life and ministry were apparently most impressive (Tomlinson, *LGC*, pp. 236-41).

The Case of the Church of God (Mountain Assembly)

But the overarching reason for the church's attraction was probably due to the general sentiment among early Pentecostals that the 'latter rain' had been poured out to break down denominational walls and barriers in order to unite God's people in one visible body of Christ – a sentiment that fit well with the message and vision of the Church of God. Consequently, many independent congregations and small groups united themselves with the church early in the twentieth century. It was the case with a small fellowship of churches in northeast Tennessee and southeast Kentucky going by the name, Church of God (now Church of God Mountain Assembly). This group, centered in Jellico, Tennessee, had been contacted apparently by J.B. Mitchell who was still working closely with Tomlinson while continuing to serve at the same time the American Bible Society.[213] Tomlinson was invited to preach at their Assembly in 1911 and made quite an impression.[214] Their Assembly agreed to send chosen messengers to the Assembly in Cleveland in January 1912 with a view for organic union. Terms were drawn up and accepted by the Jellico delegation, amidst shouts of rejoicing by the Assembly as the leaders embraced and gave to each other 'the right hand of fellowship'.[215] The Jellico messengers, however, were met at home with resistance and the union was never realized.[216] Nevertheless, several of the ministers and members joined the church separately in the ensuing months.[217]

---

[213] Perry had been appointed as overseer of Kentucky in 1911, and shortly thereafter located at London north of Jellico. Llewellyn lived near Knoxville and attended the convention with Tomlinson. But J.B. Mitchell is probably the one who made contact with the Mountain Assembly body since he was living at Jellico at that time (Tomlinson, *Diary*, October 9, 1911).

[214] *Minutes of the Fifth Annual Mountain Assembly of the Churches of God*, pp. 2-5. This Assembly was held at Siler Chapel, Polleyton, Kentucky, October 6-8, 1911. Tomlinson actually moderated the Assembly during the election of their Moderator. For Tomlinson's viewpoint, see *Diary*, October 9, 1911; he states that he gave a full report of this meeting in *COGE* (October 15, 1911, but unfortunately, this issue is not extant. See also Luther Gibson, *History of the Church of God Mountain Assembly*, 1954, pp. 8-9; and Michael Padgett, *A Goodly Heritage* (Kearney, NE: Morris Publishing, 1995), pp. 20-24.

[215] *GAM 1906-1914*, pp. 140-41.

[216] In regard to why they did not unite, see Padgett, *A Goodly Heritage*, pp. 20-24; but in addition to the issue of labor unions which Padgett's explains, the Church of God's doctrine and practice of tithing and its prohibition against the use of tobacco were primary causes.

[217] Padgett, *Goodly Heritage*, pp. 20-24.

The Evening Light and Church of God Evangel

The leaders of the church knew the value of the printed word. Tomlinson particularly was keenly aware of the value of a church paper. He had already experienced the benefits of *Samson's Foxes* (1901-1902) in his mission work at Culberson. After he joined the church in 1903, M.S. Lemons assisted him at Culberson and later in Cleveland to publish *The Way* (1904-1905). After *The Way* was discontinued, G.B. Cashwell's paper, *The Bridegroom's Messenger*, published in Atlanta beginning in 1907 became more or less the printed medium for Church of God ministers until 1910.[218] In February 1908 Tomlinson became a corresponding editor for that paper, which made Church of God ministers feel at home with *The Bridegroom's Messenger*. Tomlinson, J.B. Mitchell, W.F. Bryant, H.L. Trim, Flora Bower, Clyde Cotton, R.M. Evans, M.S. Lemons, and several other ministers and laymen contributed reports and sermons to the paper; funds were solicited also for missions and new field work to build the Church of God.[219]

By 1910 the need for a paper to represent the peculiar needs of the Church of God were pressing. After the camp meeting at Pleasant Grove in 1909 Tomlinson and the Church of God increasingly became distanced from G.B. Cashwell, F.M. Britton, J.H. King, and other Pentecostal pioneers. *The Bridegroom's Messenger* published a doctrinal definition of the Pentecostal Movement in May 1909 that included ten articles.[220] While there were nothing in those articles with which Tomlinson and other leaders in the Church of God disagreed, yet there were other teachings peculiar to the Church of God that the leaders felt needed to be proclaimed and spelled out: e.g. footwashing, against going to war, ethical standards in regard to marriage and holiness, and, above all, the doctrine of the church itself.

It became necessary, therefore, for the church to have its own paper. The *Church of God Evangel* was thus launched on March 1, 1910. Significantly it was published in its first year under the title *The Evening Light and Church of God Evangel* with the greater emphasis being on *The Evening*

---

[218] *The Way* was discontinued so that Tomlinson and Lemons and the other ministers could give themselves wholly to pastoral work and evangelism. Interestingly, they urged the ministers and members to subscribe to *The Church Herald* published by George Smith in College Mound, Missouri (*The Way* 2.9 [September 1905], p. 5). They had planned on using this medium to publish messages and reports of their work, adding 'The Herald and ourselves are combining our interests more closely'.

[219] Flora E. Bower and Zetta A. Gamble, 'Work in the Mountains of Tennessee', *TBM* (August 15, 1909), p. 2. Other issues show that funds were received.

[220] *TBM* 2.37 (May 1, 1909), p. 1.

Light.[221] This title reflected Zechariah's prophecy, 'it shall come to pass, that at evening time it shall be light' (Zech. 14.7), which was interpreted by the church's pioneers to mean that the light of the primitive church would be restored in the 'evening time', that is, in the last days, and that the last day's church was destined to fulfill all of the ancient and glorious prophecies. Like many prophetic passages, Zech. 14.1-21 encompasses the restoration and perfection of the church in this present world, and further envisions her in millennial glory. Following a conventional interpretation, Spurling thus depicted the church in this present world as the *church militant*, and envisioned her in heaven as the church *triumphant*.[222]

The restoration of the primitive church was the very premise upon which Spurling had established Christian Union in 1886, but this restoration theme would be developed more elaborately by Tomlinson and Spurling in the years to come. They would come to see the church ever more clearly in biblical prophecy and Christian history as having fallen away in the early centuries, then rising up out of the subsequent 'dark ages' to be established again in the last days – in the *evening time*. And they increasingly saw the Church of God more exclusively as that prophetic church – the City of God and Light of the World. Among a great many passages used to prove their interpretation of the fall and restoration of the church was Isa. 60.1-5.

It is likely that the name *The Evening Light and Church of God Evangel* was suggested by Spurling. He was on the committee to see about 'the propriety of starting a paper'.[223] His poem, *Gospel Evening Light*, appeared in the second issue of the paper (dated March 15, 1910) along with his message, 'The Church', which emphasized the essential principles of the Church of God's peculiar ecclesiology and restoration theme.

The inauguration of this publication was a sign that marked progress, to be sure, but also a change in the church's self-perception and approach to ministry. At that point, the church became more self-consciously sectarian and exclusive; but these traits were more particularly embodied in Tomlinson who at that very moment was sorting out in his mind the Scriptural revelation of the government of God in

---

[221] On the masthead of the paper, the title *The Evening Light* was in size three times larger than *COGE,* and in the first issue Tomlinson wrote an Apology that explained the name of the paper focusing almost entirely on the idea that the 'dark ages' had passed in recent years and the 'evening light' was now breaking through and would continue to shine ever brighter until the church completes her mission in this world.

[222] Spurling, *Lost Link*, pp. 18-19.

[223] *GAM 1906-1914*, pp. 77-79.

the earth, and the administrative structure of that government. But he had already perfectly settled in his mind one thing for certain, namely, that the Lord had ordained for His government in the earth to be supervised by a special agent – a General Overseer – appointed by God through the Holy Ghost.

Orphanage Work

At the turn of the twentieth century America still had not developed a social consciousness.[224] The tradition of rugged self-reliance remained the prevailing attitude and practice of the people in 'the land of the free and home of the brave'. This democratic disposition intended to keep the federal government weak and as much as possible out of the affairs of the people.[225] Consequently, there were few centralized support systems and no federal welfare program. Even public schools were slow in developing, especially on the frontier and in Appalachia. The responsibility of education most often fell upon the churches or community programs supported by the churches. Care for orphans and widows also depended on the compassion of the churches, for this was primarily the Lord's work, and the Lord's work was best carried out by the churches.

It is not surprising then that the care for orphans became a major concern in the Church of God early on, particularly under Tomlinson's leadership. Tomlinson and his good friend and co-worker, J.B. Mitchell, had established an orphanage at Culberson shortly after they arrived in the mountains in 1899.[226] Tomlinson was inspired by George Mueller,[227] the great orphanage builder in London, and otherwise was reared in the Quaker tradition famous for building schools, orphanages, and doing benevolent work. It was thus inevitable that Tomlinson would encourage orphanage work after he became General Overseer, for it was considered at the heart of Christian service and befitting any church worthy of the name of Christ.

Not until 1911, however, was the first attempt made for a children's home in the Church of God. This work opened in Cleveland with 15

---

[224] America's social consciousness was conceived during the Great Depression in the late 1930s and took form in the 'New Deal' plan initiated by President Franklin D. Roosevelt.

[225] Thomas Jefferson's philosophy of politics and government in this regard was representative of the American people in general; see Phillips, 'The Church of God: A Portrait of America', for the way this served as a context in the early development of the Church of God.

[226] Tomlinson, *Diary*, July 1899-1902; *Samson's Foxes* 1900-1902.

[227] Tomlinson, *Diary*, March 10, 1901.

children under the oversight of J.B. Mitchell, who was then living in Jellico, Tennessee.[228] He was appointed as the church's 'President of The Faith Orphanage and Children's Home Association'. The particular orphanage in Cleveland, however, was under the immediate supervision of W.F. Bryant and two matrons.[229] This work was short lived, however, lacking funds and a leader who felt a special call and burden for this particular kind of work. In 1912, Mattie Perry, a female evangelist and the sister of Sam C. Perry, invited the church to visit her Elhanan Training Institute and Orphanage in Marion, North Carolina. This meeting was scheduled with a view to merge the church and her Elhanan Institute.[230] The attempt failed, however, likely for the same reason that the attempt to form a union with the Mountain Assembly organization failed. In the case with the Mountain Assembly, it was made clear by the leaders of the Church of God that the union was not a merger but an incorporation of that body into the Church of God. Mattie felt the price for church government was too high to surrender her independence, imagining that a presbytery looking over her shoulder would stifle her inspiration and hinder her progress rather than aiding it. Like her brother, Sam, she was self-made and leery of any government that might usurp the authority of the Spirit and interfere with the providences of God in her work.

Ironically, it was in God's providence that Miss Lillian Trasher (1887-1961) met Mattie Perry at a train station in Asheville, North Carolina in 1904; thereafter Lillian joined Perry's staff at Elhanan and learned the ins and outs of orphanage work. Taking a break from her work there, she attended God's Bible School in Cincinnati in 1905, the same school that Tomlinson had attended a few years earlier. She returned to Elhanan and in a little while felt called of God to go to Africa as a missionary. In 1910, she sailed for Egypt with her sister, Jennie Benton, and soon was engaged in setting up the beginnings of an orphanage in the city of Assiout (located about 230 miles south of Cairo) receiving some assistance from the government of Egypt. However, authorities closed

---

[228] Mitchell was in Jellico partly in behalf of the American Bible Society, but he was still close to Tomlinson and involved in the work and mission of the Church of God. While in Jellico, he had forged a friendship with the leaders of the Mountain Assembly fellowship and arranged for a meeting between them and the leaders of the Church of God, with the expectations of forming a union.

[229] J.B. Mitchell wrote to *The Bridegroom's Messenger* (August 1, 1911) informing the readers of the opening of the institution in Cleveland and pointing out what the orphanage needed in order for it to be successful.

[230] *GAM 1906-1914*, p. 138; Mattie Perry advertised her school and home regularly in *The Bridegroom's Messenger*, 1907-1910.

the orphanage in 1911 temporarily because a child had entered the orphanage with bubonic plague.

Figure 64

W.F. BRYANT (FAR LEFT)
IN CHARGE OF THE ORPHANAGE IN CLEVELAND (1911).

After the orphanage was closed, Lillian returned to the United States to convalesce and to contemplate her future. While attending a camp meeting in Durant, Florida in 1912 where A.J. Tomlinson was the speaker, she apparently explained to the General Overseer the calling of God upon her life and of her work in Egypt; whereupon Tomlinson apparently licensed her on the spot as an evangelist in the Church of God.[231] Lillian did a little evangelistic work in the United States after that; but Egypt was calling her, and she soon returned to the Nile as a minister of the Church of God. 'Mama' as she was called in later years by the Egyptians was not sent to Egypt by the Church of God in an official capacity, nor was her orphanage established under the government of the church; yet her work was more or less assumed to be a part of

---

[231] Trasher was connected with the Church of God in Dahlonega, Georgia in 1908-1910, and it is possible that Tomlinson could have met her before the meeting in Durant; for the church in Dahlonega, most particularly in the persons of Emma L. Boyd and Ella Fry, had made an impact on the town and on the Church of God after Boyd and Fry united with the church in 1910 through the efforts of Sam C. Perry. For a brief account of this church, see Conn, *Mighty Army*, pp. 105-106.

Church of God;[232] she therefore reported regularly to the church of her work in Egypt and, correspondingly, some meager amount of funds were sent to her in the name of the church. Interestingly, Sarah A. Smith, whom we met earlier in regard to the outpourings of the Spirit at Camp Creek in North Carolina and at Epperson and Beniah in Tennessee, joined Lillian's staff in Egypt in 1910 and labored in the orphanage there until her death in 1918.[233]

In 1919 Lillian made a fateful decision. On a visit to the United States, she attended an Assemblies of God meeting and became deeply impressed by the offer of that organization to officially appoint her as a missionary to Egypt and provide substantial financial support for her orphanage. Lillian accepted the offer, turned in her license with the Church of God and joined the Assemblies of God.

Figure 65

MISS LILLIAN TRASHER
'MOTHER OF THE NILE'

There can be little doubt that Lillian's decision to leave the Church of God was influenced by Sam Perry and his sister, Mattie. We have already noticed Lillian's connection with Mattie in the Elhanan Institute. Thereafter, she formed a special friendship with the Perrys, and thus when Sam's credentials were revoked in May 1919 for contending against the government and teachings of the church, it affected Lillian. It is almost certain that Sam and Mattie disclosed their dissatisfaction with the Church of God to her, and we have every reason to believe that it was more than mere coincidence that she left the church shortly after Perry's credentials were revoked. Be that as it may, it was in the Assemblies of God that Trasher became celebrated as the 'Mother of the Nile' and her orphanage in Egypt became renown throughout the world.[234]

After the church's Faith Orphanage and Children's Home Association failed in 1911, no effort was made again until 1919 to build and support a church-sponsored orphanage. It was in the General Assembly

---

[232] This is the opinion also of Church of God historian, Dr. David Roebuck, that is, that Trasher's work in Egypt had been established early on under the auspices of the church.

[233] Smith also did some work in Jerusalem and had returned to the United States briefly before returning to Egypt to end her days in the orphanage there in 1918.

[234] Beth Baron, 'Nile Mother: Lillian Trasher and Egypt's Orphans', *Assemblies of God Heritage* (2011), pp. 31-39. Baron notes that the Episcopal Church actually added Trasher to its liturgical calendar of saints in 2009.

in 1919 during the General Overseer's annual address in regard to this subject that the Holy Spirit intervened and put His approval on the need for such an institution.

> While the [General Overseer] was speaking about the Orphanage, there was much weeping all over the building. Suddenly a sister arose saying, 'I will give one hundred dollars'. A brother arose and said, 'I know a man that will give a thousand dollars on an orphanage'. Others said they would give fifty dollars ... At this time a sister stood, holding an open Bible in her hands, speaking in tongues.[235]

Thereafter definite action was taken to commence a children's home. The home was opened on December 17, 1920 under the matronhood of Lillian Kinsey.[236] From that point the orphanage work became a permanent part of the church. Even after the need for church-sponsored orphanages diminished in the United States beginning in the 1960s, because of the enactment of federal welfare programs and stricter regulations on orphanages, still the zeal to build and support orphanages in the Church of God continued in many countries.

The Lost Link Versus *The Last Great Conflict*

Spurling had based the restoration of the church in 1886 on the idea of the 'lost link' – the love of God acted out in the form of brotherly love. This divine attribute supported all else and served as the cornerstone for Christian Union. Divine love was therefore the primary basis for the fellowship of the church, over against the idea of rigid disciplines based on legislated rules and regulations and static creedal statements. Further, the 'lost link' is why the Reformation churches had remained disconnected from the church in the New Testament; in fact the apostasy of the New Testament church in the third and fourth centuries and the subsequent development of denominationalism was the result of the 'lost link', or, to put it another way, after the passing of the apostles, the new leaders gradually departed from the fundamental principles of the faith and the mystery of Christian fellowship, and Roman Catholicism and the Protestant state churches were substituted in lieu of the true church. Spurling later formulated and systematized his ideas in *The Lost*

---

[235] This outpouring of generosity by the brothers and sisters in this Assembly, and the spiritual demonstration by the sister that seemed to indicate the approval by the Spirit upon the need to build orphanages, propelled the church forward in this endeavor (See 14th *GAM*, 1919, pp. 15, 16, 21).

[236] 'Youth Interviews Experience', *The Lighted Pathway* (July 1949), p. 14.

Link, showing that the essential marks of the church are found in the charismas of the Spirit acted out in philanthropy – in brotherly love.[237]

We have noticed that Tomlinson, after prayer and some travail in his spirit, accepted Spurling's fundamental ideas, and together these men of God and their followers went forth to build the 'church of love'.

> A land of gospel light have we,
> How thankful then ought we to be:
> What profit is that light to us,
> If now that light we fail to see?
> How shall we that light discern,
> Which only in Thy Spirit burns?
> O, Lord, each heart from darkness free,
> That it may borrow light of Thee.
> Send forth Thy law in every heart,
> The law of God to us impart,
> Like Thee, dear Father, and Thy Son,
> May we Thy children join in one.
> May now Thy holy law of love,
> Which cometh only from above,
> In strongest ties our hearts unite,
> That we may walk in gospel light.
> – R.G. Spurling[238]

Despite Spurling's intriguing hypothesis, 'the lost link' was found to be too liberal to hold together a growing organization, especially after 1906 under Tomlinson's aggressive leadership. Spurling's fundamental idea was too radically democratic to maintain order and discipline among the ever-multiplying number of ministers and churches, and too weak to provide a system of cooperation and sufficient government for an effective world outreach program. The tension between Spurling's fundamental idea in *The Lost Link* and the practical needs of an expanding worldwide church may be seen in Tomlinson's *The Last Great Conflict*. Spurling wrote as the leader of a small group of independent local churches, still very much influenced by the spirit and ideals of the Baptist tradition; whereas Tomlinson wrote as the General Overseer of an increasingly centralized body of churches with a vision for world conquest. Thus Spurling cries out for unity based on individual liberty and an independent conscience and Tomlinson cries out for unity based on

---

[237] 'Brotherly love' is the central thesis of *The Lost Link* and is set forth as the primary basis for Christian fellowship.
[238] Spurling, *Lost Link*, p. 29.

obedience to a centralized system of government and a corporate conscience formed through discussions and resolutions adopted by the General Assembly. Moreover, Tomlinson's *The Last Great Conflict* was written after the church had become fully entrenched in the holiness-Pentecostal tradition, with the dynamics of the Spirit and spiritual gifts at work; whereas *The Lost Link* was written for the most part before the church had entered into the holiness-Pentecostal tradition.

What we see then between 1886 and 1916 is Spurling's original ideal metamorphosing into the practical outworking of a growing worldwide church. Both Tomlinson's and Spurling's basic ideas had to be modified and qualified to meet the needs of an ever-expanding organization of churches with a centralized government. The best of both men's ideas were thus merged into the ever-increasing light of God's Word to form the church's unique vision and mission in the early twentieth century.[239] Tomlinson's ideals of world conquest and centralized government kept the ministers and members in the harness working together toward common goals; whereas Spurling's 'lost link' helped to keep the ministers and members sensitive to the fundamental graces of brotherly love, kindness and humility, which conditioned the church with a spirit of equality and mutual respect. Thus, while the church's work expanded to global proportions under Tomlinson's inspirational leadership, Spurling's vision of the 'lost link' and his personal gravity helped the ministers and churches to remain one 'Christian Union'.

Fire-Baptized Spirituality

If one is to understand the spirit and heartthrob of the Church of God in this early period, the spirituality of the ministers and members must be taken into account. The preaching and teaching within the church in those days called for entire consecration – utter abandonment to the sovereign will of God; which, accordingly, was believed to be necessary in order for the ministers and members to be supernaturally charged and 'fire-baptized'. Only through Jesus' fire-baptism could their faith and work be fully actualized. The emphasis in the Church of God in those days was therefore on the Holy Ghost *and fire*. Indeed, rarely was the baptism with the Holy Ghost preached without emphasizing 'the fire:' for so many of the leading ministers in those early days had been fire-baptized – Bryant, Tomlinson, Spurling, Lemons, Cotton, Bower,

---

[239] Wade H. Phillips, 'Our Rich Church of God Heritage: Born of the Spirit', *Church of God History & Heritage* (Summer 1997), pp. 1-2, 4-5.

Trim, Sallie O. Lee, C.R. Curtis, J.A. Davis, A.J. Lawson, and others – and many of them had had formal ties to the FBHA.

The people were hungry for God, and this hunger more or less defined their fellowship. They were preoccupied with the things that generated spirituality – prayer, fasting, worship, witnessing, reading, and preaching the Word of God. The saints believed their time in this world was short and thus focused their relationship on God and the church's mission, seeking to 'perfect holiness in the fear of God'. Worldliness was frivolity and foolishness to them. They had no time for worldly pleasures and worldly pursuits; for their conscience had been quickened by *the fire* of the Spirit, and their minds illuminated with the knowledge that material things 'perish with the using'. They were sober and sincere about their faith, seeking always to lay up for themselves treasures in heaven, for *the fire* burned into their souls a vision of eternal things.

Besides the fire-baptized context of their spiritual experience, the temporal circumstances in those early days made it more convenient for the church's pioneers to focus on spirituality; for there were no televisions and radios and conveniences connected with modern-day cyber-space technology – internet, cell phones, i-phones, i-pads, face book, etc. – things that consume so much of the time of contemporary Christians, distracting them from a more devoted and consecrated lifestyle.[240] It should be borne in mind also that hospitals, health care systems, and medicines in those days were scarce and primitive, and so people tended to depend more directly on God for their critical needs. In a word, they lived more soberly because they were more keenly aware of the frailty of human existence; and consequently they were more prone also to look to God for help. Both the simplicity and harshness of the times, each in its own way, caused the church's forefathers and foremothers to look to God for solace and assistance, and quickened within them a thankful heart. Neither was the spirit of antichrist prevalent in America in those days, and the church's membership in 1915 was still overwhelmingly concentrated in this nation. In the friendly atmosphere of a culture that had been founded upon and nourished by Judeo-Christian principles, and conditioned by two Great Awakenings in the previous two centuries, the seeds of the kingdom more readily germinated and produced a bountiful harvest of souls.

Again, too much emphasis cannot be placed on the holiness-Pentecostal transformation of the church in the late nineteenth and

---

[240] In contrast, see the apostles' predictions of spiritual conditions in the last days: 2 Thess. 2.3; 1 Tim. 4.1-3; 2 Tim. 3.1-5; 4.3, 4; 2 Pet. 3.3, 4.

early twentieth century, for it conditioned the spirituality of the church. The unprecedented revival at Camp Creek that had begun in 1896 was set ablaze by Irwin's fire-baptized holiness movement between 1898 and 1901. [241] Thereafter the church was immersed in the holiness-Pentecostal Gospel. Believers plunged themselves ever deeper into the life of God through Jesus' Spirit-baptism. Tomlinson's hunger for the baptism with the Holy Ghost and fire in 1907 was typical of the time. Years later he recalled, 'I was so hungry for the Holy Ghost that I scarcely cared for food, friendship or anything else. I wanted one thing – the Baptism with the Holy Ghost'.[242]

Tomlinson's baptismal experience was extraordinary but by no means unique among the church's early pioneers. During their immersion into the depths of God's power, many of church's fathers and mothers saw visions that revealed scenes in heaven and hell, including relatives and persons they had known in this life; and often they were carried through the Spirit to far away lands and saw themselves proclaiming the Gospel to the heathen and explaining the peculiar message of the Church of God to believers. Some were 'slain by the Spirit' and claimed to have levitated several feet in the air, or at least imagined that they had, floating like a cloud by the miraculous power of the Spirit. Others claimed to have been translated to distance lands by the Spirit and enabled to speak to the indigenous peoples in their own dialects. Tomlinson's Spirit-baptism in 1908, as we noticed earlier, inculcated all of these miraculous manifestations and glorious demonstrations.[243]

Tomlinson's testimony brings up another point commonly believed by Church of God pioneers, namely, that the Pentecostal baptism was not so much a one-time experience as it was the door to ever deeper experiences into the intra-Trinitarian life – into the infinite depths *of* the Father *through* the Son and *in* the Holy Ghost.[244] The saints believed in fact that one could go so deep into God so as to be able to discern the particular persons of the Trinity. This idea, as we noticed earlier, was a common practice among Wesleyan holiness people. John Fletcher, Hester Ann Rogers, and many leaders of early Methodism believed that Spirit-baptism was the means to explore the infinite depths of God.[245] Referring to Lady Maxwell, B.H. Irwin wrote in *Live Coals of Fire* that she

---

[241] See 'Fire-baptized Transformation at Camp Creek' in Chpater 3..

[242] Tomlinson, *LGC*, p. 233.

[243] See 'Completing the Pentecostal Transformation' in Chapter 4.

[244] See "Trinitarian Mysticsm," in Chapter 3; and Phillips, 'Significance of the Fire-Baptized Holiness Movement', pp. 26-28.

[245] Tomlinson acknowledges the influence of Fletcher, Bramwell, and other Wesleyan greats upon his ministry; see Tomlinson, *LGC*, p. 175.

had 'the real baptism of fire, and how the Lord did reveal Himself to her – the personal Father, the personal Holy Ghost, and the personal Son, each separately, and she was so taken into God that she knew when the Father visited her heart, and when the Son visited her heart, and when the Holy Ghost visited her heart'.[246] Irwin quoted also the Puritan divine, John Owen, to support the practice of mystical communion with God. Owen had written that 'the saints might have communion distinctly with the Father, distinctly with the Son, and distinctly with the Holy Ghost'.[247]

Was this fanaticism? On what ground? For if God is a Trinity, why could not a hungry soul go so deep into the mystery so as to be able to discern the particular persons in the Godhead. Moreover, why could not God use a person to perform miracles and do exploits in more glorious ways than one could ever imagine? What then was preventing a saint from obtaining the power to heal the sick, make the lame walk, raise the dead, and speak in any number of languages to give greater and more effectual witness to the truth and power of the Gospel of Jesus Christ? Did not Jesus say, 'He that believes on me, the works I do shall he do also; and greater works … shall he do; because I go to the Father'. And did He not promise His church that 'the gates of hell shall not prevail against it'. What then was hindering the church from conquering the world for Christ; apparently nothing but a lack of faith and a greater desire to plunge ever deeper into God.

Make no mistake, however; though the church's pioneers lived in the mystical realm of the Spirit, and were exercised in extraordinary ways, yet their experiences were what John Fletcher called a 'rational mysticism', which he explained as 'the prudent spirituality that covers the naked truth to improve her beauty, to quicken the attention of sincere seekers, to augment the pleasure of discovery, and to conceal her charms from the prying eyes of her enemies'.[248] As already noted, Fletcher employed the term 'evangelical mysticism' to explain what he considered to be a 'judicious' and 'necessary' mysticism, in contrast with philosophical and speculative mysticism, the latter of which does 'violence to sound criticism, in quitting, without reason, the literal sense of the Scriptures, and running into ridiculous and forced allegories'.[249] This was precisely

---

[246] B.H. Irwin, 'The Eradication of Sin', *LCF* (November 3, 1899), p. 5.

[247] 'Editorial', *LCF*, October 6, 1899, p. 7. Owen is here quoted but not cited. I discovered the quote in *The Works of John Owen* (16 vols.; London: The Banner of Truth Trust, 1966), II, p. 34.

[248] *Works of Fletcher*, II, p. 7.

[249] *Works of Fletcher*, II, p. 9. This was precisely the Church of God's view and experience in mysticism.

the Church of God's theology of mystical experience in the early twentieth century. The pioneers were not seduced by Eastern mysticism – by the idea of 'thinking without thoughts' and that sort of thing; for their spiritual experiences were made to conform always to reason, experience, tradition, and, above all, to the Holy Scriptures. In this sense the church was completely Wesleyan in its spirituality.

The church's fathers and mothers were therefore secure and confident in their spirituality and Pentecostal theology. As such, they were undaunted by the criticism of spiritually shallow Calvinistic ministers who doubted and denied the extraordinary manifestations of the Spirit; neither were they intimidated by the fanatical tendency within their own ranks to go to extremes in regard to their unfolding Pentecostal theology and experience. They believed that if they hungered for a deeper life in God through the Spirit, and sought for a fuller illumination of truth in regard to the government and operation of the church, that any fanaticism and irregularities in worship would be corrected and leveled-out in due time through the order and discipline of the church.[250] In regard to the charge of 'wildfire', Tomlinson answered that some 'wildfire is better than no fire at all!'

Spirituality was therefore the principal thing in the church in the late nineteenth and early twentieth century. The church's pioneers believed that the signs and gifts of the Spirit defined the church. The ministers thus endeavored to maintain a hallowed atmosphere in the church so that the Spirit of God would be free to move and operate as He willed. A section in Tomlinson's annual address in 1917 typified his many admonitions that encouraged spirituality in the church.

> Our people should be encouraged to yield to the Spirit, and even stir up the gift that is in them. Preaching is necessary, but if all of our services were given to preaching only, the spiritual fire would go out. There must be testimonies, talking in tongues, interpretations, signs, wonders, dancing, and whatever else the blessed Spirit of God dictates. Our people must be free in the Holy Ghost. This freedom

---

[250] Tomlinson encouraged the church in his annual address in 1921 to go deeper into the Word of God in order to discover new truths and open 'new mines' that will produce their 'glittering gold and glorious truths'. He explained that this disposition is what makes the Church of God different from other organizations: the fact that it is not 'staked out by a tether', nor 'limits God ... [and] His Son'. Moreover, he encouraged the church not to be intimidated by mistakes of the past, including the tendency toward fanaticism and heresy; for to 'sit still and not try to find the hidden wealth' in God's plan is more dangerous and inexcusable. He concluded, 'I have seen people who were so fearful of running into error that they sat still and would not do the things that were right' (*HAA*, I, pp. 161-62).

must not be taken away from them. A part of almost every service should be given to these free exercises in the Spirit. Then the preaching will be enjoyed better ... and do more good. The letter alone will kill, but the Spirit gives life. These outpourings serve as juice or flavoring to the Word. They are necessary for the best interests of all the children of God. It has been said that there is more liberty, and rejoicing, and love among the Church of God people than any people on earth. We must retain our reputation, and not become dead and formal. I have thought we could make the most noise, and then suddenly change to the most intense quietness above any people on earth. The Lord tells us to make a joyful noise unto Him, and He also says for us to be still and know that He is God. Thus we are changed and wafted about by the blessed Holy Ghost according to the will and Word of God.[251]

Tomlinson went on to show in this same address that the presence of the Spirit with all of His manifestations, including the *shekinah*, is the very ground and life of theocratic government. Thus in order for the church to be a true theocracy there must be the visible as well as the inner witness of the Spirit in the midst of the church. This was necessary if the church expected to bind and loose on earth what God had bound and loosed in heaven (Mt. 16.19); it must keep itself therefore buried in the bosom of God; for how else could the church discern and know the mind and will of God and make His kingdom visible in the earth (Mt. 6.11)? How else is it possible for the church to propagate and effect in earth what God had willed in heaven!

In reflecting on the Church of God's Pentecostal transformation between 1896 and 1910, two things are worthy of further examination. First, Tomlinson and many in the congregations at Camp Creek in North Carolina and in Monroe, Polk, and Bradley counties in Tennessee had leaned toward Pentecostalism even before the twentieth century; indeed, many of the church's ministers and members had been baptized with the Spirit during the outpourings at Camp Creek and at Beniah and Epperson in 1898-1900. Tomlinson reported that it is 'estimated that more than one hundred persons really received the baptism with the evidence during the revival'.[252] Yet early in the twentieth century, the

---

[251] *GAM*, 1917, p. 269
[252] Tomlinson, *LGC*, p. 212. Tomlinson himself may have witnessed speaking in tongues at Camp Creek in 1899-1902, as well as at Shiloh in Maine in 1897-1901, but at that time did not understand the significance of tongues, nor identified tongues-speech with Spirit-baptism. Moreover, since he was not present in the meetings at Camp Creek in 1896-1899, and only on occasion in 1899-1902, he had

church's pioneers were still focused on restoring the visible church based on a radical, if not rigid, ethical discipline – a discipline pursued often at the expense of spiritual and charismatic gifts. It was only after the outpouring of the Spirit during the great revival at Azusa Street in Los Angeles in 1906 that the Church of God fully embraced the theology of the Pentecostal movement, particularly in the light of tongues-speech as the initial evidence of Spirit-baptism.[253] Not until after Tomlinson invited G.B. Cashwell, the 'apostle of Pentecost in the South', to preach the Pentecostal message at the General Assembly in 1908 in Cleveland was the church identified with the Pentecostal movement.[254] Even then, as noticed earlier, the resistance of the faction led J.B. Goins and J.H. Simpson in 1909-1910 had to be overcome before the whole church was fully immersed in the movement.

Having been fully baptized with the Holy Ghost during the General Assembly in January 1908, Tomlinson that summer put up a tent in Cleveland and conducted a revival that swept the city. During the course of this crusade, which lasted for several weeks, thousands attended, hundreds were saved, about 250 were baptized with the Spirit, and more

---

to rely on the testimonies of others. He had received his information from scores of participants in the Camp Creek meetings. A close scrutiny of the records, however, indicates that the number of those who had been Spirit-baptized may have been inflated; for the distinction of speaking in tongues seems not to have been carefully considered in the estimates. Some who had been blessed or moved by the Spirit in some manner [shouting, screaming, dancing, leaping, quaking, falling to the ground] may have been counted though they had not spoken in tongues. W.F. Bryant's wife and two of his daughters, who were present in many of the meetings during the outpourings in 1896-1901, said that they had not heard tongues-speech until after they arrived in Cleveland in 1907. It may have been, however, that they simply did not recognize the phenomenon at the time; but, in any case, the testimonies of Bryant, Billy Martin, Joe Tipton, Sarah A. Smith, Emeline Allen, Margaret Melissa Murphy, Pinckney Spurling, Daniel Awrey, Stewart Irwin, and scores of others leave no doubt that a great many in the revival at Camp Creek and in Monroe, Polk, and Bradley counties actually spoke in tongues in 1899-1900.

[253] In reflecting on the 'History of Pentecost', *FS* (September 1922, pp. 5-6), it is apparent that the church had at that time submitted to conventional opinion and dated the beginning of the Pentecostal movement with the Azusa Street revival in Los Angeles in 1906. Tomlinson, even in 1912, credits W.J. Seymour, the pastor of the Azusa Street mission, with the restoration of the doctrine of speaking in tongues as the evidence of Spirit-baptism (Tomlinson, *LGC*, pp. 156-57). Assuming that he first began writing *The Last Great Conflict* in 1910-1911, he thus dates the beginning of the Pentecostal movement to 1906 by saying, 'Wonderful advances have been made in the last four years, since the falling of the "latter rain"' (Tomlinson, *LGC*, p. 102). Upon further reflection, however, the church would years later modify this view, seeing the restoration of Spirit-baptism in the fire-baptized holiness movement between 1895 and 1900, which gave the Church of God a much earlier date for its Pentecostal identity.

[254] Tomlinson, *LGC*, p. 233; *TBM* 1.6 (January 15, 1908), p. 2.

than 150 joined the church.²⁵⁵ Cleveland's *Journal and Banner* published that the religious fervor 'is at white heat' and that the Church of God had 'captured all the east and northeast of Cleveland'.²⁵⁶ Sparks from this revival ignited other revivals in the surrounding towns and merged with the Pentecostal fires that were by then blazing throughout the Southeast.²⁵⁷ Scores of evangelists joined the church in 1908-1915, finding freedom in the Pentecostal experience and haven in the church's government.

Figure 66

G.B CASHWELL

Figure 67

M.M. PINSON

Cashwell accepted Tomlinson's invitation to the Assembly in 1908, and preached twice. During Cashwell's second message, Tomlinson dropped to the floor from his seat as moderator, and was dramatically baptized with the Spirit. He claimed to have levitated in the Spirit and to have spoken at least ten languages while in an ecstasy which lasted for more than three hours. Pinson, one of the founders of the Assembly of God in 1914, attended the Assembly in 1910 but was not favorably enough impressed with the church to unite with it. Apparently he considered the Church of God to be too 'churchy' in regard to its doctrine of the church; and too rigid and narrow in regard to its teaching on sanctification and practical holiness standards.

---

²⁵⁵ Tomlinson, *Diary*, I, pp. 24-32, August 9-October 14 1908; and Conn, *Mighty Army*, pp. 86-92.
²⁵⁶ *The Journal and Banner* (September 17, 1908), p. 3.
²⁵⁷ The best source for an overview of the rapid spread of Pentecostalism throughout the Southeast is *The Bridegroom's Messenger*. This was a bi-monthly publication that G.B. Cashwell began in Atlanta in October 1907. It is a virtual journal of the Pentecostal movement in the South between 1907 and 1910.

5

DOCTRINAL TRANSFORMATION: 1886-1923

The Church of God was conceived in a Baptist womb, particularly in a Landmark [Missionary] Baptist womb, and in fact Spurling's Christian Union was more or less a reformation of the Landmark Baptist tradition. It was inevitable therefore that the Church of God would at first bear many of the characteristics of the Baptist tradition, most noticeably in regard to salvation-related and church-related themes.

Notwithstanding, Spurling's radical experiment in Christian Union and his magnanimous vision for the unity of God's people effectively modified the Church of God's resemblance to the Baptist tradition in several respects. The fact that he and his followers had freed themselves from the harness of any particular theological or denominational construct enabled them to think afresh on doctrinal themes, but at the same time it opened the door for them to be influenced by other Christian traditions and contemporary movements. And that is precisely what happened.

Was Spurling an original thinker? His major written work, *The Lost Link*, is sufficient proof that he was. And his 'Wild Sheep Union' gave him the opportunity to explore and experiment with some of his radically new ideas. We have seen, however, that his ecclesial system harbored an individualism and was so radical that it could not in any practical way fulfill his noble vision; and in fact the lack of sufficient government and discipline in Christian Union caused the fellowship to cave in on itself. There was constant confusion and dissension within the fellowship over any number of doctrinal and disciplinary issues; members inevitably wandered off and the sheep were scattered for lack of government and discipline. Simply put, the system lacked the necessary principles to enable the members to cohere together in one concrete body and to grow up together in the fullness of Christ. It became obvious soon after the first Christian Union church was set in order at Barney Creek in 1886 that Spurling's high ideals about brotherly love, equality, and mutual respect were not sufficient to sustain the fellowship of God's people; and that God has set certain rules and practical regulations in the church to yoke believers together in their worship and work.

It is almost certain that if Spurling's congregations had not been drawn into the holiness revival that swept Monroe County beginning in 1895, that Christian Union would have died out altogether. It was the new dynamic of holiness experience and holiness teachings that revived and sustained the movement between 1895 and the time that Tomlinson joined the church in 1903. As it turned out in any case, Christian Union churches at Piney Grove, Shuler Creek, and on Paul's Mountain eventually collapsed for lack of sufficient government and discipline, and a cooperative mission effort. In point of fact, after Tomlinson introduced centralized government and united the churches together under his leadership, the Christian Union congregations that refused to come under the new government became defunct. The churches at Shuler Creek and on Paul's Mountain disbanded rather quickly; and the church at Piney Grove, though sustaining itself for three generations mainly through one family, also eventually died away.

It was the personal vision and leadership ability of A.J. Tomlinson that transformed the Church of God both theologically and structurally. It would be difficult to exaggerate, in fact, the extent to which his personality and vision overwhelmed the fellowship between 1903 and 1922. Alonzo Gann, the chairman of the Better Government Committee in 1922 and one of the Twelve Elders, said that

> [Tomlinson] was the most instrumental of any human being in the Church of God, in bringing about the new lights that were shed upon the church because he acted as moderator in all Assemblies I have ever been in and used his influence in the passage of all of them. We had such confidence in him he could just say the word and we would all adhere to what he said. His influence I guess was more influential in bringing about these different determinations of the Church than all of us together. I am confident of that.[1]

Even Lee admitted that '[Tomlinson] had been responsible for the interpretations placed upon the Bible in more instances than any other one man in the church'.[2]

---

[1] Gann, 'Deposition', pp. 98-99.
[2] Lee, 'Deposition', p. 921.

It is important to grasp the significance of this, for through Tomlinson the influence of several radical Christian traditions came to bear on the theological and political development of the Church of God, including as we noticed in Chapter 4, Indiana Quakerism, Frank W. Sandford and his Shiloh community in Maine, the radical holiness preachers connected with God's Bible School in Cincinnati, A.B. Simpson and his Christian Missionary Alliance movement in New York, Benjamin Hardin Irwin's fire-baptized holiness movement through the Midwest and Southeast, and several other movements that promoted apostolic primitivism and revivalism. The ministries of John Alexander Dowie in Chicago, Charles Fox Parham in Kansas, and William Seymour in Los Angeles also affected the development of the Church of God either directly or indirectly through Tomlinson.

Having come under the influence of R.G. Spurling in 1903, the Landmark Baptist tradition now also formed part of Tomlinson's religious experience; and thus through Tomlinson the Church of God became an intriguing eclecticism. It is not too much to say in fact that Tomlinson represented a link that joined together not only Spurling and Sandford and his own Quaker tradition, but also a great chain of elements in historic Christianity. In and through him merged elements of the Anabaptist and Baptist traditions, Quakerism, late nineteenth and early twentieth-century restorationism and revivalism, the Holiness and Pentecostal Movements, and relics of many marginal, mystical, and nonconformist sects in American Christianity. The theology of Jacob Arminius and vestiges of a moderate Calvinism found place in him; traces of Puritanism were mixed with his Quaker roots; and rudiments of Lutheran Pietism may be seen in him. Further, traditional orthodoxy and radical nonconformity, Catholicism and Congregationalism, Americanism and monarchism, the Old World and the New, the American North and South, the urbane and rural Appalachia all

Figure 68
R.G. SPURLING (C. 1915)

merged in Tomlinson with their diversity of elements to form what came to be known as the Church of God.³

The Trinity

Both Spurling and Tomlinson despised deep theological reflection and blamed the church's apostasy in the fourth century on the formulation of articles of faith and the adoption of creeds. Spurling had gone so far to say that Arius should not have been disciplined by the church for merely holding that Jesus was a creature and that there was a time 'in which He was not'. Apparently, Spurling did not grasp the theological implications and practical consequences of Arius' heresy, and therefore maintained that the church had no excuse for dividing over the issue.⁴ It was probably Spurling's weakness in this regard and the fact that Christian Union allowed each man to interpret the Bible for himself, and that every person had a divine right and obligation to live according to his own conscience, that Andy Paul, whom we noticed earlier, eventually pulled away from Christian Union and formed an independent church on the basis of the 'Jesus Only' doctrine.⁵

Figure 69

MARY JANE AND A.J. TOMLINSON (C. 1918)

Tomlinson, conversely, as we have seen actually declared on one occasion that Jesus was a created being, yet in utter theological confusion otherwise praised and exalted Him as the Son of God.⁶ But for Tomlinson and most early Church of God ministers and members, Jesus' sonship did not signify equality with the Father. Somehow it was simply

---

³ Phillips, *Quakerism*, pp. 1-2.
⁴ Spurling, *Lost Link*, pp. 23-26.
⁵ See 'Christian Union on Paul's Mountain' in Chapter 2.
⁶ A.J. Tomlinson, 'Our Christmas Message', *WWM* (Dec. 21, 1940), pp. 1, 4.

held that Jesus was unique and special and to be praised and exalted but that He was something less than Almighty God! The pre-existence of Christ, the miraculous nature of His virgin birth, and the special relationship of the three Persons in one Godhead were generally accepted on the basis of the biblical revelation, but were not considered subjects open for theological debate.

A significant number of Church of God ministers and members between 1886 and 1923 therefore harbored a tri-theistic concept of God. Jesus was Lord and Savior and the Head of the church, but He was subordinate to the Father both before and after His incarnation. But notwithstanding Spurling's and Tomlinson's theological weaknesses and tritheistic leanings, the orthodox Trinitarian theology and experience of the fire-baptized movement and its influence on the church was positive and helpful. It was this deep mystical movement rooted in Wesleyan theology and experience that won out in the Church of God; for after the Church of God divided in 1923, both factions eventually adopted orthodox Trinitarian statements of faith.

The Bible

Almost all Protestant and evangelical bodies in America in the nineteenth and early twentieth century presumed the infallibility of the Bible, and the Church of God was no exception. The people in the southern Appalachian Mountains even more especially took for granted that the Bible is God's inspired Word and endeared it as such; and most of them made it the centerpiece of their homes and family life. Illustrative of this fact, thousands of photos were taken by itinerate photographers in 1895-1905 of Baptist and Church of God families in the region bordering the tri-state area of western North Carolina, eastern Tennessee, and northern Georgia; and in most of the instances, the patriarch is seated in the center of the photo holding a large family Bible surrounded by his wife and children and grandchildren.

Following in the stream of John Calvin in regard to exalting the reliability of the Bible, the Church of God believed the Bible was self-authenticating through the power and illumination of the Holy Spirit, and needed no sophisticated theological defense. Taking issue with Roman Catholics and philosophical rationalists in his day, Calvin reasoned,

> Nothing, therefore, can be more absurd than the fiction that the power of judging Scripture is in the Church, and that on her nod its certainty depends ... As to the question, How shall we be persuaded

> that it came from God without recurring to a decree of the Church? It is just the same as if it were asked, How shall we distinguish light from darkness, white from black, sweet from bitter? Scripture bears on the face of it as clear evidence of its truth ... The witness of the Spirit is superior to all arguments. God in His Word is the only adequate witness concerning Himself; and in like manner His Word will not find credence in the hearts of men until it is sealed by the witness of the Spirit. The same Spirit that spoke by the Prophets must enter our heart to convince us that they faithfully delivered the message which He gave to them. Isa. 59.21. Let this then be a settled point, that those who are inwardly taught by the Holy Spirit place firm reliance on Scripture; and that Scripture is its own evidence. And may not lawfully be subjected to proofs and arguments, but obtains by the testimony of the Spirit that confidence it which deserves.[7]

Again, as if he anticipated the error of many Quakers and spiritualists in the next century, Calvin argued,

> Those who, rejecting Scripture, imagine that they have some peculiar way of penetrating to God, are to be deemed not so much under the influence of error as madness. For certain giddy men have lately appeared, who, while they make great display of the superiority of the Spirit, reject all reading of the Scriptures themselves, and deride the simplicity of those who only delight in what they call the dead and deadly letter. But I wish they would tell me what spirit it is whose inspiration raises them to such a sublime height that they dare despise the doctrine of the Scripture as mean and childish. If they answer that it is the Spirit of Christ, their confidence is exceedingly ridiculous; since they will, I presume, admit that the apostles and other believers in the primitive Church were not illuminated by any other Spirit. None of these thereby learned to despise the Word of God, but every one was imbued with greater reverence for it, as their writings most clearly testify ... Hence it is easy to understand that we must give diligent heed both to the reading and hearing of the Scripture, if we are to obtain any benefit from the Spirit of God (just a Peter praises those who attentively study the doctrine of the prophets [2 Pet. 1.19] ... Add to this, that Paul, though he was carried up even to the third heaven, ceased not to profit by the doctrine of the law and the prophets, while, in like manner, he exhorts Timothy, a teacher of singular excellence, to give attention to reading (1 Tim.

---

[7] John Calvin, *Institutes of the Christian Religion* (Grand Rapids: Eerdmans, 1983 reprint), pp. 68-73.

4.13). And the eulogium which he pronounces on Scripture deserves to be remembered – viz., that 'it is profitable for doctrine, for reproof, for correction, and for instruction in righteousness, that the man of God may be perfect' (2 Tim. 3.16) ... Since Satan transforms himself into an angel of light, what authority can the Spirit have with us if he be not ascertained by an infallible mark? ...[so] lest Satan should insinuate himself under [the Holy Spirit's] name, He wishes us to recognize Him by the image which He stamped on the Scriptures. The author of the Scriptures cannot vary, and change in His likeness.[8]

Although John Wesley interpreted the Scriptures radically differently from Calvin, yet he agreed with him in identifying the Scriptures as the very Word of God and attributing to them the highest sense of divinity. Wesley confessed, 'I am a man of one Book'. In his *Explanatory Notes on the New Testament*, he wrote,

Concerning the Scriptures ... the word of the living God ... was committed to writing ... This is that 'word of God which remains for ever' which 'though heaven and earth shall pass away, one jot or tittle shall not pass away'. The Scripture, therefore, of Old and New Testaments is a most solid and precious system of divine truth.[9]

The Church of God as well as most Christian denominations and religious groups in America agreed with these sentiments and convictions.

American presidents and statesmen no less than Christian clergyman and average church members believed that there was a supernatural element that brought about and preserved the Bible. George Washington declared, 'Above all, the pure light of revelation has had an influence on mankind, and increased the blessings of society. It is impossible to rightly govern the world without God and the Bible'.[10] John Adams designated the Bible 'the best book in the world'.[11] John Quincy Adams noted that 'The first and almost only book deserving of universal attention is the Bible'. Henry Clay could say that it is 'the only book to give hope in darkness'.[12] Daniel Webster magnified it as 'the book of all

---

[8] Calvin, *Institutes*, pp. 84-85.
[9] John Wesley, *Explanatory Notes Upon the New Testament* (London: Epworth, 1941, reprint), p. 9.
[10] Cited in Finis Jennings Dake, *God's Plan for Man* (Lawrenceville, GA: Dake Bible Sales, Inc. 1949), p. 19.
[11] Cited in Nathan O. Hatch and Mark A Noll (eds.), *The Bible in America* (New York: Oxford University Press, 1982), p. 40.
[12] Cited in Hatch and Noll (eds.), *Bible in America*, p. 40.

others for lawyers as well as for divines'.[13] And of course the celebrated dictum of President Lincoln that attributed supreme worth to the Bible as 'the best book that God has given to man'. Franklin D. Roosevelt thus discerned the prominence and importance of the Bible in American history and American life, acknowledging, 'The influence of the Scriptures in the early days of the Republic is plainly revealed in the writing and thinking of the men who made the nation possible ... They found in the Scriptures that which shaped their course and determined their action'.[14]

National leaders knew that biblical images aroused and inspired the public spirit. Yet the celebration of the Bible was not for them merely a political scheme. They themselves were conditioned by and woven into the fabric of Old Testament themes and images, so that they could hardly avoid expressing them in their lives and work. And thus they created and developed, either consciously or unconsciously, their statecraft by the light and inspiration of the Holy Scriptures. It is not surprising, then, that Benjamin Franklin proposed to the Continental Congress that the national seal reflect an image of Moses, depicted in the books of Exodus and Numbers, leading Israel through the Red Sea to her destiny. The celebrated Jefferson, though a deist, and in part a product of the Enlightenment, suggested a similar image of Israel being led by a cloud and pillar of fire through the wilderness.[15] This strong Judeo-Christian influence little by little formed America into what one historian designated 'a nation with the soul of a church'.[16]

The Bible – the ultimate and sovereign authority of Protestant Christianity – was taken for granted in America. There were various interpretations of it, to be sure, but only men who wished to be considered infidels and fools questioned its divinity and authority. And thus most of America's founding fathers were so familiar with and influenced by biblical language and concepts---particularly the nationalism in the Old Testament---that the new nation was bound to reflect the affinity.

American children were often named for biblical characters particularly in the pre-Revolutionary era and for the first century after nationhood was constituted. Richard Spurling's grandfather, John Spurling, for

---

[13] Cited in Hatch and Noll (eds.), *Bible in America*, p. 40
[14] Cited in Dake, *God's Plan for Man*, p. 19.
[15] Hatch and Noll (eds.), *Bible in America*, p. 40.
[16] Perry C. Cotham, 'The Nation With the Soul of a Church', in *Politics, Americanism, and Christianity*, pp. 127-53; for a broader view of this concept, see Sidney F. Mead, *The Lively Experiment: The Shaping of Christianity in America* (New York: Harper and Row, 1963); and for the narrower context in the Church of God, see Phillips, *The Church of God: A Portrait of America*.

example, reproduced twenty-three children, naming the boys, Isaac, Jesse, Jeremiah, Elijah, Eli, Aaron, Levi, James, John, Andrew, and Stephen, and the girls, Mary, Anna, Elizabeth, Delilah, Sarah, and Rachel, making exception in only four instances. Except for nature's limitations, the Spurling patriarch doubtlessly would have sired namesakes for all the major personalities in Scripture. One of John Spurling's fellow Baptists actually named his daughter, *Talitha-cumi*.

Likewise, Tomlinson's ancestors in America were named Noah, Jacob, Moses, Levi, Samuel, Jesse, Josiah, Zechariah, Sarah, Esther, Dinah, and Charity, among others. His mother's name was Delilah. German and Scotch-Irish immigrants in America named their children, Uriah, Hezekiah, Obadiah, Absalom, Cyrus, Darius, Jerahmeel, Ichabod, Abel, Seth, Gideon, Asahel, Biel, Asel, Asher, Eliakim, Benoni, Azariah, Nehemiah, Eliphalet, Enos, Jehiel, Elijah, Elisha, Eli, Gideon, Ebenezer, Asa, Ephraim, Mannaseh, Eleazar, Jedidiah, Jephtha, Melchizedic, Isham, Peleg, Bethuel, Phinehas, Caleb, Elnathan, Lebbeus, Onesimus, Philemon, and other strange-sounding Hebrew, Chaldee, and Greek names, all in honor of prominent men and women in the Holy Scriptures.

Tomlinson was aware of the higher criticism movement that was just then making some headway in the universities and seminaries, but it was having no impact on the Church of God and other groups that were fully convinced of the inspiration and infallibility of the Bible. Tomlinson wrote in *The Last Great Conflict* of the 'infallible Word of God'[17] and offered scripture and verse for every teaching that he proclaimed. He wrote,

> This blessed old Book has stood the tests of ages and has been opposed in every generation since its origin, but today it has wider circulation than any time in the history of the past. If the Bible could be destroyed then we would have nothing to depend on that is infallible ...[18]

The reliability and perfection of the Bible as the revelation of God was thus never questioned in the Church of God and was never an issue. Indeed, it served as the basis for the covenant of Christian Union in 1886, the precise wording of which was examined in Chapter 1. By 1912 the formula had been modified and the candidates for membership committed themselves under the following sacred obligation:

---

[17] Tomlinson, *LGC*, p. 110.
[18] Tomlinson, *LGC*, p. 112.

> Will you sincerely promise before God and these witnesses that you will take the Bible as your guide, the New Testament as your rule of faith and practice, government and discipline and walk in the light to the best of your knowledge and ability?[19]

Before the covenant was administered to a prospective candidate, certain teachings of Jesus and the apostles considered prominent in the Scriptures were publicly read, and it was necessary for the person being received into the fellowship to accept the church's interpretation of these teachings as a rule of faith, and this in order for all of the members to have the 'same judgment', 'speak the same thing', and 'walk by the same rule'. Biblical references such as Rom. 15.6; 1 Cor. 1.10; and Phil. 3.16 were cited for authority for this practice. It was thus on this basis that the government and discipline of the church was established.

The Church

The 'founders' of the Church of God were preoccupied throughout their lives with the nature, characteristics, and mission of the church of the Bible; in fact, they saw themselves on a quest to discover and restore the Bible church in order to fulfill its prophetic mission in the world. We examined Spurling's doctrine and vision of the church in Chapters One and Two, including his experiment in Christian Union. In Chapter 3 we examined the holiness-Pentecostal transformation of the church, and in Chapter 4 we explored the initial reformation and transformation of the church under the leadership and vision of Tomlinson.

The remaining chapters of this book will analyze and critique the on-going radical transformation of the Church of God under Tomlinson's leadership and vision, which on one hand would see the church grow into a prestigious international organization, and on the other hand experience a great deal of turbulence and disharmony. The confusion and strife, as we will see further on, resulted finally in a small division in 1919-1920, which then escalated into a major spectacle and division in 1922-1923. The spectacle ended in a significant disruption followed by a bitter legal battle that would last for more than two decades.

Tomlinson's leadership radically transformed the government and polity of the church between 1903 and 1921; yet there were certain principles that remained constant and unchanged in regard to Spurling's original doctrine and vision in 1886, and these principles formed the foundation of the Church of God. Among these were the following: 1)

---

[19] Tomlinson, *LGC*, p. 218.

the church and kingdom are distinct entities: one is 'born' into the kingdom of God (Jn 3.3-8; Col. 1.13) but 'added' to the church of God (Acts 2.47; 2 Cor. 11.2); 2) the church is visible (Mt. 5.14; 1 Cor. 1.2), the kingdom invisible (Lk. 17.20, 21; Jn 3.3-8); 3) the church is God's government in the earth administrated through human instrumentality (Mt. 16.18-20; 18.15-20; Mk 13.34; Acts 1.14-22; 6.1-7; 15-16.5; Eph. 4.11-16; *et al.*); 4) the church is formed visibly by a church covenant (Exod. 19.5-8; 24.3-8; 2 Kgs 23.2-3; Isa. 62.5; Jer. 50.5; Ezek. 16.8; Jn 17.6, 8, 14; Acts 2.40-47; 2 Cor. 11.2); 5) the church is authorized and empowered to exercise discipline and to keep itself pure (Mt. 18.15-20; 1 Cor. 5.1-13; 6.1-4; *et al.*); 6) the church was ordained by God to fall and then to be restored (Song 6.10-12; Isa. 60.1-5; Zech. 14.6-8), following the pattern of her Lord who died and then came forth from the grave.[20]

Like Spurling, Tomlinson at first taught that the church began on the day of Pentecost,[21] but later he understood that the church had been established by Jesus Himself under the New Covenant before the day of Pentecost: and this became an important aspect of the doctrine of the church among his followers after the disruption in 1923.[22] Tomlinson also changed his view on the relationship between the church and the bride. Before the disruption, he boldly denied that the church was synonymous with the bride; for he understood the church apparently to be the bride-in-the-making, and therefore only a part of the church was destined to be the prophetic bride. Reflecting on an early Pentecostal writer who taught that the church and bride are synonymous, Tomlinson noted in his typical confident and critical style:

> The same writer affirms that the church is the bride and the bride is the church. If this is true, then the church must now be something different from what it was in John's day, or else a backslidden preacher or pastor has the power to divorce and cast out of the bride one who is espoused to the King, for at 3 John 9 and 10 we read, 'I wrote unto the church: but Diotrephes … casteth them out of the church'. If the church and bride are the same then it would do to have it read thus – Diotrephes casteth them out of the bride.

---

[20] Tomlinson wrote in 1912, 'The church is the body of Christ (Col. 1.24), then it is no surprise if she follow her Lord into obscurity and then make her appearance again' (Tomlinson, *LGC*, p. 146; see also pp. 147-50).

[21] Tomlinson, *LGC*, p. 154.

[22] *HAA*, III, p. 220; see also Tomlinson's tract *The Last Days Church of God* written in the early 1930s, pp. 7-9. The Scriptural references cited for the origin of the church under the New Covenant are Mk 3.13-15 and Lk. 6.12-17.

Honest, sincere and humble people can readily see the inconsistency of such teaching. This is a time when mere theories and false teachings are being exposed and the false teachers themselves put out of the ring.[23]

As late as 1926 Tomlinson was still teaching that 'the bride will be composed of only a part of the church'.[24] He apparently thought that only certain ones in the church militant would be perfected and thus be identified as the bride of Christ – the church triumphant. It was not until about 1929 that he began to modify his interpretation of the church relative to the bride, and to crystallize his doctrine of the 'Last Days Church of God'. Thereafter, he plainly stated on several occasions that the church and the bride are one and the same, and that the whole church, not just a part of it, would be perfected and presented to Christ at His appearing.[25] During a *Questions and Answers* session in the 1932 Assembly he stated, 'I have decided to talk about [the church] like the Bible says. He is going to present IT to Himself a glorious Church, and that is the whole Church'.[26]

Tomlinson's restoration view of the church was agreeable with Spurling's and the Anabaptist's view and also his traditional Quaker view – namely, that the New Testament church apostatized and needed to be restored; and this view was supported also by a large number of radical holiness-Pentecostal groups in the late nineteenth and early twentieth century. But, as we noticed in Chapter 4, none of these impacted him more than the community at Shiloh in Maine. The recurring theme in Sandford's teaching of the bride in the Song of Solomon anchored itself deep in Tomlinson's psyche. Ever after his Shiloh experience, he would glory in the prophetic vision of the church and cry out with the ancient seer, 'Return, return, O Shulamite; return, return, that we may look upon thee'.[27]

Tomlinson's vision of 'The Last Days Church of God' gradually became the driving force and prophetic burden of his life and ministry. After he discovered the church of the Bible through Spurling's teaching and had become more fully convinced by a personal revelation of the Spirit on the mountain at Camp Creek, he set out to restore the apostolic church and to spread its message to the ends of the earth.[28] He

---

[23] Tomlinson, *LGC*, p.135.
[24] *GAM*, 1926, p. 49.
[25] *HAA*, III, pp. 261-63.
[26] *GAM*, 1932, p. 53
[27] Tomlinson, *LGC*, p. 149.
[28] Tomlinson, *LGC*, pp. 154-63.

awoke each morning anxious to rebuild God's house, always looking forward with thrilling expectations through the eyes of faith to see the apostolic church unfold during his ministry. And his indefatigable energy to fulfill his vision, no less than Sandford had attempted to fulfill his at Shiloh, was contagious. Hundreds and thousands and then tens-of-thousands entered into that vision, and, like Tomlinson, gloried in it and gave their all to proclaim it to the ends of the earth!

> As the discovery was made a shout pierced through [my] soul, and almost before [I] was aware of it, [I] was ... shouting at the top of [my] voice, leaping and clapping [my] hands as [I] cried, 'The Church of God! The Church of God! From her extends all previous truths! From her comes all the laws and government we need! Away with your articles of faith! Away with your creeds! Upon "this rock" Jesus built His church, and there it is just like it was, only it had been hidden from view by the debris of the "dark ages", unbelief, and man made churches and organizations! Hallelujah! Hallelujah! Glory! Glory!' And the shouts and cries of joy were taken up by the other fruit, and echoed and re-echoed until dread consternation seized scores and hundreds of people looked on with amazement and wonder.[29]

Notwithstanding Tomlinson's zeal for the 'Great Church of God' and his self-proclaimed special agency in rediscovering the 'Last Days Church', it was his doctrine of the church in particular that was most confusing; for not only did he change his views on when the church began and its relationship to the bride, but some of his more important doctrines and illustrations were often ambiguous and confusing, if not self-contradictory. He insisted, for example, that the church is strictly visible – made up of real flesh and blood members – yet conversely he asserted that the church is a divine system constituted of doctrines and an outward structure even without real flesh and blood people. For example, in his comparison of the church to the ancient city of Pompeii, he says that just as that city was covered over with the lava from Vesuvius in the first century, so the Church of God was 'snowed under' with creeds – with men's laws and ways.[30] But just as excavations have uncovered the walls, streets, gates, and some inscriptions of the original inhabitants of the city, so the original doctrine and government of the church is being uncovered. Further, he says in regard to Pompeii, 'Its former inhabitants are gone, but the city itself is still there'. So also in

---

[29] Tomlinson, *LGC*, p. 159.
[30] A.J. Tomlinson, 'The Covering Removed', pp. 5-9.

regard to the church, he says, 'Peter and James, and John and Paul are gone, but their writings and instructions are preserved; the same form of government and everything pertaining to the building (Church) itself is sound and solid, just like it was when it was covered up centuries ago'.[31] Again he says, 'The building has been preserved, but is now being uncovered and people are now flocking to it. They see in the beautiful form just what their hearts have been craving'.[32] His reasoning here is more or less Platonic in that he sees the church as 'the building itself', which he understands to be the doctrine, government, and outward structure of the organization; and thus, though all of the people may be dead under the ashes of Vesuvius or under a spiritual cloud of apostasy, still the form of the church is somehow still there.

Tomlinson thus denied that the church ever ceased to exist. He says that the church was always there during the Dark Ages; it was just covered over with creeds and men-made traditions, etc. He insisted therefore that it was never 'overthrown' but only covered over; and he said this in order to reconcile the idea of the apostasy in 325 CE with Jesus' promise that 'the gates of hell shall not prevail against [the church]'.[33] His logic here, however, contradicted the doctrine that the church is essentially a body of 'real flesh and blood people' covenanted together in a distinct and visible government, a doctrine with which he otherwise agreed and proclaimed. If the church is in fact just as real and visible as the United States of America and formed by a verbal covenant just as real and binding as the constitution of the United States,[34] then where was this 'city set on a hill' during the Dark Ages? Where was the living body of Christ, particularly the 'members one of another?' Where was the divine government and system operating? Where were its ordained rulers holding business conferences? Where was the *ekklesia*?

If the church, as Tomlinson admits elsewhere, 'is made up of real flesh and blood people', and 'that God's church only exists where His law and government [is] observed by His children',[35] then how was it not really 'overthrown' in the days of Constantine, when it adopted the Nicene Creed in 325 CE and joined together with the state. Ironically, Tomlinson agreed with Spurling and the Anabaptists in regard to the church's apostasy in 325 CE, but he insisted contrary to Spurling and the Anabaptists that it was merely 'covered over' rather than 'overthrown'

---

[31] Tomlinson, 'Covering Removed', p. 7.
[32] Tomlinson, 'Covering Removed', p. 8.
[33] Tomlinson, 'Covering Removed', pp. 5, 9.
[34] Tomlinson, *LGC,* pp. 70-72.
[35] Tomlinson, *LGC,* p. 206.

and destroyed. But his logic here contradicted what he otherwise endeavored to maintain, namely, that the church is actually regenerate believers in covenant together and operating under the government of God, and when they are not faithful they cease to be the church. He wrote in his *The Last Great Conflict* that 'The very moment [the leaders] formulated [the first] creed and set the church upon it, that very moment it ceased to be the Church of God'.[36] Again, in reference to the adoption of the Constitution in 1921 and the subsequent reformation by his followers, he declared, 'It was a creed that wrecked us in 1921',[37] and again, 'Since the passage of this Constitution we have not been the Church of God'.[38] In his annual address in November 1923, Tomlinson referred to the *Call Council* held in Chattanooga the previous August, and noted,

> it was acknowledged that the constitution just as literally destroyed the Church of God as the Nicene Creed destroyed it in the year 325, and the only thing left for us to do was to repudiate the constitution and every other action of the past Assemblies that caused a departure from the faith and true Bible principles, and, by God's permission and help, resolve ourselves back into the Church of God under Bible rule and government.[39]

Again it is difficult, if not impossible, to reconcile Tomlinson's illustration of the church as a trunk of a tree with the branches being represented as doctrines rather than persons. This illustration becomes even more confusing because he depicts Martin Luther, John Wesley, George Fox, A.B. Simpson, and W.J. Seymour as rediscovering the most important teachings of the church, yet somehow they were not connected with the trunk of the tree.[40] They were the 'fruit of the branches' yet 'none of these men ... ever crawled back down the branches to discover, if possible, where they started from, and [thus did not] locate the trunk of the tree'.[41] Again, this illustration clashes with the original doctrine of the church as a visible body with a distinct government and discipline, making the church more or less spiritual in nature: for the branches of the tree are said to be producing fruit (illustrated in Luther, Fox, Wesley, Simpson, Seymour, *et al.*) yet this fruit did not know it was part of the tree trunk; and therefore, according to the logic, it was not

---

[36] Tomlinson, *LGC*, p. 166.
[37] Tomlinson, *Call Council*, p. 2.
[38] Tomlinson, *Call Council*, p. 7.
[39] *HAA*, I, p. 219.
[40] Tomlinson, *LGC*, pp. 155-60.
[41] Tomlinson, *LGC*, p. 157.

part of the tree. Again, the church in this sense is identified with doctrines rather than real flesh and blood persons, that is, the doctrines produced fruit but the fruit was not part of the church.

Figure 70
NORA CHAMBERS (C. 1912)

Figure 71
M.S. LEMONS AND EFFORD HAYNES (C. 1920)

Nora I. Chambers had the distinction of being licensed in the Church of God by R.G. Spurling. She had been a student and teacher at Holmes Bible School at Altamont, South Carolina. There she befriended E.J. Boehmer, both of whom were destined to become prominent leaders in Cleveland. Nora and her husband, Fred, evangelized the mountains of North Carolina, Tennessee, and Georgia in 1909-1913. They labored together on occasion with J.W. Buckalew, C.R. Curtis, and J.A. Davis, as well as with Boehmer *et al*. They were violently persecuted and suffered deprivations for the sake of the Gospel. Nora became an outstanding teacher and, accordingly, was selected in 1918 by Tomlinson and the Elders to teach in the newly established Bible Training School in Cleveland.

Lemons and Haynes teamed up for evangelistic campaigns in the South. They held tent meetings in South Carolina, Georgia, Florida, Alabama, Tennessee, and Mississippi. Haynes was a charter member of the Pentecostal Worldwide Mission Band, and shortly before its virgin voyage to the Bahamas in 1911, he married Miss Clyde Cotton. Significantly he was selected in 1919 to succeed Sam C. Perry on the prestigious Council of Twelve. Haynes was a notable singer and musician. With Lemons he edited the first Church of God songbook, 'Church of God Songs: Tears with Joy'.

Full Plan of Salvation Restored

In addition to the visible church itself being rediscovered and reestablished, with its unique form of government and polity, the full plan of salvation along the lines of Wesleyan theology and experience was restored between 1895 and 1908. It was generally concluded that 'all were born under sin' and that Jesus' death provided for a 'general atonement', which meant that 'whosoever will' could repent and be saved. This position was held by Spurling and the ministers and members in Christian Union from the beginning.[42] But after the church was swept into the Holiness Movement, salvation included not only justification [regeneration] as a crisis experience, but also sanctification as a second crisis experience – a 'second definite and instantaneous work of grace'.[43]

After William Durham in 1910 preached his famous or infamous sermon on the 'Finished Work' concept of Christ's death, and divided the Pentecostal movement into two camps – Wesleyan and non-Wesleyan – Tomlinson and the Church of God remained squarely in the camp of the Wesleyan tradition. Wesley had taught in his *Plain Account of Christian Perfection* that the blood of Christ had provided for an instantaneous experience of entire sanctification that he termed 'Christian perfection'. He had admonished believers therefore to seek for this glorious work of grace, which he adjudged to be the meaning of the apostle Paul's words – 'our old man is crucified' (Rom. 6.1-6). So whereas in regeneration one became a new creation in Christ and his actual sins were forgiven, in sanctification the root of sin was removed and one was made perfect in love! Durham, however, after having been baptized with the Spirit at the Azusa Street Mission in March 1907, returned to his church in Chicago and soon began to contradict the traditional Wesleyan view of sanctification, which flew in the face of the interpretation and experience of almost all holiness-Pentecostal churches in the early twentieth century. He apparently had reverted back to his Baptist roots in teaching that sanctification was a gradual process that began at conversion and was completed only in glorification.

---

[42] Interestingly, Spurling's original license signed by his father in 1886 specifically states that he was ordained on the basis of belief in a 'general atonement', apparently to distinguish the ministers in Christian Union over against the Primitive Baptists and 'hard shell' Calvinists.

[43] This may be seen in the resolutions adopted year after year by the General Assembly as doctrinal issues were addressed and settled. Justification and regeneration had been accepted as tenets of faith and practiced in the church since 1886 (Spurling, *Lost Link*, pp. 7-10, 44, 45); but the Holiness Church at Camp Creek set in order in May 1902 marked the church's acceptance of sanctification as a second definite and instantaneous work of grace in the heart.

Durham's doctrine – actually a Calvinistic view of the order of salvation – had a powerful effect on many reputable Pentecostal leaders who were gradually swept into the new non-Wesleyan Pentecostal movement. The most glaring effect of Durham's doctrine was in the establishment of the Assemblies of God in 1914 in Hot Springs, Arkansas. In the opening address of the convention, M.M. Pinson (who had attended the 1910 General Assembly of the Church of God as one of Tomlinson's guests) proclaimed, 'The Finished Work of Calvary'. Most early Pentecostal leaders – e.g. T.B. Barratt, C.H. Mason, J.H. King, G.B. Cashwell, W.J. Seymour, and especially Tomlinson – passionately opposed the doctrine, and many like Charles Parham and Florence Crawford categorized it as a 'doctrine of devils'.

There were other dynamic movements that taught a 'higher Christian life' and 'deeper and fuller experiences in the Holy Spirit' but denied at the same time a second instantaneous experience of entire sanctification. The most notable and influential of these was the Keswick Movement originating in England in the last half of the nineteenth century and spreading throughout Europe and the United States in the late nineteenth and early twentieth century. 'Keswickians' taught that there was a higher experience in the Spirit subsequent to regeneration, yet insisted that the sin nature in 'man' – 'the old man' – could not be eradicated but only suppressed. Pentecostals were thus divided between 'suppressionists' and 'eradicationists'. Again Tomlinson and the Church of God believed it was of paramount importance to hold to a second definite work in which the 'old man' is crucified. Tomlinson's reflection on his own experience in the cornfields of Westfield Indiana in July 1892 was his expectation for every blood-bought child of God.

> Some little time after [regeneration], I fell into a tremendous conflict with an 'old man' who gave me a violent contest. I fought him and wrestled with him day and night for several months. How to conquer him I did not know. Nobody could tell me or give me much encouragement. I had some serious thoughts of building a little booth out in the middle of a certain field, where I could be alone with God and the Bible. Nobody could help me, so I did not want to be where they were. I was making a corn crop, and I suppose I prayed in nearly every row, and nearly all over the field. Though I worked hard every day, I frequently ate but one meal a day. I remember it as if it were but yesterday. I would leave the house at night at times, and stay out and pray for hours. I searched my Bible and prayed many nights till midnight and two o'clock, and then at work again the next morning at sun up. It was hard fight, but I was determined for that 'old man'

to die. He had already given me much trouble, and I knew he would continue to do do if he was not slain. I saw it, and I knew he must be destroyed or I would be ruined, and my soul dragged down to hell by his subtile influence and cruel grasp.

At last the struggle came. It was a hand to hand fight, and the demons of hell seemed to be mustering their forces, and their ghastly forms and furious yells would no doubt have been too much for me had not the Lord of heaven sent a host of angels to assist me in that terrible hour of peril. But it was the last great conflict, and I managed, by some peculiar dexterity, to put the sword into him up to the hilt.

It was about twelve o'clock in the day. I cried out in the bitterness of my soul: 'Now! Now! You've got to give up now! Now! I felt him begin to weaken and quiver. I kept the 'Sword' right in him, and never let go. That sharp two-edged 'Sword' was doing its deadly work. I did not pity him. I showed him no quarters. There we were in that attitude when all of a sudden came from above, like a thunderbolt from the skies, a sensational power that ended the conflict, and there lay the 'old man' dead at my feet, and I was free from his grasp.[44]

We have seen that the influence of apostolic restoration movements in the late-nineteenth century merged with the church's Anabaptist and holiness roots in the early twentieth century, and by 1908 the Church of God stood in the classical holiness-Pentecostal tradition.[45] Though the church's acceptance of the new Pentecostalism was challenged in the local church in Cleveland in 1909-1910, the organization as a whole emerged from the ordeal fully committed to a baptism of divine power subsequent to sanctification, namely, the baptism with the Holy Ghost with the evidence of speaking in other tongues. It followed naturally that the full restoration of spiritual and charismatic gifts flowed naturally out of this Pentecostal theology and experience, and by the end of 1908 the Church of God was teaching 'the baptism with the Holy Ghost and speaking in tongues', 'the full restoration of the gifts to the Church', and

---

[44] Tomlinson, *LGC*, pp. 225-26.
[45] The baptism with the Holy Ghost had been widely experienced in the church since 1898; however, the doctrine of speaking in tongues as 'initial evidence' of Spirit-baptism gained acceptance only little by little between 1906 and 1908 (see *GAM 1906-1914*, pp. 35-39).

'signs following believers'. And these teachings and experiences became an integral part of the church's worship and ministry.⁴⁶

Figure 72

J.W. BUCKALEW (C. 1910)

Figure 73

MARGARET MELISSA SHEARER (C. 1900)

Buckalew's fearless aggression in proclaiming the holiness-Pentecostal Gospel won him the nickname, 'Old Rough and Ready'. The Church of God was built by men like him – men willing to sacrifice temporal comforts and pleasures to answer the call of God. He worked the cotton fields during the day to support his family and preached at night. He was severely persecuted, and on more than one occasion arrested for the sake of the Gospel. Typical of many of the church's pioneers, Buckalew was unpolished and deprived of formal education, yet he was powerfully anointed and produced much fruit for Christ and the church until his death in 1918. A drunkard, gambler, and brawler before his conversion (had been left for dead on one occasion after a fight over a gambling dispute), he was wonderfully saved under the influence of L.P. Adams, and was later baptized with the Spirit under the preaching of Miss Clyde Cotton. He joined the church on February 20, 1910. Buckalew was part of the Pentecostal Worldwide Mission

---

⁴⁶ Thus when the church published its 'prominent teachings' in the Assembly Minutes in 1913, the tenth teaching was called 'The full restoration of the gifts to the church', citing 1 Cor. 12.1, 7, 10, 28, 31; 14.1 as proof texts (*GAM 1906-1914*, p. 245).

Band that sailed to the Bahamas in 1911 to plant the Church of God in that island nation. His wife, Mattie, was also a preacher and labored faithfully by his side.

Born in 1847 in northern Georgia, Melissa [Gay, Shearer, Murphy, Tilley, Maddox] lived through the Civil War. She was raised a Baptist and was a member of the Liberty Baptist Church at Camp Creek after she married Drury Shearer in 1866. She was drawn into the holiness-Pentecostal movement when Billy Martin, Joe Tipton, and Milton McNabb brought the message to Camp Creek in 1896. The Shearer schoolhouse, where the great revival was ignited, was named in honor of her husband's family; located only a stone's throw from her mountain cottage. After Drury died in 1901, Melissa married J.C. Murphy, who was part of the fire-baptized holiness movement in Cleveland. Murphy moved in with Melissa and they hosted in their house the first Assembly in 1906. Melissa fed and entertained the 'delegates' and participated in Assembly discussions. She was a close friend of the Tomlinsons, moving with her husband to live next door to them in 1906. When the church was set in order in Cleveland in October 1906, Melissa was a charter member. Reflecting on her life, Homer Tomlinson praised her as 'a lovely and wonderful woman', comparing her to Christiana, the wife of Christian, in Bunyan's *Pilgrim's Progress*. She was a veritable jewel, a mother of Israel, exemplifying grace and holiness and demonstrating spiritual fortitude.

Apostolic Restoration

We examined earlier Frank W. Sandford's influence on Tomlinson, particularly in regard to his teaching on church leadership and on apostolic restoration as a whole. He taught a full restoration of apostolic gifts and graces. According to Sandford, the primitive church had fully apostatized to the extent that 'the light of the world seemed well nigh extinguished'. Subsequently 'the dark ages' ensued and continued, until that time that the prayer of Christ began to take effect.[47] Accordingly, the light began to reappear and the church began to be restored when Martin Luther rediscovered the doctrine of justification by faith; then was added the light of John Wesley on entire sanctification. Other great men followed who added further understanding to God's perfect plan. They brought to light the freedom of the human will, divine healing, the gifts and miracles of the Holy Spirit, and other biblical truths that had been lost or suppressed during the 'dark ages'. But this divine restoration movement was

---

[47] Sandford referred to Jesus' high priestly prayer in John 17 to support his vision of Christian unity. Accordingly, he taught boldly also that the initial restoration of the prophetic church had begun at Shiloh in 1901, and that the Shiloh saints should expect forthwith the manifestation of the full restoration of the church with all of the Pentecostal gifts and powers.

now especially reaching its climax in Sandford and his Church of the Living God at Shiloh.

A rather lengthy passage from Sandford's *Seven Years With God* deserves attention here because it reveals not only his own views, but also his influence on Tomlinson's theology of apostolic restoration. After having expounded on the power and greatness of the apostles and the primitive church, Sandford continued:

> Then gradually the power and glory of the early church departed, and amid the dark ages that followed, the light of the world seemed well nigh extinguished. The prayers of the Great Apostle above however prevailed, till gradually the church of God began to regain the truth which it had lost during these centuries of darkness. Luther was an apostle, regaining the truth of justification by faith. Wesley was another, bearing off in triumph from the battle field the doctrine of sanctification through faith. Then followed many others, some of whom are yet living, mighty men of God, contending for the sovereignty of the Creator, the freedom of the human will, healing through the prayer of faith, the healing of disease through Christ's death on the cross, the personality of the Holy Ghost, the gifts of the Spirit, the gathering of the lowest classes to the marriage supper, worldwide evangelization and, now God has called us to stand for the union of these fragmentary bits of truth in His church scripturally organized, and scripturally adjusted, 'the pillar of the truth', prepared to disciple all nations, and teach them to observe all things uttered by the Son of God and practiced by the early apostles.
>
> From the first movement, to regain the truth of justification, down to the present one to regain all truth, the apostleship of each great leader has stood for some new portion of truth; and thus each has been successively putting away defects, and correspondingly acquiring some new phase of perfection, as it made its way up to the ideal church, 'all of gold' (Zech. 4.2).
>
> This church is to be swayed by the full power of the Holy Ghost, ministered to them by 'the two witnesses' ... and slain by the Antichrist [Rev. 11.3-7]. Since the Antichrist has not yet been manifested we know that the witnesses are connected with a church *yet future*, which is to have power and glory greater than the early church, and which, having obeyed the commission given to it by our Lord before His departure, shall finally with power and great glory go to meet Him, as He comes with clouds 'in power and great glory' to meet the church.

As Luther stood for but a portion of the deep truths of God's Word, his apostleship was correspondingly incomplete. When Wesley, accepting the results of Luther's battles, added to it the glorious doctrine of sanctification by faith, his apostleship correspondingly surpassed Luther's; and so they continued, each great leader, entering into other men's labors in the past, contended during his lifetime for some great additional truth. Thus these successive men of God became more and more like the apostles of the Scriptures; and now, in a movement minutely scriptural and embracing all truth, we ought to expect the development of apostles with as much power and perception as in the days of Peter and Paul.[48]

A comparison here of Tomlinson's words in his *The Last Great Conflict* with Sandford's in *Seven Years with God* is illuminating. Bear in mind that Tomlinson was there at Shiloh for extended periods in 1897 and 1901 and heard Sandford expound on these very themes. After magnifying the apostles and the church in the New Testament, Tomlinson wrote:

> When the Church (His body) was really manifested and took His place the fruit was seen in abundance. From the church went out the teaching of repentance, as a branch from a tree, and on this branch were people who repented. Another branch was extended from the same body named baptism, another sanctification, another baptism with the Holy Ghost, another feet-washing, etc., etc. From the body (the Church) extended every line of truth and teaching that He had given them. Although His disciples were the branches while He was with them, yet when He went away and the Holy Ghost came upon them they were all baptized into one, and became the body from which all the teachings or commands branched out, and then appeared the fruit. People were converted, sanctified, baptized with the Holy Ghost and healed.

> Behold, there stands the full developed tree. First is the trunk, and from the trunk extends the branches, and upon the branches appears the leaves and luscious fruit hanging in great yellow or red clusters. The Church of God is to the gospel or doctrine taught in the Bible as the trunk or body of the tree is to the branches, leaves and fruit.

> Where did Martin Luther get the doctrine of justification by faith? From the Church of God as it was given by its members through the Bible. The branch had grown and grown and lengthened out through

---

[48] Sandford, *Seven Years With God*, pp. 136-37.

the 'dark ages' until by and by Martin Luther appeared as a cluster of fruit away out on the end of the long branch.

Where did John Wesley get the doctrine of sanctification as a definite and instantaneous experience subsequent to justification? From the Church of God. The branch had also extended away out through the darkness, and finally blossomed with George Fox, and then fruited heavily in the time of the Wesleys. These two branches have grown and borne much precious fruit ever since.

Where did Dr. Simpson get the doctrine of divine healing? Where did this branch come from? The Church of God. Hundreds, yea thousands have given up physicians, thrown away remedies, wheel chairs and crutches, and have been suspended on this wonderful branch.

Where did Dr. Seamore [sic] get the doctrine that he preached in Los Angeles, Cal., a few years ago, that not only stirred that western city and our own beloved America, but also the countries across the deep blue sea, yea, and many parts of the world. Where did he get the doctrine – the baptism with the Holy Ghost and the speaking in other tongues as the Spirit gives utterance as the evidence? From the Church of God. This branch, also, had been reaching out and growing in length until it budded, blossomed, and is to-day filled with delicious fruit. The rich experiences, the shining faces, the good clean lives, the love for one another and the lost souls of earth, the 'Go ye' spirit, tears and sacrifices, all tell the story of this special branch having life and fruitage, although thought to have died long ago and been buried with the Apostles. All these branches have been bearing fruit. Thank God.

But the wonder is that none of these men, who discovered these wonderful truths, ever crawled back down the branch to discover, if possible, where they started from, and locate the trunk of the tree. But no, they seem to have been so occupied with present surroundings and conditions, and the branches had grown so long, and through the long, long night of the 'dark ages', that the darkness was too dense and the task too great. And thus, instead of discovering the trunk of the tree, men went to work and got up articles of faith and creeds, and have tried to make out that these precious truths were doctrines of church so and so. For example: It has been said so often that 'Sanctification is a doctrine of the Methodist Church', 'Baptism by immersion is a doctrine of the Baptist church', etc., etc. None had been able to see just where the branches sprang from and to what body they were attached.

At last, after centuries of fruitage, the branch of sanctification put forth a little unassuming bud, and other little buds made their appearance about the same time. Finally the fruit appeared, and, as if they wondered and consulted with each other as to where such delicious sap and nourishment could come from, finally this least of all, and the most insignificant and uncouth in appearance, disappeared in the darkness as it went rolling and tumbling and rattling down the bark of the branch, and although the way was lonely and dark, and the obstructions thick and hard to penetrate, yet as if determined to reach the trunk or die, it kept scrambling away until finally the discovery was made, and sure enough, not only that special branch was located, but also all the others, whose tip ends had been bearing fruit, were located, and found to be fastened to and held in place by the Church of God.

As the discovery was made a shout pierced through his soul, and almost before he was aware of it, he was back again at the end of the branch, shouting at the top of his voice, and leaping and clapping his hands as he cried, 'The Church of God! The Church of God! From her extends all these precious truths! From her comes all the laws and government we need! Away with your articles of faith! Away with your creeds! Upon 'this rock' Jesus built His church, and there it is just like it was, only it has been hidden from view by the debris of the 'dark ages', unbelief, and man made churches and organizations! Hallelujah! Hallelujah! Glory! Glory!' And the shouts and cries of joy were taken up by the other fruit, and echoed and re-echoed until dread consternation seized scores and hundreds of people who looked on with amazement … As we trace every branch of truth it runs us right back to the Church of God – the body of Christ. People accept the branch or teaching of repentance, or sanctification, or the baptism with the Holy Ghost evidenced by the speaking with other tongues as the Spirit gives utterance, and divine healing, etc., then why not accept the body upon which each branch rests?[49]

What is plain to see in these passages is that Tomlinson had picked up on Sandford's historical view of restoration beginning with Luther and continuing with Wesley and others up to the brink of the twentieth century: but then he culminated the restoration movement not with

---

[49] Tomlinson, *LGC*, pp. 155-60.

Sandford and Shiloh but with himself and the Church of God in Cleveland. He is thus that 'little unassuming bud' in his metaphor in *The Last Great Conflict*, and his discovery of the Church of God is the perfection of the restoration process. It followed then that, once the Church of God was discovered and its visible structure restored – that is, its government and divine system – all of God's people could now be 'gathered together in one' and rally around her standard. For the Church of God is the trunk of the tree and eventually all of God's people will find their way to it through one of its branches – the doctrines being expounded by the Church of God or for that matter by the Methodist Church or the Baptist Church or the Quaker Church, *et al.*

'The Covering Removed'

Tomlinson's three-week visit to Shiloh in September-October 1901 coincided precisely with the time that Sandford was reaching the climax of his most intense revelatory experiences. But Tomlinson had tasted of Sandford's madness in the years leading up to that time – not only by his visits to Shiloh but through his subscription to *Tongues of Fire* and other reports being circulated through the grapevine of the holiness movement. He was fully aware of the unfolding of Sandford's vision of the Bible church and its restoration, and of Sandford's recent commission given by the Lord at Shiloh to 'Remove the covering cast over the face of all the earth'.[50]

The historical development of restoration since the days of Luther was all part of 'the covering being removed' from the truths buried beneath the rubble of the 'dark ages'. The motif of 'removing the covering', taken from Isa. 25.5, 6, was interpreted as a prophecy of the church's apostasy and restoration, but it was uniquely applied by Sandford to his developing 'white-clad army' at Shiloh. Sandford saw his movement as the instrument to fully 'destroy the face of the covering cast over all people and the veil that is spread over all nations', and he saw himself as the 'Overseer' authorized to see to its successful conclusion'.[51] Finally, Sandford believed that his church was the true church fully restored, and accordingly was the synthesizing agent of all the reformers' 'fragmentary bits of truth'. His church was 'scripturally organized, and scripturally adjusted, "the pillar and ground of the truth"'. He

---

[50] Sandford, *Art of War*, pp. 142-44.
[51] Murray, *Sublimity*, p. 503

thus came to refer to his church as 'a movement minutely scriptural and embracing all truth'.

Sandford believed that the progressive path of truth had culminated finally in his Shiloh movement. 'The Church of the Living God' had been restored, and now the door was open for it to be perfected, and part of the perfection process was to defeat the powers of Antichrist and usher in the fullness of the glorious millennium!

Tomlinson departed from Shiloh in October 1901 and soon thereafter distanced himself from Sandford and took special pains to make sure his work at Culberson was no longer identified with Shiloh. Apparently, after he had sorted out all that Sandford had taught in those three weeks in September-October in 1901, and particularly his announcement that he was 'Elijah', it was more than Tomlinson could digest. Still, however, the teachings and frantic expectations of Sandford and Shiloh remained deeply embedded in his psyche. On some points, however, he did not reject Sandford's extravagant ideas but rather reconfigured them to suit his peculiar situation in the Church of God. And thus, though he visibly separated himself from Sandford and Shiloh, yet he consciously or subconsciously reworked and transplanted many of Sandford's radical ideas and his apocalyptic vision in the Church of God.

One of Tomlinson's prominent themes was gleaned from Sandford's interpretation of Isa. 25.6, 7. Tomlinson masterfully reworked this concept to fit his scheme in the Church of God. He published his vision in tract form, which became a classic among his followers. In this tract – 'The Covering Removed' – he expounded upon the exciting themes of restoration that he had heard at Shiloh, and transplanted them in his developing work now centered in Cleveland.

The importance of the fulfillment of the prophecy of 'the covering removed' hinged on the fact God's church had to be restored in order to fulfill the ancient prophecies and to go forth into all nations to proclaim the 'all things' that Christ commanded, which included evangelizing the world (Mt. 24.14; 28.18-20); gathering into the one fold all of God's scattered sheep (Isa. 60.1-5; Jn 10.16; 11.49-52; 17.20-23); perfecting of the saints (Eph. 4.11-16; 5.26-27); being 'caught up' together with all the saints in the rapture (Jn 14.1-3; 1 Thess. 4.16-17; 1 Cor. 15.51); returning with Christ and the saints to defeat the Antichrist and his armies in the battle of Armageddon (Rev. 19.11-21); and ruling and reigning with Christ on earth in the Millennium (Dan. 7.7-14, 18, 22, 27; Rev. 20.4-8).

Modern-day Apostles

The influence of Sandford's teaching and vision may be seen all through Tomlinson's *The Last Great Conflict*. His work is more or less a compendium of Sandford's teachings at Shiloh, including the restoration of the fallen apostolic church with all of the spiritual gifts and powers – healings, miracles, etc.; perfection in holiness, and indeed perfection in all things. To some extent, Tomlinson's *The Last Great Conflict* is simply superimposed over Sandford's *Seven Years with God* and *The Art of War for the Christian Soldier*. Like Sandford at Shiloh, Tomlinson more or less nuanced his movement as the 'Restoration of All Things', and cast an apocalyptic vision for his devoted followers in the Church of God. And, like Sandford, Tomlinson proclaimed that the Church of the Living God under his inspired and divinely authorized leadership would defeat the stubborn and imminent powers of Antichrist; gather together God's people into one body; 'speedily evangelize the world;' and serve as the primary agent to rule and reign with Christ on the earth during the Millennium.[52]

Tomlinson was thus especially affected by Sandford's apocalyptic vision of end-time events, not only because the themes were so fascinating but also because Sandford himself was so powerfully persuasive and convincing that the fulfillment of these events was imminent. The 'last great conflict' was fast approaching – the clash of the armies of Antichrist with Christ and His church aided by the armies of heaven! Shirley Nelson in her *Fair, Clear and Terrible: The Story of Shiloh* captures well the spirit that engulfed the students at Shiloh in 1901,

> At Shiloh life took on such speed some students thought they could not keep rank ... They would no sooner absorb one revelation than another would call them to higher ground ... At times, Sandford confessed [that] he forgot he was still in the present, and seemed 'to be living in the millennial age'. He had begun to concentrate on the Great Tribulation, the future period of seven years on earth filled with unprecedented war, famine, and plague.[53]

The Church of the Living God at Shiloh was being prepared by God and Sandford to mount up for the last great conflict against the forces of darkness and hell; and God's 'white-clad army' was assured of victory over all opposition – 'men' and demons – in the earth, and was promised

---

[52] Tomlinson, *LGC*, pp. 116-18.
[53] Shirley Nelson, *Fair, Clear and Terrible*, p. 155.

to enter the Millennium triumphantly.[54] 'Oh, what great days ahead! Why, the millennium in all its glory is bursting upon us!'[55]

Tomlinson in the end did not buy into all that Sandford taught and forecast at Shiloh,[56] but long after his separation from him in 1902 he remained deeply affected by many of his most prominent teachings and themes; but perhaps more significantly he remained affected by his model of leadership and apocalyptic vision; and by the passion with which he imparted them to his admirers and followers at Shiloh. We have noticed many of Sandford's ideas that Tomlinson transplanted in the Church of God in its early years; but he also transplanted Sandford's frantic expectations of end-time events and his fanatical insistence on absolute abandonment to the church's mission in the world. Tomlinson wrote,

> Ease, pleasures, friends, homes and all comforts must be forsaken by those whom God calls. Money that has been hoarded up must be put into use ... It is time to leave legacies and estates for children yet unborn. Everything must be put into the one great effort to take the gospel to all the world ... To be or act contrary to this will only prove disloyalty to the Christ ... To fail to put forth every effort and bend all of our energies in that direction means to fail Him ... We are now in the time of the culmination of events. The time of the consummation.[57]

He believed also, like Sandford, that the church would go through some of the 'great storm of the tribulation',[58] and he eventually settled more or less on a mid-Tribulation view of the Rapture, though, like Sandford, it is difficult to classify his position precisely. His message in the *White Wing Messenger* in April 1930 titled, 'Getting Ready for the Lord's Return', indicates that at that time he was teaching a mid-Tribulation rapture – though he refused to be pressed for a precise position in regard to 'the exact day and hour'. Still, he asserts in this message,

> There is a difference in the coming of the Lord to resurrect the dead saints and to rapture away the Church, and the coming of Christ with

---

[54] Sandford, *Majesty of Snowing Whiteness*, pp. 34-37.
[55] Sandford, *Art of War*, p. 119.
[56] For example, Sandford believed that many of the saints at Shiloh would go through the Great Tribulation and meet the Antichrist at Armageddon; whereas Tomlinson eventually accepted the doctrine of a mid-Tribulation rapture and believed that the glorified church would return with Christ from heaven after three years and a half to defeat the Antichrist and his armies at Armageddon.
[57] Tomlinson, *LGC*, pp. 40-43.
[58] Tomlinson, *LGC*, p. 118.

His saints to reign on the earth … At His first appearing He does not come to the earth – He will come close enough to call the saints – that is, the dead saints and the Church – to Him in the air, and they soar away to the … marriage supper, where they will remain, perhaps, for three years and a half, while the tribulations are bursting forth upon the earth. Then, at the proper time, Jesus and His army will mount white horses and ride down to earth, capture and cast into the lake of fire the beast and false prophet, and the angel shall rush down from heaven about the same time and capture and bind the devil and cast him into the bottomless pit where he shall remain for a thousand years.[59]

Later he asserts, 'The coming of the Lord with His saints to earth will be the means of breaking up the tribulation period and ushering in the peaceful reign of our Lord for a thousand years …'

Sandford's expectations of success in the end-times conflict with the spirit of Antichrist and the powers of darkness depended on the appearance of modern-day apostles. Tomlinson picked up on this teaching and brought it back to his work at Culberson in 1901[60] and later used his considerable abilities in an effort to persuade the ministers and members in the Church of God to expect modern-day Apostles soon to burst on the scene in spectacular fashion and enable the church speedily to evangelize the world. In his *Last Great Conflict* he imagined, 'We are evidently entering the penumbra, and soon will break out the full wave, and the signs of an Apostle will be seen in hundreds, yea thousands of God's children as they run to and fro all over the world'.[61] He admitted in 1912 that presently

> We have teachers, pastors, evangelists, and prophets to a slight degree, but no Apostles are known yet. There is no doubt there are men living today who will develop into Apostles, but no one can palm

---

[59] A.J. Tomlinson, 'Getting Ready for the Lord's Return', *WWM* (April 26, 1930), pp. 1-3.

[60] Fresh from his trip to Shiloh and his baptism into the 'Church of the Living God' by the hands of Sandford, and having observed some 'confession meetings' orchestrated by Sandford to sift out the slackers and troublemakers at Shiloh, Tomlinson noted in his *Diary* on December 4, 1901: 'We have been having some confession meetings [at Culberson], and we are having some general sifting. One person has been asked to leave the work … Bro. Overstreet is specially exhorting every one to be true to God's apostle'. Though Tomlinson was not especially bold at this time to claim the office of apostle, he had apparently convinced Overstreet and some of the workers there that he was called to that lofty office. The 'confession meetings' were patterned after Sandford's at Shiloh.

[61] Tomlinson, *LGC*, p. 123.

himself off on us as an Apostle who is not, for the unmistakable signs will prove him the same as the sign of tongues proves the baptism with the Holy Ghost ... there are truly signs that will evidence and single out the Apostles until they cannot be hidden ... That lame man hobbling down the street yonder, see him as he limps! He must be made to walk! A few words from an Apostle, and a touch of his hand, and the old cane or crutch will be thrown aside, and the poor cripple leaping and shouting at the top of his voice, until all the folks on Main street will begin to think a lunatic has escaped from the asylum. See the poor, pitiful looking man, all humped up and drawn together, yonder in that wheel chair. What is the matter with him? Rheumatism. Incurable! Send for Peter (an apostle), let him walk beside the chair, and his shadow fall on the poor helpless invalid. All of a sudden a cry of astonishment is heard. The chair is suddenly vacated. What has happened? Only an Apostle passed by, that's all. But the whole country hears of it. Where is the Apostle? He is gone to the city of G—. Go down to the railroad station, watch every train as they come in. Help! Help! The train men are unable to handle the cripples, so they call for help. Where is he (the Apostle)? The cripples are all placed on the platform, and very soon the Apostle passes along and touches every one, and all are healed, and running and shouting until the whole city comes together and demands an explanation. Now is the opportunity. The multitudes have gathered. Upon an old goods box or an express wagon he stands to explain, when after a few words about Jesus and faith in His name, and God glorifying His Son Jesus, three, five, yea ten thousand people will surrender and accept such a Christ as that. Hallelujah!

But wait a moment! Hear! Listen! Oh, it's only a blind man! But see, he gropes his way along all in utter darkness, has not seen the light of the sun, the green vegetation, the beautiful structures, nor the faces of loved ones for years. What a pitiable sight! You must have a heart of stone if you do not pity him. The humble, loving, sympathetic Apostle comes near, and suddenly, like a flash, a stream of light appears, and those once faded, sunken eyes sparkle with delight as they once more behold the faces of friends and the beauty of nature. Noised abroad? Oh yes, and all will be healed! Glory! The sick, the deaf, the dumb, all will be healed, every one (Acts 5.12-16).

But stay! Why that weeping and screaming and people rushing in and about that house yonder? What has happened? A woman has just died, and she was the only support of an aged widowed mother. Send for Peter (the Apostle). He sees the situation. Nothing is especially strange; many have died. In fact, death is only a gateway to heaven to those who are prepared. But wait a moment, let us see what he will do. Lovingly, tenderly, gently, he puts them all out of the room and fastens the door. There he is alone with a corpse. Look in at the keyhole in the door. He kneels down and prays; then turns suddenly and takes the corpse by the hand, and says, 'Tabitha, arise' (Acts 9.40). Has anything happened? Suddenly the door is opened, and there stands she that was dead in the bloom of youth and a picture of health.

No good in that, you say? Yes, but the whole city will be stirred (Acts 9.42). The newspapers and telephones and telegraphs will herald the miracle far and wide, and thousands will believe and say good by to old forms and creeds, and will be stanch followers of Christ (Acts 9.35).

How rapidly the world will be evangelized with such as that as a daily occurrence in every country and on every island of the sea![62]

This vision by Tomlinson was more or less an extension of Sandford's vision at Shiloh which had impacted him deeply as he sat and listened to the man who was metamorphosing into the prophetic 'Elijah'. The general content of Tomlinson's message to the Church of God was Sandfordian through and through; even some of his expressions and literary phrases were almost identical to Sandford's. Compare Sandford's comments below in his *Seven Years With God* and *The Art of War For the Christian Soldier* to Tomlinson's comments and vision in *The Last Great Conflict* and his annual address in 1912. Sandford wrote,

> Since apostles are promised until we all come into unity, and we have not yet arrived at that glorious stage, we should expect such God-sent men to re-appear and lead the church out of divisions into order and harmony. We not only should expect them, but since our very perfection is dependent on upon their ministrations, we should as earnestly desire them ... Every portion of the true church should shake itself from the dust and stir itself mightily in prayer for the re-appearance of men, each of whom can truthfully sign himself 'an apostle of Jesus Christ by the will of God'.[63]

---

[62] Tomlinson, *LGC*, pp. 127-30.
[63] Sandford, *Seven Years with God*, p. 134.

There will be a 'church of gold', a company of people who will forsake every earthly thing they have to evangelize the world, a company 'fair, clear and terrible'. There will be a company of people who know divine authority and who stand in the church of God as loyal to apostles in the twentieth century as the early church was to the apostles in the first century. God will have a church against which the gates of hell shall not prevail, and he will sweep this globe with the glorious gospel of our Lord and Savior Jesus Christ until a countless multitude whom no man can number stand before the throne ... God is going to have a company that is one body, who are of 'one mind' and have 'the same judgment', and 'continue in the apostles' doctrine ...

Then is it possible that God actually, in His sovereign will and plan, desires to magnify a leader whom He appoints, and that people do not do wrong if they join in with hi and do what their Maker does? Oh, that lie of hell that has been belittling leaders! I brand it as such today. God's will is to magnify any leader that He appoints, and His pleasure is that people follow His example. You will never show any more honor to your God than you show to those whom God sends you ... God [puts] him in authority to lead the troops, and there is no reason why God should send around His orders to every private. Orders are transmitted to the commander-in-chief and by him to his subordinates; and it is your business to hear them as the oracles of God ... 'Submit yourselves' to them as they must give an account to the Divine Commander-in-chief for your obedience or disobedience.[64]

Now compare Tomlinson's remarks to the Assembly in 1912:

If you will turn to [Eph. 4.11] you will find these words, 'And he gave some apostles; and some, prophets; and some, evangelist; and some, pastors and teachers; for the perfecting of the saints, for the work of the ministry, for the edifying of the body of Christ: Till we all come in the unity of faith, and of the knowledge of the Son of God, unto a perfect man, unto the measure of the stature of the fullness of Christ'. We have acknowledged the pastors and teachers, etc., but we have failed to acknowledge the apostles. The reason has probably been because of erroneous statements of tradition, and probably because of prejudice incited by the innumerable failures of those who have called themselves apostles. We have about come to the conclusion

---

[64] Sandford, *Art of War*, pp. 61-64.

that there will be no apostles in the latter days, but in spite of the numerous failures and prejudices that may exist, this office is in the Bible. And although we may be short in understanding, yet the time has come that we must be filled with the Holy Ghost and wisdom and come to the full acknowledgement of the truth, for we cannot harmonize the Scriptures without taking all, and we can never have a complete church until we acknowledge and have a complete gospel ministry ...

Some of these times the signs of an apostle will show and he will not only speak as the oracles of God, but they will be in him and then the dead will be raised.

This subject was on my heart at the last assembly one year ago, but not quite so well matured as it is now. I have kept it to myself because the people have been saying that I wanted to make myself a king or pope, but I can keep still no longer, people or no people, for it is in God's Word, and I am seeking to please God and not men. I am not seeking for position, nor honor from men, I am zealous for God's truth and the Lord's church. The fact is, brethren, we will continue to make blunders until we acknowledge the entire Bible.

The apostles is [*sic*] the highest order of ministers outlined in the Bible, and although we are not yet able to see them, we must keep low before God and point in that direction. A man has to see his work in his mind before he can complete it. When the painter steps back from his finished picture he says, 'That is the finished picture I have had in my mind for some time'. So we must expect God to reveal His perfect plan to our minds, which will soon after be finished and in perfect working order.

We learn by types and shadows, so let us see if we cannot find a picture. Little folks have to be taught by pictures, and as we are little folks we must be taught in this way.

Where do we get a picture, or what is the type of the church of God? Answer: The church in the wilderness – the tabernacle service. The tabernacle was enclosed by four walls. The court, an open square surrounded by curtains, could be entered by all. The tabernacle itself was a tent forty-five feet long, fifteen feet wide. This was divided into two apartments, the Holy place and the most Holy. Into the first went the priests accomplishing the service of God, but into the Holy of Holies the high priest only could enter, and that only once a year. He had to wear a special robe, with the golden bells and pomegranates as a fringe at the bottom. His robe was more beautiful that the others, and he had to go through an extra cleansing of his person, and he represents the apostles of the church of God in a sense. The golden bells had to make a noise lest he die. Such a position is hardly desirable, as there is danger if he should go into the holy of holies without having on the robe of cleanliness.

Some may say 'I know now what you are aiming at, you want to organize a body like the Catholic Church;' but no, we are leaving the type and getting to the real. Where did the priests get their authority? Moses gave it to them. Moses is a type of Christ.

When Titus was left in Crete to ordain elders in every city, can you find any place where Paul, who was not a whit behind the chiefest apostles, ever instructed him to give those he ordained authority to ordain others? Then the authority was only vested in the apostles. Have we made a mistake in the past? Most assuredly, but it was because we did not have the light. The light has now come, and we must walk in it and change our customs about ordination.

We have no apostles yet, but by the help of God we can do something that will answer for the present need.[65]

In 1913 Tomlinson endorsed a book written by a young Church of God minister named Roy C. Miller, entitled, *Classified Scriptures on the Church of God and Her Teachings*, which was published by the Evangel Publishing House.[66] Miller was then serving as the overseer of Mississippi. Among the subjects which Miller outlined was the doctrine of the five-fold ministry – apostles, prophets, evangelists, pastors, and teachers (1 Cor. 12.28; Eph. 4.11); which, accordingly, the church should expect to be fully restored in the near future.

Notwithstanding Tomlinson's expectation of the office of Apostle to be restored in the Church of God, the Assembly had never addressed the issue *per se* and Tomlinson's interpretation as it turned out was never endorsed by the church. Apparently a significant number of leaders influenced the majority of the ministers and members to resist his attempt to establish modern-day apostles in the church. Tomlinson admitted that he had 'received some letters of warning and criticism' in regard to 'putting too much stress on the church and her glory and power'. But he insisted that 'It is my purpose to agitate this question until the results are seen – the church fully established with all of her former glory and

---

[65] *GAM 1906-1914*, pp. 135-37.
[66] Miller, *Classified Scriptures*.

power, gifts and graces'.⁶⁷ And in his view one of the most important gifts was the office of Apostle.

We may be sure that among those who criticized his over-emphasis on the church and the restoration of the office of Apostle was Sam C. Perry, who was probably joined in his opinion by Spurling and other men of reputation. But, in any case, whoever had written the 'letters of warning and criticism', their counsel prevailed, for Tomlinson thereafter denied the existence of modern-day apostles.⁶⁸ Interestingly, at that point he envisioned instead a system of government that was ruled by a hierarchy of Elders who in turn were subject to a God-appointed General Overseer who occupied a 'mediatory throne' at the pinnacle of the Episcopate. And amazingly, according to Tomlinson, this office was above that of an apostle! It was thus that Tomlinson dismissed the idea of restoring the apostolic office, but otherwise retained Sandford's doctrine of a unique and specially appointed and anointed commander-in-chief at the head of a hierarchy of divine authority.

The most significant adjustment that Tomlinson made in Sandford's apocalyptic scenario of end times events was in regard to the Rapture. Sandford had settled on the church going through the Great Tribulation, whereas Tomlinson joined with most classical holiness-Pentecostals at that time in the view that the church would be 'caught up' either before or out of the midst of the Great Tribulation. Still, however, he maintained Sandford's 'hurry up and get ready' theme in the Church of God, including the perspective that the church exists in a hostile world and 'should make haste' to equip itself to engage in 'the last great conflict'. Correspondingly, he carried forward also Sandford's militaristic motif, which required a regimented discipline in order to perfect the 'bride' for the soon-coming Bridegroom, that is, to qualify the bride to rule and reign with Christ on earth for a thousand years.

---

⁶⁷ Tomlinson, *LGC*, p. 124.

⁶⁸ In his annual address in 1931, he freely admitted that 'The apostles and prophets were the foundation of the church and we are at the top of the building, with the structure almost finished. Why should we want to leave off building or finishing and go back to the foundation? ... We have no desire to take the place of the apostles' (*HAA*, II, p. 127). It was doubtlessly Spurling and Perry and other respected men in the church who leveled him out in regard to the role of the office of apostle and the part it played in forming the foundation of the church.

Divine Healing[69]

Interestingly, though Tomlinson modified his view of the office of Apostle, he remained steadfast and unmovable in regard to divine healing. Instead of it being a gift exercised more or less exclusively by Apostles, it was now seen as a distinct privilege and benefit of the Atonement; and thus all believers were expected to trust in Christ the Healer, especially God's 'peculiar people' – the Church of God.[70] For Tomlinson, divine healing was to be increasingly one of the outstanding and distinguishing characteristics of the true church.

Here again, the greatest influence on Tomlinson in regard to divine healing was Sandford, and perhaps the second and third greatest influences on him either directly or indirectly were A.B. Simpson in New York and John Alexander Dowie in Zion City, Illinois.[71] But it was especially the sensationalism and flamboyancy of Sandford and Dowie that inspired Tomlinson to carry his vision of apostolic restoration to extremes. But Tomlinson was no exception, for the views of Sandford and Dowie were more or less the norm in early Pentecostalism. Seymour and the Azusa Street Mission, for example, taught that

> Sickness is born in a child just as original sin is born in a child. [Jesus] was manifested to destroy the works of the devil. Every sickness is of the devil ... God is our healer ... [but after men lost the Spirit in the Garden of Eden and went a whoring after other spirits] they turned to the arm of the flesh to find something to heal their sicknesses. Thank God we have a living Christ among us to heal our diseases. He will heal every case ... If Jesus bore our sicknesses, why should we bear them? So we get full salvation through the atonement of Jesus.[72]

Sandford had been tutored and influenced by Simpson, who perhaps more than anyone else, except for Dowie, restored and heralded the

---

[69] There is a distinction made by some scholars between divine healing and faith healing; in regard to the former God may use human instruments and medicines to assist in bringing about physical healing; the latter is by faith alone without the aids of doctors or medicine. In either case, however, the Atonement provides the dynamic remedy for healing and God is to be given all the glory. But Tomlinson and the Church of God did not make this distinction early on in the church's development, and thus divine healing and faith healing were equated; it followed then that for one to resort to doctors and medicines was seen as faithlessness and disobedience.

[70] Tomlinson, *LGC*, pp. 92-98.

[71] Homer, however, says that Tomlinson's first encounter with faith healing was in 1892 through a tract by Carrie Judd Montgomery, who had been healed in 1877.

[72] 'Healing', *AF* (September 1907), p. 2.

practice of divine healing in the latter part of the nineteenth century.⁷³ Simpson advocated divine healing as a fundamental principle of the work of the Atonement, the same as salvation for the soul.⁷⁴ This opened the door for equating healing of the body with the healing of the soul in salvation. Thus, accordingly, one was not truly saved if he did not also fully trust Christ for the healing of his body, which included denying the assistance of doctors and medicine. This radical view of healing was precisely the view that Tomlinson brought into the Church of God.

Figure 74

A.B. SIMPSON

Figure 75

JOHN ALEXANDER DOWIE

We will see in this next chapter that apparently the majority of the Twelve Elders embraced Tomlinson's view and filtered this perspective down to the majority of the ministers and members in the Church of God. It was this extreme and rigid view of divine healing that Sam C. Perry resented and rejected, which, along with other concerns and complaints, led him into a confrontation with the General Overseer and other Elders in 1919. Perry wrote in his own defense '[I reject the doctrine] that a man who has a physician when sick is an infidel'.⁷⁵

In the second Assembly in 1907 the subject of Divine Healing was addressed. The question was asked, 'Shall we use drugs in case of sick-

---

⁷³ Simpson's work was centered in Nyack, New York. The fact that he organized the Christian and Missionary Alliance and sent missionaries all over the world with the message and practice of faith healing popularized the movement.

⁷⁴ The best works on Simpson's view in the context of the Church of God is Kimberly Ervin Alexander, *Pentecostal Healing: Models in Theology and Practice* (JPTSup 29; Blandford Forum, UK: Deo Publishing, 2006), and John Christopher Thomas, *The Devil, Disease and Deliverance: Origins of Illness in New Testament Thought* (JPTSup 13; Sheffield: Sheffield Academic Press, 1998), now (Cleveland, TN: CPT Press, 2011).

⁷⁵ Perry, 'Before A.J. Tomlinson', p. 3.

ness or trust Jesus alone?' This was discussed by R.G. Spurling at some length,[76] and W.F. Bryant gave an exhortation that was attended by 'demonstrations of the Spirit in favor of taking Jesus only as our healer'. Bryant's message was then reinforced by an address by M.S. Lemons:

> What does the Bible say about taking drugs or Jesus? There's no Scripture giving man license to decide as he pleases about how to get healed. The Lord says to take Jesus only. I'd rather die a martyr and do what Jesus says, than to spend all my money for Doctors and then die and the Dr. have to be paid with the money that my wife and children ought to have. Die for the principle if needs be. A man full of faith is a pillar in the house of God. Peter and John seemed to be pillars.[77]

Following Lemons' exhortation, Tomlinson then '[concluded] the discussion earnestly and in the power of the Spirit and at a call a number came forward for healing, and as we anointed with oil and prayed, some were healed instantly according to their own testimony'.[78] This was apparently the first healing service in a General Assembly of the Church of God.

This narrow interpretation of divine healing tended to blame all sickness and disease on sin or the devil and demonic powers, and did not take into account God's universal Curse on humankind as a result of the Fall (Gen. 3.14-24), nor that God intended in one way to use the Curse for '[man's] sake' (Gen. 3.17), that is, not only did God curse the earth 'on account' of humanity's sin but on account of humanity's worth to God; and that, accordingly, pain and adversity was God's method to bring redemption and perfection to humanity through suffering.

For Tomlinson and most Church of God ministers, sin and the devil and demonic powers were the cause of sickness and disease.[79] When

---

[76] Regretfully, Spurling's commentary was not recorded, but it is likely that he offered some modifying explanation to the extreme view that Tomlinson and his followers were then advocating in the churches. He did not according to his granddaughter, Allie, who lived with him for nineteen years, denounce doctors or medicines nor was he radically opposed to consulting physicians or using medicines in some cases (Interview, July-August 1995). Since Tomlinson served as clerk of the first few Assemblies and recorded and edited the *GAM*, it is likely that he purposively omitted Spurling's remarks – if they did indeed modify his strict view on the subject – in order to encourage the ministers and members to trust God fully for physical healing and to reject the assistance of doctors and the use of medicine.

[77] *GAM 1906-1914*, pp. 36-37.

[78] *GAM 1906-1914*, p. 37.

[79] F.J. Lee in his sermon in the Assembly in 1912 on 'Demonology' (*GAM 1906-1914*, pp. 22-25), seemed to locate the source for all sickness and disease in the devil and demons; whereas Tomlinson located the root cause in the Fall of human-

Tomlinson's wife, Mary Jane, beginning in late March 1911 was overwhelmed with what apparently was either an acutely infected gall bladder or appendix, if indeed the bladder or appendix had not already burst,[80] she experienced the 'agonies of death over and over again' for more than four weeks.[81] She had lost during the ordeal about eighty pounds. Feeling obligated to uphold her husband's convictions, she had refused the services of Dr. W.H. Sullivan of Cleveland who had offered his assistance. She said, 'My husband is teaching divine healing. I am not a preacher, but I am his wife, and I feel the least I can do is stand true and trust the Lord to heal me.'[82]

Tomlinson had been in the Bahamas holding a mission campaign, and was called home because of his wife's severe illness. When he arrived, he found her in the throes of a great struggle with death. He reported that 'Eight times she had [traumatic] attacks, lasting from eight to twenty-four hours'.[83] Tomlinson believed there could be only one source in this instance – the devil and demonic powers. He reasoned that in these cases, even the child of God, like the patriarch Job, is 'delivered into the hands of Satan' to be tested and tried. The Lord allows 'the devil to settle down upon our bodies in sickness, placing his cruel fangs upon our vitals.' Tomlinson recalled,

> The worst finally came. For about ten hours we wrestled and fought against demonic powers which caused the awful suffering and most excruciating pain. Having taken no medicine that might tend to stupify [*sic*] her she was at her right mind all the time, but for hours she was like a raving maniac on account of the severest suffering and pain. She endured agony, obeyed the Word, stood the test, until the Refiner, who was standing by, saw it was enough, and bade the arch-enemy release his grasp and depart.[84]

Satanic powers were generally understood to be the active agents in sickness and disease. That God could be the source was never deeply considered, particularly in the sense that His Curse may have mutated the genetic structure of nature, including humankind's physical and ma-

---

kind (Tomlinson, *LGC*, p. 92). Sin was the essential source of sickness and disease, but it had opened the door also for demonic powers to afflict humanity (Tomlinson, *LGC*, pp. 21-22).

[80] This was the opinion of W.F. Bryant and others, who had been advised by Dr. Sullivan (Homer, *Diary*, I, p. 189).

[81] Homer, *Diary*, I, pp. 182-83.

[82] Homer, *Diary*, I, p. 183.

[83] Tomlinson, *LGC*, pp. 21-22.

[84] Tomlinson, *LGC*, p. 22.

terial make-up, which accordingly allowed for sickness and disease.[85] Neither was it considered that under the Curse the universal corruption remained in effect after Jesus made Atonement, and that, accordingly, believers remained physically subject to this corruption the same as unbelievers. In other words, the Cross made it possible that one's soul could be instantly healed and cleansed, while the body, being part of this material world remained under the Curse and was subject to sickness and disease. Thus the apostle Paul writes,

> For the creature was made subject to vanity, not willingly, but by reason of him who has subjected the same in hope. Because the creature itself shall also be delivered from the bondage of corruption into the glorious liberty of the children of God. For we know that the whole creation groans and travails in pain together until now. And not only they, but ourselves also, which have the first fruits of the Spirit, even we ourselves groan within ourselves, waiting for the adoption, to wit, the redemption of our body (Rom. 8.20-23).

Even so, God still may choose to heal instantly by faith, but He is not bound to respond on the command of humanity; that is, the prerogative to heal or not to heal or when to heal remains always with God; thus, according to the Lord's infinite wisdom and mysterious will, some believers may be healed instantly or in due course in this present world, while others may not be healed until glorification. It is true that, in any case, the death and sacrifice of Christ provides for divine healing; but the position of the Church of God in its infancy did not encourage any deeper theological reflection on the issue, nor allow for any nuanced interpretation.[86] Tomlinson's narrow and absolute view had prevailed; and it occasioned, as we will see in a moment, some grievous excesses and corresponding problems in the church, particularly in regard to the church's opposition to doctors and medicine.

---

[85] See Thomas, *The Devil, Disease and Deliverance*. Thomas concludes that the writers of the New Testament maintain that the origin of 'certain, if not the majority' of sicknesses and diseases is neutral, that is, not directly caused by God nor the devil nor sin (pp. 304-305). It follows therefore that physicians and medicine are 'an appropriate response to an infirmity in certain situations' (pp. 309, 318-19), e.g. 1 Tim. 5.23.

[86] In Jn 9.1-3 we have an instance of Jesus healing a blind man. When asked by His disciples whose sin was the cause of his blindness from birth – his parents' sin or his own – Jesus said, 'Neither this man nor his parents sinned, but this happened that the works of God might be manifest in his life'. Here then is a case where neither Satan nor sin is the source of the disease, but rather God allowed it in order to magnify His own glory and power and bring about humaniy's redemption and perfection.

Conversely, the dynamic benefit of physical healing in the Atonement had been more or less ignored or denied by the Holiness movement in favor of spiritual cleansings (regeneration and entire sanctification); and many holiness preachers and 'higher life' groups criticized 'healing services' and 'healing lines'. Simpson's faith healing movement was thus clearing new ground in the Holiness movement. His platform was the 'Four Fold Gospel', which exalted Christ as Savior, Sanctifier, Healer, and Coming King.[87] This theological perspective is clearly reflected in Tomlinson's ministry and writings,[88] and he explicitly associates Simpson with the doctrine of divine healing, saying, 'Where did Dr. Simpson get the doctrine of divine healing?'[89]

Simpson's doctrine of healing was already radical in his day compared with the majority of evangelicals, but Sandford took Simpson's views to the extreme, proclaiming and requiring at Shiloh that one should except death rather then resort to doctors and drugs.[90] The use of medicines was considered a sign of unbelief. Thus, there were no medicines in Bethesda, Sandford's hospital for the sick and afflicted. Tomlinson himself spent several days at Bethesda in September 1901, overcome of a sickness. His recovery came by prayer and faith, without the aid of medicine or professional assistance.

> I arrived here at Shiloh, Maine. September 24 ... About 3:00 p.m. of same day I was taken with a hard chill which lasted until I was piled up in bed for sometime. That night, to my utter astonishment, I found I was sick and helpless. I called for the 'elders' and they anointed me and prayed. I was then taken from Shiloh extension and brought to 'Bethesda' where I have been ever since. For about 12

---

[87] Charles Nienkirchen, 'Albert Benjamin Simpson', *Dictionary of Pentecostal and Charismatic Movements*, pp. 786, 787; H.P. Shelly, 'A.B. Simpson', *Dictionary of Christianity in America*, p. 1087.

[88] Simpson's Fourfold phraseology and platform are clearly represented in Tomlinson's writings (See Tomlinson, *LGC*, p. 102 *et al.*). After the Pentecostal movement began, Tomlinson added Christ as 'baptizer with the Holy Ghost', thus making it a Fivefold Gospel. Tomlinson was evidently seriously influenced by Simpson, the latter being the link to Sandford or vice versa. Tomlinson clearly credits Simpson with the restoration of divine healing (Tomlinson, *LGC*, p. 156); see also Homer, *The Great Vision of the Church of God*, p. 3). But Tomlinson's extremism and fanaticism in this regard were clearly reflective of Sandford and Dowie.

[89] Tomlinson, *LGC*, p. 156.

[90] Sandford was charged on more than one occasion for manslaughter; for his opposition on the inside and outside of Shiloh believed his radical view and strict discipline inside Shiloh was the cause of severe sickness and death. One teenage boy, Leander Bartlett, who died in 1904 of diphtheria became a celebrated case (Nelson, *Fair, Clear, and Terrible*, pp. 227-42).

hours the second day I suffered untold agony, nothing could relieve me. They prayed, they whispered all in vain until God said enough. The precious blood availed when God got ready and said 'enough!' I am out a little today. Praise God for raising me up. I have missed four days of the convention, but I had something better for myself.[91]

Figure 76   Figure 77
BETHESDA (C. 1900)   A.J. TOMLINSON (C. 1901)

He was not only indoctrinated by Sandford's fanatical view of divine healing but experienced the practice of it. This evidently contributed to his deep conviction that medicines were a waste of good money and that physicians were for the most part a caste of swindlers. Money spent on doctors and medicines could be better used for the furtherance of the Gospel.[92]

Ever after his Shiloh experience and indoctrination, Tomlinson would espouse and propagate divine healing, teaching or harboring a kind of dualism, that is, limiting God to work in the supernatural alone, as if He were not sovereign and holding sway over the natural as well as the supernatural, and could as readily use physicians and hospitals to serve His purpose as Gospel preachers.[93] The majority of physicians in

---

[91] Tomlinson, *Diary*, September 28, 1901. Tomlinson was at Shiloh on this occasion from September 24-October 9, 1901.

[92] Tomlinson, *LGC*, pp. 93-96, 101-102.

[93] We have elsewhere distinguished divine healing from faith healing. Faith healing is understood by some to be effected by faith alone without the aid of physicians or medicines, whereas God may employ the services of professional help and medicines as assistants in the process of divine healing. Thus in divine healing God is yet considered the ultimate source of healing, though physicians or medicines may be employed. Tomlinson did not make this distinction, and used the terms interchangeably in teaching that the practice of divine healing without any human assistance was necessary for obedience to the Gospel.

the nineteenth century in fact acknowledged that they were merely instruments in the Lord's work, and that whatever service they rendered in the process of healing infringed in no way on the Atonement of Christ, nor diminished the fact that ultimately in any case Christ is the Healer!

Tomlinson's concept of divine healing implied that medical science was something evil of itself and by nature an enemy of the Cross, and presumed also that medicines contradicted a merry heart rather than serving it.[94] This perspective on divine healing robbed God of the glory for the good that was being accomplished through the medical profession and medical science. It was an extreme view of perfectionism which left little, if any, room for anticipating glorification and the resurrection. To Tomlinson, paradise was restored immediately in Jesus' sanctifying blood and in Pentecostal glory.

Always with an eye and ear for restoration ideals, Tomlinson made divine healing one of the predominant subjects of his early ministry; for the doctrine and practice of divine healing was at the turn of the century a restoration venture. Unable to reconcile medical science and the medical profession with divine healing, Tomlinson opted for Sandford's extremely dualistic concept. His teaching on divine healing therefore reflected Sandford's fanaticism, but also his military sense of obedience and martyrdom complex.

> Teach divine healing? Yes! Practice it and no other live or die? Yes! Yes!! Amen!!! Be bolder in it than ever! This is fighting the enemy on his own territory, bearding the lion in his den, in the last great conflict. 'It is appointed unto man once to die', then bravely die for the truth, as men by the thousands have died for their country, marching right up to the roaring cannons as they belched forth their deadly carnage, merely because they have sworn to obey their captains.

---

[94] Tomlinson, *LGC*, pp. 95-96; but study Prov. 17.22, Ezek. 47.12, Rev. 3.18; *et al*. The Bible does not support the theory that it is wrong to use medicines or consult physicians. On the contrary, medicines may be a Godsend. Jesus himself did not contradict the use of medicines and physicians either in precept or example. Our Lord used on one occasion saliva, a reputed cure, to heal a blind man (Jn 9.6) and never spoke derogatorily of physicians, though on occasion he emphasized their limitations (Mk 5.25, 26; Lk. 8.43). On the contrary, Jesus would not have said, 'They that be whole need not a physician, but they that are sick' (Mt. 9.12) if He intended believers strictly to avoid physicians and medicines; neither would it seem reasonable for Him to speak in a commendable fashion of the 'good Samaritan' using oil and wine as a treatment for wounds (Lk. 10.33, 34) if He did not expect believers to do the same; nor would He have recommended 'eye salve' to the pastor and members at Laodicea so that 'you may see' (Rev. 3.18).

Dear Friend ... You surely know the Bible on this point. If you do not, then you are a very poor soldier ... Poor Christian! That has listed in his service and will not accept, learn and practice divine healing, but will resort to other means, and just as really disobey God as Adam and Eve did in the garden of Eden.

Remember we are now in the last great conflict. Now is the time to press the battle and wage a strong warfare against the devil and all his allurements and devices. Die rather than go contrary to the plain teaching in God's Word! If you should die for the truth it would be no more than thousands have done before you. Then you would obtain a better resurrection ...

Live by the Bible or die by the Bible, yea, whether we live or die, if we obey Him we are true soldiers of Jesus Christ ...[95]

Remarkably, Tomlinson was able to carry almost the whole church into his radical teaching on divine healing. F.J. Lee, who as much as anyone in the church before 1923 ascribed to Tomlinson's teachings, laid great stress on divine healing, and frequently conducted special healing services. His *Diary* is replete with instances of healing services and reports of miraculous results. And he practiced what he preached. Even on his deathbed, having been stricken with a deadly cancer of the liver, he refused medical assistance. He even sent for his close friend, J.B. Ellis, and made him promise that if he should collapse into a coma or become unconscious that he would see to it that no medicines were administered to him.[96]

A.J. Tomlinson doubtlessly rejoiced over Homer's report that, while he was serving in the war in France in 1918 and was seized with the deadly Influenza that was then sweeping the world, he had trusted God fully for his healing and refused to resort to medicines. In his typically self-exalting manner, Homer wrote, 'Compelled [by the military authorities] to go to the clinic, [I] accepted the medicine prepared, [but] when the medico was not looking emptied the glass over [my] shoulder and out the window, [and] resolved to trust wholly in the Lord for healing'. He noted further that 'many of [my] comrades at the clinic that day died shortly, but after two days [I] rose up healed, and without medicine'.[97]

The influence of Tomlinson in regard to divine healing caused or occasioned the death of some of the ministers and members, for he encouraged believers to die rather than accept the aid of physicians and

---

[95] Tomlinson, *LGC*, pp. 25-26.
[96] Conn, *Mighty Army*, p. 204.
[97] Homer, *Diary*, I, p. 253.

medical cures.⁹⁸ Such was the case apparently with the young overseer of Mississippi, Roy C. Miller (1891-1913). Miller caught a cold in a meeting in Alabama in 1912 while assisting Tomlinson on a convention tour. Pushing himself on to Mississippi without rest or medical aid, the cold apparently turned into pneumonia. Still pressing on, now suffering with fever, chills, and strenuous coughing, he finally collapsed confessing 'that if he did not get well he would die trusting God and the Bible'.⁹⁹ And true to his word, he abstained from doctors and medicines and 'died in the faith' on June 28, 1913. Just before he died, he reportedly testified of seeing angels and his last words were, 'Glory! Hallelujah!'¹⁰⁰

Tomlinson wrote the Introduction to Miller's little book, *Classified Scriptures on the Church of God and Her Teachings*, which included a brief sketch of his life and ministry. In this sketch, Tomlinson admitted that if Roy had not fully trusted God or had resorted in the least to the use of medicines he would have refused to write a tribute to him, and that 'in fact if he had yielded at the last [to medical aid any time during his sickness] it is hardly probable you would ever have seen his work in print'.¹⁰¹

The Church of God's extreme position on divine healing – or rather its extreme view against doctors and medicine – entangled the church in some legal problems. On February 9, 1915, M.S. Lemons was sent by Tomlinson to investigate a situation involving Walter Barney, from Virginia, who was charged with manslaughter for allowing his child to die without the aid of medicine or the assistance of a doctor.¹⁰² Barney subsequently was found guilty and spent five months on a prison chain gang. The state attorney reportedly admonished the jury as representatives of the state of Virginia, 'You can't afford to let this holiness movement go on – it must be put down ... It is hellish fanaticism'.¹⁰³

Roy was born in Riceville, Tennessee in 1891 and moved with his parents to Cleveland in 1902. He was drawn to the great revival in Cleveland in the summer of 1908, and after observing the manifestations of God's power was sanctified and Spirit-baptized. The young man was enthralled with Tomlinson and became a devout follower. That same year, Roy joined the Church of God, and in 1910 acknowledged his call to preach and was licensed on April 12, 1911. In October 1910 he had

---

⁹⁸ Tomlinson, *LGC*, pp. 25-26, 93-96.
⁹⁹ Miller, *Classified Scriptures*, p. 18.
¹⁰⁰ Miller, *Classified Scriptures*, p. 20.
¹⁰¹ Miller, *Classified Scriptures*, p. 11.
¹⁰² Tomlinson, *Diary*, February 20, 1915.
¹⁰³ *COGE* 6.4 (January 23, 1915), p. 2; *COGE* 6.5 (January 30, 1915), p. 2; *COGE* 6.8 (February 20, 1915), p. 2, 3; *COGE* 6.20 (May 15, 1915), p. 4.

traveled with Tomlinson and some others to Florida to conduct camp meetings. It was probably then that he met Miss Lula Williams. After the others returned, Roy remained in Florida through the winter to minister – and apparently to court the affections of Lula. In February 1911 he joined the 'Pentecostal Worldwide Mission Band' and sailed with a party of twelve, including Lula, to evangelize the Bahamas. The tour of the islands took a toll on Roy physically, but he pressed on. When the Band returned to Florida, Roy remained to evangelize the state and fortify his relationship with Lula. The couple was married during a meeting in Arcadia on July 7, 1911. Soon after this meeting, they traveled with Tomlinson to Alabama to conduct camp meetings. It was in one of these meetings that Roy contracted a cold from which he never recovered. Still, he and Lula ['Lu'] pushed on with Tomlinson to Mississippi. While there, Roy was appointed to oversee the state. Though ill, he participated in the Assembly in January 1913, and gave his report as an overseer. But his condition grew worse, and on June 28, 1913 he took his last breath in this life.

Figure 78

ROY C. AND LULA MILLER

Anything less than absolute abandonment to faith was considered by Tomlinson to be spiritually deficient and rebellious.[104] The light of the Gospel was being restored in the 'last days' and, accordingly, one could not long be considered a Christian who resorted to 'medical aid in time of sickness'.[105] For the use of medicines was clearly transgression and

---

[104] Tomlinson, *LGC*, p. 102.
[105] Tomlinson, *LGC*, p. 99.

disobedience against God's Word.[106] It was 'trampling blood' the same as murder, idolatry, hatred, and extortion.[107] Obedience to the principle and practice of divine healing was regarded as being as important as obedience to the call of salvation; and, as the light of divine healing continued to 'illuminate' the minds and hearts of Christians, the enlightened ones were obligated to abstain from all medicines and physicians in order to go to heaven.[108] Indeed, Tomlinson questioned the salvation of any person in any age that used medicine.[109] He implied that they were 'thieves and robbers' in the same fashion as others who tried to go to heaven by other means than Christ.[110] Trusting God for the healing for the body without any human or medical assistance was as necessary as trusting God for the saving of the soul. He made no allowance for the present human predicament in this world, as Paul had for one's unredeemed body (cf. Rom. 8.24-27; 2 Cor. 4.7).

Tomlinson taught and practiced divine healing until his death and encouraged others to do the same, which included abstaining from doctors and medicine. However, he did eventually mellow somewhat and relaxed his position in regard to church membership. In the General Assembly in 1917, he stated that the practice of divine healing was not a particular test for membership, but that 'It is expected that people give up their pill bags and medicine to become members …[111]

In somewhat of a defense for Tomlinson's extremism along these lines, as well as some of his contemporaries (Dowie and Sandford, e.g.), it should be noted that medical science was just developing at the turn of the century and was yet primitive in its technology and methods. There were a lot of gimmicks and chicanery, and not a few charlatans in the medical field. Dowie obviously went too far, however, in his famous sermon, 'Doctors, Drugs, and Devils; or the Foes of Christ the Healer'.[112] In this widely-circulated message, which he delivered at his Shiloh Tabernacle in Zion City in March 1896, he labeled physicians the 'Molochs of Medicine and Surgery' who 'dispense poisons under the protection of the law'.[113] His sermon was virtually a declaration of war against

---

[106] Tomlinson, *LGC*, pp. 96, 99.
[107] Tomlinson, *Diary*, July 2, 1897.
[108] Tomlinson, *LGC*, p. 101.
[109] Tomlinson, *LGC*, p. 99; see also *Samson's Foxes* (April 1901), p. 1.
[110] Tomlinson, *LGC*, p. 99.
[111] *Cyclopedic Index of Assembly Minutes*, p. 83.
[112] P.G. Chappell, 'Healing Movements', in *Dictionary of Pentecostal and Charismatic Movements*, p. 367.
[113] John Alexander Dowie, 'Doctors, Drugs, and Devils; or the Foes of Christ the Healer' (Zion, IL: Zion Printing and Publishing House, 1901).

doctors and medicine; he denied that medicine was a science, and charged that the practice was rather a delusion and deception in order to fill the pockets of those who practiced the 'witchcraft'. He proclaimed that 'doctors and devils go together' and that doctors are 'forgers of lies' who promote idolatry and lead people into worshipping 'false gods'. He berated fathers and mothers who 'like [pagan] worshippers sacrifice their children on Druid altars', and declared that physicians are 'monsters who hold in their hands deadly poisons and deadly surgical knives'. He further denounced inoculations against small pox, diphtheria, and tuberculosis, charging that they were nothing more than a scheme concocted between physicians and the state to pad the pockets of the rich.

Notwithstanding his extremism and delusional mindset, Dowie's view of doctors and medicine at the turn of the century was not unpopular among the radical evangelists of the holiness-Pentecostal movement. Certainly Tomlinson had bought into Dowie's radical views, and through him most of the ministers and members in the Church of God before 1923 made trusting God directly for healing tantamount to salvation.

Though there is no explicit evidence that Tomlinson had any direct contact with Dowie, it is almost certain that he had made his way up to Zion City to see firsthand the sensational demonstrations of healings and miracles that were being reported in Dowie's meetings. An entry in his *Diary* says that he was in Illinois in the early part of 1897 and it is likely that he had attended Dowie's meetings at that time.[114] But, in any case, he was influenced by Dowie at least indirectly through Sandford who had attended Dowie's meetings and was fascinated by what he saw; and in turn he reported the same to his followers at Shiloh. Homer says that his father 'had counseled Alexander Dowie people ... [and that] Dowie took away nearly all of the people from the mountains and moved them to Zion City, Ill., where they worked in his lace factories ... [and that later] multitudes of Dowie's people came back to the faith at the beginning back there in those mountains of western North Carolina and still believing in divine healing'.[115]

Besides these indirect connections with Dowie, Tomlinson would have been aware of Dowie's exploits through secular and religious publications that reported his sensational meetings and invectives against

---

[114] Tomlinson, *Diary*, July 2, 1897. The fact that a radical view of divine healing was on his mind when he made this entry in his *Diary* further supports the likelihood that he had visited Dowie at this time; he notes 'Trampling blood when we refuse healing for the body as well as the soul'.

[115] Homer, *Diary*, I, pp. 19-20.

physicians and medicine, for Tomlinson was an avid reader of newspapers, religious and secular.

As with most enlightened ideas, the understanding and clarity of the doctrine of divine healing opened up progressively with time. Consequently, most of the evangelists in the Healing Movement backed off from their earlier radical and absolute views. Tomlinson, however, considered any deviation from the absolute position to be 'faithlessness' and tantamount 'to [falling] back into disobedience'.[116] Thus he practiced and encouraged divine healing until his death. He did, however, relax his intensity on the subject after becoming more preoccupied in later years as a church administrator.

In reflecting on Tomlinson's teaching and practice of divine healing, it is easy to see that he carried the doctrine and practice too far, even as he did with other ideas related to ethical living. But in his favor, it seems that love for people and compassion for their needs were his strongest motivation. It is doubtful that he considered that his requirements for divine healing in many cases only put a greater hardship upon those already weak in faith and body and caused much needless deprivation and suffering. He rather thought that uncompromising firmness would give support to their faith and help them through their trial and suffering of sickness and disease. But in the final analysis, he felt that medical abstinence, even in the face of death, was necessary to authenticate the testimony of faith and therefore tantamount to justification. According to Tomlinson, God required it!

The church overall, however, by 1917 seemed to be making an effort to modify the harsh and rigid position it had taken in 1907. In the *Questions and Answers* session of the Assembly that year, the question, 'Would it be wrong for any one who is trusting in the Lord for their health to give medicine to an unsaved friend in case of sickness?' was thus answered:

> We cannot make any rigid rule regarding this matter. People must be governed by their own conscience. I could not do it [this 'I' was almost certainly Tomlinson], but others might feel obligated to do so and feel alright about it. No one should condemn another in this matter. Some may be engaged as nurses and if they give medicine let them do it, but if they feel condemned they had better get another job'.[117]

---

[116] Tomlinson, *LGC*, p. 102.
[117] *GAM*, 1917, p. 43.

In regard to denigrating and speaking abusively of physicians, it was advised, 'We should not abuse anybody. Let the world have their physicians.'

Anabaptist and Quaker Influences

The church's Anabaptist roots merged with its Wesleyan roots early in the twentieth century to inform the church's position on several key issues, including the visible nature of the church; interdisciplinary fellowship and accountability; a restoration view of the church in history and prophecy; the discipline of practical holiness; forbidding swearing and the taking of oaths even in secular court cases; separation of church and state; pacifism ('against going to war'); the practice of footwashing; and a posture of nonconformity in regard to social structures and civil regulations that tend to draw believers into fellowship with the world.

It may be seen, however, that the church's Anabaptist and Wesleyan roots were also confused with Tomlinson's Quaker roots, with the strength of one tradition winning out over the weaknesses of the others on various issues. The Anabaptist understanding of the visible church, for example, won out over the Quaker view of a spiritual church and also Wesley's confusion on the nature and purpose of the church. Quakers flatly and passionately denounced the observance of the ordinances of Baptism, the Lord's Supper, and Footwashing, and Wesley refused to administer the 'sacraments' in his Methodist movement, believing that this practice was the prerogative of his Anglican ecclesial structure;[118] whereas Anabaptists universally taught and practiced Baptism and the Lord's Supper, and many of their churches observed Footwashing. In regard to pacifism, oath-taking, and the separation of church and state, Quakers and most Wesleyans and Anabaptists were more or less agreed; in regard to the slavery issue, Quakers and Wesleyans were agreed and denounced the institution and practice; whereas some Anabaptists and especially Southern Baptists supported the institution; in point of fact, many of Richard Spurling's fellow ministers owned slaves. In regard to plainness in dress and outward adornment, Anabaptists, Quakers and early Wesleyan Methodists were more or less

---

[118] Though Wesley was highly critical of the Anglican Church, he never left it, and he was careful until very late in his life not to usurp ecclesiastical authority – e.g. in the administration of the ordinances and ordination of ministers; though he did, after coming into conflict with the Anglican hierarchy, ordain ministers. Still, it was not until 1784 (he was then 82 years of age) that he appointed superintendents to oversee the work in America.

agreed; but liberal Methodists succumbed to the powerful currents of worldliness in the nineteenth century and consequently dress among them became a non-issue.[119]

Spurling clearly understood Christian Union in 1886 to be in one sense the outgrowth and fruit of seeds planted by the Anabaptists in the previous three centuries. *The Lost Link* reads like a treatise written by Anabaptist ministers in the sixteenth and seventeenth centuries. Spurling speaks of 'our fathers in the days of Luther'[120] and locates them in the center of Anabaptist strongholds in the Piedmont Valley and Alps region of Italy, Switzerland, and Germany.[121] His narrative and poems recall the saints' bloody persecutions by political states and Protestant state churches from the sixteenth century forward to his day.[122] And he warns that without diligent watch, the American state would become a persecutor of God's people.[123]

The theology and historical narrative in *The Lost Link* is almost perfectly consistent with G.H. Orchard's *History of the Baptists*; and Orchard's aim in the nineteenth century was to show that modern-day Baptists were a continuation of historical Anabaptists, and thus that Baptists in his day were the true heirs of the primitive (apostolic) church. Ironically, the most glaring departure in Spurling's theology and historical narrative in *The Lost Link* from Orchard's history and theology is in regard to the church itself. For Spurling's aim in *The Lost Link* is to convince his readers that the primitive church apostatized in the fourth century and that God had used him to restore it in 1886. Interestingly, his view in this regard was in the mainstream of Anabaptist thought, for, as we noticed earlier, Anabaptists did not believe in succession but in the radical fall of the church in 325 CE and its radical restoration in the sixteenth century. It is thus especially ironic that Orchard and J.R. Graves and Landmark Baptists saw themselves as the heirs of Anabaptists, for historical Anabaptism clearly contradicted their basic ecclesiological premise. In any case, Spurling's restoration view of the church not only departed from Orchard and his Landmark Baptist tradition but from Baptists in general.

---

[119] Wesley taught rather conservatively in regard to dress, but he emphasized inner purity and saw holiness mainly as acts of charity and good works. The celebrated Wesleyan scholar and commentator, Adam Clarke, emphasized plainness in his renown *Commentary* and in his *Christian Theology*, a perspective that was gradually abandoned by the Methodists in the nineteenth century.

[120] Spurling, *Lost Link*, p. 39.
[121] Spurling, *Lost Link*, pp. 16, 34.
[122] Spurling, *Lost Link*, pp. 15-16, 34-35.
[123] Spurling, *Lost Link*, p. 35.

Between 1884 and 1886, after much soul-searching and an impassioned search into Christian history with his father, Spurling was convinced that the primitive church had apostatized in 325 CE under Constantine and had ceased to exist.[124] Reflecting on his search through history for the church after the fourth century, Spurling wrote,

> Down, down the history of time four centuries or more we call for God's church again. No answer comes, but from proud Rome comes the answer, saying she is the church which the gates of hell shall not prevail against. Sick with her foul breath and blood-stained hands we call to the valley of the Piedmont, then we ascend the Alps again, call for God's Church and only an imaginary answer comes. At this, many go over to ride on the beast and share in the Babylonian Captivity, under Rome or some one of her daughters. Oh, that through all these years God's people had known what Jesus meant when He said, 'Upon this rock I will build my church'.[125]

Spurling further shows that the church was still in darkness and in 'Babylonian Captivity' in 1886, and that God had imparted to him the secret to its restoration. This is his central thesis in *The Lost Link*.[126]

Before we move on to look at some of the peculiar teachings and practices that reflect the Anabaptist roots of the Church of God, we should point out that Spurling was able to write so vividly and passionately about the Anabaptist story because he believed he was an heir of that story; and though he modified the story by his peculiar vision and experience, he saw it nevertheless as continuing in him. After all, his father (b. 1810) and some of the members of Christian Union (e.g. John J. Plemons [b. 1818]) were only two generations removed from the bloody persecutions of the Anabaptists in central Europe. Some of their grandfathers and great-grandfathers had suffered under the church-state systems in England and on the European continent. Moreover, Baptists in America – especially the Landmarkers – in the late nineteenth and early twentieth century kept alive the story and embraced it as their sacred heritage. J.R. Graves, the father of Landmarkism and the most celebrat-

---

[124] Spurling, *Lost Link*, pp. 6, 15, 21.
[125] Spurling, *Lost Link*, p. 16.
[126] His dialog with the Methodist minister in *The Lost Link* (pp. 33-34) almost certainly recalls his actual dialogues in 1884-1886 with John Duggan and Jeremiah Martin, the Methodist pastors at Coker Creek (Ironsburg), with whom he had worshipped and 'taken refuge' after having been expelled from his Landmark Baptist Church at Pleasant Hill in Cherokee County, North Carolina. Here he clearly shows that neither Luther nor Calvin nor Wesley had restored the church, for God had laid this glorious task upon him and his contemporaries (pp. 39, 47-48).

ed Baptist in the South throughout much of the nineteenth century, and the man to whom Richard and his father had looked to for leadership in the 1860s and 1870s, gloried in the fact that his grandparents were among the persecuted Huguenots in southern France that 'had fled to America'.[127]

Plain Dress and Practical Holiness

Practical holiness in the Church of God meant plainness in dress, including censoring outward adornment.[128] Though nothing is explicitly stated in *The Lost Link* indicating that Christian Union denounced or discouraged the wearing of jewelry, nor had put any special emphasis on plain dress, nevertheless, Spurling's poem about 'Worldly Jack' and the 'Heavenly Bride' indicates that plainness was simply understood to be the norm in Christian Union and needed not to be explicitly stated:

> I saw the heavenly bride so fair; With lovely eyes and face, Not decked with earthly jewels rare, But full of truth and grace. The Bridegroom held her by the hand, As they walked side by side, But worldly Jack came stepping up, Upon the other side. I saw the rings upon his hand, His collars, cuffs, and ties; And when he took her by the hand, My soul was much surprised ... In all the fashions up-to-date, He decked her all so fine, And then he whispered through his teeth, 'This lovely girl is mine'. Just then a holy man of God, Came running up the way, Unto the erring bride he said, You sure have gone astray. She blushed and turned to see the one, That once walked by her side, Instead of him it was worldly Jack, [who] claimed her for his bride.

After the church came under the influence of the Holiness Movement and especially the Fire-Baptized Holiness Association, the use of cosmetics and the wearing of jewelry were especially frowned upon and censored, though an exception was made for a plain wedding band.[129] Church of God members were cautioned, however, that the wedding band should not be 'worn for ornament', and if purchased it should be inexpensive, citing Isa. 55.2 for authority. It was suggested further that if

---

[127] Burnett, *Pioneer Baptist Preachers*, p. 184. Much of Spurling's *The Lost Link* may be seen in Graves' 'Introductory Essay' to Orchard's *History of the Baptists*.
[128] Spurling, *Lost Link*, pp. 38-39.
[129] *The Book of Doctrines* (Cleveland, TN: Church of God Publishing House, 1922), pp. 124-26.

a member purchased a wedding band, it should cost no more than $5.00.[130]

The church believed it had firm footing for its stand against jewelry and outward adornment based on apostolic teachings in 1 Tim. 2.9, 10; 1 Pet. 3.3, 4; *et al.* and also the witness of the Church Fathers in the second and third centuries.[131] Generally speaking, the church's stand against expensive dress, cosmetics, jewelry, and outward adornment was seen to be consistent with the apostolic admonitions for modesty and humility (Isa. 3.16; 1 Tim. 2.9; 1 Pet. 3.3; *et al.*).

It may be observed however that the church's teaching on jewelry was seldom addressed officially or formally in its first thirty years, and was not considered a test of fellowship unless it created corresponding problems in the church – contentions, strife, divisions. The mention of jewelry in the Eighth Assembly in 1913 was a rare occasion, and even then there was not a hard line taken. Certainly it was not classified as a work of the flesh in the same sense that the use of drugs or tobacco or the manifestations of anger and malice were viewed. Tomlinson advised and cautioned the ministers and churches patiently to teach and sway the members against the wearing of gold and jewelry for adornment.[132]

After the Council of Elders was established in 1917, a number of the Elders, however, held a more rigid view in regard to jewelry and outward adornment. These Elders encouraged the Council to adopt a list of 'Instructions and Advices' for the ministers and members. This list included the following: 'Your dress should be with moderation, neat and clean, but not for show. You should never wear gold for ornament

---

[130] *Book of Doctrines*, pp. 125-26. Here it was explained that a 'little inexpensive ring that tells the story of wedlock' should be left to individual conscience.

[131] There is no lack of evidence in the Church Fathers to support the Church of God's stand in regard to plainness in dress, including prohibitions against the wearing of jewelry and cosmetics. We cite here only two sources to illustrate. Clement of Alexandria wrote, 'Let not their ears be pierced, contrary to nature, in order to attach to them earrings ... Women who wear gold seem to me to be afraid, lest, if one strip them of jewelry, they should be mistaken for servants, without their adornments' (*Early Christian Beliefs*, p. 379). 'By no manner of means are women to be allowed to uncover and exhibit any part of their persons. Otherwise, both may fall – the men being excited to look; the women, by drawing to themselves the eyes of the men (*Early Christian Beliefs*, p. 455). Tertullian wrote, 'Most women ... walk as if modesty consisted only in the bare integrity of the flesh and in turning away from actual fornication ... They wear in their gait the same appearance as do the women of the nations, [in] whom a true sense of modesty is absent ... [These] women ... earnestly desire to look pleasing even to strangers? ... and on that account take care to have [themselves] painted out, yet denying [they] have ever been an object for carnal appetite' (*Early Christians Beliefs*, pp. 455, 456).

[132] *Cyclopedic Index of Assembly Minutes*, pp. 208, 283.

or decoration. Finger rings, bracelets, earrings, necklaces, lockets, and large showy pins are unbecoming for the saints of God'.[133]

Most of those who took an extreme position on this issue had been a part of or otherwise influenced by the Fire-Baptized Holiness Association. These brethren, accordingly, not only considered wearing jewelry 'worldly', but preached and taught against women cutting their hair and wearing pants, citing Deut. 22.5 and 1 Cor. 11.5-10 as proof texts to support their censors. It was not unusual for Church of God preachers from the pulpit to mention the name 'Jezebel' and apply it to any woman who 'painted her face' and wore jewelry, and otherwise tended to usurp the authority of elders and men in the church.

Notwithstanding, the use of cosmetics and the wearing of jewelry were generally considered rather trivial points and were not problematic in the church. This was true especially in the church's formative years, for most evangelical bodies in America even in the early decades of the twentieth century frowned upon and discouraged gaudy cosmetics, extravagant and expensive apparel, and wearing of jewelry.[134] The decision among Tomlinson's followers in 1944 that drew a rigid line against the wedding band represented a major shift in the church's spirit and disposition; thereafter the wearing of gold and jewelry was considered more or less sinful!

The Church of God, like all holiness-Pentecostal bodies in the early twentieth century, also taught against card playing; discouraged and in some cases forbade its members to participate in social dances; and counseled them to stay away from theaters, secret clubs and lodge meetings, and places where alcohol is served. Tomlinson wrote,

> Not a few [church houses], whose walls used to echo the shouts of happy, well fed souls, are left for the owls and bats. Lodges and shows, base-ball games and theaters, society and dress parades are attracting the once happy church going people and commanding their money.[135]

Drinking coffee, coca-cola, and soda water was advised against, also the purchasing of life insurance policies and chewing gum were discouraged,

---

[133] *GAM*, 1917, p. 48. These 'instructions and advices', moreover, were further dogmatized and codified in the church's list of 'teachings made prominent'. It became the twenty-six teaching in the church's developing 'creed'. Isa. 55.2; 1 Pet. 3.3; 1 Jn 2.15 were cited to support the church's position.

[134] America began to be transformed in the early twentieth century by the glamorous visions of Elizabeth Arden and Helena Rubenstein, and also by the motion picture industry and developing Hollywood culture.

[135] Tomlinson, *LGC*, p. 171.

though these things were not held as a test of membership.[136] However, ministers who chewed gum were warned that the practice would prevent them from being licensed.[137]

The corporate counsel of the church further advised its members to avoid worldly literature and all kinds of entertainment that militated against spirituality and consecration in holiness, including 'skating rinks, nickelo[deons] and shows'.[138] Church of God pioneers reasoned that where there was an emphasis on heart purity and inner holiness, there should be a visible correspondence in outward appearance and behavior. 1 John 2.15-17; Jn 17.15, 16; 18.36; Gal. 1.4; and 1 Thess. 5.22 were classical texts used to support the church's position along the lines of worldliness and nonconformity.

On Oath-Taking and Swearing

Oath-taking was listed as 'against members swearing' in the church's list of 'prominent teachings' in 1915. What was in view was the Anabaptist and Quaker interpretation of Jesus' words in the Sermon on the Mount recorded in Mt. 5.33-37, and asserted again by the apostle in Jas 5.12. Again, it should be borne in mind that many of the pioneers of the Church of God were only two or three generations removed from their Anabaptist and Quaker forbearers, the latter having been persecuted by the political states and Protestant state churches in England and Europe. And they were still vividly aware that oaths and swearing were used by those systems to marginalize and persecute Christians whose supreme allegiance was to Christ, not to the existing political and ecclesiastical institutions. Thus, when temporal laws were enacted that contradicted Jesus' teachings, the church's courageous ancestors – like Shadrach, Meshach, and Abednego – stood on the Word of God

Though oaths were allowed and even commanded as a religious duty under the Old Covenant (Gen. 21.28-31; Deut. 32.40; Judg. 8.19; 1 Sam. 14.39; 20.42; Jer. 42.5), Jesus expressly forbade the practice under the New Covenant, saying 'You have heard that it has been said by them of old time, you shall not foreswear yourself [that is, you shall fulfill what you swear to] … But I say unto you, swear not at all.' As in the case of divorce and remarriage, Jesus taught a completely opposite view than what had been allowed under the Old Covenant. The teachings of 'them

---

[136] *GAM*, 1917, pp. 27-29.
[137] *GAM*, 1917, p. 28.
[138] *GAM 1906-1914*, p. 51.

of old time', referring to the Mosaic legislations, were now superseded by His teachings, which He emphasized by saying, 'I say unto you'.

The divine reasoning behind the prohibition against oath-taking and swearing was plainly revealed in Jesus' teaching. *First*, it is presumptuous of humanity and irreverent to call an infinitely perfect and holy God as a witness to his statements. Even if a person means well and believes his or her statement is true, he or she can inadvertently be in error; and thus by invoking God in his or her oath involves Him in his or her false statement. It is an arrogant presumption for a person to assert that what he or she is saying is absolutely and perfectly true – to presume infallibility. And thus we should not upon a solemn oath say anything to the effect, 'As the Lord lives' or 'I solemnly swear in His name' (Judg. 8.19; 1 Sam. 14.39 and cf. Eccl. 9.2-3). *Second*, it is certain that by swearing a person 'cannot make one hair white or black'. One can speak truth only by sanctified union with a holy God, and by maintaining a consecrated lifestyle in the Spirit – by 'living and walking in the Spirit!' And thus through divine grace and Christian integrity, God gives witness to one's testimony and actions. Swearing an oath therefore adds nothing to one's testimony; indeed, it militates against it. *Third*, oath-taking and swearing tend to disannul plain and simple truth, for under a legal oath a person tends to reason and testify from a legalistic standpoint, and thus to speak factually but not necessarily truthfully. Legal minds in fact are trained to examine a witness with this perversion in view – to draw out of a person's testimony partial facts to form a particular conclusion that they have in view, which often is a complete distortion of the truth in order to win their case. And the object in these cases most often is monetary gain and temporal advantage – not the glory of God. Jesus thus commands the believer, therefore, 'let your communication be, Yea, yea; Nay, nay: for whatsoever is more than these comes of evil'. In other words, 'let your yes be yes, and your no be no!' – speak the truth simply on your honor to the best of your knowledge with a good conscience in Christ. Thus says the apostle, 'I say the truth in Christ, I lie not, my conscience also bearing me witness in the Holy Ghost' (Rom. 9.1).

Though oath-taking had been strictly forbidden by Jesus and the apostles in the New Testament, and the early church discouraged the practice in the second and third centuries on the basis of Jesus' teachings, which Justin Martyr, Clement of Alexandria, Origin, Tertullian, Cyprian and other Church Fathers clearly show,[139] the practice never-

---

[139] Let Clement of Alexandria answer here for the Church Fathers; his words capture the essential meaning and moral authority of Jesus' commandment in Mt. 5.33-37: 'The man of proven character in such piety is far from being apt to lie and

theless was revived after the church apostatized during the reign of Constantine in the fourth century. Thereafter, the true church disappeared in the darkness of the 'Dark Ages', or, to put it another way, the apostolic church degenerated and was absorbed into Roman Catholicism.

Church of God pioneers were keenly aware of Jesus' and the apostles' teaching on swearing and oaths; and thus, following in the path of the radical Anabaptists, sought to restore the church on its original foundation: for they believed the true church must be 'subject to Christ in everything' (Eph. 5.24, 32).

The practice of oath-taking and swearing was revived in the Roman Catholic Church because her interests had become entangled with the interests of the Roman Empire; for under Constantine the church and state were wedded. Believers were thereafter drawn into a worldly system of religion mixed with politics, which like a powerful tide carried them out into a sea of idolatry and apostasy, blinding them to the essential meaning and implications of Jesus' commandments; or, to put it another way, they lost the spiritual ability to discern the 'hidden wisdom' in Jesus' teachings – became insensitive to the voice of the Spirit and the Word of God. What Spurling called a 'Christianized conscience' – a conscience formed by the teachings of Christ and the Spirit – was deformed and confused by the pagan world around them.

Augustine in the fifth century was well aware of the objections to the oath by pious believers, both within and without the pale of the Roman Church; but he nevertheless was able to open the door for its practice on a universal basis, reasoning that the oath not only glorified God but was beneficial for the state and society as a whole. Roman Catholicism thereafter used the oath and swearing to advance her agenda in co-existing and working in harmony with the various states in Europe.

The Protestant reformers and churches in the sixteenth century adopted the position of the Roman Catholic Church in regard to oath-taking. Luther believed the church existed to serve the state, and therefore put his approval on the practice and encouraged it. In spite of

---

to swear. For an oath is a decisive affirmation, with the taking of the divine name. For how can he, who is once faithful, show himself unfaithful so as to require an oath ... But he does not even swear, preferring to make averment in affirmation by 'yes' and in denial by 'no' ... it suffices, then, with him, to add to an affirmation or denial of expression, 'I speak truthfully' ... To him who lives in accordance with the extreme of truth, where, then, is the necessity for an oath? He, then, who does not even swear will be far from perjuring himself ... So he does not lie, nor does he do anything contrary to his agreements. And so he does not swear even when asked for his oath' (*Dictionary of Early Christian Beliefs*, p. 480).

the plain teachings of Jesus and the apostles on the subject, he declared in his *Greater Catechism*, 'The oath is a right good work, by which God is praised, the truth and right are confirmed, lies are stopped ... and strife is overcome, since God enters in to separate right from wrong and good from evil'.[140] Like Luther, almost all of the Protestant reformers failed to grasp the essential meaning and important implications in Jesus' teaching on oath-taking and swearing.

It was the radical reformers in the sixteenth and seventeenth centuries – Anabaptists and Quakers – who held to the standard of Jesus' teaching and refused to compromise with Roman Catholicism and the existing states of Europe. They were brutally and mercilessly persecuted for their stand; barred from voting and participating in civil events; and imprisoned on occasion and sometimes executed. But the Lord nevertheless sustained them and honored their testimony; and through their Godly and consecrated witness many of the political states in Europe and elsewhere in the world in the eighteenth and nineteenth centuries allowed Christians to simply 'affirm the truth' of their statements, rather than requiring them to swear to an oath. Included among these nations was the United States of America. Thus, in regard to the question posed in the Assembly in 1917 – 'Can we be compelled by the laws to hold up our hand and swear in court?' – the Elders gladly responded, "No. The law provides that we can affirm without holding up our hand'.[141]

The wisdom of the Wesleyan scholar and commentator, Adam Clarke, is worthy of note here. In regard to Jesus' commandment in Mt. 5.34 – 'Swear not at all' – he says, 'An oath will not bind a knave nor a liar; and an honest man needs none, for his character and conduct swear for him'. Again he observes, 'When we make any promise contrary to the command of God, taking, as a pledge of our sincerity, either God, or something belonging to him, we engage that which is not ours, without the Master's consent'.

On Footwashing

Baptism, Lord's Supper [Communion], and Footwashing ['Washing the Saints Feet'] were recognized and practiced in the Church of God from

---

[140] In his 'On War Against the Turk' he sanctions oath taking and calls for obedience to the state, even to 'the heathen emperor at Babylon' (*Works of Martin Luther* (6 Vols.; Grand Rapids, MI: Baker Book House, reprint 1982, 5.112); in 'Discussion of Confession', he claims that oaths are of 'divine law' (*Works*, 1.99).

[141] *GAM*, 1917, p. 43.

the beginning in 1886 and, interestingly, were never controversial.[142] Jesus' express command and example in Jn 13.1-17 and the apostle Paul's words in 1 Tim. 5.9, 10 were sufficient proof for the church's pioneers to adopt the practice of Footwashing as a divine ordinance. But whereas Baptism and the Lord's Supper were accepted universally by most Christian bodies, Footwashing was controversial among the high church traditions. The Roman Catholic, Greek Orthodox, and Anglican churches all denied to Footwashing the status of a sacrament or ordinance, particularly on a level equal with the Lord's Supper and Baptism; but so did the mainline Protestant bodies – Lutheranism, Presbyterianism, *et al*. Only the Anabaptists and related radical reformation groups considered Footwashing to be important enough actually to observe, and even some Anabaptists failed to grasp the significance of Jesus' teaching and personal example in regard to the subject.

The great Quaker apologist, Robert Barclay, thought it inconsistent for the Roman Catholic and Protestant churches to hold to the significance of Baptism and the Lord's Supper and yet deny the same significance to Footwashing. Though Barclay, like all Quakers, denied the need to outwardly observe the ordinances, yet he could not see the logic in observing Baptism and the Lord's Supper, while denying the same honor to Footwashing. Speaking in regard to this, he wrote,

> If we respect the nature of [Footwashing], it hath as much in it as either *baptism* or the *breaking of bread*; seeing it is an outward element of a cleansing nature, applied to the outward man, by the command and example of Christ, to signify an inward purifying. I would willingly propose this seriously to men, who will be pleased to make use of that reason and understanding that God hath given them, and not be imposed upon, nor abused by the custom or tradition of others; Whether this ceremony, if we respect either the time that it was appointed in, or the circumstance wherewith it was performed, or the command enjoining the use of it, hath not as much to recommend it for a standing ordinance of the gospel, as either water-baptism, or bread and wine, or any other of that kind? I wonder then what reason the Papists can give, why they have not numbered it among their sacraments, except merely *Voluntas Ecclesia & Traditio Patrum*.
>
> But if they say, That it is used among them, in that the Pope, and some other persons among them, use to do it once a year to some poor people; I would willingly know what reason they have why this should not be extended to all, as well as that of the eucharist (as they

---

[142] Spurling, *Lost Link*, pp. 9, 44.

term it), or whence it appears from the text, that [Do this in remembrance of me] should be interpreted that the bread and wine were every day to be taken by all priests, or the bread every day, or every week, by the people; and that that other command of Christ, Ye ought to do as I have done to you, &c. is only to be understood of the Pope, or some other persons, to be done only to a few, and that once a year? Surely there can be no other reason for this difference assigned from the text. And as to Protestants, who use not this ceremony at all, if they will but open their eyes, they may see how that by custom and tradition they are abused in this matter, as were their fathers in divers Popish traditions. For if we look into the plain scripture, what can be thence inferred to urge the one, which may not be likewise pleaded for the other; or for laying aside the one, which may not be likewise said against the continuance of the other? If they say, That the former, of washing the feet, was only a ceremony; what have they, whence they can show, that this breaking of bread is more? If they say, That the former was only a sign of humility and purifying; what have they to prove that this was more? If they say, That one was only for a time, and was no evangelical ordinance; what hath this to make it such, that the other wanted? Surely there is no way of reason to evade this; neither can any thing be alleged, that the one cease, and not the other; or the one continue, and not the other; but the mere opinion of the affirmers, which by custom, education, and tradition, hath begotten in the hearts of people a greater reverence for, and esteem of the one than the other; which if it had fallen out to be as much recommended to us by tradition, would no doubt have been as tenaciously pleaded for, as having no less foundation in scripture. But since the former, to wit, the washing of one another's feet, is justly laid aside, as not binding upon Christians; so ought also the other for the same reason.[143]

Although the interpretation and significance of Footwashing varied among the Anabaptist groups that taught and observed the ordinance, it

---

[143] Robert Barclay, *An Apology for the True Christian Divinity* (New York: Published by Samuel Wood and Sons, 1832), pp. 468-70. Barclay knew and worked with George Fox; his *Apology* was first published in 1675. John Christopher Thomas in his *Footwashing in John 13 and the Johannine Community* (Cleveland, TN: CPT Press, 2014, Second Edition) offers the best defense by a Church of God scholar for the observance of Footwashing as an ordinance. Dr Thomas refers to the early Church Fathers – Origin, Ignatius, Augustine, and especially Ambrose – to support his thesis that both the apostolic church and the church in the early centuries saw in Footwashing the elements of a 'sacrament' (pp. 182-91). But his exegesis of the biblical text in John 13 is his most effective argument.

was generally held to be symbolical of a spiritual lesson and thus by no means had any intrinsic power to bestow grace upon those who participated; nor did the practice in any way possess any religious value in and of itself; notwithstanding, many understood footwashing to be an important *symbol* of cleansing from sin, which added weight for the need to observe it. And this was the view held by the Church of God and other contemporary groups in the twentieth century that had roots in Anabaptism.[144] Further, it was commonly held by those who subscribed to its importance and sacredness that it taught believers the lessons of humility, equality, and divine service – that all of the members of the church (including the ministers) stand on equal footing before the Master, the one head of the church.[145] By observing the practice often, the members are thus kept reminded of the important aspects of the church's sacred fellowship and mission to the nations.

In regard to divine government, the ministers and members were to learn by observing Footwashing that every member is important and has a voice in decision-making; for every member is potentially sanctified and Spirit-baptized, and thus has the ability through the Spirit to discern truth and to be 'guided into all truth and righteousness'. The church was thereby enlightened and encouraged not to 'fall away' from the unique form of government in the New Testament, nor especially to adopt in the place of this primitive government some worldly type of system – monarchy, episcopacy, oligarchy, *et al.* Here we are reminded of Jesus' words,

> Jesus called [His disciples] ... and said unto them, You know that they which are accounted to rule over the Gentiles exercise lordship over them; and their great ones exercise authority upon them. But so

---

[144] Dr. Thomas makes a convincing argument in his *Footwashing in John 13 and the Johannine Community* that the ordinance of Footwashing is symbolic of forgiveness and post-conversion cleansing of sin (pp. 157-76, 189-91). It is almost certain that Spurling and Christian Union held this view in 1886, for this was a common view among Footwashing Baptists, and he was at that time not far removed from that tradition; in any case, it was not the view of the Church of God after the fellowship was swept into the Holiness movement in the 1890s, for the eradication view of sin in sanctification tended to discount the need for post-conversion forgiveness. In his chapter on 'Historical Reconstruction', Dr. Thomas aims to reestablish what he believes was the original view and practice of the New Testament church, that Footwashing included the idea of forgiveness and cleansing among the members of the church who committed sin. He suggests that this view is consistent with Mt. 16.19; Jn 20.23; *et al.*

[145] Dr. Thomas lists seven historical interpretations for the observance of Footwashing in the New Testament church (*Footwashing in John 13 and the Johannine Community*, pp. 2-7).

shall it not be among you: but whosoever will be great among you, shall be your minister: And whosoever of you will be chief, shall be servant of all. For even the Son of man came not to be ministered unto, but to minister, and to give his life a ransom for many (Mk 10.42-45).

In regard to humility, the church is reminded that genuine Christian fellowship depends on this grace; and it follows also that in order for the church to be truly lovely and beautiful and distinct from the world, the spirit of humility must be a conditioning and ruling factor.

Let this mind be in you, which was also in Christ Jesus: Who, being in the form of God, thought it not robbery to be equal with God: But made himself of no reputation, and took upon him the form of a servant, and was made in the likeness of men: And being found in fashion as a man, he humbled himself and became obedient unto death, even the death of the cross (Phil. 2.5-8).

In regard to service, the church is to be ruled by the great commandment: 'to love [our] neighbor as [ourselves]'. Here again, Jesus is our Master Teacher: 'For even as Christ pleased not himself; but, as it is written, The reproaches of them that reproached you fell on me.' And thus the apostle says, 'We then that are strong ought to bear the infirmities of the weak, and not to please ourselves. Let every one of us please his neighbor for his good to edification' (Rom. 15.1-2). And again, 'Give none offense, neither to the Jews, nor to the Gentiles, nor to the church of God: Even as I please all men in all things, not seeking mine own profit, but the profit of many, that they may be saved' (1 Cor. 10.32-33).

The theology and practice of Footwashing was introduced into the church from the beginning by Spurling; but the other charter members of Christian Union were from Landmark and Primitive Baptist backgrounds and were thus familiar with the practice. Tomlinson, however, seems to have come to the conclusion independently, though he had been in meetings with Anabaptist groups – Brethren in Christ, Mennonites, *et al.* – who taught and practiced Footwashing. The practice was thus not strange to him. While at Culberson on March 25, 1901, he recorded in his *Diary*:

After a special outpouring of the Spirit in our Sunday meeting yesterday. I could not take my breakfast as usual. At night we had special prayer ... and I read the words of Jesus that we receive the petitions we desired because we keep His commandments. I then turned, guided by the Spirit, and read where Jesus washed the disciples' feet and said, 'Ye ought to wash one another's feet'. I had never obeyed this commandment. I at once laid aside my coat, girded myself with a towel, poured water into a basin and washed the feet of the brethren present. Other members of our household became more zealous to keep the commandments.

This act by Tomlinson was especially significant in view of the strict prohibition by Quakers against the practice. Tomlinson had been baptized in October 1897 and again in 1901 at Shiloh and had been excluded from the Quaker church on that basis. In regard to his baptism, he was visited and offered some reproof and counsel by some of the ministers and members of his Quaker church in Westfield. Their counsel did not impress him much nor dim his new light on the subject. In an attempt to reprove and belittle his action, his Quaker elder referred to him as a 'water duck' and even went so far to call the apostle Peter a 'water duck'. This remark of course only strengthened Tomlinson position, for he considered it to be disrespectful and sarcastic and a rather lame defense for the Quaker position.[146]

Tomlinson's description of the Footwashing service in his home on March 25, 1901 makes it almost certain that he had been in such services before with other groups, though he had not participated; for his description of the service in his home is almost identical to the typical service in most Anabaptist churches.

> The most common mode of the observance is as follows: After the communion service is completed, one of the ministers or deacons reads and comments on John 13:1-17. Basins, usual small wooden or metal tubs, with warm water and towels have meanwhile been provided in sufficient quantity to permit a fairly rapid observance. These are placed, either in the front of the church or in the 'amen' corners, and in the 'ante-rooms', or in some cases in rows between the benches. The sexes then wash (more properly rinse or lightly touch with water) feet separately in pairs, concluding with the greeting of the holy kiss and a 'God bless you'. In some localities towels are furnished in the form of short aprons to be tied by cords around the waist, in presumed imitation of Jesus 'girding himself', though most commonly ordinary towels are used. In some congregations the practice is not pair-washing but row-washing, in which case each person washes the feet of his right-hand neighbor in turn in a continuous chain ... In the Church of God in Christ Mennonite group the ministers wash each other's feet first, and then wash the feet of all the

---

[146] Tomlinson, 'Deposition', p. 2337.

brethren in turn, the minister's wives doing the same for the sisters.[147]

This description is fitting for the way the ordinance was observed thereafter in the Church of God. To preserve the sanctity of the observance, men and women met apart, usually not in sight of each other, and then re-gathered together to be dismissed or to complete the worship service. In the Church of God, the practice of Footwashing almost without exception followed the observance of the Lord's Supper, though these ordinances were addressed in the First Assembly in 1906 and the manner in which they were to be observed was left up to the local churches.

> Communion and feet washing were duely [sic] discussed by Eld. R.G. Spurling and others, and it is the sense of this Assembly that the Communion and feet washing are taught by the New Testament Scriptures, and may be engaged in at the same service or at different times at the option of the local Churches. In order to preserved the unity of the body, and to obey the sacred Word, we recommend that every member engage in these sacred services. We further recommend that these holy ordinances be observed one or more times each year.

It should be pointed out here that the term 'ordinance' rather than 'sacrament' in regard to Baptism, the Lord's Supper and Footwashing is also of Anabaptist origin. This term was preferred because after the church went into apostasy in the early centuries, the Roman Catholic Church perverted the significance of the ordinances attaching to them magical power to convey grace.[148] The term 'sacrament' was coined to signify this perversion. Augustine said a sacrament 'is the visible form of an invisible grace', and Thomas Aquinas defined a sacrament as a 'sign

---

[147] *Mennonite Encyclopedia*, II, p. 347.

[148] Even early in the second century, there are signs that the Church Fathers were already perverting the biblical significance of the divine ordinances. It may be seen in comments by Justin Martyr, Irenaeus, Clement of Alexandria, Tertullian, *et al.* (see under 'Eucharist' in *Dictionary of Early Christian Beliefs*). Ignatius, in regard to observing the Lord's Supper, exhorted the church about 105 CE that the members should 'come together in common, and individually ... in obedience to the bishop and the presbytery with an undivided mind, breaking one and the same bread, which is the medicine of immortality, and the antidote which prevents us from dying ... [which causes] that we should live in God through Jesus Christ' (*The Anti Nicene Fathers*, I, pp. 57-58), and again, 'I desire the bread of God, the heavenly bread ... which is the flesh of Jesus Christ, the Son of God ... And I desire the drink, namely, His blood, which is incorruptible love and eternal life (pp. 76-77).

of a sacred thing in so far as it sanctifies man'. Soon after the church had fallen under Constantine in the fourth century, John Chrysostom, the celebrated patriarch of Constantinople, spoke in regards to the Lord's Supper in the following manner,

> That dreadful and mystic Table ... The Lamb for thee is slaughtered, the priest for thee contends, the spiritual fire from the sacred table ascends, the cherubim holding their stations round about, while the seraphim hovering around, and the six-winged veiling their faces, while for thee the incorporeal orders along with the priest intercede ... Not as bread should thou look at first at that, neither esteem that as wine, for not like other aliment do these descend into the draught ... Think not that you receive the divine body, as from the hand of man; but rather as the fire from the tongs of the very seraphim given to Isaiah.[149]

It was thus that Chrysostom and his predecessors and fellow priests reinvented the observance of the Lord's Supper. Through the blinding power of Satan, the observance gradually metamorphosed into a ritual of Mystery, not unlike some of the rituals in pagan traditions. The dynamic power of the new birth through simple faith in Christ was supplanted with the ritual of the 'Mystic Table'. Salvation was now appropriated through this observance rather than simple personal faith and the actual regenerating power of the Holy Spirit. In this manner, the church fell into the same error of the Jews, who had mistaken the Ark of the Covenant for the real presence of God!

The Anabaptists, thus, in order to restore apostolic faith and practice, taught that the significance of the ordinances was merely symbolic, and passionately denied that they bestowed grace upon the believer or possessed any power to save and sanctify. Indeed, most Anabaptists believed that the observance of the ordinances among Roman Catholics and the liturgical traditions was idolatrous and antichrist. Many Anabaptist leaders like Menno Simons claimed these traditions attached magical powers to the 'sacraments', and thus charged these groups with having been seduced by the spirit of witchcraft.[150] This was more or less also the position of Baptists in nineteenth and early twentieth century Appalachia and also the pioneers in the Church of God.

---

[149] Cited in Thomas Armitage, *A History of the Baptists*, II, p. 224. Chrysostom's homilies on First Cor. 11.17 and 11.28 give this same sense (*Nicene and Post-Nicene Fathers*, XII, pp. 157-68).

[150] *Mennonite Encyclopedia*, IV, p.72

Separation of Church and State

In regard to the church's relationship with the state, this issue came up very early in the General Assembly. It was resolved in 1908 that the church was 'Opposed to the union of Church and state under any circumstances'.[151] Again, that the issue came up at all in those early years reflected the church's roots in the radical reformation of the sixteenth and seventeenth centuries. It will be recalled that both Spurling and Tomlinson were students of history and knew well the plight of pious Christians wherever the state was subjected to the 'church' or the 'church' to the state. Even in the American colonies in the seventeenth and eighteenth centuries, Quakers had been executed and Baptists had been treated like 'stepchildren'. Since most of the early pioneers of the Church of God had been reared in the Baptist tradition, it was natural for them to see the importance of maintaining a separation between church and state; for many of their ancestors had been bitterly persecuted and murdered by both Roman Catholics and Protestants in Europe, and had been persecuted in the American colonies by Anglicans and Puritans. They knew what the inevitable result would be if the freedom of conscience and individual liberties were not held sacred and tenaciously embraced. Spurling warned, therefore, in *The Lost Link* about a 'political ecclesiasticism, that is, state and church united [which historically had compelled] God's people to worship idols'.[152] He further emphasized that America was not immune to becoming a tyrannical state if she were given that kind of power. He wrote, 'I turn from these awful scenes [that is, the brutal scenes of persecutions in the Middle Ages in Europe] to the fair land of America and ask, Shall this fair land ever drink the blood of God's people, at the hand of some human creed? God only knows what the law of men will do when substituted instead of God's law'.[153]

The essential principle for sixteenth-century Anabaptists according to Heinrich Bullinger, Zwingli's successor in Zurich, was religious liberty. Accordingly, the Swiss brethren taught that:

> One cannot and should not use force or compel anyone to accept the faith, for faith is a free gift of God. It is wrong to compel anyone by force or coercion to embrace the faith, or to put to death anyone for the sake of his erring faith. It is an error that in the church any sword

---

[151] *GAM 1906-1914*, p. 43.
[152] Spurling, *Lost Link*, p. 16.
[153] Spurling, *Lost Link*, p. 35.

other than the divine Word should be used. The secular kingdom should be separated from the church, and no secular ruler should exercise authority in the church. The Lord has commanded simply to preach the Gospel, not to compel anyone by force to accept it. The true church of Christ has the characteristic that it suffers and endures persecution but does not inflict persecution upon anyone.[154]

The Church of God in regard to church and state thus stood squarely in the tradition that had begun with sixteenth-century Anabaptists. The true church must be free from the state in order to rebuild God's house on the basis of personal conscience and a free moral agency of the individual members. For wherever the state and church are united, men and women are coerced into practices that violate their consciences; and this in turn results in the prostitution of the Gospel.

Figure 79
H.L. TRIM AND FLORA E. BOWER[155]
(C. 1914)   (C. 1911)

William R. Estep in telling the story of the Anabaptists in the sixteenth century in his *The Anabaptist Story* virtually mirrors the sentiments of Spurling and Tomlinson and the pioneers of the Church of God in the late nineteenth and early twentieth century. In his chapter on 'Church and State', he writes,

---

[154] Heinrich Bullinger, *Der Widertaufferen Ursprung* (Zurich, 1560), per translation in English by John Horsch, *Mennonites in Europe*, p. 325.

[155] Henagar L. Trim (1855-1935), from the Union Grove community, had been drawn into the holiness-Pentecostal movement and in 1906 became a member of the Church of God. In the second Assembly in January 1907 he was licensed as an evangelist. Flora E. [Bower] Trim (1866-1948) had attended N.J. Holmes mission school near Greeneville, South Carolina and joined the church 1906 in Cleveland. She evangelized with Tomlinson, Clyde Cotton, Nora Chambers, E.J. Boehmer, J.W. Buckalew, W.F. Bryant, and others in the mountains of East Tennessee, North Carolina, and Georgia, and also in Florida, Alabama, *et al.*, and labored in various ways to build the 'great Church of God'. It was apparently on occasion of her labors in the Cleveland area that she became acquainted with Trim. They married in 1912 [his first wife, Anna having died c. 1910), and thereafter evangelized together with a fervent zeal, residing for extended periods in Illinois, Virginia, and Alabama. When J.J. Lowman contracted a 'sickness unto death' in 1914, Trim was appointed to oversee Virginia, and remained in that position until 1916. In 1921 he was appointed to serve on the Council of Seventy.

The separation of the church and state was viewed as necessary because of the nature of the church. Only thus could the church be cleansed and freed to be the church under God. The disestablishment of the state churches was for the Anabaptists the minimum requirement in a guarantee of religious freedom. Thus the Anabaptists became the first advocates in the modern era of the disestablishment of the [state] church. They alone among the sixteenth century evangelicals made the break with the medieval pattern of church establishment. This even Calvin did not do.

Ultimately, the Anabaptists' movement for religious freedom received its greatest motivation from the conviction that faith cannot be coerced.[156]

Still the Church of God maintained a certain leveled-headedness and balance in regard to the issue. The Assembly in 1908 acknowledged the need for civil government, seeing in it a special gift of divine order to provide for civil peace and safety and to 'protect public worship'. The delegates agreed therefore that 'The church should appreciate the laws that protect public worship and should recognize the officers of the law as God's ministers'.[157] Romans 13.1-6 was cited to support the Assembly's decision. In his *The Last Great Conflict*, Tomlinson added,

We are in the world but not of the world. We are under Christ's government, but must be subject to 'the powers that be' in whatever country we are placed, except [where] the world's governments conflict with our obligations to Christ. Then Christ must be honored and obeyed rather than the world governments even at the peril of our lives (Acts 4:19; 5:29).[158]

The strong convictions voiced by the Assembly for the separation of church and state were not strange, therefore; for the majority of the ministers and members in the Church of God were descendants of seventeenth century radical, non-conformist sects that had been severely persecuted; indeed tens of thousands of their numbers had been tortured and brutally executed by the sword or burned at the stake. Again, it should be borne in mind that many Church of God pioneers were born in the early or mid-1800s. Some of their fathers and grandfathers and great uncles had fought in the Revolutionary War, envisioning a na-

---

[156] William R. Estep, *The Anabaptist Story* (Grand Rapids: Eerdmans, rev. edn, 1975), pp. 179-202.
[157] *GAM*, p. 27.
[158] Tomlinson, *LGC*, p. 73.

tion that would be founded upon religious liberty and the principle of church and state separation. Richard Spurling, the church's first ordained minister, was born in 1810 and we may be sure that his father, James, and grandfather, John, both Baptists, had shared with him tales of the persecutions that Baptists had endured in the American colonies before the United States was born and the Constitution and Bill of Rights were enacted in 1887-1889. Further we may be sure that Richard had shared these stories with Richard Green. Thus the reality of being persecuted for one's faith by the state, even in America, was still fresh in the mind of Spurling when he wrote *The Lost Link*, and also in the minds of the 'delegates' in the 1908 Assembly.

'Against Members Going to War'

When Christian Union was set in order in 1886, the majority of the members were almost certainly under the persuasion of the traditional view of a 'just war', that is, they believed Christians were obligated to support the civil state in a 'righteous cause'. Thus, the only reason that R.G. Spurling gives for his father not fighting in the Civil War is that he was 'too old to be a soldier', not that he was opposed to participating in war.[159] Some of the ministers and members in Christian Union had in fact fought in the Civil War.[160]

Figure 80
HOMER TOMLINSON
Homer served in World War I, 1918-1919

Notwithstanding, there was no official consensus on this position in Christian Union and, consistent with the prevailing rule of the fellowship, the members were free to decide either for or against participating in war according to their own consciences. However, after the church was

---

[159] *Lost Link*, p. 47.
[160] Theophilus Ellis and J.C. Murphy, both delegates to the first Assembly in 1906 were Civil War veterans; Minter Freeman in Christian Union at Piney Grove was a Civil War veteran, and there were others.

swept into the Holiness-Pentecostal movement beginning in 1898, the pacifism that permeated that movement began to affect the ministers and members in the Church of God. It was not until the outbreak of World War I in 1914, however, that the relationship between Christians and war became an issue. Gradually the church, quite apparently under the influence of A.J. Tomlinson – a former Quaker – therafter took a pacifist position in regard to war.

Quakers, unlike a large number of Baptists, were staunch pacifists and stood firmly against going to war, as well as against capital punishment and the taking of human life in any form. It was on this basis, primarily, that the teaching – 'Against members going to war' – first appeared in the church's list of Prominent Teachings in 1917, for the Assembly had not formally addressed the issue.[161] And it was Tomlinson more than anyone else who pressed for an anti-war posture in the church.[162] However the teaching came to be formally listed in 1917 *Assembly Minutes*, the church was thereafter on record as being 'Against members going to war', and from that time until 1921 the teaching remained.[163] Just as mysteriously, the teaching disappeared between 1921 and 1922 without having ever been addressed in the Assembly.[164]

There was to be sure a powerful spirit of patriotism and nationalistic fervor that swept the nation when Congress declared war against Germany on April 6, 1917; and eventually most Christians were caught up in what approximated a national hysteria. The reality of the Great War had jarred many of the ministers and members into a sense of patriotism and

---

[161] Beginning in 1917, there was the tendency of the General Overseer in counsel with the newly-adopted Council of Elders to act unilaterally in behalf of the Assembly. They had acted together without the consent of the Assembly on several issues, including in July 1922 their decision to drop the Assembly plan to send all tithes to headquarters. It is likely that the General Overseer in counsel with the Twelve Elders (or with some of them) simply assumed that the church was more or less unanimous in the sentiment that members should not go to war; but in any case, Tomlinson and most of the Elders believed that the Council was more or less ordained to speak for the church.

[162] See A.J. Tomlinson, 'President of United States Calls the People to Prayer', *COGE* 5.39 (September 26, 1914), p. 3; *idem*, 'War Notice', *COGE* 8.29 (July 28, 1917), p. 2; *idem*, 'The Awful World War', *COGE* 8.8 (February 24, 1917), p. 2; *idem*, 'The Awful War Seems Near', *COGE* 8.13 (March 31, 1917), p. 1.

[163] Thus in 1917, the church's list of Prominent Teachings totaled twenty-nine (*GAM*, 1917, p. 65). After this teaching was dropped in 1921, the list totaled only twenty-eight. However, after the church divided in 1923, Tomlinson and his followers took a strict stand against divorce and remarriage and included it in their list of 'Twenty-Nine Important Bible Truths', inserting it in place of the teaching on 'Against members going to War'.

[164] See *GAM*, 1922, p. 71.

social responsibility; but perhaps the emotional element of the war connected with American ideals – political and religious freedom, 'human rights', and the 'American Dream' – played an even greater role in causing the majority of Christians to modify their thinking in regard to war. And the thinking of Christians in general gradually affected the thinking of Christians in the Church of God. Even Tomlinson's son, Homer, went to war in 1918, serving in the French theater.

Whether it was the reality of the war itself that caused the Church of God to rethink its position, or the burden of being ostracized by American society, or simply that the church had obtained a more enlightened view on the subject, or all of the above, the church had abandoned its pacifism and nonconformist position by the Assembly in 1921.[165] Thereafter, military service, including going to war or not going to war, was left to individual conscience.

Development of a Corporate Conscience

We noticed in Chapter One that Anabaptists and Baptists in England and Europe had championed the doctrine of the inviolability of personal conscience and had transplanted this idea in the American colonies in the seventeenth century. In Chapter Two we noticed that Christian Union had carried this idea to the extreme, fostering an untenable individualism. Thus the members of Christian Union had 'equal rights and privilege to read and interpret [the Scriptures for themselves] as [their] conscience may dictate'.[166] Spurling elaborated on this point in *The Lost Link*, saying, 'Does every Christian have a right to read the Bible? If they do then is it true they have a right to believe as they understand it. To teach them if they do not practice as they believe, it is hypocrisy and a sin, so read and practice as you think will please God best'.[167] Again he argues, 'Has [not] every member equal rights and privileges to read and understand and practice God's Word as they see it?'[168]

This doctrine as a matter of course made the individual's conscience supreme. But this idea, without certain modifying and qualifying factors, is a fundamental error, for it presumes that the conscience is true and thus inviolable; whereas, the conscience merely reflects the authority by

---

[165] It is almost certain that many of the ministers and members in the Church of God did not agree with Tomlinson's pacifism, but were intimidated to voice their opinion, for in 1912-1921 few dared to disagree with the influential and powerful General Overseer.

[166] Tomlinson, *LGC*, p. 207.

[167] Spurling, *Lost Link*, p. 40.

[168] Spurling, *Lost Link*, p. 8; see also pp. 44-45.

which it is informed and governed, and that authority may be pagan or antichrist or a confused Christianity (cf. e.g. 1 Cor. 8.1-13). Nevertheless, this idea was harbored by Baptists and other radical non-conformist groups in general in the sixteenth century, which caused them to develop extremely democratic forms of government and polity, and by extension to promote the philosophy of a 'rugged individualism'. And no one took these basic ideas farther in that direction than Primitive Baptists and to some extent J.R. Graves and his Landmark Baptist movement, which was the primary influence in the lives and ministries of R.G. Spurling and his father. To emphasize the point, a Baptist friend told the writer some years ago, 'That if any two Baptists agree on anything, they are no longer Baptists!'

It was from this tradition that Spurling drew his basic theological concepts, particularly the radical ideas promoted in G.H. Orchard's *History of the Baptists*, which Graves had reprinted in Nashville and used to promote his radical democratic ideas in his Landmark movement beginning in the 1850s. But the practical consequences of this principle prevented Christian Union from being able to fulfill the very mission that its name implied – namely, to teach and inspire all of God's people to come together in one visible union, and to pull together under one divine government to fulfill the church's mission in the world.

Spurling had hoped rather naively that love alone could effect a miraculous union in one visible body of Christ. This concept, however, did not take into account that Christian fellowship must be established on an intellectual and rational basis as well as an emotional basis, that there must be a meeting of the minds as well as the hearts, a coming together of opinions as well as affections. Indeed, Baptists in general had failed to realize that the individual's conscience is fallible and, as such, cannot be trusted with supreme authority. For as the apostle Paul pointed out, the conscience may be weak and misguided (1 Corinthians 8; 1 Tim. 4.2; Eph. 4.19). As a faculty of the human mind and will, or more particularly as a mode in which these faculties act, it cannot stand alone; and in fact may cause one completely to 'miss the mark' and sin against God. The so-called 'inner voice' within man may not be the voice of God at all, but the spirit of error; it may even be demonically influenced and confused. Moreover, one's conscience may become deadened or 'seared' through disobedience and violations of the moral authority that commands it (cf. Rom. 1.21-32; Eph. 4.18-19; 1 Tim. 4.2).

As the church grew under Tomlinson into a universal body with a centralized government, Spurling's original view of individual autonomy and local church independence had to be modified. And it followed that the church had to rethink what the conscience actually is, and how it functions for individuals and the members of the church collectively. It has been rightly said that the conscience is the judicious element in human nature. It is 'not the law, not the sheriff, but the judge'.[169] The conscience (from Latin, *conscientia*, literally 'with knowledge', signifying an inner or intuitive knowledge, equivalent with the Greek word *syneidesis*) judges our thoughts and actions according to the moral or religious influence it is under. It tells us what is right and wrong according to whatever authority we hold as supreme. Thus Hindu and Mayan fathers and mothers sacrificed their children on altars to their pagan gods; and radicalized Muslims today blow up thousands of innocent people in obedience to what they believe pleases Allah, according to their interpretation of the teachings of the Koran and Hadith.[170] The Jews acting with pagan Rome crucified Jesus consistent with their conscience, that is, under misunderstandings of the Law (Mt. 21.33-42; Lk. 13.31-34), and the apostate church in the Dark Ages executed millions of pious believers on the authority of their Inquisition, fulfilling Jesus' prophecy, 'Yea, the time will come, that whosoever kills you will think that he does God service' (Jn 16.2).

Spurling was right, of course, in the sense that he held the conscience to be a valuable part of human nature and indispensable to humanity's ability to judge right and wrong (Jn 8.9; Acts 23.1; 24.16; Rom. 2.15; 13.5; 2 Cor. 1.12; 1 Tim. 1.5, 19; 3.9; *et al.*). And he knew that the conscience – the judicial or interpretative faculty or mode of the human's mind – must be informed according to God's righteous laws in Holy Scripture and be illuminated by the Holy Ghost; else, if it be informed by a pagan law or the social consensus of fallen humanity, it will feel justified in breaking the commandments of the true and living God to please a false god or misguided presumption. Thus, as one of Spurling's contemporaries wrote, 'the conscience is like one's nose, you can follow it if you first get it pointed in the right direction'. And this is agreeable

---

[169] Strong, *Systematic Theology*, p. 82

[170] So too, millions of women today ('Christian' and otherwise) abort their babies because the supreme authority that informs their conscience says it's well and good, that their bodies are their own and, accordingly, that they can do with them as they please. They refuse to acknowledge that their bodies actually belong to God, not themselves, and were created to be temples for the indwelling of the Holy Spirit (cf. (1 Cor. 6.19-20; John 14.23). They proceed therefore to disobey the moral authority of the true and living God and the plain teaching of the Holy Scriptures; choosing rather to live in conformity with laws inspired by demons or otherwise fabricated by human tradition in contradiction to the laws of God.

with the apostle's words, 'I say the truth in Christ, I lie not, my conscience bearing me witness in the Holy Ghost' (Rom. 9.1), and again, 'All scripture is ... profitable for doctrine, for reproof, for correction, for instruction in righteousness' (2 Tim. 3.16).

Our conscience must be illuminated therefore by the Holy Spirit and be informed by the moral teachings in the Word of God, and trained accordingly; indeed, the Holy Spirit and the written Word of God are understood throughout Scripture to be necessary for the conditioning of a 'pure conscience' (1 Tim. 3.9; 2 Tim. 1.3). Thus the Psalmist,

> Blessed are the undefiled ... who walk in the law of the Lord. Blessed are they who keep his testimonies, and that seek him with the whole heart ... Then shall I not be ashamed when I have respect unto to all thy commandments ... Thy testimonies are my delight and my counselors ... I will run the way of thy commandments, when thou shalt enlarge my heart ... And I will walk at liberty: for I seek thy precepts ... And I will delight myself in thy commandments, which I have loved (Ps. 119.1-6, 24, 45-48).

Still, this is where Spurling's view had to be modified: for, ultimately, the conscience must be taught and shaped by the corporate counsel of the church: for 'the church is the pillar and ground of the truth' (1 Tim. 3.15). 'Iron sharpens iron, so a man sharpens the countenance of his friend' [or 'so one sharpens another'] (Prov. 27.17), and again, 'For ... in the multitude of counselors there is safety' (24.6), and again, 'Upon this rock I will build my church ... And whatsoever you bind on earth will be bound in heaven, and whatever you loose on earth will be loosed in heaven' (Mt. 16.18-19; also 18.17-19). These principles were followed and practiced by the apostles and elders and the whole church in the New Testament; indeed, the Jerusalem Council in Acts 15 serves as a model for the church in all ages.

Spurling had come to grips apparently with the fact that he had overreacted against the human regulations imposed upon his ministry by the Landmark Baptist movement, and which in turn had caused him to lay a weak and liberal platform for Christian Union. He had established the church in 1886 on an incomplete foundation, one which could not support the House of God. What was lacking in his ecclesiology and vision for Christian Union was an understanding of one of the basic functions of the church, namely, that the ministers and members were not to stand independent of one another in mind and affections, but to study and interpret together the Holy Scriptures and illuminate one another by corporate counsel and reasoning, so that all of the ministers and members could 'see eye to eye' and walk together as one body of Christ.

As it was, the members of Christian Union had been left to themselves 'to read and practice as you think will please God best'. Thus some of the members freely used tobacco, indulged in moonshine whiskey, cursed on occasion, assembled together if they felt like it, or skipped their own services to attend another church if they chose to do so. Everyone was left to his own conscience, and the conscience of each man and woman was informed by any number of peculiar moral and religious notions conditioned by life in the isolation of the mountains.

Spurling was gradually modified by the counsel of Tomlinson, Lemons, Perry, Lee, Lawson, and others who came into the church after 1903, and apparently he came to realize that in some instances he had swung the pendulum too far to the left in reacting against Landmarkism. He was right, sure enough, that the Baptist elders would 'shake their gray heads and wave their palsied hands' and cry out 'heresy and latitudinarianism' in regard to some of his extreme liberal views.[171] But this was the same criticism that arose in the Church of God after Tomlinson and his followers came into the church, particularly after they all agreed to meet together in annual General Assemblies beginning in 1906.

Many of the leaders in the Assembly saw the weakness of Spurling's system, and in the Assembly in 1907 the subject of conscience was addressed and the system of decision-making modified. The question was raised about 'Worshiping God as conscience may dictate', but for the first time it was stated that one's personal conscience had to be 'purged, and trained according to the laws and commands of Jesus',[172] and it was apparently understood that Jesus' teachings were best understood in the counsel of the whole church assembled.[173] This subtle but significant decision represented a major shift in the decision-making process of the church and transformed the essential nature of its fellowship; for gradually after 1906, the members no longer worshipped and practiced their faith according to their independent consciences, but according to the corporate counsel and consciousness of the universal church; or, to put it another way, the individual's conscience was modified and condi-

---

[171] Spurling, *Lost Link*, pp. 39-40.
[172] *GAM 1906-1914*, p. 43.
[173] Spurling did make reference on occasion to a 'Christianized conscience' (e.g. Spurling, *Lost Link*, p. 45) by which he doubtlessly meant one purged by the teachings of Christ; still, however, his deep resentment against 'conscience binding creeds' diverted the ministers and members from counseling and agreeing together on many important biblical teachings, and this in turn prevented them from 'speaking the same thing' and 'walking by the same rule' (1 Cor. 1.10; Phil. 3.16).

tioned by the collective consciousness of the whole body. The individualism in Christian Union was thus effectively removed and the ministers and members in the Church of God thereafter sought together to understand the Mind of Christ. Accordingly, they endeavored to be 'perfectly joined together in the same mind and in the same judgment' (1 Cor. 1.10); 'to walk by the same rule' (Phil. 3.16); and to glorify God together 'with one mind and one mouth' (Rom. 15.6).

Snake Handling and Other Excesses

Spurling's covenant principle for Christian Union – that each member be given 'equal rights and privilege to read and interpret [the scriptures for oneself] as [his] conscience may dictate' – was designed to protect the individual believer from the 'tyranny of the majority',[174] and the local church against the tyranny of an episcopate or some other form of 'political ecclesiasticism'. While Spurling's motive was sincere, the principle of individual autonomy opened the door for some extreme thinking and behavior; and, accordingly, gave place to antinomian attitudes that made order and discipline in Christian Union impossible to maintain. The excess of personal liberty, over against corporate counsel and discipline, explains in part why the infant movement struggled to survive. Spurling's extreme idealism for the sacredness and inviolability of personal conscience had to yield eventually to the biblical and practical need of corporate and pastoral guidance and, at least, a modified form of centralized government.

After the members of Christian Union were swept into the holiness movement in 1895, an emotional element complicated the principle of individual autonomy. Entire sanctification created greater intimacy with God through the Spirit, which of itself was healthy for the infant movement; but some novice members of Christian Union became puffed up with pride and presumed a superior knowledge of God's will and purpose. Widespread illiteracy further encouraged them to seek for and claim direct revelations, which oftentimes were inconsistent with God's revelation in the Scriptures. It was in this manner that personal dreams, intuitions, and local superstitions tended to supplant 'the more

---

[174] The 'tyranny of the majority' is a political theory made famous, if not coined by, Alexis de Tocqueville in his *Democracy in America* (published in 1830). Though Spurling did not use the phrase verbatim, it nevertheless perfectly expressed his fear of the suppression of individual autonomy and personal conscience. See *Lost Link*, pp. 10-11, 23, 26-27, 29-30, 34-37, 40-42, 45.

sure word of prophecy', and occasioned some of the ministers and members unwittingly to relegate the Scriptures to a secondary status.

To be sure, the claims of immediate revelation from God created high-pitched religious fervor in Christian Union, which in turn helped to enlarge God's kingdom; but it also occasioned confusion within the fellowship as each person tended to do 'what was right in his own eyes'. This already difficult situation in Christian Union was all the more complicated when B.H. Irwin's fire-baptized holiness movement began to influence the churches after 1896. 'Fire-baptisms' were believed to enhance sanctified believers with extraordinary gifts of power and discernment. Experiences in 'dynamite', 'lyddite', 'selenite', and 'oxidite' were believed to elevate the saints to glorious heights in spiritual perfections. It was not until Spurling organized the Holiness Church at Camp Creek in 1902, and A.J. Tomlinson joined in 1903, that a more stable form of government and discipline began to appear. This positive development in the church's order and discipline became more solidified beginning in 1906 when the several churches began to meet annually in General Assembly.

Notwithstanding, the burning desire to restore apostolic Christianity occasioned new excesses. The belief that the restoration of apostolic Christianity would be manifested by signs and wonders equal to and greater than those recorded in the New Testament were sought for and expected.[175] This mind-set in Tomlinson became more acute after his Spirit-baptism in January 1908 and the glorious revival that swept the city of Cleveland that summer. Thereafter, Tomlinson sought for extraordinary powers and manifestations that would confirm not only his own apostolic calling and position but also the corporate identity of his followers as being the true restoration of the apostolic church. This was well and good, on one hand, as tens-of-thousands were converted, sanctified, Spirit-baptized, healed, and delivered from demonic possession; but, on the other hand, an exaggerated sense of peculiarity developed among the early pioneers of the Church of God which occasioned some lofty and extravagant views of the church, including the claim of exclusivity. Their peculiar identity with the apostolic church, in turn, occasioned other extremes; for extraordinary signs and miracles were thought necessary to support the claim, and to demonstrate the peculiar status of the Church of God before the world. This led apparently (at least in part) to the widespread practice of serpent-handling. Tomlinson exulted in his annual address in 1914:

---

[175] Tomlinson, *LGC*, pp. 232-41.

> Under the illumination of God's love and mighty power many signs and wonders have been wrought ... Wild poison serpents have been taken up and handled and fondled over almost like babies with no harm to the saints. In several instances fire has been handled with bare hands without being burned. Glory to God. Have seen no reports of anybody outside the Church of God performing this miracle. We are beginning to surpass all others in miraculous signs and wonders ...[176]

Again in 1916 he emphasized:

> And now we are following in the wake of the apostles and the early Church as if many different Churches and movements had never had an existence. And God is now just as truly confirming the Word with signs following as at the beginning. Devils are cast out, we have the new tongues, the serpents are taken up ...[177]

He concluded his annual address in 1916 in his typical cheerleading style with an array of lofty expectations:

> Upon us [the Church of God] is conferred the honor of being her worthy representatives. We must rally to the standard and place it in every hamlet, village, town and city of this lost world, to shine forth the beautiful light and show forth the signs and wonders in excess of all other institutions. Although [other institutions] do great things, we must do greater. We must surpass them all in righteousness, order, power, and glory ... The Church of God shall win Hallelujah! The Church of God shall win! ... 'Who is she that looks forth as the morning, fair as the moon, clear as the sun, and terrible as an army with banners?' The Church of God! ... The beautiful and glorious Church of God; and we are beholding her beautiful appearance as we exclaim the Church of God! The Church of God![178]

Though never officially accepted, the practice of serpent-handling was widespread in the Church of God between 1910-1930. Some of the church's most influential leaders taught or indirectly encouraged serpent-handling, including A.J. Tomlinson, F.J. Lee,[179] and J.B. Ellis. Ellis

---

[176] *HAA*, I, pp. 42-43.
[177] *HAA*, I, p. 64.
[178] *HAA*, I, pp. 77-78.
[179] Besides the explicit evidence in personal letters showing Lee's approval and admiration of the practice (e.g. 'Letter to Josh Brewer of Naugatuck, WV', dated July 30, 1925 ['F.J. Lee File', ZACG Archives], he was a member of the Publishing

actually handled snakes on occasion. He wrote to A.B. Adams on November 23, 1915 and gave three fascinating accounts of serpent handling which he had observed and in which he had personally participated:

Incident No. 1

I pitched my Gospel tent among these people [serpent-handlers] in September 1913 ... and became convinced that God really meant for His children to take up serpents so I gave myself to prayer and fasting for I felt I would need a special anointing. The third day of the meeting I noticed a wagon load of women and children coming, they were being peculiarly exercised [sic] by the Spirit. Then I noticed in the back end of the wagon a little girl had in her hands a large serpent, the child was thirteen years of age. As soon as the wagon stopped she jumped out and came running to me with it. The old serpent looked as docile as a lamb and was noozing [sic] its head around the girls ears as if it enjoyed the performance. It was with much trembling I reached out my hands to take it, it stiffened itself into a coil and made ready to bite me as though it was defending the girl and it was not until the girl rebuked it in Jesus name that it would allow me to take it without fight. After she rebuked it all fear left me and I felt a strange power coming over my body. After this it seemed to be my defender.

Incident No. 2

It was Sunday morning. We were in the midst of a warm testimony meeting. A man came down the isle [sic] with a bucket containing a large copperhead. The man lifted the lid and poured the contents into the altar. A man reached down and ran his hand under the coil of the snake and held it above his head and exhorted the people for about three minutes, set it down. Another picked it up and it bit her. They both fell to the ground as though they would be dead in a few minutes. The first man called the saints to prayer and rebuked death in the name of Jesus, instantly they sprang to their feet praising God. While all this was going on another girl was dancing up and down the isle with the serpent in her hand and biting her as fast as it could strike. She felt no harm.

Incident No. 3

It was at the 11:00 o'clock service I was about half through with my message. A lady rose in front of me and spoke a few words in

---

Committee for the *Faithful Standard* which endorsed serpent-handling). See Homer Tomlinson, 'Manifestations of the Spirit', *FS* (September 1922), p. 12).

tongues. A boy gave the interpretation as follows: 'They are coming with a rattle snake. Fear nothing. Do what I have commanded you'. Instantly 60 or 70 saints were on their feet dancing and speaking in tongues. This continued for five minutes before there was anything in sight. At last I saw a large crowd of people come around the corner of a wood into the main road. It proved to be just as the message was given. They had a large rattler with ten rattles, they also had two smaller rattlers. They had been carefully guarded by an officer and sworn witnesses to see that nothing was done to the serpents to destroy their fangs or poison. I saw the snakes bite the saints on the hands, in the face and different parts of the body. Some were bitten five times. I saw the blood from the bites mingled with the poison running down their faces and hands. I saw the poison settle in dark pools around the wounds and peel out like a blood blister in a few days. I saw one of the fangs that was picked from the hand of a girl the next day. None of them felt any pain and there was no swelling. You could feel the power like waves in the air. I could hear a rushing sound like a wind. Some were amazed, some doubted and some believed. The saints were comforted. The devil's crowd became divided among themselves and fought like wild animals.[180]

Notwithstanding, some in the church challenged the practice of serpent-handling, and by the early 1930's the phenomenon had more or less ceased to exist in the Church of God.[181] Those who persisted in snake-handling did so usually as defectors outside the order and discipline of the church, and almost invariably for the same reason that led to the practice to start with – to authenticate the claim that according to Mk 16.17-18 serpent-handling was a distinct sign of the restoration of the true apostolic church.

---

[180] 'Letter from J.B. Ellis to A.B. Adams', November 23, 1915. Written from Oneonta, Alabama ('J.B. Ellis File', ZACG Archives).

[181] Among Tomlinson's followers, however, the practice prevailed here and there as late as 1940. Mrs. A.B. Adams of the Adams Gospel Crew wrote to Tomlinson in June 1940 and reported that the practice was still being observed in Kentucky and elsewhere. She gloried in the practice, saying, 'We can find no people like our church of God people ... We saw some pictures of church of God people who were taking up serpents in one of the New Mexico daily papers, it was an inspiration to know the church people are still holding this faith in the Lord' ('Letter from Mrs. A.B. Adams to Tomlinson', from Coffeeville, MS, June 29, 1940).

Figure 81

GEORGE W. HENSLEY (CENTER) AND OTHERS
'TAKING UP SERPENTS'

Serpent handling was practiced in the Church of God as early as 1913. The photo above was taken years later, after George W. Hensley had left the Church of God and established an independent ministry. Hensley later died of a snake bite.[182]

---

[182] Hensley joined the Church of God in 1912 and evangelized in Cleveland, Birchwood, Ooltewah, and Chattanooga. In 1918 he was appointed to pastor the East Chattanooga church. Though he had been preaching for a number of years, he was not licensed until 1917. He began to 'take up serpents' apparently about 1913 and became renowned for the practice by 1914. In a meeting in the Cleveland tabernacle in 1914, he took up serpents and inspired others to do so, including M.S. Haynes, T.L. McLain, and W.S. Gentry (*Evangel*, September 12, 1914, p. 2; September 19, 1914, p. 3). Serpent handling became a sensation also in a tent meeting conducted in South Cleveland. Encouraged by Tomlinson, Ellis, and other leaders, Hensley focused his ministry on serpent handling and the particular signs in Mk 16.17, 18. Serpent handling was celebrated at the Dolley Pond church in Birchwood. This church reportedly began at Owl Holler, and Homer Tomlinson claims to have had a hand in its establishment. A.J. Tomlinson attended a meeting in this church in September 1914, and observed 'Two large rattlesnakes ... taken up by the power of God' (*Evangel*, October 4, 1914, p. 6). Hensley later backslid, left his family, remarried, and indulged in the works of the flesh. In 1921 he resigned his ministry with the Church of God and turned in his license to M.W. Letsinger, who was then

Figure 82

MINNIE PARKER HANDLING A SNAKE

Minnie Parker, in an apparent ecstasy, frames her face with a large rattlesnake.

There were other excesses and fanaticisms, to be sure, including those associated with 'handling coals of fire' and 'drinking deadly poisons'.[183] Counterfeit spirits came in among the saints to confuse genuine moves of the Spirit. These spirits were so subtle and deceptive that even some level-headed and moderate believers fell under their influence and exhibited rude and abrasive behavior. Homer Tomlinson wrote of some of the instances that he observed and were reported to him by other eyewitnesses. Some of the manifestations were reminiscent of the behavior that marked the Fire-Baptized Holiness Movement in the late nineteenth and early twentieth century in East Tennessee, western

---

serving as the overseer of Tennessee. Hensley was later restored, returned to Dolley Pond and resumed the practice serpent handling, but as an independent minister outside the government and fellowship of the Church of God.

[183] Homer, 'Manifestations of the Spirit', *FS* (September 1922), p. 12.

North Carolina, and north Georgia, and, in fact, these are the instances to which Homer may be referring in the following report.

> There are almost always some counterfeits with the genuine. Satan will mimic the ways of the Lord if he can get a hold on any who are inexperienced and do not know where to draw the line. A few years ago some strange things happened in portions of two or three states. A spirit of some kind would take possession of some in the meetings and they would single out some one in the meeting that this spirit would make them believe was a hypocrite or wrong in some way and strength would be given to take hold of that man or woman and literally carry them out of the house and throw them off like trash. The same spirit would sometimes operate on the women to pull the hair of others, snatch men's neckties, and women's pins or ribbons or lace on their dresses. So many were injured and bruised by these manifestations that people got afraid to attend the meetings. Investigations showed that there were supernatural forces at work and those exercised were enveloped with special power and strength until a two hundred pound man was picked up as easy as a little child and carried and pitched out at the door as easy as throwing out a small stick of wood. Further investigations convinced the investigators that this was not the Spirit of God, but a spirit of Satan that deceived the innocent and sincere worshippers. It had to be broken up and it was, and some who were into it are fine, gentle spirited Christians today.
>
> In weighing the results of investigations that have been made through the years of religious awakenings there is an established rule that is almost if not always safe to recognize. Manifestations that cause the one operated to become hard, rigid, extremely radical and abusive in language, and lay hold on others and use them roughly, pull their hair, beat them over the head and back, thrust them roughly out of the house, and other similar performances are not of God, but belong to the adversary. Where these manifestations are allowed to prevail no one gets saved, they do not get sanctified and filled with the Holy Ghost. The sweet and gentle Spirit of Jesus does not agree with such manifestations. But manifestations, no matter how queer they seem to be, which produce good results, – bring conviction to sinners, bless and edify the saints, and do not interfere with the rights and privileges of others, may be encouraged and the Holy Ghost honored as being responsible for them.[184]

---

[184] Homer, 'Manifestations of the Spirit', *FS* (September 1922), p. 2

In regard to these excesses, we should be careful not to judge the pioneers of the Church of God too harshly: for underneath their excesses was a fundamental desire to please and obey God fully. They acted on the courage of their convictions, and with a mind-set trained to act on impulse in obedience to God's commands. Indeed their hearts were set to teach and practice without hesitation or reservation 'all things whatsoever [that Christ had] commanded' in order to demonstrate more effectively the power of God through the Gospel. They were conditioned to act spontaneously to God's Word, whether it was revealed in Scripture or by the Spirit's illumination in their hearts. Faith and perfect love seemed to them to require a swift response to the revealed will of God. There was no time or need to reason out the 'higher ways' of God that 'were past finding out'. Like Abraham, they 'considered not' nor 'staggered not at the promise of God' (Rom. 4.19-20). If they erred, it was not by omission but by an excess of enthusiasm, which on occasion caused them to race emotionally ahead of reason. They were also confident in the foundations upon which they based their restoration movement, so that when their enthusiasm occasioned excesses and fanaticism, they trusted that 'theocratic government' would in due process restore proper order and discipline. And, as in the case of serpent-handling, the government of the church did indeed correct the excesses and made disciplinary adjustments. It was thus that the church's pioneers labored with full knowledge of their potential excesses, believing that 'wild fire was better than no fire at all', that is, that a wild fire could more easily be brought under control than to ignite a fire in a frozen tundra.[185] And thus in wisdom they allowed 'smoking flax' and supported 'bruised reeds' in order to nurse a movement whose aim was to prepare a bride for the Son of God.

Thus, we learn from the mistakes of our great fathers in the church, as well as from their positive examples. We freely admit that they had feet made of clay, and that on occasion their zeal was misguided and their perceptions of divinity imperfect. But, notwithstanding their shortcomings and excesses, they nevertheless restored and nursed for us a precious holiness-Pentecostal tradition, the core of which is perfectly divine – a rich heritage purchased by the precious blood of Jesus and which can ultimately never fail nor be destroyed.

---

[185] It was thus that Tomlinson readily used reckless and emotionally-packed phrases to spur greater zeal in his followers. His sermons and addresses were peppered with such expressions as 'reckless enthusiasm', 'reckless bravery', 'rushing heedless and reckless into the fight', and 'burst forth like wild men'.

Tobacco Controversies

We have noticed that the covenant of Christian Union allowed for each member to decide for himself or herself according 'as your conscience may dictate' in regard to almost all matters of personal behavior including the use of tobacco. It was thus that the use of tobacco in its various forms – snuff, chewing, smoking – was prevalent in and among the ministers and members of the Church of God for the first twenty years of the fellowship. However, when Christian Union came under the influence of the Holiness Movement beginning in 1895, the use of tobacco gradually developed into an issue: and the issue was the more complicated because of the individualism built into the polity and fellowship of Christian Union. The following treatise written by Tomlinson and presented to the church in his 1940 annual address thoroughly covers the history of tobacco in the Church of God and the controversies surrounding its use. However, since the treatise is so lengthy and written especially to address the particular issue of growing and selling of tobacco that arose in the 1930s among Tomlinson's followers, we will give here only that part of the treatise that pertains to the church before 1923. We should add, however, that the church's stand against the use of tobacco that had solidified into an absolute prohibition between 1906 and 1911 was one of the primary reasons that the Mountain Assembly Church of God decided finally not to unite with the Church of God in 1911-1912.[186]

A Treatise on Tobacco and Its Uses and Abuses

> This subject has been before the Assembly occasionally for thirty-five years. Even at the time of our first Assembly in 1906 some of our members used tobacco. The subject came before the Assembly for discussion for the purpose of learning whether or not it was right or wrong to use it as it was being used by many people, both men and women, and even children. It was being used by people for chewing and spitting, smoking, and some times blowing the smoke

---

[186] Mountain Assembly historian, Michael Padgett, cites the Church of God's stand against labor unions as the primary reason that prevented the union, since so many Mountain Assembly ministers and members belonged to the United Mine Workers' Union (*A Goodly Heritage*, p. 22). Notwithstanding, it is almost certain that the Church of God's strict discipline against the use of tobacco was equally a primary factor. While the Mountain Assembly drew up a resolution in 1912 against ministers using tobacco, the organization remained lenient on discipline. Padgett says in fact that the discipline of ministers was lax or non-existent, and thus even in 1915 'members as well as ministers continued to use tobacco' (p. 19).

out through their noses, snuff on sticks and swabbed in their mouths, or their lips poured full of it, pipes, cigars and cigarettes. After long discussions, prayers, reading the Bible with a desire to get information, and honest light and good understanding of the subject, it was finally agreed and fully decided that it was wrong to use it in any form. Thus the following record was made:

After due consideration, this Assembly agrees to stand with one accord in opposition to the use of tobacco in any form. It is offensive to those who do not use it; it weakens and impairs the nervous system; it is a near relative to drunkenness; a bad influence and example to the young; useless expense, the money for which ought to be used to clothe the poor, spread the gospel or make the homes of our country more comfortable. Last, we believe the use of it to be contrary to the teaching of the Scripture, and as Christ is our example we cannot believe He would use it in any form or under any circumstances.

It was further recommended and advised that the pastors and deacons of each church make special effort to use their influence against the use of tobacco, deal tenderly and lovingly with those in the Church who use it, but insist with an affectionate spirit that its use be discontinued as much as possible'.

In the minutes of the third Assembly it is shown that the tobacco subject was mentioned twice. The first mention was a question; viz., 'Does the use of tobacco disqualify a man for the office of a deacon?' The answer was simply 'Yes'.

The second mention was as follows:

It was decided that those in the Church who use tobacco should be dealt with kindly, fairly and given a little time for consideration and those who refuse to discontinue its use in a reasonable length of time be disfellowshipped'. As proof that this view was considered right, and the proper course to pursue, the following Scriptures were referred to: 'Isa. 55:2; 2 Cor. 7:1; Gal. 5:19-21; Eph. 5:3-7'.

The fourth and fifth Assemblies passed without any mention of tobacco at all. But the subject came up in the sixth. The record reads as follows: 'The subject of tobacco was considered which resulted in reading the minutes of the first Assembly. The General Overseer advised that ministers who are receiving persons as members into the Lord's Church should humbly, tenderly and lovingly advise those who might be eligible to membership, not to present themselves for membership if they use tobacco in any form unless they, in that self-same moment, decide to renounce the habit and by the grace of God declare themselves total abstainers hereafter'.

The seventh and next Assembly brought the subject in the form of a question and answer as follows: Question. 'What about selling tobacco and rolling cigars when their bread and meat depends on this labor?' Answer. 'You might do such work a little while until you can have time to change your vocation, but to continue it you will soon get under a cloud of condemnation'. Reference was then made to the sixth Assembly minutes.

The very next year, the eighth Assembly, the subject came up again. This was in the form of a question. 'Question. What must be done with a member who has the Holy Ghost and 'must have just a little bit of tobacco?' 'Answer. This question gave rise to considerable discussion and careful consideration of the tobacco subject. The sentiment of the Assembly was finally obtained and a decision made. 'All of our ministers and local churches are to refuse to accept any who use tobacco into the Church under any circumstances. Those who are already in the Church who use it are to be dealt with in love, given ample time, only a few weeks, and if they fail to abstain they are to be disfellowshipped'.

Two more Assemblies passed without anything being said about tobacco. But in the eleventh Assembly held November 1-7, 1915 the subject was brought up again. It was brought before the Assembly by a question: 'What shall be done with members of the Church that grow, sell or handle tobacco?'

There was considerable discussion on this subject. The extremes were shown on both sides. After some time was given to this discussion the General Overseer offered the following statement, which, with the amendment was accepted, and it seemed good to the Holy Ghost and to us:

It is the sense of this Assembly that our members be required to abstain from growing and selling tobacco, either owners, renters or clerks in stores, but that each one be dealt with wisely and always tenderly, and when such dealers or producers obstinately refuse to concur with the advice of the Assembly after all has been done to teach that is necessary under the surrounding circumstances connected with the individual case, then such individual should be dismissed.

Amendment to the above ruling added, that in no case should any one be finally dismissed from the Church without the approval of the state and general overseers'.

I do not find where the tobacco question has been openly discussed by the Assembly since this ruling was made. If any mention was made of the subject reference was usually made to this ruling. Although the members of the Church were forbidden to grow, sell or handle tobacco by this last ruling, more attention has been given to keeping the Church free from members who use it in any form than from growing or handling it. The obligation demands that no one be taken into membership who uses it in any form. Then after they become members and take up its use they are supposed to be dealt with properly, and if they do not leave it off they are dismissed from membership. Many have been excluded because they refused to abstain. Quite a number have been dismissed for growing and handling it, but not so many. In a good many instances, those who felt like they must grow it as a means of earning their support and livelihood they would quietly withdraw from the Church and grow their tobacco. In some instances, this class produced their tobacco, sold it and paid their tithes in the Church and attended the services as faithfully as if they were members. Such as these never used it for chewing or smoking or any other way. All this time they claimed they did this without any condemnation, and felt good because they could have money upon which to pay tithes for the support of the ministers ...[187]

The rest of this treatise was written with a view to change the church's position on members being allowed to raise and sell tobacco for good and productive purposes, such as providing insecticides and fertilizers for farmers and medicines for veterinarians. But since this issue did not trouble the church again until the 1930s, we will address that subject in its proper place in Volume II, including an examination of the remaining part of Tomlinson's *A Treatise on Tobacco* and the church's response.

---

[187] *HAA*, III, pp. 161-76.

Important Teachings Codified

In reflecting on the development of the most prominent teachings of the church before the disruption in 1923, several significant intervals stand out: *first*, the covenant of Christian Union as it stood in 1895; *second*, the first General Assembly in 1906; *third*, the court case in 1909 in which the church's position on specific teachings was emphasized; *fourth*, the Assembly in 1910; *fifth*, the Assembly in 1915; *sixth*, the Assembly in 1917; *seventh*, the Assembly in 1922.

It is difficult to know whether or not 'the basis of union as it stood in 1895'[188] was the same upon which Spurling established Christian Union in August 1886. His brief explanation in *The Lost Link* seems to indicate that some modifications had been made between 1886 and 1895. Since he often exalted Alexander Campbell as one of the 'great reformers',[189] we are inclined to think that he had come under Campbell's influence to some degree early in his ministry.[190] A case in point is where he pleads with his readers in *The Lost Link* not to settle [as he himself admittedly had] for a shallow and incomplete salvation. 'Don't do as I did. I thought repentance, faith and baptism was God's law but I find it only brings us to where we ought to keep God's law …'[191] Not only does this statement ring with the sound of Campbellism, but Spurling otherwise would have been unavoidably informed about, if not affected by, Campbellism in the 1870s and 1880s: for J.R. Graves and ministers his Landmark Movement often took Campbellism to task in the *Tennessee Baptist* and in open debates in the 1840s through the 1870s.

In any case, there are now no records of the precise basis of union in 1886 except what is indicated on Spurling's license signed by his father in September 1886 and the account given by Tomlinson in *The Last Great Conflict*.[192] From these records we learn that Spurling was basically

---

[188] Spurling, *Lost Link*, pp. 44-45.
[189] Spurling, *Lost Link*, pp. 15, 18.
[190] We noticed earlier that Spurling's father and grandfather may have come under Campbell's influence in the 1830s, either directly or indirectly when they lived in James County, Tennessee; for the Baptist churches in that region of Tennessee and Kentucky were rocked and divided by Campbell's Restoration Movement at that time. It is entirely possible that Spurling and his father pondered over Campbell's legacy again during their years of searching for the true church in 1884-1886.
[191] Spurling, *Lost Link*, p. 9. There are, however, some reflections by G.P. Spurling (Spurling's son born in 1877) on the early development of the church, both before and after it was set in order in August 1886. But there is little doctrinal content, and his account tends to collapse several events into one event that transpired over a number of years. Further, though his account is valuable, it tends to exalt and sensationalize the work of his father and thus to distort the facts somewhat.
[192] Tomlinson, *LGC*, pp. 206-209.

Arminian in faith in contrast with Calvinism, and that he believed in a general atonement rather than a limited atonement.[193] Further, Tomlinson's account of the polity and order of Christian Union is that it was in harmony with Campbell's view of the restoration of the New Testament church rather than the Baptist view of succession.[194] Also there is an extreme exaltation of the New Testament over against the Old Testament, which Spurling could have gotten from the Landmarkers as likely as from the Campbellites. Still, Spurling inaugurated his own restoration movement rather than having joined Campbell's movement; and he based his restoration venture on the exalted and unique view of love as the fundamental basis for 'Christian Union'.

Tomlinson's historical account shows that the basis for fellowship in Christian Union was extremely liberal in regard to its government and polity, leaving every minister and member free to believe and practice his or her faith according 'as [one's] conscience may dictate'.[195] Apart from what we can glean from Spurling's minister's credentials and Tomlinson's brief historical account of Christian Union in 1886, we have no other records or accounts to inform us more fully and precisely of the original foundation of Christian Union; and, therefore, we are forced to fall back on the basis of union as it stood in 1895. Significantly, the church at Piney Grove was set in order on October 8, 1897 precisely on this same 'basis of union'.

> We here give [the] agreement or basis of union as it stood in 1895. First. The New Testament is the only infallible rule of faith and practice, so we reject all other articles of faith and men-made creeds, and for the basis of our union we accept the law of love instead of faith, faith in Christ being the only faith required in the gospel and love being the commandment of Christ, by which we should know each other as His disciples.
>
> 'We further agree that the New Testament contains all things necessary for salvation and church government. So all dealings must be on gospel principles. Baptism, the Lord's supper and feet-washing, as taught in the Scriptures and that each member shall have equal rights and privileges to read, believe and practice for themselves in all matters of religion that may not prove contrary to the law of love or the

---

[193] His license in 1886 clearly states that he stood on and proclaimed a 'general atonement', and the sentiment in *The Lost Link* is Arminian rather than Calvinistic.

[194] This is further supported by Spurling throughout *The Lost Link*, e.g. pp. 13, 15-25, 31-35.

[195] Tomlinson, *LGC*, p. 207.

true spirit of Christianity. We invite to union and fellowship all persons who avow faith in Christ and love to God and His people and a willingness to live a Christian life so as not to dishonor the cause of Christ, and we exclude only for known violations of God's Word or commands.

Whereas each member shall give an account to God for themselves and a Christianized conscience is the basis of purity we do reject all conscience binding creeds as being contrary to Scripture, also to religion and love, and are in open rebellion against the constitution of our nation. Against such we do protest.[196]

The church made a significant transition between 1895 and 1902 in regard to doctrine. The fact that Spurling set in order on May 15, 1902 the Holiness Church at Camp Creek in Cherokee County, North Carolina marked the transformation of Christian Union churches into a radical holiness body, particularly because most, if not all, of the original sixteen members of the Holiness Church at Camp Creek had been definitely sanctified and Spirit-baptized under the influence of the Fire-Baptized Holiness Association. The outpourings of the Spirit and the radical perception of holiness is what at first attracted Tomlinson to the little holiness band; then, afterward, through prayer and the counsel of Spurling in regard to the Bible church, he became convinced to unite with the congregation. At that point, now under the leadership of Tomlinson, the church at Camp Creek and the several new churches and missions established by him between 1903 and 1908 transitioned into a full-blown holiness-Pentecostal fellowship.

Beginning in 1906 the several ministers and churches began to counsel together in annual General Assemblies, and through this means a number of doctrinal issues were addressed and agreed upon enabling the ministers and churches to see 'eye to eye' and 'walk by the same rule' of faith and practice; indeed, the General Assembly itself was gradually understood to be the restoration of the New Testament church's original form of government – 'the highest tribunal of authority in the church for the interpretation of the Scriptures'. Thus, the council at Jerusalem in Acts 15.1-16.5 was considered to be the model of government and decision-making for the church in any age.

This interpretation, coupled with the corresponding logic that 'church' and 'government' are more or less synonymous in meaning – that is, 'church signifies government' – prompted many of the brethren to mark the church's origin with the first General Assembly. F.J. Lee, for

---

[196] Spurling, *Lost Link*, pp. 44-45.

example, wrote, 'The Church of God, in its present existence was set in order January 26, 1906, in the home of J.C. Murphy, Cherokee County, North Carolina'.[197] Tomlinson and others believed this also, but by the time Tomlinson published in 1913 his 'BRIEF HISTORY OF THE CHURCH THAT IS NOW RECOGNIZED AS THE CHURCH OF GOD', he had established the church's origin [or restoration] with the actions of Spurling and his father at Barney Creek in Monroe County, Tennessee on August 19, 1886.[198]

An important document that sheds light on the development of doctrine and experience in the Church of God is the court case in Cleveland in August 1909 brought against 'A.J. Tomlinson, W.F. Bryant, Ringgold Wimberly, and *et al.* by M.L. Beard, G.L. Hardwick, J.F. Harrison, J.H. Hardwick, W.C. Nevin, D.A. North, C.T. Carter, J.T. Hall, J.F. Maxwell, C.L. Hardwick, and the City of Cleveland'. The Bill of Complaint was received and Injunction ordered by Judge T.M McConnell of Bradley County Chancery Court.

This court case marked a serious confrontation between the Church of God and City of Cleveland. Some of the complainants in the case – the 'good citizens of Cleveland' – one of them (Walter Rogers) being a justice of the peace, cut down the church's tent, physically removed one worshipper and forced him into the street,[199] and another, M.L. Beard, threatened one of the worshippers with a knife in his hand attempting to intimidate and terrorize the leaders of the revival and the worshippers to abandon their emotional form of worship, or at least to confine their meetings in an enclosure out of sight and sound of the city.[200] The complainants – representing themselves officially as the City of Cleveland – further warned the court that 'unless some relief was obtained from the situation ... that it was not improbable that a riot might ensue and bloodshed follow'. They pleaded with the court therefore to issue an order to the leaders of the Church of God to

> desist and refrain from continuing in a noisy, boisterous and tumultuous conduct ... and from disturbing the quietude, peace and rest of complainants; and from parading the streets of the town in said boisterous conduct, [until] late and unseemly hours at night, and [in]

---

[197] 'Letter from Lee to Mrs. W.D. Clark', Galloway, FL, dated July 13, 1926 ('F.J. Lee File', ZACG Archives).
[198] Tomlinson, *LGC*, pp. 205-209.
[199] *M.L. Beard* et al. *vs. A.J. Tomlinson* et al., p. 3.
[200] *M.L. Beard* et al. *vs. A.J. Tomlinson* et al., pp. 3-4.

unlawful conduct at the [their] tent or otherwise in the limits of said city.[201]

In answer to the Bill filed against them, Tomlinson and his followers convincingly contradicted the charges and were given opportunity to present a lengthy explanation of the essential points of their faith and practices. Further, the legal prosecution by the complainants and official representatives of the City of Cleveland only gave Tomlinson and his followers further opportunity to magnify what the Lord had being doing through them – namely, to proclaim the Gospel and build the Church of God. Working through their lawyers, Traynor and Smith, Tomlinson and his followers elaborated upon the following points of doctrine to defend their position and make their case:

Introduction

… the defendants aver that they believe in all things written in the old testament and the new; they believe in the resurrection of the dead, both the just and the unjust, and they endeavor to exercise themselves so as to have a conscience void of offense toward God and man, they believe in repentance, in the remission of sin, and especially do they believe in the following points of doctrine, to wit:

1. All under sin (Romans 3:9-10, 23).
2. Repentance (Acts 3:19; 2 Peter 3:9).
3. Justification by faith (Romans 5:1; Titus 3:7).
4. Water baptism (Matthew 28:19; Acts 2:38).
5. Sanctification (1 Thessalonians 4:3; Hebrews 13:12).
6. Baptism with the Holy Ghost (Matthew 3:11; Luke 24:49; Acts 2:38, 39).
7. Baptism with the Holy Ghost an experience for people today, the same as for the Apostles (Luke 24:49; Matthew 28:19, 20; Acts 2:39).
8. Speaking in other tongues, the evidence of the baptism of the Holy Ghost (John 15:26, 27; Acts 2:4; 10:44-46; 19:6).
9. Signs following believers (Matthew 10: 1,7,8; Mark 16:15 to 20; Acts 4:29, 30; Romans 15:18,19; 1 Corinthians 4:9; 14:22).
10. Fruits of the Spirit (Matthew 7:15, 20; John 15:2, 8; Galatians 5:22, 23).
11. Gifts of the Spirit (1 Corinthians 12:1-10).
12. Divine healing (Matthew 8:17; Luke 17:15, 16; James 5:14, 15; 1 Peter 2:24).

---

[201] 'Injunction', State of Tennessee, Chancey Court at Cleveland, August 7, 1909.

13. The Return of the Lord (Matthew 24:30; Acts 1:11; 1 Thessalonians 4:13-17).
14. The Lord's Supper (Matthew 26:26-31; 1 Corinthians 11:23-29). Washing the Saints' feet (John 13:4-15; 1 Timothy 5: 9,10).
15. Everlasting punishment for those who reject Christ (Matthew 25:41, 46; Revelation 21:8).
16. Casting out of devils (Matthew 10:8; Mark 16:17; Acts 8:7).
17. Rejoicing and praising God (Matthew 5:12; Luke 6:23; Luke 19:37-40; Acts 3: 8, 9; Acts 8:8; 1 Thessalonians 5:16; Romans 12:15; 15:10; Philippians 1:18; 3:1, 3; 4:4).
18. The fulfillment of the prophecy of joy (Acts 2:15, 18; Ephesians 5:18).[202]

This ordeal with the 'establishment in Cleveland' was one of the reasons that the church systematically outlined its basic teachings. Another reason was to provide a doctrinal criteria to examine the increasing flood of new candidates for the ministry. Thus, in the months following the confrontation with the city of Cleveland, the church more carefully and conscientiously codified the teachings that were considered prominent in the Scriptures, and that distinguished the Church of God from other religious organizations. This body of doctrine first appeared in the August 15, 1910 edition of the *Evangel* and then in the Assembly Minutes in 1911 under the heading, 'TEACHINGS'.

1. Repentance: Mark 1:15, Luke 13:3, Acts 3:19.
2. Justification: Romans: 5:1, Titus 3:7.
3. Regeneration: Titus 3:5.
4. New Birth: John 3:3; 1 Peter 1:23; 1 John 3:9.
5. Sanctification subsequent to justification: Romans 5:2; 1 Corinthians 1:30; 1Thessalonians 4:3; Hebrews 13:12.
6. Holiness: Luke 1:75; 1 Thessalonians 4:7; Hebrews 12:14.
7. Water Baptism by immersion: Matthew 28:18; Mark 1:9-10; John 3:22, 23; Acts 8:36-38.
8. Baptism with the Holy Ghost subsequent to cleansing: The enduement of power for service: Matthew 3:11; Luke 24:49-53; Acts 1:4-8.
9. The speaking in tongues as the evidence of the baptism with the Holy Ghost: John 15:26; Acts 2:4; 10: 44-46; 19:1-7.
10. The full restoration of the gifts to the Church: 1 Corinthians 12:1, 7, 10, 28, 31; 14:1.

---

[202]*M.L. Beard, et al. vs A.J. Tomlinson et al.* 1909, pp. 3-15.

11. Signs following believers: Mark 16:17-20; Romans 15:18-19; Hebrews 2:4.
12. Fruits of the Spirit: Romans 6:22; Galatians 5:17-20; Ephesians 5:9; Philippians 1:11.
13. Divine healing provided for all in the atonement: Psalm 103:3; Isaiah 53:4-5; Matthew 8:16; James 5:14-16; 1 Peter 2:24.
14. The Lord's Supper: Luke 22:17-20; 1 Corinthians 11:23-26.
15. Washing the saints' feet: John 13:4-17; 1Timothy 5:9-10.
16. Tithing and Giving: Genesis 14:18-20; 28:20-22; Malachi 3:10; Luke 11:42; 1 Corinthians 16:2; 2 Corinthians 9:6-9; Hebrews 7:4-9-21.
17. Restitution where possible: Matthew 3:8; Luke 19:9.
18. Pre-millennial second coming of Jesus:
    First, to resurrect the dead saints and to catch away the living saints to meet Him in the air: Matthew 24:27-28; 1 Corinthians 15:51-52; 1 Thessalonians 4:15-17.
    Second, to reign on the earth a thousand years: Zechariah 14:4; 1 Thessalonians 4:14; 2 Thessalonians 1:7-10; Jude 14-15; Revelation 5:10; 19:11-21; 20:4-6.
19. Resurrection: John 5:28-29; Acts 24:15; Revelation 20:5-6.
20. Eternal life for the righteous: Matthew 25:46; Luke 18:30; John 10:28; Romans 6:22; 1 John 5:11-13.
21. Eternal punishment for the wicked. No liberation no annihilation: Matthew 25:41-46; Mark 3:29; 2 Thessalonians 1:8-9; Revelation 20:10-15; 21:8.
22. Total abstinence from all liquor or strong drinks: Proverbs 20:1; 23:29-32; Isa. 28:7; 1 Corinthians 5:11; 2 Corinthians 6:10; Galatians 5:21.
23. Against the use of tobacco in any form, opium, morphine, etc,: Isa. 55:2; 1 Corinthians 10:31-32; 2 Corinthians 7:1; Ephesians 5:3-8; James 1:21.
24. Meats and drinks: Rom. 14:2-17; 1 Corinthians 8:8; 1 Timothy 4:1-5.
25. The Sabbath: Hosea 2:11; Rom. 14:5-6; Colossians 2:16-17; Romans 13:1-2.[203]

In 1915 three more teachings were added to this list, namely,

---

[203] The list of teachings were prepared by a Committee composed of A.J. Tomlinson, R.G. Spurling, M.S. Lemons, and T.L. McClain (*COGE* 1.12 (August 15, 1910), p. 3. These teachings were then brought before the Assembly and accepted as outlined by the committee, except for the term 'immersion' in regard to baptism; it was 'struck out' in favor of 'dipping' or a comparable word to signify a 'burial beneath the water' and with full understanding that this sprinkling or pouring was not an acceptable alternative (*GAM 1906-1914*, p. 87).

26. Against members wearing jewelry for ornament or decoration, such as finger rings, bracelets, earrings, lockets, etc.: Isaiah 55:2; 1 Timothy 2:9; 1 Peter 3:3.
27. Against members belonging to lodges: John 18:20; 2 Corinthians 6:14-17.
28. Against members swearing: Matthew 5:34; James 5:12.

Then in the 1917 Assembly Minutes appeared a 29th teaching that, strangely enough, was not brought before the Assembly for discussion and approval, namely, 'Against members going to war' (Exod. 20.13; 1 Chron. 28.3; Ps. 120.7; Mt. 5.38-48; 6.14, 15; 26.50-56; Lk. 22.49-52; Jn 18.10, 11, 36; Rom. 12.19).[204] Then just as puzzling, the teaching disappeared in 1921, again without having been discussed and acted on by the General Assembly.[205]

What is almost certain is that the church was being swayed by the consensus of public opinion in adding this teaching – 'Against members going to war' – to its list of 'Important Bible Truths' in 1917 and then omitting it in 1921. It was added because the general consensus in 1917 among holiness-Pentecostal believers was against Christians participating in the war.[206] The news of the atrocities in Europe had disgusted and horrified most American holiness and Pentecostals believers, particularly those who came from Quaker and Anabaptist backgrounds. It was generally accepted without a great deal of theological debate that Christians should not kill and therefore should not 'go to war'. Little or no consideration was given to Luther's and the early Reformers' concept of a 'just war'.

Further, it can hardly be overlooked that Tomlinson was the most influential man in the church and his roots were in the pacifist tradition of Quakerism. And, as we will see in the following chapters, the Church of God more or less followed the inspiration and opinions of Tomlinson until 1922. Moreover, it is likely that Homer, who entered the war in 1918, had some impact on the fact that his father modified his opinion on the issue.

---

[204] *GAM*, 1917, p. 65.
[205] *GAM*, 1921, pp. 71-72.
[206] D.J. Wilson, 'Pacifism', in *Dictionary of Pentecostal and Charismatic Movements*, pp. 658-60.

On Divorce and Remarriage

Spurling and the ministers and members in Christian Union were rather liberal in regard to divorce and marriage, leaving remarriage (while one's first companion was still living) up to the individual parties involved. This was in keeping with their liberal covenant to allow 'each man [and woman] equal rights and privilege to read and interpret for yourselves as your conscience may dictate'. Consequently, as we noticed in Chapter Two, divorce and remarriage was not uncommon among the ministers and members in Christian Union.

Notwithstanding, after the church was swept into the holiness movement beginning in 1895, and particularly after Tomlinson assumed the helm of leadership beginning in 1903, the issue of divorce and remarriage became troublesome and vigorously debated. The particular controversial point was the so-called 'exception clause' in Mt. 5.32 and 19.9 in regard to the term 'fornication'. Thus, while the general sentiment agreed that marriage is a divine institution and holy union, on par with the general consensus in the western world itself on the issue, yet the church was divided on what Jesus meant by 'except it be for fornication'.

There is no way of knowing how all of the ministers and members stood in regard to the subject in 1906, but it is almost certain that the majority still remained fairly liberal on the issue,[207] holding that each man or woman be allowed to judge for themselves in regard to the matter. Tomlinson himself, according to his own testimony,[208] was not absolutely settled on the issue early on, but nevertheless seems to have been carried by the stream of his Quaker tradition and thus held marriage in high esteem; further, his connection with Anabaptist groups and the holiness movement beginning in 1892 did nothing to diminish his high estimation of marriage as a divine institution. His position from the beginning, therefore, leaned heavily toward the idea that marriage could be dissolved only by the death of one of the partners.

Because Tomlinson's inspirational leadership and esteem in the Church of God had reached such a high level by 1912, naturally his conservative opinion on marriage carried a lot of weight, and gradually it more or less leavened the whole fellowship. But there were other holiness ministers who joined the church beginning in 1908 who held more

---

[207] Tomlinson admitted that for many years 'the party that held for remarriage when the separation was caused from fornication seemed to outnumber the other party' (*GAM*, 1922, p. 22).

[208] He admitted in his annual address in 1922 that his conservative argument on Mt. 5.32 was 'not his settled opinion' (*GAM*, 17th Assembly, p. 23).

or less to the same view – that only death could dissolve the divine institution. Thus by 1909 the issue was being hotly debated.

The subject of divorce and remarriage first came before the Assembly in January 1908 and was discussed for the better part of the day on January 10th and then again for hours in an extra session that continued until after midnight. At that point it became obvious that the church was seriously divided on the subject. The issue was further complicated because the church had committed itself to resolve issues only by unanimous agreement, and thus, being deadlocked in crossed opinions, it was finally agreed to 'table' the issue until the next Assembly in 1909. The controversial point was the so-called 'innocent party', the view that if one's spouse committed adultery, the offended party was free and justified to remarry if he or she chose to do so.

> After hours of discussion and searching of the Scripture ... a real decision was never reached, but it was finally agreed to extend the subject another year. However it was decided that there was only one cause granted for a divorce that would leave either party innocent and at liberty to marry again and that was fornication or adultery. It was advised that it was really safest for all parties to remain unmarried who were divorced for any cause. It was further decided that none who are divorced and married again are eligible [for] membership in the Lord's Church except the innocent party of Matt. 5:32 or perchance it might be the woman who was the innocent party. And these were the contraverted [sic] points that was [sic] extended for further consideration.[209]

Therefore, as the issue stood in 1908, members who were not guilty of marital infidelity were allowed to divorce and remarry and join the church, and members already in that condition were allowed to remain members.

Notwithstanding the Assembly's decision or rather indecision in regard to the so-called 'exception clause' in Mt. 5.32, many ministers would not officiate nor sanction a second marriage if the companion from a previous marriage was still alive; nor would they receive into the church one who was divorced and remarried. F.J. Lee, for example, agreed with Tomlinson that a valid marriage was 'until death', and therefore he refused to perform a marriage to a divorcee whose companion was still alive.[210] This caused a great deal of confusion and cre-

---

[209] *GAM 1906-1914*, pp. 45-47.

[210] In a letter written to Mrs. Edith Burnside of Tangerine, Florida, dated December 30, 1925, Lee explained to her that since she had married a man that had a

ated a serious impasse in the progress and unity of the church – for some were teaching and practicing one thing and some another. Indeed, no issue had ever been so controversial and explosive in the church, nor has any issue since been more troublesome and divisive. Divorce and remarriage was for the church between 1907 and 1923 what circumcision was for the church in the days of the apostles, that is, before the issue was settled in the Jerusalem Council in Acts 15.

The issue of divorce and remarriage surfaced again in the Assembly in 1909 and still again in the Assemblies in 1912, 1913, 1914, 1915, and 1917. Each time, the committee appointed to study the issue and the ministers and members were divided on the issue; thus the Assembly concluded that the 1908 Assembly decision which allowed for an 'innocent party' should remain the rule of faith and discipline. But this only perpetuated an unsatisfactory situation, one with which Tomlinson was especially dissatisfied: for he and his followers believed that a legal marriage was broken only by death and therefore that the victim of marital infidelity or divorce was yet bound to his or her covenant partner 'until death'. Adultery was thus no excuse for remarriage. The victim of adultery might divorce or separate, but according to Paul's counsel in 1 Cor. 7.10-12 the offended party must remain 'unmarried or be reconciled to [her or his companion]'.

Tomlinson saw the issue of divorce and remarriage in the church like Lincoln saw the issue of slavery in pre-Civil War America, and concluded, like Lincoln and Jesus, that 'a house divided against itself cannot stand'. It is not surprising, then, that after several years of relevant quietness on the subject, it was Tomlinson who brought up the issue again in the explosive 1922 Assembly. Already anticipating a division in the church over other issues, he decided apparently to settle all of the divisive issues together – the office of General Overseer and political structure of leadership, the Constitution, the financial system, and divorce and remarriage. His aim was to come out of the contentious atmosphere with his followers united together in spirit as well as in faith and practice – 'speaking the same thing' and 'walking by the same rule!'

---

living companion, she was therefore free to divorce him and marry her own husband, that is, to marry a man who had never been married or one whose companion was dead. Further, he acknowledged that the issue was controversial in the Church of God and that some disagreed with his strict position ('F.J. Lee File', ZACG Archives).

Figure 83

ORDAINED MINISTERS C. 1913

Top row left: C.R. Curtis; H.B. Simmons; W.S. Caruthers; A.H. Bryans; H.W. McArthur; G.T. Brouayer. Second row: T.S. Payne; R.S. Robinson; J.J. Lowman; M.S. Haynes; J.D. Simpson; F.J. Lee. Third row: V.W. Kennedy; J.B. Ellis; J.W. Buckalew; Sam C. Perry; C.C. Walker; W.R. Anderson. Fourth row: E.E. Simmons; J.C. Underwood; E.W. Anderson; W.M. Rogers; J.L. Scott; H.L. Juillerat; C.M. Padgett. Bottom row: unknown; T.R. Austin; A.J. Tomlinson; J.S. Llewellyn; unknown; M.S. Lemons

His interpretation of Jesus' words, 'except it be for fornication', in his 1922 Assembly address is rather remarkable and worth quoting here in full, for it became the established position of his followers thereafter. It may be noted, however, that his interpretation was apparently influenced by, if not altogether borrowed from, a large number of Anabaptist and holiness-Pentecostal ministers and fellowships in the late nineteenth and early twentieth century, including W.J. Seymour and the Azusa Street Mission[211] and J.H. King and the Pentecostal Holiness Church.

---

[211] Seymour explained the 'fornication' referred by Jesus in Mt. 5.32 and 19.9 and in Paul's writings identically to the way that Tomlinson explained it, namely, that fornication in these references signifies a single man or woman who marries a person who had been married before and whose husband or wife is still living

The subject of divorce and remarriage has been hanging over the Church without a settlement or an agreement for many years. There are reasons to believe that it has hung in this quiet manner long enough. In order to keep down disturbances and cross teaching on the subject the Assembly advised that the ministers refrain from teaching on the special points of difference between the two contending parties, and in the main this advice has been obeyed. Probably there have been a few instances that the advice has been ignored, but not enough to cause any serious trouble. At times some of the contending parties have become much agitated, but now all seem to be very quiet.

After much prayerful consideration I have concluded it is time to mention the subject again, enough at least to let it be known that we have not forgotten it and still intend to reach an agreement. All agree that a man and his wife may separate and not live together if they will not marry another while the other is still living when they separate for any cause than fornication. In other words it is agreed that the divorced parties must not marry again when they have separated for any cause besides fornication. But the contention arises over the words 'except it be for the cause of fornication'. One party believes the innocent party may marry again when he has put his wife away for the cause of fornication. The other party does not believe they have any right to marry when separated for any cause.

A few years ago the party that held for remarriage when the separation was caused from fornication seemed to out number the other party, but after years of study many have turned away from that idea and embraced the belief that there should be no remarriage when divorced for any cause. After watching the ebb and flow of the tide all these years I am thoroughly convinced that the party that holds for no remarriage far outnumber the others now.

(Seymour, 'To The Married', *AF* [September 1907], p. 3). Further, the 'innocent party' in a marriage (whose companion has committed adultery) has no grounds to remarry while his or her companion is still living (Seymour based this on Paul's counsel in 1 Corinthians 7). It is possible that Tomlinson based his interpretation of marriage and particularly the issue of the so-called 'innocent party' on Seymour's teaching, having been informed of his doctrine either directly through the *Apostolic Faith* paper or indirectly through others who had been influenced by Seymour's interpretation on the subject. Be that as it may, Seymour's and Tomlinson's view was held widely by many Anabaptists and holiness-Pentecostal people in the late nineteenth and early twentieth century.

It is not my purpose to discuss the subject, I only intend to state conditions. I believe there should be a coming together on this subject so that it can be discussed pro and con by our ministers in the pulpits. We cannot afford to ignore one point of teaching in the Bible much longer. The ban must be removed so the men and women may speak their convictions on the subject, but how much better will it be for all to leave the Assembly speaking the same thing on this subject than for them to go away divided, and one preacher preach it one way and one another. To teach it differently will confuse the people until they will not know what to do, and probably some will go to hell over it when if all could teach alike many may be saved.

In the past the two contending parties have been very stout against each other. I do not know how it would be now if the subject was thrown open for discussion, but I have no intention of testing it. I would rather find a middle ground and build a platform upon which all can stand. And who knows but what this may be found after years of prayer, waiting and study! Individuals of the party that holds for remarriage when separation has been caused by fornication have stated that they would submit if the word 'except' was not in the Scriptures. But 'except' is there, and we do not dare to cut it out. Now for the sake of an agreement and to start in search of a middle ground platform, suppose we leave the word 'except' right where it is and let it mean just what the remarriage party takes it to mean, but let us take the word 'fornication' and move it over a little and get a different meaning of it from what is usually accepted. Let it be fornication for a man to marry a woman who has a living husband instead of the act of adultery. Sally Pratt comes into a community, forms the acquaintance of John Jenson and they marry. Afterward it develops that Sallie Pratt has a husband somewhere that she has divorced, but now she has married John Jenson. While John Jenson and Sallie Pratt are living together they are living in adultery. But John Jenson has a perfect right to divorce or put away Sally Pratt and marry another because John Jenson put away Sallie Pratt for fornication, and now whoso marrieth Sallie Pratt which is put away doth commit adultery. Why is it that any one commits adultery who marries Sallie Pratt after she is put away? Because she already had a living husband when she married John Jenson, and it was fornication for John Jenson and Sallie Pratt to be married. Now read the text that is causing the division on the divorce and remarriage subject: 'Whosoever shall put away his wife, except it be for fornication, and shall marry another committeth adultery, and whoso marrieth her which is put away doth commit adultery'. But John Jenson is free to go and marry another because he has no wife; he only had Mr. Pratt's wife in fornication.

Please remember I am not giving this argument as my settled opinion, but only in search of a middle ground upon which the two contending parties may meet. But let me give a verse of Scripture to bear me out in the argument: 'It is reported commonly that there is fornication among you, and such fornication as is not so much as named among the Gentiles, that one should have his father's wife'. John Jenson had Mr. Pratt's wife, but here is one that has his father's wife, and this is fornication. The Gentiles had fornication among them like the case of Sallie Pratt and John Jenson, but they did not have it where a man had his father's wife. This could be taken as evidence that fornication is not the act of adultery, but a man having another man's wife. Why can we not all agree that the fornication that permit's a man to put away his wife and marry another is that where a man has another man's wife or a woman has another woman's husband? Why could not this be the middle ground platform upon which all can stand? That would explain and reconcile the word 'except' and both parties would be yielding.

It is not my purpose to force this conclusion, neither is it my purpose to open the subject for discussion further on in the Assembly, but if the two contending parties cannot make enough concessions to meet on this middle platform I do believe we should consider removing the bar which has been on the subject so long and give a chance for both parties to teach it as they see it even if it does cause some confusion: We must open the subject some way before our people so they may be able to consider both sides of the question and decide for themselves, and in this way every one can be responsible for his own acts.[212]

Tomlinson's new interpretation of the term 'fornication' and its relevance to the issue of divorce and remarriage, however, was not taken up in the 1922 Assembly; for Llewellyn and Lee and their followers remained focused on Tomlinson's 'grasp for more power' and his alleged 'financial improprieties' in order to reduce his popularity and modify his position. After the church divided in June-August 1923, Tomlinson's followers adopted his 1922 interpretation of divorce and remarriage including his explanation of the term 'fornication' used in Mt. 5.32 and 19.9; whereas the followers of the Llewellyn-Lee faction continued with

---

[212] *HAA*, I, pp. 192-94.

their 'innocent party' interpretation. This latter faction (Church of God) continued in the following years to widen their toleration of divorce and remarriage, even going so far in recent years to ordain bishops who have two or more living wives. The main body of Tomlinson's followers (Church of God of Prophecy) also modified their view of divorce and remarriage in recent years, covenanting themselves together with an increasing number of persons who have two or more living companions. Both denominations have yielded to popular opinion in redefining Jesus' and the apostles' teachings on marriage. 'You shall not follow a multitude to do evil; neither … decline after many to wrest judgment' (Exod. 23.2). 'Blessed is the man who walks not in the counsel of the ungodly …' (Ps. 1.1).

6

THE ROAD BACK TO ROME: 1912-1921

The developments that took place in the church between 1912 and 1921 are full of intrigue and complicated by crosscurrents of conflicting ideas and strong personalities. The central and most important figure in the unfolding saga was Tomlinson himself, for between 1903 and 1914 he had risen to a preeminent position in the Church of God, and his persona was highly exalted among his admirers. To some degree his prominence was deserved, for he had made many sacrifices to build the organization and he was a gifted leader; indeed, no one had contributed more to bring about the growth and prestige of the church up to that time. But the exaltation of his person and his position as 'General Overseer' became problematic, particularly after 1912. In some ways Tomlinson was an enigma: it is almost certain that the church would have not advanced as it did without him, yet it was bound to disrupt with him. He was a great and noble man and to some extent deserved to be praised; but he had feet made of clay, and the abundance of praise heaped upon his person and unique position in the church tempted his vanity and invited self-exaltation.

As we go forward to examine this period of Church of God history, it will be necessary to evaluate the impact of Tomlinson's leadership on the church both in regard to doctrine and polity and the controversies that ended in the schism in 1919-1920 and the disruption in 1923. In doing so, we will attempt as far as possible to avoid judging Tomlinson's motives and to focus on his words and actions. The writer admittedly is for many reasons an admirer of him, and thus inclined to give him the benefit of the doubt for what otherwise might seem to have been egotism and self-aggrandizement on his part.

It should be borne in mind that Tomlinson was endeavoring to reform the church on the basis of an unfolding vision – a prophetic vision of the universal nature and purpose of the church in contrast to the Baptist-type vision upon which Spurling had formed Christian Union. Moreover, we have no reason to call into question Tomlinson's sincerity in regard to his defense for the radical changes he called for in the government and polity of the church; for he insisted that the changes were necessary in order for the Church of God to conform more perfectly to the model of the New Testament church and more effectively to fulfill her global mission. Further, we have no reason to doubt that he sincerely believed that a strong man at the top of a pyramid of hierarchical authority was the true biblical order for church government and a necessary condition for a successful execution of the church's mission in the world. Bear in mind, further, that Tomlinson was attempting his quest for apostolic restoration in the Southern Appalachian Mountains – a region that was extremely hostile to the idea of a universal organization, particularly an organization ruled and maintained by men. The legacy of the 'Radical Reformation' in the sixteenth century, particularly its passionate reaction to the pope-king system of government in Europe and England, had found its greatest expression and most practical application in the American colonies in the seventeenth century. It was Anabaptists, Quakers, and Baptists who had led the way in 1787-1789 for the United States to be established on the basis of separation of church and state and the Bill of Rights, and these principles were still zealously embraced by the people of the southern Appalachians in the late nineteenth and early twentieth century.[1] The mountaineers practiced these principles in fact in the extreme, advocating and insisting upon radical democratic ideals and a 'rugged individualism'.

Tomlinson thus had his work cut out for him in his quest to reform the Church of God on the basis of a system that resembled in so many

---

[1] Space prevents here arguing the point that there was an actual and constitutional separation of church and state in the United States. But no one will dispute the fact effectively that the United States was founded more or less upon Judeo-Christian principles, and thus that there was no separation of Christianity and the state: for this was acknowledged by almost every American president and statesmen until recently. Even the Supreme Court in 1892, in the case of the *Church of the Holy Trinity vs. United States*, boldly admitted, 'Our laws and our institutions must necessarily be based upon and embody the teachings of The Redeemer of mankind. It is impossible that it should be otherwise; and in this sense and to this extent our civilization and our institutions are emphatically Christian … this is a Christian nation'. I have argued this point more fully in *The Church of God: In the Light and Shadow of America;* see also Wade H. Phillips, 'America: The Secret of Her Greatness: A Tribute and a Warning', *Voice of Zion* (July 2009, pp. 4-23); and David Barton, *Original Intent: The Courts, the Constitution &Religion* (Aledo, TX: WallBuilder Press, 1997).

ways European political and religious models – models which radical Christians in America as well as the political founders had so passionately rejected. In that context, it is amazing that Tomlinson succeeded at all; the fact that he did can only be attributed to his personal charisma and leadership abilities.

The Magnanimity of Tomlinson

In spite of the fact that Tomlinson had shortcomings and made some extravagant errors in engineering the spiritual and political development of the Church of God, both before and after the disruption in 1923, he was in many ways personally magnanimous and made many positive contributions during his tenure as General Overseer.

1) Foremost, he was a Christian, and in many respects an outstanding one. There were no flagrant sins or scandals in his life, and even the errors associated with his role as General Overseer and his over-institutionalization of the church were made mostly through unfortunate misjudgments and misinterpretations of the Scriptures. Tomlinson's life was otherwise spent in service for others and the cause in which he passionately loved – the Church of God. The first ten years of his ministry were spent sacrificially evangelizing the poor and disenfranchised, and the next ten reforming and pioneering the on-going development of Spurling's Christian Union. During those years, he and his family suffered privations and lived more meagerly than most were willing to do. Even when he became a little more affluent in later years, he paid little attention to monetary gain, and died with little of this world's goods and treasures. He worked hard and long hours, and suffered much undue criticism and persecution for the Gospel's sake. He persevered and overcame, however, as a testimony to his faith, enduring the contradiction of friends and sinners, and learning also from the chastisement of the Lord on account of his own shortcomings, theological misinterpretations, and administrative misjudgments.

2) Tomlinson should be allowed the context of his times. It is tempting through hindsight to judge a person more harshly than he or she deserves. If Martin Luther and other historic champions of the faith are not understood in the context of their times, they will scarcely be considered justified before God according to our present knowledge of salvation and understanding of God's overall plan. Tomlinson lived in an age when strong leaders were unquestioned in their respective organizations. This had been his experience nearly everywhere he turned in the late nineteenth and early twentieth century, including the ministry of

Dr. John Alexander Dowie and the Christian Catholic Church that he established in Zion City near Chicago; the ministry of Benjamin H. Irwin, the General Overseer of the Fire-Baptized Holiness Association; and especially the ministry of Frank W. Sandford and the Church of the Living God at Shiloh in Maine. He was also familiar with General William Booth's work in the Salvation Army, and with George Mueller's great orphanage network, both men being strong leaders in their respective movements. Even John Wesley was considered a near autocratic ruler in the Methodist movement. Moreover, the image of the ruling Quaker elder was strong and commanding, which formed his first impressions of leadership. Thus, it is understandable, if not justified, that Tomlinson could have conceived of himself and his position in such an exalted manner in the context of his times and experience.

Further, restoration movements were springing up all over the country at the turn of the century, and by their very natures claimed little or no connection with historic Christianity. Americans in general saw the old world of Europe and its religion as apostate, and thus interpreted the American experience as something brand new with no strings attached to the past. While this concept was necessary to correct some errors in historic Christianity, it occasioned others. Accordingly, a certain 'historylessness' or *a*historical mindset caused most Americans, both secular and religious minded, to repeat many of the errors of the past, particularly in the Christian restoration movements that sprang up at the turn of the twentieth century. And Tomlinson was integrally a part of this radical *de novo* tradition.

3) He should be understood in the context of his predicament as a novice administrator. He was inexperienced as a leader and church administrator, and was learning his trade by trial and error. Moreover, he was the most capable and gifted man in the Church of God in its earlier years, and thus the circumstances related to building up an embryonic organization more or less cast him into an overloaded position.

4) He was a highly self-motivated man, driven frantically by imminent millennial expectations. Correspondingly, he had a vision of spiritual world conquest as large and luminous as that of Frank W. Sandford, the latter of whom helped to form his worldview. In addition, the mystical impulse that he inherited from his Quaker roots and from the radical religious groups with which Providence seemed to have arranged for him to interact in his early Christian experience, encouraged the idea that he was uniquely called and anointed by God to lead the church into fulfilling its prophetic and glorious eschatology. The highly subjective atmosphere in which he found himself in the late nineteenth and early

twentieth century tended to blur his perspective of reality and himself as a leader, which contributed significantly to the agitations between himself and those with whom he worked, and to some extent to the disruptions in 1919-1920 and 1922-1923.

5) He was actually convinced that his theories and perspectives on church government and polity were the right line for the best results in the organization and the most efficient means to fulfill the church's mission. Again, it should be borne in mind that at the turn of the twentieth century – particularly in Appalachia – most enthusiastic and radicalized Christians feared 'organized religion' and fellowshipped in a rather ragged and disconcerting manner. In attempting to avoid denominationalism and especially Episcopal type governments, they formed themselves rather loosely into associations, and were thus ineffective in evangelism and missions. Allowing Tomlinson the benefit of the doubt for what motivated him, he nevertheless over-organized the church and usurped nearly totalitarian powers in order to rectify the rather ragged and inefficient conditions that he found in the Southeast. Sandford's example and teachings in regard to organizing and training ministers and members along the lines of a highly disciplined and regimented army under a strong Commander conditioned Tomlinson's perception of leadership; for, like Sandford, he despised 'headless' fellowships, and, like Sandford, he overreacted by establishing himself in a position of headship that to some extent infringed upon the headship of Christ over the church.

6) Tomlinson did not seem to realize the theological repercussions of exalting his person and position as General Overseer in relation to the office of Christ; that is, he did not grasp the way the two offices were confused, and thus took no notice of the potential Christ-substituting nature of the position. This was due in part to his fuzzy and distorted understanding of the person and office of Christ in light of the nature and work of the Trinity. Tomlinson had a more or less tri-theistic concept of God, due to his theologically-shallow Quaker background on one hand, and Sandford's perverted theological notions and messianic complex on the other. The legacy of his distorted Christology was especially noticeable in the next generation of his followers. His son, Homer, and not a few second generation leaders in the Church of God had only a vague concept of Christ's deity; some even denied it.[2]

---

[2] The writer was once confronted by a former official in one branch of the Tomlinson tradition who adamantly denied the deity of Christ, and admitted that he did not worship Him. When I asked how long he had believed that way, he said, 'Oh, since about '38' or '39'. This same man, who otherwise was a good man and a churchman, boldly contradicted the doctrine of the Trinity toward the end of his life. The writer discovered later that not a few leaders in that tradition either denied

Tomlinson's conception of Christ's sovereignty and deity, indeed his whole Christology was underdeveloped. He reasoned that Christ had 'gone' to Heaven, without properly considering His omnipresent headship in the church, and thus it seemed only normal or natural to him that a special person or 'anointed one' would take 'Jesus' place' until He returned. After this manner he tended to supplant Christ's headship with his own. This was a frightening and dangerous concept of God, of course, but nonetheless one that he espoused.[3]

7) Tomlinson alone should not be blamed for his exaltation. His followers promoted and even helped to fabricate his exalted image and position. Admirers were constantly inflating his attributes and qualities, and 'yes men' for temporal advantage stroked what they perceived in him to be a trace of vanity. F.J. Lee and M.S. Lemons, two of the most influential men in the church next to Tomlinson in its early development, fell in with Tomlinson's concepts of a hierarchical governmental system and gave several addresses supporting the office of General Overseer. Indeed, both Lee and Lemons helped develop it through Tomlinson's influence and guidance.[4] Some also with highly emotional natures confused the flesh with the Spirit, claiming to be speaking for the Holy Spirit in an ecstasy in exalting Tomlinson and his authority. The accolades and flatteries from admirers had the tendency to push the great man in the direction that he was already leaning.

The context and circumstances of Tomlinson's rise to power in the church makes his attitude and actions in regard to his position at least a little more understandable. All men are capable of the same kind of disposition in similar circumstances. Only the grace of God and lack of occasion prevent most individuals from doing the same and worse. But these considerations do not lessen the seriousness of the aberrations that

---

the deity of Christ or harbored tri-theistic concepts of God. Homer Tomlinson flagrantly denied the deity of Christ. A.J. Tomlinson himself declared that Christ was a creature in a Christmas Message in 1940. ('Our Christmas Message', *WWM*: December 21, 1940, pp. 1, 4). Nevertheless, in spite of these distorted, if not heretical, concepts of God, the official position of the Church of God of Prophecy was somehow declared Trinitarian in 1970. See 'Questions and Subjects Committee Report', Section III, *GAM*, 1970, p. 121.

[3] In *The Last Great Conflict*, Tomlinson emphasizes time and again that the church 'really took [Jesus'] place' (pp. 154-55). He even paraphrased Jesus' words to say, 'I am going away, and upon this rock I'm going to build my Church, which is to take my place when I am gone, and she shall be called my body … I have left all the laws she needs and she must not leave off any nor add any more' (p. 154).

[4] See, for example, 'Confirmation of the Actions of the Assembly' by F.J. Lee, and 'Government the Principle of the Church' by M.S. Lemons (*GAM*, 8th Assembly, 1913). Lee and Lemons also gave a vote of confidence to Tomlinson's lifetime tenure in office in the Ninth Annual Assembly, 1914.

developed relative to his person and position. The rise of the office of General Overseer with its corresponding system of government and administration, though embodied in one esteemed so highly as A.J. Tomlinson, was a serious mistake. But so was the Constitutional form of government which sought to correct it. By either system, the Church of God fell short of restoring the New Testament form of government and polity; and in fact virtually repeated many of the errors made by the Church Fathers in the early centuries in regard to the government and structure of the church. Unwittingly, the early Church Fathers paved the road to papal Rome, and Tomlinson and his followers no less unwittingly repaved that road.

Figure 84

EIGHTH ASSEMBLY, CLEVELAND, TN, JANUARY 7-12, 1913

Ten Assemblies were held here – 1908-1915, 1919. Two were held in 1913, one in January and one in November. This building was erected in 1907 on the site of what is now the North Cleveland Church of God and dedicated on September 29 of that year. A.J. Tomlinson was the first pastor. The large addition in the rear was added later to accommodate the Bible Training School and to house the students. After the new Assembly auditorium was built in 1920, this building continued to be used for the local church and Assembly activities.

Feet of Clay

Tomlinson was a gifted leader and a loving and well-intentioned man, but he was insufficient for the office that he and his followers created –

but so is any man! Thus, notwithstanding his abilities and good intentions, he led the church into some serious errors in regard to the office of General Overseer and the institution built up around it. Moreover, he more deeply entrenched those errors among his followers after the disruption in 1923 and still more so during his stroke years in 1937-1943. We will elaborate upon this period in Tomlinson's ministry in Volume II; but for the moment we will focus on the errors connected with the office of General Overseer and political development of the church between 1912 and 1923.

Besides misinterpreting the Scriptures to support the exalted office of General Overseer – an office that was virtually a figment of his imagination – there was a certain characteristic in Tomlinson's personality that made matters worse, namely, the tendency to remain fixed in his decisions even when a large number of prominent ministers disagreed with him; but more importantly he tended to exasperate a disagreement by avoiding a reasonable discussion of the matter. We saw this method employed in his confrontation with the two Baptist ministers who came to his home in Culberson in 1901. When challenged with what he had written in *Samson's Foxes* about the 'poor ignorant whites in the mountains', he refused to defend his position or to offer any further explanation for his statements, and virtually dismissed the men with an 'I love you' and an invitation to prayer. This was more or less the same attitude and strategy that he used during the controversies in 1919-1920 and again in 1922-1923. Besides being unbiblical,[5] this method of dealing with differences and disagreements frustrated and sometimes angered those who believed they had legitimate complaints; for most 'churchmen' believe that genuine mutual respect deserves a hearing of differences and a judicious answer in regard to a disagreement. 'Good understanding wins favor' (Prov. 13.15); 'Come now, and let us reason together, says the Lord' (Isa. 1.18); 'Moreover, if your brother ... shall neglect to hear you, then take with you one or two more, that in the mouth of two or three witnesses every word [or every matter] may be established' (Mt. 18.16 and cf. Deut. 19.15). 'Where no counsel is, the people fall: but in the multitude of counselors there is safety' (Prov. 11.14).

But Tomlinson resented especially being called to account by those whom he believed to be his subordinates, which in view of his lofty and unique office included every minister and member. He therefore resisted the counsel of the Elders and dismissed unilaterally their complaints. His entry in his diary reflecting on the confrontation in the infamous 'June

---

[5] Cf. e.g. Mt. 5.23, 24; 18.15-17; Acts 17.2; 18.4; 2 Tim. 2.25.

Council' in 1923 captured in a kernel his mind-set and attitude in this regard: 'F.J. Lee and M.W. Letsinger had the "gall" and audacity to call for my credentials, and try to revoke my ministry, and they themselves carried credentials signed by myself. Such inconsistencies are viewed by wise men as absurd and ridiculous.'[6]

Tomlinson's view was biased and somewhat self-preserving, to be sure; yet the overall circumstances did make Lee's and Letsinger's actions in revoking his credentials seem rather disorderly and hypocritical, if not 'absurd and ridiculous'. For their actions were in response to the quarrels and contention that had developed in 1921-1922 that were tainted by, if not rooted in, the 'works of the flesh'. Admittedly, Tomlinson's fixed posture in regard to his position as General Overseer and his refusal to relinquish any of the powers and privileges which he believed were inherent in the exalted office provoked opposition, most particularly in Llewellyn, who by the Assembly in 1922 had drawn others into a conspiracy to unseat him. Manifestly, Llewellyn and some of his cronies were operating 'in the flesh', using every available means to smear Tomlinson's good name and reputation in order to achieve their aim. Admittedly, there were grounds certainly for complaints against him, but were the shortcomings and mistakes just grounds for the actions taken against him by the Ten Elders? Even in consideration of his reluctance to surrender any ground that might curb his increasing autocracy and authority, did Tomlinson's actions rise to the level of the punishment that the Ten Elders demanded? It could be argued that even their own standards of justice, the punishment that the Ten Elders called for exceeded the transgression; for in the final analysis Tomlinson's fault amounted to little more than his determination to hold on to and perpetuate the powerful political position that he (and most of he Elders!) had managed to create. And thus in order to accomplish their 'dastardly deed', they were forced to paint him in the worse light possible, leaving the distinct impression that he was a thief and embezzler. Certainly the charge that he had extorted the church's funds and that he was orchestrating an elaborate cover-up scheme was utterly false; and doubly shameful and inexcusable was the malicious slander heralded against him from Church of God pulpits and in the *Evangel*. Indeed, the slanderers even attacked Tomlinson's wife and family.

Did something have to be done about Tomlinson's increasing authority and exalted position? Certainly, but were false accusations and slander and the Constitution the way to do it? Certainly not. Do two

---

[6] Tomlinson, *Diary*, September 10, 1923.

wrongs make a right? If the whole ordeal had been handled in the right spirit and according to biblical principles, we have every reason to believe the outcome would have been different; but as things were, the door was opened for the deceiver and enemy of the church to exploit the situation, drawing the ministers and members of the body of Christ into a war against themselves, particularly those who had failed to maintain their spiritual consecration. The result was confusion and spiritual death and destruction, and a legacy that stands forever to contradict the noble vision of 'Christian Union'.

Carried by an Ancient Current

Notwithstanding Tomlinson's particular contribution and his good intentions, he led the church into some serious errors in regard to the office of General Overseer and the institutions of government correspondent to that exalted office. There were several sources that influenced his thinking and actions in this regard, but perhaps none more than Frank W. Sandford and his Shiloh community in Maine, which has been noticed in Chapters 3 and 4. The Sandfordian influence on Tomlinson began to surface more clearly after he moved to Cleveland in December 1904. In the months ahead he was able to establish several churches and missions in and about the city. Under his influence, these churches and missions began to view Cleveland as the center or 'Shiloh' for the movement. As the embryonic organization continued to prosper and grow, and Tomlinson's stature increased, changes began to appear in his attitude and way of thinking in regard to his personal role in the administration of the church. He became more of a governor and chief executive than pleading evangelist.

By 1909 Tomlinson's disposition in regards to spiritual authority became more apparent. However good his intentions may have been, he initiated definite steps to control the organization. His means to do this was the office of General Overseer. He sought tirelessly to establish the office as autocratic in function; offering questionable interpretations of Scriptures and appealing to the writings of some early church fathers – Clement of Rome, Hegesippus, Eusebius, e.g. – to advocate an exalted seat of authority in the church, virtually a kind of popish throne.[7]

---

[7] Tomlinson was especially fond of referring to Clement of Rome and Hegesippus, whose works are quoted prolifically in Eusebius' *Ecclesiastical History*. Hegesippus' and Clement's writings, however, clearly reveal that they were already falling to the doctrine of apostolic succession and leaning toward the development of an episcopate and papal throne – ideas that Eusebius was promoting in order to

Again, however benevolent his motive may have been, control of the church through an administrative hierarchy that was headed by a specially anointed leader was in Tomlinson's mind and scheme of things very early; for he thought such a system was necessary to fulfill the mission of the church.[8] As early as 1909 he began to suggest a more prominent role for the moderator of the church's general councils. The term 'General Overseer'[9] was introduced for the first time in that same year

---

establish Constantinian Christianity and the Roman Catholic system. These early church fathers gloried in those who had fleshly connections with Christ, and exalted Jesus' brother, James, beyond anything comparable to his humble estate in the New Testament. See *Eusebius' Ecclesiastical History* (Grand Rapids: Baker Book House, 1955), pp. 76, 99, 117, 156-58, *et al*. Hegesippus, in fact, puts James squarely in the context of the ceremonial trappings of the law and the lifestyle and regulations of the Nazarite (p. 76). He even went so far to depict him in the image of the high priest; for speaking of James, he says, 'He alone was allowed to enter the sanctuary. He never wore wollen, but linen garments. He was in the habit of entering the temple alone, and was often found upon his bended knees, and interceding for the forgiveness of the people ...' (p. 76). Since Tomlinson apparently considered Hegesippus' writings authoritative, if not infallible, it is little wonder that he became confused. It is significant, as well, that his comments about Hegesippus were made in context with his 1914 annual address, which was focused on establishing the exalted office of General Overseer. Equally noteworthy is that in this same reference, he shows his consistent pattern of contradicting himself, for Hegesippus confirms otherwise what Tomlinson denied, namely, that James, the Lord's brother, was in fact an apostle, saying, 'This apostle was consecrated from his mother's womb' (p. 76).

[8] Again Tomlinson was clearly operating here under the impressions of Sandford's teachings. It will be recalled that Sandford held that the office of God's 'anointed leader' must first be established indisputably in order for a movement to succeed. 'So the very first battle to be fought is the battle of securing, training, and disciplining God's anointed leader, until Divinity can reckon him, so that whatever God wants done He can be certain it will be carried out without His purpose being turned aside by the failures of humanity' (Sandford, *Art of War*, p. 58). This was necessary, according to Sandford, in order for 'the people' to trust leadership so thoroughly that 'all you have to do is follow along with them' (*Art of War*, p. 59).

[9] The term, 'overseer', was employed by Quakers, and was thus familiar to Tomlinson early in his experience. The exalted title 'General Overseer' had been adopted by several autocratic leaders with whom Tomlinson was familiar, including John Alexander Dowie in his Zion church in Chicago (1896) and Benjamin H. Irwin in his Fire Baptized Holiness Association, headquartered in Anderson, South Carolina. William Booth had already taken the title 'General', and made it famous by the turn of the century. Tomlinson doubtlessly borrowed the title from these men and movements. He was aware of, if not personally acquainted with, Dowie and Irwin through his subscription to *The Way of Faith* religious periodical edited by J.M. Pike. Both Dowie and Irwin contributed articles and reports of their work through this holiness paper. Pike featured regular reports on Irwin's movement and progress. Abigail Cress, who faithfully supported Tomlinson at Culberson, was connected with Irwin. Otherwise, Tomlinson would have been familiar with Dowie's church in Chicago, for reports of Dowie's meetings were widespread and newsworthy; moreover, Tomlinson's home in Westfield, Indiana was by rail not far south from

and a resolution adopted to effect, 'The appointment of a General Overseer of all churches for mutual help and general information'.[10] This was briefly discussed but no action was taken at that time. However, the office of 'General Moderator' was adopted with the following resolution:

> Whereas, the following office is considered in harmony with the New Testament order and on account of the present needs for the general welfare of the churches and the promotion of the interests of the same, we hereby institute the name General Moderator, whose term of office shall commence at the closing of each yearly Assembly and expire the following year at the same time or until his successor is selected.
>
> The duties of said officer shall be as follows, to issue credentials to ministers, to keep a record of all the preachers and evangelists within the bounds of the Assembly, to look after the general interests of the churches, to fill vacancies either in person or by sending someone who in his judgment would edify the body of Christ, and to act as moderator and clerk of the General Assembly.[11]

The following year (1910) Tomlinson's desire for the title 'General Overseer' was granted by the Assembly,[12] and he was selected to serve another year. He was again chosen to serve in the years 1911 and 1912, all the time gaining more influence and prominence in the church.[13]

The years 1913 and 1914 were eventful ones in regard to the development of the office of General Overseer. In his annual address in 1913, Tomlinson began to wax bolder in regard to governmental control and authority. His approach in this direction was typically Sandfordian. He likened the church to a military institution, frequently making a sharp distinction between clergy and laity – an erroneous strategy that had been employed by some of the early church fathers in the second and third centuries in paving the road to papal Rome. The terms 'position', 'rank', 'inferior', and 'superior' are interspersed throughout his dis-

---

Chicago and it is likely that he had attended his meetings personally. In addition, Frank Sandford had attended Dowie's meetings in Chicago in 1899-1900 and had reported to his followers at Shiloh the exploits of Dowie, which was the same period that Tomlinson was under the influence and guidance of Sandford and Shiloh.

[10] *Cyclopedic Index of Assembly Minutes*, p. 16.
[11] *Cyclopedic Index of Assembly Minutes*, p. 17. There seems to have been little awareness initially, however, of the radically new direction the church was taking by instituting this office and empowering it with universal responsibilities.
[12] *Cyclopedic Index of Assembly Minutes*, p. 18.
[13] *Cyclopedic Index of Assembly Minutes*, p. 18

course.¹⁴ According to Tomlinson, every man and woman staying in his 'proper rank of position' was the answer for successful evangelization of souls and the church's perfection. Moreover, he emphasized that 'those who disregard government and authority here will hardly be given ten cities over which to rule during the glorious reign of Christ ...'¹⁵ It was after this manner that the church's authority began to approximate God's, with less and less qualification to distinguish it as being truly 'theocratic', particularly in the sense of lining up with a reasonable interpretation of the Holy Scriptures.

We have seen that Tomlinson had a preconceived notion of an exalted ecclesiastical office, which apparently had been suggested to him at first by Sandford, and afterward was reinforced for him by the writings of Clement of Rome, Hegesippus, Eusebius, and other early church fathers. He then superimposed his preconceived notions over the Holy Scriptures to establish the office of General Overseer in the Church of God. After this manner, 'government and discipline, system and authority' exercised with unquestioned authority by a God-appointed General Overseer and a hierarchy appointed by him, were Tomlinson's answer for a successful and prosperous church:

> Nothing will go successfully without government and discipline, system and authority ... I appeal to you, my dear fellow workers and noble reformers, let us dig it out and show it to an amazed multitude as we march through the land harnessed up and every man in his rank and place until His body, the church, is perfected and ready for presentation to its head.¹⁶

At the top of this rank and file institution would be the exalted office of General Overseer, which had been developing since the Assembly in 1909.¹⁷ The man holding this exalted office would come to be consid-

---

¹⁴ *Cyclopedic Index of Assembly Minutes*, p. 41.
¹⁵ *Cyclopedic Index of Assembly Minutes*, p. 41
¹⁶ *Cyclopedic Index of Assembly Minutes*, p. 42.
¹⁷ It is evident that 'General Overseer' was understood by Tomlinson to mean 'general', more in the sense of military rank and hierarchical position than pastoral oversight of the church. It may be that he meant 'general' in this latter sense also, but it is evident that he conceived the church in a militaristic and political sense, with a commanding general at the top of a chain of command. He did not hesitate to use military and political nomenclature in his messages and writings, using magisterial terms such as superiors and inferiors, ranks and subjects to support his theory. He also incorporated into his administrative system the American political ideas that had so impressed him before his conversion. Thus he spoke of the United States government often in relation to the church's polity and system of government. He likened himself to the President of the United States and the Council of Elders to his Cabinet (*Cyclopedic Index of Assembly Minutes*, p. 69). He spoke of over-

ered as a kind of head of state awaiting the return of an exiled king; or as one holding the power-of-attorney for the head of state. In any case, the man holding the office was considered to be more or less the visible head through which the Holy Ghost directed the affairs of the church on earth.

Tomlinson's flagrant use of military language and management was clearly Sandfordian. It is true that the image and metaphor of the church as a 'mighty army' was a common expression in Tomlinson's day and universally used by religious leaders. Biblical writers themselves often use the metaphor, including Jesus and Paul in the New Testament. The Salvation Army had emerged in London in 1865 and spread quickly throughout the United States having adopted an administrative system that resembled a militaristic chain of command. William Booth, its founder, had adopted the title 'General', and other officers were given the titles of 'captain', 'lieutenant', etc. Though Tomlinson and the Church of God did not adopt these titles, yet the military implication of their administrative government was taken more seriously:[18] for their officers represented a theocratic chain of command in which subordinates were to obey divinely appointed superiors in order for the church to succeed and achieve her mission in 'the last great conflict'.

Tomlinson, like his former militaristic-minded mentor, taught that the members of the church must 'learn to submit' and be trained to 'bow to authority'. He saw the church as a 'training camp' to effect these ends.[19] Ideas associated with rank, position, and authority were driven into the minds of the membership. Seldom did Tomlinson address the

---

seers as senators and noblemen, etc. This kind of mentality contributed to the idea and development of the Constitution adopted in 1921, with its opening lines, 'We, the Church of God ... In order to form a more perfect union ...' Though Tomlinson rightfully repudiated the Constitution afterward, he had ironically contributed to its influence and, as General Overseer, had personally introduced it to the Assembly and zealously called for its ratification. The American political system had been his experience and he never fully departed from it. The way he managed the General Assemblies and some conventions was much in the color and image of political rallies and conventions. The displaying and waving of banners and a kind of excitement that one might see at secular political events often filled the Tabernacle where Tomlinson moderated the services. Assembly committees – 'Ways and Means' and 'Questions and Subjects' – were clearly in the tradition of American government, and the political jargon that he used – 'wire pulling', 'filibusters', etc. – to describe the actions of his opponents also reflected the influence of the American political system.

[18] Booth, like Wesley, did not consider his movement a church, and thus did not practice the sacraments. His Salvation Army was more or less a social movement.

[19] *Cyclopedic Index of Assembly Minutes*, p. 82.

General Assembly without reserving a section for the purpose of training the minds of the delegates in disciplines of submission and obedience to authority. And seldom did he fail to mention that at the top of this authoritative system was the General Overseer, who was in turn subject ultimately only to God.[20] The church was government to Tomlinson: a corporate body with laws that are to be obeyed, and with officers to execute them.[21] In this regard, Tomlinson sounded more like a military general than a Gospel preacher or spiritual pastor. The militaristic images tended to misconstrue and distort the nature of the church, particularly in its metaphorical image as the *body of Christ*.

During these adolescent years, Tomlinson filled the young church with a sense of corporate pride. He constantly referred to his followers as the most 'noble and honorable body on earth', and exuded airs of confidence that swelled the fellowship's sense of self worth. He exclaimed, 'there had never existed so worthy and noble body as the last days Church of God', particularly when it assembled in its General Assemblies to do God's business on earth:

> The Church of God is the greatest, wisest and most glorious government that has ever been inaugurated on this earth. To be called upon, as is this honorable body and sacred Assembly, to search out and apply the laws of the greatest, wisest and most glorious government that has ever made its appearance on earth, should certainly be considered the highest honor conferred upon man ... No people on earth have ever been called upon to occupy such an exalted position.[22]

In the Eighth Annual General Assembly in 1913, Tomlinson seemed overwhelmed with a sense of self-exultation as the saints in the midst of emotional excitement and physical demonstrations once again chose him to serve as General Overseer:

> You are going out from this Assembly and the world is going to hear from you. I appreciate your love and honor, but it gets bigger when I see the Holy Ghost has made the selection. In making the selection of the man to conduct one of the great camp meetings at Durant, Fla., they wrote me that the Holy Ghost had named me as the man. This is greater than a camp meeting. If God has set His approval upon this it is a more exalted position than the one occupied by Roosevelt, Wilson, Taft, King George of England or any other great leader or ruler.

---

[20] *HAA*, I, p. 257.
[21] *Cyclopedic Index of Assembly Minutes*, p. 82.
[22] *HAA*, I, p. 24.

Although they have more people under their jurisdiction, yet this is a government and position under God, for the Holy Ghost has placed me in it as you all know.[23]

Still, Tomlinson did not believe his indisputable authority had been established clearly enough in everyone's mind. In order to nail down his position more effectively, he thus interpreted the position and authority of James, the Lord's brother, and the Jerusalem council recorded in Acts 15 to suit his own purposes. In doing so, he bestowed nearly blasphemous titles upon James, and assigned superlatives to his nature that were insulting to both James and his Lord. But this was necessary for him to secure the kind of power and influence that he desired; for he depicted himself in James' position in 'the last days Church of God'.[24]

In his annual address in 1914, Tomlinson's quest for authority and the superior position in the church reached its climax. His excited concept of the new office caused him to misinterpret the Scriptures, and on occasion to wrest them to justify and support his idiosyncratic view of 'theocratic government'. He employed the splendid craft of his pen and the eloquence and fluent power of his oratorical skills, carefully choosing certain verbs and adjectives to persuade the saints that James, the Lord's brother, had a unique and peculiar office in the primitive church. James was, in fact, Tomlinson maintained, the indisputable General Overseer. To establish this, he cleverly depicted James as belonging to a category and rank by himself, elevated higher than even apostles like Peter, James, John, and Paul. Indeed, he labored to establish the proposition that James, the Lord's brother, was not an apostle but in fact held an exalted office above all the apostles. He stressed the concept that James was superior in rank and position to everyone in the church, including the 'twelve apostles', no less than eight times. The phrase 'occupied the executive chair' is used three times in his discourse, and 'chairman', 'high position', 'superior position', 'chief executive', and 'superior in rank' are repeated several times. Earlier in his address, he went beyond the line of respectable Christian thought in depicting the character and position of the 'ever to be revered James' as a mediatorial lord over the church. He encouraged the saints to imagine,

> ... that illustrious man of God, James, the Lord's brother, as he sat upon his imperial and mediatorial throne, like Moses of fifteen cen-

---

[23] 'Address of Acceptance', *GAM*, 8th Assembly, 1913, pp. 101-103.
[24] *Cyclopedic Index of Assembly Minutes*, pp. 49, 50.

turies before, and at the proper time see him rise to his feet with holy reverence and godly dignity ...[25]

Interpreting James, the Lord's brother, in this manner approached nearly the heresy of the Roman Catholic concept of Peter and the papal throne. That system maintains that Peter was the first primate of Rome and therefore the 'chief of the apostles', himself holding the keys to the kingdom of God. By virtue of his office and primacy, he is said to have spoken *ex-cathedra* and was empowered to act in behalf of the universal church. Roman Catholics eventually declared that the pope by virtue of his office as Peter's successor spoke and acted with infallibility in all matters pertaining to faith and doctrine. After this manner they perverted Peter's role beyond any semblance to leadership in the New Testament.

Tomlinson restrained himself from using some of Rome's most flagrant language and terminology in his quasi Roman Catholic interpretation of James' position, but nevertheless he implied it on occasion and functioned on its principle.[26] In one sense he went beyond the Roman Catholics by insisting that James occupied a peculiar position above the office of an apostle. In order to substantiate this idea, he denied that James, the Lord's brother, was an apostle, and that he in fact occupied a position superior in rank to all apostles including Peter and the rest of the 'twelve'.

> As the Apostle Peter once said concerning David, 'Let me freely speak unto you of the patriarch David', I say, let me freely speak unto you of this ever to be revered and beloved James, the Lord's brother. Many believe him to have been one of the twelve apostles, but there are certain evidences given that rather show that he was not one of the 'twelve' but occupied a position superior in rank to any of them. Be that as it may it remains that he was esteemed very highly by Peter who was the very chiefest apostle, as well as by other chief men.[27]

Tomlinson further assumed that if James, the Lord's brother, was not an apostle he must therefore be above the apostles, rather than serving under them in the office of prophet, evangelist, pastor, or teacher. He further complicated his eccentric presentation of the church's adminis-

---

[25] *Cyclopedic Index of Assembly Minutes*, p. 47.
[26] For example, he did not claim infallibility and tactfully avoided assigning titles to James such as 'pope' and 'His Holiness', but he nonetheless spoke of him as that 'ever to be revered', and qualified his position to approximate that of the Roman See.
[27] *GAM*, 10th Assembly, 1914, p. 156.

trative order and James' position by admitting that Peter was 'the very chiefest apostle'. Thus if James, the Lord's brother, was superior in rank to Peter and the office of apostle, there must of necessity be another office in the church other than those mentioned by Paul in Eph. 4.11 and 1 Cor. 12.28, namely, the solitary office of 'General Overseer'. But since there is not actually a higher office in the New Testament church than that of an apostle, where did that leave Tomlinson's conception of the office of General Overseer? It was obviously a fabrication, a figment of his imagination, and by virtue of its exalted station was bound to conflict with the very office of Christ. Taking Tomlinson's thinking to its logical conclusion, it implied that James was in a superior station to Christ himself, for the writer of Hebrews declares that Christ is 'the Apostle and High Priest of our profession' (Heb. 3.1). Thus if Jesus is an apostle, and James was above all apostles, the obvious deduction would leave James in a more exalted station than even his Lord. Tomlinson did not actually believe this, of course, and thus his confusion made a complete *reductio ad absurdum* of his whole muddle-headed hypothesis concerning James and his position.

Notwithstanding, giving Tomlinson the benefit of the doubt in regards to his motive for developing James' office as he did – that is, that he truly believed the office was necessary for the right governance of the church and the fulfillment of its mission in the world – his interpretation was nevertheless enthusiasm inflamed by an exalted view of position, a position that infringed upon the headship and sovereignty of Christ.

In his zeal to establish government and order among his followers, Tomlinson invented an office impossible to find in the New Testament apart from Christ. He maintained that the office of General Overseer was unique, and that it could be filled only by one man at a given time. Thus, whereas the offices of apostle, prophet, evangelist and pastor could be filled by many persons at the same time, that is, the church could have hundreds of pastors and evangelists serving at the same time in various places, it was not so with the office of General Overseer. The man holding this exalted office was unique and positioned at the apex of an ascending hierarchy of ecclesiastical power.

Since Tomlinson labored to show that James was not an apostle, further analysis will be given here to show the contradictions and repercussions of his conclusion. First, his contention that James, the Lord's brother, was not an apostle was erroneous, for James is clearly designated as such by the apostle Paul in Gal. 1.19: 'But other of the apostles saw I none, save James the Lord's brother'. This fundamental error became all the more complicated by Tomlinson's further elaborations upon James and his office. In his 1914 address he repeatedly urged the church to return to 'apostolic teachings and apostolic practices', yet he exalted James, the Lord's brother, above the apostles, insisting that he had the final word on matters pertaining to the faith and the practices of the church. What he actually urged then was not a return to apostolic teaching and practice, but a new system comparable to the papal system of Rome.[28]

With all his insistence on returning to apostolic Christianity, Tomlinson instead injected an innovation into the church – an office above and beyond that of an apostle. The result was an autocratic monstrosity that would ever after trouble the church, contributing fundamentally to the disruptions in 1919-1920 and 1922-1923, and as we will see in Volume II to more disruptions among Tomlinson's followers in the years to come. It may be observed that in almost every quarrel in the years to come among Tomlinson's followers that ended in schism was the exaltation of leadership. In some instances, the exalted office would become vacant and a quarrel would ensue over who was the new 'anointed one'; in other cases a new self-proclaimed 'anointed one' would rise to compete with the 'anointed one' still in office – the old 'anointed one'. In every case, a schism would result, with each group making the claim to be followers of the true 'anointed one' and thus to be the true church. Interestingly, some of Tomlinson's followers remain today and continue to defend the Tomlinsonian view of the office of General Overseer with a ferocious tenacity.

It is ironic that, though Sandford's teaching on spiritual authority and mediatory leadership factored significantly into Tomlinson's interpretation of James and the office of General Overseer, he went beyond

---

[28] Tomlinson's conclusion in regards to James is not supported in Acts 15 or in the whole of the New Testament. James is not set apart and above the apostles in the Jerusalem council, nor is there a 'General Overseer' mentioned or even alluded to in all of the narration of the text. James is simply included in the references concerning 'apostles and elders' (e.g. Acts 6.2-6; 15.2, 4, 6, 22, 25-27 *et al.*). It seems that he was positioned for a time as *primus inter pares*, but his office was not preeminent nor unique. He evidently moderated the Jerusalem council and was prominent in the church, but he was not preeminent, nor unique; nor does the record show that he functioned in any manner similar to Tomlinson's conception of the office of General Overseer. He did not make universal appointments nor speak *ex cathedra* nor act *ex officio* for the whole church; nor did he act autocratically or unilaterally. Though James concluded the sentiments expressed by Peter, Paul, and Barnabas in the Acts 15 council, his personal 'judgment' was made neither unilaterally nor was considered final on the basis of a superior office. The emphasis throughout Acts is that the church 'continued steadfastly in the apostles' doctrine and fellowship' (Acts 2.42; see also Acts 15.28), not in James' or the General Overseer's doctrine and fellowship.

Sandford in developing his concept of James' position; for Sandford clearly shows that James, the Lord's brother, was in fact an apostle.[29] Sandford had justified his exalted position at Shiloh by referring to the mediatory roles of Moses and Joshua, and the monarchical position of King David rather than a New Testament figure. He considered this sufficient because he had no particular commitment to the New Testament as a rule of faith and made little distinction between the Old Economy and the New. Thereby, he was able to confuse his own position in the church at Shiloh with messianic passages in the prophets. Tomlinson, however, had covenanted himself with the Holiness Church at Camp Creek to take 'the New Testament as [his] rule of faith, practice, government and discipline', and thus he was forced to find a New Testament parallel for Moses' role in the Old Testament, that is, other than the obvious parallel of Christ himself. His answer was James, the Lord's brother. After this manner, Tomlinson contravened the new order of Christ's government and administration under the New Covenant by returning to the regimented and pre-Christian system under Moses.

Tomlinson would later deny, evidently under pressure from some horrified and disillusioned members, that he was sitting in the 'place of God' or even taking the 'place of Moses'.

> We do not interpret the meaning of theocracy as requiring one to sit in the place of God, or even to take the place of Moses, but rather one to take the place of James, the Lord's brother ...[30]

Obviously this was more rhetoric than substance, for he had already gone on record stating that James sat on an 'imperial and mediatorial throne like Moses'.[31] He further stated in the same address, in enthusiastic but illogical contradictions, that James 'evidently occupied the same position in the Church at that time that Moses occupied when Israel was signally named "The Church in the wilderness"'.[32] In this manner he juxtaposed the position of Moses in the Old Testament beside that of James in the New and beside himself in the 'last days Church of God', confusing them all with the headship of Christ over the church.

In his 1928 annual address he drew the fantastic conclusion that James not only held Moses' place but also occupied the place of Jesus: 'Jesus, the Founder and General Overseer, was the first to depart. But

---

[29] *Seven Years With God*, p. 135. So did Hegesippus whom Tomlinson quotes for authority.
[30] *HAA*, I, p. 206.
[31] *GAM*, 10th Assembly, 1914, p. 163.
[32] *GAM*, 10th Assembly, 1914, p. 156.

He finished His work and apparently arranged for and appointed His brother James to take His place as Overseer before He left ...'[33]

After this manner, Tomlinson exalted the 'ever to be revered' James beyond any semblance to the New Testament record. Grasping for some authority to support his extravagant conclusions, he quoted Clement of Rome who maintained that James 'ruled all the churches everywhere established until the day of his martyrdom'.[34]

Having established the exalted and indisputable office of James as the New Testament church's 'General Overseer', and himself in the same office in the 'last days Church of God', what remained for Tomlinson to gain absolute control of the church was a lifetime tenure in the office. This would effect and complete his desire for the preeminent position. He thus carefully guided his followers into selecting him for life.[35] His method for doing this was the power of suggestion. After having discoursed on the awesome character of James and his highly exalted position as an imperial mediator, and creating an allusion to himself as one in the same superior position, Tomlinson said:

> If this James, the Lord's brother, was not one of the 'twelve' and yet occupied a position that even they recognized, respected and submitted to, it becomes a question as to how he received his appointment and why he was placed in a position above that occupied by any of them. As this is one of the important points pertaining to God's government it becomes our duty to fathom this mystery as well as the many others that have confronted us year after year. If we acknowledge that James, the Lord's brother, was not one of the 'twelve' and yet occupied the executive chair of which there is no question, it will certainly throw a gleam of light before us that will soon reveal some mysteries that have hitherto been obscure.[36]

In this manner he endeavored to sway the people's minds to his way of conceiving the unique and mystical appointment of the General Overseer. In typical Sandfordian mysticism, Tomlinson believed that God directly appointed the General Overseer who in turn appointed subordinates to their offices. He thus acted *in persona Christi*, or rather in the place of Christ, as God's vicar on earth, and hence all authority was vested in him as the special instrument of the Spirit to dispense divine authority and wisdom; that is to say, all authority was delegated by the

---

[33] *HAA*, II, p. 17.
[34] *HAA*, I, p. 64; and see *GAM*, 12th Assembly, 1916, p. 213.
[35] *Cyclopedic Index of Assembly Minutes*, pp. 51, 52.
[36] *Cyclopedic Index of Assembly Minutes*, p. 51.

one who was especially chosen and appointed by God, namely, the General Overseer. We see then that God appointed the General Overseer and he in turn appointed everyone else. Thus after a few remarks about prayer, and in full confidence of his influence over the Assembly and its decision, Tomlinson stated, 'now is a good time to ask the Lord to give a new General Overseer'.[37] After this, Tomlinson stepped back and knelt down.

> The congregation became quiet and all seemed almost as still as death. No one spoke a word for a few moments. At length the silence was broken by Brother Lemons who said, 'Brethren, the place is vacant, let us pray for God to give us an overseer'. All fell upon their faces and cried out to God for several minutes, after this there was a great calm again. When the silence became almost painful, one spoke in tongues and the interpretation followed immediately. 'My beloved, you can't do better than what you have. Hold on to what you've got'. A joyous cry arose from almost everybody present. A second message was given and the interpretation followed. 'He has been so faithful, as he was led by me and has governed and led the little flock. So follow him as he follows me.' With this the power fell upon many and the one chosen was literally covered up by the brethren as they fell upon him and kissed him. He was so overcome that he was unable to rise for several minutes. People laughed, shouted, cried, danced, made speeches, and finally Brother Lemons took the one named by the Holy Ghost by the arm and lifted him up and led him to the stand and placed him before the great congregation who shouted their approval and greetings for several seconds.[38]

The effect of this moment on the 'delegates' is revealed by the comments of some of the more prominent men in the church at that time:

> J.A. Davis – 'I do not find in the Scriptures any change of overseer in the early Church until James died and then Paul took his place. Others endorsed this remark.'

> W.R. Anderson – 'I find that when God puts a man in a place, he holds it until he dies'.

> J.L. Scott – 'When I look at what Brother Tomlinson has done for the Church of God and the little financial support he received for himself

---

[37] *Cyclopedic Index of Assembly Minutes*, p. 51.
[38] It should be noted that Tomlinson himself was the clerk and recorder of the minutes, and thus uses the third person in speaking of himself.

and family, I can truly say, it is God that has sustained him. He has been so faithful and true and I am glad to say we have a man that never murmurs nor complains.'

F.J. Lee – 'I have known Brother Tomlinson for several years. I love him. I honor him. I honor him more because God honored him. God has given him special wisdom. I went to him with a burdened heart because it seemed the devil was going to try to make an inroad into the Assembly and cause division. My fears did not disturb him. He took it so calm and quiet that it made me feel ashamed. He quietly remarked that he had no fears and that the Church of God is not like other churches. The burden that was on my heart vanished away. There is such unity and harmony prevailing in this section that I don't see any need of ever making any change until God takes him away.'

M.S. Lemons – 'I think you can all see that God's approval is on this selection, and I don't see any use of ever saying anything more about a change.'

R.G. Spurling – 'I praise God for Brother Tomlinson. I feel toward him like a father.'

Following these remarks, there was a message in tongues with the interpretation, 'I have made this man what he is give God all the honor and not man'. Then another message in tongues with the interpretation, 'We are in harmony now. Keep your eye on me and remain in harmony.' During these emotionally charged proceedings, the General Overseer was unable to speak, so at that juncture he motioned for all to rise to their feet and dismissed the congregation. The sentiment of the entire Assembly, according to Tomlinson, was to make this selection final.[39]

The tributes lauded upon Tomlinson by some of the most prominent men in the church show clearly the high estimation in which he was held at that time, and testify to the many admirable traits of his Christian character and leadership ability. At the same time, however, it is noteworthy that the messages and interpretations in tongues that followed Tomlinson's 'Acceptance Speech' diverted attention away from him and counseled the delegates to focus on Christ. These fearful admonitions seem to have confirmed that they were true manifestations of the Holy Spirit, for Jesus said concerning the work of the Spirit, 'he shall glorify me' and 'he shall testify of me'.[40]

---

[39] *Cyclopedic Index of Assembly Minutes*, p. 52.
[40] John 16.14; 15.26.

Still, neither the people nor Tomlinson apparently comprehended the Spirit's counsel; and thus Tomlinson emerged from the 1914 Assembly magnified more than ever in the eyes of the people – and in his own estimation. The intervention of the Spirit in the selection process and the high tributes paid to him by leading men in the church seemed to have crowned him with a halo, and, as he stood before the people, his presence seemed in the view of many to be encircled with a sacred aura.

The legacy left in the Tomlinson tradition regarding the office of General Overseer has caused people to fear and tremble before the one who occupies the exalted chair. But this is considered normal given the awesome powers attached to the position – 'a position', according to Tomlinson, 'greater than the one occupied by Roosevelt, Wilson, Taft, King George of England or any other great leader or ruler'.[41]

It will be observed that the creation of the office of General Overseer by necessity of its concomitant powers and responsibilities had to inevitably supplant Christ's headship over the church. The nature of the office itself made it appear that Jesus was 'out of the picture' in the last day's Church of God, and that another was left to fill His place on earth. The fact that Jesus, even after His ascension and glorification, yet walked 'in the midst of the seven golden candlesticks' and abided in the midst where even 'two or three gathered in His name'[42] was not grasped apparently by the majority of Tomlinson's followers; nor did they grasp that Jesus may have been jealous for preeminence in His church, and for an immediate and direct sovereignty over each individual member as well as all of the members collectively. To Tomlinson, Jesus was the Alpha and Omega, but in between the Alpha and Omega God had raised up men in His place – a succession of General Overseers. Accordingly, Jesus was the head of the church, but He ruled from a great distance away through a proxy or general – a man of great nobility, unblemished character, and courage and power; a specially chosen representative of Christ on earth; a man who through his own perfection could lead others to perfection. In fine, Christ was the heavenly head who turned another head on earth, who in turn ruled the church.

There was, of course, some precedent in Scripture to think like this. Jesus had likened himself to 'a man taking a far journey, who left his house, and gave authority to his servants ... and commanded the porter to watch'.[43] Such passages regarding Christ were understood by Tomlinson apparently with a kind of monophysitic presupposition in mind.

---

[41] 'Address of Acceptance', *GAM*, 1913, pp. 101-103.
[42] Revelation 2.1; Mt. 18.20.
[43] Mark 13.34.

First, he did not grasp clearly Jesus' two natures and His eternal and omnipresent divinity in the church;[44] second, he failed to understand that such passages were meant as a way for Jesus to express His self realized humanness, without denying or confusing His deity.[45] Third, he failed to grasp that such passages were to be understood allegorically in respect to Jesus' deity, for Christ must by necessity of His indivisible nature with the Father be ever present in the church. In one sense Christ did leave 'His house', but in another sense His divinity and headship in the church made Him ever present.[46] The same Jesus that made the worlds continues ever to dwell in them and hold them together, and to know infinitely all things.[47]

By pressing too hard and literally Mk 13.34 and similar passages in respect to Jesus' finite nature, especially at the expense of His divine nature, Tomlinson allowed for the doctrine of the church's vicarious position and the exaltation of his office as General Overseer. Though his intentions may have been harmless and his motives pure, his theological and Christological weaknesses opened the door for such errors.

Notwithstanding Tomlinson's personal views, it seems that the immediate headship of Christ would have been vividly realized and recognized by the majority in the Church of God, especially in light of the church's Pentecostal theology and experience; for mainline Pentecostals held that the Holy Spirit's gifts and graces were indiscriminately operated throughout the whole body of the church. In fact, the intense spirituality and mystical nature of Pentecostalism purported to offer a more vivid and realistic revelation of Jesus Christ in the midst of the church through the baptism with the Spirit. In the heavenly atmosphere of Pentecostal restoration, it would seem to have been apparent that the church had only one 'chief executive' and only one 'throne and mediator' – the Lord Jesus Christ – whom God had ordained to be the very center of the church. Again, it would seem that the metaphor 'body of Christ' would have kept before the ministers and members of the Church of God the fact that Jesus was the very heartthrob of the church, and that His life animated the whole body and pulsated in its every muscle and joint. Yet this was not apparent to Tomlinson and his followers, which opened the door for the development of the Christ-substituting system that followed.

---

[44] Matthew 18.20; Rev. 2.1; Jn 3.13.
[45] John 1.3; Col. 1.17; Heb. 1.3.
[46] John 3.13; Rev. 1.8; 2.1.
[47] John 6.64; 23.17; Mt. 11.30.

The negligence of holding to a Christ-centered ecclesiology became the very source of the aberrations and problems that followed the Tomlinson tradition. His religious system was raised in a Christological void, theologically speaking. He and his followers professed a restoration of the apostolic church, including the efficacious restoration of the Holy Spirit's gifts and graces, but they built an organization on the presumption that the Chief Corner Stone was missing – away on 'a far journey'. And this was the misconception that caused the distortions that followed. Because the government and polity of the true Christian church was incompatible with Tomlinson's conception and practice of the office of General Overseer, the contentions and disruptions that followed in 1919-1920 and 1922-1923 were inevitable. For men beholding the face of Jesus in Pentecostal glory could not for long settle for an imperfect image of Him – a religious system that could boast only of a mere representation of Christ's headship. For the true Gospel church boasts not only of a returning Christ but of a living, dynamic, and abiding Christ![48]

If the living and dynamic presence of Christ was truly vivid in the church, what need was there further for a mediatory hierarchy; particularly a superior one positioned at the apex of a pyramid authority who merely represented on earth the headship of Christ? Wasn't Christ everywhere realized and known and felt in the presence of every moment of time and eternity? Wasn't He real and presently active in the church at that very moment? Or was Christ merely the transcending head of the church, who through the Holy Ghost guided and turned a visible head on earth who in turn guided and directed the church? The latter was in fact the prevailing rationale behind the development of the office of General Overseer and the hierarchy that ascended up to its exalted station.

The office of General Overseer recreated the image of the Hebrew high priest, and set the Church of God tradition back to a pre-Christian era, in a similar fashion that Rome did with the papal office. The idea of the office was the invention of misguided zeal, and it materialized in the vacuum of a distorted Christology. If Tomlinson would have applied his reasoning in regard to creeds to the office of General Overseer, the church might have been spared the calamities ahead. In regard to creeds, Tomlinson wrote, 'Creeds show that people are a long ways off from God, and only have a mere opinion or hearsay of Him. Israel said they

---

[48] Cf. Matthew 28.20; Jn 14.20, 23; 2 Cor. 5.17; Gal. 2.20; Col. 1.27; 2.9, 10, 19; 3.11; *et al.*

did not know what had become of Moses. To accept a creed, people say they don't know what has become of Christ.'[49]

However, somehow he failed to see that his reasoning here applied equally to the office of General Overseer: for the idea behind the office was basically that Christ had gone back to the Father and that one had been appointed 'to take His place' until He returned.

But let us see more particularly how this deistic conception of Christ came into the church, and how such a popish concept of leadership developed. We have already noticed that Tomlinson had a more or less tritheistic concept of God, and particularly a weak and confusing doctrine of Christ, the origin of which can be traced to his Quaker roots. His early work, *The Last Great Conflict*, reveals clearly that he embraced the doctrine of the Trinity;[50] but also that he conceived the Trinity in a tritheistic manner. In his limited treatment of the Godhead, he tended to separate the divine essence; and, though he acknowledged the three persons, he explained them in mechanical terms and thus distorted their nature and relationship.

> God the Father is one. God the Son is one. God the Holy Ghost is one. Every wheel in the watch is one wheel. When the wheels are all geared together properly, and the mainspring and hairspring properly adjusted and in the case wound up, we call it a watch that is running and marking time. God the Father, God the Son, and God the Holy Ghost, has each His function to perform, but these three are one.[51]

This mechanical concept of God's unity may not have been so damaging in itself, as Tomlinson yet honored the three persons in worship and the practice of his faith; yet it opened the door for a more serious flaw in his Christology. He taught that Christ was a created being in a similar fashion that Arius did in the fourth century and Joseph Smith in the nineteenth. He did not teach this as a habit, for he seldom theologized his faith, maintaining that the faith was better honored by the practice of it. He apparently was careful not to express his unorthodox views about Christ until late in his ministry. His Arianism did not show up so blatantly in his writings until a Christmas message in 1940. At that time he openly declared,

> This very Christ was God's first creation, and made the worlds for God, and was God's Son in a similar sense to the way Adam became His son. We do not celebrate His birthday in recognition of His crea-

---

[49] Tomlinson, *LGC*, p. 167.
[50] Tomlinson, *LGC*, pp. 105-107.
[51] Tomlinson, *LGC*, pp. 138-39.

tion as God's first creation, but we celebrate on account of His being born of the Virgin Mary who is spoken of as His mother. But He is the same Personage all the way through.⁵²

This rather startling admission by Tomlinson was more from confusion and theological neglect than deceit and blatant heresy; for prior to this message and in the remaining two years of his life, he maintained that Jesus was eternal and equal with God and worthy to be worshipped,⁵³ though he yet felt that he had to qualify Jesus' equality with the Father as being only in the sense that He represented God.⁵⁴ He seems simply to have failed to grasp the unity of the three Persons in one substance or nature. Tomlinson's otherwise zealous acknowledgement of Christ's deity dissociated him at least with Mormons and Jehovah Witnesses who were at the same time militantly propagating their heretical and destructive concepts of God. Tomlinson's anti-intellectualism and distaste for theology made him vulnerable to such mechanical notions about the nature and work of the Godhead. He was further confused by the rather strange mixture of religious traditions that formed his mystical mindset – traditions as diverse as the highly subjective Quaker mysticism and the radical holiness and nonconformist groups that helped to form his concept and theology of God and the church.

In the Christmas message referred to above, his Arian tendencies were confused with a kind of deism that resulted in an exalted church on earth with a visible head.

> He was once a helpless child lying in a manger, but now at the right hand of His Father in heaven, there to remain until his foes are made His footstool. I do not know what all this means, but I do know that He left the great responsibility of subjugating the world to His Church. He must have all confidence in this Church of prophecy or He would not be satisfied to sit there, as the Book declares He will, and let us do the work that is yet to be done.⁵⁵

Tomlinson's confusing theology of God opened the door for his exaggerated exaltation of the church and his Christ-substituting position as

---

⁵² Tomlinson, 'Our Christmas Message', p. 4.
⁵³ Tomlinson, 'The Enormous Price Paid For the Church', *WWM* (April 23, 1938), p. 4.
⁵⁴ Tomlinson, 'The Enormous Price Paid for the Church', p. 4. Here he states, 'Jesus who was God's personal representative in the world, and for that reason did not consider it robbery to be equal with Him'.
⁵⁵ Tomlinson, 'The Enormous Price Paid for the Church', p. 4.

General Overseer. Though, like Sandford, he always exalted the presence of the Spirit and purported that the Holy Ghost was the true Director of the church, and Christ the Head, yet he nevertheless treated Christ as a king in exile and conceived himself positioned as the head of state until the King returned. He was thus acting more or less with the 'power of attorney' in Christ's absence.

Tomlinson conceived and developed this vicarious concept not only in regard to himself and his position, but also extended it to the whole church. In reference to 2 Cor. 5.20, he wrote, 'We are marked by the apostle Paul as ambassadors for Christ. Now, an ambassador is one to serve in the place of another'.[56] While this statement was not wrong on its face, Tomlinson then pressed Paul's meaning beyond respectable theological limits, endeavoring to establish his vicarious doctrine of the church and his personal position.

> What a sacred position we occupy! How could it be more so? ... Can you fully imagine and realize what a sacred position we occupy? We are here instead of Christ. Standing here pleading with the lost world as if it was Christ Himself. Can you half comprehend this high position? In the place of God ... As I peer deeper into this wonderful position we occupy my breast heaves with emotion ... Think of yourself! What a high calling – what a high position! In God's stead![57]

Tomlinson's thinking in this regard shows how easily a truth can be pressed into an error; and helps us to understand how the Church Fathers in the early centuries drifted into error and developed the Roman Catholic system. It is an error that has been made many times by various groups in Christian history, namely, to understand oneself or one's institutions to be 'in the place of God'.

This same error permeated a large part of Pentecostalism in the early years of the movement. In the excitement of the advent of the 'latter rain outpouring' of the Spirit, a tritheistic theology tended to prevail. Without proper respect and attention being given to the essential unity of God, the Holy Spirit was singled out as immediately present in the church, with the Father and Son considered positioned rather obscurely or remotely beside each other on a throne in heaven. This concept con-

---

[56] Tomlinson, 'Our Christmas Message', p. 4. Tomlinson failed to grasp that Paul was speaking more or less allegorically and thus pressed the passage beyond the apostle's intention. He failed to notice carefully that Paul said, 'As though God did beseech you by us'. The 'as though' should have been understood as permeating the whole meaning of the passage. Two verses later Paul qualifies the passage by saying, 'We then, as workers together with him, beseech you' (2 Cor. 6.1).
[57] Tomlinson, 'Our Christmas Message', p. 4

tributed to the diminishing influence and recognition of Christ's immediate headship in the church, for if one divine person was leaving the scene of action and another coming, accordingly, in the natural way of thinking, they both could not be present at once. This concept of the Godhead was in part what gave place to the rise of Pentecostal unitarianism ('Jesus Only' doctrine) in the early twentieth century. Oneness people overreacted against tritheism and thus fell back on ancient forms of Apollinarianism, Cerinthianism, Sabellianism, and modalism. Thus, in an effort to avoid one excess and error, a door was opened for other excesses and errors.

Figure 85

TOMLINSON AS HE APPEARED IN 1913

Tomlinson wore a beard until 1905, removing it after he moved to Cleveland. He retained his mustache until c. 1918.

After this manner, the immediate headship of Christ in and through the actions and operations of the Holy Spirit was not clearly perceived in the Church of God. Rather than interpreting Christ's ascension as the means to effect His universal presence in the church through the indwelling Spirit, Jesus was considered on a 'long journey into a far country' and would not return for an extended time, namely, until after the church got her work done on earth. Moreover, since the Holy Spirit was invisible, and since human nature and especially the carnal nature require visible images, the absence of Christ's physical presence opened the door for men to be exalted in His place. Thus the Pentecostal movement entertained and recognized all sorts of Christ substitutes in their sects and denominations, sometimes under the title of apostle or prophet, sometimes in the claims of prophetic personages like Elijah or one of the two witnesses in the book of Revelation, and sometimes under the titles of executive headship – 'General Overseer', 'Chief Bishop', and so on.[58]

---

[58] In the Tomlinson tradition alone, Homer eventually claimed to be 'The King of all Nations of Men;' Grady R. Kent took the title of 'Chief Bishop' and later claimed to be 'John the Revelator' and 'St. John II'. Tomlinson himself claimed to be the unnamed person and 'man of prophecy' in Isa. 66.2 and Jer. 30.21, besides taking the exalted title of 'General Overseer'.

Accordingly, the idea of a visible and powerful head over the church was the firm conviction and teaching of A.J. Tomlinson. Throughout his ministry he would reveal ever more clearly his thinking along these lines. He believed that Christ was actually absent, and in the vacuum of His absence he himself was divinely chosen and positioned by the Spirit to be the head of the church on earth. In this manner he tended to identify his office as General Overseer with the office Christ and *vice versa*. Thus, he did not flinch in bestowing the title of General Overseer upon Christ and adopting that title to identify also his own office. In his 1928 annual address, he declared that Christ at first 'reserved the position as General Overseer for Himself', however, before He vacated the office and ascended to the Father, He apparently arranged for the office to be filled by His brother, James.

> Jesus, the Founder and General Overseer, was the first to depart. But He finished His work and apparently arranged for and appointed His brother James to take His place as Overseer before He left ...[59]

As James was in Jesus' place and Tomlinson was in James' place, the juxtaposition naturally put Tomlinson in Christ's place as the head of the church. If this papist concept had not been made clear enough by his 1914 annual address and in subsequent addresses, the 'Declaration' made on June 27, 1923, four days after his infamous impeachment by the 'Ten Elders', made his position absolutely clear:

> Whereas, according to the Scriptures, the original and only Church of God was established with Jesus Christ as the Great Head of the Church, and after Christ ascended to His Throne on High, there was a General Overseer selected to direct the affairs of the Church under the guidance of the Holy Ghost ...[60]

Tomlinson clearly espoused the idea that another man was appointed by God to 'take Christ's place' on earth in His absence. He developed this notion in order to establish his own position as General Overseer in the present generation of the church. For after James was martyred, and the ensuing period of the 'Dark Ages' was fulfilled, the church arose in the 'last days' with a new General Overseer:

> In a little while Stephen was slain, then the Apostle James and others followed in quick succession until all of that generation were gone ...

---

[59] *HAA*, II, p. 17.
[60] Declaration made on June 27, 1923 and signed by A.J. Tomlinson (Church of God, Bureau of Information, A.J. Lawson, General Manager, Cleveland, Tennessee).

And now after an interval of fifteen hundred and ninety three years it has come our turn ...[61]

Tomlinson's Autocracy

Once the position of General Overseer had been established and Tomlinson began to operate according to its prescribed powers and responsibilities, some began to question the wisdom of assigning so much authority to a mere mortal man.[62] Gradually a large number of the ministers and members began to realize that the vast array of powers and duties accorded to the office could be filled by no one other than Christ himself. Once this began to dawn on some of the leaders, talk began to circulate as to how the church might hold the General Overseer in check and to limit the powers of his office. This led to some internal strife that soon began to surface. Even some Elders and leaders who had recommended his lifetime appointment realized that they had acted in haste, and some began to call for modifications or qualifications to be made in regard to 'the exalted position'. As early as 1912, mention had been made of dictatorial rule and lordship. J.W. Buckalew mentioned in the Ninth Assembly in November 1913 that 'Reports have gone out that Brother Tomlinson has put himself in this place to rule over us'.[63] By 1914, Tomlinson apparently had been likened to a dictator and despot by some of the ministers and members. He himself acknowledged that even in 1911 and perhaps earlier some were accusing him of setting himself up as 'a king or pope'.[64] As the tide of criticism continued to rise against his posture over the church, Tomlinson took the offensive to defend his position. His statement in his 1915 annual address is typical: 'I wish it to be distinctly understood now and forever that your General Overseer is a servant of God and of the Lord Jesus Christ ... and not a despotic ruler'.[65] Again in his annual address in 1922, he stated, 'The enemy has had his machine guns of opposition aimed at this position for years', and then he went on to reveal a rather startling rationale in regard to the

---

[61] *HAA*, II, p. 17.
[62] Were not the limitations attached to His human form – His 'fashion as a man' (Phil. 2.7) – the main reason in fact that Christ returned to the Father and subsequently sent the Holy Ghost? 'It is expedient for you that I go away: for if I go not away, the Comforter will not come unto you; but if I depart, I will send him unto you ...' (Jn 16.7-14). Jesus' human nature limited His ability to function as a visible administrator on a universal scale; it localized and therefore limited His abilities.
[63] *GAM*, p. 145.
[64] *GAM 1906-1914*, p. 136.
[65] *HAA*, I, p. 47.

death of James, the Lord's brother. He reasoned that James was martyred not for his testimony of Christ but as an act of violence 'against the position he occupied'.[66]

Between 1914 and 1916 a ground swell of concern arose over the office of General Overseer, which many perceived to approximate a 'Pentecostal pope'. An ever-increasing number began to call for a balance of power. Some suggested a counseling body that could share the burden of leadership and executive decision-making in the church. Tomlinson himself had introduced the idea of 'councilors' in his annual address in 1915 in seeking to restore the New Testament pattern and order of government for the church.[67] He based his thinking in this regard as always first on Moses and the 'church in the wilderness', that is, the position of Moses was preeminent in the church and the twelve tribal heads and seventy elders served under him. He then endeavored to reconcile that system with the twelve apostles in the New Testament church and the 'seventy' that had been appointed and sent out by Christ recorded in Luke 10.[68] Thus, the elders in the New Testament church, or 'councilors' as Tomlinson called them, were to correspond in some way with the tribal leaders and seventy elders in the Old Testament church.[69] This enabled Tomlinson to maintain that any type of counseling body – if the Assembly should adopt one – would be subservient to the General Overseer, for, accordingly, the General Overseer's position in the New Testament church was the same as Moses' position in the Old Testament church.

We have no reason to doubt the sincerity of Tomlinson's claim that, in suggesting some type of counseling body of elders to assist in leadership and decision-making in the church, he was seeking to discover and restore the 'perfect system of government' for the church; but it is apparent also that his interpretation of the elders or 'councilors' in the New Testament who were to 'cluster around "James" [the General Overseer]' was to quiet some of the criticism then making the rounds that his position and authority approximated that of a dictator or pope.

---

[66] *HAA*, I, p. 201.

[67] *HAA*, I, pp. 54-56.

[68] In regard to establishing the church on the basis of the government and pattern of the 'church in the wilderness', or the Old Testament church, this was as much the conviction and teaching of M.S. Lemons and F.J. Lee as it was Tomlinson, though the influence of the latter was greater. See addresses by Lemons – 'Government the Principal of the Church (*GAM 1906-1914*, pp. 204-206), and an address by Lee – 'Confirmation of Actions of Past Assemblies' (*GAM 1906-1914*, pp. 180-89.

[69] See Exod. 24.1, 9; Num. 11.16-25, and Tomlinson's references in his 1915 annual address.

Council of Elders

Tomlinson had left open for further discussion the precise identity of the elders or 'councilors' who had formed James' 'cabinet'; but he had pretty much narrowed the number to either twelve or seventy. For whatever reason, the Assembly in 1916 preferred the number twelve and resolved to create a twelve man council to help guide and administrate the affairs of the growing organization, and to help limit and balance the inherent powers of Tomlinson's office, that is, to hold in check the General Overseer's tendency to act unilaterally.[70] Accordingly, the Council of Elders by March of the next year was fully formed.[71]

Tomlinson, however, did not perceive the purpose of the Council of Elders in the same way that some of the twelve elders did, that is, as an arm of government to help balance out the office of General Overseer and to guide and govern the church. Rather, he saw the Council of Elders as merely an advisory council that 'sat before him' and which he might call into session 'when he deemed it necessary on account of some important business pending'.[72] Again, according to Tomlinson, the Council was 'only meant ... for a strength and stay for the General Overseer', and thus any 'measures framed [by the Council] for presentation to the Assembly' necessarily had to come 'by and through the General Overseer'.[73] In a word, the 'counselors were not a body unto themselves to represent the people, but selected to serve as counselors and assistants to the General Overseer'. He did admit that the Council was appointed to exercise certain authority, but it is clear that he understood the Council's actions to be always subject to his approval; for according to Tomlinson, 'theocratic government' depended on the anointed General Overseer being able finally to govern and act unilaterally directly under God, and thus always to have the final word in matters of faith and divine government. He based this on James' dictum in the Jerusalem council in Acts 15, 'Wherefore my sentence is' (v. 19), and also according to the 'mediatory role of Moses' in the church in the desert.

Tomlinson at first endeavored to work with the Council, but soon felt his autocratic style encroached upon.[74] Even from the outset in 1917 he resented the method by which the members were appointed.

---

[70] *GAM*, 12th Assembly, 1916, pp. 241, 242; see also *Cyclopedic Index of Assembly Minutes*, 1906-1949, 'Bible Plans of Order: Section 2', pp. 62, 63.
[71] *GAM*, 13th Assembly, pp. 275-76.
[72] *HAA*, I, p. 68.
[73] *HAA*, I, p.118.
[74] *HAA*, I, pp. 206-208.

The plan called for the General Overseer to appoint two of the Council members and the three together to appoint the remaining ten.⁷⁵ He accepted this plan but only against what he believed was his better judgment, for he and some others thought it more in line with the Scriptures for the General Overseer unilaterally to appoint all of the members of the Council. He explained later,

> At the time, some were in favor of following the plan shown plainly in the Bible as they thought, viz., the General Overseer select his own counselors, but others, who reasoned that in order to save the General Overseer from certain criticism and accusations then going the rounds, thought it best to have it the way that it was finally agreed upon.⁷⁶

In his annual address in 1922 he waxed bolder, declaring that the plan implemented in 1917 was un-Scriptural – 'No trace of such a method can be found between the lids of the Sacred Lawbook'. He insisted therefore that the plan be modified in favor of the General Overseer making the appointments for the sake of 'theocracy', that is, that God should be allowed to make the appointments through the anointed General Overseer. Oddly enough, he then drew a parallel between the President of the United States being allowed to unilaterally appoint his cabinet and the General Overseer being allowed to appoint the Council of Elders.

> The President of the United States of America has been honored by a republic with more rights and authority than that. It is in his power to select every member of his cabinet. Men may be recommended to him by others, but it is his to select from these recommended. I can't think of it being Scriptural for the General Overseer of the great Church of God to have less authority in selecting his counselors than the President of the United States.⁷⁷

It was strange enough that in attempting to establish a theocracy Tomlinson pointed to the democratic-republican system of the United States, but he also failed to point out that most of the prominent members of the President's cabinet are approved by the Senate, and further that the President, Vice-President, and the whole Presidential cabinet are held in check to one degree or another in the exercise of their powers by the House and Senate.

---

⁷⁵ *HAA*, I, p. 207.
⁷⁶ *HAA*, I, p. 207.
⁷⁷ *HAA*, I, pp. 207-208.

Figure 86

COUNCIL OF ELDERS

Back row, from left: S.O. Gillaspie; M.S. Haynes; J.S. Llewellyn; S.W. Latimer; T.L. McLain; J.B. Ellis; E.J. Boehmer; Front row, from left: T.S. Payne; M.S. Lemons; George T. Brouayer; F.J. Lee; Sam C. Perry; Tomlinson far right kneeling.

Having accepted the inevitability of the Council of Twelve and the selection process, Tomlinson's political savvy moved him immediately after the formation of the Council to use it to heighten further the already exalted image of his position. He drew a parallel between Christ and the Twelve Apostles and himself and the Twelve Elders, again creating a Christological allusion to the office of General Overseer.

> When Jesus was here He called twelve men to be with Him, and when James, the Lord's brother, was called and chosen to occupy the chief executive's chair it appears that ... there were elders ... who sat before him in council and deliberation.[78]

It was the illusion of a powerful mythological office, and of himself as the one especially anointed to fill it, that created the rub between himself and some of the leading men in the church. The Council of Elders was bound therefore to create still more friction in the developing

---

[78] *HAA*, I, p. 68.

saga, not only because there were strong men on the Council who would stand up to Tomlinson, but who would inevitably be tempted with material advantages and position and power, and, as a matter of course, would jockey against one another for preeminence; indeed, some had already shown a weakness for temporal power and a propensity toward mammon.

The creation of the office of General Overseer with its array of powers and lifetime appointment in 1914, and the creation of the Council of Elders in 1916, show how far the church had moved away from Spurling's vision in 1886. The pendulum had swung from one extreme to the other. By 1917, Tomlinson and the chief men in the church were virtually paving an Episcopal road back to Rome. Tomlinson at that point was fully aware of the radically new direction the church was taking. He intended it so. In his 1916 annual address, he acknowledged,

> We have been following too closely, I fear, after the idea of each church being an independent government of its own and bordering on to [*sic*] independent democracy instead of real Bible theocracy. But there is a company of men assembled who are determined to uncover the entire principles of God's government. Traditions, former practices and customs, ideas and opinions must be dispensed with and all such give place to the open Word of God.[79]

The question that preoccupied the General Assemblies between 1911 and 1923 was not so much 'if' or 'how' the church should be ruled but 'who' should rule it. There were few leaders left in those days who saw any virtue in Spurling's Baptist-like theology of church government, particularly in his warnings against centralization and Episcopal hierarchy; indeed there were apparently few prominent men remaining who were even aware of Spurling's contribution to the restoration of the church between 1886 and 1903. His congregational principles were thus all but forgotten by 1917 and this disconnect with Spurling opened the door for the development of a highly centralized system and a hierarchical structure. Thus, though Spurling's system admittedly was inadequate and fostered a chaotic individualism, Tomlinson's and the Elder's system was virtually paving a road back to Rome. Tomlinson in particular saw no middle ground upon which to stand between Spurling's system and the papal-type Episcopal system that he was constructing. What was being sacrificed in the radical turn of events was the principle of individual dignity and freedom, and the collective wisdom and spirituality of the entire body of the church. A true biblical theocracy was there

---

[79] *HAA*, I, pp. 70-71.

somewhere between the two extremes; but Tomlinson and his followers unwittingly were being guided by the same spirit of error that had permeated the church in the second and third centuries, that had led the church fathers to pave the road to Rome.

Spurling had warned against 'political ecclesiasticism' in *The Lost Link*.[80] While he believed that all Christians and churches in Christ should be united or 'unionized', he clung to the principles of the independence of the local church and the preeminence of individual conscience. Any counsel and coordination between churches were by mutual consent in the spirit of brotherly love, and therefore no ruling authority among and between the churches was necessary. He maintained that a corporate system of churches, united together by a centralized council or conference and authorized to impose binding laws and rules, would negate or impair freedom, equality, and real Christian fellowship; further, where a highly centralized system of churches was effected, carnal and ambitious men would naturally aspire to headship of the organization. He further maintained that this would encourage jealousy, strife, malice, and every degenerate and evil desire. Ministers would see each other with envious eyes in varied ranks and elevations and with inferior and superior stations and positions, which in turn would lead again to the investiture of a pope and an Episcopal hierarchy.

We have noticed that Spurling was influenced by Baptist historian, G.H. Orchard, particularly in his *History of the Baptists*. He cites him several times in *The Lost Link* to support his warnings against man-made councils, creeds, and church hierarchies.[81] In regard to the latter, Orchard wrote,

> The officer formerly known by the name of elder, bishop, or presbyter (terms synonymous in the New Testament) became now distinguished by the elevation of the bishop above his brethren, and each of the above terms was carried out into a distinction of the places of the Christian church. The minister, whose congregation increased from the suburbs of his town and vicinage around, considered the parts from which his charge emanated as territories marking the boundary of his authority; and all those presbyters sent by him into surrounding stations ... acknowledged the pastor ... as bishop of the district ... Associations of ministers and churches, which at first were formed in Greece, became common throughout the empire. These mutual unions for the management of spiritual affairs led to the

---

[80] Spurling, *Lost Link*, pp. 18, 22, 23, 34, 35.
[81] Spurling, *Lost Link*, pp. 34, 35, and cf. Orchard, *History*, pp. 22, 110, 175.

choice of a president, which aided distinction amongst the ministers. In those degenerating times, aspiring men saw each other in varied elevations; consequently jealousy, ambition, and strife ensued, and every evil work followed. The ... distinctions and superior stations ... at last became vested in the metropolitan minister. Places of distinction to which ministers were eligible, prompted the ambitious to use every device to gain the ascendant position ...[82]

Figure 87

FIRST SESSION OF ELDERS' COUNCIL – OCTOBER 4-17, 1917

Standing, left to right: M.S. Lemons; T.S. Payne; T.L. McLain; F.J. Lee; Sam C. Perry; George T. Bouayer; E.J. Boehmer; J.B. Ellis; S.W. Latimer; S.O. Gillaspie; J.S. Llewellyn; M.S. Haynes; seated in front: General Overseer, A.J. Tomlinson; Secretary, Blanche Koon.

It was thus that the Baptist tradition and Orchard in particular formed Spurling's view of church polity and government, namely, a radical congregationalism and rugged individualism. Consistent with his view of church government and polity, he harbored also a low opinion of a man's ability – even a spiritual man's ability – to hold a superior office in a hierarchical structure without becoming corrupted with pride and self-exaltation.

Even if Spurling was extreme in his views, still there is something to be gained in considering his suspicions of a church hierarchy, for much

---

[82] Orchard, *History*, pp. 28-29.

of what followed in the Church of God between 1916 and 1923 succumbed to the very evils that he had warned against, namely, envious and ambitious men seeking for power and superior stations in the church, who in turn corrupt the government and discipline of the church and ruin the sweet fellowship of the Spirit that was established initially between the ministers and members.

Cleveland – Seat of the 'Theocratic Government'

At the same time that Tomlinson was establishing his concept of 'theocratic government' and locating it particularly in himself – that is, in the one whom the Holy Ghost had appointed and anointed to be General Overseer – he was also establishing Cleveland as the geographical seat of divine government. Again, his thinking along these lines was typically Sandfordian, for the Shiloh commander had instilled deeply in Tomlinson's mind two indispensable principles during his attendance at the 'Holy Ghost and Us' Bible School, namely, that in order to establish a stable and effective church movement two factors are necessary: first, the establishment of 'the man of God' with unquestionable authority and, second, the establishment of a 'divinely chosen center' or headquarters for the movement.[83]

According to Sandford, and by extension according to Tomlinson, a headquarters was necessary for the purpose of control by the 'chief executive' or 'the man of God'. In order to convince his followers of this concept, Sandford always went to the Bible, but especially to the Old Economy under Moses and Joshua. The place that God had chosen for 'the whole congregation of Israel' was 'Shiloh' (Josh. 18.1), hence the name of Sandford's headquarters. Later the headquarters for the 'church in the wilderness' under Joshua would be moved to Jerusalem, a few miles distance from Shiloh. Always under military motifs, Sandford showed that in order for a movement to be successful in its conquest to evangelize the world and unify God's people in one concrete community, it must have a center like Israel under Joshua. This was always without exception God's way of working. 'And now they proceed to do what God always does as a means to the continuation of a victory – they proceed to establish a center'.[84]

It was thus that Sandford declared, unapologetically, that this 'center' was necessary 'to control the people'. He did not flinch in his use of mil-

---

[83] Sandford, *Art of War*, p. 136.
[84] Sandford, *Art of War*, p. 136.

itary language: it was as natural to his way of thinking as pastoral was to Jesus' and John's way of thinking.

> Never until God gets a center from which He can work has He been able to control the people who believe in Him. Satan had a 'seat' in the time of the seven early churches and God Almighty has a seat on earth where He plants His authority and where He authorizes men to act for Him.[85]

Once 'Shiloh' had been established as the place where God put His name, there could be no question as to the authority of the man of God in charge – the man whom God authorizes to 'act for Him'. Thus all schisms and divisions must be denounced in order to maintain the unity of God's people. Ever the commander and general, Sandford taught his followers to fight to maintain a strict uniformity and obedience to headquarters objectives and orders. He compared the tribes of Israel with the denominations of Christianity and denounced the divisions:

> The secret of awful failure today all over the world is a tribe of Methodists here, a tribe of Baptists there, a half tribe of Presbyterians yonder, a little company of holiness people, and a few mission workers, and so forth here and there until the whole mass of Christianity is divided up into thousands of little cliques, sects, and divisions, while God's Word solemnly declares, 'There shall be one Church, one Body'.[86]

Then, in accordance with his craft, he pointed to his exclusive church as 'The Restoration of Unity' and the headquarters of the company of the elect.

> I am so glad He has planted His name on earth once more; and He is slowly but surely securing a company of people who say, 'We will not have fellowship whatever with any company of people that refuse to stand for 'one Church' – 'one faith, one baptism, one God and Father of us all', and 'one Word by which we go, the Scriptures, to make us perfect' ...[87]
>
> AND THERE WILL BE ONE CHURCH, FAIR, CLEAR AND TERRIBLE, AND ONE LORD TO RULE OVER IT, WHILE HE HIMSELF WILL APPOINT APOSTLES, PROPHETS, PASTORS

---

[85] Sandford, *Art of War*, p. 137.
[86] Sandford, *Art of War*, p. 142.
[87] Sandford, *Art of War*, p. 142.

AND TEACHERS TO CONTROL THAT CHURCH. THANK GOD FOR THE HARBINGER OF GLAD DAYS AHEAD. [88]

After Tomlinson had moved to Cleveland, the influence of Sandford's teaching in regard to a center for the church began to emerge more plainly in his teaching and preaching. And this became more evident after the General Assemblies began to be held there in 1907. Tomlinson explained in his sixth annual address in 1915,

> But the all important matter that concerns us is to discover that system and order that prevailed in the time of the apostles and made them able to so expand and publish abroad that every creature under heaven heard the preaching of this glorious gospel. We are truly under obligations to discover and put in operation that system of government that was operated so effectively by James and the apostles of our Lord and Saviour Jesus Christ and their zealous, self-sacrificing co-workers ... From the limited history given in the Bible we glean a few thoughts that are worthy of consideration. The first point to which we wish to call attention is that the center, or seat of government, was Jerusalem. 'Beginning at Jerusalem', is a familiar term used by our Lord Himself. The preaching was to have its beginning there; the Holy Ghost was to be given there; they were to begin their witnessing there. All this was fulfilled just as Jesus had given orders. A little later when the persecutions arose so tremendously, and the church at Jerusalem was the main target for the enemy, the members 'were all scattered abroad throughout the regions of Judaea and Samaria, EXCEPT THE APOSTLES. See the pillars of the Church clinging invincibly to their seat of government. They could die there, but they would not be driven away ... As long as the apostles lived, and for some years following Jerusalem was recognized as the one center around which clustered all churches far and near ... In the history of Israel under the first three kings, Saul, David and Solomon, the kingdom was ONE and had ONE seat of government. The place was changed, but the government was ONE. Saul had his capital at Gibeah, and David moved it to Jerusalem. But when the kingdom was divided under Rehoboam and Jeroboam, then there were two kingdoms. The one that revolted and pulled away from Jerusalem was designated as the northern kingdom. The place where God had set His name was at Jerusalem. Thither came the worshipers year after year to present themselves before God ... Under Solomon's reign

---

[88] Sandford, *Art of War*, p. 143.

there was instituted the complete temple worship patterned after the plan given Moses for the tabernacle service. One capital city and one place of worship ...[89]

Having established in the minds of the ministers and members that Jerusalem was the center of government for the New Testament church, Tomlinson proceeded to create the impression that Cleveland was the 'Jerusalem' for the last day's Church of God. The Jerusalem in Palestine was thus merely a symbol for the center of the church, so that wherever the ruling government of the Church of God was, there was 'Jerusalem'. But Tomlinson was not alone in this presumption, Lemons and other prominent ministers believed that Cleveland had been set apart and exalted by God to be the center for God's church in the last days.[90]

After the disruption in 1923, Tomlinson would further develop the idea of a divinely-chosen center of government for the church. He cited Isa. 49.13-23 and other passages to support the view that the New Testament church having been established in Palestine in the first century, was predicted in prophecy to 'fall away' and be covered with spiritual darkness (Isa. 60.2; 2 Thess. 2.2-8; Rev. 2.5; *et al.*) and then be restored centuries later in a land 'far away' from the 'land of [its] destruction' (Isa. 49.19; cf. also 52.1-10; 59.19-21; 60. 1-5, 14, 21; 61.2-5; 62.1-7; *et al.*).

> We are cutting ourselves loose from [traditions] as fast as we can ... to launch out into the deep as did Christopher Columbus when he left the shores of Europe and started on his western journey ... And by his venturing out into the unknown against all the influences that would have held him back, the 'new world' was discovered upon which it was destined that the Lord's Church should be rebuilded upon its own heap. And how great is the wisdom of God in reestablishing His Church – His Holy Arm – in a country that has been attracting the eyes of the people of all nations and climes for many centuries ... Is it not a fact that all nations of the world are almost involuntarily looking to the United States of America for examples, for patterns, for aid and assistance in one way or another? Why, then, is it not perfectly logical, as well as Scriptural, for this to be the country in which the ENSIGN of the Church of God is to be lifted up first? This is a long distance from the place where Isaiah prophesied when he said the ensign would be lifted up some place afar off from

---

[89] *HAA*, I, pp. 51-53.
[90] It is likely, however, that Lemons and other ministers were merely parroting Tomlinson's view.

where he was when he uttered the prophecy ... There are other Scriptures that indicate that Palestine is not to be the place for the capital of the world for the Church of God in the last days ... The wise men came to Jerusalem to find Jesus, but they had to go down to the little town of Bethlehem before they found Him ... Perhaps it is not so contrary to reason after all that God would choose the little city of Cleveland, Tenn., USA to be the capital of the world for the Church of God in the latter days, and from thence stretch forth His strong and mighty arm to the nations'.[91]

Tomlinson made it clear to his followers that he believed Cleveland was chosen by God to be the world headquarters for the Church of God. He had billboard signs posted at each end of the city advertising 'Cleveland: World Capitol for the Church of God'. On April 16, 1935 he declared in a speech to the Chamber of Commerce that it seems to be 'the Lord's plan and will for Cleveland to be regarded ... as the capital of the world for the Church of God'. He went on to exult in the growth and development of the church, saying,

> This is not a little despised work that is being done in a corner. Behold it is worldwide, and already declarations have been made that our flag shall float over every country of the world ... In conclusion I shout, hurrah for our Cleveland, the capital of the world for the Church of God.[92]

In his annual address that year in September, he said, 'It is evident that from this time Cleveland will become more prominent in being recognized as the capital of the world as we continue our great work by means of the new and improved methods of procedure ...'[93]

A Developing Exclusivity

There was a propensity toward exclusiveness in the church in the very beginning, based on the principles upon which Spurling had established Christian Union: namely, 1) that the church is visible, 2) that it is God's government in the earth, and 3) that God is calling all of His children into one Christian Union. Further, Spurling had emphasized as early as 1908 in an Assembly address that there is 'a germ of life in the true

---

[91] *HAA*, II, pp. 236-37.
[92] *HAA*, II, p. 238.
[93] *HAA*, II, p. 240.

Church that is not in men's organizations'.⁹⁴ Still, Spurling had managed to avoid a strict exclusivity on the basis that the church in this present dispensation is *something-in-the-making*. He used the 'the temple of old' to illustrate his point, that is, that just as the temple was not complete until every stone was cut and fitted in its place, so the church is not complete until 'every stone [or saint] is ... fit perfectly in the church triumphant'.⁹⁵ In his theology of the church, exclusiveness would be realized therefore only when the church had successfully fulfilled her mission in this world; or, in other words, it was more or less synonymous with the church's perfection and eschatological fulfillment.

Tomlinson, however, did not see the church as *something-in-the-making*, but rather as a government as real as the government of the United States'; and, as such, once constituted, it was as complete as it would ever be.⁹⁶ The addition of new citizens did not modify the United States in the least, neither did new additions make the Church of God any more or less the church. It was therefore inevitable that exclusivity would be defined ever more narrowly as the church progressed under Tomlinson's guidance. By 1912, the sentiments of the overseer of North Carolina, C.R. Curtis, in his report to the Assembly, were on the lips of the majority of the ministers and members, namely, that the Church of God is 'the true and only church'.⁹⁷

As the church increased in numbers and material assets and developed a degree of political sophistication, a sense of institutional pride swelled in the breasts of the ministers and members. And this mind-set increased proportionately with the growth and prestige of the organization. In time, Tomlinson would declare as boldly as Sandford had at Shiloh that the Church of God of which he was General Overseer was the exclusive custodian of the whole truth, and that all other Christians and Christian groups would eventually look to his corporate fellowship for the full light of the Gospel. This attitude in Tomlinson and his fol-

---

⁹⁴ *GAM 1906-1914*, p. 45.

⁹⁵ Spurling, *Lost Link*, pp. 18, 19.

⁹⁶ 'The Church of God is just as real as the government of the United States. Its laws are on the statute books, they can be obeyed or violated' (Evans, *God's Anointed – Prophet of Wisdom*, p. 89). Tomlinson said that he had argued this point with Spurling and Bryant and others in the Holiness Church at Camp Creek on the morning that he joined the church on June 13, 1903. 'I then asked if they were willing to take me in with the understanding that it is the Church of God – not going to be but is the Church of God' (Evans, *God's Anointed – Prophet of Wisdom*, p. 41; see also pp. 33, 42-43; and Tomlinson, *LGC*, pp. 68-72). Obviously, he was taking issue with Spurling's doctrine that the church is something-in-the-making (Spurling, *Lost Link*, pp. 18-19).

⁹⁷ *GAM 1906-1914*, p. 128.

lowers would become more pronounced after the disruption in the early 1920s,[98] and even more so after the Burger Mountain tradition developed in the early 1940s, which we will elaborate upon more fully in Volume II.[99]

We have noticed that there was a certain inclination toward an exclusive ecclesiology present in the church from the beginning, inherent in the idea that the church is a visible government in the earth. But once Tomlinson combined visibility with universality, and defined the church in terms of a corporation or institution -- as something already completed – the development of an exclusive ecclesiology was inevitable. But more so, when Tomlinson began to perceive and define the church as a centrally controlled institution, with a solitary and unique leader positioned at the apex of a pyramid of administrative authority, exclusivity was unavoidable. Thus, the Church of God's strict exclusiveness developed proportionately with the development of the office of General Overseer and the ecclesial system correlated to it.

There were ways, of course, to explain the church in terms of its visible and universal nature without pressing so hard on the idea of exclusiveness, and without compromising with the myth of a spiritual or invisible church; but Tomlinson and the other leaders at that time apparently had not advanced that far in their thinking; or perhaps it was because they had acquired such deep affections and jealousy for the prophetic vision of the church that they became unwilling to entertain a slightly modified view. To them, the church was a beautiful, visible bride – 'the only one of her mother'[100] – and they were bound and determined to love her and to be faithful to her!

---

[98] The transition from his former Quakerism to a fully ecumenical commitment is clearly represented in an early message that was published in *The Bridegroom's Messenger*, the paper inaugurated and edited by G.B. Cashwell in Atlanta beginning in 1907. Entitled 'Unity of the Faith', his message emphasized the visible unity of believers based primarily on Eph. 4.13 and Jn 17.20, 21. Yet Tomlinson was not sure at that time whether this unity could be obtained in this life; only that one should strive for it (*TBM* [April 1, 1908], p. 2). The influence of Sandford's teachings and also elements of his former Quakerism are apparent in this message.

[99] The Burger Mountain tradition was the basis for the development of the world-famous 216 acre 'Fields of the Wood' Bible Park located in Cherokee County, North Carolina.

[100] Song of Solomon 6.10.

Growing Dissatisfaction

Despite the fact that Tomlinson, Llewellyn, Lee, Lemons, and a number of other prominent leaders were enthralled with the numerical growth and political and material developments in the church, quite a number of other ministers were disturbed by the church's focus on these developments. Among these were Sam C. Perry, J.L. Scott, and A.H. Bryans, the former a member of the powerful Council of Twelve, the latter two prominent bishops serving on Assembly committees. First of all, they rejected categorically the concept of the church as a political or mechanical system, and especially the spirit in which this concept was being promoted and pushed through in the church. Beginning about 1911 Tomlinson became preoccupied and captivated by the idea that there was a 'perfect system of government' in the New Testament, and once it was discovered and implemented the church could then be perfected and complete her mission in the world. His comments in his annual address in 1915 were typical of his thinking along these lines:

> We have given some time in studying government and system, but at this Assembly we see the need of combining the two [to study] systematic government. In God's universe He ... governs all His worlds and planets with their suns and moons, but ... a collision has never been known. We feel safe in saying that He has planned for no less order and system for His Church, so there will be no collision or clashes among the members. This perfect order is indicated by Paul in his first epistle to the church at Corinth. Under the ... imperfect system we have been following we are obliged to confess with a feeling of embarrassment that there have been some slight clashes among the members, and even the ministers, which have brought some reproach upon the dear and blessed Church that we love so well. This ought not to be. We are here to learn, if possible, that perfect system of government by which this may be avoided. We want to learn how every member can stay in his place so perfectly that, like all the planets of God's universe in their orbits, there will be such perfect harmony that there will not even be any danger of collision. We fully believe this perfect order and system is marked out in the Bible we love and cherish so much. God help us to find it. I say again from the very deepest recesses of my heart, God help us to find it. I believe I voice the sentiments of the throbbing hearts in this presence when I make one more earnest appeal to the Source of knowledge, wisdom, and

power, and say, God help us find it, and then be willing to follow it when it is discovered.[101]

He pushed this theme incessantly in his annual addresses and in the *Evangel* endeavoring to create in the saints a hunger to discover and establish the 'perfect system'. But the more he pushed this vision, the more it was resented and rejected by men like Perry, Scott, and Bryans. Again, not only was the principle resented but also the spirit that drove it. Tomlinson's comment in his 1916 annual address was doubtlessly aimed at men like Perry and Scott. In calling for submission and cooperation with his plan and vision for the 'perfect money system', he said, 'There is one thing we can all do if nothing else. We can be men and women for God, instead of a crowd of spoiled babies, crying around and whining because we cannot have our own pettish ways ... Perfect organization and concerted action will save souls, and house them in the great Church of God ... No unity, no organization, no system, no obedience, no concerted action will damn souls in the abyss of everlasting punishment by the millions'.[102]

Again, we can sympathize somewhat with Tomlinson's desire to see a well ordered and disciplined organization so that 'great things can be accomplished for God', but he, as well as Lee, Lemons, Llewellyn, and others pushed the idea to the extreme. What was sacrificed in searching for the 'perfect system' was the original love and fellowship of the ministers and members. How could men who were apparently so deeply spiritual and endowed with spiritual wisdom not see that Christian unity is essentially a spiritual matter; and that wherever spirituality and consecration are lacking, no institution or outward structure is sufficient to fill the vacuum? But that seems to have been the mindset of Tomlinson and those in harness with him at that critical juncture in the church's development. The result was that institutionalism trumped spirituality and genuine Christian fellowship, and consequently the ministers and members failed to continue to 'endeavor to keep the unity of the Spirit in the bond of peace'. Tomlinson's vision of a 'perfect well-ordered system' tended to supplant the need to depend on the presence and graces of the Holy Ghost to unify and inspire the church. This was the complaint of men like Perry and Scott, and before these men had come along it had been from the beginning the stern warning of R.G. Spurling.

> The Lord promised to give His Spirit to His people and what we want is perfect love to God and each other and perfect liberty ... Liberty of

---

[101] *HAA*, I, p. 57.
[102] *HAA*, I, pp. 75-76.

the soul is the breath and element of that religion inculcated in the New Testament and has been and will be preserved only by those who descend from all governments devised by human policy ... Liberty is what God's people want and must have it at any cost or hypocrisy will soon invade the church.[103]

The Case of Sam C. Perry

Samuel Clement Perry (1875-1960) rose rapidly to prominence after he joined the church in 1909.[104] Having had considerable experience in the ministry in the Holiness tradition, Tomlinson licensed him on the spot as a bishop during the great Pleasant Grove Camp Meeting that he conducted in Durant, Florida in May 1909. Comparatively well-educated,[105] Perry immediately became instrumental in helping to inaugurate the *Evangel* in 1910, and served in 1910-1916 as a field editor (special correspondent) and member of the Editorial and Publications Board. He was also a prolific writer and contributed regularly to the *Evangel*. Spurling, who got acquainted with him shortly after he joined the church, considered him and Tomlinson to be the 'topmost flowers' in the church 'both in general ability and spirituality'.[106] In 1911 he was appointed with six others to serve in the newly created office of state overseer, being assigned to Kentucky in 1911-1913. In 1916 he was appointed as overseer of Florida, and in 1917 was selected to serve at the same time on the newly created Council of Elders.

Notwithstanding his rise to prominence, Perry had become increasingly dissatisfied and unsettled by the institutionalization of the church under Tomlinson. He held virtually a congregational view of church government and polity, and thus disagreed with centralized authority, particularly the militaristic image of Cleveland as a 'headquarters'. But he especially despised the growing concept of exclusivity and what he perceived to be an ever-increasing sense of institutional pride. And he was

---

[103] Spurling, *Lost Link*, p. 42

[104] According to Tomlinson, who was the principle speaker in those powerful Pentecostal meetings, 64 joined the church on May 28th, and about 35 more on May 29th (Tomlinson, *Diary*, May 28-29, 1909). While in Florida, he also established churches in Tampa and Jacksonville and received about 70 more into the church.

[105] The assumption by Conn that Perry was the first college man in the church (Conn, *Mighty Army*, pp. 122-23) is inaccurate. J.B. Mitchell had attended Oberlin College in the 1850s and had been taught by Charles Finney.

[106] 'Letter to Perry', July 23, 1919, p. 2 ('Sam Perry File', ZACG Archives).

not shy to point out his disappointment in some of the leaders who gloated over and exaggerated reports of success.[107]

At some point, Perry had become disgruntled and disagreeable, if not embittered, particularly against Tomlinson and some of the leaders on the Elders' Council. This may be seen in the tone and content of his four-page tract that he published in May 1919: 'BEFORE A.J. TOMLINSON AND THE ELDERS' COUNCIL'. He resented Tomlinson's cheerleading style of leadership and his boasting in regard to the accomplishments of the Church of God; charging that reports in the *Evangel* were exaggerated and, even if true, were 'unwise, misleading and out of keeping with the meek and humble spirit of Jesus'.[108] He also categorically rejected the fanaticism of Tomlinson and Lee and others in regard to faith healing, particularly the assertion that 'A man who has a physician when sick is an infidel'.[109]

Perry's disillusionment and disgruntled disposition seems to have grown proportionately with the rise of Tomlinson's popularity and the office of General Overseer, particularly after 1912, and also with the increasing emphasis on the church as a concrete visible organization to the exclusion of an invisible or spiritual church. He especially despised the theological definition of the church held by Tomlinson, Lee, Lemons, and others, namely, that 'CHURCH MEANS GOVERNMENT'.[110]

We may be fairly certain that one of the voices that criticized the developing office of General Overseer after 1912, comparing the office to that of a 'king or pope', was Perry's.[111] After being called to account by Tomlinson and the Council of Elders in May 1919 for his unruliness and insubordination, he recorded his response to the charges in his tract,

---

[107] Sam C. Perry, 'BEFORE A.J. TOMLINSON AND THE ELDERS' COUNCIL', pp. 3-4 ('Sam Perry File', ZACG Archives).

[108] Perry, 'BEFORE A.J. TOMLINSON', p. 3.

[109] Perry, 'BEFORE A.J. TOMLINSON', p. 3.

[110] 'I object to the idea that the Church of God or body of Jesus is only a VISIBLE THING that a man can organize. I believe in the great invisible body of Jesus that embraces all the faithful from the beginning until Jesus comes ... I object to the idea that CHURCH MEANS GOVERNMENT ... (Perry, 'BEFORE A.J. TOMLINSON', pp. 1-2).

[111] We may assume this for the following reasons: 1) because of the objections he raised to the office recorded in 'BEFORE A.J. TOMLINSON', p. 2) because when most of the other prominent leaders in the church, e.g. Lemons and Lee, were endorsing and praising Tomlinson and the office, Perry was noticeably silent; 3) because Perry was a man of bold convictions and had remained to a great degree under the influence of the free holiness church tradition.

'BEFORE A.J. TOMLINSON AND THE ELDER'S COUNCIL'.[112] In regard to Tomlinson and the office of General Overseer, he wrote,

> I object to a system whose head (one man) must have a full financial report monthly from all the churches and ministers, but who makes no such reports of his affairs ... I object to a system with one man for a life time as its head, over all finances, ministers, and officers, and every interest of the church ... I object to a general overseer and editor of our church paper having authority to always do and say whatever he pleases, without question, while others have no such privileges. Are the interests of Jesus safe in such hands?[113]

He proceeded in the defense of his actions to attempt to dismantle the whole ecclesiological and practical framework of the church that had developed under Tomlinson's leadership, namely, the office of General Overseer and the system correlated to it; but more particularly he opposed the ever-tightening centralization of authority at 'headquarters' and the developing Episcopal hierarchy that culminated at its highest point in Tomlinson's exalted position, and in Tomlinson himself.[114]

On reflection, it is clear that Perry had some legitimate complaints, particularly in regard to the fanatical tendencies existing at the time and the rigid way the government and discipline of the church were being developed, and also in regard to the harshness and lack of genuine affection expressed on the part of some of the church's chief officers. In a lengthy letter almost certainly written by R.G. Spurling[115] dated July 23,

---

[112] Perry's complaints are systematically laid out in this four-page tract, which records the charges made against him by the Elders' Council, and his defense during his trial on May 14, 1919 in Cleveland.

[113] Perry, 'BEFORE A.J. TOMLINSON', p. 4.

[114] Church of God of Prophecy historian, Charles T. Davidson, reported that he and Bishop Vernon H. Smith visited Perry near Portsmouth, Virginia in the summer of 1934, and that he was at that time still bitter toward Tomlinson and those in sympathy with him (*Upon This Rock*, I, p. 504).

[115] This letter consisting of 21 handwritten pages bears unquestionably the marks of Spurling's teachings, fatherly command, pastoral disposition – particularly in regard to love and gentle moral suasion – and his style of composition. But unquestionably the letter was rewritten by the hand of A.J. Tomlinson. Why? We suggest three possible reasons: 1) Though Spurling was a man of deep thought and exhibited mature spiritual judgment, his grammar and spelling were atrocious, on the level of a second-grader: and thus Tomlinson endeavored to make his composition more readable; 2) Tomlinson had great admiration and respect for Spurling, holding him as a father, and knew also that his opinions carried weight with a number of others in the church; 3) Tomlinson considered the letter to be rather personal, certainly not an open letter, and thus did not hand it over to his secretary to be typewritten, intending perhaps to share it with the members on the Elders' Council who had committed themselves to work with utmost confidentiality, a

1919 and addressed to Perry and Tomlinson in response to Perry's tract, 'BEFORE A.J. TOMLINSON AND THE ELDERS' COUNCIL', the writer, under great heaviness because of the developing divisions and bitter arguments going on in the church, points out the wrongs done by both sides, and calls for restitutions and reconciliation to be made on the basis of love and forgiveness. As a loving and pleading father, Spurling reproves Perry for his failure to cooperate with the General Overseer and the Elders' Council, and for distorting the doctrine of the visible church and separating himself from the fellowship of it. Conversely, he chides Tomlinson and the Elders for governing the church with an 'iron hand' instead of love and tender affections, and for defining the church too strictly in terms of government, and also for not conducting (according to the complaints in Perry's tract), the council meeting on May 14, 1919 according to fair and just principles.

Tomlinson responded to Spurling's letter, and apparently convinced him that Perry's complaints were distorted and slanted to justify his rebellion; and, while he acknowledged that mistakes were made and a harsh spirit was sometimes manifested at headquarters by certain Elders on the Council which we may assume included Llewellyn and Lemons,[116] he maintained that he and the majority of the Elders had counseled with Perry in grace and with meekness in trying to reconcile him. Spurling responded to Tomlinson in a letter dated August 2, 1919:

> I received your good letter today and read it through with special care, and was not surprised at your attitude on the different questions referred to in my joint letter to you and Brother Perry ... As I said before, Brother Tomlinson, I was sure I knew where you stood on every part of the questions involved before, and now I know it, and am happy to know it. There is no further chance for doubt. I believe every member of the Church that has the work at heart has perfect

---

commitment that had prompted Perry's charge of 'doing things in secret'. The rewritten version of the letter is perhaps also the reason it is not signed – Tomlinson perhaps avoiding the possibility of a forgery charge. Further, it is possible that Tomlinson got permission from Spurling to rewrite his letter. But, in any case, the fact that Tomlinson rewrote the letter in his own hand opens the door to certain suspicions: 1) Did he translate it accurately? 2) Did he edit it to put himself and the Elders in a better light in the controversy? 3) Did he intend to use it to help justify the actions of himself and the Elders' Council in the discipline of Perry?

[116] Llewellyn and Lemons especially were at odds with Perry and pressing for him to be brought to account for his actions and disciplined. Llewellyn was the first to lodge charges against him (Tomlinson, 'Deposition', p. 2383), and he was appointed 'to arrange in order a list of charges against Sam C. Perry, and present them to the Council' (Tomlinson, 'Deposition', p. 1801).

confidence in you to do the very best you can and know, and that you are ready to amend mistakes when found ... I feel so delighted to find you as you are in every way, and I am sure you will lead us as near right as possible ... I hope the entire church will continue to pray for Brother Perry to see his error.[117]

We may conclude that, though Perry had some legitimate concerns and complaints, he had no good excuse for his actions in refusing to cooperate with the reporting system of the church, and more especially was to be blamed for attempting to lead the ministers and churches in Florida in his rebellion. On these points, Spurling wrote,

> Now you object to the compulsory reporting and financial system. If those systems are not what they ought to be, you should have remained in the fold and endeavored to assist in getting them to what they ought to be. I object to some things too, but continue to trust they will be made right. And they will if we stay in our place and do what is Scriptural ... So you should have reported and instructed all others to have promptly done the same.[118]

How much stock Perry put in Spurling's counsel we do not know, but in the final analysis he rejected it;[119] and he refused to submit to the authority of Tomlinson and the Elders' Council and thus left the church. He argued that he had 'waited for years to see the work 'RISE AND SHINE', but that he had been grievously disappointed, and in fact that contrariwise 'the church, in general, is on the spiritual decline [and] backsliding ... [and] what little spiritual light it has is going out'.[120] Besides the fact that the light of Christ in the church was going out, according to Perry, he boasted that he would not 'submit to men who are

---

[117] Interestingly, this letter was rewritten by Tomlinson apparently to make it legible for public consumption. In doing so, Tomlinson opened the door for criticism: particularly the accusation that he may have edited the letter to put himself and his actions in a more favorable light.

[118] Spurling, 'Letter to Perry and Tomlinson', pp. 12-14.

[119] It is likely that Perry considered Spurling to be rather naive and uninformed in regard to what was going on at 'headquarters', and thus did not esteem very highly his counsel. Spurling's letter to Perry and Tomlinson does indeed reveal a certain naiveté in Spurling in regard to Tomlinson and the direction he was leading the church. Further, he does not seem to have grasped the implications of Tomlinson's claims for his exalted office, nor that Tomlinson (particularly between 1900 and 1920) questioned a believer's salvation if he resorted to a physician or medicine. Tomlinson and Spurling had formed a deep emotional bond in the early days of the church, which endeared Tomlinson to the elder. This endearment seems to have clouded Spurling's ability to be objective in judging Tomlinson's leadership.

[120] Perry, 'BEFORE A.J. TOMLINSON', p. 4.

forcing and urging human order, system and rule that destroys individual freedom and liberty in the Spirit'.[121]

Interestingly, Spurling's response to Perry in regard to an invisible or spiritual church shows that he had not modified his view of the Bible church since 1886, and, further, that the doctrine of a so-called spiritual church was still incomprehensible to him, though he seems to have left open for further study the idea that part of the church may be in heaven – that is, that the *church militant* (on earth) and the *church triumphant* (in heaven) are one and the same. But, in any case, he emphasized that our present work and concern is with the church on earth.

> It behooves all God's children to carry out the Scriptural program. And ... all should assist in the work of maintaining the Church on earth to do business for God. And those who shirk that duty will certainly suffer loss ... You cannot minimize the Church on earth where God's business is carried on without displeasing God, and consequently suffer loss for disobedience. You say you don't want to be in bondage. If you call doing God's work in a Scriptural way bondage, I am sorry for you, or any one else in that fix'.[122]

Spurling also pointed out to Perry that, while the church on earth has invisible characteristics within it and should manifest a pious and deep spirituality, it is strictly visible in nature.[123] Further, he made it plain that one is 'born into the family of God [but is] added to or [joined to] the business church on earth'.[124] Finally, in regard to Perry's argument for a spiritual church composed of all born again believers, Spurling concluded,

> So, Brother Perry, you fail to make a case against the Church of God in that way, and you must acknowledge that your excuse for acting as you have and causing so much trouble has been prompted either by malice against the brethren, or personal ambition, or love of money ...[125]

---

[121] Perry, 'BRFORE A.J. TOMLINSON', p. 4. Perry evangelized independently thereafter in Florida for a few years, then joined the Assemblies of God in 1923. In 1934 he joined the Church of God and served on the Board of Directors for Lee University (then called Bible Training School) in 1936-1938. However, he left the Church of God in 1940 and according to reports remained an independent minister until his death in 1960.

[122] Spurling, 'Letter to Perry and Tomlinson', pp. 10-11.
[123] Spurling, 'Letter to Perry and Tomlinson', pp. 5-6.
[124] Spurling, 'Letter to Perry and Tomlinson', p. 7.
[125] Spurling, 'Letter to Perry and Tomlinson', p. 6.

J.L. Scott's Reformation

Though Perry was the highest ranking officer in the church in 1919 to oppose Tomlinson's authority and the centralization of the church, he was by no means alone in his sentiments. Prominent ministers like J.L. Scott[126] and A.H. Bryans had in recent months boldly lifted their voices to register their complaints against Tomlinson's autocracy and exalted position and the developing centralized system. Though these ministers and others in sympathy with them had organized no formal league between themselves, yet they had the same mind and judgment in regard to the issues that Perry had raised and made public in his tract, 'BEFORE A.J. TOMLINSON AND THE ELDERS' COUNCIL'. Perry in fact quoted Bryans to support his views and actions in separating himself from the church:

> We desire only true unity, liberty, and peace. We are aware of the fact that SUBMISSION TO EVERY right or wrong RULING of the assembly would produce an external form of unity and peace, but such submission would not produce inward peace, nor give us that liberty for which we are contending, inasmuch as it would compel us to stifle our convictions, silence the voice of conscience, surrender our God-given right of private judgment, ignore the leading of the infallible guide (the Holy Ghost) and go out to preach under FALSE PRETENSES. Brethren, such a sacrifice is too great.[127]

Notwithstanding the apparent dissatisfaction that was escalating among a growing number of ministers and members in the church, Tomlinson maintained that the numerical and monetary growth of the church in recent years, along with the manifestations and demonstrations of the Spirit in worship services signified God's approval on the system of government that had been constructed; and, consequently, he became impervious to any criticism against his exalted position and the developing headquarters system.

> In our searching of the Scriptures we have found James, the Lord's brother, occupying the executive chair under God, and the twelve apostles of the Lord in submission to Him, and they recognized Him

---

[126] Scott was the prominent pastor at Ridgedale in Chattanooga and had served on Assembly committees, including the committee to 'consider plans for Foreign Mission work'. Bryans, from Hayesville, North Carolina, had served as overseer of North Carolina and also as chairman of the committee to consider plans for Foreign Mission work. Scott and Bryans had thus become well acquainted and had worked together in close Christian fraternity.

[127] Perry, 'BEFORE A.J. TOMLINSON', p. 4.

as their superior in governmental affairs. This same order is recognized by ancient history. And from ancient history we glean much valuable information that leads us to believe that under the apostles were others occupying subordinate positions of trust and authority. All of these gleanings from ancient history and what we get from the Scriptures, both the Old and New Testament, lead us to the conclusion that the Church of God is theocratic in government. We have been following this order to the very best of our understanding and ability for years. The Church has prospered and grown numerically almost beyond our expectations under this rule. We believe we have God's approval upon the system practiced and described. He sets His approval upon it by pouring out the Holy Spirit upon our services and by demonstrating His power in the salvation of souls, healing and miracles, and the signs are following the Church of God to a greater degree than any other people on earth.[128]

The growth of the church was indeed impressive and exciting; increasing from a handful of churches in 1906 with twenty-one delegates in the first Assembly to 12,341 members and 690 ministers in 425 churches in 1919.[129] Added to the growing excitement was the fact that Tomlinson had reconvened the Assembly in Cleveland that same year, after it had been conducted in Harriman, Tennessee in 1916-1917 and had been canceled in 1918 due to the worldwide Influenza Epidemic. Also, plans were made that year to build a permanent Assembly Tabernacle and to make the city of Cleveland the 'permanent headquarters for the Church of God'.[130] This was realized in 1920, and the Assembly met for the first time that year in its new Assembly Auditorium on Montgomery Avenue.[131]

Still, ignoring the complaints of Scott and other ministers did not make the problems go away. The criticism against centralizing the government and authority of the church in a headquarters' system continued to mount, particularly because that system was being executed more or less unilaterally by the General Overseer with the backing of the most influential members on the Council of Twelve, which in turn was creating an ever-widening gap between a developing episcopacy and the rest of the church, reminiscent of the error in the second and third centuries

---

[128] *HAA*, I, p. 147
[129] 'Statistical Report', *GAM*, 14th Assembly, pp. 57-79.
[130] *GAM*, 14th Assembly, 1919, 'Prefatory Notes'.
[131] The Assembly Auditorium was not quite complete, but nevertheless it was dedicated with an elaborate program of celebration and the Assembly was convened there.

that had divided the church between 'clergy' and 'laity' and paved the road to Roman Catholicism.

Figure 88
SAM C. PERRY

Figure 89
J.L. SCOTT

Figure 90
A.H. BRYANS

It was this system and the refusal to modify it that prompted J.L. Scott to reform with other dissidents in Chattanooga in 1919. Scott and his followers organized sometime between the time that Perry had been disciplined in May 1919 and the entry in Tomlinson's *Diary* for August 12, 1919.[132] They apparently saw the hand writing on the wall in regard to their own destiny: for they held to the same views that Perry had expressed in his 'BEFORE A.J. TOMLINSON AND THE ELDERS' COUNCIL'. When confronted by his state overseer, J.S. Llewellyn,[133] and asked to resign, he declined and proceeded to divide the local church at Ridgedale.[134] Scott and his followers refused to vacate the large, nice building that had been dedicated sometime earlier by Tomlinson, and proceeded to initiate a lawsuit to obtain ownership of the property, winning the decision of the court in 1922.

Scott's influence reached beyond the Ridgedale church. Soon after he had divided the local church in Chattanooga, he acquired followers in three other states. In a convention in June 1920, Scott and his followers formed a denomination and chose the name 'The Original Church of God' to express their faith and intentions. They believed that the church under Tomlinson's leadership had been slipping off the rock of its original charter and principles for several years, particularly in the move to centralize the local churches under an Episcopal hierarchy headed by the

---

[132] Tomlinson reported in his August 12, 1919 entry in his *Diary* that 'Sam C. Perry and J.L. Scott have been discontinued from their ministry in the church and are giving us some little trouble'.

[133] Llewellyn acted in counsel with the General Overseer.

[134] Homer, *Diary*, I, p. 262.

General Overseer.[135] The reasons for their reformation were plainly stated in the minutes of their June 1920 convention:

> We do not believe in any man being the head of the Church of God; 2) We do not believe in State overseers, District overseers, nor overseers over tens, as they now have them in each local church as Governors, bosses or rulers of the Church of God; 3) We do not believe in the Elders as they have them to enforce their new laws and governments ... 4) We do not believe in the late form of appointing pastors, but ... the old form of each church selecting and calling its own pastor ...[136]

Added to this dissatisfaction was the growing sentiment among some leaders to make tithing compulsory and centralized. In their organizational convention, Scott and his followers called attention to the church's 16th teaching:

> Tithing is voluntary. We stand on the original way of paying tithes, as on the other questions, doctrines, etc. Each member should pay tithes into the local treasury where they hold their membership. Deacons shall have charge of the tithe treasure ... The pastor's need shall be supplied first ... and the remaining tithes shall belong to the local church in which they are paid, and will be at the disposal of the said church ... We object to one-tenth of all tithes being sent to so-called HEAD QUARTERS ... We also object to the remaining tithes left in the treasury, after the pastor is supplied, BELONGING to Head Quarters.[137]

To Scott and the small number of ministers and members in East Tennessee, Georgia, Alabama and Kentucky who stood with him, these developments in the church were gross acts of apostasy that could not be tolerated. They declared independence and began their reform movement based more on Spurling's ecclesial principles in Christian Union, particularly in regard to local church autonomy and individual liberty. It seems almost certain in fact that Scott and his followers were encouraged in their actions by the sympathies of Spurling toward some of their complaints.[138]

---

[135] *Minutes of the Convention of The Original Church of God*, June 19, 1920, pp. 7-8.
[136] *Minutes of the Convention of The Original Church of God*, June 19, 1920, pp. 4-5.
[137] *Minutes of the Convention of The Original Church of God*, June 19, 1920, pp. 4-5.
[138] Perry had been called to account on some indiscretion by the Elders' Council. Lee noted that 'We dealt with Perry for much less than what Tomlinson has done' ('Letter from Lee to S.O. Gillaspie', shortly after the June Council in 1923

The Case of R.G. Spurling

We noticed in Spurling's letter to Perry and Tomlinson in July 1919 that he had disapproved of Perry's separation from the church at that time, yet he had sympathized with many of his complaints and acknowledged, 'I object to some things too'. His objections apparently became stronger in the course of the next year, and particularly after Scott and others left the church and formed a new organization in Chattanooga in June 1920.

Figure 91

R.G. SPURLING AS HE APPEARED C. 1916

By 1921 Spurling was clearly at odds with the direction that Tomlinson and the Elders were taking the church, yet he seems to have remained with the organization (at least nominally) until matters grew worse. He had apparently turned in his license to Tomlinson after the Assembly in 1920.[139] That year he had been offended for not being allowed to sell his newly published *The Lost Link* at the Assembly.[140] Still, there is no official record showing that his license had been revoked until 1925, and that action was taken by the Llewellyn-Lee faction, not by Tomlinson and his followers.[141]

Apparently Tomlinson's great admiration and deep affection

['F.J. Lee File', ZACG Archives]). This disciplinary action doubtlessly influenced Perry's move.

[139] 'Letter to Tomlinson', December 1, 1931 ['R.G. Spurling File', ZACG Archives]. We may assume this also on the basis that his name had been dropped from list of ministers in the *GAM* in 1920.

[140] 'Letters from Spurling to Tomlinson', December 1, 1931, and Tomlinson to Spurling, January 13, 1931 ['R.G. Spurling File', ZACG Archives]. It seems to have been understood between Tomlinson and Spurling that it was certain of the Elders who had objected so strenuously to his book; but obviously the central theme of *The Lost Link* was also diametrically opposed to the direction Tomlinson was taking the church.

[141] 'Letter from F.J. Lee to John C. Jernigan', June 16, 1925 ['F.J. Lee File', ZACG Archives]; and see Phillips, 'Transformed Tomlinson', pp. 28-29.

for Spurling would not allow him to revoke his license on the grounds of his complaint. It is probable that he held his license in his personal care, hoping that his hurt would heal and that they could be reconciled. It is likely that the 'Ten Elders' faction were unaware that Spurling had turned in his license to Tomlinson, and thus Lee [General Overseer] and John C. Jernigan, pastor of Copper Hill, Tennessee where Spurling's membership was, assumed that he was still a minister in the church, and thus acted accordingly. In any case, the actions of the 'Ten Elders' was irrelevant to Spurling and also to Tomlinson and his followers.

It is almost certain that Spurling joined Scott's group in 1922.[142] He had become increasingly disillusioned with the developing power structure in Cleveland and the over-centralization of the organization, and particularly the ever-increasing lordship spirit manifested by some of the ruling Elders, two of which he had in mind were almost certainly Llewellyn and Lemons. He had counseled with Brouayer and others and expressed his disdain for 'ecclesiastical bosses'.

Christianized Communism

A catalyst to the eventual disruption of the church in 1923 was the revised financial system adopted by the Assembly in 1920. In spite of the solemn protests against a centralized financial system by men like Perry, Scott, and Bryans, with the resulting schisms, Tomlinson and the Elders pushed forward with their radical plan. This system required all tithes from the local churches to be sent directly to world headquarters in Cleveland where they would be distributed by a seven-man committee as the needs became apparent.[143] The system evidently was to work as a kind of Christianized communism with a highly idealistic egalitarianism in view.

Tomlinson had prepared the church for this system in his annual address in October 1919 under the heading, 'Equal Distribution'.[144] Moreover, he seems to have suggested in his annual address in 1916 that as the church progressed in her judicial search into the Scriptures, particularly in the Old Testament, the perfect financial system '[would] be materialized'. It would be a 'plan to equalize the benefits derived from

---

[142] *Certificate of Ordination* signed by Scott in 1922 with the official seal of The Original Church of God ('J.L. Scott File', ZACG Archives]; and Spurling's name is listed as one of the principal members in chartering the Original Church of God in 1922.
[143] *GAM*, 1920, p. 19.
[144] *HAA*, I, p. 107.

the preaching of the gospel' and to 'make possible a just and equal distribution of the bread of life'.[145] Indeed, *The Last Great Conflict* shows that the seed for this financial plan had been planted in Tomlinson's mind as early as 1909[146] – and perhaps much earlier than that if, as we suspect, it had been first planted in his mind by Sandford while he was at Shiloh in 1897-1901. In any case, now in 1920 in his annual address he shared his vision more plainly and boldly, systematically laying it out for the whole church to see – a radical centralizing system that had in view a kind of Christianized communism. But it is almost certain that he was assisted in his thinking in this regard by J.S. Llewellyn and perhaps even moreso by F.J. Lee, for first of all Lee zealously defended the system in 1920-1922, and, secondly, Tomlinson in his annual address in 1921 denied that he was the chief architect of the system and wholly responsible for suggesting it to the Assembly; it was rather the result of a 'current working its way through the minds of our people',[147] a 'sentiment' among many in the church that 'may be stronger than some of us realize'.[148] Further, Tomlinson had built up expectations among the Elders that one or more of them might be chosen to reveal a more perfect financial plan to the church:

> I fully believe that the Holy Ghost will use some one, or more of these wise counsellors, to point out to the balance of us the very beautiful blazing system for which we have been searching and praying. What could be more beautiful – what could be more grand and glorious – than to discover a money system that surpasses all the wisdom of men! We are destined to find it. The prophecy has gone forth and cannot fail. It will take this beautiful system to so attract the people that they will bring their silver and gold with them as they come and cast it into the treasury of the Lord.[149]

This expectation of Tomlinson for a 'wise counselor' to be revealed seems to have been answered by Lee in his lengthy discourse in the 1920 Assembly titled, 'Efficient Organization'. Speaking in particular about a complete and more perfect financial system for the church, he elaborated upon what Tomlinson had earlier in the week suggested in

---

[145] *HAA*, I, pp. 75-77.
[146] Tomlinson, *LGC*, pp. 196-201. He reveals on p. 201 that this financial plan or 'money system' had been gradually developing in his mind 'for more than three years', but noted, 'this is the first time I have ventured to place it before the public in its fullness'.
[147] *HAA*, I, p.135.
[148] *HAA*, I, p.169.
[149] *HAA*, I, p. 76

his annual address in regard to Abraham paying tithes to Melchisedec, and virtually laid out systematically the radical plan that was adopted later in that Assembly. Lee, however, unlike Tomlinson, insisted that Melchisedec was in fact Christ himself, rather than a type. He reasoned that as Melchisedec was Christ and Abraham paid tithes to Him, then all should pay tithes to Christ. Then, anticipating the question, 'How may I pay my tithes to Jesus', Lee responded,

> [Jesus] says, the church is My body. Bring ye all the tithes to the store house. We leap entirely over the Levitical priesthood to Christ who appeared away back with our faithful father, Abraham, and taught him the lesson on tithes, by receiving them, so our father is to teach us the lesson by the things he did – by paying the tithes of ALL, not here and there wherever it pleased him but he brought all the tithes and presented them to Melchisedec's person. We are able to do the same, but the church is His body. Now, like the circulation of the corpuscles, let it go first into the lower ventricle (the local church treasury), then let it contract and force through space to the upper ventricle, the general treasury. It, in turn, will contract and force it out to the body that every organ in need shall be supplied. What a beautiful system! Efficient Organization.[150]

Earlier in this message, Lee had drawn an analogy between the organization of the human body and the centralized financial system that he was suggesting for the church. In rather convoluted logic, he pointed to 'the main leading officials of the church' as the heart and center of the body of Christ;[151] his reasoning then proceeded as follows: the heart has two receptacles – the lower and upper ventricles – but when the blood comes first into the lower ventricle, it then

> contracts at once and forces [the blood] out through the lungs ... into the upper ventricle ... [which] then contracts and forces [the blood] out all the way through the whole body, thereby nourishing the

---

[150] *GAM*, 15th Assembly, p. 39. But the idea that Melchisedek represents Christ, and that, in the absence of Christ, the church is His representative body on earth was also plainly stated by Tomlinson in *LGC*, pp. 196-200.

[151] The idea that the leading officials represented the center of the church was also apparently borrowed by Lee from Tomlinson. In *LGC*, Tomlinson stated, 'Jesus Himself, the head of the church, had ascended to the Father, but the church, which is His body, was on earth, and the apostles were the officers of the church, then it is easily seen that all the offerings were laid at the apostles' feet, as that was the only way to give literally to the High Priest ... All literal offerings were made to His body, the church, of which the apostles were chief' (p. 197).

different organs of the body. This seems to be Christ's plan to keep the life giving flow to His body, the church.[152]

He thus concluded that God's financial plan for the church is revealed plainly by the heart and flow of blood in the human body, and thus, accordingly, the tithes should be paid into the local churches (the lower ventrical) and then the local church treasuries should be emptied into the general treasury at headquarters (the upper ventrical).

In view of Lee's discourse, it is difficult to say with certainty between Lee and Tomlinson who had the greater influence on the other in regard to the new financial system, but it was most likely Tomlinson, for Lee generally developed ideas that were first suggested to him by Tomlinson. Reflecting on Tomlinson's leadership and predominance in this regard, Alonzo Gann, who was chairman of the Better Government Committee and one of the Twelve Elders in 1923, said that Tomlinson was

> the most instrumental of any human being in the Church of God, in bringing about new light [in the church] ... he acted as moderator in all Assemblies ... and used his influence in them. We had such confidence in him he could just say the word and we would adhere to what he said. His influence I guess was more influential in bringing about the different determinations of the Church of God than all of us put together. I am confident of that.[153]

In any case, there is no question that Tomlinson was the first to suggest and lay out the general principles for the financial system in *The Last Great Conflict*. But Lee seems to have pushed the idea of sending all the tithes to headquarters to its final conclusion with his analogy of the function of the heart in the human body. But according to protocol, it was left to the General Overseer to be the prime mover of the new system and to introduce it to the Assembly for consideration.

Now Tomlinson knew the subject of tithing and finances in general were sensitive issues – particularly during the hard times that most Americans were facing in 1920; and thus in introducing the system he chose his words carefully to guide the minds of the people to his way of thinking. He thus spoke of centralizing all tithes into a 'General Headquarters Treasury' in terms of an incentive plan according to the [ministers] needs and the efficiency of their work, and the responsibility of the position in which they serve'.[154] Further, in order to avoid jolting the saints' emotions too abruptly with the idea of this 'more perfect

---

[152] *GAM*, 15th Assembly, pp. 37-38.
[153] Gann, 'Deposition', p. 99.
[154] *HAA*, I, p. 135.

financial system', he eased his way step by step into the subject. His address along these lines is worth quoting at length in order to be able to grasp his rationale and tactfulness:

> We are thoroughly convinced that all should pay one tenth of their income to the Lord, and we are just as fully convinced that the tithes are to be paid to the Church of God – the Body of Christ – and not handed around promiscuously according to your own feelings or notion. We are fully convinced that the Church of God is the storehouse into which all tithes are to be brought. I do not think this point is questioned at all. But there may be some other points in connection with the present financial system that are not so clear. And even if there are no amendments or improvements to make it will be good for us to look deeper into the subject. If we have reached the end of it we will stop and be satisfied, and follow the same order we have been following for nearly three years. But here is the question. Some believe we have not yet arrived at the proper plan for distribution. Some think it is a mistake for the Overseers of the states to draw from the nine-tenths in the local treasuries. They say it looks too much like taking out the second tithe. Although they know it is not meant for the second tithe, yet it has the appearance of it. And thus they feel we have not yet reached the standard.
>
> In raising the question the people have no disposition to rebel. They do not raise the question to create any dissatisfaction; they want only to find the Bible standard, and if this is it, they are willing to submit and go on with the practice. And if it is not the standard we all want to drop this plan and go on to the standard as soon as we know the next step to take. We are all interested in this subject and all we want is the very right thing. We are not prejudiced. We have no intention of working for any selfish interest. We do not form factions and try to run some scheme through by 'wirepulling' and advantage. We are honest. We are sincere. We do not mean to make laws; we only mean to search out the laws that are already made and marked out in the Scriptures and put them into practice. This is our desire in reaching the standard for the financial system.
>
> There is another current working its way through ... our people concerning the financial system. There may not be much said about it, but I am sure there is a good deal of thought about it. If I should mention it here surely no one will take offense at it. I do no want to offend any one. I want to bless and help and encourage. I want to speak words of edification and comfort. It is my desire to keep mov-

ing toward the complete Bible standard. But it is not my purpose to speak from a personal point of view at this time. I am only to speak now of a sentiment among our people, and it may be stronger than some of us realize. That sentiment is in favor of a General Headquarters Treasury into which all the tithes are to be placed, with seven men to regulate and make, or order, the distribution among the ministers according to their needs and the efficiency of their work, and the responsibility of the position in which they serve.

And this may be the Scriptural system. And the Scriptural system is what we are driving for. We want to make the goal at this Assembly. If this is it I'm sure the Lord will let us see eye to eye about it, and when we make the decision it will seem good to the Holy Ghost and us.

To adopt this system would mean quite a change, but changes are often good for us, and especially so when we change from bad to good or from good to better or best. If this plan is accepted the tithe of tithes would drop off. That which appears to be a second tithe paid to the State Overseer would disappear. The charge of following the law in this respect could not be made any more. It would land us back to our father Abraham and Melchizedec. Abraham paid tithes to Melchizedec, and Melchizedec was a 'priest of the most high God, and Christ was made a high priest forever after the order of Melchizedec.

The Levitical law said a tithe of the tithes, also called the heave offering, should be given to the high priest, but Abraham paid all the tithes to Melchizedec instead of a tithe of the tithes. When the priesthood was changed from the order of Levi and Aaron, back to the order of Melchizedec, it was necessary to change the law. This is clearly stated at Heb. 7:12. 'For the priesthood being changed, there is made of necessity a change also of the law'. The change then with respect to the tithes is apparent. No more heave offering. No more tithe of tithes, but all the tithes given to our High Priest – Jesus. And since the Church is the Body of Christ, the tithes are to be paid to the Church. This special point has been taught for years. But now, since Abraham paid all the tithes to Melchizedec, this surely puts the tithes all in one place with no tithe of tithes. Then the distribution can be made with perfect safety, and give no chance for a surplus to pile up unused unless there is really more than it takes to supply all the ministers. At any rate there would be none tied up where it could not be gotten to when needed.

This plan would solve some serious problems. It would prevent a surplus from accumulating in the tithe of tithes treasury which could not be used for the common ministry. It would prevent a surplus from accumulating in the local treasuries where it could not be gotten to supply some of the ministers that were in want. It would remove the temptation for ministers to 'feel led to go' to a certain place where they had heard the treasury was well filled. They would be just as ready to go to some neglected field of labor as to a place that has been well supplied with ministers. It would solve the evangelistic and new work problem. In fact, it would be a strong incentive and stimulus to the spread of the gospel into new fields as well as to build up the work among the poor and at places that are weak and almost ready to die. It would stop such questions as, 'Will I get my car fare? Will they give me support for my family? How much does that church pay? How much money do you have in the treasury? Can't you give me a little more this time? Can't you let me have it all this time, as I am in special need this week?' And it will stop the saying, 'Brother M___ went to the churches ahead of me and got all the tithes in the treasury and when I got there they had nothing to give me. Brother Z___ has the favor of the treasurer of the church at S___ and when he goes there he gets a good lift'.

These may not be bad questions and statements, but I'm sure we can spend our time and breath to better advantage than in such meditations or expressions. And if it is according to the Bible to have all the tithes come to one common center and paid out in first class systematic order every one of us will be in favor of it. This subject will be given further attention on in the Assembly. We are all anxious to reach the perfect Bible system that will bring joy and perfect satisfaction.[155]

In advocating for this radically new financial system, we have no reason to question Tomlinson's sincerity; for he seems to have truly believed it was the 'Scriptural system' and therefore would produce the best possible results for all concerned in the church. But, here again, as in other instances, it is difficult not to see the influence of Sandford on him in regard to this form of government and operation; for he had been indoctrinated as a young man by the Shiloh commander and witnessed first hand how he had organized his followers into a highly centralized cultish system, which included centralizing the finances of the

---

[155] *HAA*, I, pp. 134-36.

church and dispersing them at his own discretion.[156] But it is possible also that Tomlinson may have been influenced by the political and social movements of the day, including the rising tide of communism and the developing fascist states in Europe, for he kept a keen eye on world events and the developing political systems. Bolshevism and various forms of fascism were in the air in 1917-20, and Tomlinson admired powerful men who sat as heads of centrally controlled political and religious systems. Even as late as 1934 he acknowledged with a certain naiveté that he admired 'great men' like Mussolini, Hitler, and the Roman pope 'who sat as heads [of nations and governments] and held the reigns of government in their hands'.[157] Be that as it may, Tomlinson claimed to be guided only by the Holy Ghost and the Word of God in calling for all tithes to be sent to Headquarters and dispersed at the discretion of a financial board or committee.

Still, it is amazing that when the General Overseer finally brought up the new financial system for the Assembly's consideration, it passed without a dissenting voice.[158] How could such a radical system have been adopted? We suggest three primary reasons: First, because Tomlinson and some of the most powerful men on the Elders' Council had managed in the past year to silence certain voices and purge the church of men like Perry, Scott, and Bryans; and thus the spirit of dissent had been more or less suppressed. Second, Tomlinson, Lee, Lemons, Llewellyn, McLain, and other leaders had proceeded to preach incessantly against heretics and seditions on one hand,[159] and the virtues of a regimented obedience to church authority on the other. Tomlinson, for example, concluded his discourse on 'Church Government' in his 1920 annual address, saying,

> What is the use of having government if we are not loyal to its laws? It was on account of the disloyalty and disobedience of the captains over thousands and the captains over hundreds that Moses was angry at them on one occasion. And this caused him to give them some sharp orders. These officers refused to respect the counsel and orders

---

[156] Centralizing all finances at Shiloh naturally followed Sandford's militaristic concept of the church as an army – an army with a centralized headquarters headed by a commander-general. But unlike Sandford, Tomlinson did not use the finances to purchase luxuries and special comforts for himself, though his unilateral handling of the church's tithes would eventually occasion some of his friends to turn on him and slander him as being a charlatan and embezzler and even attempt to send him to prison.

[157] *HAA*, II, p. 198.

[158] *GAM*, 15th Assembly, 1920, pp. 43, 44.

[159] See, e.g. Tomlinson's 1919 annual address, *HAA*, I, pp. 115-16.

of their superiors. And such as this will always have a demoralizing effect. Saul lost his kingdom because he refused to obey the instructions of his Superior. These things are written for our learning. And we are learning obedience and loyalty so that we may have God's approval on our service for him'.[160]

Figure 92

ASSEMBLY IN SESSION C. 1920

Later in that same Assembly, J.S. Llewellyn's preached a message, titled, 'The Church a Distinct Government', in which he boldly asserted,

> The meaning of the word government is exercise of authority; administration of law ... We have people today (spiritually speaking) who oppose government, they are spiritual anarchists. As a general thing when people speak against government, there is something dead up the branch. Look at a church without government, the fact is, it is no church. A church without government has no authority – how can she do business? The Bible says that an elder who rules well is worthy of double honor. If there is no government, who is he to rule over? When you get the real liberty which the Bible speaks about, you feel good in your heart by being ruled by those who have rule over you ... Some say they accept the idea of God ruling but let man be out of it ... How can matters be adjusted when there is no authority, no con-

---

[160] *HAA*, I, p. 148.

trol, no direction? Why did Paul say to obey them that have the rule over you and submit yourselves ...[161]

But there was also a third possible reason that the new legislation passed. Astonishing as it may seem, the people actually accepted Tomlinson's and Lee's new light on Melchisedec, namely, that Melchisedec represented the church, the body of Christ, and particularly Headquarters; and thus as Abraham paid *all tithes* to Melchisedec so now under the New Covenant *all tithes* should be paid into the General Church Treasury. Moreover, this new system was according to Tomlinson and other witnesses manifestly approved by the Holy Ghost.

Thus, having been convinced by the General Overseer and Lee and other distinguished men on the Elders' Council and, interestingly enough, also by Spurling,[162] and by manifestations of the Holy Ghost including ecstatic messages in tongues with interpretations[163] that indicated this new financial system was the 'the plan of God', the Assembly left it up to the General Overseer and his twelve councilors to work out the details. But actually the details had already been settled in the General Overseer's address, namely, that all tithes were to be sent to Cleveland and put into a 'General Headquarters Treasury' under the oversight of seven men appointed to 'regulate and make, or order, the distribution among the ministers according to their needs and the efficiency of their work, and the responsibility of the position in which they serve'. Significantly, however, the General Overseer and the Council of Elders failed to comply with the Assembly's plan for a seven-man committee to oversee the finances, and the Elders encouraged the General Overseer to take it upon himself to disburse the funds as he deemed wise and necessary.[164]

Personally overseeing and dispersing the tithes proved to be a grave mistake on Tomlinson's part, for as the needs were great everywhere and the funds limited, he was bound to be put in a bad light. Some of

---

[161] *GAM*, 15th Assembly, pp. 46, 47.

[162] Spurling: 'I believe the system suggested to us by Brother Tomlinson in his Annual Address is the Bible order, I heartily endorse it' (*GAM*, 15th Assembly, p. 43).

[163] *GAM*, 15th Assembly, p. 19. The first message in tongues was interpreted to say: 'This is My plan. Stand true and look to Me ...' The second message was, 'There have been many confusions. The gospel must be carried to every nation ... I am glad I have a few who will follow My Word'.

[164] Tomlinson acknowledged in his annual address in 1921 that he and the members of the Elders' Council took it upon themselves not to appoint a seven-man committee (*HAA*, I, p. 170); further, he admitted in his *Dairy* [September 2, 1921 entry] that in the absence of this committee he had been personally distributing the tithes 'since January'.

the pastors received little assistance from the tithe fund, while others received no tithes at all. Yet some others apparently received more than their share, or so it seemed.[165] As some fared better than others, Tomlinson seemed to be showing respect to persons and lording over the funds. The post-war depression that was devastating the South at that time made the situation even more sensitive. Worse yet, Tomlinson used some of the tithes [$19,000] to help pay the debt on the newly built 4,000 seat Assembly auditorium and dispersed some also for the *Evangel* and Publishing House deficit, which by 1920 was nearly $23,000.00.[166] These unilateral decisions were unwise, to be sure, and gave occasion [when they were discovered] for doubts to be cast on Tomlinson's integrity and honesty.[167] Discontent began to mount over the management of the finances, particularly by some of the ministers in Cleveland.[168]

Over the next year, the General Overseer continued to defend the new financial system in the *Evangel* and on the field, and so did Lee and other members of the Elders' Council. But their efforts were like beating a dead horse; for the funds simply were not there to accomplish what Tomlinson and the Elders had promised, namely, an inflow of prosperity and an equitable distribution of funds. It was becoming obvious to an increasing number of ministers that the favor of God was not on this new financial system – that communism, even under the cloak of the venerable Melchizedec, invoked God's judgment rather than His blessings.

But this new financial system was part and parcel of a larger overarching problem, namely, a system of government and discipline that was infringing upon the sovereignty of Christ over the ministers and churches. The ever-increasing centralization of authority was being developed on the presumption that Christ was out of the picture, and that the church was acting in His place on earth. While a surface reading of certain Scriptures may seem to indicate and justify such a system, e.g. Mt. 5.14-16; 16.19; Mk 13.34; Jn 20.23; Acts 3.21; 4.32; 2 Cor. 5.18-20, a deeper understanding of these passages on balance with other Scriptures

---

[165] Davidson, *Rock*, I, pp. 566-67; Conn, *Mighty Army*, p. 160.

[166] He confessed later [in his annual address in 1922] that in order to save the Publishing House and the church from bankruptcy, and to meet the notes due on the orphanage property and new auditorium, he had been little by little using the tithes designated for the ministers.

[167] Tomlinson's actions did not impact the church until later in the year, and particularly at the Assembly in 1921.

[168] E.L. Simmons, *History of the Church of God* (Cleveland, TN: Church of God Publishing House, 1938), p. 38.

rightly divided shows plainly not only that the headship of Christ is ever present in the church in the Holy Ghost (cf. Mt. 28.20; Heb. 13.5; Jn 16.13-16), but that the spiritual dynamics of the church under the New Covenant militates against any system not centered in the living, present Christ. Even after Jesus ascended to the Father, He continued to 'walk in the midst of the [churches]' (Rev. 2.1), and to rule all of the ministers and members collectively and individually. Indeed, the system that Tomlinson and the Elders were attempting to build flew in the face of the apostle Paul's teachings and warnings: cf. Eph. 1.17-23; 3.17-21; 5.24-32; Colossians 1.15-19, 27-29; 2.8-10, 18, 19; *et al.*, for Christ is never out of the picture, nor has He ever appointed any person or any group of persons to 'take His place' or to 'act with the power of attorney' in His absence. The reason for this is plain on its face: for the finite headship of 'men' must inevitably and unavoidably come into conflict with the infinite wisdom and headship of Christ. The church – the whole body of ministers and members together – therefore, rather than standing in the place of Christ, is called and ordained and filled with the Spirit visibly to embody the ever-present Christ, to be a 'city upon a hill' through which the light and wisdom of Christ might shine out to the world (Isa. 60.1-5; Mt. 5.14-16; Eph. 1.3-6, 13-23). The church acts *with* Christ through the Holy Ghost (1 Cor. 3.9; 2 Cor. 6.1; Eph. 2.13-22), not *for* Him in a plenipotentiary sense, the latter of which smacks more of Roman Catholicism and the papacy than of the 'church of the living God'.

The new financial plan was therefore a disaster – doomed by the Lord from the outset, along with the whole system of government and authority that was centered in a General Overseer who purportedly had been specially appointed by God to take Jesus' place until He returned![169] Again, we have no reason to question the sincerity of Tomlinson and Lee and others in introducing the new financial system, but it should have been despised rather than admired: for it was a serious error which was despised by God himself. The church did indeed finally awaken to the error, but not before the usurping system had infected a large number of ministers and members with distrust, suspicion, and murmuring. More seriously, the new financial system created confusion and gave occasion for the chief leaders in the church to turn on each other; for when the system failed, the leaders began to blame each other, and what followed was the unraveling of the fellowship. The unbiblical system opened the floodgates of the church to the works of the flesh; for in the vacuum where love and Christian graces and mutual respect

---

[169] *HAA*, II, p. 17; 'Our Christmas Message', *WWM* (December 21, 1941), p. 4; Phillips, 'Quakerism', pp. 14-25.

once flourished, strife (variance), rivalries (emulations), anger, hatefulness, slander, and evil speaking came pouring into the church.

Beholding the chaos and internal strife in the church at that time, Spurling pleaded in his letter to Tomlinson and Perry,

> Dear Brethren, I have seen the dear Church of God suffer so much, and so often, at the hands of Satan by using the topmost flowers among God's people to carry on his infamous plots … Every hard lick the church has had to suffer has been struck by God's own people, which has robbed it of much good it could have accomplished. And now the very essence of the church, or the strongest men of the church are at variance, separated with a wedge driven home by Satan himself. Oh, he is so subtle![170]

Later in this letter, after having reproved the wrongs apparently done by those on both sides of the controversy, he concluded,

> Now dear brethren, can you not see that all have done some things wrong? And won't you sincerely seek the love of each other, and the right, and do right, so that you will be a unit, and in the real Church of God? Take the pains to understand each other, and love with a real Church of God love. Will you please pardon me for worrying you so? But I could not get these things off of my mind. And now I feel greatly releaved [sic], and leave it with you and God. Do remember that you cannot trifle with the real Church of God. It is the body of Christ. Come together and build up and not tear down what little that has been built up.[171]

It is almost certain that the 'Supplement' in *The Lost Link* was added by Spurling after he had written his letter to Perry and Tomlinson, probably sometime between August 1919 and the time the book was published in 1920. His aim was to reprove the errors that were then escalating and tearing the church apart – particularly the desire for position, temporal power, and money. He was beholding the very things that he had warned against in *The Lost Link* take hold of some of the 'topmost flowers' in the Church of God. He saw the grappling for power and position connected with the office of General Overseer and the prestigious seats on the Council of Twelve, and it was becoming more apparent that the move to centralize all tithes in Cleveland, in a General Headquarters Treasury, was tainted by greed and love for money. Spurling had already denounced a 'gluttonous ministry' in *The Lost Link*, and

---

[170] Spurling, 'Letter to Perry and Tomlinson', pp. 1-2.
[171] Spurling, 'Letter to Perry and Tomlinson', pp. 20-21.

had warned against allowing a 'political ecclesiasticism' to creep into the church; but his 'Supplement' focused particularly on the apparent fault that had developed in the leadership of the church in 1917-1920, namely, maneuvering and manipulating for the sake of position and material gain. Interestingly, he cites 1 Sam. 2.17 and 2 Kgs 5.2-26 to make his case. In the first instance, the sons of Eli were guilty of taking more of the offerings of the people than their allotted portion, committing themselves to use force if necessary to fulfill their avaricious appetites; in the second instance, Gehazi, the servant of the prophet Elisha, was blinded by his greed for money and material possessions, which in turn caused him to lie and cheat to obtain the gold and fine garments of Naaman. In both instances, God poured out severe judgment.

Spurling concluded his reproving remarks and warnings against God's impending judgment in the form of a poem:

> Go work in my vineyard today,
> The Master is calling for you;
> Why ask your poor brethren to pay?
> The Master will give you your due.
> The clusters are falling today,
> That should have been gathered by you,
> But when the harvest is past,
> What use has the Master for you?
> The wolves have now entered the flock,
> The hirelings are hasting to flee;
> Before the great raid can be stopped,
> I fear much destruction we'll see.
> The flock now is starving for food,
> The fleece you're longing to shear;
> But they that are perished and gone,
> Your labors can never restore.
> The people their offerings abhor,
> Because of the yearning for coin;
> Remember the sons of Eli,
> And fear lest their fate should be thine.
> Oh, Lord, do Thou pity Thy poor,
> And into Thy vineyard now send,
> Men like Peter and Paul,
> Unbought by the wages of men.[172]

---

[172] Spurling, *Lost Link*, pp. 36-37.

Granted, Spurling was critiquing the situation in the church at that time from a position extremely left of center, which he had inherited from his mountain Baptist tradition. He had never fully believed that tithing was a New Testament teaching, but had more or less gone along with the majority of the ministers and the church to preserve the order and unity of the fellowship. In a letter addressed to Tomlinson dated December 1, 1931, he confessed, 'I have tried for years to believe in tithing, but the more I hear it preached and written on, the further I am driven from it'.[173] Even so, he continued to encourage fellowship and Christian Union based on the freedom of each person's conscience. As long as tithing was not made compulsory, he was able to live with the differences of opinion on the subject; in fact, he even went so far to say that even if the church's rule on tithing was an ordinance of men, it should be complied with according to apostolic teaching, for Peter says to 'submit to every ordinance of man' and Paul says to 'pay tribute' to God's ministers.[174] But when the centralized system was adopted in 1920 and the Elders began to urge, if not force, the ministers to comply with the doctrine of tithing, he proclaimed 'the boat left me',[175] and 'for conscience sake' he confessed that he could no longer go along with the leadership of the church, particularly with the spirit that tended to force compliance with the decisions of the Council of Twelve and Assembly rulings.

We will return to Spurling in a moment, but for now suffice it say that his objections and actions more than anyone else's drew a distinct line of demarcation between the original church founded in 1886 and the one that had developed under Tomlinson's leadership after 1903, and which stood in the place of the original in 1920-1922. The radical changes that had developed between 1909 and 1921 left only a continuity of organization, not a continuity of the spirit, faith, and essential principles of the original church; in fact the original church had been supplanted gradually by the high churchism of Tomlinson and the leading Elders on the Council.

It was inevitable that the whole system – the office of General Overseer and the vicarious system proceeding from it – that had developed under Tomlinson's administration would collapse and fall: for spiritual 'men' with Bibles in hand were bound eventually to see the errors. The

---

[173] Spurling, 'Letter to Tomlinson, December 1, 1931', p. 2 ('R.G. Spurling File', ZACG Archives).
[174] Spurling, 'Letter to Tomlinson, December 1, 1931', p. 2. Spurling was in reference to 1 Pet. 2.13 and Rom. 13.4-7.
[175] Spurling, 'Letter to Tomlinson, December 1, 1931', p. 1.

contentions that followed the adoption of the overly-centralized institution were also inevitable, and the schisms in 1919-1920 and the disruption in 1923 were unavoidable; for 'men' beholding the face of Jesus in the dynamic atmosphere of Pentecostal glory, in mystical intimacy with the Spirit and in the mirror of prophetic revelation, could not for long settle for an imperfect and lopsided image of Him, nor remain in a religious system that boasted of being in the place of Christ. The true Gospel church looks not only for a returning Christ but entertains an ever-abiding Christ – an unchangeable and [ever-present God-man], One who may be known by His inspired autobiography as well as by the Spirit's testimony in the heart'.[176]

Some Further Reflections on the Church's Experiment in 'Christian Communism'

For all of the admirable and praiseworthy things that might be said in behalf of the Church of God's pioneers, particularly in regard to their deep spirituality and self-sacrificing dedication, it is rather mind-boggling that they could have conceived and developed a system of government and discipline that depended so much on political expedients and mechanics. They saw in the New Testament church the communal spirit, and thought apparently that it could be politically harnessed and formed into a mechanical system. They failed somehow to comprehend that a Christianized communism could work only by grace and faith and spiritual liberty, and therefore could not be legislated nor superficially produced by formal rules and regulations and human ingenuity and machinations. The apostle Paul's reproving question to the churches in Galatia could as well have been asked of the Church of God in 1920: 'O foolish Galatians, who has bewitched you ... having begun in the Spirit, are you now made perfect by the flesh?'

The plain truth of the matter is that for all their searching for the 'perfect system' in the New Testament, it was not there. What is revealed in the New Testament is not a perfect system but perfect principles – principles that are dependent on the inspiration and unction of the Holy Ghost for their execution and fruitfulness. In a word, only the Holy Ghost can form and operate a true, spiritual communalism. What might be called 'Christian communism' is nothing more or less than the simple and natural expression of Christian graces working their way out

---

[176] Phillips, 'Quakerism', p. 26.

of regenerate and consecrated saints into material blessings for the whole body of Christ.

The ideal and essential principles of a Christianized communism were laid out in *The Lost Link*, namely, a genuine philanthropy motivated by the love of God to create Christian Union. But whereas Spurling had discerned the true essence of Christian communism, he did not grasp the church's responsibility in procreating a practical system to enhance and cultivate the graces and gifts of the Spirit to benefit and edify all concerned, that is, he did not fully comprehend the indispensability of men in the process. Tomlinson and his followers, conversely, believed that God had designed a perfect form of external government and polity for the church, and, once discovered, the ministers and members could be pressured, if not forced, politically and mechanically to comply with the rules and regulations of the system; and that this process would finally invoke God's favor and create a euphoric atmosphere in the church. Being untaught and inexperienced, Tomlinson and his followers did not realize that this system resembled more the one taught by Karl Marx than the one taught by Jesus. It could produce only a communized form of 'Christianity', not a true and efficacious form of Christian communalism.

Significantly, Tomlinson admitted that the Church of God's financial system could not be found in the New Testament, including the new system adopted in 1920, and thus he and the Elders were forced to revert to the Old Testament to find support for it. Said he,

> The twenty-seven books of the New Testament do not furnish sufficient instructions on this particular subject to enable us to institute the perfect system, but we have a description of the 'Church in the wilderness', from which to draw information, so that we believe the system can be and will be materialized'.[177]

Again, in referring to the financial system in the New Testament, he said, 'The sands of time seem to have covered up the line marked out by the apostles, but the corner stones [the regulations laid out for the "church in the wilderness"] are still standing – the old landmarks still remain'.[178]

It was under this kind of reasoning that Tomlinson and his followers sought to find the perfect financial system for the church, just as they had sought to find the perfect system of church government and discipline in the 'church in the wilderness'. Under these impressions, they

---

[177] *HAA*, I, p. 75.
[178] *HAA*, I, p. 75.

endeavored to put 'new wine in old bottles' – or, perhaps more accurately, to superimpose the dynamic of the New Covenant church over the Old Covenant system.

Council of Seventy

Following the same line of reasoning that had brought about the office of General Overseer and the Council of Elders, Tomlinson recommended to the Assembly in 1921 a new arm of government which he intimated had 'flashed' upon his mind by the Spirit while meditating 'upon a plan to give the Church new life and make it seem more secure for the last days voyage'. The words that flashed upon his mind with great 'force' were 'Other Seventy'.[179]

It had been suggested even in 1916 that members should be added gradually to the Council of Twelve until the number reached seventy. But somehow, according to Tomlinson, he and the twelve elders never felt impressed to add another member to the Council, and he intimated that it was because God was guiding them into the more perfect system, a divinely designed and foreordained system in which two councils of government would assist the General Overseer – a Council of Twelve and a Council of Seventy.[180] He imagined that as Moses had chosen and appointed seventy in the 'church in the wilderness', so the 'other seventy' that the Lord had appointed in Lk. 10.1 was in fact a form of government, rather than simply evangelists appointed to proclaim the Gospel. Further, he declared that Jesus had 'raised [these seventy members] to a rank almost equal with that of the twelve, separate and apart from the common everyday disciples'.[181]

Significantly, Tomlinson said he had come to the conclusion after 'looking deeper into the Scriptures' that 'the twelve' should serve as his immediate counselors, and that the twelve and seventy together in joint council with the Genera Overseer should compose the 'official part of the General Assembly'.[182] He then made the astonishing claim that 'this is in harmony with the General Assembly that . . . was the highest tribunal [of authority] in the days of the early Church while the apostles still remained'.[183] He then cited the actions by the apostles and elders in Acts 15 as indisputable proof for this system – 'that the official Assem-

---

[179] *HAA*, I, p. 164.
[180] *HAA*, I, p. 164.
[181] *HAA*, I, p. 164
[182] *HAA*, I, p. 164
[183] *HAA*, I, p. 165

bly is composed of both the twelve and seventy, presided over by the General Overseer, making a total of eighty three vested with official authority ...'[184]

It had become the practice of Tomlinson to assign subjects to be considered by the Assembly to certain members on the Council of Twelve,[185] most often to Lee, Lemons, and Llewellyn who were prominent and gifted speakers. Lee was thus appointed to address and support the idea of the Council of Seventy. His assigned subject was 'Puissant Organization – Going the Bible Way'. Always creative, if not sound and accurate, Lee as usual referred to the 'church in the wilderness' to support the proposed system.

> I believe that Jesus, in launching this great gospel movement, did it in harmony with that which was prefigured in Israel. He first appointed twelve men, then later seventy. Why not fifty or sixty? Because that would not have been in harmony with the type and examples given in Israel, but seventy elders were appointed, they returned and reported that the spirit of the position was on them.[186]

He then explained that the twelve wells and seventy palm trees at Elim in Exod. 15.27 were a perfect type of the government of the church – Moses prefiguring the General Overseer, the twelve wells the elders on the Council of Twelve, and the seventy palm tress the elders who would compose the Council of Seventy.[187] He further endeavored to establish with mind-boggling logic that the palm tress received their life and sustenance from the twelve wells, typifying that the Council of Twelve is the superior body of government – both in regard to position and spiritual giftedness – and the Council of Seventy the inferior body, the latter being in subjection to the former and both in subjection to 'Moses' – the General Overseer.[188] Further, he endorsed Tomlinson's notion that the spirit and enablement for the prestigious positions on the councils would come after the men were appointed, not before – 'I was struck with the thought Brother Tomlinson gave, that the spirit of the position comes upon a man after he is appointed to the position'.[189]

---

[184] *HAA*, I, p. 165
[185] Lee, 'Deposition', p. 921; Tomlinson, 'Deposition', pp. 2545-46.
[186] *GAM*, 1921, p. 46.
[187] *GAM*, 1921, pp. 45-46.
[188] *GAM*, 1921, pp. 46-47.
[189] *GAM*, 1921, p. 46.

Courts of Justice

The church was further institutionalized with the adoption of a court system in 1921. This system was hierarchical in structure, rising from the local church (lower court), to the state office (court of appeals), to general headquarters (Supreme Court). The system already existed in embryonic form under the oversight of the chief bishops, for a person who felt that he or she had been tried unfairly before the local church, could appeal to the State Overseer to rectify any perceived wrongs or unfair decisions, and, if still not satisfied, the complainant could appeal finally to the General Overseer for a rehearing of his or her case.

Apparently, however, a large number of complaints had been launched against the old system, particularly because the court of appeals at the state level was composed of only one judge, and so also the supreme court in Cleveland, namely, the General Overseer. It had been recommended therefore that a bishop in each particular state and one of the members on the Council of Twelve serve with the state overseer to compose the court of appeals. Likewise, it was recommended that the supreme court be composed of three or five judges to assist the General Overseer in making just and equitable decisions. Tomlinson noted in his annual address, 'This system recommended is meant to make a way for perfect satisfaction in everything'.[190]

Tomlinson assigned M.S. Lemons to elaborate upon the subject of the Courts of Justice before the Assembly in order to make a case for its adoption. The speaker opened his discourse by citing 1 Cor. 6.1-5 to establish the principle of judgment and justice in the church, then referred almost entirely to Old Testament scriptures to establish the system of the Courts of Justice, citing particularly Exod. 18.13-27; Deut. 1.15, 16; 16.18; 19.18; Judg. 2.16-19; 2 Sam. 15.15; 2 Chron. 19.1-11; Isa. 1.25-27. He reasoned from the standpoint that since the 'saints shall judge the world', the church should in this present world be exemplary in developing a court system to judge in truth and righteousness – and thereby fulfill the prophecy, 'thou shalt be called, the city of righteousness, the faithful city' (Isa. 1.26). Alluding to the exclusiveness of the church, he proclaimed boldly, 'We have a government that can rule the world ... We can settle everything ourselves'.[191]

---

[190] *HAA*, I, p. 162.
[191] *GAM*, 1921, p. 35.

Following a 'message of prophecy in English'[192] by a certain sister and some further comments by Lemons, Tomlinson spoke at some length on the subject. He addressed again the theme of perfection, but added a peculiar aspect to the doctrine, namely, he tended to transubstantiate the attributes and work of Spirit to the church. He emphasized that when the church finds and restores the perfect system, that although the particular persons in the divine offices of the church may not be perfect, yet they will be empowered to make perfect decisions because the offices are divine and holy. Astonishingly, he declared,

> There is such a thing as getting so perfect before God that when He puts us in a position, the spirit of that position will come upon us. We may not be absolutely perfect but we are so near perfect that when we touch the right key we hear from heaven ... When these judges are put in place and it seems good to the Holy Ghost and us a dove-like spirit will come over us. The Spirit of the Lord came upon the seventy, Num. 11:16, 17, because they were placed in their position by God.[193]

Tomlinson's reasoning here is remarkably similar to the Roman Catholic doctrine of the 'charism of infallibility'. The teaching of Rome in this regard is that officers of the church in communion with the pope when speaking *ex cathedra*, that is, when speaking in behalf of the church in regard to making moral or doctrinal judgments, are empowered through a charism of the Spirit or special anointing to preach and teach infallibly. The person holding a divine office and the bishops together in magisterial council are thus 'immunized against error'.[194]

Though Tomlinson did not fully develop the idea nor use the term, 'charism of infallibility', yet his vision and mission to find and restore the perfect theocratic organization and system laid the foundation for the doctrine. His exaltation of the church as an outward institution was not a whit less than the boasts of the bishops of Rome. He sincerely believed that there is a perfect outward form of divine organization and government – 'a perfect pattern of theocracy and divine order' – and, once it was discovered and restored, the ministers and members would

---

[192] Apparently what is signified by this term – 'a message of prophecy in English' – was that a prophetic message was given out directly in English in distinction from a message in unknown tongues with interpretation.

[193] *GAM*, 1921, p. 35.

[194] Richard. P. McBrien (gen. ed.) *Encyclopedia of Catholicism* (New York: HarperCollins Publishers, 1995), p. 664.

be empowered through that system to function perfectly – to make perfect decisions; for the 'spirit of the position will come upon us'.

The church could thus, according to Tomlinson, look forward to perfect judgment and satisfaction in cases of dispute, for the prophetic Word had promised, 'And I will restore thy judges as at the first, and thy counselors as at the beginning: afterward thou shalt be called, The city of righteousness, the faithful city' (Isa. 1.26).[195] The Courts of Justice were thus being recommended 'to make a way for perfect satisfaction in everything'.[196]

Is there such a thing as the 'charism of infallibility?' Without question there is, for millions of witnesses could be brought to bear upon this fact, having seen the anointing come upon a preacher to interpret and proclaim truth infallibly. It is no less than what the apostle John exclaims, 'But the anointing which you have received of him abides in you, and you need not that any man teach you: but as the same anointing teaches you of all things, and is truth, and is no lie, and even as it has taught you, you shall abide in him' (1 Jn 2.27). But can this anointing, this 'charism of infallibility' be applied to the offices and particular institutions of the church? Is the church literally, without qualification, the incarnation of God or an extension of the incarnation of Christ? Can the attributes and gifts of the Spirit be transubstantiated to an institution? Do holy offices sanctify and perfect the actions of unholy men? Quite obviously not: for the councils and particular arms of government in the Church of God no less than those in the Roman Catholic Church have on many occasions contradicted this presumption.

Notwithstanding, this was the philosophy that captivated the mind of Tomlinson and those under his influence in the years leading up to the disruption in 1923, and no less so than in the minds of many of the great bishops in the second and third centuries which shipwrecked the early church and gave rise to Roman Catholicism.

Politics and Militarism

It was inevitable that the more the church was thought of in militaristic terms and formed into the likeness of a political institution, the farther it would be removed from its humble beginnings in Christian Union. The concept of 'superiors', 'inferiors', 'generals', 'officers', and 'subordinates' tended to minimize, if not destroy, the dignity of non-officers and less

---

[195] *GAM*, 1921, p. 35.
[196] *HAA*, I, p. 162.

gifted members. There was an ever-increasing tendency to exalt the bishopric and to distinguish between elders and those whom Tomlinson called 'common disciples'. There seems to have been little or no awareness that this trend reflected the error of the church in the second, third, and fourth centuries, that of gradually separating the 'clergy' from the 'laity' and laying a foundation for an episcopacy.

It was thus that corporatism, institutionalism and episcopalism tended to supplant genuine fellowship and the intimacy of intra-communion in the Spirit. The concept of the church as 'God's government for His people' tended to eclipse the image of the church as the 'body of Christ'. Under the influence of the statecraft that this idea inspired, the ministers and members tended to see themselves as having been constituted together merely on the basis of an outward covenant, and, as such, to be standing in relation to one another in a military or political formation rather than as saints dynamically fitted together by the Holy Ghost in love, and existing together as 'members one of another'. This view of the church as a political institution trumped the apostle's view of the church of 'an habitation of God through the Spirit' (Eph. 2.22).

It is no wonder then that the ministers and members under these impressions began to function like a common political body or military regiment. Tomlinson would describe the actions and tactics of those who opposed him in the coming months as 'wire pulling' and 'filibustering', language buried deep in his psyche, borne from the days of his political activism in Indiana and carried forward into the Church of God under his leadership. In the atmosphere of this political climate, some of Tomlinson's followers, ironically, became more politically-inclined and motivated than he himself, which, as we will see in a moment, lent itself to the further corruption and disintegration of the church. Still, it was Tomlinson more than anyone else who had introduced politics into the church, and all of the ministers and members wound up living and suffering with the consequences.

Two other significant measures were introduced and adopted by the Assembly in 1920 that should be mentioned here, namely, a Declaration or Manifesto and the Exchange and Indemnity Department.

The Declaration

A precursor to the infamous Constitution was adopted in the Assembly in 1920. It was conceived and drawn up by J.S. Llewellyn, assisted by Tomlinson, to solidify the legal standing of the church in the event of lawsuits and legal battles that might have to be litigated and settled in civil courts. The fact that the church lost its property at Ridgedale in Chattanooga when J.L. Scott and his followers brought suit against the church and won the case in 1919-1922, was enough to convince Llewellyn that the church's form of government from a legal standpoint was weak and inadequate.[197] He argued that the church was not only in jeopardy of losing more local church properties but all of the property at headquarters.[198] He then convinced Tomlinson of the same, and the Declaration was drawn up and presented to the Assembly. Llewellyn first suggested and drew up the Declaration, but Tomlinson admitted that he assisted 'in getting it up in shape'.

Llewellyn, being the primary author of the Declaration, was permitted to read it before the Assembly, and it was accepted by unanimous agreement. Coincidentally, it was read twice before the Assembly so that, according to legal precedence, its official status would not be challenged by the courts in the event of any civil litigation. The Declaration was composed of Six Articles and signed by A.J. Tomlinson, General Overseer, E.J. Boehmer, clerk:

> Be it known to all people everywhere that we, the General Assembly of the Churches of God, now convened in business conference, at Headquarters in the city of Cleveland, Tenn., set forth the following declaration:

> FIRST. That the minutes of all previous Assemblies are a true official record in substance and in fact as kept by the authorized clerks by said Assembly, and published by those fully and legally authorized to do so, and not the product or individual statements of A.J. Tomlinson, the General Overseer.

> SECOND. That the names of all the local churches recorded in various minutes including this one are the result of the faithful services of the ministers and representatives of the General Assembly and when thus received by the said representatives of the General Assemby, they then became and composed a part of the General Assembly. We, therefore, do not recognize the right of any local church to withdraw from the General Assembly as a whole, but those who prove disloyal to the Government and teachings as promulgated from time to time by the General Assembly or otherwise disorderly are to

---

[197] Llewellyn, 'Deposition', pp. 1058-64
[198] Tomlinson, 'Preparation Notes', p. 19; Llewellyn, however, under oath endeavored to conceal or blur the fact that he was the prime architect and mover of the Declaration and the Constitution (Llewellyn, 'Deposition', pp. 1061-68).

be dealt with in individual manner and excluded as a member of said church.

THIRD. That all the ministers, whether General Overseer, elders, bishops, deacons, or evangelists have been and are construed legal representatives of the Church of God while in harmony with its government and teaching.

FOURTH. That the General Assembly of the Church of God is that organized body with full power and authority to designate the teaching, government, principles and practices of all the local churches composing said Assembly.

FIFTH. That the name of this church is the Church of God which is sometimes referred to as, with headquarters at Cleveland, Tenn., only with the purpose of distinguishing it from other churches calling themselves the Church of God, but that it is no part of its name.

SIXTH. That one of the first principles accepted in the earliest history of its organization was that we accept the whole Bible rightly divided, which is today one of its most sacred principles, therefore we meet together in annual conference to search the Scriptures and put them into practice. Our teachings and faith are the same as originally accepted in its original organization and all of the changes in government and management have been duly authorized by the General Assembly in its various annual sessions.

This read and unanimously approved by the Fifteenth Annual Assembly of the Churches of God on the 8th day of November, 1920.[199]

In order to insure that the Declaration would be binding and recognized by the courts of the land, and to centralize and universalize further the church, Tomlinson in counsel with the Elders recommended also to the Assembly in 1920 that the names of all the members of each local church be registered at Headquarters. This church directory was also conceived by Llewellyn, but Tomlinson assisted him in giving it shape and called it a 'Manifesto'.[200] Following the Assembly, Tomlinson sent a letter to all the churches, which required the members by their signatures to affirm the Declaration and commit themselves fully and heartily to the centralized government of the church.

---

[199] *GAM*, 1920, p. 50.
[200] Tomlinson, 'Preparation Notes', p. 18.

Whereas, this local church has been subject to the government, teachings, principles and practices as promulgated from time to time by the said general assembly of the Churches of God, whereas, the said General Assembly which convened in Cleveland, Tenn., November 3 to 9th, 1920 did unanimously adopt a certain declaration which appears on page 50 of the minutes of the General Assembly, which we heartily endorse, approve, and in which we concur'.[201]

Tomlinson later admitted that he had failed to see how drastically the Declaration had changed the government and spirit of the church, particularly in regard to binding the ministers and members and local properties to the General Assembly, and that the General Assembly thereafter stood virtually in lieu of the church itself. Again, the Declaration was the precursor to the Constitution that was adopted in the next Assembly in 1921, which will be examined in its proper place. Suffice it here to note that the Constitution still more radically transformed the government of the church, making the Council of Twelve and the Council of Seventy in joint session with the General Overseer the 'official Assembly', and these 'legally authorized officials' according to Article 4, Section 6 were fully empowered 'to designate rules of government, teachings and principles for the local churches'.[202] Further, the name of the church according to Article 1, Section 1 of the Constitution was changed from the Church of God to the 'General Assembly of the Churches of God'.

It does not seem too much to say, in fact, that the church as it developed between 1912 and 1922 resembled the Roman Catholic Church more than Christian Union, particularly in view of the development of the exalted office of General Overseer, the establishment of an Episcopal hierarchy, the Council of Elders, the Council of Seventy, Supreme Court Judges, and in general the developing universality and centralization of the whole organization.

Exchange and Indemnity Department

In order to generate some finance for Headquarters' operations and to help pay for the new Assembly Auditorium and the Orphanage houses, the General Overseer recommended in his Annual Address in 1919 that the church adopt some plan to get money flowing into Headquarters. Again, strangely enough, Tomlinson referred to the system of the Roman

---

[201] Llewellyn, 'Deposition', p. 1078.
[202] See also Article 2, Sections 2-6.

Catholic Church as a model to follow in regard to a Headquarters system and how to acquire money for use in Cleveland.

> What has been the secret of the success of the Roman Catholic Church as they are gaining all the time? Surely it is not their spirituality. It certainly cannot be God's special favor bestowed upon them. It must be the careful arrangement of their financial system which places money at headquarters ...[203]

Tomlinson admitted that Llewellyn assisted him in planning the Exchange and Indemnity Department and that the Council of Elders had approved of it. There was also a Loan Department created in conjunction with the Evangel Publishing House. The idea of the Loan Department was first conceived in the latter part of 1919 when several members of the church had offered to loan money to the church to help with the financial obligations at Headquarters, and some had mentioned that they were willing to 'exchange property' to assist the church; indeed, there were a number of members living in other states who desired to move to Cleveland to be near the headquarters of the great Church of God.[204] The Loan Department was apparently to work like an 'insurance company', according to Llewellyn,[205] in which the lenders would be indemnified or protected against loss of property or cash loans. Significantly, Tomlinson noted,

> In talking over the matter with J.S. Llewellyn especially, we went over the ground of what could be done in the way of starting up a general business that would be helpful to the members of the church, and the church. This was discussed freely between us from time to time but not being especially developed until the early part of 1920 when we decided to launch what we called the Exchange and Indemnity Department of the Church of God Evangel.[206]

---

[203] *GAM*, 1919, pp. 32, 33.
[204] Llewellyn, 'Deposition', p. 1060
[205] Tomlinson said Llewellyn had 'mentioned that it would be a good idea to arrange for the church of God to carry an insurance of property as well as a trade business ('Preparation Notes', p. 61). Note: Tomlinson's notes in preparation for his legal deposition in the lawsuit in 1924 are hereafter designated as 'Preparation Notes'. These preparation notes refer to a number of preliminary questions that his lawyers had given him to think about anticipating questions that would be raised by the prosecution. His answers and comments in these Preparation Notes have been a valuable source in writing this section of the history of the church. The Prepartion Notes consists of 92 pages.
[206] Tomlinson, 'Preparation Notes', p. 61.

Tomlinson further admitted that the name, Exchange and Indemnity Department of the Church of God Evangel, was chosen so that it would not have to have Assembly approval, that is, it could be organized and begin operations as part of the Evangel Publishing House which already had Assembly approval.[207] This scheme to institute what was virtually a banking system in the church and to do so without Assembly approval – by actually circumventing the authority of the Assembly – would come back to haunt Tomlinson and give occasion for his adversaries to accuse him of a number of violations including usurping his authority and acting unilaterally.

One of the operations of this department was the 'Loan Fund' sometimes referred to as the 'Loan Department'. This was fully explained to the Council of Elders in the September meeting in 1920 and after a great deal of discussion was 'unanimously agreed upon'.[208] This department was thus launched after the Elders' Council meeting in September 1920. Thereafter, apparently a substantial number of ministers and members made loans and were given certificates of receipt signed by A.J. Tomlinson, Editor and Publisher of the *Evangel*. Among these were several of the Elders including E.J. Boehmer, T.L. McLain, and J.B. Ellis.[209]

---

[207] Tomlinson, 'Preparation Notes', p. 61.
[208] Llewellyn, 'Deposition', p. 1059; Tomlinson, 'Preparation Notes', p. 62.
[209] Tomlinson, 'Preparation Notes', p. 63.

7

ANATOMY OF A DISRUPTION: 1920-1923

The events that unfolded in 1920-1923 are packed with intrigue and curious twists and turns. The church's leaders entered this period with thrilling expectations of increasing blessings and material progress, anticipating that the Church of God was on the precipice of experiencing a number of glorious prophetic fulfillments. But as things turned out, what had begun with expectations of heavenly glory and divine visitations ended in a bitter and shameful disruption. 'The watchmen had failed to stand their watch … and the wise men had fallen to sleep!' (Isa. 29.9-14; 56.10).

There were other periods, to be sure, in which discord was sown and dissensions ended in schism. We have noticed the division in 1909-1910 led by J.H. Simpson and John B. Goins over Spirit-baptism and speaking in tongues and the recent schism in 1919-1920 led by J.L. Scott in opposition to the centralization of the church, but never until 1922 had the General Overseer been so bitterly and widely opposed by such a large number in leadership, including 'chief men among the brethren'. Moreover, no disagreements had ever produced so much slander and malicious gossip by the developing factions. Like the sudden appearance of a mighty tsunami, the still young organization was flooded with a tide of carnality. Envy, jealousy, evil speaking, bitterness, vengeance, hatred, and confusion infected and sickened a large part of the body; and true to the warnings of the apostles, the works of the flesh did their deadly work in the midst of the darkness.[1] Sadder yet, men holding some of the highest positions in the church were the source of the vile contagion, which as a matter of course spread everywhere they went. Thousands of

---

[1] Cf. Jas 3.13-16; Eph. 4.29-32; Heb. 12.15; Gal. 2.11-13; 5.15.

precious souls were disillusioned by the quarrels and evil deeds, and hundreds of these left the Church of God; and some also left Christ.

Looking back, we can see plainly that mistakes were made by those on all sides of the issues; however, some mistakes were simply human misjudgments in regard to administrative decisions and political strategies; others were caused by misinterpreting the Scriptures; and still others were occasioned by men inexperienced in churchmanship. But some mistakes – indeed the most damaging ones – were caused by men driven by worldly ambitions and temporal pursuits, whom the Serpent exploited in an effort to destroy the church.

The troubles that led to the disruption in 1923 actually began in 1912 when the General Overseer began to magnify his office. He admitted that he had restrained himself in the previous Assembly from suggesting the need for modern-day apostles and a hierarchical form of government because 'the people have been saying that I wanted to make myself a king or pope'.[2] But after having declared his intention in the Assembly in 1912, he continued in 1913-1914 to expand the powers and privileges of the office of General Overseer beyond any semblance to leadership in the New Testament church.

Tomlinson finally defined the position of General Overseer as being unique and set apart in a special way by the Holy Ghost for a special purpose. The implication in his assertions was that God had set in the church first the office of General Overseer, after that apostles, prophets, evangelists, pastors and teachers. Moreover, he guided the people in 1913-1914 through his annual addresses and 'table talk' discussions to appoint him for life in the office.[3] This lifetime appointment was the second most flagrant error he made in regard to the office of General Overseer; the first being his claim that the office was an 'imperial and

---

[2] *GAM 1906-1914*, p. 136.

[3] It may be argued whether or not the church freely selected Tomlinson for life in the office. A few of the ministers in 1913-1914, to be sure, suggested his lifetime appointment; and some believed – none more than Tomlinson himself – that the Holy Ghost had appointed him for life; but others did not think the office itself nor a lifetime appointment were wise or consistent with leadership in the New Testament. Among these were Spurling, Scott, Perry, Llewellyn, *et al.* And it is apparent that soon after the Assembly in 1914, a large number, if not the majority, of the leadership were uncomfortable with the extent of the powers of the office and the lifetime tenure. Further, it is apparent that Tomlinson in his charismatic way guided the proceedings in the selection process in order to achieve the outcome he desired, and he had also a hand in the way the *Minutes* were written in regard to the proceedings, that is, the *Minutes* corresponded with his particular interpretation of the proceedings. This is not to say that he flagrantly schemed for the office, but he believed he was called and anointed to lead the church and thus tended to guide the proceedings toward the inevitable outcome.

mediatorial throne'. The creation of this mythological office was the basis for Tomlinson's elder son, Homer, to claim in the late 1950s and 1960s that he was ordained by God to be 'King of all Nations of Men'. Outrageous as it was, Homer's claim was actually only a small step up from his father's perception of the office of General Overseer. Homer's fantastic claims to be the 'King of the World' will be elaborated upon in Volume II.

The Rise of J.S. Llewellyn

In the months following the schism by J.L. Scott and his followers and the adoption of the new revised financial plan in 1920, matters grew worse in the struggle for position and power, and for what form of government the church should practice. Tomlinson continued to gain influence and prestige in the church, but certain other men also had been increasing in influence and stature among the people, namely, F.J. Lee, M.S. Lemons, J.S. Llewellyn, T.L. McLain (Lee's brother-in-law), J.B. Ellis, and S.W. Latimer, all of whom sat on the Council of Twelve; and there were other men also rising to prominence – J.W. Culpepper, M.W. Letsinger, J.A. Self, E.L. Simmons, T.S. Payne, A.J. Lawson, George T. Brouayer, S.O. Gillaspie, Efford Haynes, G.A. Fore, R.P. Johnson, J.H. Walker, S.J. Heath, John C. Jernigan, Alonzo Gann, W.H. Cross, J.A. Davis, E.C. Clark, F.W. Gammon, I.C. Barrett, et. al. – most of whom were appointed to the newly created Council of Seventy, and some of these would eventually hold the highest offices in the church.

Among those rising to prominence, none were more bold, aggressive, and zealous than J.S. Llewellyn (1878-1934), and perhaps none more able and talented in regard to legal matters, finance, and business management than Llewellyn. He had a background in business; was comparably well educated for a Church of God minister; and had been a zealous evangelist for the church in the Knoxville region of East Tennessee, particularly in the Harriman, Oak Ridge, and Chandler vicinities near his home in Byington. Homer Tomlinson had befriended Llewellyn during his college days at the University of Tennessee in 1911-1913, and had joined with him in holding some revival meetings in and about Knox County. Reflecting on those times years later, Homer wrote that Llewellyn was an outstanding preacher and offered promise as a future leader in the church. He noted also that he had established a church in Oak Ridge near where the famous nuclear plant would be constructed years later contributing to the creation of the first Atomic Bomb.[4] Reminiscing further on his earlier friendship and labors in the ministry with Llewellyn, he acknowledged, 'I loved and honored him very much'.[5]

Notwithstanding that Llewellyn's friendship with Homer perhaps helped him to catch the eye of the General Overseer, it was his fruitful labors as an evangelist for the church and his potential as a leader that prompted Tomlinson to appoint him as overseer of Kentucky in the Eighth Assembly in January 1913. Thereafter Llewellyn became a prominent speaker in the Assemblies and served on important Assembly committees. In 1915 he was appointed to oversee Georgia, and in 1917 was selected to serve on the newly created Council of Elders. In addition to obtaining a seat on this powerful and influential Council, he was appointed to oversee the churches in Tennessee in 1919.

Figure 93

BISHOPS IN ATTENDANCE AT THE ASSEMBLY IN 1913
(LLEWELLYN IS KNEELING BESIDE TOMLINSON, THIRD FROM THE RIGHT)

Like Tomlinson, Llewellyn was an enigma; he was indeed a capable preacher and business manager, and gloried in the government and vi-

---

[4] Tomlinson, *Shout of a King*, p. 52.
[5] Tomlinson, *Shout of a King*, p. 52.

sion of the 'great Church of God', which of course helped to endear him to Tomlinson; but he was not a man who adorned in any outstanding way the Christian graces, nor made any great effort to live by the apostle's counsel to 'be gentle, showing all meekness to all men'. Lee, who would join with him in 1923 to unseat Tomlinson as General Overseer, admitted that he was 'hard' and used 'ridged terms'.[6] He had a reputation for being impatient and harsh, including at home with his family, and had left behind at Byington, his hometown (located about forty miles northeast of Harriman), reports of being less than honest in his business dealings. Many reputable ministers and members did not believe he was 'fit to be a bishop' according to the apostle's requirements in 1 Timothy 3, including several of the ministers and members in his local church at Chandler's View, Tennessee. His request for transfer to Harriman on April 16, 1916 was therefore denied for the following reasons:

> 1) J.S. Llewellyn is not in fellowship nor good standing with the church; 2) Disloyal as a member and bishop; 3) Guilty of lying; 4) Manifest a bad spirit at times; 5) Does not fill the requirements for a bishop ... is greedy of 'filthy lucre'!; he is not 'patient' in his home and with other people; his notoriety as a 'brawler!'; he does not have a 'good report' of them which are without or within.[7]

The document stating these charges was signed by the pastor at Chandler's View, M.W. Letsinger, who later became overseer of Tennessee and editor of the *Evangel*. The charges were also signed by the clerk, J.M Scarbrough, Bishop M.H. Koon, his sister, Blanche (who would later serve as Tomlinson's secretary), W.M. Freels (a prominent deacon), and two other members.[8] According to Tomlinson, Letsinger

---

[6] 'Letter from Lee to Tomlinson', December 28, 1922 ['F.J.Lee File', ZACG Archives]). Lee attempted to excuse Llewellyn, however, on the grounds of Tomlinson's superior attitude in regard to his position as General Overseer and especially because Tomlinson was uncooperative with the investigation against him in 1922-1923.

[7] *Church of God at Chandler's View vs. J.S. Llewellyn* (ZACG Archives).

[8] One of these members was Mollie McClure. She wrote a lengthy letter to the General Overseer dated June 2, 1916 ('J.S. Llewellyn File', ZACG Archives), stating among other things that Llewellyn and his wife 'had one brawl in the neighborhood that caused quite a sensation', and that he is 'by no means backward in accusing his sisters in the church of lying – He told me that Sister Cotton had lied – If he hears anything that has been said about him he manifests a very un-Christian spirit. I thought the preacher was to be an example to the flock, but if the members were to manifest the spirit that he manifests sometimes, it would be bad'. She concluded the letter with a plea for Tomlinson to intervene in the matter.

said further that '[Llewellyn] had never been the right kind of man' and that he had confronted him 'to his face many times' in regard to his behavior and 'crooked' business dealings.[9]

Notwithstanding these charges and accusations, and the fact that the state overseer, George T. Brouayer, had stood with Letsinger and other complainants in the Chandler's View Church against Llewellyn,[10] Tomlinson intervened in the matter by request of Llewellyn and all of the parties involved. He interceded first by correspondence and then also finally in person. Llewellyn had denied all the charges in letters to Tomlinson, claiming that it was a 'malicious prosecution' by the 'click' that ran the Chandler's View Church. He also produced a letter by E.J. Allen, a deacon of the church at Harriman, which praised him, stating in particular that the church at Harriman would not have a building in which to worship had it not been for Llewellyn's hard work and supervision.[11] Further, Llewellyn said the church at Harriman had made its own investigation of him (by order of the board of deacons and the assistant pastor) and had found him to be of good Christian character and had requested for him to be received into the fellowship at Harriman.

After making some investigation and hearing the grievances on both sides, Tomlinson sided with Llewellyn in the matter, particularly because Letsinger and the Chandler's View Church as a whole were not willing to bring charges against him in a formal business meeting. It seems also that most of the complaints against Llewellyn were in regard to incidents that had happened before he was ordained in September 1912, which Tomlinson adjudged at the present time – more than three years later – to be irrelevant. Tomlinson's explanation in a letter to Letsinger dated May 22, 1916 pointed out that the pastor and complainants at Chandler's View had not followed the proper principles and procedures to try the case justly, and apparently on this basis Letsinger and the other brethren at Chandler's View after some consideration decided to drop the case and to grant Llewellyn's transfer to Harriman. The following

---

[9] Tomlinson recorded Letsinger's accusations against Llewellyn on his official stationary as General Overseer, dated March 1923 ('J.S. Llewellyn File', ZACG Archives).

[10] In a letter written to Tomlinson from White Stone, Georgia dated April 25, 1916, Llewellyn appealed for help from Tomlinson, saying, 'Bro. Brouayer had written them [the church] ... and made himself a party with them. I therefore waive any consideration of this cause from before him and submit the matter to you for final consideration with full confidence' ('J.S. Llewellyn File', ZACG Archives).

[11] 'Letter addressed to Tomlinson', dated July 1916 ('J.S. Llewellyn File', ZACG Archives).

paragraph in Tomlinson's letter to Letsinger captures his overall judgment of the matter.

> In reference to some of those things that you mentioned that took place before he was ordained, I cannot pay any attention to them because the Church passed them by when they recommended him for the ministry and I cannot take them up now after several years of waiting. It occurs to my mind that as there was nothing sufficiently bad to keep him out of the ministry at that time that such should not now be brought up to prevent him having a transfer. If there has anything so wrong been done since, it should have been taken up and settled before he asked for a transfer. Also it should have been taken up before he was appointed state overseer. I thought he was in good standing in every way or I should not have given him the appointment.[12]

It seems that Tomlinson investigated the case thoroughly, and gave his judgment of the matter based on what he considered to be fair to all concerned, and best for the Church of God. But was he completely impartial? He admitted that he had a great deal of confidence in Llewellyn, and the indications in his correspondence with Llewellyn and others are that he thought the charges and accusations against him were exaggerated, amounting to no more than minor indiscretions committed in the past and, for the most part, best forgiven and forgotten. But the fact that Llewellyn had been under general appointment since 1913, working closely with Tomlinson as a state overseer and serving presently as overseer of Georgia, also complicated the situation. Further, Tomlinson was depending on Llewellyn to prepare the W.C.T.U. Temple at Harriman for the next General Assembly, which was to convene in September only a few months hence. Reflecting on Llewellyn years later and his relationship to Tomlinson, F.J. Lee said, '[Tomlinson] looked upon Llewellyn as a special friend and right hand man'.[13]

Still, Tomlinson would live to regret his promotion of Llewellyn and his part in getting him exonerated in this case. Notwithstanding his skills as a businessman and builder and his zeal for the 'great Church of God', it turned out that the ministers and members at Chandler's View had discovered his true spirit and summed up his character. In the years to come, Llewellyn would justify by his words and actions the charges and accusations that had been brought against him by Letsinger, Koon,

---

[12] 'Letter from Tomlinson to Letsinger', dated May 22, 1916 ('J.S. Llewellyn File', ZACG Archives).

[13] Lee, 'Deposition', p. 705.

Freel, and others in 1916. When the split came in 1923, W.M. Freels, the reputable deacon at Chandler's View, wrote to Tomlinson that he had been warned of this 'evil doer' and that he was the 'master mind' of the church's tragedy.[14] Another brother, A.C. Kelly, from Canton, Tennessee, said he had known and worked with Llewellyn for many years and that he had always been a troublemaker – that 'his maxim is to rule or ruin' and that '[he] does not care one iota for the Church of God, nor the people therewith connected. He does not care for the sheep, except the wool on their backs …'[15]

During his rise to prominence, Llewellyn became bolder and more presumptuous in his opinions in regard to the on-going development of the church. His legalistic mindset and business background led him naturally to interject ideas that would further institutionalize and politicize the church, some of which, ironically, corresponded with Tomlinson's ideas, and in other instances modified the concepts of the General Overseer.[16] Certainly the political ideas that Tomlinson weaved into the on-going development of the church helped to form young men like Llewellyn into a political mold, which in turn conditioned them to think and act more like politicians and *hommes d'affaires* than pastors and 'men of the cloth'. Thus, unwittingly, Tomlinson's political-militaristic slant on church government invited disaster, encouraging men like Llewellyn who were already bent in that direction.

Tomlinson's firm disposition about his exalted position irritated the relationship between himself and some of the Elders, to be sure, and most particularly Llewellyn. As early as 1913, during a discussion in which some were advocating that the General Overseer appoint the pastors instead of the state overseers, Llewellyn remarked, 'There is a way of doing the right thing in the wrong way. In the multitude of counselors there is safety. If we are not careful now we will make one of the greatest mistakes ever made. We can't object to the ability of our general overseer, but it would be putting too much on him'.[17] These

---

[14] 'Letter from Freels to Tomlinson', dated August 28, 1924 (Llewellyn File, ZACG Archives).

[15] This letter was sent to Tomlinson, dated July 7, 1923 (Llewellyn File, ZACG Archives).

[16] As early as 1913 Llewellyn was taking a lead in discussing many of the important issues coming up in the Assemblies. In the 9th Assembly in November 1913, he joined the General Overseer in promoting 'system and order in every department of the Lord's work'. Then, interestingly, he noted further, '… the wealthy people are forming themselves into trusts and combines, and the poorer classes into labor unions. Everything seems to be systematized except a few Pentecostal and holiness people' (*GAM* 1906-1914, pp. 268-69).

[17] *GAM* 1906-1914, p. 267.

comments revealed a certain mindset in Llewellyn in regard to the office of General Overseer, namely, that the office and officer were subject to the Assembly and other officers in the church. We might well suspect then that, as Tomlinson pressed to adorn himself with papal-like powers, Llewellyn was resisting all along. It will be noticed that in the next Assembly in 1914, when others were praising the General Overseer and intimating that he should be selected for life, including Lee and Lemons, that Llewellyn was silent.[18]

Llewellyn had come to despise Tomlinson's superior attitude and posture over the church, and labored untiringly to modify the 'exalted office' and Tomlinson's connection with it; but, at the same time, he sought with equal zeal to enhance his own stature, always jockeying for higher positions and grasping for more power. He had by 1919 ascended to the highest and most prestigious office in Tennessee – state overseer; and since 1917 had sat on the Council of Elders, managing in those two years to wield a superior influence even among some of the members on the Elders' Council. He had also held the office of General Trustee since 1916. By 1920, he had obtained also the important position of Foreign Missionary Treasurer, and, if all that was not enough, he had appointed himself in his capacity as the overseer of Tennessee to pastor the prestigious church in Cleveland. Not content, he managed also to get himself appointed as one of five Directors for Bible Training School, sat as one of the seven Judges on the Supreme Court and served also on the Orphanage Committee. He was also under contract with the church to construct the new Assembly auditorium and the Orphanage house.

There seemed to be no quenching of Llewellyn's thirst for position and power and material gain. Though he never explicitly admitted that he coveted the office of General Overseer, yet the circumstantial evidence is so overwhelming that one would be rather naïve to think otherwise. Be that as it may, once he realized that obtaining the highest office in the church was out of his reach, his political sophistication and business acumen enabled him to scheme to obtain part of Tomlinson's power. His maneuvering toward this end was to persuade the most influential men in the church, including other members on the Elders Council, that the powers and multiple positions inherent in the office of General Overseer needed to be diversified. Tomlinson would thus need to be divested of some of his powers and responsibilities and new offices created to accomplish this purpose. He thus suggested and lob-

---

[18] *GAM 1906-1914*, pp. 314-15. It may be noticed as well that Sam C. Perry was silent.

bied for the idea that other men be appointed to do the work of Editor and Publisher of the *Evangel* and Superintendent of the Bible School, and that these same men be selected by the General Assembly rather than by the General Overseer. Further, he suggested that the men selected for these offices should together serve with the General Overseer as an Executive Council, and so diversify all the more the executive power that had been concentrated in Tomlinson himself, including the appointment of national and state overseers and Assembly committeemen, and the appropriation and disbursements of general funds. It was in this way that Llewellyn maneuvered to get his fingers on the purse strings of the church, and to obtain a position to oversee the management and disbursements of the General Treasury.

We have noticed that a door had been opened for Llewellyn toward this end when J.L. Scott and his followers left the church in 1919 and in the ensuing months won the legal dispute over the local property at Ridgedale in Chattanooga. Llewellyn at the time was the overseer of Tennessee and, as such, was personally involved in the case. Tomlinson said later that Llewellyn began to say at that time that the church's 'order of business did not amount to anything and recommended a new order'.[19] He further suggested that the church needed 'chartered' and that all of its official statements and procedures needed to be 'patented' or 'copyrighted'.[20]

The legal victory of Scott gave Llewellyn plenty of latitude for his argument. He had increasingly thereafter criticized and belittled the church's business procedures and operations as being poor and inadequate, and did it in a way that reflected on Tomlinson's abilities and oversight of the church. Indeed, he had suggested that Tomlinson should serve more particularly in a spiritual and pastoral capacity, and leave the business end of the church to men like himself.[21] Further, as the new financial system – the Christianized communism – continued to fail to meet the needs of the ministers and their families, a flood of complaints came into Headquarters and many of them were registered against the chief leaders of the church. Under tremendous pressure, the Elders – particularly Llewellyn, Lemons, Ellis, and McLain – began to turn on Tomlinson and blame him for the failure, although Llewellyn and Lee and the whole Council were as much to blame for the design and adoption of the new system as Tomlinson.

---

[19] Tomlinson, *Call Council*, p. 7.
[20] Tomlinson, *Call Council*, p. 7.
[21] Homer, *Diary*, II, pp. 19-21; Tomlinson, 'Preparation Notes', pp. 16-64; Davidson, *Upon This Rock*, I, p. 608.

The Elders made a serious and costly mistake, as we noticed earlier, by not following through on the Assembly resolution to appoint a seven-man committee to distribute the tithes, and Tomlinson made an even greater mistake by taking it upon himself to perform this task unilaterally,[22] and more importantly to take it upon himself to use the tithes to pay off the debts on the new Assembly Auditorium and Publishing House.[23] This gave occasion for the more aggressive Elders, led by Llewellyn and Lemons, to charge Tomlinson with misappropriation of funds, and opened the door for the legal investigation of Tomlinson and the confusion that was to follow in the months ahead.

In a letter addressed to 'A.J. Tomlinson, General Overseer, Cleveland, Tennessee', dated March 28, 1921, four members of the Elders' Council – Llewellyn, Lemons, Ellis, and McLain – took it upon themselves to urge Tomlinson in language with threatening overtones to call a special meeting of the Council

> ... for the consideration of important matters that may be brought before them. We do this on account of the deep concern that we have for the welfare of the church and in view of the fact that there is a growing and wide spread dissatisfaction on account of some recent developments of vital interests of the Church. Some of the practices and costoms [sic] are ceriously [sic] questioned from a legal standpoint, and the general interest of the church demands adjustment of matters in question.[24]

This was the first clear signal that an uprising was in-the-making against Tomlinson and his autocratic authority, and the first indication of how far Llewellyn and Lemons and those under their influence were prepared to go to overturn the system of government that Tomlinson had established between 1910 and 1914, namely, a system almost completely under the thumb of the General Overseer. But while these Elders had legitimate concerns, the principal leaders had allowed a malicious spirit to take hold of them, and it was this spirit that desired not only to unseat Tomlinson from his exalted position, but to destroy in the process his influence and Christian reputation.

---

[22] Though denied by Llewellyn and Lemons, Tomlinson said in his deposition that 'They had put upon me the handling of the money against my will but I submitted' ('Preparation Notes', p. 26).

[23] Tomlinson and A.J. Lawson declared that the Elders in council had given the General Overseer the right to borrow from one fund to assist another when necessary, but this assertion was contested by the Lee-Llewellyn faction in the lawsuit (see *Opinion*, pp. 2-4; Tomlinson, 'Preparation Notes', pp. 25-26).

[24] Davidson, *Upon This Rock*, I, p. 543.

It was about this time that Llewellyn began to show his true colors, namely, that below the surface he was a man with mammon in his eye. He loved positional power, too – 'to be in the driver's seat' – for position served well to obtain financial gain. He had always been driven by the three G's – God, Gold, and Glory – but 'Gold' had managed apparently to excite and win over his deepest passions. Ambitious and always looking for a lucrative opportunity – even if the opportunity subjected him to the temptation of 'filthy lucre' – he had spoken to Tomlinson about starting a 'Sears Roebuck' type of mail order business for the church under the name of 'Golden Rule Supply Company', with himself as president and treasurer of the company. He desired the endorsement of the General Overseer and permission to use the *Evangel* to advertise it: for this would open the door to the membership of the church, which in 1922 approximated about 20,000 potential customers. His sales pitch to Tomlinson was that the profits would be used for missionary outreach. Tomlinson, however, in order to avoid a confrontation or ugly disagreement with him over the matter seems to have at first simply avoided giving his consent to the project, or else had tactfully turned down the proposal in language that Llewellyn did not comprehend.[25] There is every reason to believe that Tomlinson suspected the whole enterprise was nothing more than another scheme by Llewellyn to make gain for himself: and therefore he either ignored or turned down his proposal on the principle that individuals should not be allowed to use the *Evangel* to promote private businesses and enterprises.[26] In either case, what is almost certain is that Tomlinson would have been reluctant to turn over to Llewellyn a business endorsed by the church that was not under the direct supervision of the General Overseer.

However that may have been, Llewellyn, never easily discouraged and always bold and persistent, was determined to inaugurate his enterprise with or without Tomlinson's approval, and did so in December 1921. The *Cleveland Herald* featured an article on its front page advertising the 'Golden Rule Supply Company'. It was established with Llewellyn as president and acting treasurer, D.W. Haworth as secretary, and

---

[25] It is difficult to reconcile the conflicting statements in regard to whether or not Tomlinson approved of the project. Llewellyn said that he had, Homer and his father said that he had not. The preponderance of evidence seems to indicate that Tomlinson at first avoided turning Llewellyn's proposal down flatly, but afterward was forced to be more decisive when Llewellyn pressed the issue.

[26] A complaint was registered, however, that he had allowed his close friend and confidant, A.J. Lawson, to do that very thing – to promote his real-estate business in the *Evangel*. And was not the Exchange and Indemnity Department more or less the same thing, except it was under Tomlinson's direct supervision?

Avery D. Evans and W.M. 'Will' Chester as incorporators.[27] Haworth, Evans, and Chester were employed in the Evangel Publishing House, the latter as a bookkeeper for Tomlinson, and Evans, intriguingly, had recently married Tomlinson's daughter, Iris Marie.[28] In his book, *Cleveland The Beautiful*, William R. Snell made note that the 'Golden Rule Supply Company was chartered in 1921 as a mail order company, which operated out of its Benton Pike location formerly occupied by the Cleveland Buggy Works. Capitalized at $30,000 the company was led by J.S. Llewellyn'.[29]

In the summer of 1922, Llewellyn made a trip to New York to solicit the cooperation of Tomlinson's son, Homer, to promote the Golden Rule Supply Company. He offered to make him Vice-President of the company with a 'fancy salary' in exchange for his influence and endorsement, and assured him that his father had approved of the project.[30] Stunned and sickened by what he perceived to be an apparent scheme, Homer that same night called his father and rehearsed what 'Joe' had told him. His father denied it, saying, 'The idea, did he talk about that? Of course we cannot go into that'.[31] The next morning Homer told Llewellyn about his conversation with his father and that the General Overseer had denied giving him consent to go forward with the company under the auspices of the church. Irate and infuriated, Llewellyn immediately left by train for Cleveland and went straight to Tomlinson's office to vent his anger and frustration. According to the reports of Homer and his father, Llewellyn 'thrust his fist under A.J. Tomlinson's chin, and the first words he said were, "I'll break you for this"'.[32]

There is every reason to believe that the reports that Tomlinson and Homer gave of the incident are true and un-exaggerated, for many witnesses left testimony of Llewellyn acting in a similar manner in connection with other incidents in his past, and he would still again manifest this same anger and assertiveness in the events leading up to the 1922 Assembly and during the business sessions in that particular Assembly. Much like M.S. Lemons, whom we will notice again in a moment, Llew-

---

[27] *Cleveland Herald*, December 23, 1921, p. 1.
[28] On June 16, 1920 (Bradley County Marriage Records, Book 14, p. 321); the wedding, coincidentally, was officiated by Llewellyn, and witnessed by W.M. Chester.
[29] William R. Snell, *Cleveland The Beautiful* (Nashville: Williams Printing Company, 1986), p. 341.
[30] Tomlinson, *Shout of the King*, pp. 52-53.
[31] Tomlinson, *Shout of the King*, p. 53.
[32] Tomlinson, *Shout of the King*, p. 53.

ellyn became more forceful and brutish, unable to suppress the fleshly nature that was driving him.

In regard to Llewellyn's weakness for 'filthy lucre' and using the church for his own profit, the *Opinion* of the Appellate court speaks for itself. In the case of the *Church of God vs. A.J. Tomlinson, et al.* July 3, 1925, which Llewellyn and his faction initiated in the first place, the court concluded,

> The record shows that Mr. Llewellyn did not hesitate to combine business with his religion, much to the profit of his business; as stated before, he was paid $3000, but claims to have donated to the church $500 of this money as a gift ... Mr. Llewellyn also came to Knoxville and traded in certain property of his own for certain printing presses and equipment which he knew the Church of God anticipated buying, and he immediately sold the printing press and equipment to the Church of God. The record does not show his profit on this transaction. Mr Llewellyn states that he sold the church a second-hand truck worth $1600 for $1100, but that he donated $500 of this purchase price to the church. On cross-examination he admits that his truck only originally cost him $1100, and that he sold it to the church for the original price ... Mr Llewellyn admits that he, as an officer of the church, declined to pay the holder of a certificate $500 because the courts had not finally determined the liability of the church, but he advised the holder that he could trade it to an automobile dealer for a Ford car, which he did, and Mr Llewellyn admits that he obtained a commission from the Ford dealer by the sale of the Ford car and that he later cashed the $500 certifcate and is now holding it as a trustee of the church, we assume, on the theory that it makes a difference who holds the certificates in the case the court holds the church liable therefore.[33]

The court's *Opinion* goes on to show several transactions made by Llewellyn through the church for his own profit. And still more to the point, another report says, 'J.S. Llewellyn wanted A.J. Tomlinson to let him start a merchandise business – with THE CHURCH OF GOD MEMBERS AS HIS SPECIAL CUSTOMERS'. A.J. Tomlinson turned him down FLAT, with the statement that 'The Church of God shall not be commercialized to any persons [sic] advantage'.[34] He also had re-

---

[33] *Opinion*, p. 9.
[34] This was a statement by Homer; but even if true, it is almost certain according to the preponderance of testimony that Tomlinson did not at first turn Llewel-

ceived thousands of dollars for his part in building the orphanage house and the Assembly auditorium on the pretense, according to the court record, that he was an 'architect, while as a matter of fact he was only a common carpenter'.³⁵

Figure 94   Figure 95

J.S. LLEWELLYN AND HOMER TOMLINSON AS THEY APPEARED C. 1921

We will return again to Llewellyn in a moment, but it is important here to point out that the letter composed by the four Elders – Lemons, Ellis, McLain, and Llewellyn – and sent to Tomlinson in March 1921 urging him in threatening language to call a special meeting of the Elders Council, gave indication of the spiritually brutal confrontation to come. Further, it revealed implicitly that these Elders suspected, if they had not already concluded in their minds, criminal wrong-doing on Tomlinson's part, namely, that he was embezzling funds. It is not surprising then that the style and tone of the letter marked a change in their attitude toward Tomlinson – an attitude that would progressively degenerate into a presumptuous and disrespectful disposition toward his person and office.

It was not until Tomlinson actually called the Council together on September 8, 1921, however, that these four elders, especially Llewellyn and Lemons, made their complaints public and demanded answers to what appeared to be discrepancies in regard to the receipts and disbursements of monies connected with the Evangel Publishing House, including the Exchange and Indemnity Department, the Loan department, and the Bible Correspondence Course that had been inaugurated in September 1919 under the direction of Homer. In the course of the

---

lyn down 'FLAT', but seems to have been forced to this conclusion by Llewellyn's persistence.

³⁵ *Opinion*, p. 8; see also Tomlinson, 'Preparation Notes', p. 16.

meeting, they created an air of suspicion and left the distinct impression by their questions and remarks that Tomlinson and his son, Homer, had used some of the funds for their personal benefit. Llewellyn had often in fact complained because Tomlinson had sent Homer blank checks to purchase materials and supplies in New York for the Publishing House in Cleveland.[36] He also complained about the amount that Tomlinson's daughter, Iris, received as a worker in the Evangel office, though in 1919 it was only $15 per week.[37]

Suffice it for the moment to point out that the civil courts in the months and years ahead would prove beyond any doubt that Tomlinson had not embezzled funds, nor had used his office in any way for personal gain; far from it, he had given his life and material substance to build and advance the Church of God. If the least little effort had been made by the suspicious Elders to examine carefully the facts of the matter, they would have discovered this to their entire satisfaction; but they chose rather to think the worst of Tomlinson and rushed to judgment, even to the extent, according to the court record, of 'attempting to indict and send Tomlinson to the penitentiary'.[38] It is true that Tomlinson's poor bookkeeping practices[39] and tendency to think and act unilaterally gave occasion for suspicion and the forthcoming accusations, particularly on the part of some already resentful of his air of superiority and autonomous way of working. If the brethren on both sides could have only recalled Spurling's counsel and pleadings in *The Lost Link,* things almost certainly would have turned out differently – for the better; brotherly love and grace and fairness would have triumphed over evil suspicions, whisperings, and slanders. But, alas, Tomlinson and the Elders had forbidden Spurling to sell *The Lost Link* at the Assembly in 1920, for by that time they had removed themselves far from the wisdom and essential principles contained in the little book. Tragically, *The Lost Link* had been more or less lost again, at least at Headquarters. The light of love and hope for Christian Union was little by little eclipsed by what Spurling called 'political ecclesiasticism'. The grand institution – 'the great Church of God' – that Tomlinson and the Elders were build-

---

[36] Tomlinson, 'Preparation Notes', p. 69: 'Llewellyn kept fussing and growling at me about Homer's drawing and signing the checks as he did that I stopped that and at Llewellyn's suggestion signed the blank checks and sent them to Homer to fill in the names, amounts and dates, and this is how came me to sign the checks'.

[37] Llewellyn, 'Deposition, pp. 1039-42; Tomlinson, 'Preparation Notes', p. 14.

[38] *Opinion*, p. 9.

[39] *Opinion*, p. 3. The court accepted the judgment of the auditor's report in regard to Tomlinson's bookkeeping, admitting 'that he did not understand bookkeeping, and as a result, his bookkeeping was crude and laborious'.

ing, and in which they so zealously exulted, was just then beginning to block the light emanating from the Sun of Righteousness, depriving to some extent the ministers and members of His divine energy, and a lost world from receiving His glorious salvation.

Notwithstanding these developing conditions, the contentions were still more or less contained in Cleveland in the latter part of 1921, having not yet spread to the majority of the ministers and members on the field. There was, to be sure, some general dissatisfaction and serious concern in regard to the inadequacy of the new financial system – the church's experiment in a kind of Christianized communism – but the complaints and concerns seem to have waned for the moment as the saints gathered from across the United States and Canada and the Bahamas and British West Indies for the annual Assembly in Cleveland on November 2-8, 1921. They brought to the great conclave their prophetic vision and Spirit-filled expectations of a glorious church untainted by the darkness – by the evil thoughts and schemes – that had entered into the hearts of a few of the leaders at Headquarters. Reflecting on that Assembly a few weeks later, Tomlinson wrote that '[the meeting] beggars description … [for] the glory of the Lord and the display of His power … prevailed throughout the whole from beginning to end'. Though always the cheerleader and tending to see things through 'rose-colored lenses', he insisted that it was

> the greatest and most wonderful Assembly I have ever witnessed … God was there and everybody knew it. The great love of God dominated in every service, and the fellowship of saints was extremely pleasant, and all were happy and in touch with the bell-cords of heaven. It was surely like heaven to be there.[40]

The heavenly atmosphere in the 1921 Assembly, however, existed but for a moment; for heaven was actually in the hearts of the people, and thus when the saints returned to their local churches the glory went with them. Moreover, notwithstanding the heavenly atmosphere that had prevailed during the Assembly week, and the glory that had descended upon the people as they magnified and worshipped the Lord, they had unwittingly contributed to and participated in a grave mistake: namely, they agreed in the business sessions to adopt the Constitution. This legal monstrosity was conceived with a political scheme in mind, namely, to divest Tomlinson of most of the powers and privileges connected with his position as General Overseer, and to bring all of the

---

[40] 'Prefatory Notes', *GAM*, 1921.

ministers and members of the local churches under an Episcopal oligarchy. Did the human authors of the Constitution understand all of the ramifications of what they had written? Probably not; but certainly Satan did! And the Dragon was its essential author.

The Constitution

Tomlinson's description of the 1921 Assembly in his 'Prefatory Notes' was therefore even more amazing in view of the fact that the infamous Constitution was introduced and adopted in that Assembly. We have noticed that Llewellyn had convinced Tomlinson and the rest of the Elders on the Council in the months leading up to the 1921 Assembly that a Constitution was necessary in order to prevent ministers and local churches from pulling out of the organization and taking their properties with them. He insisted also that Headquarters was in jeopardy of losing its 'property at Cleveland if anybody wanted ... to contest it'. The experience at Ridgedale in Chattanooga gave him plenty of leverage to advance his argument.[41]

Llewellyn's argument had prevailed already to the extent that a Declaration was adopted in the 1920 Assembly, which in some particulars was similar in content to the forthcoming Constitution, most especially in regard to binding the local churches and their properties to the centralized authority of the church – the General Assembly. But the Constitution was much more sophisticated and involved; indeed, though Llewellyn and Lee and other Elders insisted then and later that the Constitution changed nothing in regard to the church's teachings and government,[42] it very obviously did; even on its face, the Constitution transformed the nature and government of the church, and prepared the way for Llewellyn and his followers to divest Tomlinson of his multiple positions and autonomous powers, and also his claim to a lifetime appointment. Further, it made a way for other changes and modifications to be made in the Constitution in Article 8, Section 2, which provided for amendments.

At the same time, despite Llewellyn's denials, the Constitution virtually disenfranchised the great majority of the ministers and members from the decision-making process of the church, particularly in regard to what would be finally passed. For under Article 4, Section 6, the Council of Twelve and Council of Seventy in joint session with the General

---

[41] Tomlinson, 'Preparation Notes', p. 19.
[42] Llewellyn, 'Deposition', pp. 1059-70.

Overseer composed the 'official Assembly' and were empowered to act with 'full power and authority to designate rules of government, teachings and principles for the local churches'. Further, this 'official Assembly' was duly recognized and authorized to act even if a large number of the Council of Elders and Council of Seventy did not answer a summons for a joint session; thus whether 83 men or 20 men participated, those present duly 'constituted a quorum'. Conceivably, therefore, two or three men could constitute a quorum and function as the 'official Assembly'. Behold how far the church had moved from the principles of Christian Union!

Further, whether it was 83 or 63 or 23 that constituted the quorum, the 'official Assembly' was much more likely to be manipulated and controlled by a few forceful and intimidating church bosses – dominating mafia-type godfathers – men like Diotrephes in 3 John 9, 10 'who loves to have the preeminence'. And even if those in charge were gentle men with good intentions, the new Constitutional form of government was most obviously at variance with the New Testament, particularly the church council in Acts 15.12, 22, 23, 25-28, and also at variance with the prophetic wisdom that 'in the multitude of counselors there is safety' (Prov. 11.14; 15.22; 24.6; cp. also 1 Kgs 12.1).

In addition, Article 8, Section 1 was included in part in anticipation of acting upon what Llewellyn had been promoting for several months, namely, that Tomlinson should be divested of some of his responsibilities and privileges, including acting as Editor and Publisher of the Evangel and Superintendent of Bible Training School. As well, Article 4, Section 10 was included in part to divest him of his lifetime tenure as General Overseer. While Llewellyn's thinking along these lines was technically right, for certainly Tomlinson wielded too much authority and influence, yet his motive was not pure. Llewellyn's aim, which would be proven in the months and years ahead, was to divest Tomlinson of most of his powers and privileges in order to invest himself with those same powers. The appellate court's review of the case in 1925, which based its *Opinion* on the sworn depositions of Tomlinson and the major players in the lawsuit – Llewellyn, Lee, Lemons, *et al.* – makes this perfectly clear.

> By reason of the facts to be hereinafter recounted, Mr. Llewellyn has wrested control of the church properties and is now occupying the chief position, or the position of greatest influence in the church. This was made possible by the adoption of the Constitution and a certain

investigation conducted by Mr. Llewellyn in conjunction with other elders ...[43]

The court also discerned perfectly in light of the evidence that the church's 'controversies evolve around the personalities of two men, A.J. Tomlinson ... and J.S. Llewellyn'.[44] But here we are jumping ahead in our narrative, so let us return to see how the Constitution came to be written and by whom.

Llewellyn had pressed incessantly since at least mid-1920 for a Constitution to be drafted and presented to the Assembly. His persistence finally prevailed and the subject was given due consideration in the Elders' Council in September 1921. It was decided in that meeting for a committee to be appointed to draft a Constitution and then allow sufficient time for the General Overseer and all of the Elders to go over the document to determine whether or not it should be presented to the Assembly for consideration. In compliance, Tomlinson appointed J.S. Llewellyn, F.J. Lee, and M.S. Lemons to compose this committee.[45]

Llewellyn, however, was the main architect of the document, which he apparently had already more or less written before the September meeting;[46] for, first of all, most of the Constitution already existed in kernel in the Declaration that he had written and that was adopted in the 1920 Assembly; and second, almost single-handedly he had lobbied for the Constitution since that time, and had been arguing for months for the very additions and modifications that appeared in the Constitution, particularly the articles that relegated all of the ministers and members of the church to an 'official Assembly' composed of only the Council of Twelve and Council of Seventy in joint session with the General Overseer. In any case, the Constitution was drafted and presented for the first time to the General Overseer and the whole Elders' Council for their consideration during the Assembly in November 1921. In a room located off the main auditorium, the General Overseer and Council of Twelve according to Tomlinson 'read over the constitution hastily and agreed to present it to the assembly'.[47] Strangely enough, the Constitution was introduced and adopted as one of the last items of business on

---

[43] *Opinion*, p. 1.
[44] *Opinion*, p. 1.
[45] Tomlinson, 'Preparation Notes', p. 20.
[46] As well, it is almost certain that Llewellyn had consulted legal counsel in drafting the Constitution. He had in 1920 advised Tomlinson 'that a certain lawyer in Chattanooga had very kindly and politely offered his services to help us remodel our government completely and make it dependable' (Tomlinson, 'Preparation Notes', p. 20).
[47] Tomlinson, 'Preparation Notes', p. 20.

the last day of the Assembly, November 8, 1921, the same day the Declaration was adopted the year before.

According to procedure, the General Overseer introduced the Constitution to the Assembly: 'The elders in council with the General Overseer have concluded there is need of a constitution for the Church of God'. He then proceeded to assure the ministers and members that the Constitution is not 'setting forth any laws or creeds that are binding us ... only that which we have been practicing for years',[48] and read the entire document to the Assembly. After he had read the lengthy Preamble and Eight Articles and all of the Sub-Sections, he opened the floor for questions and comments. Accordingly, there were 'a few questions, explanations, and deep consideration'. T.A. Richard, from Nashville, who was in that same Assembly appointed to the newly-created Council of Seventy, made a motion to accept the Constitution as read, and it was adopted unanimously. Apparently a holy hush had come over the Assembly at that moment, for the General Overseer acknowledged the special presence of the Lord, and said, 'it seeming good to us and the Holy Ghost, let us all kneel before the Lord and reverence Him'.[49] Then 'after prayer all stood and praised God', and 'while the orchestra played, the General Overseer exclaimed, 'BEHOLD, WHAT GOD HATH WROUGHT'.'[50]

Tomlinson would in the months and years ahead lament that he had anything to do with the Constitution, and especially that he had introduced it to the Assembly and also used his influence to mislead the saints in accepting it.

> I state with some embarrassment, that I had not given [the Constitution] any special thought or consideration. My reason for having the part in it [that] I did, was because of the confidence I had in the brethren, who were so desirous to have the constitution and [I thought they] had given it all the necessary attention ... especially J.S. Llewellyn. I had obtained the information that it ... did not set forth any laws or creeds that were binding us but merely setting forth in plainer statements what we have been practicing for years. In my

---

[48] *GAM*, 1921, p. 60.
[49] *GAM*, 1921, p. 65.
[50] *GAM*, 1921, p. 65. A legend among Tomlinson's followers that he merely signified by the expression, 'BEHOLD, WHAT GOD HATH WROUGHT', that an unusual quietness had come over the Assembly, rather than that God had approved of the Constitution is suspect and, in fact, incredible, for Tomlinson had just said, 'it seeming good to us and the Holy Ghost' (Compare Tomlinson's comments in the actual *Minutes* with Davidson, *Upon This Rock*, I, p. 562).

statement in presenting the constitution, I was honest and sincere and as matters had been explained to me about [civil] litigations, I supposed it was for protection, and for that reason I accepted and recommended it to the assembly.[51]

The following is the Constitution as it was approved in the 1921 Assembly without the amendments added in the following Assembly:

Preamble

We, the Church of God, the ministry and membership of the General Assembly of the General Assembly of the Churches of God in conference assembled at Cleveland, Tenn.

In order to form a more perfect union, establish the principles of Theocratic Government, set forth the teaching, principles and practices as heretofore interpreted by the General Assembly as further herein provided and for the general welfare of its membership; do ordain and establish this constitution for the General Assembly of the Churches of God.

ARTICLE 1.

Purpose of Organization

Section 1. This organization is and shall be known as the General Assembly of the Churches of God.

Section 2. The object and purpose of this organization is to propagate the doctrine, principles and practices of the Church of God, as set forth in the New Testament, as interpreted by the legally authorized officials of this organization, which interpretations may be found in the minutes of the annual sessions of the General Assembly, also filed at the business headquarters of the Church of God.

Section 3. To promulgate rules and regulations to govern the local churches of said organization, and otherwise promote the general interest of the General Assembly.

Section 4. To search out the Bible plans of government and discipline and interpret the same.

Section 5. To provide a general government in which is vested full power and authority to dictate and promulgate rules and regulations

---

[51] Tomlinson, 'Preparation Notes', p. 22.

from time to time to govern the local churches composing said Assembly.

Section 6. To provide a general convocation for the mutual fellowship, spiritual development and general welfare of its membership.

ARTICLE 2

Membership

Section 1. The Membership of the General Assembly is and shall be composed of all the local churches as recorded in the minutes of said Assemblies.

Section 2. When a new church is set in order by any legally authorized minister of the Church of God, this new church as a product of his labor becomes a member of the General Assembly and shall be subject to the government, teachings, principles, and practices as promulgated from time to time by said General Assembly.

Section 3. No local church shall withdraw from the General Assembly as a whole, but such individual members of said local church who may become disloyal or otherwise disorderly, shall be dealt with and excluded from membership in such local church.

ARTICLE 3

Government

Section 1. The government of this organization is and shall be Theocratic in form, as interpreted by its officials.

ARTICLE 4

Officers

Section 1. The officers of the General Assembly of the Churches of God are and shall consist of General Overseer, general secretary, council of twelve elders and other seventy elders, presbytery, state overseers and trustees.

Section 2. The duties of the General Overseer shall be the general supervision of all the work of the general Assembly, and to sit as chairman of said Assembly when in session.

Section 3. The duties of the general secretary shall be to keep a careful record of the General Assembly, and act in conjunction with the General Overseer in execution of any and all legal documents authorized by the General Assembly.

Section 4. The duties and powers of the council of the twelve elders shall be to consider all questions that may properly come before them pertaining to the general interest and welfare of the Church of God. It is, and shall so be understood, that the twelve in conjunction with the General Overseer shall be the supreme council.

Section 5. The duties of the seventy elders shall be to faithfully represent the government and teaching of the Church of God in their various fields of labor, and to sit in joint session with the twelve in the Assembly to make final decision on all questions that shall come before said Assembly.

Section 6. The twelve elders and the seventy elders shall together with the General Overseer be understood and so construed to be the official Assembly while in joint session, which shall have full power and authority to designated rules of government, teachings, and principles for the local churches, those present to constitute a quorum.

Section 7. The duties of the trustees of the General Assembly is and shall be to hold in trust all property belonging to the General Assembly for the full use and benefit of said Assembly, and to see that no property or part of the same shall be converted to any other use than that which is in harmony with the plan and purposes, government and teachings of said General Assembly.

Section 8. The presbytery and their duties:

The General Overseer and the state overseer shall constitute the presbytery in the respective states or provinces, who, after all investigations necessary and other proceedings provided and authorized by the General Assembly shall have full power and authority to license or ordain candidates for the ministry.

It is further understood that it shall be within the power of the presbytery to take final action in revoking the license or ordination of any minister for any reason or cause satisfactory to themselves.

Section 9. The duties of the state overseer is and shall be to have the oversight of his state and territory and as much as possible conduct or order a general evangelistic campaign over his state during the year. To see that every church is supplied with a pastor as much as lieth [*sic*] in his power. In short, oversee every interest of the work in his territory.

Section 10. The term of all officials shall be fixed by the General Assembly while in session.

Section 11. Any official is subject to impeachment for an offence rendering him unworthy of the position that he occupies.

ARTICLE 5

Judicial

Section 1. There shall be a supreme judicial body composed of seven of the twelve elders who shall decide all matters which shall properly come before them, whose decision shall be final.

Section 2. There shall be a judicial body who shall sit in the various states where churches are established, to consider all matters coming under their jurisdiction, said body shall be composed of the state overseer, one of the seventy elders, and one bishop.

Section 3. It shall be the duty of the board designated in section 2 of this article to examine all candidates for the ministry, and if satisfactory they shall refer them to the presbytery for license or ordination.

Section 4. It shall be the duty of the board designated in section 3 of this article to try all ministers for any offence committed within the state where they shall convene; if, for any reason their decision should be unsatisfactory to either of the litigants, he shall have right to appeal to the body mentioned in section 1 of this article.

Section 5. It is and shall be within the power of the local church to try its members for any offence contrary to the government, teachings, principles or practices of the Church of God. Their jurisdiction, however, is limited to lay members only.

Section 6. No business conference or any act shall be legal unless presided over by a legally authorized moderator.

Section 7. Any lay member of the local church who has been tried for any offense and convicted and excommunicated who, for any reason, may feel that he has been improperly or illegally dealt with, shall have the right to appeal from such decision to the body set forth in section 2 of this article. And if, for any reason, he may be dissatisfied with the decision of this body, he shall have right to appeal to the body set forth in section 1 of this article.

Also if there be a litigation between two or more members of a local church, and if, for any reason, they be dissatisfied with the decision of the local church, they may have a right to appeal to the board set forth in section 2 of this article, and if, for any reason, they should be dissatisfied with the decision of the board set forth in section 2 they may have right to appeal to the board set forth in section 1 of this article.

ARTICLE 6

Finance

Section 1. It is and shall be recognized as an accepted principle, and a part of God's financial plan

that all membership shall pay tithes of their net earnings or income.

Section 2. It is and shall be ordained that the tithes are for the support of the ministry only.

Section 3. For the love of the gospel and the general welfare of the Church it shall be the duty of the membership to make free-will offerings from time to time as the needs may require.

Section 4. It shall be the duty of all persons intrusted with finance belonging to the Church of God

for any purpose, as treasurer of said church, to deposit the same in a reliable bank to the credit of the Church of God.

Section 5. The power to regulate and operate the financial system shall be vested in the supreme council.

ARTICLE 7

Education

Section 1. A Bible Training School shall be maintained as long as advisable, for the education of our ministers and workers, which shall include the extension department of the Bible Training Correspondence Course and any other educational pursuits that the General Assembly may from time to time deem necessary.

ARTICLE 8

Amendments

Section 1. As the work of this organization progresses, and the number of Churches increase, the General Assembly may create new and other positions and fill them as needs may require.

Section 2. This constitution may be amended by a unanimous agreement of the official Assembly in any regular session.

Roots of Revolution

Tomlinson claimed that he did not give 'any special thought or consideration' to the Constitution before introducing it to the Assembly, and only 'awoke to its real significance in February 1922, three months after it had been adopted'.[52] But it is difficult to accept that he did not see the glaring statements that were aimed at reducing the powers of his office and radically transforming the government and operations of the church. For, first of all, he read the Constitution to the Assembly; second, he moderated a discussion of the entire document on the Assembly floor and admitted that it had been '[deeply considered];'[53] third, he stated that in any case he never intended to 'enforce the Constitution' if it came into conflict with former practices in the church.[54]

Taking at face value the bishop's statement – 'I had never given it any special thought or consideration' – he could only have meant, in light of all the evidence, that he had not fully grasped all of the implications of the Constitution, and that he had not decided on what was the wisest and most tactful way to respond to it, that is, he had not thought through what course to take to get the Constitution overturned. Even in February 1922, after he had committed himself 'to get rid of it', he thought it best in order to avoid creating 'any disturbance' to 'pass it over until the next Assembly'. However, he admitted that he had mentioned his intentions to 'S.W. Latimer and perhaps a few others',[55] namely, to revolt against the Constitution and try to get it abrogated. He said later that, 'When I saw [the Constitution for what it is] my first impulse was to take matters in hand in true revolutionary style and combat the thing, but a more mature judgment decided on a better course'.[56] As it turned out, this more 'mature judgment' was simply to wait until the next Assembly, for in that more favorable setting he had the advantage as General Overseer and was more likely to succeed to 'start the revolution' and 'combat the thing'.

On reflection, it is plain to see that, though Tomlinson had endeavored to avoid 'any disturbance' in the church prematurely, the revolution had virtually begun in February 1922. Once Latimer or one of the others in whom Tomlinson had confided had informed Llewellyn of the General Overseer's intentions to overturn the Constitution, the war was vir-

---

[52] Tomlinson, 'Preparation notes', p. 22; Tomlinson, *Call Council*, p. 7.
[53] *GAM*, 1921, p. 60.
[54] Tomlinson, 'Preparation Notes', pp. 23-24.
[55] Tomlinson, 'Preparation Notes', p. 23.
[56] Tomlinson, *Call Council*, p. 7.

tually declared – either Tomlinson or the Constitution had to go! Tomlinson said later in his court deposition, 'J.S. Llewellyn must have known I was taking this stand against the Constitution, and this brought about his 14 Points in the following June'.[57] These 14 Points contained apparently in essence the 15 charges that would be laid against Tomlinson by the Ten Elders' in the June Council in the following year, which we will elaborate upon in a moment.

It will be recalled that during the interval between the time that the Constitution was adopted in November 1921 and when Llewellyn sent Lemons in June 1922 to deliver his 14 points to Tomlinson's office,[58] that Llewellyn had made a trip to New York to recruit Homer as vice-president of his newly launched Golden Rule Supply Company. When Homer refused his offer and revealed to Llewellyn that his father claimed to have flatly rejected supporting the company under the auspices of the church, Llewellyn was infuriated and returned to Cleveland immediately to see Tomlinson about the matter. During the confrontation, Llewellyn exclaimed in the heat of anger, 'I'll break you for this'.[59] We may be sure that Llewellyn's 14 Points was his answer in part to this embittered promise.

The Faithful Standard

Before we move on to examine the significance of the Elders' Council in September 1922, we should pause to notice a significant advancement for the church initiated in April 1922, namely, the launching of *The Faithful Standard* magazine printed by the Church of God Publishing House. The masthead stated the nature and aim of the magazine – 'Monthly Journal of Full Salvation' – and included the Publishing Committee, namely, F.J. Lee, T.S. Payne, M.S. Lemons, A.J. Lawson, and George T. Brouayer, all of whom, except Lawson, were on the Elders' Council.

The *Faithful Standard* was on average a 28-page periodical designed to complement the *Evangel*. Tomlinson was duly acknowledged as the Editor and Publisher of the magazine, but for all intents and purposes his son, Homer, was its actual editor and publisher, and also its chief writer and contributor. Significantly, inasmuch that the *Faithful Standard* was not the official voice of the church, it carried many theological articles and messages that were of a speculative nature, particularly personal in-

---

[57] Tomlinson, 'Preparation Notes', p. 23.
[58] Llewellyn, 'Deposition', p. 991.
[59] Tomlinson, *Shout of a King*, pp. 52-53.

terpretations of apocalyptic events and prophetical writings. In a word, *The Faithful Standard* provided Homer a format to express his prolific pen and apocalyptic imagination.

The magazine also contained soul-stirring evangelistic messages by various Church of God authors including F.J. Lee, M.S. Lemons, and T.S. Payne. Homer wrote lengthy and invaluable narratives of the church's early beginnings at Camp Creek and Culberson, and also narratives of the Pentecostal outpourings in the late nineteenth- and early twentieth century that are filled with details and insights about the church's early beginnings that can be found nowhere else. In addition, the magazine carried full-page and small advertisements, including A.J. Lawson's real estate business, R.E. Winsett's song books and sheet music, and Merchants Bank of Cleveland.

Notwithstanding the extremely valuable contribution *The Faithful Standard* made to the ministry of the church, only eight issues were published – April-November 1922.[60] The magazine supported itself with subscriptions and paid 'ads' and Tomlinson reported verbally in the Assembly that it showed a net profit of $60. However, later when it was learned that the magazine may have actually profited $200 per month, it gave further occasion for the Llewellyn-Lee faction to charge him with embezzlement.[61] The appellate court in 1925 adjudged the difference in the reports to be simply one of Tomlinson's 'exaggerated promoting ideas not based upon the facts', and thus ruled in this instance that his exaggeration 'casts no light upon the real issues on the lawsuit'.[62] The Llewellyn-Lee faction nevertheless made the most of the error during the course of the church's investigation and trial in June 1923 in prosecuting Tomlinson, and it remained an issue during the civil court trials that followed in 1924-1927.

---

[60] After Llewellyn was appointed as Editor and Publisher in December 1, 1922, *The Faithful Standard* was discontinued by the church, but Homer resumed the magazine in September 1923 after the disruption in July-August under the auspices of the Faithful Standard Publishing Company in New York. Homer was appointed by his father as the business manager, and published two issues in September and October, but only the October issue is extant.

[61] Llewellyn and Lee continued to press this point, demanding to know what happened with the apparent $200 per month profit, since Tomlinson did not report it. Tomlinson's answer was that his report of $60 was just an estimate and that he really had no solid grounds for having reported that amount, and that, in any case, all of the profits whatever they actually amounted to, were used in the interests of the church.

[62] *Opinion*, p. 9.

An Explosive Elders' Council

The regular meeting of the Elders' Council in September 1922 opened in the usual manner with introductory remarks by the General Overseer. Then the resignation of Bishop M.S. Haynes was taken up. Haynes, who had served on the Council of Elders since its inception in 1917 and also as overseer of Louisiana for several years, had 'fallen into reproach on account of some of his conduct'.[63] He had acknowledged his faults and the Council accepted his resignation. It was then acknowledged that a 'spirit of dissension' existed among the members within the Council itself, and that in order for the General Overseer and the Elders to proceed to do the Lord's business 'a great deal of time [should be spent] in prayer [so] the dissension might be cleared'. This effort was emphasized by several of the Elders, especially F.J. Lee.[64]

Accordingly, seasons of prayer continued for several days, but then Llewellyn, anxious to announce publicly his 14 Points and to begin his informal prosecution of Tomlinson, said the prayer time had 'become wearisome'[65] and pressed the General Overseer to get on with the business at hand. Indeed, he was already agitated because he felt that Tomlinson had treated his 14 Points with 'silent contempt'.[66] He then told the Elders publicly about his 14 Points and asked Tomlinson if he had the document on hand. Tomlinson replied that it was locked up in the safe in his office. Now anxious to discover what Llewellyn's 14 Points contained, the Elders who were not privy to the charges asked Tomlinson to bring the document to the next session of the meeting. This was done and the secretary, E.J. Boehmer, proceeded to read the 14 Points. The Elders then advised Tomlinson to respond to each of the 14 Points. He complied, and a great deal of discussion followed; and inasmuch as some of the matters involved Publishing House transactions and funds, the Publishing Committee was called together and asked to respond to some of Tomlinson explanations. It was at that time that M.S. Lemons broke in with a 'tirade of abusive words' accusing Tomlinson, as Editor and Publisher of the *Evangel* as well as General Overseer and Superintendent of Bible Training School, of 'mismanagement, misappropriation of funds, and a number of other things'. Lemons' comments were quite obviously anticipated by Llewellyn and in part at least inspired by him. For Lemons, who had for many years been an

---

[63] Tomlinson, 'Preparation Notes', p. 24. His use of tobacco was one aspect of his questionable conduct.
[64] Tomlinson, 'Preparation Notes', p. 24.
[65] Llewellyn, 'Deposition', p. 992.
[66] Llewellyn, 'Deposition', p. 992

admirer and devout follower of Tomlinson, had become in recent months a pawn in the hands of Llewellyn, and thus, whether unwittingly or with malice aforethought, he became a corroborator with Llewellyn to fulfill the latter's threat to 'break' Tomlinson.

In the midst of the Publishing Committee meeting, Tomlinson admitted in tears that he had concealed from the Elders and all of the brethren some important actions on his part, namely, that he had used $19,000 of the tithe fund to pay bills on Headquarters properties. This sent shock waves through the committeemen – Lee, Lawson, Lemons, McLain, and Brouayer – for he had on the previous day left the distinct impression that he had paid the ministers on the field the tithes that had come into the General Treasury as 'far as it would go',[67] even 'to the very last dollar'.[68] In view of this alarming admission, the Publishing Committee decided that he needed to confess his actions to all of the Twelve Elders and that the matter should be taken up by the Council.

When the Publishing Committee was dismissed and the Elders' Council resumed, Tomlinson attempted to explain the shortages in the tithe fund and the inconsistencies in the Publishing House reports, including the questions that had been raised in regard to the Exchange and Indemnity department, the Bible School Correspondence courses, and the *Faithful Standard.*

He acknowledged that he had diverted funds from the tithe fund but only to pay debts due on the new Assembly auditorium, orphanage building, and publishing house business, and this was 'to save the church and business from bankruptcy and financial ruin'.[69] It was in the midst of attempting to give a full account of his actions, affirming fully that he acted only in the interests of the church that he, according to his own testimony, 'broke over and cried like a baby'. He admitted that 'I suppose I lost my manliness for a little while'[70] but insisted that his tears and extreme sobbing were not from guilt but from being accused of what seemed to him to be unthinkable – that he and his family who had given everything to build the 'great Church of God' could be charged with abusing the church for personal gain. He was shocked by the abuse from men in whom he had put so much trust and confidence. Further, to show his sincerity in his admission or 'confession' for misappropriating part of the tithe fund to pay the church's bills, he reasoned with the brethren between sobs that if it was such a crime to use the ministers'

---

[67] Tomlinson, 'Preparation Notes', pp. 24-27; Llewellyn, 'Deposition', p. 993
[68] Llewellyn, 'Deposition', p. 993; Lee, 'Deposition', p. 676.
[69] Tomlinson, 'Preparation Notes', p. 25.
[70] Tomlinson, 'Preparation Notes', p. 26.

money to pay other bills [as Llewellyn and Lemons had indicated] then he was willing to give up his property, home and all if it took that to set things right, confessing in apparent earnest, 'I want to get to heaven'.

Figure 96

THE TWELVE ELDERS

Efford Haynes was selected to succeed Sam C. Perry on the Council after he was disciplined in 1919, and Alonzo Gann replaced M.S. Haynes after he resigned in 1922.

In the midst of Tomlinson's outbursts of crying, Llewellyn and the other Elders accepted his penitent spirit and acknowledgment of mishandling the tithes, and also of concealing it from them and the other brethren. Llewellyn said that his tearful confession was so traumatic that it seemed, 'to be dangerous, and I feared for him, he wept very bitterly, and he kept on crying …'[71] It was in the midst of this emotional outburst that the Elders, including Llewellyn and Ellis, also began to cry and seemed to sympathize with his sorrow. Llewellyn and Ellis in fact when over and 'picked him up off the floor, and told him to get up, it could be fixed some way'. And, further, they encouraged him that if he would make the confession in the same way to the Assembly 'we believe that after all everything could be tided over all right'.[72] Tomlinson, however, believed that their actions were hypocritical. He said, 'the two men [Llewellyn and Ellis] did pick me up and expressed their sympathy for me, but I knew right then it was only for a show'.[73] What is obvious upon reflection of all the evidence is that Llewellyn and his followers and Tomlinson and his followers interpreted the tearful outburst and emotional collapse of Tomlinson completely differently. Llewellyn and those in sympathy with him believed they had broken the spirit of Tomlinson – his 'hard and stubborn disposition'[74] – and that he would now be more cooperative with them, if not completely submissive; whereas, Tomlinson was grieved because he perceived the confrontation to be abusive and unjust, and anticipated that the present differences between the brethren would result finally in an outright visible separation.[75]

Tomlinson of course did desire to 'make things right to go to heaven', if indeed he had done wrong morally as the three Elders had claimed, but he was equally concerned on account of Llewellyn's and Lemons' threats to prosecute him in the criminal courts and have him sent to the penitentiary. Did Llewellyn and Lemons and others in fact threaten him with criminal prosecution? Let the court record speak for itself. The *Opinion* of the appellate court in ruling in favor of Tomlinson issued a stinging reprimand to Llewellyn and his followers in this regard, saying,

> There is no question but what [Tomlinson's enemies] have used this purported audit as a means to destroy his influence with many of his church members and to brand him as a dishonest man. Had they spent more time in an earnest investigation of the facts and less in conference with the attorney-general in an attempt to indict and send

---

[71] Llewellyn, 'Deposition', p. 994.
[72] Llewellyn, 'Deposition', pp. 994-95.
[73] Tomlinson, 'Preparation Notes', p. 27.
[74] Llewellyn, 'Deposition', p. 995.
[75] Tomlinson, 'Preparation Notes', p. 27: 'My heart was broken over the way the brethren were treating me than over the money proposition (after we had been such old friends for years)'.

Tomlinson to the penitentiary, the real facts could have been known, if facts were being sought for.[76]

In regard to the scenario of events that took place in 1922-1923, Tomlinson said that, even before the September 1922 session of the Elders' Council, his 'confidence had been shaken in some of the [Elders]', primarily because 'two or three of them had and did talk to me as if I were a dog ... [and] on that special day in September I took abuse that was almost more than I could bear'.[77] The three men he referred to were Llewellyn, Lemons, and Ellis and in that order in regard to the intensity of their resentment and verbal abuse and increasing opposition to him.[78]

But Tomlinson also made four other admissions in his deposition before the Court that are particularly noteworthy to gain insight into what caused the disruption of the church in 1923. In the course of the Elders Council meeting in September 1922, when he was being charged with serious felonious crimes and threatened with legal action to send him to the penitentiary and possibly the 'chain gang', he said, 'The whole thing dawned on me what they had been drawing me into for years and culminated in that constitution'. Accordingly, they were drawing him into a scheme to divest him of his position and authority, and to revolutionize the government and polity of the church. Second, he admitted that in the midst of the abusive talk and threats made against him, 'Right then our fellowship was broken but I did not know it then'.[79] Third, he acknowledged that he had broken off communications with them: for the more 'they talked to me as if I were a dog ... the less I said ... then I quit telling them anything'.[80] Finally, he confessed that his relationship with these brethren was so damaged that he considered them hypocrites and that 'I could hardly bear for them to touch me. I could only compare their action to the Judas kiss.'[81]

---

[76] *Opinion*, p. 9.
[77] Tomlinson, 'Preparation Notes', p. 26.
[78] The opinion of A.J. Lawson in regard to these three men – all of whom he had closely worked with and knew fairly well – was that Ellis was the more moderate and least aggressive of the three. Even in regard to the infamous June Council, Lawson testified that Ellis had not 'acted as bad as the other two' (Lawson, 'Deposition', p. 1579); and Lawson's testimony seems to agree with the preponderance of testimony from others, namely, that Ellis was generally more mild and even tempered than Llewellyn and Lemons.
[79] Tomlinson, 'Preparation Notes', p. 27.
[80] Tomlinson, 'Preparation Notes', p. 26.
[81] Tomlinson, 'Preparation Notes', p. 27.

On reflection, we can now see that everything that followed the Assembly in 1922 and led up to the events in June-July 1923 were more or less formalities leading to an inevitable conclusion. The disruption of the church happened virtually in the September 1922 meeting of the Elders Council, insofar as genuine fellowship and brotherly love are concerned. But the seeds of the division were sown still much earlier, namely, with the establishment of the office of General Overseer, and more particularly in the way that Tomlinson defined the office in his annual addresses in 1912-1914 and afterward in the way he exercised the powers and privileges thereof.

It was inevitable as the church grew and expanded that strong and intelligent men would rise up against such a powerful and exalted position. The root problem therefore ran deeper than the personality clashes that developed between the brethren in 1922-1923, and even deeper than all of the outbursts of carnality and unsupported claims of embezzlement and dishonesty against Tomlinson. Cut through all of the personality differences and manifest works of the flesh, and there existed still the taproot of the problem: namely, Tomlinson believed that he was God's special agent on earth, and that he had been uniquely appointed and manifestly exalted by the Holy Ghost to fill an exalted position in the church for life.

Contentions, disruptions, and divisions were therefore inevitable; for even good men were bound to rise up against the development of such a superior position, particularly as it was so fragrantly pressed into a Christ-substituting posture. During the same years that Tomlinson was forming the office of General Overseer, certain other men had come to believe just as strongly that the office was unbiblical and unwise – even popish; and these men rose up to deny the office as it had been defined by Tomlinson, and thus demanded that it be modified. This was the crux of the contentions and root cause of the eventual disruption in 1923. The office of General Overseer, as understood and practiced by Tomlinson and his followers, was just as unbiblical and unwise as the Constitution; and in fact there probably would not have been a Constitution if the office of General Overseer had not been created and adorned as it was in 1912-1914, exalted even above the offices of the Twelve Apostles,[82] being boldly proclaimed by Tomlinson as being an 'imperial and mediatory throne',[83] a position in the church on earth 'to take Jesus' place' until He returned from heaven.[84]

---

[82] *HAA*, I, pp. 37-40.
[83] *HAA*, I, p. 40.
[84] *HAA*, II, p. 17; Phillips, *Quakerism*, pp. 17-23.

But was it the superior and exalted office that men reacted against, or was it a superior disposition in Tomlinson? Did the idea of such an exalted position and the fact that he believed he was divinely called to fill it, cause him to become exalted? Did all of the accolades that his brethren had heaped upon him somehow contribute to a superior attitude in him? What affect did it have on Tomlinson that on so many occasions through the years a large number of ministers and members, who were presumably under the influence of the Spirit, exalted him? – for messages in unknown tongues with interpretations were often given out in the Assemblies and other meetings that magnified his person and office. What affect did these manifestations have on him, and on others who witnessed the various demonstrations? Did a superior disposition in Tomlinson cause him to develop the office of General Overseer, or did the exalted office gradually condition in him a superior attitude?

We noticed earlier, that as early as 1894 Tomlinson claimed to have a special call upon his life to head a company of believers to evangelize the world, and also that he had come under the influence of men like Frank W. Sandford who had messianic complexes. Admittedly, he admired men in powerful political positions, even heads of states: men like King George, Hitler, and Mussolini. Certainly he believed he was a man of destiny, and, as we will see further into this history, he believed he was a man of prophetic destiny, and eventually came to believe that he was the unnamed person in Isa. 66.2 and Jer. 30.21.[85] Finally, he would claim that without him there would be no Church of God.[86]

Without attempting to psychoanalyze him, it seems that Tomlinson, for whatever reasons, believed that God had exalted and placed him at the head of God's people, and he was determined to fulfill the obligations that the Almighty had put upon him. Accordingly, it followed quite naturally that he believed also that God had qualified him with special gifts to fulfill his extraordinary appointment – to judge God's people and to know uniquely and especially what was best for them. His self-perceived superiority, or at least his belief that he was in a superior position in the church, meant that everyone else was inferior or in an

---

[85] Evans, *God's Anointed – Prophet of Wisdom*, p. 9.
[86] Tomlinson's rationale was that God foreordained him to restore the church, and therefore it could not have been accomplished without him. 'I can say as well as Paul that for this reason God raised me up. Why not? Who else did it? Who else could do it? Like the Apostle Paul, "I magnify my office". And like John the Baptist, I was just a voice crying in the wilderness. You never saw my name in [the Bible], but without a name I was there … Where would [the Church of God] have been if it hadn't been for me? … You are all Church of God because I am' (Evans, *God's Anointed – Prophet of Wisdom*, p. 13).

inferior position. He thus had no peers and did not know how to relate to other leaders in the church as equals. He thus felt insulted and encroached upon when his poor bookkeeping and office management was called into question by his inferiors. This disposition in Tomlinson created the rub between him and some of his brethren, and would contribute substantially to the disruption in 1923.

Figure 97

FROM LEFT: J.S. LLEWELLYN, T.S. PAYNE, F.J. LEE C. 1923

Still, Tomlinson's shortcomings and errors were no excuse for the carnal reaction against him in 1922-1923. The onslaught of slander against him and his family, the false accusations, the threats, the trumped up charges of embezzlement, the cruel threats of legal action and imprisonment, and finally the mob attempt to destroy him by so many of the Elders and those under their influence. Some of them – beginning with Llewellyn – acknowledged this later on and made things right with Tomlinson before they went to meet their Maker. Ironically, we have no record that Tomlinson apologized to anyone for his part in the disruption, nor that he ever entertained the thought that he had anything to make right with any of the Elders. What apologies he did make were left-handed – that is, he confessed abstractly to the church collectively and maintained that what he had done was for the good of the church, to save the church, and, as we will see in a moment, this attitude in Tomlinson all the more infuriated Llewellyn, Lemons, and Lee.

Before we move on, one more significant measure was taken in the September Council meeting. The Elders at the hest of Llewellyn suggested that a committee be appointed to examine the books and business of the Publishing House and financial affairs of Headquarters. Tomlinson proceeded to appoint the committee, naming F.J. Lee, J.B. Ellis, and S.W. Latimer. But Llewellyn immediately rose to his feet and objected on the ground that it was out of order for Tomlinson to appoint a committee that would be investigating his affairs: for he would be tempted to choose men who might show favor to him. Tomlinson yielded, and the Elders together chose three in the manner of a lottery, that is, each one wrote out three names on a piece of paper and put them in a hat that was in turn given to the clerk to read. The three that received the highest number of votes were thus selected; not surprisingly, Llewellyn was added to the committee and Latimer's name dropped.[87]

A Combative Assembly

Tomlinson had made up his mind in February 1922 to endeavor to get rid of the Constitution and restore the church to its original order of government and operations, that is, to the order that had developed between 1906 and 1920, and more particularly to the order that had established him in the superior and exalted position, and that had vested him virtually with totalitarian powers. But after giving the matter some thought, he surmised that he would have the advantage to combat Llewellyn and his followers before the whole church in the next Assembly, for his position as General Overseer loomed larger in that setting, giving him as moderator of the Assembly the 'bully pulpit': and so he determined to bide his time until then. But, unexpectedly, Llewellyn trumped his plan and 'fired the first shot' in the Elders' Council in September, which as it turned out gave Llewellyn and his followers the advantage.

Notwithstanding that Llewellyn virtually declared war in the September Council, Tomlinson pressed his agenda to overturn the Constitution in his annual address. This was virtually an impossible task under the circumstances, for in addition to the arduous task of confronting the Elders and the church about the Constitution, he had to confess his misappropriation of the ministers' tithe fund, for he had promised the brethren in the September Council that he would do this in the Assembly. This was a tall order for Tomlinson to fulfill – to confess that he had unilaterally misdirected the ministers' tithes, depriving them to some extent of their livelihood, and at the same time to ask them to trust his

---

[87] Tomlinson, 'Preparation Notes', p. 28; Llewellyn, 'Deposition', p. 996.

judgment wholeheartedly in regard to doing away with the Constitution, particularly in view of the fact that he had introduced it in the previous Assembly and had persuasively endorsed it. In situations like this, however, Tomlinson was at his best, especially when he stood before the Assembly in his awesome position as General Overseer.

Not surprisingly, Tomlinson's annual address was a masterpiece in his attempt to explain why he misdirected the ministers' tithes and at the same time reinforce his standing among the people. He had prayed and prepared himself well and apparently thought through carefully how his address should unfold, envisioning also how it would be received by the 'common people' with whom he was so popular. He first exalted the church in the Bible, and then proceeded to exalt the church that was present in that Assembly, proclaiming that the ministers and members gathered there were the actual restoration and continuation of that same noble body that had gathered for the Jerusalem council in Acts 15. Significantly, though flagrantly in error, he referred to the New Testament church as having been 'nobly begun by James and his faithful subjects'.[88] This was of course to reinforce his position: for he claimed to be sitting on James' 'imperial and mediatorial throne'. He then planted the idea in the minds of the people that because it is God's church, the devil would put it in the minds of some men – 'wolves in sheep clothing' – to attempt to 'take the place of God's appointed leaders … and start something of their own and draw off followers after them from the Church'.[89]

Carefully disclosing point by point what he had carefully thought through and planned out, Tomlinson then took up one of his favorite subjects, *theocracy*, and attempted to reinforce the idea that a true theocracy – over against democracies and worldly forms of government – signifies God ruling through a specially anointed General Overseer. 'We must still hold to the form given to us by James, the Lord's brother, when he said, "It seemed good to the Holy Ghost and us".'[90] And he continued, 'In their Assembly, under James's administration the councilors counseled, but they were very careful to have the "seemed good to the Holy Ghost" in their final settlement'. He then drew an analogy to himself as a captain or 'pilot of a ship at the wheel [with] his eye on the compass', who suddenly discovers 'that the vessel [is] out of its course, and if it [continues] in that direction [will] soon strike the rocks and go down'. So the captain 'searched for the cause and soon found that a very

---

[88] *HAA*, I, p. 181.
[89] *HAA*, I, p. 182.
[90] *HAA*, I, p. 183.

small piece of metal had fallen down close to the magnetic needle and caused the slightest variation, but enough to wreck the vessel if it ... was not removed before the rocks were reached'. He concluded his analogy by saying, 'Indeed it is no child's play to pilot the great Church of God over the rugged sea and follow the instructions of the chart and the pointing of the magnetic needle'.[91]

A little later in his address, Tomlinson would direct a specific section wholly to the office of General Overseer, and structure it in such a way to insinuate that some of the Elders, under the influence of Satan, 'had their machine guns of opposition aimed at this position for years'. Then he made the remarkable statement that 'James, the Lord's brother, who was evidently the first General Overseer by divine appointment, was finally beaten to death with a club ... [not] because of personal ... ill will against him, but because of the position that he occupied'.[92] And he further stated,

> By making mention of the position in the high and ennobling terms that I do, I would not have you think I do it to attract honor to myself, but I do it for the purpose of preserving the dignity of the office. This office must be kept sacred no matter who the divinely appointed person is that occupies it. I am only doing my Scriptural and Christian duty when I attempt to hold it up to its exalted standard ... At times I was overwhelmed with awe because of the glimpses I got of the grandeur and sacredness of the new position ... [But] it was not until the year 1913, that there was any appearance of a divine appointment more than by the common way of looking at things – God's providences. But in that year there was special manifestations of the Spirit that operated in the selection,[93] that brought expressions from many of the brethren which in effect were that the matter of who should be General Overseer should not be discussed.

He then endeavored to reinforce the idea that he had been appointed by the Holy Ghost for life in his position, and that this had been duly acknowledged by the church; and thus, regardless of some 'puny little clause or section in our constitution',[94] the appointment of God should be honored over and above the displeasure and contrary views of men. Going back to his address in the order that he presented it, Tomlinson then in his typical optimistic and cheerleading style of speaking, at-

---

[91] *HAA*, I, p. 184.
[92] *HAA*, I, p. 201.
[93] *HAA*, I, p. 202.
[94] *HAA*, I, pp. 202-203.

tempted to encourage the people – in spite of the cloud hanging over the Assembly because of shortages in the tithe fund and rumors of financial corruption – to enjoy the fellowship of one another, and to allow their 'hearts to beat in unison ... [without] discord or missing notes ... [without hindering] the flow of Christian love ... [and without] grating on the nerves because of some mishap or misdoing'.[95] It was as if he was acknowledging that he had learned a painful lesson: that the over-institutionalization of the church in previous years had ruined the fellowship of the church.

Continuing to unfold his address toward his ultimate aim – to abrogate the Constitution and reestablish his exalted position – he berated legalism and Spirit-less institutions and called on the church to plunge fully and wholeheartedly into a deeper spirituality, and especially for the ministers to become 'a flame of fire' and draw out of the Scriptures through the Holy Ghost the deep mysteries of the Gospel so that the Church of God can indeed be 'the fellowship of the mystery'.[96]

Having set the stage, he then began to address the issues that were on his heart, that he believed needed to be modified or abrogated; he began with Judges and Courts of Justice and then the Constitution. When he came to the Constitution, he knew what he was going to call for would surprise and shock a great many, and present a sobering and serious proposition, so much so that he acknowledged, 'I may lose my standing in the Church of God that I love so well – it may be the cause of many thousands turning against me – but I fear God and must stand for my convictions if I have to be turned off alone'. He continued,

> I want to say it kindly [and] reverently and without any reflection on anyone more than myself. I consider that we made a grave mistake one year ago when we adopted what we called our constitution. When I awoke to what we had done in the early part of this year, I became frightened and I have never been free from this scare. I am afraid God has been plaguing us to bring us back to our senses. Nearly all of the churches have had trouble this year, more or less, in one way and another. Scarcely one has escaped. And to my knowledge, this has been the direct cause of some of the trouble, and in other instances it has been the indirect cause of trouble. I feel that the fair face of the Body of Christ has been marred. I speak from my heart, and I am so grieved over it that I have often trembled like a leaf. It puts a spirit of weeping in my soul. You may think I am foolish and fogy, and I may

---

[95] *HAA*, I, p. 186.
[96] *HAA*, I, p. 187.

be one lone man ...but I have not arrived at my conclusion in a day nor a week. I have held it before me and prayed over it for almost nine months. I can't get away from it. I almost rebelled against making mention of it here, but I'm afraid not to do it. I must be free to hold up the blessed old Bible and declare as of yore, that this is our only rule of faith and practice. As it is I can't do it, and this has been the very cause of trouble in some places this year – they felt compelled to lay down the sacred Book of all books and take up the constitution or be counted disloyal. Can this state of affairs continue? Shall we pile the old Book aside after it has piloted us successfully through so many battles for the past twenty years? Shall we substitute human laws for our guidance in preference to the sacred, inspired laws of God? ... What can be done? There is only one thing to do – and I may lose my position for saying it – and that is to abrogate the whole thing and make a record to that effect and, as far as possible, even erase it from our memory, and once more raise the Book high up in the air and declare: 'THIS IS OUR ONLY RULE OF FAITH AND PRACTICE'. No discipline but this – this blessed old Book – how I love it today! I feel that some may feel that I have lost my head, but whether I have or not, this comes right out of my heart. It will be the duty of the committee on better government to consider this subject and bring it to the Assembly for their final consideration and disposition.

Tomlinson did not know what kind of reaction his bold ultimatum would receive, but he had prepared himself for the worst, even the possibility of being rejected by many thousands and perhaps 'turned off alone'. Indeed, it is clear that he had already contemplated a revolution and had resigned himself to start over again, if need be, with those of 'like precious faith'. Having now adopted a disposition toward this end, he waxed still bolder and called for the Committee for Better Government and the Assembly to reconsider the way the members of the Council of Twelve were selected and appointed. He boldly asked the committee to modify the process adopted in 1917 and to empower the General Overseer to unilaterally appoint all the members of the Council. It will be recalled that the practice since 1917 had been for the General Overseer to appoint the first two men on the Council, and the two with the General Overseer to select the remaining ten.

Sandwiched in between his call to abrogate the Constitution and his request for the Assembly to empower him to appoint the whole Council of Elders unilaterally, he attempted to explain his actions in diverting funds from the tithe fund to pay the notes on the new Assembly auditorium and the Publishing House. But rather than admitting that he had done wrong in assuming the authority to divert the funds, and in concealing his actions from the Twelve Elders and the church, he depicted himself rather in the role of a champion to save the church.

> Now here is what I want to say just as close up to you as I can. In order to save the Church and Publishing house from bankruptcy I felt compelled to use some of the tithes. I decided that I would rather suffer the shame and reproach of whatever would be heaped upon me, and risk incurring the ill will of all the ministers, than for the shame and reproach of bankruptcy to be heaped upon the Church. In other words, I loved the reputation of the Church better than my own. I have almost given my life for the Church this year. And I suppose I have given my position, but I have saved the reputation of the Church and that is consolation and happiness to me to this day. No matter what may follow and how you may deal with me, or what the future may be, I have bridged the awful chasm with the risk of being looked upon as dishonest and saved the day – the Evangel still soars over the world to its thousands of lovers, and the wheels of the Publishing House still roll …
>
> If you will only be patient with me I will tell you all. It was this way. Just before the Assembly some bills had to be paid, and I borrowed the sum of $6000.00 on my own responsibility to carry us over the Assembly with a hope that there would be enough sales of books, subscriptions for the paper, donations and other helps to pay it back. But the hard times had struck our people and the Assembly failed to net the amount needed. Then trouble came sure enough. But I held on to God, talked to some of the brethren about it, and kept up a good face to the bank – and I say to the credit of those bankers that their patience and leniency can scarcely be duplicated anywhere in the world by businessmen. They ran the risk of sacrificing their reputation as bankers to save me and the Church of God. The Merchants Bank of this city must ever by recognized as the Church's benefactor and savior from a financial viewpoint.
>
> But at last I saw my way to pay this off. Some good loans were sent and some extra sales of Sunday school literature and other things made me able to wipe out three thousand dollars at one swipe. In just a few weeks the other was wiped out, but this time I had to use some of the tithes to finish it up. I did it then with a hope that I would be able to replace it by the time the checks were ready to go out, but it failed. A little later, a number of notes on the orphanage property and

the auditorium property came due, besides a lot of bills and dues on both that had to be taken care of, besides the insurance and running expenses of the Publishing House and the payments of the machinery. All of this required thousands of dollars, but I only used the tithes a little at a time, each time with a hope that I would get enough back in a few days to replace them and save the ministers as well as the Publishing House and Church. But, as often, it failed, and I was so distressed at times that I was almost sick. And all this time I had to keep the business going.

A careful record has been kept which shows the exact amount due each minister, and this can be paid when the Evangel debt is met. However, quite a number of the ministers have already gladly donated everything due them to the Publishing House debt, and I believe most of the others will gladly do the same thing when they thoroughly understand the situation. I have shared with the others in this sacrifice. According to the allotment there is due me six hundred dollars that I have not taken out. This is much more that is due any other minister. I am willing to give it all for the sacred cause I love – to help keep the Publishing House going. I always feel better in sharing in the sacrifices of my brethren. More may be said on this subject when the financial report is given.[97]

When Tomlinson finished his address that had continued well into the afternoon, he called the people to prayer. It was at this moment that the great majority of the ministers and members rose to their feet and rushed to the platform to shower him with their affections and to reassure him of their support.[98] Amidst shouting and various manifestations of the Spirit, they cheered and shook the hand of the man who had 'saved the day ... and the church'.[99] Then, again, after giving his financial report on the last day of the Assembly, most of the ministers following the lead of Tomlinson agreed to apply the tithes due them to the indebtedness.

---

[97] *HAA*, I, p. 200.
[98] All of the histories on both sides of the division after 1923 show that the emotional outpouring and positive response to Tomlinson's explanation for diverting the tithes to pay bills at headquarters was at the conclusion of his annual address, e.g. Conn, *Mighty Army*, p. 172; Davidson, *Upon This Rock*, I, p. 590; but Tomlinson reported to the court in 1924 that it was upon giving his financial report as Editor and Publisher a few days after his annual address ('Preparation Notes', p. 30). It is apparent, however, that the people responded in such a way on both occasions, that is, during his annual address and later during his financial report.
[99] *HAA*, I, pp. 200-201.

Llewellyn and those under his influence – Lemons, Lee, Ellis, *et al.* – were furious: they felt that Tomlinson had betrayed them; for in the Elders' Council meeting in September he had humbled himself and acknowledged his wrongs, and promised to acknowledge the same before the Assembly in November. But when the time came, Tomlinson rather interpreted his actions and the whole ordeal in a way that made him appear to be a hero and the savior of the church. Even the Appellate court that ruled in Tomlinson's favor in 1925 admitted,

> It is true he was not humble as on the former occasion, or confessed that he had violated the criminal laws, but he stated what he did and his purpose in doing it. He was able to carry the members with him, and after much singing and speaking in unknown tongues the assembly came to order and ratified the action of the general overseer and authorized him to give each minister credit as a donation to the church; but this action did not satisfy the elders. His confession was not made in the spirit expected, and as Mr. Llewellyn states 'he undertook to either tide the thing over rather than come out with it like he did at the elders' meeting, so it looked like he was about to build up a pretty strong hold.[100]

But the truth of the matter, as it would continue to unfold in the weeks and months ahead, would show that the Elders – first Llewellyn, Lemons, and Ellis, and afterward Lee, McLain, *et al.* – were not simply trying to correct certain irregularities in regard to the finances and business operations of the church, but were conspiring together to destroy Tomlinson and anyone who sympathized with him. They wanted him on his knees begging to retain his position in the church and being thankful that they had not sent him to the penitentiary; or, otherwise, they wanted him out of office altogether and even out of the church.

Thus, when Tomlinson completed his address, and the great majority of the people rushed to the platform to embrace and rally around the General Overseer, Llewellyn, Lemons, and Ellis and their followers were at the same time plotting their strategy; being now more determined than ever to prosecute their aims – to divest Tomlinson of most of his powers and privileges, and to transfer these powers and responsibilities to other men; and, whether they intended to do so or not, they were in the process recreating the church in the image of an Episcopal oligarchy.

Now in order to achieve their aims, Llewellyn and his followers knew it would be necessary to amend the Constitution and create two new

---

[100] *Opinion*, p. 4.

offices in the church, and, more importantly, to specify that the men filling these offices be appointed by the Elders Council with the approval of the 'official Assembly'. And perhaps even more importantly, they realized that Tomlinson himself would have to be discredited, for they knew his popularity with the people in general would thwart their scheme. Thus, rather than yielding to Tomlinson's pressing demand for more power, Llewellyn went to the Committee on Better Government, which was meeting in the Evangel Publishing House while worship services and other programs were still going on in the new Assembly auditorium. There, in a forceful and passionate spirit, he rehearsed before this committee his 14 points, charging Tomlinson with ignoring and failing to comply with the terms of the Constitution, and accusing him also of incompetence and embezzlement; further, he had coined the phrase and peddled the idea that the Church of God was being run by the 'Tomlinson family machine'. By this term he implied that Tomlinson was nepotistic and that his family was involved with him in a ring of corruption – including his wife, Mary Jane, daughter, Iris, son-in-law, A.D. Evans, and youngest son, Milton, all of whom worked at the Publishing House in Cleveland. Further, though Homer lived in New York he more than anyone else in the family was involved in the interests of the Publishing House, being the principal writer and editor of the Bible Correspondence Course and also virtual editor of the *Faithful Standard* magazine: and in those capacities he had been authorized by his father to write checks for the church.

It will be recalled that Llewellyn had fallen out with Homer after the latter had refused his offer earlier that year to be vice-president of his Golden Rule Supply Company, and also because he had decisively sided with his father in the developing power struggle in the church. Whether or not Llewellyn actually believed that the Tomlinson family – particularly A.J. and Homer – were embezzlers, he nevertheless left that distinct impression in his remarks before the Twelve and Seventy and the Committee on Better Government; and a little later, he with others formally charged Tomlinson before the church and the courts of the land with embezzlement.

It is apparent that Llewellyn and some of his cronies wanted to believe that Tomlinson was a crook, for a root of bitterness had entered into their hearts and they had become angry and vengeful. Llewellyn implied that Homer was his father's primary partner in a ring of financial corruption,[101] and bragged that that was the reason he had 'stood

---

[101] Llewellyn, 'Deposition', pp. 991-93, 1038-40; Tomlinson, 'Preparation Notes', pp. 13-16, 60-76; Homer, *Diary*, 2.32.

against giving [Tomlinson] any greater authority or power' and had insisted that the Constitution be amended to reduce his powers.[102] When Alonzo Gann, the chairmen of the Committee on Better Government realized the gravity of the situation and the far-reaching implications of Llewellyn's 14 Points, he advised that his complaints and charges be presented before the Twelve Elders and the Seventy together with the Better Government Committee.

Gann with Tomlinson's permission invited the Twelve and Seventy to meet at the old church house to hear the case, and to assist the Committee on Better Government to formulate its report to the Assembly. A large number attended, but, as expected, Llewellyn held the floor and was the principal speaker. After fully vented his frustrations for more than two hours and having made his case against Tomlinson, attacking his family in the process – 'the Tomlinson family machine' – remarkably his counsel prevailed in the meeting on every issue: for the committee amended their original report and recommended that two new offices be created in the church, namely, Editor and Publisher of the *Evangel* and Superintendent of Education. More significantly, the committee agreed that the men holding these offices serve with the General Overseer as an Executive Council. Further, the committee denied the General Overseer's request to abrogate the Constitution, recommending rather that it remain the same except for the new amendments, and also recommended that the appointment system for the Twelve Elders remain the same, thus denying Tomlinson's request for the privilege to unilaterally appoint the Council.

In unprecedented fashion, Tomlinson in cooperation with the Committee on Better Government had Llewellyn read his lengthy amendment to the Assembly.

> Whereas, we have pledged ourselves to walk in the light as it was shed on our pathway and that it has been our cherished principle to accept the whole Bible rightly divided and especially the New Testament for our government and discipline. We find that the duties and the responsibilities were judiciously distributed among various officials that they might share the burden of government together in order that the safety of the government might be preserved and the interest of the people protected for it is written, in the multitude of councilors there is safety.

---

[102] Llewellyn, 'Deposition', p. 999.

We, therefore, advise the official assembly as provided in our constitution and that in accordance with our constitution, article 8, section 1, that we create the office of Editor and Publisher whose duty shall be to edit our publications and be general supervisor of our printing plant and be the treasurer of all the funds belonging to the general organization, except tithes of the tithes for any and all purposes, who shall deposit all of said funds in a reliable bank to the credit of the Church of God and as treasurer of said Church of God and he shall keep a careful record of all said funds and pay all bills over $1.00 by check and file all bank settlements and make them a part of his records. He shall be the supervisor of all the work at business headquarters except as herein after provided.

We further advise that the General Assembly create the office of Superintendent of Education who shall have the general supervision of all our work of education. We further advise that, from and after the assembly that it shall be the imperative duty of the General Overseer to travel over the states and oversee the work in general, hold state conventions and sit in council with the overseers of the respective states on their fields of labor and give all matters of importance his personal attention.

We further advise and recommend that the General Overseer, the Editor and Publisher, and the Superintendent of Education shall form an Executive Council who shall council together on all matters of general interest to the Church of God and any and all departments of the Church work, such as selecting teachers, managers, clerks, book-keepers, etc., and that no investment improvement, or new enterprise, or anything that would in any wise burden incumber [*sic*] or obligate the Church of God in any of its departments in a moral or legal way without the approval of the Executive Council and that no appropriation of any funds belonging to the Church of God outside of the regular authorized channel shall be made without the approval of the said council.

We further advise that each of the officials composing the said Executive Council shall be selected by the official assembly for a term of one year, beginning with this assembly. The selection to be made in harmony with Acts 1:23-26. We advise that competent men be selected for these positions that it may be said of these as was of James, Cephas and John who seemed to be pillars.

We further advise and recommend that the overseers of states be appointed by the Executive Council and it shall be the duty of the Executive Council to plan the work of the assembly such as making the necessary arrangements and arrange programs and other necessary work. We further advise that the publishing committee be discontinued and their work left to the Executive Council.

We further advise that the twelve elders including the Executive Council shall meet not less than once each year and consider all the business affairs of the Church and give such counsel and advise as in their judgment they may deem necessary for the general welfare of the Church, and make such recommendations to the General Assembly as they may deem necessary.

We further advise that the General Secretary be the treasurer of the tithes of tithes who shall handle the same in accordance with the provisions of our Constitution together with the requirements herein provided.[103]

After Llewellyn read his amendment before the Assembly, a great deal of discussion followed interspersed with emotional outbursts and a great deal of speaking in tongues. Several women were exercised by the 'Spirit' and gave out messages and interpretations in tongues which prompted others to denounce them on the basis of the church's teaching that women should be silent in business sessions.[104] Tomlinson, however, encouraged the practice, and justified his actions as moderator on the basis that he was endeavoring to create an atmosphere in which the Spirit would be free to move and work among the saints.[105] Llewellyn and his followers, however, believed it was a tactic employed by Tomlinson to create disorder and confusion in order to prevent the passage of the amendment. One of the Elders thus suggested that the church was under 'petticoat government', and Ellis in particular said something to the effect that the business at hand had been put off long enough by 'bonnets and shawls and shouting'.[106]

---

[103] *GAM*, 1922, pp. 49-50.
[104] T.A. Richards, 'Deposition', pp. 47-48.
[105] Interestingly, Tomlinson in his *The Last Great Conflict* denounces not only women speaking in business but talking in tongues in a way to influence the church's judicial function. 'There were no women speaking in the council at Jerusalem: no talking in tongues. They were a judicial body searching for and applying the laws to a particular case' (Tomlinson, *LGC*, p. 71). Tomlinson's vacillation in this regard gave occasion for his opponents to accuse him of allowing spiritual manifestations only when it served to forward his interests and particular agenda.
[106] W.M. Lowman, 'Deposition', pp. 968-69.

The controversy over Llewellyn's proposed amendement became more confusing and disorderly when two and three persons at the same time were allowed to take the floor and, being caught up in the excitement of the controversy, would talk over each other to advance their point of view. Llewellyn, Lemons, Ellis, and W.F. Bryant were particularly haughty and aggressive in their effort to push through the amendment. Tomlinson testified that 'J.S. Llewellyn, J.B. Ellis and M.S. Lemons were prominent in taking part in the discussion, and at times about took the gavel out of my hands. It was very hard to preserve order, and it was not uncommon for these three to break in and speak without any recognition from the chair at all ... I didn't know what was coming next'.[107] Ellis especially became presumptuous and bold during the proceedings. Tomlinson noted, 'At one time I recall that I was considerably tempted just to hand the gavel over to J.B. Ellis [and step out of the way], as he seemed to be taking such a prominent part in managing the affairs'.[108] J.P. Hughes, Lee's son-in-law, said that Llewellyn and those under his influence had caused the most disorderly and chaotic business session he had ever witnessed in an Assembly.[109]

In the midst of the chaos, Llewellyn, Lemons, and Ellis were intimidating some of the people who were not in favor of the amendment, endeavoring to discourage them from participating in the discussions. Lemons, for example, said to a man who had asked for scripture and verse in regard to the proposed recommendation for an Executive Council, 'that if I was as ignorant as that, I would come to Bible school and learn something'.[110] Some who stood against and questioned the amendment were called 'Joree hunters' and told to 'go back to the briar patches' where they came from.[111] This slur[112] caught on and was used

---

[107] Tomlinson, 'Deposition', p. 1940.
[108] Tomlinson, 'Deposition', pp. 1940-41.
[109] Hughes, 'Deposition', pp. 1025-29.
[110] Richards, 'Deposition', p. 49; Hughes, 'Deposition', p. 1029; J.O. Hamilton, 'Deposition', pp. 843-45. The man was either Winfred Thompson from Louisiana or a Brother Edmunds from Illinois – both were called down by Llewellyn, Ellis, and Lemons. In any case, the brother's response to Lemons was reportedly, 'You have insulted me by calling me an ignoramus' (Hughes, 'Deposition', p. 1030).
[111] Hughes, 'Deposition', p. 1027; Guy Marlowe, 'Deposition', p. 740; J.O. Hamilton, 'Deposition', pp. 843-45; Lemons denied that he had used the term, but several witnesses declared under threat of pujury that they had heard him.
[112] The 'Joree' or Towhee is a bird of the bushlands known throughout the southeast in the United States. It is also called the 'ground robin'. Smaller than the common robin, it is hatched in a ground nest and loves to scratch about on the ground hunting for insects, and as he hunts he kicks up dead leaves and earth rubbish creating a disturbance, and often is noisy as he scratches and digs for his food. The Joree rarely flies like other birds and when he does it is not so graceful; and he

a number of times in the 1922 Assembly to make those who did not agree with Llewellyn and his followers feel inferior and unworthy to participate in the discussions.[113] The debate and confusion went on for several hours until finally Tomlinson, as moderator, suspended the discussion until the next morning.

That evening Llewellyn, Lemons, and Ellis apparently discussed the situation and planned a strategy for the next morning. As soon as Tomlinson opened the session, Ellis addressed the chair and asked to be recognized. He then proceeded to make a short speech about the importance of the Twelve and Seventy and emphasized that the Constitution had distinguished them as the 'official Assembly' to decide all matters.[114] He then proceeded with the assistance of the ushers to have the Seventy seated together in the front of the platform to give them a place of prominence and to distinguish them from the rest of the congregation. Then he made a roll call of the Twelve and Seventy to further distinguish them as the 'official Assembly' and as a means to intimidate the rest of the congregation and inform them that they had no part in the final decision-making process and the resolutions adopted.

Sensing the gravity of the situation and realizing the revolutionary changes that the amendment would create, Tomlinson called the Assembly to prayer. As moderator he had purposed to refrain from interacting on the subject, but he was also endeavoring to slow down the proceedings in hopes that the Holy Ghost would move upon some of the brethren to oppose Llewellyn's plan.[115] While in prayer, according to Tomlinson and many other witnesses, Llewellyn came up to Tomlinson in a rage and interrupted him.

> After the subject was discussed for some little time, I called all to prayer as had been our custom for years. When the measure was before the house for consideration and during the prayer, I was aroused or stopped from my prayer by feeling the air pressed to the side of my head; as I opened my eyes, I saw a fist shaking at the side of my head

---

most often flies only high enough to mount a briar bush. This seems to have been the significance of the slur in the Assembly in 1922 – to trivialize and render insignificant the comments of those who questioned or opposed the amendment.

[113] Hughes, 'Deposition', pp. 1027, 1221-22. Hughes said it had become a 'by-word' in the Assembly.

[114] Tomlinson, 'Deposition', pp. 1931-33; Lowman, 'Deposition', p. 932.

[115] Tomlinson, 'Deposition', pp. 1941-43; Richards, 'Deposition', p. 50.

and heard Llewellyn say: 'How dare you block this measure. You shall not do it'. and as I turned my face ... I saw he was in a rage ...[116]

Llewellyn acknowledged the incident, but denied that he was angry and explained that he had shaken his fist only as a gesture of his earnestness to force Tomlinson as moderator to recognize Lemons and Ellis and others who were in favor of the amendment: for it was obvious, according to Llewellyn, that Tomlinson was attempting to block its passage in the Assembly.[117] Tomlinson, conversely, accused Llewellyn and his followers of 'working schemes and wire pulling' to accomplish their 'dastardly deeds'.[118]

Remarkably, though many of the leaders of the church knew Tomlinson was opposed to the amendment, the 'official Assembly' after a little further discussion accepted the committee's report. Just as remarkably, Tomlinson did not raise his voice against the amendment, though his voice alone could have prevented its passage because the General Overseer was part of the 'official Assembly' and, according to the Constitution, Article 8, Section 2, this body was required to act with unanimity in order to amend the Constitution.

Why didn't Tomlinson oppose the amendment? He later admitted that at that time he was himself confused and intimidated, and that, frankly, he did not know what to do. He was afraid that any action on his part would disrupt and divide the church right then and there.[119] And besides that, he admitted, he had been advised by F.J. Lee 'that those men intended to carry [their plan] through ... or else burst the Assembly and the church wide open'. Lee had advised and encouraged him therefore 'to try to be as easy as possible, [so that] maybe we could work it out later, and ... not have a separation'.[120] Explaining his actions or lack of action a little later, Tomlinson said, '[so] not wanting to be too headstrong and run things my way too much, I just let it drift'.[121]

Tomlinson's decision to 'tide things over' was one that he would come grievously to regret. He confessed that he wished many times he had rejected Lee's counsel and opposed Llewellyn and his forces and the

---

[116] Tomlinson, 'Preparation Notes', p. 36; Lowman, 'Deposition', p. 932; Gillaspie, 'Deposition', pp. 448-49; Brouayer, 'Deposition', pp. 1449-50; Lawson, 'Deposition', p. 1574.
[117] Llewellyn, 'Deposition', pp. 1115-18.
[118] Tomlinson, 'Preparation Notes', p. 36. Even his comments in his annual address in regard to 'wirepulling' (*HAA*, I, pp. 204-205) were obviously aimed at Llewellyn, Lemons, Ellis, and their followers.
[119] Tomlinson, 'Deposition', pp. 1941-42.
[120] Tomlinson, 'Deposition', p. 1942.
[121] Tomlinson, 'Deposition', p. 1942.

amendment right then and there on the Assembly floor![122] And on reflection, it would have probably served more favorably for him and his followers if he had taken his stand at that moment, for in the Assembly he had the 'bully pulpit' and was a master in getting the people in general to see things his way. But he did not take his stand then and there – and so we are left to wonder how things would have unfolded if he had.

The passage of the amendment, and other items in the Better Government Committee's report that had Llewellyn's mark on them, amounted to nothing less than a complete revolution of the government of the church. What Tomlinson had preached and labored to establish since 1912, namely, the office of General Overseer and the system of government built down from that exalted position, was overturned. The content of the amendment and the manner in which it was presented and passed by the 'official Assembly' revealed the stature that Llewellyn had attained in the eyes of many of the leaders, if not the church in general. Many thought that the amendment just made good sense, as well as being more biblical, particularly in regard to the three-man Executive Council over against an exalted and solitary leader who ruled virtually with unquestioned authority. But it is apparent also that several influential men wanted Llewellyn himself to be one of the men to form the newly created Executive Council, for he had demonstrated his ability and strength not only to correct some of the business irregularities at Headquarters but to stand up to Tomlinson. Thus, when the Twelve Elders met that morning – shortly after the committee's report had been accepted – to confer together and recommend the three men to form the Executive Council, it was a foregone conclusion that Llewellyn would be the new Editor and Publisher,[123] and it was just as likely that F.J. Lee would be selected as the new Superintendent of Education, for he was held in high esteem as a biblical scholar and had been involved in the work of the Bible Training School.[124] It was also unthinkable at that moment that anyone but Tomlinson would be considered for the office of General Overseer, though it was strange that he was considered at all:

---

[122] Tomlinson: 'I have wished several times that we had gone ahead and had the burst up, and we would have been better off than we are now ('Deposition', p. 1963).

[123] Interestingly, Lee and Ellis wanted A.J. Lawson to be the Editor and Publisher (Hughes, 'Deposition', p. 1225; Lawson, Deposition', pp. 1586-88); but inasmuch as Lee was not so vocal and insistent about the matter, the more aggressive and wily Llewellyn was able to manipulate his way into the position – and with the position he was able to control the properties and the finances.

[124] He was in fact chairman of the Publishing Committee and answered most of the questions that came into the offices in regard to the Bible lessons.

for since 1913 he had maintained that his appointment had been made by the Holy Ghost for life, and thereafter he did not allow his appointment to be reconsidered.

Not only had the 'official Assembly' by accepting the committee's report reduced the term of the office of General Overseer to one year, it had gutted the powers and privileges of the office. In a flash, the office was no longer what it had been: but also the church was no longer what it had been: for it was now for the first time ruled by an oligarchy. This was the first Assembly in which a large part of the ministers and members were discouraged from speaking and addressing issues, and certainly the first Assembly in which they were ruled out of the final decision-making process. Though most of the people did not comprehend the extent of their decision to accept the Constitution the year before in 1921, particularly in regard to the 'official Assembly' as defined in Article 4, Section 6 which transformed the government of the church into an oligarchy, they now came face to face with it in 1922 and experienced the devastating significance of their decision. But neither did the great majority of the people realize the consequences of accepting Llewellyn's amendment in 1922, which amendment not only dethroned Tomlinson but also relegated him more or less to the office of a glorified evangelist. Homer Tomlinson, though prejudiced in favor of his father, gave a more or less accurate assessment of what took place in the Assembly in 1922 and the events leading up to that time, particularly in regard to the report by the Committee on Better Government.

> Many matters were involved at this Assembly [1922], and it was these J.S. Llewellyn had taken to use to gather the leadership to himself, sowing discord against A.J. Tomlinson. He had encouraged the centralization of all church funds, church titles for local property, and the adoption of a constitution and by-laws, following other churches. He had encouraged the appointment of twelve elders and a body of seventy to govern the church, and as one of the elders, and general missionary treasurer with his office at headquarters, he stood like Absalom at the door, and went everywhere criticizing A.J. Tomlinson, and seeking to introduce what he called business methods. A.J. Tomlinson had been alright to build the organization, but now it needed more guidance from businessmen, Llewellyn would say. One thing that had been adopted upon J.S. Llewellyn's urging was to have all tithes sent to headquarters, and then distributed about equally to all ministers ... The 1921-22 temporary set-back in the U.S. affected the income of the church to some extent [and the tithes were used by the General Overseer to pay the bills on the Auditorium, and the en-

larged publishing house and printing plant] ... J.S. Llewellyn used this situation in a political sort of way, that he could have handled it better, and had himself put in, at the 1922 General Assembly, as treasurer, and editor and publisher ... A complete change was instituted, whereby J.S. Llewellyn as publisher, F.J. Lee as Director of Education, and A.J. Tomlinson as General Overseer would comprise a committee to conduct the affairs of the church, instead of having the General Overseer lead as in the past. J.S. Llewellyn had succeeded in getting A.J. Tomlinson out of office, and F.J. Lee siding with him, they could and did together begin to tell A.J. Tomlinson what he should do and not do ... [that] he should go out on the field.[125]

Tomlinson Resigns

It is true that Tomlinson retained the exalted title of 'General Overseer', but the office was a mere skeleton of what it had been; in effect, the 'official Assembly' had 'dethroned' him in favor of a three-man Executive Committee to rule the church; which, considering the differences in personalities, dispositions, and theological variations of the three men selected was nothing less than the creation of a 'three-headed monster'. This would become more especially noticeable in the spring of 1923 when it looked inevitable that Tomlinson would be impeached and that Lee would be the most likely candidate to succeed him as General Overseer. But on this development we will elaborate further in a moment. In any case, to place Tomlinson and Llewellyn together as equals at the head of the church was an unwise and unworkable decision – a recipe for disaster. For Tomlinson was not about to accept Llewellyn as his peer (nor anyone else for that matter); for, after all, he had signed Llewellyn's license and since 1913 had appointed him to his positions; Llewellyn, conversely, was not satisfied merely to neuter Tomlinson, he was determined to destroy his reputation and influence altogether. He had promised Tomlinson in the spring of 1922 that he would 'break him', and only a few weeks later boasted that he would 'have [him] out of that office if it cost him every cent he was worth'.[126]

Being driven by a carnal motive, if not an evil spirit, Llewellyn indulged his prideful notion and thereafter boldly manifested a contemptuous spirit. His boast that he would have Tomlinson 'out of that office

---

[125] Homer, *Diary*, II, pp. 21-22.
[126] Tomlinson, *Diary*, February 19, 1923. Tomlinson recalled Llewellyn's threatening words on several occasions with only slight modification of expression and no difference in meaning (e.g. Tomlinson, 'Deposition', p. 2302).

if it cost him every cent he had through the courts' was made in the heat of a disagreement in June 1922 over the management of the Evangel Office. Llewellyn had insisted that one of the sisters working in the publishing house should be removed from her position and fired as an employee, for he maintained that she was incompetent. Tomlinson, however, being the editor and publisher of the *Evangel*, refused Llewellyn's counsel on this occasion and the latter took it as an insult. In fact, it infuriated Llewellyn, and in response he worked unscrupulously to incite a strike among some of the other employees in the publishing house. Within a few days, one of the women – who as we will see in a moment was apparently a pawn in the hand of Llewellyn – handed Tomlinson a typewritten paper with the signatures of five or six other women who worked in the plant. The document threatened him with the alternative that if this particular woman was not fired, the others were going to quit. But rather than yielding to their threat, Tomlinson counseled them to go back to work and to allow him as editor and publisher to deal with the matter. The women submitted for the rest of the shift; however they did not show up for work the next morning and Tomlinson was forced to gather workers from other departments to get out the next edition of the *Evangel* and to complete some other pressing printing jobs. The delay and disturbance caused by the strike cost the church, according to Tomlinson, somewhere between $900 and $3000.[127]

Tomlinson suspected all along that it was Llewellyn behind the scheme, assisted possibly by Lemons, for when Tomlinson said to the woman that 'I don't believe you are responsible for this', she admitted, 'yes, there is somebody back of it' and that 'some of the Elders were backing her in regard to [the matter]'.[128] And though Llewellyn denied it and endeavored to intimidate the woman from accusing him, she had already confessed to some others that it was Llewellyn in particular that had put her up to it.[129] Tomlinson did not make any accusations, but about a week later the same woman who had brought him the paper with the signatures of the other strikers on it called him up on the phone and asked for her job back. When Tomlinson informed her that her services were not needed at that time, he received forthwith a call from Llewellyn himself.[130] In a loud and boisterous voice that could be heard

---

[127] Tomlinson, 'Deposition', pp. 2301-02. In his *Diary* entry for February 19, 1923, Tomlinson estimated that it may have cost the church about $3000 but in his court deposition in November 1924 he used the more conservative figures of between $900 and $1500.

[128] Tomlinson, 'Deposition', p. 2301.

[129] Tomlinson, *Diary*, February 19, 1923.

[130] Tomlinson, 'Deposition', p. 2302.

by others working in the room, he criticized the way Tomlinson ran the office and particularly how he had managed the recent strike. That is when he made his infamous threat: 'I will have you out of that office if it costs every cent I have ...'[131] Tomlinson assumed at the time that Llewellyn was in reference to the Evangel Office,[132] but later thought perhaps that he had in mind the office of General Overseer. Llewellyn likely had both offices in mind since at that time the office of Editor and Publisher as well as Superintendent of Bible Training School were one and the same with the office of General Overseer.

Quite apparently Llewellyn had been backsliding and yielding to the works of the flesh for several months, if not years, for his actions at that time and later among his peers in his own faction betrayed his true motives. Satan used the occasion of his unconsecrated state to enlist him as his assistant to persecute and impeach Tomlinson and his followers. Llewellyn's resentment and spite for Tomlinson grew in his soul like a leprosy, and the contagion spread throughout the church. With carnal, if not diabolical skill, he painted Tomlinson as a selfish and unscrupulous villain; and, amazingly, he succeeded to turn the great majority of the people against him. It was an incredible accomplishment considering that the people had for many years learned to love and trust Tomlinson, knowing that he had spent his life and everything he had to build the Church of God. Even Lemons, though under Llewellyn's spell and serving as his chief henchman in the campaign against Tomlinson, when asked about Tomlinson's dedication, admitted under threat of perjury that Tomlinson 'was as faithful man as I ever saw without any exceptions',[133] and acknowledged also that 'he had spent his life, ever since he moved to Cleveland, day and night in building up the church and its property'.[134] But here we are jumping ahead of our narrative; we will return in a moment to the frame-up and prosecution of Tomlinson.

Tomlinson saw the futility of the new government – particularly the institution of the Executive Council – knew it was unworkable, and had already determined that if the committee's report was passed with Llewellyn's amendment, he would resign. That same afternoon, after the Tithe Report was given, Tomlinson announced his resignation 'to take effect as soon as his successor was installed'.[135] He noted in his *Diary* that he took this action as a means to protest against the Elders' 'wire-

---

[131] Tomlinson, 'Deposition', p. 2302.
[132] Tomlinson, 'Deposition', p. 2299.
[133] Lemons, 'Deposition', p. 486.
[134] Lemons, 'Deposition', p. 487.
[135] *GAM*, 1922, p. 52.

working, trickery, and political chicanery ... and because the Assembly had accepted their dastardly acts'.[136]

Figure 98

M.S. LEMONS C. 1922

Figure 99

A.J. LAWSON

Lemons became one of Tomlinson's most fierce opponents, Lawson one of his most loyal supporters.

The General Overseer's resignation stunned the Assembly, for the great majority of the people did not comprehend the implications of the report, and were not aware of the deep divide existing among the leaders at Headquarters. Ironically, however, Tomlinson's resignation infuriated Llewellyn and Lemons and a few others under their influence: for they wanted Tomlinson to pay for his 'crimes' and believed his resignation was only a trick to escape his much deserved punishment.[137] Lemons, under Llewellyn's spell, seems to have been genuinely convinced that Tomlinson had stolen thousands of dollars and pocketed it for his personal use; and he wanted him to remain in the church to pay back what he had stolen.[138] He seems also to have sincerely believed that if he did not separate himself from Tomlinson, he could be linked with him legally as a partner in the scandal, if indeed the matter was brought to court and Tomlinson was found guilty. This was a widespread rumor in fact at the time; and thus, through this method of fear-mongering, Llewellyn and Lemons and their close associates had convinced a great many to turn on Tomlinson.[139]

---

[136] Tomlinson, *Diary*, February 19, 1923.
[137] Lemons, 'Deposition', pp. 430-37.
[138] Lemons, 'Deposition', pp. 437, 498-502.
[139] Lemons was not alone in promoting this fear-mongering. J.N. Martin, a deacon in the Ridgedale church in Chattanooga who had been especially supportive of his pastor, J.P. Hughes, Lee's son-in-law, after having made several trips to Cleveland had been convinced that 'if he stood with A.J. Tomlinson he would go to

Being convinced that Tomlinson was guilty of embezzlement, Lemons was enraged when Tomlinson in his annual address 'tried to cover it all up' and to convince the Assembly that 'we were all wrong, and that he was the only one right'.[140] And his anger was only the more intensified when the people in response to the General Overseer's address began to sing, shout, rejoice, applaud in the Spirit, and to crowd around him for almost two hours to shake his hand and kiss and embrace him.

Plainly, Llewellyn and Lemons and some others had allowed 'the flesh' to creep into their hearts, and under the power of carnal impulses could not conceal their jealousy, envy, and malice. And a few, like Llewellyn and Lemons, unable to contain their rage, vocalized and acted out what was hidden in their souls.[141] In the midst of the jubilation by the great majority of the people in response to Tomlinson's explanation, Lemons stood up on the Assembly floor before more than two thousand people and railed against him with language that had never been heard on the sacred floor of the General Assembly of the Church of God; indeed, seldom had such a tirade of verbal abuse been heard on the floor of the United States Congress. In a most unbecoming spirit, certainly unbefitting a Christian, he defamed and accused the General Overseer of moral and legal transgressions and threatened to put him 'behind bars'.[142] This in turn raised a storm of protest and criticism against Lemons and others who had spouted similar obscenities and created such a disturbance that Tomlinson was forced to call them down and restore order in the house.

When order was restored, some, including ironically F.J. Lee and J.B. Ellis,[143] pleaded with Tomlinson to reconsider his resignation and remain the General Overseer: not so much because they had deep affections for Tomlinson or were sympathetic with his complaints, but rather because they were afraid that Llewellyn would be elected in his place, for at that moment he was looming as a spiritual giant in the eyes of many.

---

the penitentiary'. He thus stood up in a meeting and declared he was going to stand with the Elders (Hughes, 'Deposition', p. 1095).

[140] Lemons, 'Deposition', p. 435.
[141] Lemons, 'Deposition', pp. 461-63.
[142] Tomlinson, *Diary*, February 19, 1923. Tomlinson's description of Lemons' words and actions were not exaggerated, for many witnesses testified that Lemons did the same and worse, e.g. S.O. Gillaspie, J.A. Davis, Lillie Duggar, C.T. Anderson, and A.J. Lawson. Even Lemons himself, after having denied several times during his disposition that he had endeavored to get an indictment against Tomlinson, finally admitted under pressure from the defense attorney and blurted out that he in fact had, saying, 'Sure, I do, yes sir, I aim to do it' (Lemons, 'Deposition', p. 500).
[143] Davidson, *Upon This Rock*, I, p. 604.

But none of the leaders at headquarters, except perhaps Lemons, wanted Llewellyn in that position.[144] Llewellyn was alright to help get Tomlinson straightened out but not to take his place. When Tomlinson saw that it seemed to be the overwhelming consensus of the Assembly for him to remain as General Overseer, he said he would reconsider his resignation and 'inform the Assembly of his decision [in the evening service]'.[145]

Meanwhile Tomlinson went home, and soon a great crowd gathered outside his house on Gaut Street pleading with him to remain the church's General Overseer.[146] This was balm for his wounded heart and allowed a ray of light to burst through the darkness that had clouded his mind and pressed his spirit; he sensed in the midst of such a display of affection and admiration that if he kept fighting on perhaps the tide could be turned back to the way things had been. He said later, 'The reason I withdrew my resignation was because so many begged me to continue and I hoped we would be able to straighten out matters and get together within another year'.[147] Thus, in the service that evening at 8.00 p.m. he announced to the Assembly that 'Since it seems you all want me and are not willing to let me go, I withdraw my resignation and will serve you another year in the capacity of General Overseer'. This was received with great relief and the people stood to express their appreciation.[148]

Nothing Actually Settled

The Assembly appeared to end on a good note, with the General Overseer agreeing to remain in office, and with the financial and business irregularities at Headquarters apparently having been corrected. Thus, most of the ministers and members went back to the fields eager to build the great Church of God and to spread the holiness-Pentecostal mes-

---

[144] According to Lawson, Ellis was especially concerned that Llewellyn would become the Editor and Publisher if Lawson turned down the position. He said, 'If we put J.S. Llewellyn in, we are a ruined people' (Lawson, 'Deposition', p. 1588). J.R. Kinser who was an eyewitness to this scene in the 1922 Assembly, and later became general treasurer among Tomlinson's followers, told this writer in 1983 that F.J. Lee had pleaded with Tomlinson not to resign for he believed Llewellyn would be elected in his place, and that this would not be good for the church. See also Davidson, *Upon This Rock*, I, p. 603.

[145] *GAM*, 1922, p. 52.

[146] Tomlinson, *Diary*, February 19, 1923; Tomlinson, *Shout of a King*, p. 160; Homer, *Diary*, II, p. 20.

[147] Tomlinson, 'Preparation Notes', p. 36.

[148] *GAM*, 1922, p. 58.

sage.[149] But, still, nothing had been settled among the leaders at Headquarters. Tomlinson had agreed to remain General Overseer only to fight the measures that had been adopted at the Assembly and to seek to get them overturned – to restore the church to its former government and order. But just as determined were Llewellyn and his followers to see that the measures adopted become the fixed rule of the church. The new Editor and Publisher, having taken over the duties of that position on December 1, 1922, immediately set out to use the Publishing House to promote his agenda. One of the first things Llewellyn did was to see that the Minutes of the Assembly were edited to discount Tomlinson's influence and to reinforce the Constitution and the new measures adopted in the recent Assembly, particularly the new government that had been spelled out in his amendment and adopted as part of the report by the Committee on Better Government.

> We are closing the minutes of the 17th Annual Assembly of the Church of God and sending them forth with the hope that they will be carefully read and understood and prove to a blessing to many.
>
> The General Overseer's Annual Address is not to be understood or construed as a part of the action of the Assembly, but only as a recommendation and suggestion for action.
>
> The reader's attention is especially called to the report of the committee on Better Government and the amendment thereto, which was adopted by the Assembly which action placed a new endorsement on our constitution with some amendments to conform to the report of the committee on better government and some other matters.
>
> The reader would do well to observe that it has long since been decided that customs and practices establish constitution and laws. Therefore, to abolish our constitution would virtually repeal every action and dissolve the entire organization. A careful study of the constitution and its amendments together with the book of minutes which can be had at this office is respectfully advised.[150]

---

[149] Some, however, went home disturbed because of the actions and the ill-tempered spirit manifested by Llewellyn, Lemons, and Ellis and a few others, sensing also that these men represented the potential for more trouble in the church in the weeks and months ahead.

[150] *GAM*, 1922, p. 106.

The New Government – A Freakish Arrangement

The die had been cast. The war was on, led by two immutable and irreconcilable forces – Tomlinson and Llewellyn. Both men were strong-minded, if not stubborn, and each was as convinced as the other that his vision was from God and was true to the Scriptures. Tomlinson was fully convinced that the church needed a Moses at the helm, and Llewellyn and his followers were just as sure that the church needed a Peter, James, and John – a threesome at the helm. The irony is that the views of both men twisted the meaning of the Scriptures to support their biases, and neither allowed for a middle ground between the two views. Tomlinson's view had created a popish, Christ-substituting type of position, Llewellyn's view created a freakish three-headed monster. It was naively presumed by Llewellyn and his followers that the three men composing the Executive Council could stand together as equals in position and work together as if they were one man. Thus, whereas Tomlinson's view infringed upon the headship of Christ over the church, Llewellyn's view infringed upon the glory of the Trinity: for only the Father, Son, and Holy Ghost were capable of fulfilling the expectations of the newly-created Executive Council – of perfectly working together with one mind! Even in nature, any creature with two heads is considered a freak – an accident in the natural order of things. Certainly, the Scriptures give no support for such a calamitous system – a three-headed system of government – and, thus, Llewellyn's attempt to classify the relationship of James, Cephas [Peter] and John in this way was clearly erroneous and bogus; for there is no evidence that these apostles stood together as equals in position and formed some type of Executive Council in the New Testament church; nor did they perform together in the way that Llewellyn's amendment called for:

> [to select] teachers, managers, clerks, book-keepers, etc. and that no investment, improvement, or new enterprise, or anything that would in any wise burden, incumber [sic] or obligate the Church of God in any of its departments in a moral or legal way without the approval of the Executive Council and that no appropriation of any funds belonging to the Church of God outside of the regular authorized channel shall be made without the approval of the said council ... We further advise and recommend that the overseers of states be appointed by the Executive Council and it shall be the duty of the Executive Council to plan the work of the assembly such as making the necessary arrangements and arrange programs and other necessary

work. We further advise that the publishing committee be discontinued and their work left to the Executive Council.

While James, Peter, and John were 'pillars' in the church and were all apostles, they did not hold the same position. Clearly James, the Lord's brother, was held in highest esteem among the apostles and elders (Acts 12.17; 15.13-22; 21.18; 1 Cor. 15.7; Gal. 1.19; 2.9-12; *et al.*) and recognized apparently as the presiding bishop in Jerusalem, and thus moderated the general assembly recorded in Acts 15 and pronounced the decisive judgment (vv. 13-22). Jesus had said, 'whosoever will be chief among you, let him be your servant' (Mt. 20.27), and apparently James, the Lord's brother, was considered to be 'chief' among the brethren until his martyrdom in 62 CE.[151] Thus, though James did not 'sit upon an imperial and mediatorial throne' as Tomlinson had vainly imagined, nor had wielded the kind of power that Tomlinson asserted, still he held a position greater than the one to which Llewellyn was attempting to relegate Tomlinson. For as Hughes, Lee's son-in-law, reasoned: if Llewellyn's amendment in regard to the Executive Council was a better form of government for the church, then James' dictum in Acts 15.19 – 'My decision is' – should rather read, 'Our decision is'.[152]

It perhaps should be noted further that the James who formed with Peter and John the inner circle among the Twelve during Jesus' earthly ministry (Mt. 17.1-9; Mk 5.37; 14.33; *et al.*), is not the same James mentioned as a 'pillar' in Gal. 2.9. The former was the son of Zebedee and brother of John (Mt. 4.21; 10.2), the latter the son of Joseph and Mary, and thus the half-brother of Jesus (Mt. 13.55; Mk 6.3); and it was this James – called 'James the Just' in early church history – who had risen to such distinction and eminence after Jesus' resurrection and return to the Father.

To complicate matters further, Tomlinson in his reaction against Llewellyn's amendment denied that the James who is called a 'pillar' in Gal. 2.9 is the same James who is elsewhere called the Lord's brother; he assumed rather that he was one of the two James' among the original Twelve Apostles. For said he, 'In the first place ... Peter, James, and John were looked upon as pillars, and this James referred to there was the apostle James, and not him that is spoken of as James, the Lord's brother ...' Then in response to his attorney's question – 'As I under-

---

[151] For a compelling argument in regard to the eminence of James, the Lord's brother, and his position in the New Testament church, see Robert Eisenman, *James The Brother of Jesus* (New York: Penguin Group, 1998).
[152] Hughes, 'Deposition', p. 1072.

stand [it] then, James, Peter and John who were mentioned as pillars in the Church meant a different James from the one who was general overseer of the church?' – Tomlinson answered, 'Yes sir'.[153]

Tomlinson reasoned that if the James referred to in Gal. 2.9 with Peter and John was the Lord's brother, it would have blurred his distinction and diminished his authority as General Overseer in the primitive church, and, consequently, would have lowered his position – making him equal in position with Peter and John. But the very fact that the apostle Paul here mentions James first in this passage – before Peter and John – was apparently to acknowledge his preeminence, that he did in fact hold the most prominent position in the church. Be that as it may, other Scriptural references show plainly that this same James, the Lord's brother, held a superior position in the church (Acts 12.17; 15.13-22; 21.18; *et al.*). Ironically, Tomlinson had used these same Scriptures in his annual addresses in 1913-1914 to establish the office of General Overseer. Tomlinson therefore gained nothing by disputing that this particular James in Gal. 2.9 was the Lord's brother: and in fact he could have argued his case for the preeminence of the General Overseer over the other two men on the Executive Council by showing that this James was in fact the Lord's brother, and that he had held a superior position in the government of the New Testament church, even over Peter and John.

But Tomlinson did not argue the point and, in fact, strangely enough, was rather passive during the whole procedure while this issue was being debated on the Assembly floor. As noted earlier, he acknowledged later that he did not take an active part in the proceedings, other than moderating, on the counsel of F.J. Lee who had convinced him that Llewellyn and his followers were determined to push the measure through one way or another, even if it disrupted the church; and on Lee's counsel, namely, that if he would show patience through the Assembly and afterward bide his time, he felt sure that Llewellyn and his followers would mellow and things could be put back in order at Headquarters in due time.

It was thus that Tomlinson allowed on his part for the new government to be instituted. But very soon he would realize that if Lee's advice was not deceptive or ill-given, it was at best unwise and misleading. Tomlinson afterward wished a thousand times that he had confronted the situation there on the Assembly floor, in front of all the people, rather than leaving himself more or less in the hands of his opponents at Headquarters, particularly since he was now expected to act in harmony

---

[153] Tomlinson, 'Deposition', p. 1995.

with the new government, that is, to submit to the counsel of Llewellyn and Lee.

Again, in light of the differences in personalities and the begrudgements that had developed between Tomlinson on the one hand and Llewellyn and Lee on the other, the new Executive Council was an impractical ideal – an unworkable union. Even if the three men selected had been mild-mannered and congenial, the failure to acknowledge and designate one of them as the chief executive was a recipe for confusion, contention, and disaster. But as things were, the contention and friction was inevitable; for two of the men – Tomlinson and Llewellyn – were equally strong-minded and each one believed he was appointed by God and knew what was best for the church. But again the best of men could not have fulfilled the hopeful expectations of Llewellyn's government; it was an impossible proposition: for a tribe must have a chief; a company a CEO; an army a commanding general; a city a mayor; a national government a prime minister; a school a principal; a team a head coach; etc.

The seemingly meekest man among the three selected for the Executive Council was Lee, who until the Assembly in 1922 had stood firm with Tomlinson; but gradually he had come under the influence of Llewellyn and became critical of Tomlinson's 'incompetence as a businessman', and saw his posture over the church as being popish. He also echoed Llewellyn's criticism of the 'Tomlinson family machine' and began to circulate that some of Tomlinson's children were crooked. In a letter to S.O. Gillaspie, Lee wrote, 'You know I was once teeth and toe nail with [Tomlinson], but I tell you I was made to see things differently'.[154] In another place, he admits, 'I had my eyes opened'.[155] There is no question as to who opened his eyes, nor what Llewellyn had made him to see. The Tomlinson 'family machine' had to be broken up! Thus, what Lee once admired in Tomlinson – his wise and courageous leadership and self-sacrificing nature as a servant of the church – he had come to interpret rather as self-aggrandizement and crafty manipulation for self-serving interests. He now resented Tomlinson's habit of treating the church as if he owned it and his tendency to act unilaterally with little or no accountability. He thus joined in the movement to impeach

---

[154] 'Letter from Lee to Gillaspie', c. late June or early July 1923 ['F.J. Lee File', ZACG Archives]. Lee had been in the middle of the road in the developing contention until after the Assembly in 1922. Tomlinson acknowledged as late as January 1923 that he did not know where Lee stood between the factions.

[155] Tomlinson, 'Deposition', p. 2520. Lee admitted that his own family was turning against him for supporting Tomlinson, and that 'they were praying for him to get his eyes opened so he could see [Tomlinson] like they saw [him]'.

Tomlinson and cast him out of the church, that is, out of the Llewellyn faction of the broken body.

After the Assembly, Tomlinson left Cleveland and Headquarters in the hands of Llewellyn and Lee and, according to his new job description, set out to fulfill his 'imperative duty' to travel over the states and oversee the work in general. He closed his house and took his wife, Mary Jane, and stenographer, Maud Pangle, and headed northeast through Tennessee, North Carolina, and Virginia, en route to New York to stay with Homer for awhile. In Asheville, he was joined by his faithful secretary, Lillie Duggar. Along the way he preached, dedicated church buildings, attended conventions and met with some of his strongest supporters to reflect on the events of the recent Assembly and to counsel together with them about the future of the church.[156] When he arrived at Homer's, his daughter, Iris, son-in-law, Avery, youngest son, Milton, were already there, and in a little while he was joined also by Gillaspie, one of the Twelve Elders and overseer of Illinois. S.W. Latimer had also been invited to the meeting but was unable to make the trip.

With these friends and co-workers he discussed some primary plans in regard to going forward under the present circumstances in the church including assuming personal responsibility for publishing and promoting the *Faithful Standard* magazine, which Llewellyn in his new capacity as Editor and Publisher refused to publish as an item of the church; and he was supported in this decision by Lee. It was published therefore in New York by Tomlinson and was put virtually under the editorship and management of Homer.[157] Tomlinson also prepared to launch, when the circumstances became expedient, the United Bible Institute, using the materials that Homer had written and prepared for the Bible Training School. Moving in rapid stride, they soon organized the Faithful Standard Company, and by March 1923 were selling stock in the enterprise.[158]

The developments related to the *Faithful Standard* and Bible Training School became more significant in the ensuing months, particularly

---

[156] For example, he met with George T. Brouayer in Canton, North Carolina for a convention. Brouayer was one of the Twelve Elders and overseer of North Carolina and would remain faithful to Tomlinson during the disruption, being also impeached and tried with him and S.O. Gillaspie by the Ten Elders in the June Council and pronounced guilty as charged by the Supreme Court in July.

[157] Tomlinson, *Diary*, February 19, 1923.

[158] Interestingly, Gillaspie and Brouayer were two of original stockholders in the company, having purchased stock sometime in the spring of 1923 (Homer, 'Deposition', p. 152; Tomlinson, 'Deposition', pp. 2477-79; Lee, 'Deposition', pp. 709-11).

when Llewellyn and Lee and their followers discovered that Homer and his father had the Bible Correspondence lessons and the *Faithful Standard* copyrighted in their names;[159] and they had received a letter from Homer in January 1923 warning that they could be held accountable for 'outright theft' if they continued to use the lesson materials without permission.[160] This was considered to be a serious breach of trust by Llewellyn and his followers and was one of the 'misdeeds' that began to sway moderate Elders against Tomlinson. Lee for one, having already been shocked by Tomlinson's admission that he had misapplied the tithe money,[161] now began to suspect that Tomlinson might be at his core a hypocrite and 'crooked'.[162] Lemons held that 'the fat had been in the fire' since the September 1922 Council meeting and that every new revelation of apparent impropriety only made the fire 'hotter' and more difficult to contain.[163] It seemed obvious to these Elders that Tomlinson was arranging to set up a rival system within the church and attempting to draw away disciples after himself; in effect, 'to start a new church, and to call it the Church of God!'[164]

After a few days in New York, Tomlinson sent his family back to Cleveland, while he remained to pray and chart his own course for the future of the church. During his retreat at Homer's, Tomlinson recovered from the shock of the events that had transpired the previous year, and emerged with a renewed zeal and powerful determination to pursue his vision of the church. He confided to Homer, 'Twenty years from now, we'll look back on this experience and tell the story of it, of how the Lord helped us'.[165] Under fresh inspiration and with his countenance lighted up again, he soon was off with Avery and Iris for an extended trip to the Bahamas, remaining there for almost a month. He traveled with the overseer, Milton Padgett, and praised his abilities as an overseer, but was badly mistaken in thinking that '[Padgett is loyal] to me as General Overseer:'[166] for when the disruption came a few months later, Padgett sided with the Llewellyn faction.

---

[159] Homer, 'Deposition', pp. 124-39.

[160] Homer, 'Deposition', p. 152.

[161] Lee said the admission of this by Tomlinson 'shook me almost to the bottom' (Lee, 'Deposition', p. 681).

[162] Lee, 'Deposition', pp. 845-76; 'Letter from Lee to Alford Collins' (September 10, 1925): 'Tomlinson walked crooked, misplaced money, [sent] out false reports and statements and otherwise [defrauded] the church ...'

[163] Lemons, 'Deposition', p. 454.

[164] Lee, 'Deposition', pp. 695-96; Payne, 'Deposition', pp. 112-13.

[165] Homer, *Diary*, II, p. 25.

[166] Tomlinson, *Diary*, March 12, 1923.

Figure 100

TOMLINSON, LLEWELLYN, AND LEE FORMED THE EXECUTIVE COUNCIL

Tomlinson departed the Bahamas on March 6, 1923 and spent the next two months preaching and attending conventions starting in Miami and going to various cities in Florida, then turning north to hold meetings in Georgia, South Carolina, and Virginia. At Hazlehurst, Georgia, he met with S.W. Latimer, who was the overseer of Georgia as well as one of the Twelve Elders and one of the Supreme Court judges. He had considered him a good friend and close confidant and a wise and able minister.[167] They discussed the recent accusations made against him by the Investigation Committee – Llewellyn, Lee, and Ellis – of misappropriating the tithe money but also possibly of having embezzled a great deal of money: for rumors were already circulating that the auditor was showing a shortage of thousands of dollars in the church's accounts, and the church accounts were in Tomlinson's name.[168] He confided to Latimer also that he was 'almost sure [the church was headed for] a division' and named a number of people 'he thought would stand with us solid'.[169] But as it was in the case with Padgett in the Bahamas and a number of other leaders in the church, Tomlinson misjudged Latimer. As we will see in a moment, when the real test came, Latimer stood with Llewellyn, Lee, and seven other Elders and went through the motions with them of impeaching Tomlinson.

Significantly, soon after the Assembly, C.T. Anderson, an evangelist from Wimauma, Florida had written to Tomlinson and suggested that charges be brought against Llewellyn, Ellis, and Lemons for their behavior and disorderliness in the Assembly in November.[170] Tomlinson immediately saw in this proposal the means for a counter-attack against

---

[167] Tomlinson, 'Preparation Notes', p. 53.
[168] Latimer, 'Deposition', pp. 265-76.
[169] Latimer, 'Deposition', p. 276.
[170] Tomlinson, 'Preparation Notes', p. 51.

his opponents. He asked Anderson to come from Florida to be with him in the convention at Hazlehurst, which was in charge of Latimer. There, he counseled with Latimer, Anderson, and the local pastor, S.J. Heath and together they planned a counter-attack against Llewellyn and his followers. Tomlinson suggested that Anderson write up the charges and send them to Latimer to sign, and they would proceed from there. Latimer later admitted under the threat of perjury that they had 'talked about getting charges presented at the opening of [the June Council], so that [Llewellyn, Lemons, and Ellis] would be [silenced]'.[171] He further advised Tomlinson that he 'would have to filibuster the thing over to get it before the house ... [because a good many were sure to oppose the tactic]'.[172]

Still, though Latimer had helped Tomlinson to plan the strategy to bring the charges against Llewellyn, Lemons and Ellis in the June Council, he would later when the real test came side with Lee and the other Elders in declaring that the charges were 'brought prematurely' before the Council, and that, for the time being, they should be set aside in order to deal first with the charges against Tomlinson.[173] Tomlinson and some other sympathizers accepted this proposition on the basis that T.S. Payne promised publicly that he would see that Llewellyn, Lee, and Ellis would be dealt with after the business at hand with Tomlinson was settled.[174] Payne, however, transgressed against his promise a few days later siding with Lee, Latimer, and four other Elders in exonerating the three Elders.

It was apparently a predisposed strategy of Lee and the others to free Llewellyn, Lemons, and Ellis in order that they might act with them in prosecuting the case against Tomlinson and the two Elders who were standing with him – George T. Brouayer and S.O. Gillaspie; for otherwise the prosecution had no semblance of legitimacy. Even so, it was a travesty of justice and of righteousness: for, taking all of the evidence into consideration, any fair-minded person could see that Tomlinson had given his life and material substance to build up the church, and had even sacrificed to a great degree the comforts of his family in order to do so. And even if Tomlinson were guilty of some of the charges made by the Investigation Committee, certainly Brouayer and Gillaspie were not; in fact, both men had impeccable records. Their only 'crime' was

---

[171] Latimer, 'Deposition', p. 278.
[172] Latimer, 'Deposition', p. 278; Tomlinson, 'Preparation Notes', pp. 51-53.
[173] Tomlinson, 'Preparation Notes', p. 48; Hughes, 'Deposition', pp. 1409-10.
[174] Payne, 'Deposition', p. 187: 'I made the statement if they were exonerated I would bring charges against those fellows myself, yes sir, I made that statement'.

standing with Tomlinson and requiring the Investigation Committee to give sufficient proof for their accusation of embezzlement and other charges against Tomlinson, and to justify their actions in prosecuting him.

But back to Latimer for a moment. If Tomlinson had been able to peer deeper into the man, he would have discovered something more of his mindset and true character. Even in the meeting at Hazlehurst, Latimer had indicated how he would stand in the up-coming June Council when his strategy would actually be tested, namely, that he would preempt the Investigation Committee's report by bringing charges first against Llewellyn, Lemons, and Ellis; for when Tomlinson asked him to sign the charges drawn up by Anderson and to distribute them to the brethren, he declined on the grounds that he sat on the Council of Twelve and the Supreme Court and therefore could not 'conscientiously take part in the filing of charges against [Llewellyn, Ellis, and Lemons] and then sit at the hearing of the evidence and pass on the case'.[175] Latimer, who would become General Overseer of the Llewellyn faction after Lee died in October 1928, apparently had a bit of 'politician' in him, and accordingly was careful to make decisions that served his promising career as much or more than justice and righteousness.

Even so, allowing him the benefit of the doubt, Latimer may have sincerely desired to stand by Tomlinson as far as possible, but at a deeper level of consciousness was already beginning to question Tomlinson's integrity, for he was receiving through the 'grapevine' reports that the Investigation Committee was discovering huge shortages in the church's funds, and it was looking as if Tomlinson and his son Homer were partners in an embezzlement scheme.[176] This news weighed more heavily on Latimer because Lee, whom he highly regarded, had turned on Tomlinson and was by April 1923 becoming bolder in his slanders against him, even accusing him and members of his family of lying, stealing, cheating, deceiving, and defrauding; in a word, of being 'crooked'.[177]

---

[175] Latimer, 'Deposition', p. 266.
[176] Homer, *Diary*, II, p. 32.
[177] Lee would repeat these slanders in numerous correspondences, both verbal and in writing, for years to come: for example in his 'Letter to R.P. Johnson' (January 24, 1925), he said, 'Tomlinson claimed ... to entirely answer the Auditor's report ... [but] three of the ledgers and one day book were missing. They have done something with these books to keep our auditor from finding those checks that he is holding credit for. I just consider this a greater fraud than taking money'. In a 'Letter to Alford Collins' (September 10, 1925), he wrote, 'Tomlinson walked crooked, misplaced money, [sent] out false reports and statements and otherwise [defrauded] the church, and would not control his children, who were some of them

Still, Latimer left the impression with Tomlinson in the April and May meetings in Georgia and Alabama that he was standing with him; and, perhaps, struggling through his doubts and fears, he was hoping that Tomlinson would be able to clear himself and remain the General Overseer. He therefore agreed to meet with him in Birmingham in the middle of May and counseled with him about how to get the charges against the three Elders before the Elders' Council and the church.

Figure 101

S.W. LATIMER

Figure 102

S.J. HEATH AND WIFE, ANNIE

While in Birmingham, Tomlinson showed Latimer the report of the 'audit' made by the Lee H. Battle Audit Company of Chattanooga, which the Investigation Committee had hired. It was anything but a true audit; even the company's auditor, H.D. Blackwell, denied that it was a thorough report, for several day books and ledgers were missing and, besides, a proper audit would take many weeks and a lot of money that the church did not have. Nevertheless, the audit company showed in its initial discoveries a shortage in the church's accounts of over $14,000. A.J. Lawson, one of Tomlinson's closest friends and advisers, and a prominent businessman in Cleveland, said he did not think the auditor's report was 'worth the paper is was written on'.[178] Others, however,

---

living very crooked lives, so God turned against him like He did Eli'. In a 'Letter to Myrtle Clendon' (May 13, 1926), he wrote, 'We had to deal with Tomlinson for his misdeeds [and some of his followers] for living crooked lives'. In a 'Letter to Addie Hunter' (May 1, 1926), he wrote, '[Tomlinson would be fighting the Constitution] today if he had not been overtaken in some of his crookedness'. And in a 'Letter to A.J. Grannum' (December 13, 1926), he declared, 'Tomlinson [was turned out of the Church] for his crookedness'.

[178] Latimer, 'Deposition', p. 275.

counseled Tomlinson to take the report seriously, for it left the impression that the shortage was due to embezzlement.[179]

Tomlinson had been uncooperative with the Investigation Committee, felt reproached by the investigation, and deeply resented the committee for probing into his affairs. The Committee believed his uncooperativeness was due to arrogance, and was a desperate effort to conceal evidence that might be self-incriminating. Tomlinson, conversely, believed the investigation was being pursued with a critical and prejudiced spirit: and that the committeemen were now, quite obviously, endeavoring to frame a case against him for legal purposes. He was right, of course. What Llewellyn and Lemons had in mind all along, others like F.J. Lee were now of the same mind, namely, to prosecute him in their religious court and also if need be in the federal courts.[180] Llewellyn and Lemons had already threatened to take him to court and to see him 'behind bars',[181] and this seemed all the more their aim in January 1923 since they had hired an outside professional company to examine his books and financial records; Tomlinson, in fact, had confided to Latimer that he thought they might even succeed in their prosecution if the courts – church and civil – went strictly by the books without allowing him to explain any apparent shortages and bookkeeping discrepancies that on the surface might give the appearance of impropriety or fraud.[182]

Notwithstanding his reluctance to cooperate with the Investigation Committee, Latimer advised him to return to Cleveland to defend himself, especially because Lee, Llewellyn, and the committee had advised him that it would be in his best interest to be there.[183] He further ad-

---

[179] Evans, Tomlinson's son-in-law, was with him and Latimer in the Birmingham meeting, and had gone to see a lawyer in Birmingham. The lawyer advised him, as Latimer had already, to obtain professional counsel and prepare for a legal defense (Latimer, 'Deposition', p. 275).

[180] In a letter to Tomlinson, dated April 13, 1923, Lee warned him that he was 'laying traps for yourself in the Federal courts' ('F.J. Lee File', ZACG Archives).

[181] Lemons at first, under oath, vehemently denied that he had made this statement, but then under pressure from Tomlinson's attorney, Westerberg, admitted that he intended to have him indicted. Lemons' reluctance to admit the truth, his contradictory statements, and his obvious antagonism against Tomlinson during the trial prompted Judge Murray to say to Lemons on one occasion, 'I am satisfied you would testify to anything' (Lemons, 'Deposition', p. 455). Further, several witnesses heard Lemons on other occasions say that he wanted Tomlinson behind bars. A.J. Lawson testified that Lemons had made that statement in his office in 1924 (Lawson, 'Deposition', p. 1591), and H.R. Clark, who had worked with Llewellyn and Lemons in the publishing house, testified that he heard Lemons say, 'I don't care what becomes of the church, all I want to do is to put Tomlinson behind the bars with the rest of the criminals' (Clark, 'Deposition', p. 1684).

[182] Tomlinson, 'Preparation Notes', p. 54; Latimer, 'Deposition', p. 273.

[183] Latimer, 'Deposition', p. 271.

vised him that since he was now under a cloud of suspicion for wrongdoing, that it would be necessary first to get that cloud removed and then 'all the other matters would adjust themselves'.[184] Latimer even volunteered to go to the conventions in Augusta, Georgia and Columbia, South Carolina to represent him if he would attend to business in Cleveland with the other two members of the Executive Council.[185] But after thinking over the situation, Tomlinson decided to ignore, if not defy, the Investigation Committee and the other two members of the Executive Council and proceeded to fulfill his appointments on the field. He would thereafter set himself for a confrontation with the Investigation Committee and Elders in an open meeting that was scheduled to begin on June 12th in the Assembly auditorium in Cleveland.

The Frame-Up

A few weeks after the Assembly in November 1922, Tomlinson, according to his new job description in the Constitution, set out to 'travel over the states and oversee the work in general, hold state conventions and sit in council with the overseers of the respective states on their fields of labor and give all matters of importance his personal attention'. Ironically, this job description – 'to give all matters of importance his personal attention' – meant in Tomlinson's opinion that he should do everything in his power to overturn the Constitution and the new government adopted in the recent Assembly and to start a revolution.

Not many weeks after Tomlinson left Cleveland on December 9, 1922, however, he began to receive news that Llewellyn and Lemons and others were accusing him of having embezzled thousands of dollars of the church's money, and portraying him as being especially cold and cruel for using the ministers' tithes for his own benefit and for the comforts of his family, while many of the ministers and their families on the field were suffering. After this manner, Llewellyn and his followers incited anger and bitterness against Tomlinson among those who were susceptible to such hearsay and malicious gossip, and who were untaught in biblical ethics and proper business procedures for church discipline (Mt. 18.15-20; Jn 20.23; 1 Tim. 5.19). Certainly the accusations had not been proven before the church nor had 'every word [been] established in the mouth of two or three witnesses'.

---

[184] Latimer, 'Deposition', p. 279.
[185] Latimer, 'Deposition', p. 272.

It was thus that Llewellyn and his followers began a smear campaign against Tomlinson and his family, preempting a just and fair hearing; and when the trial actually came in June there existed already a prejudiced spirit against him and his family. It did not matter that Tomlinson had fully explained and more or less proven in the September Council in 1922 and in the Assembly in November that he had used the tithes to pay off the debts of the church's properties in Cleveland and that he and his family had suffered as much or more as any of the ministers; nor did it seem to matter to the Ten Elders that the great majority of the Assembly had genuinely forgiven him for using the tithes to pay the bills at Headquarters and to save the church from bankruptcy. In fact, Llewellyn and his followers made every effort to cover up or play-down the fact that the great majority of the people had in fact praised Tomlinson for his actions – for 'loving the reputation of the Church of God more than his own'.[186] Indeed, the enthusiastic response of the people to Tomlinson's explanation seemed only to deepen Llewellyn's resentment of him, for he believed Tomlinson was 'pulling the wool over the eyes of the sheep'. He proceeded with Lemons, McLain, Ellis, W.F. Bryant, and scores of others to launch a smear campaign against him, the talking points of which were that Tomlinson's explanations and 'smooth way of talking' was merely a cover-up for his greed and crime of embezzlement. The campaign was largely successful; the whole church was gradually leavened with the gossip and slander and consequently a great many now imagined that the General Overseer was 'a thief and a rogue'.[187]

It would be proven in time that all of the suspicions and accusations of embezzlement, fraud, and extortion were unfounded, and that Llewellyn, Lee, and Ellis had 'rushed to judgment' or 'jumped to conclusions' in their investigation. But, still, even after some of their initial suspicions had been laid to rest by the facts, Llewellyn, Lee, and Ellis pressed on

---

[186] In preparing the *Minutes* of the 1922 Assembly, for example, Llewellyn had worked with Boehmer to make sure the reports were left out of the *Minutes* which showed that the great majority of the people had forgiven Tomlinson and had volunteered enthusiastically to apply what tithes were due to them to the Headquarters' debts.

[187] It is apparent in Lemons' court deposition that he was acting according to the information given to him and interpreted by Llewellyn, for, when pressed by Tomlinson's defense attorney in July 1924, he revealed that he had little knowledge of the actual facts and figures of the case (Lemons, 'Deposition', pp. 458-67). It is apparent that Bryant also had little knowledge of the actual facts, and that Lemons' opinions and malicious spirit had infected him. These men with others proceeded to slander Tomlinson's name and reputation, as well as his entire family's reputation, and to drag them through the mud. But the main well from which Tomlinson's critics and slanderers drank was J.S. Llewellyn.

willingly, if not hoping, to prove some degree of financial corruption and cover-up, and they eventually persuaded other members on the Elders' Council to join them in their unjust and hypocritical prosecution of Tomlinson. Worse yet, they defamed and impeached Brouayer and Gillaspie – both good men with impeccable records – for 'aiding and abetting' Tomlinson; and they did not stop there, but went after everyone who disagreed with and opposed their actions. Lee concluded that everyone who stood with or sympathized with Tomlinson was guilty of unfaithfulness, disloyalty, and sedition and needed to be excluded from the church.[188]

Further, it would be proven in court that the Elders did in fact know about the Evangel Loan Department, and had approved of it; for this information was recorded in the minutes of the Elders' Council meetings in 1920-1921. Several of the Elders – Lemons and Payne, for example – had endeavored in fact to get people to deposit their money in the church rather than the secular banks, in order to help build the Church of God rather than the banks of the world.[189] McLain, Llewellyn, and Boehmer even held certificates for Evangel loans.[190] The Elders, at least some of them including Llewellyn, also knew that some of the tithe fund had been used to pay on the Assembly auditorium and Publishing House debts and had approved of the practice.[191] Lee had even recommended in the Elders' Council in November 10-13, 1920 that 'Brother Tomlinson oversee the treasury and give him the privilege to call on any of the elders to help him, and if he needs more office help, let him get it'; and 'all agreed' to Lee's suggestion.[192] Yet these Elders shamelessly made it appear that they were completely surprised by these practices in order to paint Tomlinson as a villain and oust him from office, and finally to exclude him altogether from the Llewellyn-Lee faction of the church. These same tactics had been used more or less several times since the Elders' Council in September 1922 in order to diminish Tomlinson's powers and responsibilities and to separate him from the financial and business operations of the church.

---

[188] Lee, 'Deposition', pp. 775-80.
[189] Tomlinson, 'Deposition', pp. 1795-831. We do not have access to the records of the Elders' Councils, but the attorney quotes from these *Minutes* in Tomlinson's deposition.
[190] Tomlinson, 'Deposition', pp. 1825-26.
[191] *Minutes of the Elders Council*, September 1920 (cited by the court in Tomlinson, 'Deposition', pp. 1833, 1838.
[192] *Minutes of Elders Council*, November 10-13, 1920 (cited by the court in Tomlinson, 'Deposition', pp. 1836-38).

Was Tomlinson blameless in the painful and reproachful ordeal? Quite the contrary, in fact, the root cause was his magnification of the office of General Overseer and his tendency to set himself apart and above the rest of the church. And, further, he was to be blamed to some degree for the poor bookkeeping records and for his unilateral actions in misdirecting such a large portion of the ministers' tithes, and, further, for not making himself accountable to his peers – to the Elders. Even his good friend and ally, A.J. Lawson, admitted, 'Brother Tomlinson made many mistakes'.[193] But, still, the Elders could have more readily and justly accused him of heresy, usurpation, sedition, or the spirit of lordship than of fraud and embezzlement. The latter charges were quite absurd in view of the man's proven history of self-sacrificing service to the church and the fact that he was a relatively poor man – certainly a man of very modest means. Even the Appellate Court in 1925, after hearing all of the evidence, ruled in its *Opinion* that

> About ten years before this trouble he had inherited about $2000, which he invested in property in Cleveland, notwithstanding enormous sums had gone through his hands, he now possesses only the property which he purchased with the money given him, and which he found necessary to mortgage in order to send his son through the University of Tennessee. Had he been a defaulter and a dishonest man, it is indeed doubtful whether the church would have had the valuable property which he has created for it, and whether he would have been the poor man that he is. It is unreasonable to say that of all the funds which had passed through his hands, and which he charged himself on the books, he appropriated the funds derived from the notes given at the bank.[194]

The court's *Opinion* went on to address the Llewellyn faction's complaints about the apparent inconsistencies in statements about the finances of the *Faithful Standard*, the Evangel Loan Department, the Exchange and Indemnity business, etc. and found that the complainants 'have failed to establish a shortage of any amount due from A.J. Tomlinson to the Church of God'.[195] It is true that the Supreme Court of Tennessee overturned the Appellate court's decision and ruled in favor of the Llewellyn faction, but only in regard to awarding the name and

---

[193] 'Letter from A.J. Lawson to T.A. Richard', July 17, 1923 ('Bureau of Information File', ZACG Archives).
[194] *Opinion*, pp. 8-9.
[195] *Opinion*, p. 9.

Figure 103

Tomlinson family and son-in-law, Horace D. Hughes, console each other at the gravesite of Halcy shortly after her death on January 14, 1920. Halcy Olive [Tomlinson] Hughes died in Chattanooga of complications during childbirth. She was an outstanding Christian woman. *Back row*: A.D. Evans, Iris [Tomlinson] Evans, Homer A. Tomlinson [kneeling], Marie [Wunch] Tomlinson, A. J. Tomlinson, Milton Tomlinson. *In front*: Mary Jane Tomlinson; to her right, Horace D. Hughes. Coincidentally, Horace was the older brother of Jesse Hughes, the husband of F.J. Lee's daughter Nellie.

property of the church to that faction: it did not overturn the Appellate court's *Opinion* that Tomlinson did not steal, extort, or embezzle the church's money; nor did it overturn the court's acknowledgement and even praise of Tomlinson for his untiring efforts and self-sacrifices to build the Church of God.

Nevertheless, by the time the courts had exonerated Tomlinson of embezzlement and financial corruption, the damage had been done: Llewellyn and Lee and their associates had sown to the wind their tale of corruption against Tomlinson and his family; and, further, they continued in the years to come to do everything in their power to ruin his reputation and destroy his influence.

The Twelve Elders – Divided Loyalties

The original twelve members of the Elders' Council were selected in 1917; but between October of that year and the June Council in 1923, fourteen had served on the Council, though only twelve at any one time. In 1919, Efford Haynes, the brother of M.S. Haynes, was selected to succeed Sam C. Perry who had been dismissed from the Council in May 1919 for reasons already noticed. Then in the Elders' Council in September 1922, M.S. Haynes confessed to certain moral improprieties and voluntarily tendered his resignation. Alonzo Gann, a prominent pastor in Atlanta, Georgia and one of the Seventy and chairman of the Better Government Committee was selected following the 1922 General Assembly to succeed Haynes.

The original twelve Elders were F.J. Lee, T.L. McLain, M.S. Lemons, J.S. Llewellyn, T.S. Payne, J.B. Ellis, Sam C. Perry, M.S. Haynes, George T. Brouayer, S.W. Latimer, E.J. Boehmer, and S.O. Gillaspie. These Elders by 1920 had become divided in opinion on several doctrinal issues including the nature and characteristics of the Bible church, marriage, and the order of salvation. Their differences in regard to the order of salvation was over how to identify the two works of grace – regeneration and sanctification – relative to the term, 'new birth'.[196] The differences in regard to marriage were primarily over the idea of a so-called 'innocent party' based on Jesus words in Mt. 5.32 and 19.9. Some -- like Tomlinson, Lee, Gillaspie, and Brouayer -- held that the marriage bond was indissoluble while either party remained alive; others, like Llewellyn, Perry, and Latimer believed that adultery was grounds for divorce and remarriage.

---

[196] T.L. McLain for one was fairly convinced that the new birth and sanctification were the same experience and therefore that one was not born again until he was instantaneously sanctified subsequent to regeneration (Hughes, Deposition', pp. 981-82, 1115). This had been an issue of some contention that came up in Eighth Assembly in 1913, which apparently J.W. Buckalew as well as McLain and others favored (*GAM 1906-1914*, p. 227). The sense of Tomlinson and Lee and others was that it was not worth pursuing and that 'it should not be taught either in private or public'. McLain reportedly 'told Tomlinson that he was waiting to be convinced' but there is no evidence that he ever was satisfied, though he conceded not to make an issue of his personal view of the matter (Hughes, 'Deposition', p. 1115). We have noticed that Sam C. Perry adamantly opposed the church's interpretation that the Bible church is 'God's government on earth', and disagreed with the teaching that the church is a distinct visible and corporate body. Perry also with some others believed in the 'innocent party' in regard to divorce and remarriage, whereas Tomlinson and his followers on the Council believed that the marriage covenant was dissolved only by death – that not even unfaithfulness was a just cause for divorce and remarriage.

Perhaps, however, the most fundamental difference among the Elders was the nature of the church's government, particularly in regard to the office of General Overseer. Tomlinson's theology of the office of General Overseer and particularly his personal attachment to it eventually divided the members of the Council. It was Llewellyn who at first began to take issue with Tomlinson's interpretation of the office and his self-perceived special appointment for life in the office; and he in turn eventually swayed others to his way of thinking. Lemons acknowledged that by 1920 the Elders were divided in their loyalties to Tomlinson – seven standing with him and five against.[197] The five who opposed him were Llewellyn, Haynes, Lemons, McLain, and Ellis. But this division among the Elders was not at first so visible, nor had the five solidified any specific plan to effect the changes they had in mind; nor had they become militant in their views. In Tomlinson's opinion, it was not until the September 1922 Elders' Council that the division became obvious. He said, 'I think [that] was the first council … where there was a distinct division … It was plainly shown in that council that there were two factions'.[198] Lee acknowledged the same. He noted that of the twelve elders in the September Council, seven were remaining loyal to Tomlinson, namely, Latimer, Payne, Boehmer, Gillaspie, Brouayer, M.S. Haynes, and himself.[199] As events unfolded in the ensuing months, the differences between the Elders became more pronounced and their passions more inflamed. Lemons claimed that Gillaspie and Brouayer were passionately against him, and styled them as being 'bloodthirsty'.[200]

Interestingly, after M.S. Haynes acknowledged his improprieties and asked forgiveness and tendered his resignation in the September Council in 1922, he warned in a kind of 'farewell address' that there were two factions existing in the church, and proceeded to 'prophesy' that if the opposing parties were not reconciled that a division was inevitable.[201] We can surmise that he had had conversations with his brother, Efford, who stood on one side and he himself on the other in regard to the developing rift.[202] And we may assume that similar conversations had

---

[197] Lemons, 'Deposition', pp. 476-78.
[198] Tomlinson, 'Deposition', p. 1886.
[199] Lee, 'Deposition', p. 691.
[200] Lemons, 'Deposition', p. 478.
[201] Tomlinson, 'Deposition', pp. 1886-87.
[202] This was the judgment of Tomlinson's attorney, Westerberg, upon hearing the evidence in the case. The fact that M.S. Haynes in the Elders' Council in September 1922 had said, 'Don't raise your hands against God's anointed … God put Brother Tomlinson in this place, you had better let the Lord deal with [him] and not

gone on between Lee and his brother-in-law, McLain, the latter opposing Tomlinson and the other being a devout follower of the General Overseer. Lee admitted that he was 'intimately associated' with Tomlinson and was 'one of his faithful followers'.[203] It was on that basis that Llewellyn as well as McLain and his wife, Alora (the sister of F.J. Lee), mentioned to Lee that they were praying for 'his eyes to be opened'.[204]

With the resignation of M.S. Haynes, who had been an admirer and follower of the General Overseer, Tomlinson declared that 'there was a distinct line drawn with five [Elders] on the one side and six on the other side'.[205] Tomlinson noted that 'I noticed that the 6 usually kept close to me and showed their fellowship, love, and tenderness ... I knew they were 'sticking to me', and [were] very much opposed to the spirit and ways of the other five brethren'.[206] In an attempt to distinguish the character of his opponents, he noted, 'Two of the five had but little to say, [whereas] Llewellyn, Lemons, and Ellis were very free to speak. [But I had] an inner understanding that [Efford] Haynes and T.L. McLain ... were just as strong [against me] as the others'.[207]

By January 1923, however, Tomlinson sensed that the balance of opinion in his favor among the Elders had tilted the other way. He was getting bits of information that Lee and Payne were being swayed by Llewellyn's attitude and opinions and were turning against him. On January 13, 1923, he wrote to E.J. Boehmer confidentially that he was still counting on his loyalty as well as that of Latimer, Gillaspie and Brouayer.[208] Apparently by that time, he believed the scales had tipped to seven against him and only four 'sticking to him'. Intriguingly, Gann, who had been selected to replace M.S. Haynes in the November Council meeting following the Assembly, was not notified that he had been ap-

---

you', seemed to have indicated that he was well aware of the plans laid by Llewellyn and his brother, Efford, and their associates (Tomlinson, 'Deposition', p. 1901).

[203] Lee, 'Deposition', p. 678.

[204] Lee, 'Deposition', p. 679; Tomlinson noted that Lee had gone 'through some little persecution because he had been standing with me, and his own people had about turned against him and they had told him they were praying that he might get his eyes open so he could see me like they saw me ...' (Tomlinson, 'Deposition', p. 2520).

[205] Tomlinson, 'Deposition', p. 1887.

[206] Tomlinson, 'Deposition', p. 1890.

[207] Tomlinson, 'Deposition', p. 1890.

[208] He noted further in his letter to Boehmer, 'Brother Latimer, Brother Gillaspie and Brother Brouayer are standing right with me in this matter, and of course, you are' (Tomlinson, 'Deposition', p. 1964).

pointed to a seat on the Council until the June Council in 1923.[209] Gann reasoned that he had been 'kept in the dark' in regard to his appointment because the Council was divided and Tomlinson knew that he had since the Assembly come under the influence of Llewellyn and his followers. Gann noted 'I came [to the Council] in good grace at a bad time'.[210]

Gann had been very much pro Tomlinson until the Assembly in 1922. Up to that point, he admitted that he had been like almost everyone else in the church: a zealous and devout follower of the General Overseer. He noted that Tomlinson's influence was so great that when 'he piped we danced', and when 'he sniffed, we sneezed'.[211] He declared that Tomlinson's contribution to the church was far greater that any other person in the church and more or less immeasurable.

> I consider he was the most instrumental of any human being in the Church of God, in bringing about the new lights that were shed upon the church because he acted as moderator in all Assemblies I have ever been in and used his influence in the passage of all of them. We had such confidence in him he could just say the word and we would adhere to what he said. His influence I guess was more influential in bringing about these different determinations of the Church of God than all of us together. I am confident of that.[212]

Gann's estimate of Tomlinson was no more than that of Walter E. Rogers and thousands of others at that time both within and without the church. Rogers was an old friend and business associate of Tomlinson and in 1916 had become the owner and publisher of *The Cleveland Banner*. He had worked with Tomlinson in printing *The Way* when the latter had first moved to Cleveland in 1904 and later assisted him in publishing the *Evangel*. When asked on one occasion to assess Tomlinson's importance in regard to the early development and growth of the Church of God, he declared, 'He was the whole cheese'.[213]

---

[209] Though he had been appointed either at the end of the Assembly in 1922 or in the Elders' Council in November following the Assembly, he was not officially notified until June (Gann, 'Deposition', p. 139).

[210] Gann, 'Deposition', p. 140.

[211] Gann, 'Deposition', p. 99.

[212] Gann, 'Deposition', pp. 98-99.

[213] Rogers, 'Deposition', p. 384.

Notwithstanding the admiration and zealous allegiance that Gann had had for Tomlinson, the slanderous campaign of Llewellyn and his followers had reached his ears and had some affect upon him. But it was not until he arrived in Cleveland and began to interact with Llewellyn and his associates that his esteem for the General Overseer was effectively diminished. The atmosphere at Headquarters and the turn of events in the Assembly in 1922 had jolted his naïve and idealistic con-

Figure 104

A.D. EVANS AND WIFE, IRIS [TOMLINSON] EVANS

Avery Denver Evans and Tomlinson's daughter, Iris Marie, were married on June 16, 1920. Llewellyn performed the wedding in the local church in Cleveland. They both worked in the Evangel Office and were completely loyal to Tomlinson until his death in 1943. Evans had considerable abilities as a writer and was adept in business matters, and thus became a right-hand-man for Tomlinson after the disruption in 1923. Iris worked by his side, and was a loyal and efficient servant for her father.

cept of the man who sat at the pinnacle of God's government on earth. Somewhat in the manner of the young monk from Wittenberg who had visited Rome four centuries earlier,[214] Gann was disillusioned by what he saw and heard in Cleveland. Inundated by the slanderous reports of Llewellyn, Lemons and others, he began to see Tomlinson as a corrupt pope proclaiming papal edicts, spouting out divine commands and using his position to get wealthy!

The rumors and false reports that followed the Investigation Committee in the months ahead pushed Gann more adamantly and forcefully in the camp of Tomlinson's opponents. He was soon following the beat of Llewellyn's drum and doing his bidding. As chairman of the Better Government Committee, he became one of the most vocal and influen-

---

[214] Martin Luther, not long after his visit to Rome, posted his 95 Theses on the door of the cathedral in Wittenberg in 1517 and set in motion the Protestant Reformation.

tial voices for the Constitution, the Executive Council, and the new government.[215] And, though he was but a rookie on the Council of Twelve, he became one of the leaders in prosecuting and impeaching Tomlinson.[216]

The Case of J.S. Llewellyn

We have peered a great deal into the mindset and character of Llewellyn in the ten years between 1912 and 1923 and have seen that he had some outstanding traits and abilities; and, on the basis of his abilities and indefatigable energy, he rose to become one of the chief leaders in the church. When he moved to Cleveland in 1919, he reported to Tomlinson that his father had been a magistrate, a justice of the peace, and that consequently he had had access to law books and court proceedings and had obtained considerable experience in legal matters.[217] Accordingly, Tomlinson had come to depend on Llewellyn more than any other minister in the church in regard to business and legal matters.[218] Further, he had by 1920 come to depend on him to oversee a large part of the work in general, which had prompted Lee's comment that Llewellyn had become Tomlinson's 'right-hand man'.

But in the course of working so closely with Tomlinson, and having been appointed over so many major projects in the church, Llewellyn became 'puffed up' and began to see Tomlinson as inept and incompetent, particularly in regard to the business aspects of the church. And inasmuch as he became vocal about his opinions, it created a rub between himself and the General Overseer which eventually degenerated into mutual contempt.

But there was another angle to their relationship that may help to explain how their friendship had fallen apart. It is apparent that Llewellyn had early on looked on Tomlinson somewhat as a father in the faith; for Tomlinson was fifteen years his senior and had brought him along to where he was in the church.[219] But Tomlinson also had come to depend

---

[215] Gann, 'Deposition', pp. 106-42, 967-76.
[216] Gann, 'Deposition', pp. 976-85.
[217] Tomlinson, 'Deposition', p. 1861. Llewellyn's writings and work bore out his testimony in this regard.
[218] 'I told him repeatedly I didn't know anything about law, and lawsuits ... and that I would have to depend upon others, and as he seemed to understand such things, of course, I would have to trust him about it' (Tomlinson, 'Deposition', p. 1860).
[219] Llewellyn, however, does not seem to have been pulled in by the Tomlinson mystique like Lee and most of the other ministers and members in the church.

on his natural son, Homer, particularly in regard to the publishing work and business aspects of the church. And inasmuch as the business and publishing interests were dear to Llewellyn, it gave occasion for jealousy and emulation to find place in his heart. It is apparent that a rivalry developed between Homer and Llewellyn; and the rivalry was inflamed all the more when Tomlinson sided with Homer against Llewellyn in the dispute over the Golden Rule Supply Company.

It was from this perspective that Llewellyn began boldly and publicly to campaign against the 'Tomlinson family machine'.[220] Everywhere he went over the country, he touted that 'Tomlinson was running a family machine'.[221] And he left the distinct impression that the Tomlinson family was conspiring together and embezzling the church's money.[222] Whether or not he really believed this or was simply overcome by spite and a destructive spirit, God knows; but in any case he was able to convince a great many that Tomlinson and his family were embezzlers and crooked, and those infected by his malicious tale in turn helped to spread the slander over the country.

There is another factor that may help to explain Llewellyn's growing contempt for Tomlinson. He had little or no interest in the church before he united with it. For all intents and purposes, the church began for Llewellyn when he joined it. When questioned about how the church developed and stood historically on certain issues, his standard answer was: 'Well, that was further back than I am acquainted'.[223] The significance of this is that he did not appreciate the sacrifices and labors of those who had paved the way before he came along. He knew little or nothing about Spurling's paramount contribution in the founding and early development of the church, and disagreed in principle almost entirely with his central theme in *The Lost Link*. Neither did he appreciate the early ministry of Tomlinson, nor comprehend the sacrifices and labors that his family had made in the early days of the church. He seems to have placed no value on the fact that, after Tomlinson came to Cleveland, he and his family had labored for years without pay to estab-

---

[220] There is a of volume evidence on both sides of the controversy that prove this point, including the testimony of Llewellyn himself.

[221] Tomlinson, 'Deposition', p. 1926.

[222] Even in his testimony before the court, he left this distinct impression and came close to declaring it emphatically (Llewellyn, 'Deposition', pp. 1234-46, 1277-78, 1281-82). Further, his '14 points' composed in June 1922 and later the charges he wrote up in the June Council in 1923 and the charges brought before the grand jury of the chancery court in Cleveland show indisputable evidence of this fact.

[223] Llewellyn, 'Deposition', pp. 1314-15.

lish the church and to build up its publishing interests and Headquarters system. Nor did he appreciate that the Tomlinson house had been during all those years virtually open to the church at large: that Ambrose and Mary Jane had fed and entertained scores of guests in their home on a regular basis, and that frequently ten or more guests spent a night or two in their house, and some stayed for weeks at a time. Moreover, Llewellyn seemed unable to appreciate that Tomlinson himself, far more than any other minister in the church, was responsible for the church's transformation into a worldwide organization; and that this great achievement was in large measure at his personal expense and the sacrifice of his family.

Considering the Tomlinson family's monumental contribution to the early development of the church, it is understandable that as the church grew and realized a degree of financial success that Tomlinson thought his family deserved to receive some pay for their services. He could not fathom anyone begrudging his son-in-law and children that small token of gratitude. It is true of course that his children were not professionals nor especially skilled and trained for the particular work in which they were engaged, yet Tomlinson believed they had earned some degree of respect and the right to be employed in the publishing house and to be paid for their work.

Nevertheless, Llewellyn and Lemons and those under their influence did begrudge the fact that Tomlinson had employed his children and son-in-law, A.D. Evans. And their envy and resentment caused them to become critical, and this spirit in turn drove them to find fault in Tomlinson and his family. When Llewellyn, Lemons, and Lee had discovered that Homer had received approximately $200 over a period of about three years for his services, they accused Tomlinson of lying and making fraudulent statements because he had maintained that Homer was not employed by the church and had not received any money for his services. They magnified the oversight (or discrepancy as the case may have been) and used it as evidence in their quest to prove that Tomlinson and his family were crooks and embezzlers.[224] At that point, Llewellyn and his followers had become faultfinders, rather than men who were as they claimed 'always [trying] to help the church ... and protect its interests'.[225] Indeed, for all the hoopla and hoo-ha made over the 'Tomlinson family machine', Llewellyn, shortly after he became the editor and publisher in December 1922, hired Lemons' daughter, his own son, Paul

---

[224] Lee, 'Deposition', pp. 722-23.
[225] Llewellyn, 'Deposition', p. 1266.

and T.S. Payne's son, Raburn, and placed them in strategic positions in the publishing house.[226] And McLain's daughter was employed also in the publishing house. It is difficult here not to recall Jesus' words, 'For with what judgment you judge, you will be judged … And why behold the mote [the speck of sawdust] in your brother's eye, but consider not the beam [log] in your own eye? … You hypocrite, first [remove] the [log] in your own eye; and then you will see clearly to [remove] the speck [from] your brother's eye' (Mt. 7.1-5).

It should be reported here also that for all of Llewellyn's boastfulness about his business and publishing skills and his complaints about Tomlinson's lack thereof, and his scandalous remarks about the incompetence of Tomlinson's family, that the publishing interests of the church declined steadily year after year under his management. E.L. Simmons acknowledged in his *History of the Church of God*, that

> The publishing interests did not do well through these years of reconstruction. Though the business seems to have been handled in a better way, the gross business done was below what it had been before the trouble came. A report in the [1922 *Assembly Minutes*] shows a gross business of $32,537.97 done by the Publishing House for that Assembly year. [After Llewellyn took over in December 1923 and served for five years], the gross receipts reported in 1927 were $24,083,01. This was more than $8000.00 decrease in business.[227]

Simmons then adds with a seemingly note of contempt, 'For several reasons this man [Llewellyn] became dissatisfactory and at the Assembly of 1927 a publishing committee was chosen, whose duty it was to hire an Editor and Publisher'.[228]

The Case of F.J. Lee

Notwithstanding Llewellyn's boldness and determination to 'break' Tomlinson and to 'get him out of that office', he would have not succeeded if he had not won over F.J. Lee to his way of thinking. We have noticed that Lee according to his own testimony was 'tooth and toe nail' with Tomlinson before the Assembly in 1922 and that he 'could not bear the idea of dropping him'.[229] His confidence in Tomlinson, however,

---

[226] Llewellyn, 'Deposition', pp. 1240-42.
[227] Simmons, *History of the Church of God*, p. 46.
[228] Simmons, *History of the Church of God*, p. 46.
[229] Lee, 'Deposition', p. 794.

was somewhat 'shaken' in the Elders Council in September 1922. Lee recalled in court that 'when Brother Llewellyn stood at one end of a big table ... and Brother Tomlinson at the other, and [Llewellyn] asked him if he had sent [the tithes] out in accordance with the way the Council had figured it up ... and he said ... I have'; but then the next day when [Tomlinson] admitted 'that he had used $19,000 in the wrong channel ... it so affected me, it looked like I could hardly stand to go further with him'. Still, however, 'I held on to him to the Assembly, hoping that he might make the thing good, but it got worse and worse'.[230]

Lee's way of thinking took a radical turn at the Assembly in 1922, particularly after Tomlinson had failed – in Lee's opinion – truly to confess before the Assembly that he had misdirected the tithe money to pay off the Assembly auditorium and publishing house debts. What Lee wanted was not an explanation out of Tomlinson but a confession that he had betrayed the trust of the church and dishonored the office of General Overseer. He seemed to have wanted to see him on his knees again sobbing and pleading for forgiveness like he had before the Twelve Elders in the September meeting![231] Quite obviously Lee's attitude had changed. He was not the same meek and mild-mannered young man that had been Spirit-baptized in 1908 and joined the Church of God in 1911: and certainly not the same F.J. Lee who had admired and worked with Tomlinson so closely for the past ten years. It is apparent that the influence of Llewellyn was making its mark on him, affecting his actions as well as his thinking. After all, he had been in harness with Llewellyn since they were selected in the September Council in 1922 to

---

[230] Lee, 'Deposition', p. 795.
[231] Lee, 'Deposition', pp. 698-99, 822. He said Tomlinson 'only made a partial confession', and that 'instead of being penitent and submissive' and 'making confessions' he was 'reaching for more power'. Lee reluctantly admitted in his deposition that Tomlinson in fact had explained to the Assembly that he had misdirected some of the tithes to save the church from bankruptcy and that he had asked the Assembly to forgive him. Like in the instances with Llewellyn and Lemons, the lawyer had to drag the truth out of Lee ('Deposition', pp. 823-24). Tomlinson's lawyer pointed out further that there was evidently a scheme to doctor up and edit the Assembly Minutes to deceive the ministers and members who had not attended the Assembly: for Tomlinson's explanation before the Assembly and the people's favorable response to him were omitted. But not only were the minutes of the Assembly edited with a bias but also the minutes of the June Council, in addition to all of the false reports and slanders against Tomlinson's character that went out from the Llewellyn-Lee camp.

serve together with J.B. Ellis to investigate Tomlinson's books and financial affairs; and then two months later in the General Assembly were again yoked together, this time with Tomlinson to serve on the newly-created Executive Council.

Tomlinson had always praised the piety of Lee and was careful not to criticize him; but after the June Council and disruption in 1923, he said it was obvious that Lee had been all along 'carrying water on both shoulders', that is, that 'although he tried to make out he was in favor of me ... he was more in favor with them'.[232] Homer wrote to Lee on January 6, 1922 praising him as having been for almost 15 years his 'ideal of a perfect Christian' but lamenting the fact that he had fallen in cahoots with Llewellyn and others to overthrow his father.[233] Jesse P. Hughes admitted that his father-in-law was 'under Llewellyn's thumb' and had joined Llewellyn in scheming to get Tomlinson out of office.[234] Even W.G. Rembert, who was during the June Council serving as the overseer of Ohio, railed against Lee, calling him a 'traitor' and a 'snake in the grass' for working 'under cover' against the General Overseer.[235]

After the Executive Council was created by Llewellyn's amendment to the Constitution in 1922, and Tomlinson was accordingly relegated to the role of a glorified evangelist on the field, Llewellyn was left in the driver's seat in Cleveland. Lee was there too, of course, but he was no match for the wily Llewellyn who knew how to manipulate the circumstances to achieve his personal aims, which in this instance was to fulfill his promises to Tomlinson, namely, that he would 'break' him and 'get him out of office if it cost him every cent he was worth'.

In the ensuing months, the spirit of Llewellyn was manifestly upon Lee: he became legalistic and prosecutorial, seeking to find fault in Tomlinson. In many instances where Tomlinson could have been given the benefit of the doubt in the mere appearance of impropriety, Lee now saw 'fraud', 'false reports', 'embezzlement', and an elaborate 'cover-up scheme'. Thus, together with Llewellyn and Ellis and others, he gathered 'evidence' to build a case against the General Overseer. He even threatened and warned Tomlinson in a letter that 'you are laying traps for yourself in the Federal courts'.[236]

---

[232] Tomlinson, 'Deposition', p. 2544.
[233] Homer, 'Deposition', p. 87.
[234] Lee, 'Deposition', p. 871.
[235] Anderson, 'Deposition', pp. 301, 304. Rembert, however, soon recanted and sided with the Llewellyn-Lee faction.
[236] 'Letter from Lee to Tomlinson', dated April 13, 1923 ('F.J. Lee File', ZACG Archives).

Was there an ulterior motive in Lee in seeking to 'dethrone' Tomlinson? Was he merely 'looking out for the interests of the church', as Llewellyn had said, and endeavoring to 'protect the church' against a corrupt pope-like figure? Or had Lee become tainted by the idea and flattery of friends that he should be the General Overseer? Did he join with Llewellyn to 'dethrone' Tomlinson only to be 'enthroned' himself?

Figure 105

THE EVANGEL OFFICES AND PUBLISHING HOUSE AS THEY APPEARED IN 1920

Tomlinson and the Office and Publishing House workers posed for this photo (Tomlinson is far left, his wife, Mary Jane, is standing in front of him, and Nora Chambers is standing next to her, arms locked with the first lady. The Evangel Office and Publishing House became the center of executive activities in the church between 1913 and 1923. At first, the facility was a small one story structure. It was built in 1913 on property purchased by Tomlinson and sold to the church without a profit. In 1917, more printing machinery was purchased and a two-story addition was attached to the rear. In 1918, more equipment was purchased and the original structure was widened and a second story added. In 1919, a three-story annex was added to the existing structure at the rear. The third story was used for Bible Training School.

That Lee's head had been turned by the idea of becoming General Overseer was the opinion of a great many who knew him well and who had lived through the ordeal in 1922-1923. J.R. Kinser, who had worked in the Evangel Publishing House in 1920-1923 and knew all of the leaders of both factions well, and who later served for many years as General Treasurer for the Tomlinson faction, told this writer that he believed

Lee was a good man but that he had become influenced by the flattery of those who claimed that he would make a better General Overseer than Tomlinson, and that he should accept the office to save the church.[237]

A.J. Lawson's remarks about Lee during the ordeal were stronger and more hard-hitting than Kinser's. Lawson knew Lee intimately and had worked closely with him on the Publishing Committee and on other church-related projects. He had even held Lee in his arms while the latter was being baptized with the Holy Ghost during the tent meeting in Cleveland in 1908. They once thought very highly of each other; Lee had even tried to get Lawson to accept the position of editor and publisher for the *Evangel* in the Assembly in 1922, preferring him at that time over Llewellyn. But Lawson saw a change take place in Lee in 1922-1923. He wrote,

> Was [Tomlinson] put down and out legally? No sir, a thousand times NO SIR! He was ... pretendingly [*sic*] put out by those who have been looking with the eagle's eye for years to ... put him out [of office] and get one in who was not so spiritual. You say, Is not F.J. Lee a spiritual man? Not by any means now. He has seen the day that he had God's presence with him in power but not for many months.
>
> Brother Lee received the Holy Ghost in my arms, and for many years God used him in a wonderful way, but he became puffed up by listening to the applause of men, and with regret I say, he is not a man for the responsibility of the office of General Overseer of the Churches of God, and we who are standing on the real doctrines of the Church of God ... do NOT recognize him as any part of an overseer. Brother A.J. Tomlinson is still the General Overseer of the Churches of God just as he has been for years.
>
> Brother F.J. Lee is now recognized as the General Overseer of the organization known as the General Assembly of the Churches of God, which is a split off from the Church of God, split by allowing the constitution to come in, and take the place of the Bible to an ex-

---

[237] Interview in June 1983. I was privileged to know and work with Kinser for several years in the church's International Offices on Keith Street in Cleveland. He was a saintly man and careful to speak. I include his comments here because they represent the prevailing opinion of many of Tomlinson's followers who lived and worked through the clamorous and disruptive period.

tent by saying that the Official Assembly ... shall constitute a law making body for their organization.[238]

But the most scathing retaliation to Lee's words and actions came from his son-in-law, Jesse P. Hughes, who in November 1923 aligned himself with Tomlinson and was appointed to pastor the local church in Cleveland. He wrote a number of bold and revealing letters and pamphlets to defend the position of Tomlinson and to expose those who opposed him. The occasion for the following letter, written to Lee by Hughes and made public, was in response to an article Lee had published in the September 1, 1923 issue of the *Evangel*. Under the title 'Contentions Sometimes a Good Thing', Lee denounced everyone who had not lined up with the judgment of the Ten Elders to impeach Tomlinson and to scandalize his name and reputation. He called them 'dead carcasses'. Hughes prefaced his remarks by saying that 'as far as I know there is no personal differences between my father-in-law and me, but religiously there has risen a mountain between us. I shall continue to respect him as a father in family relations, but I cannot endorse his work in the church here of late'.

> MR. F.J. Lee,
>
> I have just read your article in the *Evangel* ... You infer that you and your ecclesiastical ring are the Church of God exclusive, and those that do not line up with you are carcasses that the commotion (church row) has thrown out on the shore. Now ... you know that I can prove the guilt of some of those who have placed you in your so-called position as General Overseer, but they are your right hand men and you persist in covering their rotten lives and call those who do not line up with such, 'Dead carcasses thrown out on the shore'.
>
> I must say to you that none of your hard sayings ... can move me from the position I have taken, only to steer my bark as far from your ring as possible. I know that you have a few so called elders who will try to hold up your hands and hiss you on in your fight in trying to slur and belittle those who have come out of Babylon ... to get a following and a good paying position, and seek to put down and excel the man who has given his all to bring the church to the place where it could support its ministers and officers ...

---

[238] A.J. Lawson, 'You Have Heard So Much – But Read This And Be Honest With You Own Heart', *Church of God Bureau of Information* (ZACG Archives).

You have proved to my mind that when you were told by some that they intended to make you General Overseer, and that you had knocked yourself out of a good position by favoring Tomlinson, you let it puff you up ... and let them make you General Overseer of their ring ... If you believed that God had anything to do with you being made General Overseer and that He had put Brother T. out, you would not be so afraid ... and slip in and try to divide his flock, and turn Brother Tomlinson's friends against him.

Now, if you and your ring leaders are not cowards, come out in the open and make your attacks like men, and not fly upon your fellow-man because you have the advantage of him, because of a little money that we have all helped to accumulate that you have access to, and can use to send men to do your dirty work. Yes, and quit making ambush of the *Evangel* that we have all worked so hard for, and give others a chance to defend themselves against your cowardly and unmanly attacks ... why do you want to take the advantage of your brother, and even your son-in-law because you have access to space in the paper and he has not? I contend that the *Evangel* is as much mine as yours or any other individual. I have worked for it because it was the organ of the Church and I am as much in the Church as I ever was, and I challenge you or any other man to prove that I am not ... The fight or revolution that is now on is a church affair, and the church paper should be granted both sides to defend themselves, and then let the public make their own decision as to which way they will go. But you folks have the advantage because of the frame up at last Assembly to make J.S. L [Llewellyn] editor and publisher, and like cowards you are hiding behind ambush (*The Evangel*) and firing on every one that does not line up with you ... I reckon you thought that you could indirectly attack me and I would not catch it, but I would have you know that there are some more 'eagle eyes' besides those of J.S.L. that you dote on so much, and that they are in good use. While it is true that you were ashamed to use my name in your sugar-coated article, but it is publicly known that I was the first to come out of Babylon and declare that I would not affiliate with either side, and you make special mention of that class standing off and crowing and say that they are like the dead carcasses that have been thrown out on the shore. But I would have you to know that I have not been thrown out, but I came out of my own accord over your insisting my not resigning my position and making my reports to your Headquarters with the promise of your favor in getting good paying churches. I still have your letter which will speak for itself. Now, since I was the first to come out as I did, it is plain to be seen that I am the 'Rooster' that you have referred to, and that ... you aimed your pop-gun at me. But I will say that if you expected it to bring lasting results you should have loaded it with truth and consistency and not have wrested God's Word to make it gain your point and meet your demand.[239]

Notwithstanding the bold and sometimes scathing remarks leveled against Lee among Tomlinson's followers after the disruption, he was praised and hailed as the savior of the church by many within his own faction. Needing a hero in the midst of the awful calamity, each side tended to exaggerate the character and attributes of the man whom they placed at the helm of leadership. Thus, Tomlinson's followers saw their man as 'Moses', and the Llewellyn-Lee faction saw in Lee a 'Joshua', particularly because Moses had in one instance displeased and failed the Lord and Joshua had succeeded him as the exalted leader of God's church – 'the church in the wilderness'. Further, the image of Moses and Joshua seemed fitting because Tomlinson had created and filled the office of General Overseer since 1909 and Lee had been his admirer and student, and one of his most capable and dependable co-workers.

Figure 106

F.J. LEE AND WIFE, EVA, AND JESSE P. HUGHES AND WIFE, NELLIE (C. 1919)

Lee's first wife, Nora [Million], died in August 1912. He married Eva [Townsend] in June 1913. Hughes became a stalwart supporter of Tomlin-

---

[239] J.P. Hughes, 'A Letter of Facts and Plain Statements', *Church of God Bureau of Information* (ZACG Archives). Hughes would reconcile with his father-in-law before the latter's death in October 1928 and, interestingly, take a stand against Tomlinson and his followers just as boldly as he had the Ten Elders faction in the years following the disruption.

son in 1922-1923 and took a bold and decisive stand against his father-in-law and the Ten Elders faction. After the division in 1923, he was appointed to pastor the Cleveland church [the Tomlinson faction]; his wife, Nellie [Lee's daughter], served as church clerk and secretary.

There was, however, an important distinction between the two men: Lee was not the leader that Tomlinson was, and he was no 'Joshua'. If Tomlinson had not already built up the church and established its government and infrastructure, there would have been no church for Lee to lead, and no high office for him to occupy: and it is certain that he could not have accomplished what Tomlinson had if he had been in his shoes. Indeed, it was because of Tomlinson's sacrifices, charismatic leadership, and faithful labors in building up the organization that Lee was able to succeed at all. And even though Lee had favored modifying the office of General Overseer, he benefited from Tomlinson's embellishment of it. In one sense, he merely moved into the exalted position that the dynamic leader had formerly occupied.

But Lee also fell short in another aspect in comparison with the image of Tomlinson. The latter had become a father-figure in the church, whereas Lee was seen more or less as one of his boys; indeed, the fatherly image of the man holding the office of General Overseer was forever lost in the Llewellyn-Lee faction. But for the moment in 1923 and until his death in 1928, Lee was weighted down with the awesome image of leadership that Tomlinson had created.

The fact that Tomlinson had already firmly established the office of General Overseer gave Lee a great advantage upon his selection in July 1923: for he was certain to be admired merely on the basis of occupying the exalted office. Further, he was more or less assured to have the cooperation of the people, especially at that critical juncture when the people so desperately wanted stability and harmony and to put an end to the confusion and strife. Moreover, Lee was willing to do what Tomlinson was not, namely, to play second fiddle to Llewellyn, or at least to tolerate in him what Tomlinson was not willing to do. Ironically, it was in this intriguing manner that he was in some ways better suited for the position than Tomlinson, or perhaps it was that he was better suited for the immediate exigencies among those in his faction. The fact that he was not as gifted as Tomlinson made him less assertive and more willing to cooperate with others in leadership and executive decision-making.

There are many indications that Lee, like Tomlinson, was a good man – a prayerful, God-fearing man with sincere convictions and deeply held spiritual values. And there is no question that his esteemed stature in the eyes of the ministers and members helped to stabilize the situation in his part of the broken body, and that he guided his followers through the troubled waters ahead – until his death in 1928. And perhaps for these reasons, the honor bestowed upon his memory is somewhat deserved. But again, like Tomlinson, Lee had feet made of clay; he stumbled in some respects and doubtlessly regretted many of his words and actions, particularly his persecution and merciless slander against Tomlinson and his family during the awful ordeal of the disruption and its ugly aftermath.[240]

The Case of E.J. Boehmer

Edward John Boehmer (1881-1953) was an important figure in the church during the disruptive period in 1920-1923. He had been appointed in 1917 to a seat on the Council of Elders, and in 1921 was elected to serve as General Secretary and also as clerk of the General Assemblies and Elders' Councils. In addition, he was appointed by Tomlinson in 1921 to serve as one of the Supreme Court Judges.

Boehmer is also one of the unsung pioneers who helped to launch the Pentecostal Movement in the early twentieth century. Having moved from Missouri to Pasadena, California in 1900, he got involved in the pre-Pentecostal prayer meetings and revivals in that city. In 1905 he joined with Frank Bartleman as a prayer partner to help 'pray down' a revival in Los Angeles equal to the one that had been experienced in Wales since 1904 under the leadership of Evan Roberts. Bartleman, who became the foremost chronicler of the great outpouring of the Spirit at Azusa Street beginning in April 1906, was convinced that the Spirit-filled and agonizing prayers of Boehmer and himself had contributed substantially to igniting that great revival.[241]

Boehmer was Spirit-baptized and spoke in tongues in August 1907 at the Azusa Street mission, and like the majority who 'got their Pentecost' in that great meeting, he began to preach and promote the embryonic Pentecostal Movement. By 1910 he had made his way to Cleveland and joined the Church of God, becoming an admirer and follower of Tomlinson.

---

[240] We have cited elsewhere in this chapter many of Lee's slanderous remarks and legalistic actions. Interestingly, though Llewellyn and Lemons would eventually reconcile with Tomlinson, there is no record that Lee did so. Perhaps he believed his words and actions were justified. The full truth will probably never be known.

[241] Frank Bartleman, *Azusa Street* (New Kensington, PA: Whitaker House, 1982), pp. 15-71.

The significance of E.J. Boehmer during the disruption of the church in 1923 is that he represents the ministers who were swayed to one degree or another to stand with a certain side of the contention on the basis of monetary gain and temporal advantage. He had stood with Tomlinson faithfully even through the early months in 1923; but gradually he came under Llewellyn's influence, and as he listened to the spin that Llewellyn and Lee and others were putting on the Auditor's report and other finance-related matters, he began to entertain doubts about Tomlinson's character. Like Lee, he would eventually profess that he had gotten 'his eyes opened'. He wrote to his good friend, J.A. Davis, in August 1923 that he was determined to continue to 'preach the Church of God as strong as ever', but that he was 'going to speak more of Jesus as the head and not magnify men like we have been doing'.[242]

Sometime between late June and August, Boehmer wrote another letter to Davis[243] – the latter was then serving as the overseer of Virginia and was a zealous supporter of Tomlinson – to inform him that recent discoveries including Tomlinson's checkbook showed plainly that he was not guilty of embezzlement nor had used the church's money to pay his own debts. He admitted, however, perhaps unwittingly, that he was willing to sell out to the Llewellyn-Lee faction against Tomlinson in order to keep his job as General Secretary and his seats on the Council of Twelve and the Supreme Court.

> Bro. Davis, there has been lots said about Bro. Tomlinson that is untrue. We thought Bro. Tomlinson had taken the Church of God's money to pay his own debts, but we have found out better. We found his own checkbook here where he had paid his own bills ... and there are lots of other things coming to light the same way. This is a bad thing and somebody is going to die over this. I hardly know what to do sometimes. I love Bro. Tomlinson and hate to take a stand against him, but if I stand with him I will lose my job and I have got a good job which you know, so I hardly know what to do.[244]

---

[242] Davis, 'Deposition', p. 42.

[243] Boehmer kept up a regular correspondence with Davis; he had written to him at least ten letters between June and September (Davis, 'Deposition', pp. 5-14).

[244] Unfortunately, this letter has been lost, but its substance was retained vividly in the memory of W.M. Lowman who was then serving as the pastor of the church in Pulaski, Virginia. Davis had shown him Boehmer's letter and allowed him to read it through twice during a three-week revival that he held in Pulaski. Significantly, Davis also stayed with Lowman in his home during that three-week period (Lowman, 'Deposition', pp. 937-44; Davis, 'Deposition', pp. 4-15). Davis disputed the exact wording that Lowman had recalled, but the preponderance of evidence comes down heavily on the side of Lowman's testimony, leaving little doubt that he had

Many of Tomlinson's followers judged Boehmer's words – 'This is a bad thing and somebody is going to die over this' – as being prophetic, predicting divine judgment against Tomlinson's opponents; and this perception was strengthened after Lee and W.M. Letsinger – who had agreed together in their official capacities to revoke Tomlinson's license[245] – were dead literally within a few years, and Llewellyn and Lemons were dead spiritually. Lee had been consumed by a ravenous cancer and died mercifully on October 28, 1928; then little more than two years later Letsinger committed suicide in a most gruesome manner: putting his forehead against the end of the barrel of a shotgun and pulling the trigger.[246]

Figure 107
M.W. LETSINGER[247]
(C. 1930)

Homer's comments in the *Diary of A.J. Tomlinson* are typical of what many of Tomlinson's followers spread over the country in the years ahead. Referring to his father's persecutors, he wrote:

> But their end was already in sight. Soon J.S. Llewellyn, who led the whole thing, would himself be cast out, then losing all he had, and he had been rich, would be taken by fearful disease, and pleading with A.J. Tomlinson over and over again for forgiveness. W.M. Letsinger, their

---

read Boehmer's letter and recalled accurately the substance of it. A hand-written copy of Lowman's recollection of the letter is in ZACG Archives. The credulity of Lowman's testimony is further supported by his exemplary Christian character; he had an impeccable reputation for honesty.

[245] Lee was General Overseer and Letsinger the state overseer of Tennessee (the latter having succeeded Llewellyn in 1921); they thus formed the presbytery to revoke Tomlinson's credentials.

[246] This was reported on the front page of the *Cleveland Daily Banner*, February 2, 1931, p. 1. It was of course difficult for his family to accept, and was embarrassing for the Church of God, for Letsinger was at that time serving as the Editor and Manager of the *Evangel*. Both the family and the Church of God tried to soften the shock of the tragedy by reporting that his death may have been an accident, but the official investigators and the county coroner reported that all of the evidence pointed to a suicide.

[247] M.W. Letsinger had had an illustrative ministry in the church. We first noticed him in the dispute with Llewellyn in 1916 at the Chandler's View church near Knoxville where he served as pastor. He was pro-Tomlinson until the dispute arose in 1922. Thereafter he followed the counsel of the Llewellyn-Lee faction. He served on the Committee for Better Government in 1922; was appointed to serve as overseer of Tennessee in 1921-1924; the Council of Seventy in 1921-1927; Editor and Publisher 1928-1931; and served on the General Executive Committee 1927-1929, 1930-1931.

treasurer committed suicide. F.J. Lee had been a tool for J.S. Llewellyn. He would mercifully die. It wouldn't be long. This was a labor for the anointed of the Lord, not for just anyone who saw it as big business and could get possession of it by wire-working. J.B. Ellis, who boasted he could 'see' the shortages in A.J. Tomlinson's accounts lost the sight of both eyes, disease making it necessary to remove the eyeballs. M.S. Lemons apologized publicly, before the General Assembly, asked forgiveness, consented that God was with A.J. Tomlinson, yet lives though not able to see for many years.[248]

Boehmer himself, however, went on to have a noteworthy career as General Secretary and Treasurer with his faction of the broken body. Retiring in the Assembly in 1946, he was praised by the then present General Overseer, John C. Jernigan:

> No man in the history of the Church of God has ever retired with greater honors than E.J. Boehmer. No man has ever held the confidence of the Church in general to a greater degree than he ... His honesty has never been questioned and his character has ever been above reproach, without a stain upon it.[249]

Tomlinson's followers of course were of a different opinion, particularly among those who were immediately affected by the disruption. But the high tributes paid to Boehmer in later years were perhaps justly due; even his stand against Tomlinson was understandable amidst the confusion and cloud of uncertainty created by Llewellyn and his associates, and which were all the more complicated by Tomlinson's revolutionary reactions.

The Case of M.S. Lemons

Sterling Major Lemons (1869-1955) had served with Tomlinson for twenty years in close Christian fraternity. He had been raised in a Baptist church near Cleveland, and in 1899-1900 was swept into the Fire-Baptized Holiness Movement through the influence of Robert Frank Porter.[250] He joined the Holiness Church at Camp Creek in 1903

---

[248] Homer, *Diary*, II, p. 55. Homer fails to mention, however, that George T. Brouayer, one of Tomlinson's most devout defenders, fell off his house roof in 1929 and died shortly afterwards of the injuries.

[249] *GAM*, 1946, p. 25.

[250] Porter was the head of the Fire-Baptized movement in Tennessee, and had officiated Lemons' marriage to Mattie Carver in 1899. Mattie had preceded Lemons in joining the Fire-Baptized movement. Porter had assisted Spurling in organizing the Holiness Church at Camp Creek in May 1902 and had participated in the ordination of W.F. Bryant on that same day.

shortly after Tomlinson, and with him had sacrificed and suffered privations and persecutions in order to build the Church of God. He had baptized Tomlinson's wife, Mary Jane, shortly after she joined the church in the summer of 1903.[251] Together with Bryant and J.B. Mitchell, and sometimes R.G. Spurling, Tomlinson and Lemons had walked for miles to pray for the sick; to distribute Christian literature and Bibles; and to preach the Gospel. In 1904-1905 they had worked together to publish *The Way*, and traveled together to Birmingham Alabama in 1907 to seek for the baptism with the Spirit during M.M. Pinson's revival.[252]

Tomlinson had considered Lemons to be one of his closest friends and co-workers, so close that some accused him of making Lemons one of his 'pets'.[253] On more than one occasion, he had stood security for Lemons on bank notes to tide him over during difficult economic times,[254] and in one exceptional instance in 1913 had even appointed him as the assistant General Overseer.[255] Nevertheless, Lemons had allowed himself to be poisoned by Llewellyn's venom and joined in the movement to unseat Tomlinson, manifesting in his words and actions a carnal attitude that he regretted later.[256] Somewhere along the line he apparently had become self-deceived, unaware that he was displaying the signs of a backslidden condition. Like Samson, he 'wist not that the Lord was departed from him'. Only a few months after the church divided in 1923, reports of various sorts of misconduct on his part began to pour into the General Offices of the Llewellyn-Lee faction; and complaints and charges plagued his life and ministry for years to come. The charges ranged from 'immoral conduct', 'disorderly conduct with the

---

[251] Mary Jane, like her husband, had been a Quaker and had up to that point rejected the ordinance of baptism.

[252] Bryant/Lemons interview, pp. 15-16; *The Bridegroom's Messenger* carried reports of the revival in Birmingham (December 1, 1907; January 1, 1908).

[253] Tomlinson: 'I had been somewhat accused by some of my friends as having him as one of my pets, as I would not only give money to him nearly every time he would come to the office, but at different times loaned him money and paid him in advance, more than was due him …' (Tomlinson, 'Deposition', p. 1971).

[254] Tomlinson, 'Deposition', p. 1972.

[255] *GAM 1906-1914*, p. 235. This position existed only for one year.

[256] We have noticed that Lemons threatened Tomlinson with imprisonment and railed against him in the 1922 Assembly and in the June Council in 1923 ('Letter from C.T. Anderson to F.J. Lee', December 16, 1922; C.T. Anderson, 'Charges', June, 1923; Tomlinson, *Diary*, February 19, 1923). These actions were doubtlessly inspired in part by Llewellyn's influence. Lemons later made restitution to Tomlinson for his threats and for initiating the lawsuit (Tomlinson, *Diary*, August 13, 1930). We have every reason to believe Tomlinson's accounts of these incidents, for they were confirmed by a large number of witnesses, though a bias for Tomlinson may have colored some of the reports in his favor.

opposite sex', 'sedition', 'disloyalty', 'sowing discord', 'threatening to go to law with his brethren', 'falsifying', 'slander', etc.[257] He was known to rail against and slander the general officials of the Llewellyn-Lee faction including the Council of Twelve, no less than he had Tomlinson and his followers before the church divided in 1923. His credentials were revoked by the Llewellyn-Lee faction on two occasions.[258] Latimer, who followed Lee as General Overseer in 1928, wrote Lemons in May 1929 in a reproving manner: 'It is almost too bad to mention, to think that a man that had been a minister as long as you have should be called into question on things like this'.[259]

How did it happen? What caused Lemons to fall? Backsliding involves a degree of mystery, to be sure: 'Yet I planted thee a noble vine, wholly a right seed: how then are thou turned into the degenerate plant of a strange vine?' (Jer. 2.21). Certainly Lemons, having been instrumental in the early development and growth of the church, had become a target for 'the fiery darts of the devil'. Failing to keep a diligent watch over his own soul, he allowed the thief to enter and steal away the gifts and graces that Christ had bestowed upon him. Perhaps in irony his fall had something to do with the developing growth and prestige of the church; for as the church expanded and attracted gifted and capable ministers, his services did not seem to be needed as much as they once had; nor did his abilities stand out as conspicuously as they once had. Perhaps his fall had something to do with the special status that he had had with the General Overseer – being 'one of his pets' – and as the church flourished and the gifts and abilities of the new leaders excelled his own, he sensed that his importance in the eyes of Tomlinson and others was diminishing and his popularity in the church was fading, and, consequently, he allowed resentment and envy to fill his heart.

Be that as it may, we may be sure that his apostasy was caused in part by the corrupt influence of Llewellyn. 'Blessed is the man that walks not in the counsel of the ungodly ... nor sits in the seat of the scornful' (Ps. 1.1). It is apparent that Llewellyn was himself in the motion of backsliding during the course of his persecution and prosecution of Tomlinson; for his 'old man' showed up in the following months and years on several occasions among those whom he had led into the disruption, and even his relationship with his closet associates afterwards deteriorated

---

[257] M.S. Lemons File (Ministers' Personal Files, Church of God International Offices).
[258] M.S. Lemons File.
[259] S.W. Latimer letter to M.S. Lemons, May 29, 1929: (Ministers' Personal Files, Church of God International Offices).

until it was necessary to terminate him as editor and publisher of the *Evangel* on October 24, 1927.

So caught up in his scheme to oust Tomlinson from office and to empower himself, Llewellyn could not prevent the works of the flesh from manifesting themselves and exposing his true character. Even while being deposed under oath in 1924, after initiating the court proceedings against Tomlinson and his followers, he could not contain his arrogant and contemptuous spirit. His haughty attitude on the witness stand was so prevalent and his answers so wily and evasive, that Judge Murray on one occasion blurted out, 'I am not going to argue with you, I will not take any of your impudence ... I will take this stick and maul all the top of your head off if you insult me'.[260]

It is no wonder that only a few days after Lee's death in October 1928, his successor, S.W. Latimer, revoked Llewellyn's credentials for being contentious and unwilling to submit to authority and cooperate with the government and order of the church. Interestingly, however, these were the same characteristics that Latimer and the other nine Elders had tolerated and even applauded in Llewellyn in the course of prosecuting Tomlinson and painting him as an unscrupulous villain. The specified charges against Llewellyn were 'disloyalty – failing to pay tithes, etc.'.[261] Noteworthy as well was the action of Latimer in revoking the ministry of Lemons on some of the very same grounds – 'slander', 'sowing discord', 'threatening to go to law with his brethren', etc. – which he previously, as one of the Ten Elders and one of the seven Supreme Judges, had overlooked in Lemons when they were working together 'so nicely' to impeach Tomlinson.

To Lemons' credit, after being disciplined by his own faction of the broken body, he began to mellow in his spirit and sober to the eternal realities that he had preached for so many years, namely, that there is a heaven to gain and a hell to shun! He repented and confessed openly of many of his sins and mistakes, and also made amends with Tomlinson and his followers. On August 12, 1930 he paid a visit to Tomlinson's house and spent a great part of the day and evening acknowledging that he had done wrong in 1922-1923, and according to credible reports apparently made a sincere effort to reconcile with the man with whom he had labored so earnestly to help build the Church of God in those early

---

[260] Llewellyn, 'Deposition', pp. 1249-50.

[261] J.S. Llewellyn File (Ministers' Personal Files, Church of God International Offices). His license was revoked on October 31, 1928.

years.[262] He also spoke before the General Assembly of Tomlinson's followers in 1930, asked forgiveness for his part in the disruption and acknowledged that the Lord was with Brother Tomlinson.[263] Still, however, it is clear that he did not agree with Tomlinson's view on many particulars including the exalted office of General Overseer, nor did he approve of many of the things that Tomlinson had done during the disruption; and thus he remained with the Llewellyn-Lee faction until his death.

The Case of W.F. Bryant

In his *Diary* entry for February 19, 1923, Tomlinson reflected on the ordeal of the past year and noted,

> Last year was an awful year ... I did my work with an aching heart because of four men, all of whom I had always considered my best and most-to-be-depended-on friends, rose up against me and made it awful hard on me. These men I hate to name them, but I feel I must, were M.S. Lemons, J.S. Llewellyn, J.B. Ellis, and I might also add, W.F. Bryant.

We noticed earlier that Bryant along with Tomlinson and Lemons had sacrificed a great deal together in the early years (1900-1910) to evangelize the lost and advance the Church of God movement. In those days, Bryant was an influential and respected father in the church. Though his abilities were limited and his manners unpolished, Tomlinson admired his courage and determination and especially his power with God; and thus depended on him to help spread the message of holiness and divine healing and to assist him in advancing the unfolding vision of 'the great Church of God'. When the office of state overseer was created in 1911, Tomlinson appointed him as the overseer of Tennessee (1911-1912) and later as the overseer of Kentucky (1914-1918). Though he was overlooked when the members of the Council of Elders were selected in 1917, he nevertheless was appointed in 1921 to the newly created Council of Seventy, holding that position until the Llewellyn-Lee faction abolished that arm of government in 1929.

---

[262] Tomlinson, *Diary*, August 13, 1930. 'One of the callers yesterday was M.S. Lemons, who came to confess he had done wrong in acting as he did in 1922, and in assisting in starting a lawsuit, and asked me to forgive him. He came again to my home last night and talked a long time, and seems to have a penitent spirit, and shows a desire to make amends for his wrongs ...'

[263] Homer, *Diary*, II, p. 55.

Bryant had been good friends with Tomlinson since the latter had arrived in the mountains in 1899. Through his association with Tomlinson and their experience together, he had gained a great deal of respect in the church and was held in high esteem. Tomlinson's influence on Bryant was so great that the latter moved to Cleveland to be near him in 1906, uprooting his long family tradition in the mountains to work with the man whom apparently had the vision for world conquest and the future of the Church of God. However, he became disgruntled after his prominence in leadership began to fade in 1917. His last appointment as a state overseer was in 1917, and about that same time Tomlinson had quit sending him out to represent Headquarters in conventions. It is not surprising then that personal invitations from overseers and pastors to preach in their churches also fell off to almost nothing.

The reasons that Tomlinson quit using him are fairly clear. Bryant could not read and write and was not especially gifted as a speaker.[264] By 1917 his limited abilities and lack of polish prevented him from being able to meet the growing demands on leadership in the church. Many overseers in fact asked specifically that he not be appointed to their field of labor.[265] Tomlinson kept these things from Bryant, to avoid hurting him. This made it seem as if Tomlinson had something against him, or in Bryant's words, 'When the Church of God was small and requests would come in for ministers [Tomlinson] would send me, and I would go. Now that the church is big … he don't send me any more. I was good enough then, but I ain't good enough now.'[266] The situation doubtlessly influenced him in 1922-1923 to join in the movement to prosecute Tomlinson and finally remove him from office and revoke his ministry.

In addition to these circumstances, Bryant had fallen into a rather shady situation in 1919 and had made some rather unforntunate decisions. He had for many years received clothes and dry goods by mail and rail from members and friends of the church for orphans and for the poor in the mountains. The times being hard economically, coupled with the fact that he was receiving next to nothing from the ministry, Bryant yielded to the tempter and sold and used some of the clothes for his own benefit.[267] This was reported to Tomlinson and the Elders and some action was demanded. When confronted with the situation, Bryant

---

[264] Only after some 'great effort' he learned to read a little in the Bible and managed to write his name (Homer, *Diary*, II, p. 35).
[265] Homer, *Diary*, II, pp. 34-35.
[266] Homer, *Diary*, II, p. 34.
[267] Tomlinson, 'Deposition', pp. 1812-13; Lawson, 'Deposition', pp. 1628-29.

confessed and asked forgiveness. The case thereupon was dropped after some reproof and his promise that he would not again stoop to the practice.[268]

Now after Bryant had learned that Tomlinson had used some of the tithe money – including some due to him[269] – he became disappointed in him, and more especially because Llewellyn and Lemons and some others had convinced him that Tomlinson had used thousands of dollars of the tithe money for his own benefit; and his suspicions were only more heightened because he knew that his church in Somerset, Kentucky had sent to Headquarters the amount of $48.04 in May 1922, and yet Tomlinson had told him 'there is nothing in the treasury for you'.[270] Still more, Tomlinson's secretary, Lillie Duggar, confirmed to him that the tithes from Somerset had been sent in to the general treasury.[271] Accordingly, he now believed Tomlinson was not only a criminal but a blatant hypocrite; for he estimated that Tomlinson had done worse than he had in selling the orphans' clothes and goods and using the money for himself. Like Lemons, he had admired and trusted Tomlinson, and had put a great deal of confidence in him. He also was especially proud of the ex-Quaker because he had with Spurling personally introduced him to the Church of God, and with Spurling had formed a presbytery in June 1903 to ordain him. He had watched him grow and rise to prominence, even preeminence in the church. He recalled how they had in those early years worshipped together in his little cottage in the mountains, sacrificed and struggled together in the ministry – in the day when there was no money and no property to wrangle over; and he recalled how their families had been the best of friends and their children had grown up together. It is not strange, then, that the fall of Tomlinson, as Bryant and others imagined it, caused something also to fall in them.

---

[268] This was not the first time that Bryant had been charged with this practice. He had been reprimanded in 1909 and again in 1913 for the same thing, and threatened on one occasion with criminal action (*Bradley County Journal*, January 28, 1913; 'Holiness Church Row Before Magistrates', *Journal*, December 28, 1909, p. 1; Lawson, 'Deposition', pp. 1628-29). In his defense, it may be said that he had for years labored and distributed these dry goods to the poor in the mountains, and often at his own expense. Perhaps he believed that the minister is worthy to 'partake of the benefit', 'to reap of [their] carnal things', to 'live of the things of the temple', and that 'the laborer is worthy of his reward' (1 Cor. 9.9-14; 1 Tim. 5.18). Thus, he may have reasoned that when he and his family had needs, he was worthy 'to partake of the benefit'.

[269] W.F. Bryant, 'Deposition', pp. 1325-26.

[270] Bryant, 'Deposition', p. 1326.

[271] Bryant, 'Deposition', p. 1326.

Though Bryant would later deny it, the evidence shows that he had allowed bitterness and a vindictive spirit to enter his heart, particularly against Tomlinson; for he tended to blame him for his struggles especially during those difficult years in the early 1920s. Like Llewellyn and Lemons and those under their influence, he wanted Tomlinson to pay for his crimes, or at least to fall on his knees before the whole church weeping and begging for forgiveness like he had heard that he had done in the Elders' meeting in September 1922. Having once admired Tomlinson's polished manners and leadership abilities and his willingness to take charge and lead the way forward, Bryant now saw his old friend as an autocrat and popish dictator, and as a man using the church for his own benefit. He said on one occasion, 'When A.J. Tomlinson went into anything he had to be the head. I have been acquainted with [him] for a long time'.[272]

Notwithstanding the fact that Bryant had rebelled against and slandered Tomlinson, he had done it mainly under the influence of Lemons and some of the other Elders, all of whom had drunk from the polluted well of Llewellyn. Bryant, like so many others, believed the evil reports that Llewellyn, Lemons, Ellis, McLain, and later Lee and other Elders had circulated against Tomlinson. To Bryant's credit, when Tomlinson gave his financial report and explanation in the 1922 Assembly, he was the first to jump to his feet and rush up to the platform to forgive him, and also to ask for forgiveness for slandering him;[273] and further, like the great majority of the ministers, he expressed his willingness to donate his part of the tithe to the debt.[274]

Perhaps more could have been done in those early years to honor Bryant for his great pioneer spirit and the contribution he had made in the early development of the church, but at that stage in the church's early history there had not developed an appreciation for the church's pioneers. He would, however, be highly honored in his twilight years by the Llewellyn-Lee faction of the church for his pioneer work in helping to establish and build the Church of God.

---

[272] Bryant/Lemons interview, p. 10.
[273] Bryant, 'Deposition', p. 1322.
[274] J.P. Hughes, 'Deposition', p. 1037 – 'About the first thing I noticed was W.F. Bryant jumped across the platform and took him [Tomlinson] by the hand and says, "I will give my part of it, I want you to forgive me for what I have said about you"'. Several more witnesses testified that they heard Bryant say these same words and to ask for forgiveness. Bryant acknowledged the same in his own testimony before the court, but softened and colored his remarks in his favor, for by that time (almost two years after the fact) he had again joined with Tomlinson's opponents to prosecute and impeach him (Bryant, 'Deposition', pp. 1332-34).

The Case of A.J. Lawson

Andrew Johnson Lawson (1869-1948) was converted in 1886 and joined the Friendship Baptist Church near Cleveland. Soon he came under the influence of holiness preaching and was definitely sanctified on May 8, 1888. After being excluded from the Baptist church on charges of heresy, he united with the Methodist church at Union Grove. But while the Methodists tolerated holiness teachings, they did not fully agree with them, particularly the radical teachings of the holiness movement that swept the area in the 1890s. Lawson thus joined the East Tennessee Holiness Association.[275]

In 1898-1900 the Fire-Baptized Holiness Movement swept the area and Lawson came under the influence of that movement whose General Overseer was Benjamin Hardin Irwin whom we met in Chapter 3. Lawson's brother, Perry, and sister-in-law, Dolly, donated 75 acres of land in 1899 upon which to build an International Headquarters for the Fire-Baptized Holiness Association and a 'School of Prophets' to train their ministers and missionaries.[276]

When Tomlinson moved to Cleveland in December 1904, it was not long before the paths of Lawson and Tomlinson crossed. Lawson in fact lived only two miles from where Tomlinson purchased his house on Gaut Street in Cleveland, and he and Tomlinson maintained this proximity to one another for the next forty years.[277]

Holding holiness in common, Lawson attended between 1905 and 1907 many meetings conducted by Tomlinson and became familiar with his life and ministry. He admired him but disagreed with his view on the Bible church. Tomlinson, however, finally persuaded him that his vision of the prophetic church was true, and in January 1908 Lawson laid his hand on the Bible and repeated the words of the sacred covenant and joined the Church of God.[278] He was later baptized with the Spirit, ordained as a deacon, and became one of the church's most faithful supporters and one of Tomlinson's special partners in ministry.

Lawson was a real estate dealer in and about Cleveland, not a preacher; but in his roles as a deacon in the church and a successful and

---

[275] Lawson, 'Deposition', pp. 1545-1546.
[276] Dolly was the true spiritual connection with the Fire-Baptized movement. Perry apparently merely consented to her wishes. In any case, within a few months, Irwin fell from grace and the Fire-Baptized Holiness Association was debilitated. The vision for an international center in Cleveland died with Irwin's fall, and the land reverted back to the ownership of the Lawsons.
[277] Lawson, 'Deposition', p. 1545.
[278] Lawson, 'Deposition', p. 1546; Davidson, *Upon This Rock*, III, p. 413.

reputable businessman in Cleveland, he became a great help to Tomlinson and the latter learned to depend a great deal on him. Lawson introduced him to many important businessmen in Cleveland and vouched for his integrity and dependability, which enabled Tomlinson to secure banks loans, buy property, and do other business in the interests of the Church of God. He also connected him with other holiness leaders, like J.F. Loomis of Chattanooga, who was both the president of Loomis & Hart Manufacturing Company and also the president of the East Tennessee Holiness Association.[279] Loomis coincidentally donated the land upon which the first Church of God tabernacle was built in 1907.[280]

Lawson labored faithfully with Tomlinson as a helper to build the Church of God from nothing to become a great institution. He knew as well as anyone the sacrifices that Tomlinson and his family had made to get the Church of God off the ground, and he greatly appreciated and admired Tomlinson's untiring and faithful efforts.

The significance of Lawson during the disruption and its aftermath is that he was typical of a large number of faithful followers of Tomlinson who maintained an unshakable confidence in him and an undying sense of loyalty to him. To Lawson and thousands of others, Tomlinson was just what he said he was – the anointed General Overseer placed in his exalted position by the Holy Ghost for life! But Tomlinson was also a 'father' in the faith to the thousands of his loyal followers, and this caused them to have a deeply affectionate attachment to him. Indeed, many of them, like Lawson, believed it was their solemn duty to defend him 'tooth and toe nail' against all of his critics.

The affections and inordinate esteem that Tomlinson's followers had for him, in fact, caused them to tend to be bitter and unforgiving toward his opponents, and deceived them into believing that they were justified in retaliating against his critics and persecutors. This can be seen so clearly in the letters and pamphlets publishing by the *Church of God Bureau of Information* that was inaugurated in August 1923 and managed by Lawson. Even as late as 1927, Lawson responded to a letter by C.T. Anderson, who had suggested that some overtures might be made with the Ten Elders' faction toward some possible healing and reconciliation:

My dear Brother Anderson:

I was sure glad to get your letter but sorry to learn of the friction … between you and the Kentucky people … but one thing I will be frank to answer you on and that is that [it is] impossible to come to-

---

[279] Lawson, 'Deposition', p. 1547.
[280] Lawson, 'Deposition', p. 1547.

gether with that Gang. When I say that Gang I have no reference to hundreds, yes thousands of good, pure, true-hearted children of God who are standing with Llewellyn-Lee. But the greatest surprise to me in all my life is to think that you, a man I have always looked on as a good true child of God with good sound judgment, looking at that undermining trick of the Old Big devil himself in those sugar-coated words ... F.J. Lee, T.S. Payne, S.W. Latimer, and I will say all of these would be willing to die any kind of death if they would be assured that by their death they would stop A.J. Tomlinson from going on with God's work. This may look like a hard saying to you but I know it is not imagination, or guess work of mine but it is the truth. I might some time become willing to line up with the Campbellites or the good Baptists, or the Methodists, but never unless F.J. Lee, J.S. Llewellyn, T.S. Payne and S.W. Latimer repent and confess to the willful lies they have and are today circulating on Brother Tomlinson. I can stand all they say about me and forgive them without their asking, but when it comes to willful lying on the one who made the Church of God all that she is by yielding himself to God and suffering for Him, then they will have to make me know they have truly repented.[281]

It would be difficult to overestimate the admiration that men like Lawson had for Tomlinson, and conversely to exaggerate the disappointment, if not disdain, they had for men like Llewellyn, Lemons, Lee, Payne, Latimer, and others whom they perceived as being unjust and even vile in their treatment of Tomlinson. True, their estimation of Tomlinson was too high, bordering in some cases on worship; but they knew what he had accomplished; that he far more than anyone else had labored and sacrificed to build the Church of God. To Tomlinson's faithful followers, the actions of the Ten Elders were nothing less than a mutiny! Accordingly, Llewellyn, Lemons, Lee, and the others were guilty of treason and sedition: for they had raised up against the duly constituted authority of God Himself represented in Tomlinson.

Being so affectionately attached to Tomlinson and his image, Lawson and many like him could not entertain any fault in Tomlinson, particularly any shortcomings that called for his impeachment and excommunication from the church. It was impossible for them to grasp that Tomlinson was in part to be blamed for the disruption. Even if he had fallen short in some of his decisions and actions, it was only because he had

---

[281] 'Lawson to Anderson', dated January 15, 1927 ('C.T. Anderson File', ZACG Archives).

depleted himself physically and mentally to build God's house. And indeed he had!

Notwithstanding the fact is the church had outgrown the Tomlinson family's dominance over the church, and the autocratic leadership style of Tomlinson himself. Something had to be done in regard to Tomlinson's autocracy; it remained only to choose the proper channel and wisest course to make the necessary adjustments. Unfortunately, the proper channel and wisest course was not taken.

The June Council

After five months on the field, Tomlinson came back to Cleveland in early May 1923 to meet with Llewellyn and Lee – the other two members of the newly-formed Executive Council – to discuss their increasing differences and apparent misunderstandings in regard to the 'agreements' they had made in their meeting in December. Their disagreements in particular were in regard to Tomlinson's expenses incurred while laboring in the field and his promise to collect offerings for the various departments of the church and to send them into Headquarters.[282] They also discussed briefly the work of the Investigation Committee and the on-going audit of his books by the Lee H. Battle Company. It was at that time that they scheduled the June Council and agreed for it to be an open meeting to include not only the Twelve and Seventy but also whoever else desired to attend.[283] This arrangement was simply a way of going forward against the bitter and growing disagreements between the three men and the factions developing around their disagreements. The June

---

[282] Tomlinson noted, 'This disagreement between Llewellyn, Lee and myself got so strong that I finally made a proposition to them ... that I would be willing to count up the whole amount [of the offerings] I had received personally, and for my personal benefit and personal gifts, and let them make a check from the tithe fund and let that whole check go for the paying of some of the orphanage bills and other things and would not raise any further disturbance about my expenses that they had not met. This amounted to between $400 and $500 which was done, and those bills were paid, and still they lacked about $300 of paying my expenses, as I had understood their agreement in the first place. Agreements with three men, when the three men don't *get along* together good don't amount to much anyway' (Tomlinson, 'Deposition', p. 2163). The suspicion of Llewellyn and Lee was that Tomlinson was receiving money for *Evangel* subscriptions and orphanage donations and other monies for Headquarters and was using these funds for his personal use. Tomlinson denied this vehemently, and there is no evidence to support the suspicions of Llewellyn and Lee.

[283] This was announced in the *Evangel*, and Jesse P. Hughes, Lee's son-in-law, was present when the three men on the Executive Council agreed to it (Hughes, 'Deposition', p. 1075).

Council was set virtually to be a show-down between Llewellyn and Lee and their followers on one side and Tomlinson and his followers on the other.

Anticipating the show-down in the June Council, each side planned their strategy and were predisposed to carry it out. Tomlinson had made up his mind as early as January 1923 that the time had come to 'expose these men to the very depths'[284] if they persisted, according to his way of thinking, in unjustly and illegally opposing him as General Overseer. As already noticed, part of his scheme was to give the floor at the proper time to C.T. Anderson to bring charges against Llewellyn, Lemons, and Ellis for their disorderly conduct during the Assembly and for manifesting a blatant disrespect for him personally and showing contempt for his office as General Overseer.[285] These charges were in turn to silence Llewellyn and his followers and prevent them from pursuing their plan to make Tomlinson the focus of the meeting and ultimately to bring charges against him for his alleged wrongdoings. Further, in order to effect the ends that he had in mind, Tomlinson established at the opening of the Council some strict Parliamentary procedures and guidelines in order to keep the focus on the charges against his opponents rather than himself.[286]

Llewellyn and his followers considered Tomlinson's moderation of the meeting a travesty of justice, complaining that he was using or rather

---

[284] Boehmer, the General Secretary, had written to him on January 12, 1923 informing him that Llewellyn, Lee, and others were raising objections to publishing his annual address in the *GAM* (Tomlinson, 'Deposition', p. 1959). He responded boldly and with a passionate assertiveness: 'First, I will say, I want the full address printed in the minutes, and with no explanatory note following. The minutes of the Assembly will be sufficient to explain.' He then added, 'I think I have been bearing with these men just about long enough. If they finally refuse to put [my address] in the minutes, just as it was given in the Assembly, I shall print it myself and will give the reason ... I feel I owe this to the church ...' (Tomlinson, 'Deposition', pp. 1960-61).

[285] Anderson, 'Deposition', pp. 237-54, 291-303. This scheme was first suggested by Anderson in a letter to Tomlinson sent shortly after the Assembly in November 1922 and gradually materialized in the following months. The charges were written up by Anderson and edited in part by Tomlinson and reached their final form by about the end of April. The plan to bring them up at the June Council was finalized in Tomlinson's house on the morning of June 12, 1923. The Council was opened that evening in the Assembly auditorium in Cleveland. The specific charges have been preserved in a document put out by the Tomlinson faction's *Bureau of Information*. See 'Charges', *Church of God Bureau of Information*, A.J. Lawson, Manager.

[286] Tomlinson denied that his intention in giving Anderson the floor was to silence his opposition, but the evidence is overwhelming that this was the primary object of pressing for the charges in the June Council.

misusing his position to achieve his own aims in the Council. And doubtlessly this was the case. Parliamentary procedures were twisted by Tomlinson to attain the outcome he desired. Even the Appellate Court that otherwise ruled in Tomlinson's favor saw it that way:

> The Llewellyn faction complained bitterly because of the rulings of the chief overseer in not permitting them to refer to him and sustaining points of order to every telling point made in their speeches. There is no justification for the conduct of the general overseer, and it can be explained upon no other theory than that he lost his head when he discovered the elders were against him and were attempting to checkmate him by a summary removal.[287]

The court then made the following observation: 'The conduct of the general overseer on this occasion ... injured no one but Tomlinson and gave the opposite faction the advantage in pressing their charges and in convincing the members of the justice of the same'.[288]

The strategy of Tomlinson and his followers had become well-known to Llewellyn and his followers at least by April 1923. Anderson had written to Lee in December and again apparently in April of his intention to bring charges against the three Elders, and of course Latimer had communicated with Llewellyn and Lee about the matter after his meeting with Tomlinson and Anderson in the convention at Hazelhurst, Georgia in the latter part of March or first of April, and in their follow-up meeting in Birmingham, Alabama in May. By that time Tomlinson was carrying with him in his travels a copy of the charges against the three Elders and sharing with the overseers and pastors his plans for the June Council.[289] He was also soliciting signatures of all who agreed with the charges. The list of signatures are intriguing; they include a future General Overseer in the Llewellyn-Lee faction, H.L. Chesser, and several prominent overseers and pastors and members of

---

[287] *Opinion*, p. 4.
[288] *Opinion*, p. 4.
[289] T.A. Richards, the overseer of Louisiana in 1922, who was at the time standing with Tomlinson, testified that Tomlinson had shown him a copy of the charges which he had in hand during his convention in Louisiana about a week or so before the June Council. He stated further that Tomlinson's plan was to 'silence those elders – Llewellyn, Lemons and Ellis' (Richards, 'Deposition', pp. 52-54). J.A. Davis, the overseer of Virginia, who was at the time standing with Tomlinson, testified that he had attended the meeting in his house on the morning of June 12th and that Tomlinson had rehearsed with those present the procedure to follow when the Council was opened that evening to give priority to the charges against Llewellyn, Lemons and Ellis in order 'to silence these brothers so they could not bring charges against him during the council' (Davis, 'Deposition', pp. 6-8).

the Council of Seventy.[290] The final list presented at the June Council included seventy signatures: C.T. Anderson, J.I. Baldree, P.W. Chesser, H.L. Chesser, W.R. Sexton, J.M. Baldree, O.N. Yingst, L.E. Camp, J.L. Dorman, W.T. Jackson, R.B. Spring, G.R. Sanders, T.P. Douglas, W.S. Pinder, R.L. Carroll, G.B. Langford, Newton Harrell, J.H. Pierce, C.H. Randell, Guy Marlow, James Daniel, W.H. Prewitt, G.G. Williams, H.R. Jacobs, J.T. Priest, J.O. Hamilton, E.C. Rider, W.G. Rembert, Geo. T. Stargel, Perry Kimlin, F.W. Stone, J.M. Mullen, W.L. Bass, F.D. Hardee, Dock Hardee, R.L. Crisp, T.L. Little, C.H. Deans, A.M. Brantly, I.H. Hinton, G.B. Holder, D.F. King, W.M. Brannett, M.A. Chapman, Jesse Ballers, L.F. McCarson, C.Z. Chapman, T.M. Sensing, C.C. McGowan, W.J. McCormick, A.W. Sanders, J.A. Davis, F.J. Crowder, Geo. T. Brouayer, E.J. Hanks, L.L. Turner, J.R. Smith, J.H. Curry, R. Williams, Fred Beneby, David Le Fleure, G.C. Sapp, Thos. J. Richardson. [291]

Besides those who signed the specified charges against the three Elders, there were a large number who sympathized with the charges but were not aware of the document or else had not had the opportunity to sign it. Some of those who spoke in the Council in favor of the charges were A.J. Lawson, Homer A. Tomlinson, Jesse P. Hughes (Lee's son-in-law), J.N. Hurley, A.D. Evans (Tomlinson's son-in-law), E.L. Pinkley, W.G. Rembert, T.A. Richard, H.A. Pressgrove, and J.A. Wilkerson (the grandfather of the celebrated evangelist, David Wilkerson).[292] And of course there were two members on the Council of Twelve who spoke boldly in favor of the charges, George T. Brouayer and S.O. Gillaspie.

The document of charges against Llewellyn, Lemons, and Ellis captures the essential issues and virtually embodies the overall case of Tomlinson and his followers leading up to the disruption in June-August 1923; indeed, one could not truly appreciate the Tomlinson side's passion and convictions about their differences with the other side without actually reading the document. We thus present it here in its fullness along with an Introductory Note written by A.J. Lawson. This Introduction is significant because it lays out from the perspective of Tomlinson and his followers the scenario of events that transpired from the As-

---

[290] Chesser served as General Overseer in 1948-1952; members of the Council of Seventy who signed the charges or spoke openly in favor of them were: J.A. Davis, E.L. Pinkley, T.A. Richard, W.G. Rembert, H.A. Pressgrove, C.H. Randell, Guy Marlow, J.O. Hamilton, David Le Fleuer, F.J. Crowder, J.T. Priest, E.C. Rider, J.W. Mullen, L.L. Turner, J.H. Curry, and T.J. Richardson.

[291] Anderson, 'Deposition', pp. 240-41; see also 'Charges', *Church of God, Bureau of Information*, p. 4.

[292] Marlow, 'Deposition', p. 781.

sembly in 1922 to the June Council in 1923. Further, it is basically true to the facts and the way the events unfolded, notwithstanding that it is tainted with a bias for Tomlinson and tends to color with impunity his participation in the scheme; particularly the fact that Tomlinson clearly encouraged Anderson to write up the charges against the Elders and even furnished him information to embellish the report. Tomlinson without question helped to stage how the charges would be presented in the June Council.

Introductory Note

Directly after the annual Assembly last year – 1922, C.T. Anderson began to agitate this matter and in a few months after he returned [home], he says that he wrote up the charges against the Elders therein named, but did not present it owing to the fact that the General Overseer did no [*sic*] approve of it.

When the Hazlehurst, Ga., convention came off in the spring, C.T. Anderson went up to the meeting and together with S.W. Latimer and S. J. Heath decided on a course to pursue. When it was presented to Brother Latimer he was very enthusiastic and urged Brother Anderson to circulate it, and solemnly pledged his support.

At this meeting Brother Anderson obtained additional charges and it was decided to also incorporate them. And Brother Anderson was asked to write the charges and include this new evidence. He has the first M.S. in his possession yet.

This was done in the presence of Brother Tomlinson, but he plainly told them he would not have anything to do with getting it out, more than to give the information that was asked of him.

It was clearly understood that these charges were to be presented at the first meeting of the Elders Council, but at that time it was not known when the Council would meet, and Brother Latimer promised in all earnestness that he would back it with all his energy when it came up. He never did make a statement to the contrary. And it was expected he would be as good as his word, or at least if he thought it were wrong to tell Brother Anderson not to present it.

It was presented by Brother Anderson to the Elders Council on June 12, 1923, and read by the General Secretary, and spoken to by about twenty-five who favored it, having seventy signatures of brethren whose names are attached hereto.

We present it to the public just as it was presented to the Council. It consumed about ten hours to get through with the introductory speeches. Finally the matter was given to the defense and after a short debate submitted it to the other nine Elders for their consideration and decision.

There were no objections to the charges except that they were brought prematurely, and they agreed that the charges would be presented at the proper time and these three men dealt with properly. T.S. Payne solemnly pledged himself to bring the matter up even should others fail. The matter was never brought up again.

The Elders meeting continued in session several days trying to draw the two Elders that stood for Brother Tomlinson away, but when they could not do this they closed their meeting pending the decision of Brother Tomlinson, but when Brother Gillaspie and Brouayer were out they called a secret council and did not let these two men know about it and hatched up charges against them.

Charges

To the Elders of the General Assembly of the Church of God, Cleveland, Tenn.:

Whereas, the Church of God has recognized A.J. Tomlinson as having been made General Overseer over the Church of God by the Holy Ghost (Acts 20:28; 1 Cor. 12:28), and in his exalted position we feel that due honor and respect should be accorded him at all times and on all occasions, and

Whereas, Brother Tomlinson presented some things in his annual address before the Seventeenth Annual Assembly that were unusual, among other things the appropriation of tithes to other than the usual disbursement, and

Whereas, the Assembly noted this and unanimously agreed to accept the expenditures as it stood, and to forgive Brother Tomlinson's unavoidable misdirection of funds, and

Whereas, no one objected to the plea for forgiveness, all felt that the matter had been laid to rest, but when Brother Tomlinson saw fit to tender his resignation the matter was again resurrected and in abusive and vindictive language our General Overseer had to bear indignities publicly hurled at him as few criminals have had to bear, and

Whereas, the language employed and the extreme viciousness of deliverance, together with a very excited and enraged personage, we feel is unbecoming to any person who bears the gentle name of a Christian, and

Whereas, M.S. Lemons, J.S. Llewellyn and J.B. Ellis were most prominent by their wire pulling and chicanery, passed certain measures in the Seventeenth Annual Assembly which were both unscriptural and not pleasing to the Holy Ghost, and

Whereas, one of these men went to our interpreter and so intimated him that he was miserable during the entire Assembly, said man having in a manner given him orders not to attempt to give any interpretations during the entire Assembly, and

Whereas, these men so intimidated one of the committees that they could not act in the capacity as being free men before the Lord which prevented them from making their report to the Assembly as they wished, and

Whereas, said J.S. Llewellyn in a discourse of two hours or more in length before the Eleven and Seventy in joint session, used such words and terms in trying to ruin the influence of the General Overseer and his family, that were unbecoming for a gentleman, or a political trickster, and much less for one professing the Christian religion, and

Whereas, by these open and boisterous discourses said Lemons, Ellis and Llewellyn have proven themselves to be brawlers and contentious, which renders them all unfit to be bishops in the Church of God and therefore they are not fit to be elders and councilors, and

Whereas, the Assembly was forced by these men into cold formal business that kept the Spirit grieved, and the saints in tears most of the time because of grief, and at one time when the General Overseer called the Assembly to prayer about a measure which has been his custom for seventeen years, J.S. Llewellyn rushed up to the General Overseer in a rage, where he was praying, and shook his fist close by the side of his head and roared out: 'How dare you block the passage of this measure in any such a way? You dare, not do it! You shall not do it!' and would not pray, but turned pale like he was mad and walked the floor while the praying was going on, and

Whereas, many of the ministers were so disturbed and discouraged because of the measures passed by the influence of these men, and the way the Assembly ended, that many of them could not go to their respective fields of labor with any degree of victory and joy, to toil and labor for the Church of God, and many said they did not know how to preach the Church of God any more while such men are allowed to be in control, and

Whereas, these and other dissatisfactions existing caused by these aforesaid men which renders them unqualified to take active part in the governing of the Church of God, many of which would surprise the thousands of members of the Church of God if divulged and which will be if circumstances compel such action, and

Whereas, they kept the General Overseer grieved to such an extent for nine months or more prior to the Assembly that he was not able to render his best services as editor and publisher nor in his position as General Overseer, and

Whereas, the General Overseer has never made any defence [*sic*], neither has he offered any resistance to their railings, brawlings, misrepresentations and accusations, we feel that it has come time for definite action to not only vindicate our General Overseer and family, but to rid the Church of God of such unscrupulous and unprincipled men, so that it may go on in good order and fellowship as it used to years ago when every action that was taken in the Assembly could be recognized by an expression from all, 'It seems good to the Holy Ghost and us', but alas, in the last Assembly there seemed to be not God in the passage of any measure, and

Whereas, on the seventh day of November, 1922, on the last day of the Assembly, A.J. Tomlinson offered his resignation as General Overseer, as a protest against the passage of certain measures and to show his disapproval of the business part of the Assembly and how the Holy Spirit was ruled out of it, said resignation was not accepted, but contrariwise two or three special actions were taken which kept him in the place by unanimous vote and one voice and acclamation, and since he finally consented to remain he is still the General Overseer of the Church of God everywhere established with headquarters at Cleveland, Tenn., and

Whereas, it has been the privilege of some of us to study the general parliamentary usages in both religious and secular public gatherings, but we have never seen such humiliating confusion in any place as was practiced by these aforesaid men on our General Overseer as chairman of the Assembly of the Churches of God, and

Whereas, these aforesaid men not only publicly humiliated our General Overseer, but defamed the Holy Ghost in open defiance to Paul's specific injunction, 'Forbid not to speak with tongues', therefore

Be it resolved, that these men, namely M.S. Lemons, J.S. Llewellyn and J.B. Ellis for all these sacreligious [sic] indignities heaped upon our kind and patient General Overseer, as well as putting Lord Jesus to an open shame, should have a sharp rebuke administered, and that there be no more recurrence of a like disgrace on the Church of God, that these men be divested of all station of honor and trust in the Church of God, and a charge of disloyalty be presented to their respective places of local membership, for action in the Church.

To the Elders of the General Assembly of the Church of God, Cleveland, Tenn.:

If by any means, whether by testimony or otherwise, it is discovered that any others of the twelve have been accomplices with the men in question, M.S. Lemons, J.S. Llewellyn and J.B. Ellis, in carrying into effect things contained in these charges such shall be placed under question and charges of a similar nature preferred against them. This also to apply to other ministers and members in proportion to their guilt.[293]

Notwithstanding the complaints made against the three Elders by the followers of Tomlinson, and the sentiments expressed in their defense by a few in the Llewellyn-Lee faction,[294] all of which consumed some

---

[293] 'Charges', *Church of God Bureau of Information*, p. 4.

[294] Of the number that spoke in behalf of the three Elders were Lee and Latimer (Marlow, 'Deposition', p. 745; Lee, 'Deposition', pp. 934-39; Hughes, 'Deposition', pp. 1080-81), which was an indication or sign of things to come, namely, that the Ten Elders had planned apparently to exonerate the three Elders all along; after all, Llewellyn and Lee had been working together side by side at Headquarters since the Executive Council was appointed at the Assembly in November 1922, and Lee had gradually come to see things Llewellyn's way since the Council meeting in the previous September. As the two chief officers of the church stationed in Cleveland (Tomlinson having been relegated more or less to the field), Llewellyn and Lee were in constant communication with the other Elders. They knew exactly how things stood and had planned their strategy to counteract Tomlinson's plans in the June Council. Moreover, it seems apparent that the appearance and actions of the overseer of Florida, John L. Stephens, to oppose the actions of Anderson in the meeting were pre-planned. Stephens had followed Lee as the overseer of Florida in 1922 and had been appointed to his position on Lee's recommendation to Tomlinson. Stephens had worked closely with Lee – the latter having served in Florida as overseer in 1919-1922 – and the two had become good friends. As things unfolded in the months leading up to the June Council, Stephens took a decided stand for the Llewellyn-Lee faction and Anderson for the Tomlinson faction (Anderson, 'Depo-

ten hours and carried the meeting into the afternoon of the next day, the matter was then turned over to the other nine Elders for their consideration and decision. They with the General Overseer met separately in a room off the auditorium, and after some 'three or four hours' they concluded that the charges were brought before the Council illegally, that is, out of order; for it was argued that the June Council was called primarily

Figure 108

THE NEW ASSEMBLY AUDITORIUM (1920)

The new Assembly auditorium stood as a symbol of the church's progress, but the cost of constructing it (1919-1920) became a financial burden and a bone of contention among the leaders of the church in 1921-1923.

to hear the report of the Investigation Committee in regard to Tomlinson's affairs relative to the church's finances, which included the auditor's report and the alleged shortages in the church's accounts. Tomlin-

---

sition', pp. 258-60; Hughes, 'Deposition', p. 1080; Gillaspie, 'Deposition', pp. 482-83). It is not surprising then that Stephens – who was Anderson's state overseer – attempted to block Anderson's right to bring charges against these Elders by accusing him of misconduct while he served as a pastor and district overseer in Florida. Tomlinson, however, ruled that the meeting was focused for the time being on the charges brought against the three Elders, and thus that Anderson was free to speak and act in the meeting. As it turned out, no formal charges had been brought against Anderson by any of the churches in Florida before the June Council.

son maintained that the charges against the three Elders were legal but conceded that perhaps that they had been 'brought prematurely' before the Council.[295] This term – 'brought prematurely' – was accepted by the nine Elders and it was agreed by all present that the charges would be pursued sometime after the business at hand when Tomlinson was resolved and the cloud over him was lifted.

When the Elders returned to the auditorium and gave their report, it was accepted by Tomlinson's supporters only on the basis that T.S. Payne had promised that he would, as one of the Twelve, see to it that the charges against the three Elders were pursued after the issues with Tomlinson were settled; in fact, Payne stated boldly that 'if they [the three Elders] were exonerated I [will] bring charges against those fellows myself'.[296] This was obviously an insincere gesture, if not a set-up in order to get on with the business of trying Tomlinson, for the three Elders offered little or no defense for themselves and did not deny the charges, which was completely uncharacteristic of their personalities and aggressive dispositions. They apparently had been assured of the outcome, and on that basis submitted themselves to the judgment of Lee and the other Elders on the Council.[297] According to the scheme, the three Elders were a couple of days later exonerated of all charges, which then made them eligible to join with Lee and the others in prosecuting Tomlinson and the two Elders standing with him. Llewellyn was of course especially needed, if not indispensable in the prosecution of Tomlinson, for he had been building a case against him since June 1922, and had been leading in the prosecution of him since September 1922; and with his legal background and personal vendetta against Tomlinson was recognized as the one best suited to formulate the decisive charges against Tomlinson in the June Council in 1923.

---

[295] The best and most detailed report of this meeting and the results are given by Gann in his testimony. He alone shows that the term 'premature' was suggested by Tomlinson but that the majority of the Elders thought the action against the three Elders was illegal (Gann, 'Deposition', pp. 980-84).

[296] This is well supported by many witnesses and is admitted by Payne himself (Payne, 'Deposition', p. 187).

[297] Payne, 'Deposition', pp. 186-88. All of them in fact more or less admitted their guilt, though they colored their acts as being rather insignificant. Llewellyn said that his harshness and blunt speeches that attacked Tomlinson and his family were 'just Joe being Joe', and Lemons rather pretentiously at one point 'threw up his hands and said, I'm guilty' (Randell, 'Deposition', pp. 631-32; Marlow, 'Deposition', 744-46; Hamilton, 'Deposition', pp. 857-59. Ellis, however, did not admit to any guilt nor offer any defense for himself, for he apparently anticipated the outcome in his favor and thus simply submitted himself to the judgment of the other Elders.

After the Elders had succeeded to put the focus back on Tomlinson rather than Llewellyn, Lemons, and Ellis, they then returned to the Assembly auditorium and proceeded to what they considered to be the trial of the General Overseer. Tomlinson, however, denied that it was a trial and argued that the Council provided merely a forum for the issues and differences between himself and the brethren to be clarified and worked out to the satisfaction of both sides: for he and his followers held that only God and the General Assembly could hold him accountable and remove him from his exalted office.[298] The meeting then proceeded on that basis, that is, with the powerful crosscurrents created by the two opinions.

After being reassembled in the auditorium, Tomlinson then called the meeting to order. At that point, Llewellyn immediately rose to his feet and protested against Tomlinson remaining the moderator since he was the one being tried; for then, after all, he would be trying his own case. After some resistance, Tomlinson conceded to the suggestion and Efford Haynes was selected to fill the chair. Tomlinson then in one of his dramatic and theatrical moves went to Haynes and led him to the stand to install him, as it were, momentarily in the moderator's chair. This gesture by Tomlinson – an unprecedented action in the church's history – was to suggest that as General Overseer he was still ultimately in charge. Reflecting later on the ordeal, Lee said Tomlinson was like 'a drowning man grabbing at a straw'.

Immediately thereupon the report of the auditor representing the Lee H. Battle Audit Company was read which showed an alleged financial

---

[298] Tomlinson and some of his followers in fact maintained that no one but God could remove him from office; and they insisted in this view even in the event that the General Overseer might become corrupt. Tomlinson cited the case of King David, saying, 'Under the old Scripture, King David became very corrupt, and God sent a prophet to him, gave him to understand what he should be and do, and brought him under conviction and he repented and went on with his kingdom' (Tomlinson, 'Deposition', p. 2088). In his annual address in 1922, Tomlinson made his position perfectly plain: God had put him in office and only God could rightfully take him out. In his view, not even the Assembly could take him out without '[mocking the work of God]' (*HAA*, I, p. 203). He had stated on more than one occasion that he was 'more or less subject to the Assembly' (e.g. in his Introduction to his annual address in 1915), but he apparently meant 'less'. The actions in 1921-1923 proved this, for the Assembly had approved of the Constitution which Tomlinson refused to uphold and live under. Evidence is everywhere in his own writings that he believed the office of General Overseer was above the Assembly, and he practiced the government of the church on that basis. The notion that the General Overseer was subject to the Assembly was superficial in any case: for the Assembly is more or less a faceless body without some Ruling Elders empowered to act for the Assembly. This was in part the reason for the Council of Elders, Council of Seventy, and body of Presbyters.

shortage in the church's funds and a number of inconsistencies on Tomlinson's books and ledgers. In addition, Lee raised issues regarding inconsistencies and contradictions connected with the Bible Training School, the *Faithful Standard* magazine, and the Orphanage fund. In fact, all of the issues that had been raised since the September Council in 1922 surfaced again in this meeting, including Tomlinson's misapplication of the tithes in 1921-1922 to pay off the debts of the auditorium and Evangel publishing house. The next two days were consumed with these issues, with Tomlinson and then his son, Homer, endeavoring to explain and reconcile the apparent contradictions and inconsistencies. The two men held the floor for the better part of two days. Gillaspie and Brouayer who sat on the Council of Twelve spoke on Tomlinson's behalf, and some others also spoke in his defense including his son-in-law, A.D. Evans who worked in the publishing house; and a number of others who served on the Council of Seventy also spoke in his favor. Some of the witnesses endeavored to add light on some of the issues raised, while others simply spoke sympathetically of the overloaded burden that Tomlinson was shouldering as General Overseer, which, they contended, might cause any man to err in judgment and make mistakes.

In the course of the meeting, Lemons said that some of Tomlinson's explanations were self-contradictory and ambiguous, and that Tomlinson reminded him of the man who said 'he loved mutton but didn't care much for sheep meat'.[299] But, as we have seen, almost all of Lemons' observations were colored with his developing contempt for Tomlinson; and thus whatever explanation Tomlinson offered in regard to the financial reports and related matters were considered by Lemons to be a cover-up scheme rather than a reasonable answer, and consequently his actions were inexcusable. He had already manifested before the whole church his disdain for Tomlinson and was on record stating that he wanted him 'behind bars'. He was thus proceeding in the trial on that prejudiced basis, maintaining that Tomlinson was guilty until proven innocent. Tomlinson, conversely, styled himself in his remarks as a martyr. In his defense, he told 'a story about an old mule that had fallen into a well and the owner decided that since he was not worth the cost of

---

[299] This same expression was used by the members of the Supreme Council in a letter to Tomlinson, dated July 26, 1923. The statement was made particularly in regard to Tomlinson taking issue with the designation used for the church in the Constitution, 'The General Assembly of the Churches of God' over against the traditional name 'Church of God'. The Council responded, 'This technical question reminds us of a fellow that didn't like mutton, but was very fond of sheep meat' ('Supreme Council to Tomlinson', July 26, 1923, p. 4).

getting him out he would fill up the well and let the mule stay in the bottom thereof. Accordingly he began to dump rocks and earth in on top of the mule, and [the mule] shook it off and got on top of it until he finally walked out at the top and began grazing as if nothing had ever happened'.[300] He then told the opposing Elders 'go ahead and cover me up and bruise me all [you can], but in due time I [will] walk out on top and go on grazing as if nothing had ever happened'.[301]

When all of the issues in regard to Tomlinson's affairs as General Overseer were addressed, including the issues raised in his connection with the publishing house, orphanage funds, Bible Training School, the Correspondence course, the Exchange & Indemnity Department, the Loan Department, and the *Faithful Standard* magazine, the Elders then retired to the Evangel building to reflect on the evidence. It was anticipated, however, that they would consult with Tomlinson again if any further questions arose, or any further clarifications were needed. But as things turned out, they did not consult with Tomlinson again nor allow him any further opportunity to defend himself or offer any further explanation in regard to their charges, and proceeded to render their guilty judgment against him and the two Elders standing with him.

The judgment of the ten Elders was a foregone conclusion, for in the months leading up to the June Council the radicals (Llewellyn, Lemons, Ellis, McLain, Haynes) and moderates (Lee, Boehmer, Latimer, Payne, Gann) had coalesced around the leadership of Lee: and together they had become firmly convinced of Tomlinson's guilt and the need to remove him from office. Lee had attempted also to persuade the two dissenting Elders – Gillaspie and Brouayer – of Tomlinson's 'wrongdoing' and 'crookedness' but had failed. He admitted that Brouayer and Gillaspie 'were pretty rigid [for Tomlinson]'.[302] Even after the June Council and before the charges against Tomlinson had been turned over to the church's Supreme Court in July, Lee wrote to Gillaspie urging him to 'reconsider your actions in standing with [Tomlinson] and stand with the Council'. His letter to Gillaspie is worth quoting here at some length, for it gives insight into Lee's craftiness and the skills he had used apparently to persuade some of the other more moderate Elders to turn on Tomlinson and unite together with him and the radicals to suspend Tomlinson's ministry and ultimately to revoke his credentials and exclude him from the church.

---

[300] Tomlinson, *Answering the Call*, pp. 22-23.
[301] Tomlinson, *Answering the Call*, p. 23.
[302] Lee, 'Deposition', p. 936.

Dear Bro:

Somehow I just felt like I ought to write you a few lines. Brother I have always looked on you as a man of God and I really believe you fully intend to do right and I believe you have the same opinion of me, but brother you heard me say in the Council that I wouldn't stand for Tomlinson no more than any other man that has done wrong, so brother the thing come out … I can't feel yet that you will willingly endorse the things that came out on him. He is saying now the audit is no good because the auditor said it was a preliminary examination of the books. He did make a preliminary examination … but it was before he began the audit. Brother I will say this because I believe you are good and honest 'he is like a drowning man grabbing at a straw'. I really believe he is going to fall down in his plans … to do away with the two last Assemblies, just like he failed in his efforts this last council. Now brother I feel like you ought to reconsider your actions in standing with him, and stand with the council. You know I was once teeth and toenail with him, but I tell you I was made to see things differently. I feel like if I could or should cover up the things I know about him just because of sympathy and his smooth way of expressing himself, I would be held responsible before God. God won't stand for wrong doing in a high official no more than he would a little ignorant negro. We dealt with Perry for much less that what Tomlinson has done. Well I will say no more about this, but want to tell you that I have always loved brother Galaspie [*sic*] and I can't bear the thought of you not walking with us any more.

I have heard that you said that the greatest difficulty you have of being with the other side is the harsh spirit. Now brother you never heard a more railing speech than Anderson made, also Broughyer [*sic*] and many others. Now while Llewellyn was hard, you must remember that for months he plead [*sic*] with brother Tomlinson to make these things right, but couldn't get him to move a peg. He finally decided that he was going to use more ridged terms. I'm sure that if we had continued to pat him on the head and say smothe [*sic*] words to him he would have been in office today if he hadn't been in the receivers hands. Brother we need … men with real backbone to stand out ridged against wrong whoever it is in. Jesus turned over the money tables and talked hard to the folks, even whipped them. The spirit of

Jesus is not always smothe [sic] words. Some how I feel like you are reconsidering some things.

Would be glad to hear from you.

Yours sincerely, F.J. Lee[303]

Intriguingly, this letter was written after Lee and the other nine Elders had charged Gillaspie 'with aiding and abetting the said A.J. Tomlinson in the principal part of his illegal acts ... and embarrassing the deliberations of the council in their [sic] efforts to investigate the serious complaints against A.J. Tomlinson, also manifesting a contentious spirit which is foreign to our Holy Religion ...'[304] It is difficult to reconcile Lee's charges in the June Council with his praise and admiration of Gillaspie in his personal letter to him a few days later. The apparent contradiction between his words and actions seems to justify the opinion of Tomlinson's followers that Lee was under Llewellyn's influence. Jesse P. Hughes, whom we have noticed was one of the brightest and most promising young pastors in the church, regretted that his father-in-law was 'under [Llewellyn's] thumb'.[305]

Figure 109
S.O. GILLESPIE

Figure 110
GEORGE T. BROUAYER

However one may interpret Lee's growing partnership with Llewellyn, there is no question that the latter was the virtual leader of the Ten

---

[303] 'F.J. Lee to S.O. Gillespie' ('F.J. Lee File', ZACG Archives). This letter is not dated, but the content shows that it was written not too long after the June Council was concluded and well before the impeachment charges were put before the Supreme Court on July 26th.

[304] *Proceedings*, p. 11. How could Gillespie be a 'man of God' and honest, etc. as Lee admits in this letter, and yet at the same time charge him with 'aiding and abetting Tomlinson in his illegal acts' and 'manifesting a contentious spirit', etc.

[305] Lee, 'Deposition', p. 871.

Elders' faction, particularly in regard to the business operations of the church and the prosecution of Tomlinson and his followers. 'Politics makes strange bedfellows'. It is true that Lee and Llewellyn were miles apart in their personalities and dispositions: Lee being mild-mannered and widely acclaimed as a model Christian, circumspect in his walk and speech, while Llewellyn was boisterous, blunt, aggressive, legalistic, and had a reputation of being rather shady in his business dealings. Thus, while the moderate Elders had come to sympathize with some of the complaints of Llewellyn and his followers against Tomlinson, they could not identify with the 'harsh spirit' and 'ridged terms' that generally characterized that faction. It is almost certain that if Lee had not turned against Tomlinson, neither would have Latimer, Boehmer, Payne, and Gann. So Lee led the way for the moderates to join with the extremists against Tomlinson. But, again, to follow Lee in the stand against Tomlinson was virtually to follow Llewellyn: for Llewellyn's bold and aggressive nature would settle for nothing less than to reorganize the government and operations of the church according to his own vision and, ultimately, under his own management.

Lee had admitted that Llewellyn had a 'harsh spirit' and 'used ridged terms' and that he himself had experienced personally the impact of his verbal abuse and brutal attacks. He had remained in his office on more than one occasion weeping after having been assaulted verbally by Llewellyn, and apparently had learned, to some extent, to cower to his wishes and demands.[306] Lee even admitted to Tomlinson in December 1922 that he was under a great deal of pressure from Llewellyn to pursue the investigation of his financial affairs more vigorously. Tomlinson wrote back to Lee in a letter dated January 1, 1923 that he sympathized with his position, noting, 'Yes, I see the situation you are in, you are under bonds of the man whose name you mentioned and you are afraid of his ire'.[307] Perhaps Tomlinson was right: Lee simply could not muster the courage to stand up to Llewellyn. Yet, giving him the benefit of the doubt, it was Lee's way to 'try to get along' and to yield or submit himself wherever possible for the sake of peace and unity. In any case, and however one may interpret Lee's motives and actions, to yield to Llewellyn's demands was bound to lead the church in the wrong direction,

---

[306] In his witness before the court, Tomlinson said, 'F.J. Lee told me he had taken abuse [from Llewellyn] and it had been so severe at times that he had cried' (Tomlinson, 'Deposition', p. 2157).

[307] This letter was filed as Exhibit B in Lee's deposition before the court in January 1924. We do not have Lee's letter, but Tomlinson testified in court that the man whose name Lee mentioned was Llewellyn. See Tomlinson, 'Deposition', p. 2157.

for Llewellyn was neither pastoral in nature nor spiritually-minded; indeed, he was rather hard and legalistic and operated more in the spirit of a secular business manager and corporate executive than a pastor and gentle bishop. But more so, he had a promise to keep to Tomlinson: 'I will break you ... and get you out of that office!' His words and actions in 1922-1923 only supported the accusation that had followed him since his early days among the saints in the Knoxville area, namely, that his disposition was to either 'rule or ruin'.

Still, Lee sat at the head of the Council of Elders, notwithstanding that Haynes had been selected to moderate the June Council while the matters in dispute in regard to Tomlinson were being considered. But neither Lee's nor Haynes' influence was superior in the meeting; rather it was Llewellyn's spirit and agenda that prevailed, particularly his 14 points and the additional evidence that had surfaced during the work of the Investigation Committee between September 1922 and June 1923. Further, he was the most vocal and aggressive man on the Investigation Committee. He had made the arrangements with the Lee H. Battle Audit Company to examine Tomlinson's financial affairs, and, as the new Editor and Publisher of the *Evangel*, he had worked personally and closely with the audit company's representative, H.D. Blackwell; supplying him with Tomlinson's books and ledgers and offering him whatever information he needed to assess the situation and to make his report; and one may be sure that Llewellyn did everything in his power to make Blackwell a part of his investigation team. Tomlinson of course had Llewellyn in mind when he said, 'I do not consider this Auditor's report to be unbiased. I mean by this that there is a streak of somebody's influence all through it.'[308]

After a few days of discussion and deliberations, it was clear that the Twelve Elders were divided into two parts with each side fixed in its opinion. Ten stood on one side and two on the other – the two being Gillaspie and Brouayer. It was at that point that some unprecedented steps were taken; in fact, the whole ordeal was unprecedented, for no General Overseer had ever been impeached and tried. The Ten Elders thus decided to make up their own rules as they went along; and in some instances they contradicted standing rules in order to prosecute their aims. It had been a sacred principle, for example, to settle issues in the Council by unanimous agreement, particularly in cases where discipline and possibly exclusion were required. But since Gillaspie and Brouayer were settled in their opinion, namely, that the so-called 'evidence' against

---

[308] Tomlinson, 'Preparation Notes', p. 11.

Tomlinson had fallen short in their judgment of proving him guilty of any financial or moral corruption, the Ten Elders decided to hold these two Elders in contempt for siding with Tomlinson, and made the astounding claim that because the two Elders had disagreed with them, they were guilty of 'aiding and abetting' Tomlinson in his actions.

Charging Gillaspie and Brouayer with Tomlinson was the Ten Elders' method to achieve unanimity in their 'judicious' deliberations! And we may assume that because of the manifest disposition of Llewellyn, Lemons, Ellis, McLain, Haynes, and now Lee, that if there were others who had sided with Tomlinson in the matter they also would have been charged with 'aiding and abetting him' in his 'crimes' and 'crookedness'. That was in fact the case as we will see in a moment.

The actions of these Ten Elders would have been laughable if they had not been so flagrantly unjust and egregious. Even the court system of secular states require unanimity of Twelve Jurors to find a man guilty of a crime, and if the jurors fail to obtain unanimity the case is dismissed. But an alien spirit or attitude entered among the Ten Elders that clouded their judgment and their role as Council members. They proceeded to take matters into their own hands, making up the rules as they went along to achieve their goal, which included not only impeaching Tomlinson but then acting on their own charges to suspend his ministry and his pay – his livelihood – and this in order ultimately to establish a new government for the church under the Constitution with new leaders at the helm.

Thus, on June 21st, ten days into the meeting of the Council, the Ten Elders articulated their charges against Tomlinson, and also charged the other two members of the Council – Gillaspie and Brouayer – for disagreeing with them, and went through the motions of suspending their ministries as well as their pay. They then proceeded to articulate and systematize the charges into an official document. Now in order for the Ten Elders to accomplish their sordid purpose, Ellis requested Gillaspie and Brouayer to absent themselves from the last two days of the meeting inasmuch as charges were also being brought against them for standing with Tomlinson; and we have every reason to believe that Ellis was encouraged by some of the other Elders to do so. At that point, Gillaspie and Brouayer saw the hopelessness of the situation, and proceeded to reaffirm boldly their loyalty to Tomlinson and committed themselves to chart another course for the church. Within a few days following the Council, as we will see in a moment, they in counsel with Tomlinson and others denounced the legality of the proceedings of the Ten Elders and proclaimed their intention to restore the church under the oversight of Tomlinson according to the government and polity of the church before the Constitution had been adopted.

Tomlinson Charged

Llewellyn of course was the primary author of the fifteen charges against Tomlinson, and crafted them as follows:

1. Failing to turn over to the proper officials all funds that should have been in his hands at the close of the General Assembly, November, 1922.

2. Misappropriating contrary to the purpose for which it was raised, approximately $3,900.00 of Orphanage money and thereby depriving them of the necessary support and leaving the treasury destitute of funds to meet urgent bills made by him.

3. Misapplying other funds amounting to several thousand dollars contrary to the purpose for which it was raised and the intention for which it was to be applied.

4. Ignoring and refusing to discharge his official duties as General Overseer and member of the Executive Council, by refusing to cooperate in the manner prescribed by the General Assembly.

5. Forfeiting agreements made in Supreme Council and Executive Council and ignoring the same.

6. Copywriting certain publications belonging to the Church of God in his own name and for permitting his son, Homer A. Tomlinson, to copyright a part of the lessons of the Bible Correspondence School owned by the Church of God, and for undertaking to aid him in establishing legal claims for publications owned by the Church of God, after making repeated statements that it was the property of the Church.

7. Making misleading statements or allowing same to be made over his signature that were calculated to unduly influence and financially injure any who might be influenced by such statements.

8. Making conflicting reports to the General Assembly and the board of directors of the Bible Training School and prospective investors.

9. Attempting and undertaking to establish other publishing interests and correspondence school that is calculated to be in opposition and antagonistic to that owned and controlled by the Church of God.

10. Failing to account for a considerable shortage in his accounts and failing to give satisfactory explanation for same.

11. Employing unfair, unjust, and illegal means to block the way of a fair investigation of his affairs and business relations with the Church by circulating petitions and framing charges against certain ministers and officials who sought to protect the interest of the Church and its members and friends.

12. Unbecoming conduct in presiding as chairman over a council in which he himself was a party to the litigation. And showing partiality by allowing those favored to him to slander and criticize in a very unbecoming manner without restraint and then refusing the opposite side equal liberty in defending themselves against such evil and unjust use and abuse. It is further alleged that on account of this unfair and unjust conduct it has rendered him unworthy of the honor of presiding over such a meeting and that it has brought shame and disgrace on the dignity of the position that he undertakes to occupy.

13. Condemning some of the rules of government as passed and outlined by the General Assembly in its regular session and allowing those under him to do the same and using his influence in a very disloyal manner against the action of the General Assembly, while said rules and principles of government are in full force and effect.

14. Refusing to cooperate with those associated with him in lifting the burdens of debt off the Church of God Publishing House but at the same time using his energies and influence against it and causing others so to do and promoting his own private interest by putting on a stock selling campaign, for the promotion of a separate enterprise now owned by the Church but calculated to be antagonistic to the Interest and welfare of the Church in its various departments. This was done while on salary paid him by the Church of God. In view of this fact it should be so construed that it is a misappropriation of his time, energy, and influence which should have been used in favor of the Church of God in its various departments, according to agreements made by him in Executive Council.

15. Holding secret councils and conspiring and seeking to influence others to rebel and oppose certain actions of the General Assembly and to embarrass certain positions created and filled by the said General Assembly.

Reflecting on the Charges

It may be observed, first of all, that the Ten Elders assumed authority that they did not have. Even within the context of the Constitution, it would have been more appropriate and consistent with that document to have acted with the Council of Seventy and other officers of the church in judging Tomlinson's affairs in his capacity as General Overseer (see, Article 4, Sections 1-8). Moreover, the last paragraph of Section 8 indicates that the most appropriate body to have judged and disciplined Tomlinson's ministry was the Presbytery – the overseers of the respective states and provinces. That paragraph reads: 'It is further understood that it shall be within the power of the presbytery to take final action in revoking the license or ordination of any minister for any reason or cause satisfactory to themselves'. And since the minister in this case was the General Overseer, it would have been wiser and more just for the Ten Elders to have called together the overseers and to have presented their charges against Tomlinson to them, and to have allowed them to have '[taken] the final action' in trying and judging him. This would have been wiser and more just particularly in view of the fact that the Council of Elders was divided in its opinion and the Supreme Court was made up entirely of members who represented only one side of that opinion.

The body of presbyters was in fact the precise system that was in place to examine and discipline the General Overseer before the Constitution had been adopted, and this system seems to have been retained in Article 4, Section 8 of the Constitution. This system had been designated in the Eighth Assembly in 1913, namely, to select a new General Overseer in the event that 'the office for any reason was declared vacant'.[309] It would have been wiser therefore, it seems, to have followed through with this system, for then the whole body of the church would have been represented more or less in the body of presbyters, and the church in general would have been better informed of the complaints and issues involved in the several cases presented in the June Council in 1923, that is, in the case against the three Elders (Llewellyn, Lemons, and Ellis) and the case against Tomlinson and Brouayer and Gillaspie. If this had been done, it might have possibly prevented a disruption and certainly would have alleviated a great deal of confusion and needless speculation and slanderous accusations. But it seems that this was the

---

[309] *GAM 1906-1914*, pp. 190-91 – 'We further recommend that if at any time there comes a need by disability from any cause, and the Office of General Overseer should be declared vacant, a General Overseer should be selected by the State Overseers to fill the office until the next Assembly'.

very reason the Ten Elders assumed the authority to try Tomlinson and to suspend his ministry and pay: they were determined to have things their own way!

Second, the Ten Elders not only did not follow the old system of government but highjacked the existing system under the Constitution, pushing through their judgment over against the adamant dissent of Gillaspie and Brouayer and a large number of Elders who sat on the Council of Seventy and some other ministers who had spoken earlier in the Council on Tomlinson's behalf. The Ten Elders thus not only failed to honor and to act on the principle of unanimity in their own Council – the Council of Twelve – but also manipulated the proceedings of the June Council so that their decision would be final. For though they claimed that the final decision rested with the seven judges on the Supreme Court, it was a pretentious gesture, if not hypocritical, for the seven Supreme Court Judges – F.J. Lee, J.S. Llewellyn, M.S. Lemons, T.L. McLain, S.W. Latimer, J.B. Ellis, and E.J. Boehmer – were also seven of the Ten Elders who had brought the charges against Tomlinson in the June Council. And, moreover, the three Elders among the Ten Elders who were not Supreme Judges agreed with the seven. Further, four of the Judges – Llewellyn, Lemons, Ellis, and McLain – had been the most vocal and aggressive hounds of Tomlinson since June 1922. But on this travesty of justice and inadequate and absurd system of government we will elaborate further in a moment.

Acting on the principle of unanimity was a sacred tradition in the church and was carried over into the Constitution both in spirit and principle, except that the Constitution took the prerogative of final decision-making out of the hands of the traditional Assembly and placed it in the 'official assembly', namely, in the Council of Twelve and Council of Seventy in joint counsel with the General Overseer. The principle and even the term 'unanimous agreement' is used in Article 8, Section 2 of the Constitution. Lee and most of the leading Elders even during the court proceedings in 1924-1927 all testified that they agreed with the principle of unanimity and endeavored to operate the government of the church on that basis;[310] which of course made their actions and final decision during the June Council self-contradictory as well as unjust: for they negated the judgment of the Seventy[311] and virtually the whole

---

[310] Lee, Deposition', p. 915: 'Unanimous agreement [is our] custom ... and that is still the custom'.

[311] Interestingly, before Lee and the Ten Elders decided to take things into their own hands, Lee explained that the purpose of the Seventy was to make church decisions 'more legal' and insisted that the Twelve and Seventy acting together in

church in their actions and even acted against the judgment of two of their own Council members – Gillaspie and Brouayer[312] – and, further, charged these two Elders with 'acting shamefully' and 'obstructing justice' simply because they did not agree with the other ten Council members.[313]

Third, it is plain to see that the Ten Elders – being led by Llewellyn and Lee – had become hardened and legalistic in their views against Tomlinson, and leaned more toward faultfinding than seeking for justice. They had desired for Tomlinson to 'confess' and acknowledge his 'wrongdoing' and 'misconduct' to the Assembly in 1922 rather than 'explain away' his misappropriation of the tithes; and, in fact, Llewellyn and Lemons were infuriated over the matter and their anger in time affected the other Elders. And even though the great majority of the elders and people in the Assembly forgave Tomlinson and even applauded him for his actions and endeavored to lay the matter to rest, Llewellyn, Lemons, Ellis, and later Lee kept the matter alive and convinced the other Elders among the Ten to make it one of the charges against Tomlinson. In fact, the first three charges of the fifteen against Tomlinson had to do with misappropriation and misapplication of funds, although it had been accepted by the great majority in the Assembly that his motive for misappropriating or misapplying the funds was for the sake of the church, not for any personal gain; and the great majority of the people had expressed their sympathy with his position in the matter and were apparently convinced that he did indeed 'love the church so much' that he misdirected the ministers' tithes only to 'save the Church of God from bankruptcy', and that he had acted 'at the risk of his own welfare and reputation' to do so.

It is equally clear that the Ten Elders made mountains out of mole hills on several issues. Many of their complaints were simply based on the difference between the way Tomlinson thought and expressed himself, and the way Llewellyn and Lee thought and expressed themselves. According to the old adage, Tomlinson tended to see the glass half full,

---

unanimity was a better governmental system than the Twelve acting alone (Lee, 'Deposition', pp. 787-88; and see his Assembly address on the subject).

[312] Lee, 'Deposition', pp. 826-27.

[313] Lee acknowledged with approval that Mary Jane Tomlinson was excluded from the church simply because she was 'allied with her husband' and 'standing with her husband'. And he admitted further that Tomlinson's son-in-law, A.D. Evans, his wife, Iris, A.J. Lawson, and others were excluded from the church only on the basis that they were 'standing with Tomlinson' and 'defending him' therefore standing against the Ten Elders and 'the main body of the church' (Lee, 'Deposition', pp. 775-80). Lee even revoked his son-in-law's credentials because he 'was whole-souled with Tomlinson' (Lee, 'Deposition', p. 782).

whereas Llewellyn tended to see the same glass half empty. Tomlinson was extremely optimistic, and his leadership style tended toward cheerleading; thus, admittedly, he often magnified or exaggerated the church's progress in expectation of success; whereas Llewellyn was more legalistic and formal in business and thus more precise in keeping financial books and framing language for official records. Lee conversely was actually much different in personality and style than both Tomlinson and Llewellyn, but intriguingly he had become aligned with Llewellyn against Tomlinson, and thus what he now denounced in Tomlinson he tolerated and even praised in Llewellyn. The developing spiritual division between Tomlinson on the one side and Llewellyn-Lee on the other caused each side to magnify the shortcomings and peculiarities of the other; whereas, before the rift had developed between them, they had in fact overlooked many of the things they now claimed to be morally corrupt and even criminal. Each side now believed that they could not work with the other, and each saw the other as being stubborn and contentious. But it was the Llewellyn-Lee faction that took the initiative to formulate their petty differences into formal charges of 'misconduct', 'misleading statements', and 'making conflicting reports'.

Still further, the Ten Elders – led primarily by Llewellyn and Lee – had formulated charges in regard to certain other issues that were highly conjectural and disputed by Tomlinson and the other two Elders; for example, the fifth charge: 'Forfeiture of agreements made in Supreme Council and Executive Council'. Some of the language in the so-called 'agreements' in the Supreme Council (the Elders' Council) was so vague that no one could be rightly judged and condemned for understanding the 'agreements' one way or another.[314] And the so-called 'agreements' between the three on the Executive Council were always between Tomlinson on the one side and Llewellyn and Lee on the other, and since no minutes or records were kept of their meetings, the disputes could not be proven one way or the other by the other Elders. The Ten Elders simply accepted Lee's and Llewellyn's testimony over against Tomlinson's, and, moreover, did not allow Tomlinson sufficient time to respond to the charges: for after the charges were written up and presented to him on June 21st, the Ten Elders declared the Council closed at 9.20 p.m. and by the next evening had dispersed and went back to their respective fields of labor.

---

[314] The minutes of the Elders' Councils (Supreme Council) simply did not state the so-called agreements in technical and precise language, for no one had anticipated the forthcoming disputes and legal battles between the General Overseer and the Elders, and the Elders between themselves.

Notwithstanding the faults and actions of the Ten Elders, Tomlinson was by the end of the Assembly in November 1922 fully convinced that a division was inevitable, and by the end of December of that same year was planning a revolution and making some initial moves toward that end. Ironically, his actions in this regard gave his opposition some legitimate grounds to bring formal charges against him; for, until that time, the complaints of the Elders – particularly, Llewellyn, Lemons, Ellis, and McLain – were superficial and rather petty, as well as unofficial, and probably would not have been upheld by the majority of the Elders on the Council nor by the church's judicial system. Tomlinson was not, in fact, an embezzler nor in any way a morally corrupt man. But he was a dreamer, somewhat unorthodox, and tended toward fanaticism. He saw himself in a peculiar light, and acted under the illusion that he was specially ordained by God as the visible head of the church on earth. His misapprehension of reality – of failing to judge properly his common call in the ministry and his position in the church – caused him to act unilaterally and to see his office as 'a supreme and mediatorial throne'. He believed he had been appointed by the Holy Ghost to be the General Overseer for life, and, as such, felt it was incumbent upon him to take matters into his own hands to save the great Church of God from men who, either purposely or unwittingly, were adopting measures to destroy the church. Accordingly, his actions and statements beginning in December 1922 and leading up to the June Council in 1923, not only united the Ten Elders together against him but justified many of their charges and complaints, particularly in regard to his plan to inaugurate the Faithful Standard Publishing Company and the United Bible Institute and set them over against the Evangel Publishing House and Bible Training School, the latter of which were now under the supervision of Lee and Llewellyn. Moreover, Tomlinson began to sell stock in February 1923 in the Faithful Standard Publishing Company to ministers and members in the church, and he had the *Faithful Standard* magazine copyrighted in his own name, just as he had allowed his son Homer sometime earlier to copyright the Bible Training Correspondence lessons in his own name.[315]

---

[315] We learn from Homer's correspondence with his father that the copyright scheme was altogether Homer's idea. In a letter to his father dated March 11, 1922, he wrote, 'I think there are many reasons why it is important that the *Faithful Standard* be copyrighted. It costs only $12.00 a year, but it means a lot. I wish you would copyright it in your own name, not in the name of THE CHURCH OF GOD PUBLISHING HOUSE, or the Church of God. If it should turn out to be so good that people are cribbing our stuff, we are just out. If some pretentious person should try to "take over" the *Faithful Standard* sometime, there is a copyright in your

Tomlinson vehemently denied that he was leaving the Church of God and starting another church, but his denials were based on his belief that Llewellyn and his followers had led the church into serious error – even a 'departure from the faith' – and, therefore, that he was merely restoring the church of the Bible rather than starting something new. Tomlinson freely admitted that he had helped to cause the 'falling away', but that in his capacity as General Overseer God had awakened him to the fact, and that he was now led by the Spirit to correct the errors and restore the church. He thus, rather conveniently, fell back on some of Spurling's principles in Christian Union, namely, 1) the anti-creedalism; 2) the emphasis on personal freedom and fellowship in love over legalism and institutionalism; 3) the primacy and autonomy of the local churches; 4) the 'right of way for the leadership of the Holy Ghost and conscience;' and 5) especially the idea that 'God's church only [exists] where His law and government [is] observed by His children'.[316]

Tomlinson thus made the startling claim in the months leading up to the June Council in 1923 that with the adoption of the Constitution in 1921 the church had ceased to be the Church of God of the Bible.[317] It had become just another 'man-handled' denomination. After all of his annual addresses which emphasized the need for universal rules and regulations, a centralized corporate structure, and a military-type of obedience to its chief officers, he now claimed that the local churches – not Headquarters – were the embodiment of 'the faith' and the pillar of 'theocratic government', and that Assembly 'rulings' were merely suggestive and certainly not be enforced upon the ministers and local churches. This was his new way of interpreting the polity and government of the church; and just as he had insisted on obedience and conformity to the centralized system that had been built up between 1912 and 1921, he now insisted on liberty of individual conscience and that the local churches be considered more or less autonomous. But his re-

---

name': ('Homer Tomlinson File', ZACG Archives). In another letter addressed to his father dated September 22, 1922, he wrote, 'As you know I personally hold the copyright on the Correspondence Course, every single part of it. That means that no man can take it away from me, without laying himself criminally and civilly liable. That means also I can personally control the names that are identified with it' ('Homer Tomlinson File', ZACG Archives).

[316] Tomlinson, *LGC*, p. 206.

[317] *August Council*, p. 5. Reflecting on this Council three months later in his annual address to the General Assembly, Tomlinson said, 'In this conference it was acknowledged that the constitution just as literally destroyed the Church of God as the Nicene Creed destroyed it in the year 325, and the only thing left for us to do was repudiate [it] and ... resolve ourselves back into the Church of God under the Bible rule and government' (*HAA*, I, p. 219).

turn to Spurlingian-type principles was short lived; in the months and years ahead he would again form his followers into a highly centralized system under a hierarchical Episcopal-type of administration that culminated in the exalted office of General Overseer.[318]

It may be seen that Tomlinson's new modified understanding of the church was remarkably similar to Spurling's original order in Christian Union. The one thing that did not change in Tomlinson's doctrine of church government, however, was his view of the exalted office of General Overseer. This was in fact the real crux of the matter in the dispute that finally disrupted the church: namely, Tomlinson's view of the office of General Overseer as a unique and solitary position at the head of the church on earth over against the Ten Elders' view of the Constitutional system; or, to put it another way, the one faction advocated a popish-type office and system over against a system of government that answered finally to a Supreme Council. The arguments hinged on government in the hands of one man or government in the hands of a few men – a monarchy over against an oligarchy.

The dispute between the factions was at its core that simple. It was a power struggle. Tomlinson believed the faith and government of the church was in his hands as God's 'anointed – prophet of wisdom', and therefore to defect from his authority disqualified a body of believers from actually being the church. Whereas, Llewellyn and Lee and the rest of the Ten Elders saw the church more as a legal corporation under a contract or Constitution, and they made their complaints against Tomlinson and his followers on that basis – and finally charged them for refusing to adhere to the Constitution. In their view the legal corporation had adopted the Council of Elders (1917), the Council of Seventy (1921), the Supreme Court (1921), and the Constitution (1921) with all of its binding Articles, including the new Executive Council and other offices adopted as part of Llewellyn's amendment in 1922. The true church therefore was represented only in those who adhered to the Constitution and the institutions of government that had been adopted beginning in 1917. Accordingly, Tomlinson and the other two Elders on the Council – Brouayer and Gillaspie – as well as Lee's son-in-law, Jesse P. Hughes, C.T. Anderson, A.J. Lawson, Tomlinson son-in-law, A.D.

---

[318] The fact that Tomlinson, soon after the disruption in June-August 1923, led his followers again into a strict centralized form of government under the exalted office of General Overseer gives cause for one to question his sincerity. His return to Spurlingian principles seems to have been merely a convenience for the time being in order to dismantle the Executive Council, the Council of Elders, the Council of Seventy, and the Supreme Court in order to restore his preeminence over the church and his ability to act autonomously.

Evans, Tomlinson's wife, Mary Jane, and their children, Iris and Homer, and every other minister and member who sympathized with Tomlinson were considered equally guilty with him for 'aiding and abetting him' and 'becoming a party to a conspiracy to thwart the purposes of the Council [of Elders]'.[319] In other words, the Ten Elders and the true Church of God were one and the same.

Precisely contrariwise, Tomlinson and his followers believed the church had apostatized under the terms of the Constitution, and more especially because the Ten Elders and their followers did not give heed to the counsel of the anointed General Overseer once he had been awakened by the Holy Ghost to the essential errors in the 'heretical document'.[320]

'Declaration of Independence'

Since his annual address in November 1922, Tomlinson had emphasized that the church had been for 'three or fours years … slowly drifting toward making the Assembly a legislative body rather than judicial only'.[321] He asserted further that the adoption of the Constitution in particular in 1921 was a 'grave mistake', an error so egregious and displeasing to the Lord that it had to be immediately recognized and repudiated if the church expected to retain His favor. Indeed, the Constitution should be 'as far as possible even [erased] from our memory'.[322]

Tomlinson framed his argument on the basis that the Constitution had supplanted the Bible as the ultimate authority in the church, most particularly in regard to the anointed office of General Overseer, and further that the Ten Elders and their followers had overruled the Holy Ghost in His manifest selection of Tomlinson in that position for life. That was the real crux of the matter for Tomlinson and his followers – not so much the Constitution over against the Bible but the Constitution over against the office of General Overseer as perceived by Tomlinson and established in 1912-1914. In the Declaration of Independence (see below) that he drafted, interestingly enough, a few days before

---

[319] *Proceedings*, p. 11.
[320] In his annual address in November 1923, he said, 'Every advice and recommendation of the General Overseer was ignored, although he was, under God, looking after the best interests of the Church of God that had been so sacred to him for more than seventeen years' (*HAA*, I, pp. 218-19).
[321] *HAA*, I, p. 197
[322] *HAA*, I, p. 199

the June Council in 1923 had concluded,[323] the exalted powers and responsibilities of the General Overseer were again emphasized:

> Whereas, according to the Scriptures, the original and only Church of God was established with Jesus Christ as the Great Head of the Church, and after Christ ascended to His Throne on High, there was a General Overseer selected to direct the affairs of the Church under the guidance of the Holy Ghost, and this has been the continued practice of the true Church of God, until, in a moment of darkness, a man-made creed or constitution was accepted by the Assembly to rule the Church instead of the Government of God'.

Between the Assembly in 1922 and the June Council in 1923, the Ten Elders and their followers had crystallized their view of leadership in the church, which included favoring a three-man Executive Council over the exalted office of General Overseer, but also relegating the authority of the Assembly to merely a nominal status in favor of an Episcopacy – an 'official Assembly' made up more or less of ruling bishops. In regard to this latter point, Lee and the Ten Elders vehemently denied it but the Constitution on its face speaks for itself, and the Assembly in 1922 acted under that rule of faith and procedure. Even after the Constitution was abandoned by the Llewellyn-Lee faction in 1926, an Episcopal system of authority relegated the Assembly more or less to a body of on-lookers.

Both sides having thus hardened in their opinions, and having developed irreconcilable differences and dispositions, Tomlinson and some of his followers got together a few days after the June Council to discuss and tweak the final draft of the 'Declaration of Independence'.[324] This term was chosen decidedly to reflect on the United States' Declaration of Independence and particularly the rationale in Jefferson's opening words, 'When, in the course of human events, it becomes necessary for one people to dissolve the political bands which have connected them with another ... and that they should declare the causes which impel them to the separation'. Referring to the Ten Elders and their actions in the June Council, Tomlinson wrote,

---

[323] Significantly, Tomlinson admitted that during the latter part of the June Council he 'seemed to realize [the inevitable]' and thus 'prepared the declaration'. He likened the document to the Declaration of Independence and the overall situation in the church to the Revolutionary War (Tomlinson, 'Deposition', p. 2084).

[324] The final draft of the 'Declaration of Independence' was prepared on June 27, 1923, but it was more or less completed before the June Council had ended on June 21st.

I regard all of their proceedings as unjust and illegal, and I have utterly ignored the whole thing ... because they became so corrupt in their proceedings and work. Having no other recourse for adjustment I with others prepared a **declaration of independence**, dismissed these men from their positions, to which I had had a part in appointing them, and thus started a revolution to save the church of God from wreck and ruin.[325]

Within the Declaration itself, Tomlinson and his followers endeavored to modify the spirit of the division by referring to the strife and separation between Abraham and Lot recorded in Gen. 13.7-12, noting in particular the words of Abraham: 'Let there be no strife, I pray thee, between me and thee, and between my herdsmen and thy herdsmen; for we be brethren'. But clearly Tomlinson and his followers saw themselves in the image of Abraham and his herdsmen and the Ten Elders and their followers in the image of Lot and his herdsmen, particularly because 'Abraham dwelled in Canaan ['the Promise Land'] ... and Lot ... pitched his tent toward Sodom'. It may be observed that, in any case, the reference to Abraham and Lot was more rhetorical than substantial, for the division was bitter and hateful and engendered resentment and malice which spilled over into the next two generations.

The disruption was thus in spirit more comparable to the Revolutionary War between Britain and the American Colonies, and this was the primary image that Tomlinson used in the future when reflecting on the division in his messages and annual addresses. He most often called it a 'revolution'.[326] A 'Declaration of Independence' was thus descriptive of the actions taken by Tomlinson and his followers, and in their view fitting for the occasion.

---

[325] Tomlinson, *Diary*, September 10, 1923; *idem*, 'Deposition', pp. 2084-85.

[326] Referring to the Call Council in August 1923 in his annual address that same year, Tomlinson said, 'In this conference ... we resolved ourselves back into the Church of God ... and thus the revolutionary campaign was opened. Only one in that conference has turned traitor, and his name has gone down in disgrace alongside the name of Benedict Arnold who turned traitor in the revolution between America and England in the eighteenth century'. The 'traitor' was apparently T.A. Richard of Louisiana, whom Tomlinson, Brouayer and Gillaspie had selected in the August Council to replace one of the Ten Elders who had vacated his office. During the state marches and reports in the Assembly of the Llewellyn-Lee faction, Richard apologized, saying, 'I had an influence thrown around me that many did not have. What I did against the Church I did ignorantly, and have been heartily sorry. And if my letter of confession did not cover all of the ground, I am ready to do anything that is required of me. After I got back on the main line God began to bless my labors' (*GAM*, 18th Assembly, p. 9).

The Declaration

Inasmuch as differences and dissensions have arisen among certain of the Elders and Members of the Church over the government of the Church of God, much of which has been occasioned by the acceptance of a man-made constitution at the 1921 and 1922 Assemblies instead of relying solely on the Government of God as set out in the Scriptures and previously practiced by the Church of God, WE, the undersigned members of the Church of God make the following Declaration: –

Whereas the Constitution accepted at the 1921 Assembly and amended at the 1922 Assembly is contrary to the Word of God, the fundamental doctrines of the Church of God and the elemental principles of Theocratic Government, in that the constitution undertakes to create a general form of government with a delegated power to certain officials to dictate and promulgate rules for the government of the Assembly as well as local churches in direct conflict with the teachings of the Scriptures, and the long established practice of the Church of God that all matters of government should come before the Assembly and be discussed with love, humility and meekness and be settled by mutual agreement in love, and harmony under the guidance of the Holy Ghost according to the Scriptures; And,

Whereas an extended search of the Scriptures and a deliberate and careful consideration of the teachings of Jesus Christ and the Apostles prove that the true government of the Church of God is strictly theocratic in principle, and that the members are to be so closely united that it can be said of them, that they are one heart and one soul, that they are all to speak the same thing and have no division, and are to be perfectly joined together in the same mind and the same judgment and to continue steadfastly in the Apostles' doctrine of the early Church; And,

Whereas, according to the Scriptures, the original and only Church of God was established with Jesus Christ as the Great Head of the Church, and after Christ ascended to His Throne on High, there was a General Overseer selected to direct the affairs of the Church under the guidance of the Holy Ghost, and this has been the continued practice of the true Church of God, until, in a moment of darkness, a man-made creed or constitution was accepted by the Assembly to rule the Church instead of the Government of God; And,

Whereas, the Constitution has cast an almost impenetrable cloud over the Church of God, and has caused certain of the Elders to depart from the true and accepted doctrines of the theocratic Church Government under the guidance of the Holy Ghost, and has caused them to follow a man-made creed instead of the Word of God as laid down in the Blessed Bible according to the accepted interpretation by the Church of God; And,

Whereas, our eyes have been opened and by a careful search of the Scriptures and earnest prayers to God we have become enlightened as to the dangers and pitfalls that confront the Church of God, and the time has come when we must either be bound, body and soul, by a man-made constitution and creed, or else we must repudiate the same and cling to the laws of Jesus Christ and the Government of God on which the Church of God was established.

NOW THEREFORE, we declared that we stand for the Church of God as originally organized and as set out in the New Testament, that we believe in the government of the Church as established by the Assemblies prior to the adoption of the Constitution which undertakes to set up iron-clad rules and regulations for the government of the Church instead of the Word of God as set out in the Scriptures and the accepted interpretation thereof Excepting, however, the money system and Declaration at the 15th Assembly.

We further declare that we repudiated and denounce the Constitution accepted at the 1921 Assembly and amended at the 1922 Assembly as the same is substituted for the Word of God as the ruling Spirit of the Church; and we affirm that no man-made creed can or should dictate the policies and doctrines of the Church, but God shall be given a free hand to guide and rule the Church of God and its members until that Great Day shall come when we who remain steadfast in the faith shall sit on the right hand of God.

We further declare that the man-made constitution is a yoke of bondage thrust upon the members of the Church of God in a moment of darkness and we call upon the members to throw off this burdensome yoke and unite in one body and soul to worship God according to the New Testament and the long established teachings of the Church of God.

We further declare that according to the Scriptures and the established practice of the Church of God, that the Assembly is not a legislative body but is rather a judicial body, one that searches out the law and offices made and created by the early Church of God as conducted by the Apostles, and we aver that the Assembly of 1922 had no power or authority to create an Executive Council to dictate and manage the affairs of the Church of God, as the government of God set out in the Scriptures and accepted by the established Church of God provides that the General Overseer shall have full power and authority to direct and manage the affairs of the Church when the Assembly is not in session.

We therefore call upon the General Overseer to take charge of and direct the affairs of the Church of God in accordance with the established practice of the Church of God with the established practice of the Church prior to the enactment of a constitution, and to perform his duties as defined by the Scriptures.

We feel that we must cling to the Bible for our laws if we keep in favor with God, and we declare that the Church of God was established on the Bible as the Word of God and in conformity with the teachings of the New Testament and the rules and practices of the Apostles in the interpretation of the Scriptures. But to the Elders who desire to turn away from the Blessed Bible and the fundamental principles and doctrines of the Church of God and seek to be governed by a man-made constitution instead of the Word of God: we say: as Abraham said to Lot, 'Let there be no strife between me and thee, between my herdmen and thy herdmen, separate thyself in order that we may stand by the true doctrines and teachings of the Church of God and continue to receive its spiritual benefits.

We further declare that we adhere to the true teachings and doctrines of the Church of God and take the Blessed Bible as our only Rule of Faith and Practice, and, like the prophet Isaiah, 'we feel that the Spirit of the Lord God is upon us, because the Lord has anointed us to preach good tidings unto the meek, he hath sent us to bind up the broken hearted, proclaim liberty to the captive and the opening of the prison to them that are bound'.

And WE, like the Apostles of old, will go forth into the world and carry on the work of the established Church of God unfettered and unhampered by any man-made constitution or creed.

A.J. Tomlinson H.A. Pressgrove
Geo. T. Brouayer J. F. Dover
S.O. Gillaspie A.J. Lawson

The July Councils

After the Elders' Council ended on June 21st, the seven Supreme Court judges agreed to convene on July 26th to hear the impeachment charges filed by the Ten Elders against Tomlinson, Brouayer, and Gillaspie. Meanwhile, the Ten Elders urged Tomlinson to produce any evidence that might overturn the charges that he was responsible and accountable for the shortages in the church accounts – allegedly more than $14,000 – and further to produce any evidence to overturn the other 15 charges which included 'misappropriations' and 'misapplications' of the church's funds, 'disloyalty', 'official misconduct', 'forfeiture of agreements', 'misleading statements', 'holding secret councils', 'conspiracy and rebellion against the General Assembly', 'unbecoming conduct', and generally for bringing 'shame and disgrace on the dignity of the position that he undertakes to occupy'.

Tomlinson, apparently after counseling with Gillaspie and Brouayer, and also Homer, A.J. Lawson, Jesse P. Hughes, C.T. Anderson, and others, responded to Llewellyn and the rest of the Ten Elders by letter and informed them that their actions were illegal, and that, in any case, the business of the Council was left unfinished. He thus scheduled a meeting of the Elders' Council for July 24th to complete the business, and also apparently to preempt the meeting of the Supreme Court on July 26th. He wrote a letter dated June 25, 1923 specifically addressed to Llewellyn, apparently to imply that Llewellyn was the representative head of the Ten Elders:

> Since the business that was to come before the Council which was called in session June 12th, was not completed, and considering the matter of dismissal, I conclude that it has not yet closed, but since the brethren have dispersed I have decided to give them a little space of time to come together again and finish up the business. Therefore, I send out this special notice and call.
>
> You will be expected to meet again on July 24th, 1923, in Cleveland, Tenn., the hour to be named after the arrival of the councilors.
>
> There are some matters of the utmost importance in the interest of the Church of God to be considered. By giving this much time I trust you will be able to make all arrangements so it will not unduly inconvenience you to be in Cleveland at the time named above.
>
> With due regards, I remain
>
> Yours truly,
>
> A.J. Tomlinson

Llewellyn and Lee as members of the Executive Council responded to Tomlinson's letter the next day and categorically denied that he had the right to call such a meeting. They based their complaint on two reasons: he was under impeachment charges, and he had not consulted with the other two members on the Executive Council.[327] Obviously, the two sides were at loggerheads and the division was virtually already sealed; yet each side went through the motions and formalities of legally condemning the other side and justifying their own actions.

Tomlinson met with Brouayer and Gillaspie in his home on July 24th and there waited in vain for the other members of the Council of Elders to show up for the meeting. After several hours of 'watching thereto with prayer', Tomlinson called the Council to order and the three of them proceeded on their own. They pronounced themselves to be a quorum and thus conducted business as usual under the authority of the General Overseer.[328] In the course of the meeting, they determined that the Ten Elders by refusing to attend the meeting were disloyal and disobedient and had vacated their positions. The General Overseer was then advised by the Council to notify the Ten Elders that in vacating their seats on the Council, they 'had also vacated any other office in the Church to which they had been appointed'. Official notification was then given and the judgment of the Council made public:

TO THE FAITHFUL AND LOYAL MEMBERS OF THE CHURCH OF GOD

Notice is hereby given that the Council of the Elders held in Cleveland, Tennessee on the 24th day of July, 1923, agreement was mutually reached by the General Overseer and loyal Elders in Council, in accordance with the doctrines of the apostles and practices of the

---

[327] *Proceedings*, pp. 14-16.
[328] The meeting was considered duly called because the General Overseer had called it according to established practice and also according to the Constitution, Article 4, Sections 1, 6, and lawful and orderly because Gillaspie, Brouayer and Tomlinson formed a quorum of the Council. The Ten Elders denied the orderliness of the meeting on the grounds that they had agreed among themselves in Council that at least nine members were required to make a quorum, and that they had not been given adequate notification of the place and time of the meeting. Tomlinson and his followers, however, maintained that the Elders had been properly notified and that they simply had boycotted the meeting. Lee and the rest of the Ten Elders in fact admitted that they had no intention of attending the meeting, having fully determined that Tomlinson had no right to call such a meeting nor that he and the other two Elders had any right to perform any official acts because they were under impeachment charges.

Church of God, that the Declaration signed by many of the members of the Church of God truthfully sets out the teachings of the Church of God, and the action in repudiating the man-made creed or constitution is fully in accord with the Scriptures, for the Church of God is God's Government for His own people and we can have no Guide but the Holy Ghost and the Word of God.

Certain of the Elders refused to attend the Council but boldly declared their allegiance to that organized body provided for in their 'Constitution' under the name of 'General Assembly of the Churches of God' to be the dictator of the teachings and principles of the Church and the maker of the laws for the local churches in the place of God's laws and government.

After long prayers for guidance by the Holy Ghost and deliberate consideration, the General Overseer and Elders in Council in perfect harmony and agreement concluded that the hereinafter named Elders had renounced the Church of God and had accepted the General Assembly with its Constitution as their faith and practice instead of God's Government set out in the Holy Scriptures as the only true faith and practice of the Church of God, and that by their disloyal conduct and teachings the following named have vacated their office as Elders in the Church of God, to-wit: –

J.B. ELLIS, J.S. LLEWELLYN, T.L. MCLAIN, M.S. LEMONS, F.J. LEE, S.W. LATIMER, E.J. BOEHMER, A GANN, E. HAYNES AND T.S. PAYNE, and the Council further agreed that as each of the above named had refused to discuss their disloyalty to the Church of God with the Council that each of them be notified that by their refusal to continue the teachings and doctrines of the Church of God as laid down in the Blessed Bible, and by their heresy in insisting that they, as members of the 'Official Assembly' created by their constitution, were the lawmakers of the Church of God and that all must follow their laws instead of the Word of God, that they had thereby vacated their office of elders.

It was also mutually settled and agreed by the Council that it became the duty of the General Overseer to notify each of the above named Elders that by vacating their respective offices of Elders in the Church of God, they had also vacated any other office in the Church to which they had been appointed; and the General Overseer was directed to immediately notify them of the action of this Council and to also notify the true and loyal members of the Church of God that the following offices in the Church of God are vacant, to-wit: –

TEN ELDERS – Offices vacated by T.S. Payne, E. Haynes, A. Gann, E.J. Boehmer, S.W. Latimer, F.J. Lee, M.S. Lemons, T.L. McLain, S.W. Latimer, J.B. Ellis, E.J.S. Llewellyn.

SEVEN JUDGES – Offices vacated by M.S. Lemons, F.J. Lee, J.S. Llewellyn, T.L. McLain, S.W. Latimer, J.B. Ellis, E.J. Boehmer.

DIRECTORS OF BIBLE TRAINING SCHOOL – vacated by J.S. Llewellyn, E. Haynes, T.L. McLain, F.J. Lee, M.S. Lemons.

HOME MISSIONARY SECRETARY – vacated by T.L. McLain

FOREIGN MISSIONARY SECRETARY – vacated by J.S. Llewellyn

ORPHANAGE COMMITTEE – vacated by T.L. McLain, J.S. Llewellyn, E.J. Boehmer.

And that such of these offices now vacant, as may be found in the Scriptures be filled in accordance with the teachings and practices of the Church of God from loyal, qualified men who love the Church of God.

The forgoing findings and decisions reached by the General Overseer and Council of Elders are presented to the members of the Church for consideration so that each member may determine whether he or she will continue with the Church of God, adhering to God's law and God's Word, instead of the man-made creed adopted at the Assembly.

We love the Church of God, we know it is God's government for His people, and that His Church cannot fail, and we will not falter but will continue to follow in the wake of the Apostles and the early Church, and we call on all true lovers of the Church of God to join with us in serving under God's government so that we may all once more speak the same thing and be so perfectly joined together in the same mind and the same judgment that it will be said of us: 'They are of one heart and one soul'.

Let us all join together, unhampered by a burdensome constitution, so that we can truthfully say: 'Lord, we will follow Thee whithersoever thou goest', for 'Thou art the way, the truth and the light'.

We are glad we are back on the right road and traveling God's way for we have repudiated man's creed and constitution.

A.J. Tomlinson, General Overseer
S.O. Gillaspie, Elder
Geo. T. Brouayer, Elder

Two days later, the Supreme Court of the Llewellyn-Lee faction met on July 26th and acted on the Council of Elders charges of impeachment against A.J. Tomlinson, S.O. Gillaspie, and George T. Brouayer. The charges were filed by Alonzo Gann, T.S. Payne, and Efford Haynes, all members of the Elders Council:

Announcement of Decision of the Supreme Judges – Court of Justice

These defendants are charged with repeated violations of the rules and government of the Church of God as shown in the charges to which reference is here made. The complaints were filed and restraint sought from further injurious violations which were granted on June 21, 1923. These defendants were restrained from any further official duties or ministerial activities on the date above mentioned.

These defendants were duly notified of the sitting of the supreme judges, the time and place of the hearing, also to appear and answer the complaints filed against them and that default by them, the charges would be taken as confessed. These defendants failed to appear or file any pleadings, therefore the charges were sustained and taken as confessed.

The final order of impeachment was made and the three defendants so judged as guilty of the complaints filed and by this decision are removed from any and all positions of honor or trust and any and all positions occupied by them in the Church of God are judged vacant.

It is further judged and so decided that the ministry of each of them shall be revoked and their credentials declared void.

The undersigned Supreme Judges – Court of Justice was duly appointed as provided by the Assembly of the Church of God to serve as Supreme Judges till the close of the Assembly of 1923 (see page 106 of the minutes of the Seventeenth Annual Assembly of the Church of God, held at Cleveland, Tennessee, November 1-7, 1922.) For further authority see page 62 of the same minutes Section One, which reads as follows: 'There shall be a Supreme Judicial body composed of seven of the twelve Elders who shall decide all matters which shall properly come before them, whose decision shall be final'. These complaints was (were) filed and jurisdiction waved of any other judicial body or council claiming jurisdiction. On page 61 of the same minutes, Section Eleven, 'Any official is subject to impeachment, for an offense rendering him unworthy of the position that he occupies'. In view of the authorities referred to, it is judged that these three defendants having confessed to the charges by their default in refusing to appear and make defense that they are unworthy of the respective positions that they have hitherto occupied.

C.T. Anderson also included in the complaints filed but due and sufficient notice not yet served, his case is deferred until a later date.

The undersigned all concurring in the conclusions and decisions reached as above set forth.

SIGNED BY:

M.S. Lemons   J.B. Ellis
S.W. Latimer   E.J. Boehmer
F.J. Lee
T.L. McLain
J.S. Llewellyn

Significantly, following the 'final order of impeachment' and the verdict of 'guilty' as charged, Tomlinson, Brouayer, and Gillaspie were 'removed from any and all positions of honor or trust and ... the ministry of each of them ... revoked and their credentials declared void'. The Supreme Court Judges then elected F.J. Lee as General Overseer 'to fill the unexpired term of Tomlinson', which according to Llewellyn's amendment to the Constitution was fixed 'for a term of one year' beginning and ending with the annual Assembly. The offices purported to have been vacated by Brouayer and Gillaspie were not filled until the Assembly of the Llewellyn-Lee faction which convened November 1-7, 1923. On the second day of the Assembly, Lee's election was confirmed, and later G.A. Fore and John Attey were selected to replace Brouayer and Gillaspie on the Supreme Council. Interestingly, Lee in his acceptance speech as General Overseer praised Llewellyn for his abilities and hard work and added 'I have never associated with a man more congenial than Brother Llewellyn. We have worked together nicely'.[329]

---

[329] *GAM*, 18th Assembly, November 1-7, 1923, p. 16.

This 'congeniality', however, was short-lived; for in the following months and years, the relationship between Llewellyn and Lee and other Elders in the General Offices became strained; inevitably Llewellyn's spirit of lordship and bent toward preeminence became intolerable. Lee would learn what Tomlinson and others already had: that agreement with Llewellyn meant cowering to his wishes and implementing his plans.

What seems apparent in reviewing the historical records is that the relationship between Lee and Llewellyn was rather pretentious: it had been formed on the basis of convenience in 1922-1923 to work together against a common opponent – Tomlinson and his followers. But once Tomlinson and his loyalists were out of the way, the friendship and closeness between the two men quickly faded. The 'old Joe' began to surface again with his old disposition to 'rule or ruin', along with his old habits to contend and intimidate in order to have his own way. The 'old Joe' simply had to be in the driver's seat. But while this spirit was tolerated and even encouraged in him in the struggle with Tomlinson, it was now denounced by Lee and the new leaders at their Headquarters – Ellis, Payne, Latimer, Boehmer, Letsinger, *et al.* His refusal to cooperate with authority and submit to counsel led to the termination of his services and ministry on October 24, 1927. He subsequently began with the assistance of his son Paul to publish a secular newspaper in Cleveland called the *Cleveland Tribune*. He remained outside the pale of Christian fellowship for a number of years, fell seriously ill in the early 1930s and, as noted earlier, made restitutions with Tomlinson and his followers before his death in 1934 – and also apparently, according to Ellis, 'made things right' with some of the Elders in his faction.

We notice earlier that the pronouncement of the Supreme Court in upholding the impeachment charges against Tomlinson, Brouayer, and Gillaspie was simply a rubber stamp of the decision already made by Ten Elders in the June Council, for seven of the Ten Elders made up the Supreme Court. Lee was apparently typical of the other Judges who seemed to be blinded to the absurdity of this system – a system in which the same Elders who drew up the charges of impeachment were then ordered to turn around and judge their own judgments. Lee in particular spoke of this 'judicious' process as if he were under a delusion, testifying in court that Tomlinson's 'case was finally turned over to the judges, and they made their decision, [and] it was taken out of the hands of the Council'.[330] His ability to speak of the judges as 'they' in a detached way,

---

[330] Lee, 'Deposition', p. 767.

as if he were not one of them, was indeed strange; and it was equally strange that he could ignore the fact that the judgment of the Supreme Court was predetermined by the opinion of the Ten Elders – that the judgment was in fact one and the same as the Council's.

Figure 111

MEETING OF THE ELDERS [LLEWELLYN-LEE FACTION] (AUGUST 1923)

Seated at the desk, from left: F.J. Lee, Efford Haynes, Alonzo Gann, M.S Lemons, J.S. Llewellyn. Sitting on floor to Llewellyn's right, J.B. Ellis; in the center, E.J. Boehmer; Standing in back, fourth from left, Nora Chambers; fifth from right, W.F. Bryant.

Still, though the relationship between the Council of Elders and the Supreme Court was unwise, if not absurd, in regard to a system of justice, it was a system in which Tomlinson helped to establish. Further, he alone selected the seven Judges, although he was bound by Article 5, Section 1 of the Constitution to appoint them from among the Twelve Elders. Too bad for him and his followers that he did not choose Gillaspie and Brouayer as judges instead of Llewellyn and Lemons! If he had, the history of the Church of God would read radically different.

Clearly the intrusion of politics had influenced and flawed the creation of the church's justice system; and assigning seats on the Supreme Court to men like Llewellyn and Lemons only made matters that much worse; in fact, their appointments were sure to mock justice: for they had by their words and actions before and after the Assembly in 1922 disqualified themselves from such high and noble positions. We have seen that a great number of elders and members in the church had expressed a deep sense of outrage in regard to their behavior in the Assembly in 1922 and in the months leading up to the June Council in 1923. It is difficult to exaggerate how ridiculous it was for these men to sit in judgment against Tomlinson. A.J. Lawson had remarked that the appointment of these men to sit on the Supreme Court was one of the costly mistakes that Tomlinson had made during the contentious period. Referring to 1 Cor. 6.4, he said, '[Tomlinson] certainly did not go by the teachings of Paul, for [Paul said] when we set one to judge, to take the least esteemed among you, [whereas] Brother Tomlinson took those [who] were at that time highly esteemed ... who are now ... sending out misrepresentations to turn the people from [him]'.[331] Lawson did not realize apparently, however, that Tomlinson was bound by the Constitution to appoint the judges from the body of the Twelve Elders; and, one wonders in any case if he would have complained if Tomlinson had chosen Gillaspie and Brouayer to be judges instead of Llewellyn and Lemons.

The August Council

Several significant steps were taken by Tomlinson and his followers in the Call Council held in Chattanooga on August 8-10, 1923.[332] Foremost was the reestablishment of Tomlinson to a position of preeminence. It may be observed that between the Council on July 24th and the Call Council in August, Tomlinson became more radical in his aims and purposes and seized the opportunity of the Call Council to persuade his followers to abrogate not only the Constitution but also the Council of Seventy and the Supreme Court: for those institutions were incompatible with his view of the office of General Overseer, for they infringed upon his God-ordained authority and preeminent posture over the church.

Interestingly, however, Tomlinson retained the Council of Elders and reverted to the former appointment system to replace the Ten Elders

---

[331] 'Letter written by Lawson to T.A. Richard', dated July 17, 1923 (*Church of God Bureau of Information*).

[332] This Council was held in the home of H.A. Pressgrove at 2301 Vance Avenue in Chattanooga, and was opened for business at 2.45 pm on August 8, 1923. Pressgrove had served as overseer of Mississippi in 1920-1922 and had recently moved to Chattanooga.

who had vacated their offices, that is, he appointed Gillaspie and Brouayer and the three of them together appointed the other ten new members to the Council – namely, C.H. Randall, H.A. Pressgrove, J.H. Brooks, J.N. Hurley, J.O. Hamilton, Guy Marlow, T.A. Richard, J.A. Wilkerson, G.T. Stargel, and T.J. Richardson.[333]

The reason that the Council of Elders was retained is clear: Tomlinson had obtained legal counsel – namely, the thirty-five-year-old George E. Westerberg and Judge G.B. Murray – anticipating the forthcoming lawsuit initiated by the Llewellyn-Lee faction.[334] Westerberg addressed the Call Council and laid out a basic strategy to follow in defending the case. After having studied the minutes of several of the recent Assemblies, he concluded that the church had beginning in 1920 'thrown aside the New Testament and adopted man-made rules. This cut out any member of the Church, outside of the Elders to set a single construction on the Scriptures ... I find that the Church stuck to the same course until the year 1920, when they started away and in 1921 they went away from the Church of God'.[335]

When Tomlinson asked him before the Council, 'What steps should be taken, shall we reorganize or go ahead?' Westerberg advised, 'You should reorganize so far as filling the vacancies of those going out, but not drop your former standing. At least make temporary appointments until the Assembly'.[336] The legal strategy was thus to show that the church had transgressed against itself and broken its own sacred principles in adopting the Declaration in 1920 and the Constitution in 1921 and also the Council of Seventy and Supreme Court in the same year. But where did that leave the Council of Twelve among Tomlinson and his followers, particularly in view of the fact that the Council was considered to be an imposition upon the God-given authority of the exalted General Overseer and his ability to act freely and unilaterally by the immediate counsel of the Holy Spirit? Obviously the Council of Twelve was retained only as a temporary measure until it could be removed in

---

[333] Following the appointment of the Council of Elders, Tomlinson proceeded to fill several other positions 'that had been vacated' by the Elders, including, Bible Training School Directors – George T. Brouayer, S.O. Gillaspie, C.H. Randall, H.A. Pressgrove, J.O. Hamilton; Orphanage Committee – T.A. Richard, J.N. Hurley, Guy Marlow; Foreign Mission Secretary – H.A. Pressgrove; Home Mission Secretary – J.A. Wilkerson; Publishing Committee – A.J. Lawson, George T. Brouayer, S.O. Gillaspie, H.H. Irwin, J.F. Dover.

[334] The suit was initiated on February 26, 1924 and an injunction served on Tomlinson and his followers by the Bradley County Chancery Court. The case was styled *Church of God vs. A.J. Tomlinson, et al.* and the File Number assigned was 1891.

[335] Tomlinson, *Call Council*, pp. 18-19.

[336] Tomlinson, *Call Council*, p. 18.

proper order in the next Assembly, which was the case as we will see in a moment. The appointment of the Twelve in the Call Council was thus rather superficial and merely an accommodation in anticipation of the forthcoming litigation before the secular courts. Accordingly, the Council of Twelve among Tomlinson and his followers existed only for three months – until the Assembly in November 1923 – and even then was merely a nominal body: for the members of the Council did not meet nor act together on any issue in any official capacity during those three months.

With the Council of Twelve, Council of Seventy, and Supreme Court now out of the way, Tomlinson was free to act and practice the exalted office of General Overseer as he had envisioned and formed it in 1912-1914, and he was free again to pursue his vision of the glorious Church of God as he saw it in the prophetic Scriptures. Of course, his vision of the church and his peculiar calling and exalted position as 'God's Anointed – Prophet of Wisdom' were inextricably tied together.

Tomlinson's preeminence was settled as soon as the Call Council was officially opened on August 8th. T.A. Richard, then serving as overseer of Louisiana said, 'This body fully recognizes you, A.J. Tomlinson, as General Overseer and there is no need to select anyone else or to reselect you'.[337] The minutes of the meeting show that 'all those present agreed heartily'. T.J. Richardson then emphasized significantly 'that we recognize Brother Tomlinson as our God appointed leader'. Accordingly, Tomlinson was back in the driver's seat and proceeded to govern the church unencumbered and unimpeded, for all of his opposition had been removed from office in the July Council and he was now giving no quarters for any new opposition.[338] Further, to ensure that the church would go forward without hindrance or controversy under his chairmanship and oversight, he required full cooperation in regard to his

---

[337] Tomlinson, *Call Council*, p. 3. Richard coincidently was the 'Benedict Arnold' that Tomlinson mentions in his annual address to the Assembly in November. Between the August Council and the Assembly, Richard had come under the influence of the Llewellyn-Lee faction's newly-appointed overseer of Louisiana, T.S. Payne. He 'saw the error of his way' and wrote a letter of confession and apologized before the General Assembly on November 1, 1923 (*GAM*, 18th Assembly, p. 9).

[338] C.T. Anderson, appointed secretary at the Call Council in Chattanooga in August 8, 1923, testified that D.W. Haworth and Walter Hindman of the Llewellyn-Lee faction attended the meeting in August; but suspecting that they were there to 'molest the meeting', Tomlinson and his associates asked them to leave. Anderson noted that 'The General Overseer had made the statement that none were welcome to the meeting that came for anything but harmony, love, [and] unity, and for that reason and because the report was that these gentlemen were not there for that purpose, we asked them … not to be present to interfere with the meeting'.

stated aims, and employed the intimidating tactic to label anyone who opposed his position as a 'Benedict Arnold'.[339] He emphasized further, 'I want to refer to some things for our benefit ... [for] so many started out with us and have turned traitor. And now I want us to come to the point where we will be established and none of us turn traitor ... It is like this, if I am going to be forsaken I want you to forsake me now, not go on with me a few months, or for a time and then drop me. Some have come to me recently and have as good as sworn allegiance and then turned away. I do not want that now.'[340]

The second most significant step taken in the Call Council was to inaugurate the *Church of God Bureau of Information*. A.J. Lawson, who had been appointed as General Treasurer earlier in the Council, was appointed as General Manager of the Bureau of Information. Since Tomlinson and his followers were now deprived of the use of the *Evangel*, the purpose of this institution was to provide a medium to publish articles, reports, letters and tracts to rebut and refute the reports that were being circulated by the Llewellyn-Lee faction in the *Evangel* and in other official and unofficial correspondence, many of which were distorted and malicious slanders being spread from minister to minister and church to church with increasing injury to Tomlinson and his followers.

But the Bureau of Information also represented a change in attitude and policy among Tomlinson and his followers. For until this time, Tomlinson had more or less encouraged a turn-the-other-cheek policy. Even in his opening statement in the Call Council he said, 'We have shown that we would rather suffer the wrong than do wrong ... Many of us feel that we have been wronged, and God knows we have, but we must suffer these things. We could do things to rectify the wrong ... but for us to ... bear these things is better'.[341] However, Brouayer, Lawson, Anderson, Hughes, and others advised him to go on the offensive in the 'fight' against the Ten Elders and their followers, and their counsel finally prevailed. Accordingly, Lawson immediately began to circulate a number of reports, letters and leaflets written by him and Tomlinson and others that addressed all of the arguments and disputed issues in the contentious ordeal. Lee's son-in-law, Jesse P. Hughes, wrote some of the most hard-hitting responses to the false reports and accusations circulated by the Llewellyn-Lee faction. Included in his counterattack, he

---

[339] Tomlinson would use this term often in messages and annual addresses to intimidate his followers not to resist his leadership and visionary aims, and to insure their loyalty also to the rulings of the Assembly, the latter of which were more or less identical with his own.
[340] Tomlinson, *Call Council*, p. 4.
[341] Tomlinson, *Call Council*, p. 1.

made public a scathing rebuke that he had written to his father-in-law – 'A Letter of Facts and Plain Statements' – contradicting and reproving him for articles that he had published in the *Evangel* in September 1923.

In a pamphlet called 'Facts With Figures'[342] dated June 17, 1924, Hughes ably exposed several of the distortions put out by the Llewellyn-Lee camp, particularly in regard to exaggerating their financial growth and progress, the very thing that the Ten Elders had accused Tomlinson of doing while he was in office. Moreover, he showed that the flow of tithes into Headquarters had actually decreased, yet the leading Elders were still receiving the 'lion's share' of the tithes. He made public the fact that for the month of May 1924 J.S. Llewellyn was paid $140.00, T.S. Payne $133.57, J.B. Ellis $125.00, etc. and concluded, 'Now my dear reader, I am sure that you can begin to see who is getting the most money and that the desire for 'Filthy Lucre' is the cause of all the trouble in the church'.[343]

Hughes concluded his 'Facts with Figures' treatise by exposing the fact that the Llewellyn-Lee faction had failed in their attempt to indict Tomlinson in the Circuit Court for embezzlement – the grand jury seeing no evidence for such a case – but that the Bradley County Chancery Court had allowed the Ten Elders to enter a suit against Tomlinson and his followers for the name of the church and the ownership of the property. Llewellyn denied that his side had formally charged Tomlinson with embezzlement, yet, as Hughes eloquently showed, the evidence was too overwhelming to believe Llewellyn's denial, including the fact that the grand jury had subpoenaed at least four of the Elders to testify apparently on those very grounds. Hughes wrote that Llewellyn is 'trying to cover up their attempt to indict Brother Tomlinson on the accusations that they themselves have so publicly made against him', namely, that he was a crook and embezzler. Then he asks,

> Who is responsible for the report being out that A.J. Tomlinson is a thief and has embezzled the Church's money? In their bill that they have filed in chancery court, which is affirmed by M.S. Lemons, they aver that he has embezzled the Church's money to the extent of many thousands of dollars. They have also circulated various reports that made some think that Brother Tomlinson was a criminal and that they could put him in the penitentiary.[344]

---

[342] J.P. Hughes, 'Facts with Figures' (*Church of God Bureau of Information*).
[343] Hughes, 'Facts with Figures', pp. 1-2.
[344] Hughes, 'Facts with Figures', pp. 3-4.

Tomlinson boldly admitted that the actions taken by him and his followers inaugurated nothing less than a full-blown revolution, and he likened their efforts to America's Revolutionary War against Britain in the 1770s. The *Church of God Bureau of Information* was instituted under this motif, that is, from the perspective of a declaration of war! The title of the sermon that Tomlinson assigned to Guy Marlow to preach in the next Assembly – 'On the Warpath in This Revolution' – represented the new policy of Tomlinson and his followers. In effect, the Bureau of Information was a counterattack by Tomlinson's soldiers – his 'bravados' as he fancied them – in a war that they claimed had been initiated by Llewellyn and his followers.

The new 'fight back' policy by Tomlinson and his followers ensured that the war would no longer be one-sided, but also that the fight between the factions would become a public spectacle. In fact, the lawsuit initiated by the Llewellyn-Lee faction stands as one of the longest court litigations in Tennessee history – a legal argument that began in 1923 and did not end in the courts until 1952.

The final significant thing that transpired in the Call Council was the adoption of an official church paper. This had been discussed at some length and all agreed on the need for a regular publication to replace the *Evangel*. During an earlier session in the Council in which prayer was being made in particular for a name for the paper, a certain brother related that he had received a vision or vivid impression from the Lord. He gave this testimony: '[I saw] the name of the paper in the most beautiful form ... [it] appeared in arched form, THE WHITE WING MESSENGER, with a beautiful dove bearing an olive branch in its claws just beneath the arch'.[345] Intriguingly, this term, 'White Wing Messenger', and similar terms had been used by Brouayer and others through the years in reference to the *Evangel*.[346] But now that the *Evangel*

---

[345] Tomlinson, *Call Council*, p. 23. George T. Brouayer has been credited in some historical accounts as having received this vision or revelation. Perhaps the source of these accounts was Brouayer's comments in the Assembly in 1920: 'I don't believe there is anybody who loves the *Evangel* more than I do. I have prayed much for this wonderful White-winged Messenger. I well remember the beautiful vision God gave me years ago concerning this paper', (*GAM*, 1920, p. 41). But Tomlinson denied that it was Brouayer who testified in the August Council in 1923 about having a vision of the paper, and in fact that Brouayer had suggested another name for the paper. Further, he distinctly recalled that it was another gentleman with whom he was not well acquainted that had testified about the name for the paper (Tomlinson, 'Deposition', pp. 2484-85). The fact that the gentleman was not well known is apparently the reason his name was not recorded in the *Minutes*.

[346] Lawson, 'Deposition', 1667; Tomlinson, 'Deposition', pp. 2484-85. Interestingly, Tomlinson admits that at first the name did not appeal to him; but, inas-

had become the official organ for the Llewellyn–Lee faction and, consequently, according to Tomlinson and his followers, was now corrupted by the doctrines of the Ten Elders and the government connected with the Constitution, it seemed perfectly in order for the church's new publication to be called *The White Wing Messenger*, particularly since the Holy Ghost had apparently manifestly set His seal upon it through divine revelation. The new publication was accepted unanimously with the sentiment 'that it seems good to the Holy Ghost and us that our paper be called, The White Wing Messenger'.[347] Accordingly, the first issue rolled off the presses on September 15, 1923.

One last thing should be noticed here that showed up in this Call Council that negatively affected Tomlinson and his followers for the next three decades, namely, an anti-intellectual disposition. This was occasioned by Tomlinson and some of his associates blaming the disruption of the church in large part on the arrogance of educated men. Tomlinson explained,

> Too much stress no doubt has been laid on education. We need education but we need God more than we need education. And because some have not much education is no reason God is not with them, or that they have not wisdom ... If you ... have felt cramped because you lack education I want you to get out of it and feel free.[348]

Later that year in his annual address before the Assembly he asserted,

> There has been a spirit working among us for years that has been making a gap between the educated and those who have been deprived of educational advantages. This spirit has the tendency to crush down the uneducated and prevent them from having anything to say in the Assembly. I have battled this spirit all these years, and now I am going to come out boldly and declare myself for the common people.[349]

While Tomlinson perhaps meant well, his words caused a negative impression to permeate the church in regard to formal education. Tomlinson had unwittingly pitted education over against God and true spirituality. He remarked, 'we need education but we need God more ... because some have not education is no reason God is not with them ...

---

much as he was not that concerned about it, he simply went along with the consensus of opinion (Tomlinson, 'Deposition', p. 2485).

[347] Tomlinson, *Call Council*, p. 24.
[348] Tomlinson, *Call Council*, p. 3.
[349] *HAA*, I, pp. 223-24.

If you have felt cramped because you lack education I want you to get out of it and feel free'. However good were his intentions, thereafter formal education was generally considered dangerous or else a waste of time and money that could be better spent on evangelism and building the great Church of God. It would not be until 1941 with the institution of Bible Training Camp (BTC) that any formal and systematic effort was made to correct this negative image of education; and even BTC was hardly worthy of the name of education, since the students were not taught to think for themselves but merely to parrot established doctrine and practices. This actually stifled intellectual development and more or less rubber-stamped the next generation of leaders. It was not until 1955 with the establishment of Tomlinson Memorial School – the precursor of Tomlinson College established in 1966 – that education worthy of the name was given any serious consideration among Tomlinson's followers, and, even then, it was not well supported.

Meanwhile the Llewellyn-Lee faction pushed forward the vision that was first mentioned in 1911, namely, an agenda that put a premium on education and especially an educated ministry. That year it was recommended that a board of education be constituted and a building erected for 'an institution of learning for the training of workers ... to make them efficient'. At the same time, a 'general school or college work was duly discussed'.[350] This vision for a college began to be fulfilled in January 1918 with the establishment of Bible Training School (BTS) under the oversight of Tomlinson. After the disruption in 1923, BTS was continued by the Llewellyn-Lee faction under the oversight of J.B. Ellis, who served only briefly, giving way to the superintendency of T.S. Payne. Beginning in 1930, BTS was expanded considerably both numerically and scholastically under the considerable abilities and zealous efforts of J.H. Walker and then Zeno C. Tharp. Eventually extension schools were established in several regions in the United States and around the world. The name of the main school in Cleveland was changed in 1941 to Bible Training School and College, and then changed again in 1947 to Lee College (now Lee University) in honor of F.J. Lee.

September-October Events

Between the Council conducted by Tomlinson and his followers in August and the two General Assemblies held by the warring factions in

---

[350] *GAM*, 1906-1914, pp. 94-95, 97, 103.

November, the split in the church had become more visible and emphatic. Tomlinson had virtually reorganized with his followers in the August Council in Chattanooga,[351] filling the vacancies of a number of general offices – Bible Training School directors, Orphanage and Publishing Committees, and Foreign and Home Mission secretaries, and also reaffirmed the appointment of a number of loyal state overseers whom he noted in his *Diary* had 'stuck by me'. He also commissioned a number of other ministers to go back to their respective fields of labor to help win back and reorganize members who had become confused or had defected to the Llewellyn-Lee side.[352]

Figure 112

THE SUNNYSIDE MISSION

The Sunnyside mission on the east side of Cleveland had been established through the initial efforts of Mary Jane Tomlinson beginning c. 1914. During the course of the disruptive events in 1922-1923, Tomlinson and his followers in Cleveland began to meet in this mission to worship and counsel together to rebuild the great Church of God. In the photo kneeling far right is A.D. Evans, far left wife, Iris Marie [Tomlinson] Evans.

In Cleveland, Tomlinson and his followers, being now deprived of the use of the church's buildings and facilities, began 'immediately following the June Council' to meet and conduct services on a regular basis

---

[351] Tomlinson's lawyers, however, argued before the Supreme Court of Tennessee that the division actually occurred in the July 24th Council meeting ('Church of God, et als. vs. AJ. Tomlinson, et als.', p. 7).

[352] Tomlinson, *Call Council*, pp. 20-23.

at the Sunnyside mission on the east side of town.[353] In September, they purchased a piece of property on the corner of Central Avenue and Short Street and in October began to build a tabernacle for a local church but more especially to accommodate the next General Assembly which was scheduled for November 22-27, 1923.[354] Apparently just before this Assembly, J.P. Hughes, Lee's son-in-law, was appointed to pastor the church in Cleveland. Hughes subsequently moved to Cleveland from Chattanooga in early December, and in the first business conference held in January, his wife, Nellie Marie (Lee's daughter), was appointed as the treasurer and began to raise funds to build the new tabernacle.[355]

Interestingly, the Llewellyn-Lee faction denied that there had been a split or disruption in the church. In the Assembly in 1923, T.S. Payne declared in his address on the 'Model Church' that 'Some may speak about a division or split in the Church, but I will say that we have never recognized a split in the Church and never will'.[356] In response to a letter from Mrs. Myrtle Clendon in West Virginia, Lee wrote, 'In the first place we don't consider that there really has been a split in the church. We only had to deal with Tomlinson for his misdeeds and also dealt with some others because they stood with him'.[357] Conn in his history, says,

> From the time A.J. Tomlinson was impeached from office and expelled from the Church, matters grew worse in Cleveland. The repudiated Overseer and a few of his followers moved to another part of town and erected a tabernacle under the name of the Church of God. The Church admitted to no split or division, since no appreciable number had been lost; and those who began the new tabernacle in Cleveland were mostly men who, for various reasons, were out of

---

[353] Lawson, 'Deposition', pp. 1567-68, 1637-39, 1671, 1677; Tomlinson, 'Deposition', p. 2091. Co-incidentally this mission had been started several years earlier by Tomlinson's wife, Mary Jane. Sunnyside was near the place called at that time, Big Springs.

[354] Lawson, 'Deposition', p. 1676. There on that vacant lot, Tomlinson and Lawson and others met for an outdoor service on September 30th, and the people were so enthusiastic that a conference was called and the church was set in order; and trustees were selected: A.J. Lawson, J.R. Kinser, C. D. Keeney, a Bro. Parker, and C.T. Broyles. Lawson was also selected to serve as secretary and treasurer. Interestingly, after Lawson was appointed to the office of General Treasurer in the Assembly, F.J. Lee's daughter, Nellie, succeeded him as the treasurer of the local church in Cleveland, and her husband, J.P. Hughes, was appointed to the pastorate.

[355] Lawson, 'Deposition', p. 1669.

[356] *GAM*, 18th Assembly, 1923, p. 26.

[357] 'Letter from F.J. Lee to Myrtle Clendon', Winden, WV dated May 13, 1925.

harmony with the Church. There was no secession, therefore, no split – which remains the attitude of the Church of God today.

But the leaders in the Llewellyn-Lee faction were denying the facts on their face; and their followers continued to deny the obvious in the years following. Even in 1955 when Conn's history was published, they were still denying the obvious, both in regard to the number of the ministers and members who remained loyal to Tomlinson and in regard to the original principles upon which the church had been established. For not only had two of the Twelve Elders sided with Tomlinson but at least ten of the Seventy Elders; and there were a number of state overseers who remained true to Tomlinson. Interestingly, Conn acknowledges that several overseers allied themselves with Tomlinson including 'The Overseer of Kentucky, C.H. Randall, [who] carried with him a few churches and members … [and that] the work in the Dakotas was ravaged, leaving very little for the Church of God there'.[358] Yet he says, 'All in all, the Church suffered no great loss in numbers'. But he could say this only by ignoring the fact that most of the ministers and churches in the Bahama Islands remained loyal to Tomlinson, or soon afterward came over to his side, and more than a hundred members and friends in the Cleveland church reorganized with Tomlinson. Moreover, under the pastoral leadership of J.P. Hughes, and afterwards under the leadership of David Wilkerson's grandfather, J.A. Wilkerson, the Cleveland church flourished and within two years had about 200 in attendance – most of whom had been a part of the church before the split occurred. In the Assembly in late November, Tomlinson appointed 20 overseers to govern established churches in 30 states and also the Bahamas, and by 1925 well more than 1000 attended the Assembly, most of which had been in the church before the disruption occurred.[359]

Meanwhile, across the railroad tracks from where Tomlinson and his followers were planning to build their new tabernacle on Central Avenue, the new pastor of the church in Cleveland for the Llewellyn-Lee faction called a conference to excommunicate Tomlinson and Lawson and their families with others for 'aiding and abetting' Tomlinson or for being in sympathy with his actions. The new pastor of the Llewellyn-Lee faction was none other than J.B. Ellis. The business conference was held on September 10, 1923 and the church proceeded to act on the charges

---

[358] Conn, *Mighty Army*, p. 180.
[359] The record showed 1042 registered with 832 of these from out of town. There were 210 registered within the city of Cleveland and a large number attended evening services who did not register (*GAM*, 20th Assembly, 1925, 'Prefatory Notes').

brought against these brethren. When asked what Mary Jane Tomlinson and Lula Lawson and others had done to deserve excommunication, the answer was simply that they stood with the former General Overseer in his misdeeds and rebellion.

Tomlinson and his followers denounced the legitimacy of the actions of the Llewellyn-Lee faction, and Llewellyn and his followers denounced the actions of the Tomlinson faction. Each anathematized the other and denied the other the divine right to call their faction the Church of God.[360] George T. Brouayer's wife, Delia, in response to a letter from the Llewellyn faction in regard to charges being brought against her, wrote, 'I would rather have my name on the Ku Klux roll than on this church'.[361] And Lawson's wife, Lula, according to Llewellyn, said she and her family 'would rather have their names on a billboard than on their church roll'.[362]

Interestingly, Lee read a prepared document before the General Assembly on November 2, 1923 in regard to the charges and actions taken by the Ten Elders and the Supreme Court in revoking Tomlinson's and Brouayer's credentials and the actions of the local church in Cleveland in excommunicating them. He then asked the Assembly to 'ratify and concur in all the actions and proceedings herein set forth'.[363] Tomlinson and his followers likewise in their Assembly two weeks later endorsed the actions taken in their July and August Councils, repealing the 1920 Declaration, repudiating the 1921 Constitution and the adoption of the Executive Council in 1922, and abrogated also the State Board of Judges and the Supreme Court 'and other matters that may have a tendency to add to or take away from the New Testament'.[364] In his typical dramatic style, Tomlinson asked the Assembly to stand who favored the report presented by the Committee on Bible Government, and then 'in solemn tones slowly spoke as he looked at his watch and asked the secretary to

---

[360] Lawson's said that those who were standing with the Llewellyn faction 'were not the true Church of God, and no part of the true Church of God' (Lawson, 'Deposition', p. 1673). When asked if F.J. Lee was a member of the Church of God, his son-in-law, J.P. Hughes, said, '[he is] a member of the Llewellyn faction', and when pressed for a further explanation answered, '[he is] not a true member of the true Church of God, he departed from it by adopting the Constitution ... [and] when he joined hands with Llewellyn' (Hughes, 'Deposition', pp. 1187-88). And the Llewellyn faction believed just as emphatically that Tomlinson and his followers had departed from the faith and were not the true Church of God.

[361] Brouayer, 'Deposition', p. 1524.
[362] Llewellyn, 'Deposition', p. 1025.
[363] *GAM*, 18th Assembly: November 1-7, 1923, pp. 28-29 (Llewellyn faction).
[364] *GAM*, 18th Assembly: November 22-27, 1923, pp. 13-16, 21 (Tomlinson faction).

take note: "At 4:30 P.M., Nov. 23, 1923, the Assembly shook off the galling yoke of the constitution and went free. And by the help of the Lord this shall be forever".[365] In response to this dramatic act,

> A mighty shout of joy went up from the saints when they realized they were free from bondage ... And as the rejoicing went on, a sister went up to Brother Tomlinson and placed a Bible in his hand and raised his arm up. Then she took the Bible from his hand and placed it under his feet. Then she took it from the floor and placed it on the altar rail where all could see and had him mount upon it and stand in view of the people while they shouted and rejoiced. The demonstration of power kept up until 5:00 P. M.

Separate General Assemblies

The church had come together in the 1922 Assembly generally troubled in spirit and divided in opinion, especially among the leaders at Headquarters; yet, still, the ministers and members were one visible and undivided body, and were acting together under one government. But in the ensuing months, the quarrel between the factions gradually degenerated into bitterness and hatefulness and, being unable or unwilling to reconcile their differences, the quarrel became a public spectacle and ended in a reproachful division. At that point, the war was then being waged more on the basis of personal grudges and hurts than biblical and spiritual principles. And thus rather than grieving over the calamity, each side went forward rejoicing that it was free and loosed from the other, and each side managed somehow in their separate Assemblies to emphasize the love of God and the ideal of Christian unity.

The absence of sorrow and grief in each faction over the division is rather remarkable, particularly because the fellowship had been founded in 1886 upon the ideal of love in Christian Union and had since that time continued to emphasize the need for divine love and God's call for Christian union. Noticeably missing in each faction's view of Christian Union, however, was Spurling's theology and principles laid out in *The Lost Link*. Quite obviously the 'lost link' had been lost again.

Interestingly, it seems that each side purposely avoided addressing the glaring issue of the reproachful separation, except to drive home the final nails in that part of the body of Christ that the other believed needed to be crucified. In the midst of the calamity, each side rejoiced in typical Pentecostal fashion – with shouting, dancing in the Spirit, and

---

[365] *GAM*, 18th Assembly: November 22-27, 1923, p. 16 (Tomlinson faction).

speaking in tongues – because the carnal element had been purged from the great Church of God.

In the Introductory of the 1923 Assembly Minutes of the Llewellyn faction, we read that in the opening service Efford Haynes led in singing the old hymn, 'What A Friend We Have In Jesus'. The account then continues,

> It was indeed wonderful to hear almost every voice in that great audience singing of that precious Friend ... Truly God set His seal of approval upon us ... Oh such shining faces. Truly it could be said, 'The Lord is in His holy temple. Many saints had been praying during the past year that God might be with us in a marked way and have His way in this Assembly. It can be truly said that it is wonderful for brethren to dwell together in unity. The oil of gladness was poured upon our heads as the distilling of the dew of Hermon.

In his closing remarks to the Assembly, Lee, the new General Overseer, said,

> Everybody has decided that this Assembly has been marvelous; has been wonderful. Everybody has been enjoying it ... This is a time we will never forget ... There is nothing to make us discouraged. Everything looks favorable ... You are all going away with a smile and with renewed courage. We cannot estimate what this Assembly has been worth to us ... For months thousands have been heavy hearted ... Your prayers have reached heaven ... were heard ... All realize that there is a brighter day for the Church of God ... There is a great future for us, and we ought ... to go right on into the deeper things of God. [366]

Down the street two weeks later,

> Representatives of the great Church of God began to assemble at the newly created tabernacle in Cleveland for the Eighteenth Annual Assembly of the Church of God. There was a buoyant spirit that pervaded the place, and as shining faces and happy hearts greeted each other, anon there would be an overflow and a burst of happy praises ascend as holy incense ... [then] there burst forth one great volume of happy voices that rang out as one great happy voice ... Brother Tomlinson, our General Overseer ... suggested the song, 'In the Sweet Bye and Bye'. Then from a packed audience echoed and reechoed through the holy atmosphere the many voices mingling as

---

[366] *GAM*, 18th Assembly: November 1-7, 1923, pp. 59-60 (Llewellyn faction).

the sound of many waters ... As the singing continued the heavens seemed to bend low and kiss the earth. It was wonderful to hear the people shout and praise the Lord ... There was a wonderful demonstration of the Spirit as saints shouted and danced under the downpour of the mighty Holy Ghost.[367]

Then in the closing moments of this opening service,

> A wonderful message in tongues was given. Part of [which was as] follows: 'Wilt thou follow Me? Go down in the dust before Me. I will call thee out ... Follow the way of the cross. Thou art dearer to Me than the apple of My eye. Love, love, love shall overcome. Thou canst get strength from Me. I have great things for thee. I have called, thou has heard, thou hast listened. Keep the Wolf from among you. My people! My People! My chosen ones, I love you!'

Summary Reflection

The question is inevitably raised by those who read about this calamitous episode in Church of God history, 'What could have been done to have avoided such a spiteful quarrel and reproachful division?' Certainly there were mistakes made on both sides and to one degree or other each faction was to be blamed for the disruption. The writer lamented this fact more than twenty years ago in a paper presented to the Society of Pentecostal Studies:

> I wish I could say that this group or that group was a continuation of what Spurling had originated, and what he had envisioned for Christian Union and the Holiness Church at Camp Creek. But this would not be so. Though Tomlinson's opponents succeeded in modifying the office of General Overseer, they had to articulate a document called the Constitution to do it. This instrument was as foreign to the Gospel Church and Spurling's ecclesiology as Tomlinson's exalted position.[368]

The core of the quarrel between Llewellyn and Tomlinson and their followers was rooted, on one hand, in Tomlinson's view of his unique and special calling as 'God's anointed leader' and in the corresponding development of the exalted office of General Overseer, and, on the other hand, in ambitious men who insisted – even if it disrupted the church

---

[367] *GAM*, 18th Assembly: November 22-27, 1923, pp. 1-2 (Tomlinson faction).
[368] Phillips, *Quakerism*, pp. 26-29.

– to modify Tomlinson's position and powers in order to exalt their own status and to acquire power. But conflicting personalities and the works of the flesh complicated the situation. Tomlinson was to be blamed for treating the church as if he owned it, particularly in the years leading up to the disruption. It is true that no one had sacrificed for and contributed as much to the growth and development of the church as he and his family had, and thus it is understandable, if not excusable, that he felt some sense of entitlement; but his reluctance to yield to the counsel and pleadings of his brethren to modify the exalted powers of his office and his unilateral way of working was unacceptable, particularly to capable men who came along as the church developed and who in their own right were gifted and empowered by the Spirit to fill their place in the church.

Still, the situation in 1922-1923 was the more complicated because the primary leader who initiated the resistance against Tomlinson was J.S. Llewellyn, and the first convert he won to his cause was M.S. Lemons. These men were the least suited for the task of reforming and modifying Tomlinson and the administrative structure of the church, particularly in the early 1920s, for they were by then slipping in their personal spirituality and consecration. We are reminded here of the apostle's admonitions: 'And the servant of the Lord must not strive; but be gentle unto all men, apt to teach, patient, in meekness instructing those who oppose themselves' (2 Tim. 2.24-25). 'You which are spiritual, restore such an one in the spirit of meekness; considering yourselves, lest you also be tempted. Bear one another burdens, and so fulfill the law of Christ' (Gal. 6.1-2). Quite obviously Llewellyn and Lemons blatantly transgressed these apostolic instructions and were miserably deficient in the graces of meekness, gentleness, and patience; and even more regretfully they had lost again the very substance of *The Lost Link*.

Notwithstanding, Llewellyn and his followers had some legitimate complaints, but, whether out of frustration and impatience or else arrogance and malcontent, they approached Tomlinson with a tone of contempt and disrespect. Tomlinson in turn deeply resented their harsh tones and demanding and contentious spirit. Further, Llewellyn and his followers did not address properly and officially the core issue of their differences with Tomlinson, namely, his exalted powers and responsibilities. Rather than confront him and the church as a whole with the fact that the exalted office of General Overseer was popish, and that it had been created on the basis of a misinterpretation of the Scriptures, they conjured up the Constitution – which was equally unscriptural and troublesome – in order accomplish their aim, namely, to curb Tomlinson's powers and to increase their own. Then when Tomlinson rebelled against the Constitution in order to restore his exalted powers and privileges, Llewellyn and his followers launched a malicious attack against his character and slandered his family and, as we will see in Volume II, even attempted to have him imprisoned.

Again, Llewellyn and his associates – Lemons, Ellis, McLain, and Haynes, and later Lee, Boehmer, Latimer, Payne, and Gann – had some legitimate complaints; but they launched their attack on Tomlinson on the bogus charge that he was a crook and embezzler, and that his family had conspired with him to form a ring of corruption. Tomlinson was partly right in his assessment that 'It was not the financial situation that brought this thing [the disruption] about, but it came in handy to get rid of me'.[369] And his observation in another place was also partly true, that it 'Looks like the big boys [are] trying to turn their father out of house and home'.[370] Certainly the tale of embezzlement and financial crookedness was a malicious slander – a distinct evil perpetrated against a good and honest man, howbeit an imperfect one.

On Tomlinson's part, his hurt occasioned some deep resentment in him, and beginning in December 1923 he began to fight back – to revolt – and consequently he added to the already chaotic situation in the church. If it was in his mind all along to revolt, which apparently it was at least by February 1922 according to his own admission,[371] then it would have been wiser and perhaps less contentious and bitter to have made his stand in the Assembly in November 1922. But as we noticed earlier, he had allowed Lee and some others to talk him out of it on the presumption that the differences between the factions could be ironed out and settled satisfactory after the Assembly – without a disruption. But as things happened, the situation rather deteriorated into a bitter contention. Each side then entrenched themselves in their positions and sought to win converts to their cause, committing themselves to overcome the opposing faction – even by questionable tactics if necessary – and to reorganize the church with brethren of 'like precious faith'.

---

[369] Tomlinson, *Call Council*, p. 7. In his 'Preparation Notes', Tomlinson noted, 'I felt all the time that I was in the hands of schemers, who were scheming to get me out and to get the property out of my hands and management for the church of God' ('Preparation Notes', p. 54).

[370] 'Preparation Notes', p. 58.

[371] Homer thus states plainly that his father actually, if not officially, started over again in February 1923 (Homer, *Diary*, II, pp. 23-25).

What Could Have Been Done?

Could anything have been done to prevent the disruption? Perhaps not. Perhaps it was inevitable in view of the fact that each side believed their perspective on the situation was true and right, and because each side consequently felt justified and even obligated to resist with a holy determination any attempt to modify their point of view. Tomlinson was perfectly convinced in his mind that the exalted office of General Overseer was biblical and absolutely necessary for the proper operation of 'theocratic government'; and Llewellyn and his followers were just as convinced that the office was a figment of Tomlinson's imagination and an imposition on the spirit and process of church government in the New Testament. Inevitably, each side, as they endeavored to disarm and dismantle their opponent's system and to justify their own, complicated the dissension all the more and each side tended to add insult to injury in warring against the other. Men who once loved and praised each other now criticized, defamed, and sometimes brutally slandered the other. The primary aggressors were Llewellyn and his followers, and the meanest spirit was most often manifested by representatives of that faction, but Tomlinson in his decision and strategy to revolt and fight back led his followers into a spiteful retaliation that only added shame to the already shameful and reproachful spectacle.

It seems to this writer that the only way for the quarrel to have been settled peacefully and without a disruption – if indeed it were possible at all – was for the Ten Elders to have registered their complaints and charges against Tomlinson before the larger body of the church, preferably before the Council of Seventy and the general body of presbyters – the state overseers – and to allow that body to hear all of the evidence and to try the case. It is possible that in that 'multitude of counselors' reason may have had a better chance to prevail, particularly among those who 'did not have a dog in the fight', so to speak, that is, who did not have anything to gain by overthrowing Tomlinson or by modifying his position. It is possible that in that larger body of counselors, among those who were able to be less passionate and thus more level-headed about the arguments, that a wiser and more equitable outcome could have been achieved, certainly a more God-pleasing and charitable outcome.

Still, this conclusion is highly speculative considering all of the factors involved. Could Tomlinson have been persuaded by reason and sound biblical interpretation that his view of the exalted office was distorted and needed modified. It is unlikely, for he believed his view was a divine revelation and that he had been appointed to his position distinctly by the Holy Ghost for life! But if he could have been convinced, we will never know: for the Ten Elders usurped their authority and took matters into their own hands; and, consequently, we are left forever with the indelible impression that they acted – at least some of them – not in the best interests of the church but to serve their own selfish interests. Certainly not all of the Elders are to be blamed equally: for it is apparent that the majority of the Ten Elders were led down the road they took first by Llewellyn and later by the partnership formed between Llewellyn and Lee.

It would have been well if the calamity could have just faded into oblivion and that the whole unfortunate episode could have been forgotten; but regretfully the evils of the scandal and the carnal characteristics of the partisan ordeal were passed on to the factions' descendants and perpetuated for three more generations. Neither side thereafter represented a shining model of the New Testament church: Tomlinson restored and perpetuated his papal-like office among his followers and, being unchecked in his opinions and unilateral actions, led his admirers thereafter into some silly adventures and peculiar aberrations of the faith. The Llewellyn-Lee faction, conversely, departed altogether from some of the most essential and important features of Spurling's vision, for example, 1) the theology of the visible church as God's government in the earth [in contrast with the myth of a so-called spiritual or 'invisible church']; 2) the sacred principle of a church covenant as the means to form God's visible church; 3) certain important distinctions between the church and the kingdom; 4) the prophetic vision of the church embedded in the writings of the prophets and apostles, and particularly the vision of Christian Union over against religious denominationalism. Ironically, these features were preserved more or less among Tomlinson and his followers.

In the end, what ultimately matters is not how we have judged the words and actions leading up to the disruption in 1923, and the actions and reactions by both sides in the years following, but how the Righteous and Eternal Judge decides on these matters, and particularly on the manners of those involved. We know that the Lord judges according to His own righteous principles and spiritual laws; and that He weighs men's words and actions more on the basis of moral and spiritual substance than on official and legal formalities. 'The Lord sees not as man sees; for man looks on the outward appearance, but the Lord looks on the heart' (1 Sam. 16.7). He condemns an impure heart more readily than a confused mind, and metes out judgment against the works of the flesh, while excusing mental errors and forgiving penitent hearts. On this basis, we rest our case in this historical review. Who but our all-knowing and righteous Lord can know perfectly what was in the hearts and minds of all concerned in the awful disruption in 1923? In the end, we all stand naked before the fiery and piercing eyes of Him who says, 'I know thy works' (Rev. 2.2, 9, 13, 19; 3.1, 8, 15).

C.T. Davidson wrote with a distinct bias for the Tomlinson tradition in his *Upon This Rock;* yet perhaps both sides can agree with his closing remarks in Volume I and his magnanimous wish:

> There [were] many mistakes made on both sides of the disruption and we all regret them and remember them in grim retrospect. God help us all to walk more softly, more carefully, and try to remember the peace that Jesus Christ brought to us ... The disruption in the Church was unfortunate, and the reactions and repercussions are embarrassing ... The separation came. It was heart-rending, but maybe this is the way it had to be then ... But it does not have to continue to be this way if the 'fight in men' is subdued by the fresh-flowing blood of Jesus Christ. He declared ' ... there shall be one fold, and one shepherd' (Jn 10.16) ... Maybe it had to be this way ... maybe both churches will reach thousands of souls and lead them to Christ, which otherwise may never have been reached. Let them solve those problems they are able to solve ... then be big enough to leave the impossibles to God![372]

---

[372] Davidson, *Upon This Rock*, I, p. 648.

Bibliography

Primary Sources

1. Collections
Assemblies of God Archives, Springfield, Missouri.
Bradley County, TN: Courthouse Records; Marriage, Deed, Court, Tax, Federal Census Records.
Central Files and Records of the Church of God, Cleveland, Tennessee.
Cherokee County, NC: Courthouse records; Marriage, Deed, Court, Tax, Federal Census Records.
Fannin County, GA: Courthouse Records; Marriage, Deed, Court, Tax, Federal Census Records.
Hal Bernard Dixon, Jr. Pentecostal Research Center, Cleveland, Tennessee
Historical Society. Cleveland, TN.
Monroe County, TN: Courthouse Records; Marriage, Deed, Court, Tax, Federal Census Records.
Polk County, TN: Courthouse Records; Marriage, Deed, Court, Tax, Federal Census Records.
Wade H. Phillips' Collection, Cleveland, Tennessee.
William Squires Library, Lee University, Cleveland, Tennessee.
Zion Assembly Church of God Library & Archives, Cleveland, Tennessee.

2. Autobiographies, Biographies, and Memoirs
Abbott, Joe, *The Forgotten Church* (n.p., 1963), WHPC.
Buckalew, J.W, *Incidents in the Life of J.W. Buckalew* (Cleveland, TN: COGPH, 1920).
Duggar, Lillian, *A.J. Tomlinson: Former General Overseer of the Church of God* (Cleveland, TN: WWPH, 1964).
Ellis, James Benton, *Blazing the Gospel Trail* (Cleveland, TN: COGPH, 1941).
Elrod, Tom N., 'Testimonies', in *Minutes, Fields of the Wood Programs*, 1944-1950, WHPC.
Fox, George, *Works of George Fox, A Journal or Historical Account of the Life, Travels, and Sufferings* (2 Vols; Philadelphia: Marcus T. C. Gould and Isaac T. Hopper, 1831).
Hawk, Mary Etta, *History of the Ironsburg United Methodist Church* (unpublished, n.d.).
Hawk, Charles Timothy, *Journal 1906-1913* (ZACG Archives).
Kilpatrick, A.E., *Thoughts and Memoirs 1888-1980* (n.p., n.d.), WHPC.
Lee, Mrs. Flavius J., *Life Sketches of F.J. Lee* (Cleveland, TN: COGPH, 1929).
Miller, Roy C., *Classified Scriptures of the Church of God and Her Teachings* (Cleveland, TN: COGPH, 1913).
Robins, Roger, *A.J. Tomlinson Plainfolk Modernist* (Oxford University Press, 2004).
Spurling, G. Pinckney, *Biographical Sketch of Reverend R.G. Spurling* (n.p., n.d), WHPC.
Tomlinson, A.J., *Answering the Call of God* (Cleveland, TN: WWPH, 1933).
—*God's Anointed, Prophet of Wisdom* (Cleveland, TN: WWPH, 1943).
—*The Last Great Conflict* (Cleveland, TN: WWPH, 1913).
—'R.G. Spurling Passes Over the Tide', WWM (June 22, 1935), p. 1.

—A Brief History of Mission Work 1907 (ZACG Archives).

3. Diaries, Correspondence, Minutes
Baptist Church Minutes
    Clear Creek, 1852-1900
    Holly Springs, 1899-1910.
    Liberty, 1848-1905.
    Pleasant Hill, 1875-1908.
    Springtown, 1844-1900.
    Union, 1848-1860.
    Zion Hill, 1845-1910.
Baptist Association Minutes
    Clinton, 1853-1864.
    Eastanallee, 1870-1900.
    Liberty and Ducktown, 1858-1910.
    Sweetwater, 1830-1920.
    Stockton Valley, 1832-1835.
Bradley County Chancery Court: Case Number 1981.
Bradley County Chancery Court of Appeals, July 3, 1925.
Bryant, W.F., Jr. *Personal Correspondence*, 1949. WHPC.
Church of God Minutes
    Called Council held at Chattanooga, TN: August 8-10, 1923. WHPC.
    Council of Twelve (Elders' Council) *Minutes*, 1916-1925 (Qutote in Bradley County Chancery Court Record)
    Cyclopedia Index of Minutes. Cleveland Tennessee. WWPH, 1949.
    Executive Council (Supreme Council) *Minutes*, 1916-1925.
    General Assembly. *Minutes of the General Assembly of The Church of God* (Vols. 1-61; Cleveland, TN: COGPH, 1906-1925).
Church of God (Mountain Assembly), *Minutes* 1907-1912, 1934 (Jellico, TN: Xerox Copies) WHPC.
Church of God of Prophecy. *These Necessary Things* (Cleveland, TN: WWPH, 1968).
Church of God of Prophecy Minutes
    General Assembly Minutes 1906-1914 (Photographic Copies of Originals) (WWPH, 1990).
    Minutes of the General Assembly (Cleveland, TN: WWPH, 1906-96).
    Overseers' Meeting, Minutes, for the selection of interim General Overseer, April 30-May 2, 1990. WHPC.
    Study of the Office of General Overseer (Committee Report, 1991).
    These Necessary Things (Cleveland, TN: WWPH, 1968).
Lee, Flavius J., *Diary*. WHPC.
—*Executive Correspondence*, 1924-1926. WHPC.
Padgett, Carl, *Diaries*. 1907-1965. WHPC.
Spurling, R.G., *Personal Letters*, 1930-1932. WHPC.
—*The Lost Link* (Turtletown, TN: self-published, 1920).
—*The Lost Link* (Fragments of Original Manuscript), 1897, Photocopy. WHPC.
Spurling, H.G. Pinkney, *Personal Letters*. 1929-1949. WHPC.
Tennessee Supreme Court: Case Number 1891, 1927.

The Original Church of God; *Convention Minutes, June 19, 1920* (Ridgedale, TN). WHPC.
Tomlinson, A.J., *Diary*. (Original Manuscript).
—*Executive Correspondence*, 1921-1924. WHPC.
—*Personal Report*, 1904. WHPC.
—Personal Letters, 1930-1932.WHPC.
Tomlinson, Halcy Olive, *Our Sister Halcy* (Cleveland, TN: WWPH, 1974).
Tomlinson, Homer A. (ed.), *Diary of A.J. Tomlinson* (3 Vols.; New York: Ryder Press, 1949).
Tomlinson, Milton A., *Executive Correspondence*, 1944-1952. WHPC.

4. Genealogies
Bryant, William Franklin, Jr.
Coleman, Jesse
Elrod, Tom N.
Freeman, Andrew
Freeman, Minter
Hamby, Family
Hamby, Killis
Kilpatrick Family, William
McNabb Family
McNabb, Edmond
McNabb, Elias Milton
Plemons, John Paul
Raper Family, Glen T.
Spurling, Daniel Eli Love
Spurling, John
Spurling, Nathan
Spurling, Richard
Spurling, Richard Green
Tomlinson and Kellum Families
Tomlinson, A.J.

5. Interviews
Bryant, W.F., by Geneva Carroll, 1949. WHPC.
Bryant, W.F., by H.L.Chesser, 1949. WHPC.
Davidson, C.T., by Wade Phillips, 1982-1984.
Davis, Greta, by Wade H. Phillips, 1992.
Dockery, Loweta, by Wade H. Phillips, 1991-1996.
Freeman, Charlie, by Wade H. Phillips, 1992-1993.
Griffith, E. H., by Wade H. Phillips, 1982-1987.
Jones, Nora (Bryant), by Wade H. Phillips, 1985, 1990, 1992.
Kelly, Neil, by Wade H. Phillips, 1992-1995.
Kimsey, Alga B., by Wade H. Phillips, October 1996, March 1998.
Kinser, J.R., by Wade H. Phillips, 1982-1987
Ledford, Allie (Spurling), by Wade H. Phillips, 1983-1996.
Lemons, M.S., by H.L.Chesser, 1949. WHPC.
Plemons, Ruth, by Wade H. Phillips, 1991-1998, 2003, 2010.

Prock, Joshua, by Wade H. Phillips, 1992-1995.
Sheffield, Fina [Tilley], by Wade H. Phillips, 1990-1992.
Tomlinson, M.A., by Wade H. Phillips, 1982-1990.

6. Periodicals
Assemblies of God Heritage, Springfield, MO, 2011.
Church of God Evangel, Cleveland, TN: COGPH, 1910-1926.
Church of God History and Heritage, Cleveland, TN: Pathway Press, 1997-2004.
God's Revivalist, Cincinnati, OH, 1895-1905.
Lighted Pathway, Cleveland, TN: COGPH, 1929-1930.
Live Coals of Fire, Lincoln, NB, 1899-1900.
Samson's Foxes, 1900-1902.
The Apostolic Faith, Los Angeles, 1906-1908.
The Bridegroom's Messenger, Atlanta, GA, 1907-1910.
The Church Herald, March 1, 1907.
The Evening Light, Cleveland, TN, 1993-1997.
The Faithful Standard, Cleveland, TN, 1922-1923.
The Joyful News, Cleveland, TN, 1938-1950.
The Vision Speaks, Cleveland, TN, 1957-1963.
The Way, Culberson, NC and Cleveland, TN, l904-1905.
The Way of Faith, Columbia, SC, 1895-1900.
The White Wing Messenger, Cleveland, TN, 1923-1997.
Tennessee Baptist, Nashville, TN, July 23, 1853.
Voice of Zion, Cleveland, TN, 2005-2009.

7. Newspapers
Bradley County Journal, 1908-1910.
Cleveland Daily Banner, 1912-1952.
Cleveland Herald, 1914-1925.
Clinton Gazette, l891.
Chattanooga Free Press, 1938
Chattanooga News, 1936
Chattanooga Times, 1952.

8. Magazines
Newsweek
New Yorker

9. Tracts and Bulletins
'Biblical Wonder of the Twentieth Century'
Fields of the Wood
'The Covering Removed'
'The Last Days Church of God'
'The Message by Wings'
'Twenty-Nine Prominent Teachings'
Wings of Prophecy Evangelistic Association
Wings of Prophecy Monthly Bulletin

10. Books
Evans, A.D., *Church Business Guide* (Cleveland, TN: WWPH, 1933).
Evans, A.D. (ed.), God's Anointed – Prophet of Wisdom (Cleveland, TN: WWPH, 1943).
Lemons, M.S., *History of the Church of God* (Unpublished Manuscript, 1935).
Kent, Grady R., *Flogged by the Ku Klux Klan* (Cleveland, TN: WWPH, 1942).
Miller, Roy C., *Classified Scriptures of the Church of God* (Cleveland, TN: Press of Church of God Evangel, 1913).
Spurling, R.G., *The Lost Link* (Turtletown, TN: 1920).
Tomlinson, A.J., *The Last Great Conflict* (Cleveland, TN: Press of Walter E. Rogers, 1913).
—*Historical Annual Addresses* (3 Vols.; Cleveland, TN: WWPH, 1970).
—*God's Twentieth Century Pioneer* (Cleveland, TN: WWPH, 1962).
Tomlinson, Homer A., *Mountain of the Lord's House* (n.p., 1942). WHPC.
—*Great Speckled Bird* (n.p., 1941). WHPC.
—*Shout of a King* (n.p., 1968).
—*Great Vision of the Church of God* (1939).
—*Amazing Fulfillments of Prophecy* (Cleveland, TN: WWPH, 1934).
Tomlinson, M.A., *Basic Bible Beliefs* (Cleveland, TN: WWPH, 1961).
—*The Glorious Church of God* (Cleveland, TN: WWPH, 1968).

Secondary Sources

1. Theses and Papers
Bell, Marty G., 'James Robinson Graves and the Rhetoric of Demagogy: Primitivism and Democracy in Old Landmarkism' (Ph.D. Dissertation, Vanderbilt University, 1990).
Hunter, Harold, 'Spirit Baptism and the 1896 Revival in Cherokee County, North Carolina', *Pneuma* 5 (Fall 1983), pp. 1-17.
—'Beniah, TN: A Case of the Vanishing Flame' (Copy of Manuscript, 1994). WHPC.
Murray, Ann Elizabeth, 'Days of Perplexity: World War I and the Church of God' (MA Thesis, University of Tennessee at Chattanooga, 1982).
Phillips, Wade H., 'America: The Secret of Her Greatness: A Tribute and a Warning', *Voice of Zion* (July 2009), p. 6.
—'The Church of God: A Portrait of America' (MDiv Thesis, Church of God School of Theology, 1993).
—'The Church of God: In the Light and Shadow of America' (Thesis in partial fulfillment of Masters of Divinity degree. Church of God School of Theology. 1991).
—'The Corruption of the Noble Vine' (MDiv paper, Church of God School of Theology, 1990).
—'The First General Assembly: The Move Toward Centralized Government', *Church of God History & Heritage* (Winter Issue 2006), p. 2.
—'The Life and Times of Richard Spurling', *Church of God History & Heritage* (Summer/Fall 2002), pp. 6-7.

—'Our Rich Church of God Heritage: Born of the Spirit', in *Church of God History & Heritage* (Cleveland, TN: Pathway Press, Summer 1997).
—'A Prophetic Cry for Restoration' (Sermon delivered to the Church of God School of Theology, February, 1995).
—'Quakerism and Frank W. Sandford: Major Influences that Transformed A.J. Tomlinson and the Church of God' (Paper presented to the Twenty-First Annual Meeting of the Society for Pentecostal Studies, Lakeland, FL, 1991).
—'Richard Spurling and the Baptist Roots of the Church of God' (Paper presented to the Twenty-Third Annual Meeting of the Society for Pentecostal Studies, Guadalajara, Mexico, November 11-13, 1993).

2. Books

Alexander, Kimberly Ervin, *Pentecostal Healing: Models in Theology and Practice* (JPTSup 29; Blandford Forum, UK: Deo Publishing, 2006).
Anderson, Robert Mapes, *Vision of the Disinherited: The Making of American Pentecostalism* (New York: Oxford University Press, 1979).
Asplund, John, *The Universal Register of the Baptist Denomination in North America 1790-1794* (New York: Arno Press, 1980).
Barclay, Robert, *An Apology for the True Christian Divinity* (New York: Samuel Wood and Sons, 1832).
Barnes, W.W., *The Southern Baptist Convention* (Nashville, TN: Broadman Press, 1845–1953).
Bartleman, Frank, *Azusa Street* (S. Plainfield, NJ: Bridge Publishing, 1980).
Barton, David, *Original Intent: The Courts, the Constitution & Religion* (Aledo, TX: WallBuilder Press, 1997).
Benedict, David, *A General History of the Baptist Denomination* (2 Vols.; Boston: Lincoln and Edmunds, 1813).
—*Fifty Years Among the Baptists* (New York: Sheldon & Company, 1860).
Bercot, David W. (ed.), *A Dictionary of Early Christian Beliefs* (Peabody, MA: Hendrickson Publishers, 1998).
Braithwaite, William C., *The Beginnings of Quakerism [1912] and The Second Period of Quakerism [1919]* (2 vols.; London: Macmillan and Company, 1961).
Brooks, John P., *The Divine Church* (El Dorado Springs, MO: Witt Printing Company, 1891).
Burnett, J.J., *Sketches of Tennessee's Pioneer Baptist Preachers* (Johnson City: The Overmountain Press, 1919; Reprint 1985).
Burrage, Champlin, *The Church Covenant Idea: Its Origin and Its Development* (Philadelphia: American Publication Society, 1904).
Burgess, Stanley M. and Gary B. McGee (eds.), *Dictionary of Pentecostal and Charismatic Movements* (Grand Rapids, MI: Zondervan Publishing House, 1988).
Cairnes, Earle E., *Christianity Through The Centuries* (Grand Rapids, MI: Zondervan, 1954).
Calvin, John, *Institutes of the Christian Religion* (Grand Rapids: Eerdmans, 1983).
Campbell, Joseph E., *The Pentecostal Holiness Church* (Franklin Springs, GA: The Publishing House of the Pentecostal Holiness Church, 1898–1948).
Cawthorn, C.P. and N.L. Warnell, *Pioneer Baptist Church Records of South-Central Kentucky and the Upper Cumberlands of Tennessee, 1799-1899* (Published by the Authors, 1985).

Cherry, Conrad, *God's New Israel: Religious Interpretations of American Destiny* (Englewood Cliff, NJ: Prentice-Hall, 1971).
Christian, John T., *A History of the Baptists* (Texarkana, AR: American Baptist Association, 1922).
Clark, Elmer T., *The Small Sects in America* (New York: Abingdon-Cokebury Press, 1937).
Clarke, Adam, *Commentary* (6 vols.; Nashville: Abingdon Press, 1830).
Conn, Charles W., *Like A Mighty Army: A History of the Church of God* (Cleveland, TN: Pathway Press, l955).
—*Cradle of Pentecost* (Cleveland, TN: Pathway Press, 1981).
Cotham, Perry C., *Politics, Americanism, and Christianity* (Grand Rapids: Baker Book House, 1976).
—*The Nation With the Soul of a Church, in Politics, Americanism, and Christianity* (Grand Rapids: Baker Book House, 1976).
Cowen, Clarence Eugene, *A History of the Church of God [Holiness]* (Overland Park, KS: Herald and Banner Press, 1949).
Crews, Mickey, *The Church of God: A Social History* (Knoxville: The University Tennessee Press, 1990).
Dake, Finis Jennings, *God s Plan for Man* (Lawrenceville, GA: Dake Bible Sales, 1949).
Davidson, Charles T., *Upon This Rock* (3 Vols.; Cleveland, TN: WWPH, 1973).
—*Fields of the Wood* (Cleveland, TN: WWPH, l948).
—*America's Unusual Spot* (Cleveland, TN: WWPH, 1954).
Dawson, Joseph Martin, *Baptists and the American Republic* (Nashville: Broadman Press, 1956).
Dayton, Donald W., *Theological Roots of Pentecostalism* (Peabody MA: Hendrickson Publishers, 1987).
Deweese, Charles, *Baptist Church Covenants* (Nashville: Broadman Press, 1990).
Dowie, John Alexander, *Doctors, Drugs, and Devils; or the foes of Christ the Healer* (Zion, IL: Zion Printing and Publishing House, 1901).
Dorgan, Howard, *Giving Glory to God in Appalachia* (Knoxville: The University of Tennessee Press, 1987).
Edwards, Morgan, *Materials Towards A History of the Baptists* (2 Vols.; Danielville, GA: Heritage Papers, 1984; Reprint, University of Tennessee Press, 1987).
Eidsmore, John, *Christianity and the Constitution* (Grand Rapids, MI: Baker, 1987).
Eisenman, Robert, *James the Brother of Jesus* (New York, NY: Penguin Books, 1997).
Estep, William, *The Anabaptist Story* (Grand Rapids, MI: Eerdmans, 1975).
Eusebius, *Eusebius' Ecclesiastical History* (Grand Rapids, MI: Baker, 1955).
Finger, Thomas N., *A Contemporary Anabaptist Theology* (Downers Grove, IL: InterVarsity Press, 2004).
Fletcher, John, *The Works of the Reverend John Fletcher* (4 vols.; Salem, OH: Schmul Publishers, 1974).
Frend, W.H.C., *The Rise of Christianity* (Philadelphia: Fortress Press, 1984).
Frodsham, Stanley H., *With Signs Following* (Springfield, MO: Gospel Publishing House, 1946).
Gibson, Luther, *History of the Church of God Mountain Assembly* (Published by the Author, 1954).

Goff, James R. Jr., *Fields White Unto Harvest* (Fayetteville: The University of Arkansas Press, 1988).

Graves, J.R., *Old Landmarkism What Is It?* (Texarkana, TX: Bogard Press, 1880).

Hailey, O.L., *J.R. Graves: Life, Times and Teachings* (History and Archives Committee State Association of Missionary Baptist Churches of Arkansas, 1929).

Hamm, Thomas D., *The Transformation of American Quakerism Orthodox Friends, 1800-1907* (Bloomington: Indiana University Press, 1988).

Hatch, Nathan O. and Mark A. Noll (eds.), *The Bible in America* (New York: Oxford University Press, 1982).

The Heritage of Cherokee County, North Carolina (3 vols.; Winston-Salem, NC: The History Division of the Hunter Publishing, 1987).

Heritage Papers 1984 (University of Tennessee Press, 1987).

Hughes, Richard T. (ed.), *The Primitive Church in The Modern World* (Urbana, IL: University of Illnois Press, 1995).

Hutton, Edith W., *A Promise of Good Things to Come, Longfield Baptist Church* (Oak Ridge, TN: Adroit, Inc., 1982).

Inaugural Addresses of the Presidents of the United States (Washington, DC: United States Government Printing Office, 1974).

Jones, Rufus, *The Latter Periods of Quakerism* (London: Macmillan and Company Limited, 1921).

Kendrick, Klaude, *The Promise Fulfilled* (Springfield, MI: Gospel Publishing House, 1961).

Kirshon, John W. (ed. in chief), *Chronicle of America* (Farnborough, Hampshire, England: Chronicle Communications Ltd, 1989).

Krahn, Cornelius (ed.), *The Mennonite Encyclopedia* (4 Vols.; Scottdale, PA: The Mennonite Publishing House, 1955).

Lacy, Eric R., *Antebellum Tennessee: A Documentary History* (Johnson City, TN: The Overmountain Press, 1969).

Latourette, Kenneth Scott, *A History of Christianity* (2 Vols.; New York: Harper & Row Publishers, 1953).

Lawrence, B.F., *The Apostolic Faith Restored* (St. Louis: Gospel Publishing House, 1916).

Lillard, Roy G., *The History of Polk County, Tennessee 1839-1999* (Maryville, TN: Stinnett Printing Company, 1999).

Luther, Martin, *Works of Martin Luther* (6 vols.; repr.; Grand Rapids, MI: Baker Book House, 1982).

McBeth, Leon H., *The Baptist Heritage* (Nashville: Broadman Press, 1987).

—*A Sourcebook for Baptist Heritage* (Nashville, TN: Broadman Press, 1990).

McClung, Grant L. (ed.), *Azusa Street and Beyond* (South Plainfield, NJ: Bridge Publishing, Inc., 1986).

Mead, Frank. S., *Handbook of Denominations in the United States* (Nashville: Abingdon Press, 1951).

Mead, Sidney F., *The Lively Experiment: The Shaping of Christianity in America* (New York: Harper and Row, 1963).

Murray, Frank S., *Sublimity of Faith* (Amherst, NH: The Kingdom Press, 1981).

Nelson, Shirley, *Fair, Clear, and Terrible: The Story of Shiloh* (Latham, NY: British American Publishing, 1989).

Orchard, G.H., *History of Baptists* (Texarkana, TX: Bogard Press, 1987).

Owen, John, *The Works of John Owen* (16 vols.; repr.; London: The Banner of Truth Trust, 1966)..

Padgett, Michael, *A Goodly Heritage* (Kearney, NE: Morris Publishing, 1995).

Parham, Charles F., *Voice Crying in the Wilderness* (Baxter Springs, KS: Parham, 2nd edn, 1910).

Parham, Sarah E., *The Life of Charles F. Parham* (Joplin, MO: Tri-State Printing, 1930).

Paschal, G.W., *History of North Carolina Baptists* (2 Vols.; Raliegh, NC: Edwards and Broughton Co., 1930).

Pendleton, J.M., *Why I Am a Baptist* (Nashville: Baptist Publishing House, 1853).

Phillips, Wade H., *Mysterious Babylon and the Church of God* (Cleveland TN: WWPH, 1982).

—*The Nature of the Church* (Cleveland, TN: WWPH, 1989).

—*The Church in History and Prophecy* (Cleveland, TN: WWPH, 1990).

Purefoy, Geo[rge] W., *A History of the Sandy Creek Baptist Association, From its Organization in A.D. 1758, to A.D. 1858* (New York: Arno Press, 1980).

Qualben, Lars P., *A History of the Christian Church* (Nashville, TN: Thomas Nelson, 1942).

Ray, D.B., *Baptist Succession: A Handbook of Baptist History* (Oklahoma City: Published by the Author, 1912).

—*Textbook on Campbellism* (St Louis, MO: St. Louis Baptist Publishing Company, 1881).

Reid, Daniel G., Robert D. Linder, Bruce L. Shelley, and Harry S. Stout, *Dictionary of Christianity in America* (Downers Grove, IL: InterVarsity Press, 1990).

Sandford, Frank W., *Seven Years With God* (Mount Vernon, NH: The Kingdom Press, 1957).

—*Majesty of Snowing Whiteness* (Amherst, NH: The Kingdom Press, 1963).

—*Art of War* (Amherst, NH: The Kingdom Press, 1966).

Sands, Sarah G. Cox, *History of Monroe County, Tennessee* (4 vols.; Baltimore, MD: Gateway Press, 1980).

Schaff, Philip, *History of the Christian Church* (8 Vols.; Grand Rapids: MI: Eerdmans, 1910).

Sheldon, Henry C., *History of the Christian Church* (Peabody, MA: Hendrickson, 1988).

Simmons, E.L., *History of the Church of God* (Cleveland, TN: COGPH, 1938).

Spencer, J.H., *A History of Kentucky Baptists* (2 Vols.; Cincinnati: J.R. Baurnes, 1885).

Strong, Augustus Hopkins, *Systematic Theology* (Valley Forge, PA: Judson Press, 1907).

Synan, Vinson, *The Holiness-Pentecostal Movement in the United States* (Grand Rapids, MI: Eerdmans, 1971).

Thomas, John Christopher, *The Devil, Disease and Deliverance: Origins of Illness in New Testament Thought* (JPTSup 13; Sheffield: Sheffield Academic Press, 1998).

—*Footwashing in John 13 and the Johannine Community* (Cleveland, TN: CPT Press, 2nd edn, 2014).

Toomey, Glenn A., *History of the Sweetwater Association and Affiliated Churches 1830-1980* (Published by Author, 1980).

Trueblood, D. Elton, *The People Called Quakers* (Richmond, IN: Religious Society of Friends, 1975).
Wardin, Albert W. Jr., *Tennessee Baptists: A Comprehensive History 1779–1999* (Brentwood, TN: Tennessee Convention, 1999).
Wesley, John, *Explanatory Notes Upon the New Testament* (London: Epworth, 1941).
Whitley, W.T., *The Works of John Smyth* (Cambridge University Press, 1915).
Wittlinger, Carlton O., *Quest for Piety and Obedience: The Story of the Brethren in Christ* (Nappanee, IN: Evangel Press, 1978).
Wood, Dillard L. and William H. Preskitt Jr., *Baptized With Fire: A History of the Pentecostal Fire-Baptized Holiness Church* (Franklin Springs, GA: Advocate Press, 1983).

Index of Biblical (and Other Ancient) References

Genesis

3.14-24	311
3.17	311
14.18-20	369
15.18-21	xviii
21.28-31	329
28.16, 17	233
28.20-22	369

Exodus

15.27	456
18.13-27	457
19.5-8	52, 283
20.13	370
23.2	378
24.1, 9	411
24.6-8	52, 283

Leviticus

24.2-4	198

Numbers

11.16-25	411, 458

Deuteronomy

1.15-16	457
16.18	457
19.15	386
19.18	457
22.5	328
32.40	329

Judges

2.16-19	457
7.3	157
8.19	329, 330

1 Samuel

14.39	329, 330
16.7	8, 634
20.42	329

2 Samuel

2.17	451
15.15	457

1 Kings

12.1	484

2 Kings

5.2-26	451
11.17-18	52
23.1-3	52

1 Chronicles

28.3	370

2 Chronicles

19.1-11	457

Psalms

1.1	378, 565
30.11	6
45.6-15	xxii, 5
50.3	1
72.16	66, 67
87.3	xxii
89.34	45
102.13-14	5, 66
103.3	369
110.3	122
119.1-6	348
119.24	348
119.45-48	348
120.7	370

Proverbs

11.14	386, 484
13.15	386
15.22	484
17.22	316
20.1	369
22.28	19
23.10	19
23.29-32	369
24.6	348, 484
27.17	348

Ecclesiastes

9.2-3	330

Song

6.9-10	xxii, 6, 424
6.10-12	283
6.13	5

Isaiah

1.18	386
1.25-27	457, 459
2.23	xvii, 66
3.16	327
9.6	95
11.11	66
25.7	216, 298, 299
28.7	369
29.9-14	466
49.18-22	xviii, 421
51.1-3	xviii
52.1	421
54.2	xviii
54.3	xvii
55.2	326, 367, 369, 370
55.11	45
56.10	466
59.19	xvii, 4, 421
59.21	277
60.1-5	xvii, xxii, 5, 56, 258, 299, 421, 449
60.1-21	xviii, 1, 283, 421
61.25	421
62.1-7	421

Index of Biblical (and Other Ancient) References

62.5	283, 421	*Malachi*		28.20	404, 449
65.8-10	xviii	3.10	369	*Mark*	
65.17-25	xviii				
66.2	174, 411, 501	*Matthew*		1.9-10	369
66.8	67	3.8	369	1.15	369
		3.11	120, 127, 367, 369	3.13-15	283, 448
Jeremiah				3.29	369
2.21	565	4.21	528	5.37	528
6.16	19	5.12	367	6.33	528
18.7	5	5.14	210, 283, 448, 449	10.42-45	336
23.3	66			13.34	283, 402, 403
30.21	174, 411, 501	5.23-24	386	14.33	528
31.7-13	66	5.25-26	316	16.17-18	355, 367, 368, 369
42.5	329	5.32	371, 372, 374, 377, 543		
50.5	283			*Luke*	
		5.33-37	329, 370	1.75	369
Ezekiel		5.38-48	370	6.23	368
16.8	52, 283	6.11	270	6.12-17	66, 283
37.3-11	5	6.14-15	370	6.13	66
47.12	316	7.15-17	367, 551	8.43	316
		8.16	369	10.33-34	316
Daniel		8.17	367	11.42	105, 369
2.34	67	10.1, 7, 8	367, 368	13.3	369
7.7-14	299	10.2	528	13.13-34	347
7.18-27	299	13.55	528	14.16-24	43
		16.19	270, 283, 335, 348, 448, 528	17.15-16	367
Hosea				17.20	283
2.11	369	17.1-9	528	17.21	210
		18.15-20	120, 283, 348, 386, 402, 403, 529	18.30	369
Joel				19.9	369
2.28-32	xvii, xix, 120			19.37-40	368
		19.9	377, 543	22.17-20	369
Amos		20.27	528	22.49-52	370
9.11	66	21.33-42	347	24.49-53	367, 369
		21.43	5		
Micah		22.2-14	43	*John*	
2.12	66	23.23	105	1.3	403
		24.14	299	3.3-8	283, 369
Habakkuk		24.2228	369	3.13	403
2.2-3	xxiii, 5	24.30	368	3.22-23	369
		25.6-10	5	5.28-29	369
Zechariah		25.41	368, 369	6.64	403
4.2	294	26.26-31	368	8.9	347
14.1-21	258	26.50-56	370	9.1-3	313
14.4	369	28.19	xix, 299, 367, 369	9.6	316
14.6-7	xvii, 1, 56, 258, 283				

10.16	7, 216, 299, 635	9.35	303	1.10	282, 350
		9.40	303	1.30	369
10.28	369	9.42	303	3.9	449
11.30	403	10.44-48	367, 369	3.10	xix
11.49-52	7, 216, 299	12.17	528, 529	4.9	367
13.4-15	368, 369	15-16.5	223, 230, 246, 283, 365, 397	5.1-13	283, 369
14.1-3	299			6.1-4	283, 457
14.20, 23	403	15.12-28	484, 528, 529	7.1	369
15.2, 8	367	15.16	66	7.1-10	373, 375
15.26-27	367, 369, 401	15.28	120, 232, 397, 484	8	346
16.2	347			8.1-13	345, 369
16.7-14	401, 410	16.4-5	120	9.7-14	105, 569
16.13-16	449	17.2	386	10.31-32	369
17.	293	18.4	386	11.5-10	328
17.6, 8, 14	283	19.1-7	367, 369	11.19	xx
17.15-16	329	20.28	579	11.23-29	368, 369
17.20-23	7, 216, 299, 424	20.29-31	5	12.1-10,	292, 367, 369
		21.18	528, 529	12.14	122
18.10-11,	370	23.1	347	12.28	292, 307, 367, 396, 579
18.36	370	24.15-16	347, 369		
20.23	336, 448, 538			14.1	292, 369
		Romans		14.2	137, 143
Acts		1.21-32	346	14.22	367
1.4-8	369	2.15	347	14.28	232
1.8	130	3.9-10, 23	367	15.7	528
1.11	368	4.19-20	358	15.51-52	299, 369
1.15-26	120, 283, 513	5.1-2	369	16.2	369
2.1-21	120, 126, 127, 134, 138	5.6	367		
		6.22	369	*2 Corinthians*	
2.4	367, 369	8.20-23	313	1.12	347
2.14-18	xviii, 368	8.24-27	320	4.7	320
2.38-39	xviii, 367	9.1	348	5.17	404
2.40-47	283	9.29	66	5.20	407, 449
2.47	283	11.19-24	5	6.1	407, 449
3.8-9	368	12.15	368	6.9	66
3.19	367, 369	12.19	370	6.10	369
3.21	2, 5, 448	13.1-6	342, 369	6.14-17	370
4.19	342	13.5	347	7.1	360
4.29-30	367	14.2-17	369	9.6-9	369
4.32	448	14.4-5	369	11.2	283
5.12-16	303	15.6	282, 350		
5.26	342	15.10	368	*Galatians*	
5.35-39	46	15.17-20	367, 369	1.4	329
6.1-7	283, 397	16.17	239	1.19	396, 528
8.7	368			2.4	210
8.8	368	*1 Corinthians*		2.9-12	528, 529
8.36-38	369	1.2	283	2.11-13	466

Index of Biblical (and Other Ancient) References

2.20	404	1.25-29	xix, 404, 449	7.4-9, 21	369
3.1-3	5	2.9-10, 19	404, 449	7.12	443
4.4	5	2.16-17	369, 449	11.13	233
4.19	5	2.19	105	11.10	233
4.27	xviii	3.11	404	12.14	369
5.15	466	3.14	208	12.15	466
5.19-21	360, 369			13.5	449
5.22-23	367			13.12	367, 369
6.1-2	631				

1 Thessalonians

4.3	367, 369
4.7	369
4.14	369
4.16-17	xix, 6, 299, 368, 369
5.16	368
5.22	329

Ephesians

1.3-6	449
1.10	216
1:13-23	449
2.11-19	6, 7, 216, 449
2.13-22	449
2.20	xix
3.5	216
3.5-10	1
3.6	6
3.17-21	449
4.13	424
4.18-19	346
4.11-16	xix, 7, 105, 283, 299, 305, 307, 346, 396
4.29-32	466
5.3-8	360, 369
5.9	369
5.18	368
5.24-32	xix, 299, 331, 449

James

1.21	369
3.13-16	466
5.12	329, 370
5.14-15	367, 369

2 Thessalonians

1.7-10	369
2.1-12	56, 421
2.3	266

1 Peter

1.23	369
2.9	52, 327
2.24	367, 369
3.3	327, 370

1 Timothy

2.9	370
2.11	232
3.9	348
3.15	348
4.1-3	266, 346, 369
5.9-10	368, 369
5.17-18	105, 569
5.19	538
5.23	313

2 Peter

1.19	278
2.1-10	5
3.3-4	266

3.9 367

1 John

2.15-17	329
2.27	459
3.9	369
5.11-13	369

Philippians

1.11	369
1.18	368
1.27	xix
2.7	410
3.1-3	368
3.12-16	xix
3.16	282, 350
4.4-6	7, 368

2 Timothy

1.5	347
2.9	327
2.24-25	386, 631
3.1-5	266, 348
3.9	347
3.16	279, 348
4.3	278
4.3-4	266

3 John

9-10	210, 484

Jude

3-4	5, 210
14-15	369

Titus

3.5	369
3.7	367, 369

Colossians

1.13	283
1.15-19	449
1.17	403
1.24	283

Hebrews

1.3	403
3.1	386

Revelation

1.8	403
2.1	402, 449
2.2	635
2.5	5, 421
2.9	635
2.13	635
2.2, 9, 13, 19	635
3.1, 8, 15	635

3.12	60	21.8	368, 369	Clement of Alexandria	
3.18	316	21.9-11	xv	2.246	327
5.10	369			2.270	327
7.14	xix	*Early Christian Fathers*		2.275	327
11.3-7	294			2.257	331
17.5	57, 145	Eusebius			
19.7	xv, xix, xxii	EH		Tertullian	
19.7-9	145	2.1.3-4	389	3.23	328
19.11-14	145, 299, 369	2.9.1-4	389	4.18-19	
20.4-8	299, 369	2.23.1-15	389		
20.10-15	369	3.16.1	389	Ignatius	
				I, 57-58	339

General Index

Abercrombie, H. Balford   62, 231
Adams, A.B.   353, 359
Adams, John   279
Adams, John Q.   279
Adams, L.P.   240, 292
Agee, Alfred   17, 22, 23
Aikman, Ralph   241, 242
Allen, E.J.   471
Allen, Emeline (Emelyne)   x, 158, 160, 271
Allen, Ethel   129
Allen, Ross   x, 158, 160
Alexander, Erwin   310
Alexander the Great   122
Alexander, Kimberly E.   641
Aledander, John   174, 320, 642
Ambrose   334
American Bible Society 4, 176, 187, 215, 256, 260
American Tract Society   4, 187
Anabaptists   1, 3, 47, 51, 55-57, 275, 284, 286, 291, 323-325, 329, 331-338, 340-342, 345, 370, 371, 374, 375, 380, 643
Anderson, C.T.   524, 533, 534, 564, 572, 573, 575, 577, 578, 582, 588, 601, 608, 613, 618, 619
Anderson, Dolly   189, 192
Anderson, E.W.   374
Anderson, Iowa Aletha   189, 190
Anderson, Milt   193
Anderson, S.D. 189, 190
Anderson, Tinch   23
Anderson, Nettie   193
Anderson, W.R.   374, 400
Anglican Church   58, 323, 333
Anglo-Israelism   142
Antichrist   58, 168, 227, 266, 294, 299, 300-302, 339, 345
Apostolic Faith, The   137, 139, 140, 141, 143, 339, 375

Apostles, modern-day   119, 300
Appalachian Mountains   9, 118, 187, 276, 380
Aquinas, Thomas   338
Arminianism   13
Arminius, Jacob   275
Associations, Baptists 24
—Clinton   17, 24, 22, 23,
—Liberty & Ducktown   110, 113-117, 119, 156, 157, 160, 162, 163, 203, 204
—Eastanallee   27, 29, 36, 39, 45, 69, 70, 161
—Holston   14, 15
—Northern   18
—Powell Valley   18
—Sandy Creek   15, 18
—Stockton Valley   16, 17, 53
—Sweetwater   24, 25, 27, 29, 35-37, 70, 161, 162
—Tennessee   25
Associations, Holiness
—Fire-baptized Holiness   326, 328, 364
—East Tennessee Holiness   25, 39
—National Holiness   120, 130
Atonement, doctrine of   13, 22, 24, 289, 309, 310, 313, 314, 316, 364
Augustine   331, 334, 338
Austin, T.R.   375
Awrey, Daniel   140, 271
Azusa Street Mission (Los Angeles)   137-140, 142, 143, 233, 234, 271, 289, 309, 374, 560, 641, 643
Backus, Issac   12
Bahamas   248-252, 254, 288, 293, 312, 319, 482, 532-534, 626,
Ballew, Gussie   187, 189-92, 204
Ballew, John W.   187, 189-191, 204
Baptist Denominations

—Landmark   93, 95, 113, 161, 226, 248, 273, 275, 324, 325, 336, 345, 348, 350, 364, 640, 643,
—Primitive   17, 25, 74, 93, 95, 289, 336, 345
—Regular   v, 12-14
—Separate   v, 12-14, 18, 27, 55
—Southern   19-20, 35, 37-39, 161, 323, 642
—United   v, 12-15, 17-18, 21, 28
Baptist Churches (local)
—Clear Creek   16-17, 22, 53, 637
—Coker Creek   30
—Cog Hill   45
—Culberson   203
—Friendship   119, 161, 571
—Hiwassee Union   45
—Holly Springs   68, 69-72, 74, 82, 85-87, 89-91, 109, 114, 162, 637
—Liberty   38, 41, 110-111, 115-116, 119, 155-157, 160-164, 203, 663
—Pleasant Hill   110, 112, 116, 118, 156, 160, 162-64, 170, 203, 325, 637
—Poplar Cove   15-17, 22, 53
—New Hope   17, 53
—Rural Vale   87, 109
—Salem   15, 22
—Shady Grove   27, 193, 203
—Spring Creek   23-27, 30, 74, 107
—Springtown   24, 30, 74, 637
—Union   16, 22, 637
—Wolf River   x, 16
—Zion   22
—Zion Hill   75, 82, 119, 156, 161, 637
Baldree, J.I.   577
Baldree, J.M.   577
Ballers, Jesse   577
Baptism, doctrine of   322, 332-34, 337, 338, 363, 364, 366, 368, 369
Baptism with the Holy Spirit/Holy Ghost, doctrine of   126, 138, 141, 143, 149, 234, 238, 244, 367-368
Barney Creek   v, 37-38, 41, 64, 69, 72, 74, 76-84, 90, 94, 96, 98, 103, 106-109, 168, 171, 218, 224, 274, 366
Barney, Walter   318
Barr, Edmond S.   251-252
Barr, Rebecca   251-252
Barratt, T.B.   290
Barron, George C.
Bartleman, Frank W.   201, 233, 560, 641
Bass, W.L.   577
Battle, Lee H., Audit Company   536, 574, 585, 591
Beard, M.L.   366, 368
Beneby, Fred   577
Benedict, David   13-14, 18, 48-49, 641
Beniah   135, 140-141, 153, 155, 262, 270, 640
Bethesda (Maine)   xi, 314-315
Bill of Rights (United States)   12, 58, 180, 343, 380
Bible Training School   288, 385, 432, 474, 484, 491, 495, 518, 522, 531, 554, 585-586, 593, 599, 611, 623, 624
Blackwell, H.D.   537, 591
Boehmer, E.J.   viii, 255, 288, 341, 414, 417, 461, 465, 495, 497, 539, 540, 543-545, 560, 563, 575, 587, 589-591, 595-596, 604, 607, 608-610, 612-614, 615, 617, 619, 621, 627, 631
Bootright, Chesley   17
Bower, Flora   xi, 250, 253, 255, 257, 266, 341
Bowers, Dorcas [Freeman]   x, 86, 88, 90
Boyd, Emma L.   261
Brantly, A.M.   577
Brannett, W.M.   577
Bramwell, William   146, 268
Brethren in Christ   118, 174, 188, 193, 336, 645
Brewer, Josh   352
Briant, Gamaliel   28
Britton, F.M.   250, 252, 257
Brooks, J.H.   617

Brooks, John P.   226, 641
Brouayer, Delia   627
Brouayer, George T.   xi, 374, 414, 438, 468, 471, 493, 496, 497, 517, 531, 534, 540, 543-545, 563, 577, 586, 587, 589, 591, 595, 604, 607, 608-610, 612-614, 617, 619, 621, 627
Brown, Johnnie   231
Broyles, C.T.   625
Bryan, William Jennings   181
Bryans, A.H.   xii, 374, 425, 427, 433, 435, 438, 445
Bryant, Agnes   170, 231
Bryant, [Bru]Nettie   114, 117, 156, 158, 159, 170, 193, 204, 231
Bryant, Julius L.   170, 189, 192, 193
Bryant, Luther   170, 189, 192
Bryant, Nancy   157
Bryant, Nora   114, 159, 170, 214, 638
Bryant, William Franklin, Sr.   112, 114
Bryant, William Franklin, Jr.   viii, x, xi, 28, 62, 63, 84, 86, 106, 110-119, 136, 139-147, 152-154, 156-159, 162, 167-171, 189, 192-194, 196, 204-06, 208-15, 219, 220, 224, 231, 235, 239-41, 250, 253, 257, 260-261, 266, 271, 311, 312, 341, 366, 423, 515, 539, 563, 564, 567-70, 615, 637, 638
Bryant, W.G. 'Gay'   159
Buck, Charles   58
Buckalew, J.W. xi, 253, 255, 288, 292, 341, 374, 410, 543, 636
Bullinger, Heinrich   340, 341
Burger Mountain   212, 215-216, 424
Burnett, J.J.   14-15, 22, 25, 34, 35, 48-50, 57, 161, 163, 326, 641
Bureau of Information, Church of God   469, 541, 556, 558, 572, 575, 577, 582, 616, 619-621
Burroughs, Homer   191, 207
Calvinism   13, 25, 124, 275, 364
Calvin, John   277-279, 325, 342, 641

Campbell, Alexander 4, 16, 53, 56, 122, 363
Campbell, Joseph E.   129, 250, 641
Campbellism/Campbellites   16, 20, 52-56, 361, 364, 573, 644
Camp Creek   vi, xi, 41, 74, 75, 96, 107, 110-112, 116-18, 124, 136, 139-141, 143, 152-55, 157-59, 164, 166-71, 183, 192-94, 203-05, 207-10, 212, 214, 216-18, 222-24, 227, 231, 238, 262, 267, 270, 284, 289, 293, 351, 365, 398, 423, 494, 563, 630
Camp, L.E.   577
Cane Ridge Revival   18
Carradine, Beverly   200
Carrol, Geneva   106, 638
Carrol, R.L.   577
Carter, C.T.   366
Caruthers, W.S.   374
Carver, Mattie   563
Cashwell, G.B.   xi, 234-236, 250, 257, 271-272, 290, 424
Chambers, Fred G.   255
Chambers, Nora   xi, 62, 255, 288, 341, 554, 615
Chapman, C.Z.   577
Chapman, M.A.   577
Chappell, P.G. 320
Chesser, H.L. 106-107, 139, 196, 235, 576-577, 638
Chesser, P.W.   577
Christian Apostolic Church   141
Christian Communism   viii, 438-54
Church Covenant   xxi, 50-51, 84, 97, 102, 210, 227, 229, 240, 283, 634, 641-642
Church and State Separation   vii, 12, 47, 56, 111, 180, 211, 323, 331, 340-343, 380
Church Herald, The   227-229, 257, 639
Churches of Christ   53
Church of the Living God   195, 198, 201, 213, 294, 299, 300, 302, 382

Church of God Evangel, The   vii, 257, 258, 464, 639,
Church of God (Holiness)   vi, 226
Church of God (Mountain Assembly)   vii, 256, 637
Civil War   2, 9, 16, 23, 26, 29, 38, 70, 80, 85, 110, 162, 163, 190, 293, 343, 373
Clark, Dougan   188
Clark, E.C.   468
Clark, Elmer T.   123, 642
Clark, H.R.   537
Clarke, Adam   xviii, 324, 332, 642
Clay, Henry   279
Clayton, Elijah   24, 27-29, 34, 37, 161-63
Clement of Alexandria   327, 330
Clement of Rome   388, 91, 399
Clendon, Myrtle   536, 625
Cleveland Banner   75, 546
Cleveland The Beautiful   478
Cleveland Herald   240, 477, 478, 638
Cleveland Tribune   614
Clinton Gassette   23
Coco Creek/Coker Creek   30, 38, 64, 76, 78, 79, 81, 84, 106, 108, 140, 153, 221, 325
Cole, Texas Missouri   75, 82
Cole, Thomas   75
Coleman, Jesse   157, 252, 638
Coleman, Lucy   157, 231
Coleman, Luther   157
Coleman, Viney Josephine   124
Coleman, W. M.   231
Conn, Charles W.   68-69, 116, 157-158, 166, 192, 250-251, 266, 272, 317, 427, 448, 511, 625-626, 642
Constantine the Great   47, 56, 211, 325, 331, 339
Constitution of the United States   12, 180, 286, 343, 365, 380, 641, 642
Constitution of the Church of God   179, 287, 373, 387, 392, 460, 463, 483-632

Cotton, Clyde   xi, 249, 253, 255, 257, 266, 288, 292, 341, 470
Corporate Conscience, development of   345-371
Council of Elders   vi, xii, 251, 328, 344, 391, 412-14, 428, 448, 455, 464, 465, 467, 474, 484, 495, 507, 560, 567, 585, 591, 596, 601, 609, 612, 616, 617
Council of Seventy   viii, 179, 341, 455-456, 463, 468, 484, 486-487, 562, 568, 577-578, 586-587, 595, 596, 601, 616-619, 634
Courts of Justice   viii, 457-59, 506
Cowen, Clarence Eugene   226, 642
Cramblit, P.E.   241
Cress, Abigail   xi, 188, 193, 389
Crittenden, Eva M.[Simpson]   239-240
Cross, W.H.   468
Crowder, F.J.   577
Cumberland Mountains   14, 18, 28, 54, 69, 81
Culpepper, J.W   468.
Curry, J.H.   577
Curtis, C.R.   255, 266, 288, 374, 423
Cyprian   330
Dake, Finis Jennings   279, 642
Daniel, James   577
Dark Ages   1, 4, 5, 56, 58, 59, 98, 108, 250, 285, 286, 293, 294, 296-98, 336, 347, 409
Davidson, Charles T.   68-69, 116, 129, 166, 181, 429, 448, 475-476, 486, 509, 524-525, 572, 635, 638, 642
Davis, Greta   17, 638
Davis, J.A.   255, 266, 288, 400, 468, 524, 561, 576-577
Davis, W.H.   202
Dayton, A.C.   19
Dayton, Donald   642
Deans, C.H.   577
Declaration   viii, 460-63, 484-86, 606, 617, 620, 627
Declaration of Independence of the United States   603

Declaration of Independence of Tomlinson and his followers viii, 409, 602-05, 610
Defriese, Emma 121
Dehart Cemetery 27, 69, 70, 91, 219
Dehart, Mary 30, 70
Dehart, William J. 70, 71
De Renty, Monsieur 146
Diotrephes 283, 484
Disciples of Christ 53
Divine Healing vii, 149, 293, 296-297, 309-318, 320-322, 367, 369, 567
Divorce and Remarriage vii, 90, 99, 123, 179, 283, 329, 344, 371-373, 475-478, 543
Dorgan, Howard 33, 34, 642
Dorman, J.L. 577
Douglas, T.P. 577
Dover, J.F. 607, 617
Dowie, John Alexander 124, 141, 143, 156, 171, 174, 201, 246, 275, 309, 310, 321, 382, 389,
Dry Creek 25-26, 74, 85, 90-91, 106-107, 109, 219
Duggan, John F.M. 78, 80, 106, 325
Duggar, Lillie 68, 70, 185, 241, 242, 524, 530, 569, 636
Dull, John E. 127-128, 130-131
Durham, William H. 289-290
Edwards, Jonathan 4
Edwards, Morgan 14, 51, 642
Elhanan Training Institute and Orphanage 260, 262
Ellis, J.B. 255, 317, 352-355, 374, 414, 417, 475-476, 497-500, 503, 510, 514-17, 524-526, 533-535, 539, 543-545, 553, 559, 563, 567, 570, 575-578, 580, 582-584, 587, 592, 595-597, 599, 610-613, 620, 626, 632, 636
Ellis, Nancy S. 231
Ellis, Theophilus 231, 343
Ellison, John 231
Elrod, Tom N. 231, 636, 638

Episcopalism 20, 52, 54-56, 79, 95, 102, 145, 153, 220, 221, 225, 232, 244, 248, 262, 383, 414, 415, 429, 435, 460, 463, 483, 510, 601, 603
Eusebius 244, 388-389, 391, 642
Evangel Publishing House 307, 464, 465, 478, 480, 511, 554, 586, 599
Evans, A.D. 423, 478, 501, 511, 532, 538, 547, 550, 577, 586, 597, 624, 640
Evans, Iris 532, 547, 597, 624
Evans, Larkin x, 87, 89,
Evans, R.M. xi, 249, 251-255, 257
Evangelical Visitor, The 174, 188, 189
Evening Light vii, 257-258, 639
Exchange and Indemnity Department viii, 460, 463-465, 477-480, 496, 541, 587
Exclusivity viii, 39, 46, 56, 147, 351, 422-424, 427
Executive Council xii, 475, 512-15, 518, 522, 527-30, 533, 538, 548, 553, 574, 582, 593-594, 598, 601, 603, 607, 609, 627, 637
Faithful Standard , The 139, 206-207, 353, 493-494, 496, 511, 531, 532, 541, 586-587, 599, 639
Faithful Standard Company 531
Faith Orphanage and Children's Home Association xi, 260-262
Fanaticism vi, 137, 165-168, 206, 242, 268-269, 314, 316, 318, 356, 358, 428, 599
Fenelon 123, 146
Finney, Charles 175, 427
Fletcher, John 130, 145-149, 175, 267-269, 642
Flint Hill Schoolhouse 78, 80
Florida Holiness Camp-meeting 249, 250
Footwashing vii, 13-14, 26, 56, 100, 227, 258, 323, 332-338, 644
Four-fold Gospel 187
Fox, George 53, 174-78, 296, 334, 636
Freels, W.M. 470, 472-73

Freeman, Andrew   85-86, 108, 218, 224, 230-231, 638
Freeman, Charlie   85-87, 90, 99, 104, 107, 230
Freeman, Dorcas   x, 86, 88, 108
Freeman, George   86, 88
Freeman, James   x, 86, 89, 108
Freeman, Minter   85, 90, 95, 343
Freeman, Sarah   86
Freeman, William Thomas   86-87
Frost, Joshua   x, 17-18, 21-23, 26
Fry, Ella   261
Fuller, Andrew   22, 25
Gambrell, J.B.   47, 48
Gammon, F.W.   577
Gann, Alonzo   274, 441, 468, 497, 512, 543, 590, 612, 615
Gentry, W.S.   355
Gibson, Luther   256, 643
Giddens, Luther   256, 643
Gillespie/Gillaspie, S.O.   255, 414, 417, 436, 468, 497, 524, 530-531, 534, 545, 577, 607, 611, 617
Gleason, Ralph   194
Gleason, William   196
God's Bible School
Goff, James R. Jr.   136, 643
Goins, John B.   233, 238, 240, 271, 466
Goins, J.L.
Golden Rule Supply Company   477, 478, 493, 511, 549
Graves, J.R.   19-24, 35-36, 38, 41, 55, 91, 324-325, 344, 363, 640, 643
Great Awakening   12, 266
God's Revivalist   175, 177, 639
Gulledge, Maude   207
Gurney, Joseph John   176
Hall, J.T.   366
Haines, John   245
Hamby, Alexander ('Elic')   157, 169, 224, 231, 235
Hamby, Barbara Melinda   37, 38, 160, 182
Hamby, Billy   106, 108, 110, 119, 164, 171
Hamby, David   155

Hamby, Callie   115
Hamby, E. Kilas [Killis]   638
Hamby, Elizabeth (Dockery)   83
Hamby, Sallie   231
Hamby, Zilphia [Shearer]   155
Hamilton, J.O.   515, 577
Hanks, E.J.   577
Hardwick, C.L.   366
Hardwick, G.L.   366
Hardwick, J.H.   366
Hardee, F.D.   577
Hardee, Dock   577
Harrell, Newton   577
Harle, C.W.
Harrison, J.F.   366
Haun, Mary   85
Hawk, Charles Timothy   106, 219
Hawk, Mary Etta   78, 637
Haworth, D.W.   477, 478, 618
Heath, S.J.   468, 534, 536, 578
Heath Annie   xii, 536
Hedgecock, David E.   70
Hegessippus   244, 388-389, 391
Haynes, Clyde   253, 255
Haynes, Efford   253, 255, 288, 468, 497, 543, 585, 610-612, 615, 629
Haynes, M.S.   355, 374, 414, 417, 495, 497, 543-545
Hensley, George W.   xii, 355
Hensley, Rastes   158
Hickey, W.H.   155-157
Hickey, Laura   155-157, 204
Higdon, M.C. (Michael Columbus)   22, 24, 27-28, 34-35, 37, 74, 161, 163
Higdon, T.A.   162
Hills, A.M.   174, 177, 200
Hillview   249, 252
Hinton, I.H.   577
Hodges, Rebecca   90
Holder, G.B.   576
Holston Methodist Conference   14, 15, 78, 79, 153
'Holy Ghost and Us' Bible School   174, 177, 198, 215, 249, 251, 260, 288, 385, 474, 475, 484, 491, 495,

518, 522, 531, 554, 586, 587, 593, 599, 611, 617, 623, 624
Howell, Robert   35, 38-40
Hughes, Horace   542
Hughes, Halcy (Tomlinson)
Hughes, J.P.   515, 523, 542, 553, 556, 558, 570, 574, 577, 589, 601, 608, 619-620, 625-627
Hughes, Nellie (Lee)
Hurley, J.N.   577, 617
Hyatt, Carl   190-191
Hyatt, Ella [Withrow]   189-191
Irons, Alvin   75
Ignatius   334, 338
Irenaeus   338
Irons, Susannah C.   76
Irwin, Benjamin Hardin   119, 121, 123, 137, 143, 188, 194, 204, 211, 268, 275, 351, 389, 570
Irwin, H.H.   617
Irwin, Stewart Toomes   134, 140, 234, 271
Jackson, Andrew   163
Jackson, W.T.   577
Jacobs, H.R.   577
Jefferson, Thomas   12, 183, 259, 280, 603
Jernigan, John C.   116, 117, 437, 438, 468, 563
Jesus Only, doctrine of   91, 276, 408
Johnson, R.P.   468, 535
Jones, Nora   62, 114, 159, 170, 214, 255, 288, 341, 554, 558, 615, 638,
Jones, Rufus R.   114, 176, 177, 212, 231, 643
Joree Hunters   515
Journal and Banner   242, 272
Juillerat, L. Howard   374
Justification, Doctrine of   144, 149, 227-228, 244, 289, 293-296, 322, 367-368
Justin Martyr   334, 338
Kelly, A.C.   473
Kelly, Neill   76, 77, 79, 638
Keeney, C.D.
Kennedy, V.W.   373

Kiergan, A.M.   226, 228
Keswick Movement   291
Kilpatrick, A. E.   158, 636
Kilpatrick, Betty (Coleman)   157
Kilpatrick, M. D. ('Uncle Dick')   157, 189
Kilpatrick, T.C.   222
Kimbrough, I.B. (Isaac Barton)   25, 26
Kimlin, Perry   577
Kimsey, William Scott   37, 160, 161, 162, 163, 164, 165, 170
King, D.F.
King, J.H.   148
Kinser, J.R.   525, 554, 555, 625
Kinsey, Lillian   263
Kipling, Rudyard   183
Knapp, Martin Wells   174, 177, 187, 194, 200, 249
Koon, Blanche   417
Koon, M.H.   470
Ku Klux Klan   157, 627, 640
Landmarkism   19-21, 37, 38-40, 46, 49-56, 59, 64-65, 93, 161, 325, 349, 640, 643
Langford, G.B.   577
Last Great Conflict, The   5, 67-69, 96, 97, 103, 108, 120, 185, 206, 208, 218, 250, 263-265, 271, 281, 287, 298, 300, 302, 304, 342, 363, 384, 405, 439, 441, 514, 640
Latimer, S.W.   417, 468, 492, 497, 503, 533-537, 543-545, 538, 565, 566, 573, 576, 578, 587, 590, 596, 610-614, 632
Lawson, A.J.   239, 241, 266, 349, 409, 468, 477, 493-494, 496, 499, 517-518, 523-524, 525, 536-537, 541, 555, 556, 568, 569, 571, 572, 573, 577, 597, 601, 607-608, 616, 619, 621, 625-626
Lawson, Cynthia 'Dollie' [Curry]   121
Lawson, Lula   627
Lawson, Perry Neptune   121
Ledford, Allie (Spurling)   9, 43, 69, 83-84, 159, 638

Ledford, Sandford   159
Lee, Eva [Townsend]   558
Lee, F. J.   224, 245, 255,   311, 317, 352, 365, 372-374, 384, 387, 401, 411, 414, 417, 468, 470, 472, 485, 494-495, 502-503, 517-520, 524-525, 529, 533, 537, 542-543, 545, 555-556, 558-559, 563, 572-573, 589, 596, 610-611, 613, 615
Lee, Nora [Million]   558
Lee, Sallie O.   255, 266
Lee, William Carroll   162
Le Fleue, David   577
Leland, John   12
Lemons, Mattie [Carver]   154, 563
Lemons, M.S.   3, 62-63, 83, 141, 154, 159, 167-169, 196, 200, 209, 212, 217, 219, 221, 223-226, 229-231, 235, 238-242, 245, 247, 255, 257,   266, 288, 318, 369, 374, 384, 400-401, 411, 414, 417, 421, 425-426, 428, 434, 438, 445, 456-458, 468, 474-476, 478, 480, 484, 493-499, 502, 510, 515-517, 520-524, 532-540, 545, 547, 550, 554, 560, 562-567, 569-570, 573, 575, 582, 584, 586-587, 592, 595-597, 599, 611, 613-616, 620, 631, 632, 638, 640
Letsinger, M.W.   355, 387, 468, 470-472, 562, 614
Liberty Baptist Church   38, 110, 114-115, 155-157, 160, 163, 293
Lincoln, Abraham
Little, Frank H   47
Live Coals of Fire   120, 121, 125, 129, 131, 136, 138, 145, 148, 150, 151, 154, 166, 238, 268, 639
Llewellyn, J.S.   253, 255, 256, 329, 374, 377, 387, 414, 417, 425-439, 446, 456, 457, 461-486, 492-499, 502, 503, 510-533, 535, 537, 538-570, 573-577, 580, 582, 584-585, 587-604, 608, 609-627, 629-634
Lighted Pathway, The   3, 139, 168, 263, 639

Loan Department   464, 465, 480, 540, 541, 587
Loftis, Mary Adeline 'Addie'   64, 74-75, 82
Loftis, Margaret [Pemons]   74-75
Loftis, Texas Missouri   75, 82
Loftis, William 'Bill'   74-75
Loomis, F.J.   239
Loomis, J.F.   572
Lord's Supper, doctrine of   100, 228, 332, 333, 338, 339, 364, 368, 369,
Lowman, J.J.   341, 374
Lowman, W.M.   314, 561
Lost Link, The   2-5,   8-11, 26-27, 32, 41, 43-47, 51-60, 62, 65-66, 68, 79, 80-81, 91-92, 94, 96, 98-102, 104, 163, 210, 218, 226, 258, 263, 264, 276, 289, 324-326, 340, 343, 345,   349-350, 363-364, 416, 423, 426, 437, 450-451, 454, 481, 548, 628, 631, 637, 640
Lutheranism   20, 78, 145
Luther, Martin   287, 294-296, 381, 548, 644
Manifest Destiny   183
Manifesto   460, 462
Marlowe, Guy   575
Martin, Callie   115, 121, 141, 158
Martin, Jeremiah C.   64, 78, 80
Martin, J.N.   523
Martin, William B. 'Billy'   3, 64, 80, 106-109, 112, 115, 119, 121, 139, 140-141, 152-154, 158, 194, 200, 249, 271, 287, 293, 295-296, 325
Mason, C.H.   290
Mayfield, Charles S.
Maxwell, J.F.   366
Maxwell, Lady   146, 268
McAllister, R.R.   192, 204, 207
McAllister, John Milton   207, 208
McArthur, H.W.   374
McCarson, L.F   577
McClure, Mollie   470
McConnell, Judge T.M   366
McCormick, W.J.   577
McGowan, C.C.   577

McGraw, W.D.   191
McKinley, William   125, 182, 184
McLain, Alora (Lee)   545
McLain, T.L.   6, 195, 255, 355, 415, 417, 445, 468, 475-476, 481, 495, 497, 510, 539, 540, 543-545, 551, 570, 587, 592, 599, 610-613, 632
McNabb, Edmund   110, 638
McNabb, Elias Milton   110, 119, 124, 140, 141, 152, 164, 172, 235, 238, 243, 293, 638
McNabb, Viney Josephine   124
McNabb, Henry Clay   124 234
McNabb [Simpson] Mamie   124
McNabb [Simpson] Minnie   124, 238
McNabb, William Oliver   124
Mennonites   3, 336, 341
Merritt, Stephen   174, 187, 195, 281
Methodism   20, 21, 35-36, 43, 53-55, 79, 80, 102, 149, 267
Methodist Churches   2-3, 42, 55, 80, 101, 106, 112, 153-156, 253, 297, 299
—Ironsburg   78-79, 80-81, 106, 219, 636
—Reid's Chapel   118, 119
—Coco Creek   3, 78-79, 108, 219
Millennium/Millennialism   198, 299- 301
Miller, Roy C.   252-253, 255, 307, 318-319, 637, 640
Miller, Lula   319
Mitchell, John B.   118, 175, 187-188, 205, 256-257, 259-260, 427, 564
Mitchell, Nancy Sue   64
Montgomery, Carrie Judd   309
Montgomery, W.A.   36, 37, 49
Mormons   4, 182, 406
Mueller, George   175, 188, 259, 382
Mulkey, William R.   37, 38
Mullen, J.W.   578
Murphy, J.C.   155, 157, 222-224, 293, 343, 366
Murray, Frank S.   196, 643

Murray, Judge G. Bancroft   537, 566, 617
Mysticism   145, 148, 267
  Rational   148, 269, 347, 404, 410, 442, 501, 603
  Trinitarian   145, 147, 268
  Orthodox   277
National Holiness Association   120, 130
Nelson, Shirley   194, 300, 301
Night Raiders
  Night Caps   157, 158
Nevin, W.C.   366
Non-Conformity, doctrine of   56
Norman, Nancy   22, 64
North, D.A.   366
Oath Taking/Swearing   329-332
Opinion of Appellate Court   479, 484, 495, 499, 501, 541-542, 576
Orchard, G.H.   20-21, 58, 94, 324, 346, 416, 643
Origin   330, 334
Orphanage Work   205, 228, 259, 260, 263
Overstreet, James H.   191
Overstreet, Eliza   193
Owen, John   146, 268, 644
Padgett, Carl M.   251, 374, 637
Padgett, Milton   532
Padgett, Michael   256, 359, 644
Parham, C.F. (Charles Fox)   126-28, 136, 137, 139-44, 211, 275, 290, 644
Park, E.A.   93
Parker, Minnie   124, 356
Patrick, Noah   241, 242
Patrick, Joe   241
Paul, Andy   76, 86, 87, 90, 91, 95, 99, 107, 276
Paul, John   74, 75
Paul, Penelope Josephine ('Aunt Nep')   76, 77, 82, 90
Paul, Sarah   86
Paul's Mountain   87, 90, 91, 94, 98, 218, 219, 274, 275, 276
Payne, T.S.   374, 414, 417, 468, 494, 497, 502, 532-535, 540, 544-545,

551, 573, 579, 584, 610-612, 614, 618, 620, 623, 625, 632
Pendleton, James Madison   19, 20, 28, 39, 50, 55, 644
Penn, William   175, 180, 181
Pentecostal Holiness Advocate   156
Pentecostal Worldwide Mission Band   186, 254, 288, 319
Pentecostalism, modern origin disputed   136-144
Perry, Mattie   260, 262
Perry, Sam C.   3, 62-63, 122, 224, 249, 250-254, 256, 260, 262, 288, 308, 310, 349, 375, 415, 425, 426-433, 435-438, 446, 450, 474, 497, 543, 571, 573, 577, 589, 642, 643
Phillips, Wade H.   2, 12, 60, 265, 380, 636, 638, 640, 644
Pickett, J.J.   200
Pierce, J.H.   577
Pietism   276
Pike, J.M.   119, 174, 234, 235, 236, 237, 389
Pinder, W.S   577.
Piney Grove   84-92, 94, 95, 98, 99, 105-108, 117, 171, 218, 219, 224, 274, 343, 364
Pinkerton, R.A. 'Albert'   112
Pinkley, E.L.   577
Pinson, M.M.   4, 235, 250, 290, 564
Plainness and Modesty, doctrine of   176, 178, 204, 324, 326-328
Pleasant Hill Baptist Church   vi, x, 37-40, 83, 102, 109-112, 115, 156, 160, 162-164, 204, 325, 637
Plemons, John J.   5, 64, 74-75
Plemons, John Paul   64, 74-75, 82, 98
Plemons, Margaret   75-76
Plemons, Melinda   64, 74-75, 82, 98
Plemons, Polly   64, 75-76
Porter, Robert Frank   3, 106-107, 115, 119, 139, 152, 155, 168, 563
Pressgrove, H.A.   577, 607, 616-617
Presbyterians   4, 52, 54, 56, 244, 419
Prewitt, W.H.   577

Priest, J.T.   577
Prock, John   89
Prock, Joshua   90, 99, 639
Protestants   4, 57, 334
Puritans   3-4, 58, 340
Quakers   1, 3, 57, 175-178, 180, 211, 213, 215, 278, 332-333, 337, 340, 343, 380, 389, 645
Quakerism   53, 100, 174, 176-177, 194-195, 211, 244, 248, 275-276, 370, 424, 450, 453, 500, 630, 641-643
Quinn, George   159
Randall, C.H.   262, 617
Rapture, doctrine of   299, 301, 308
Red Knobs   249, 253
Regeneration, Doctrine of   227, 368
Rees, Seth Cook   177, 178, 187, 194, 200,
Rembert, W.G.   553, 577
Richards, Ellis   576
Richards, T.A.   514-516, 576
Richardson, T.J.   576-577, 617-618
Robertson, Ethel [Simpson]   239
Robinson, A.E.   131
Robinson, Bud   174, 177
Robinson [Roberson], Hayes   157, 170, 374
Robinson, [Lou] Ella [Bryant]   170, 231
Roebuck, David   262
Roman Catholic Church   46, 52, 98, 331, 338-339, 460, 463, 464
Rogers, Amber   157
Rogers, H.G.   236
Rogers, Hester Ann   146, 267
Rogers, Walter E.   5, 366, 540, 547,
Roosevelt, Franklin D.   259
Roosevelt, Theodore   183, 280
Rose, Gideon   281
Rose, Zechariah   23-24, 34-35, 50, 161-162
Russell, J.S. (T.S.)   25
Sanctification, doctrine of   xxiii, 13, 64, 109, 111, 115, 127, 136-138, 145, 148-149, 155-156, 163,

166-167, 170, 177, 185, 188, 195, 211, 228, 233-235, 272, 289-198, 297, 314, 335, 350, 367-368, 544
Sanders, A.W.   577
Sanders, G.R.   577
Sandford, Frank W.   127, 137, 143, 174, 178, 187-188, 194-196, 201, 211, 221, 275
Sapp, G.C.   577
Scarbrough, J.M.   470
Scott, J.L.   62-63, 375, 400, 425, 433, 435, 438, 461, 466, 468, 474
Scott, Walter
Self, J.A.   468
Sensing, T.M.   577
Separatists   3
Sexton, W.R.   577
Seymour, W.J.   126, 137, 233, 271, 275, 287, 290, 374
Shearer, Drury   155, 222, 293
Shearer, Evert   157
Shearer, Laura   155, 157
Shearer, Margaret Melissa   155, 292
Shearer, Osco   157, 158
Shearer Schoolhouse   64, 111, 112, 116, 139, 152, 154, 156, 160, 165, 293
Shiloh (Maine)   137, 143, 174-175, 187, 194-201, 211, 213, 215-217, 221-222, 246, 271, 275, 284-285, 293-294, 298-302, 304, 314-315, 320-321, 337, 382, 388, 390, 398, 418-419, 423, 439, 444-445, 643
Shoal Creek   157, 160, 192, 203
Shruggs, John   25
Shulamite   56, 285
Shuler Creek   83-84, 94, 105, 274
Simmons, E.E.   374
Simmons, E.L   68, 69, 448, 468, 552, 644
Simpson, A.B.   175, 187, 194-195, 201,
Simpson, J.D.   374
Simpson, J.H.   217, 224, 233, 235, 238, 239, 240, 243,
Simpson, Julia   222, 240
Simpson, Minnie   124

Smalling, Thomas   25
Smalling, Nancy [Mitchell]   64, 80
Smith, George   229, 257
Smith, J.R.   405, 577
Smith, Sarah A.   107, 139, 140, 141, 154, 158, 262, 271,
Smyth, John   51
Snake-handling   xi, 350, 352 357
Snead, Robert   25
Snell, William R.   478
Speaking in Tongues   33, 78, 107-108, 110, 126-127, 134, 136-144, 158, 233, 238, 242, 271-272, 367-368
Spring Creek Baptist Church   23-30, 74
Spring, R.B.   107, 577
Spurling, Andrew   29-30, 70, 71
Spurling, Anne   26, 30
Spurling, Barbara Emmaline   83
Spurling, Barbara Melinda   37, 64, 65, 83
Spurling, Clark   23
Spurling, Colonel   30, 70
Spurling, Daniel E.   23, 29-30, 70-71, 91, 163
Spurling, Elijah   12, 281
Spurling Frances [Francis]   16, 17, 27, 69
Spurling, G.P. (Pinckney)   10, 64, 65, 77-79, 107, 271, 363
Spurling, Hicks L.   18, 23, 25, 69, 76
Spurling, Hiram   x, 9, 23, 30, 37, 81, 89
Spurling, John   14, 280, 281, 638
Spurling, James   14, 16-18, 27, 69
Spurling, James, J.   26, 27
Spurling, Jeremiah   12, 18, 281
Spurling, Killis   83
Spurling, Lewis   27, 70
Spurling, Mary   30, 70
Spurling, Nancy   30
Spurling, Nancy Jane   22, 26-27, 64, 69, 91, 162
Spurling, Nancy Sue   64, 80
Spurling, Nathan   25, 30, 69, 70, 163, 638

Spurling, R.G.   viii, x, xi, xii, xxiii, 8-12, 15, 18, 21, 23, 27-31, 34-39, 41, 44, 52-53, 56-59, 63-72, 76, 78-85, 92, 96, 101, 105, 110, 154, 159-161, 167, 170, 175, 179, 182, 184, 211, 224, 226, 231, 244, 248, 264, 275, 288, 311, 338, 343, 345, 369, 401, 426, 430, 437, 452, 464, 636
Spurling, Richard   v, x, 11, 12, 14-16, 25, 27, 29, 45, 64, 67-69, 75-76, 84-92, 95-96, 114, 160, 162-163, 280, 323, 343, 638, 640, 641
Spurling, Richard Eli   83
Spurling, Sarah   83
Spurling, William A.   23, 29-30, 69, 70, 163
Stargel, George T.   577, 617
Stearns, Shubal   14
Steer Creek   26-27, 68-69, 74, 85, 90, 91, 106, 108, 219
Stewart, James M.
Stiles, Milas   76
Stone, F.W.   577
Strong, Augustus H.   92-93, 644
Sullivan, W.H.   312
Sunnyside Mission   624, 625
Tennessee Baptist, The   14, 22, 645
Tertullian   327, 330, 338
Tharp, Zeno   623
Thomas, John Christopher   310, 334,
Thomas, David   51
Thompson, Winford   515
Thompson, Ester Melinda   74
Tilley, Elihu   76
Tilley, Fina   76-77, 639
Tilley, Lewis   76
Tilley, William A.   76
Tipton, Eglantine   87
Tipton, Eliza   89
Tipton, Joseph M.   87, 89, 90, 106, 109, 113, 119, 139, 141, 152, 164, 219, 224, 271, 293
Tocqueville, Alexis de   3, 350

Tomlinson, A.J.   xi, xv, 5, 32, 62-63, 68-69, 87, 96, 117-118, 120, 155, 173-176, 184, 190, 192, 231-234, 237, 241, 243, 248, 253, 255, 261, 274-276, 285, 302, 310, 315, 317, 343-344, 351-352, 355, 366-369, 374, 384, 385, 409-410, 417-418, 434, 461, 465, 476-478, 485, 519-21, 523, 531, 532, 555, 562-563, 570, 573, 579, 581, 589, 606, 608, 612, 617, 619-620, 625, 636, 638
Tomlinson, A.K.   175, 176
Tomlinson, Delilah   176, 181
Tomlinson, Halcy   xii, 184, 190, 204, 208, 542, 638
Tomlinson, Homer   xi, xii, 32-33, 117, 139, 174, 177, 184, 195, 204, 208, 217, 220, 242, 245, 249-251, 293, 309, 313, 317, 321, 343, 345, 353-357, 370, 383-384, 408, 435, 468-469, 475-481, 493, 494, 511, 519-520, 525, 531-532, 535, 542, 549-550, 553, 562-563, 567-568, 577, 586, 593, 595, 599, 601, 602, 608, 632, 638, 640
Tomlinson, Iris   xii, 184, 189, 208, 478, 481, 511, 531-532, 547, 597, 602, 624
Tomlinson, Mary Jane   xi, 83, 176, 182, 184, 189, 191, 192, 204, 217, 241, 249, 276, 312, 531, 532, 550, 554, 564, 597, 602, 624, 625, 627
Tomlinson, Milton   176
Tomlinson, Milton A.   208, 542
Tomlinson, Robert   175, 176
Tomlinson, William   175
Trasher, Lillian   141, 260, 262
Trim, H. L.   239, 255, 257, 341
Trim, Flora. E.   341
Turner, L.L.   577, 603
Underwood, J.C.   374
Unicoi Mountains   8
Verduin, Leonard   47, 48
Waldrop, Joab   95
Waldrop, Omia (Spurling)   89

Walker, C.C.   374
Walker, J.H.   468, 623
Waters, Jennie   131
Watson, George D.   174, 177, 187, 194, 200, 208
Watters, Mattie   131, 133
W.C.T.U (Harriman Temple)   472
Webster, Daniel   279
Wells, E.D.   146
Westfield Union Academy   180, 245, 249, 251
Wesley, John   175, 279, 288, 295, 296, 382
Westerburg, George D.   537, 544, 617
White, Fanny L.   78, 107
White, Henry H.   78
White Wing Messenger   63, 301, 621, 622
Whitsett, William H.   39
Wilkerson, David   577, 627
Wilkerson, J. A.   577, 617, 626
Williams, G.G.   577
Williams, Lula   253, 255, 319
Williams, R.   577
Williams, Roger   13, 72
Willis, A.K.   131
Winsett, R.E.   494
Winthrop, John   3
Withrow, Ella   189-191
Withrow, James   207
Withrow, Oscar   217
Witt, Hezekiah   78
Witt, Mary Letitia   80
Wimberly, Ringgold   366
Wingo, P.A.   241
Yingst, O.N.   577
Zion Asssembly Church of God   xvi, xxi, 2, 10, 160, 636
Zwingli, Hudreich   340

www.ingramcontent.com/pod-product-compliance
Lightning Source LLC
Chambersburg PA
CBHW050157240426
43671CB00013B/2156